PSYCHI᷈

AND SUPER]

PHENOMENA

THEIR OBSERVATION AND EXPERIMENTATION

BY

DR. PAUL JOIRE

Professor at the Psycho-Physiological Institute of France
President of the Société Universelle d'Études Psychiques

TRANSLATED BY DUDLEY WRIGHT

WITH 22 ILLUSTRATIONS

British Library Cataloguing-in-Publication Data
A catalogue record for this book is available from
the British Library

PREFACE

THE thorough study of Hypnotism has drawn attention to phenomena which seem, on the one hand, only to be the continuation of hypnotic phenomena, and, on the other, to be connected with faculties of the human mind hitherto unknown.

These phenomena are, first of all, those of mental suggestion and thought-transmission, which we have studied in our *Traité de l'Hypnotisme*.

In other cases, we have witnessed phenomena of lucidity in certain subjects placed in a condition of deep somnambulism. In studying lucidity more closely we noticed that certain special circumstances, and in particular a methodical training, develop this faculty in a singular manner in those endowed with it.

The investigator is thus led to inquire whether this faculty of lucidity does not sometimes appear spontaneously, in the same way as we witness spontaneous somnambulism in connection with induced somnambulism. He then finds a certain number of cases of telepathy which seem to be closely connected with the instances of lucidity.

After embarking upon the study of telepathy it is not long before we become convinced that the phenomena of this category are very complex.

In fact, while certain instances of telepathy are only the mental perception of a fact that has occurred at a distance, there are others in which this perception is accompanied by an hallucination, and sometimes this hallucination is collective.

At other times, hallucination is no longer a sufficient explanation, because the phenomenon has left permanent traces—the displacement of objects, impressions, objective and undeniable traces that a force accompanied the telepathic vision.

If we wish to transfer these phenomena we have observed to the domain of experiment, we find, among some subjects, in certain of the hypnotic conditions we have described, phenomena of externalisation—externalisation of sensibility and of force.

We have thus brought under our observation the chain which seems to connect hypnotic and psychical phenomena.

On the other hand, in entering upon the study of the whole of psychical phenomena, we easily witness a natural progression from the most simple phenomena up to the most complex.

All these phenomena are connected one with another, in a continuous manner, in such a way that we are convinced that the phenomena are undoubtedly of the same order, in spite of their apparent diversity and complexity in manifestation.

We may take abnormal dreams for our starting-point, dreams with manifestation of lucidity, and premonitory dreams, which lead us to telepathic dreams. We then come to telepathic phenomena with apparitions, telepathic phenomena in a waking state, and to collective telepathic visions.

Without going beyond telepathy, we find some instances where telepathic visions have left objective traces of their existence. We are thus forced to ask ourselves if thought is quite as abstract a phenomenon as we have hitherto believed it to be, and if, in certain instances, it is not capable of creating a durable entity possessing independent force.

We are thus led to examine the experiments made in the photography of thought.

Beginning with phenomena of the same character, brought into the domain of experiment, we find facts similar to those of telepathy in crystal-gazing, and amongst those of crystal-gazing we find some which present the characteristics of lucidity.

Lucidity appears to be a special faculty in certain subjects, and we see that we may search for and experiment with it in the somnambulistic condition.

Lucidity is also shown in other circumstances, and that, without somnambulism having been induced in the subject, but spontaneously exhibited. These facts are connected, by their spontaneity, with the phenomena of lucidity observed by means of crystal-gazing.

We now come to the phenomena of externalisation, which in hypnology we connect with the mediumistic states. The first of these phenomena is that of externalisation of sensibility.

We pass from this to more advanced phenomena—we observe the externalisation of force, movement of objects without contact, raps and various noises; finally, the creation of a form having its own objectivity and capable of developing a special force, although always in relation with that of the medium. Hence the most complex phenomenon of all, viz. Materialisation.

"I confess that I do not see why the very existence of an invisible world may not in part depend on the personal response which any of us may make to the religious appeal. God Himself, in short, may draw vital strength and increase of very being from our fidelity. For my own part I do not know what the sweat and blood and tragedy of this life mean, if they mean anything short of this. If this life be not a real fight, in which something is eternally gained for the universe by success, it is no better than a game of private theatricals from which one may withdraw at will. But it *feels* like a real fight—as if there were something really wild in the universe which we, with all our idealities and faithlessness, are needed to redeem; and first of all to redeem our own hearts from atheisms and fears. . . ."

WILLIAM JAMES.

CONTENTS

PSYCHICAL PHENOMENA

CHAPTER I

PSYCHICAL PHENOMENA IN GENERAL

CERTAIN strange phenomena, which occur from time to time, have, by reason of their mysterious appearance the power of forcibly impressing the imagination of the multitude.

The sphere in which they are produced, and the manner in which they are presented, have the effect of adding, often largely, to their importance, and of causing them to undergo singular transformations. The newspapers seize upon these sensational facts with great avidity, and relate them with a profusion of details, more or less correct, but always skilfully arranged, so as to add further to the effect already produced.

Among the people who have come into closer contact with these facts, or have been more or less actively concerned with them, there are always to be found a certain number who purposely add to the scenic effect, whether it be to serve well-defined interests, or whether they are led on in spite of themselves to supplement the truth by mirages produced by their own imagination.

The facts in themselves are sometimes very simple whether they come within the category of those which we observe spontaneously in unhealthy persons, or whether they are of the class of induced hypnotic phenomena. These are, for example, the phenomena of lethargy and catalepsy and hallucinations, which may become more complicated through collective or repeated hallucinations.

A

But such facts only now astonish a small number of persons, who are entirely ignorant of modern scientific discoveries : it is not of them we desire to speak.

There are sometimes even stranger phenomena, more difficult to explain and to verify, and in which, consequently, exaggeration and fraud have free play ; these may be visual phenomena which do not come within the class of hallucinations of which mention has already been made ; or they may be phenomena of a purely psychical character, such as the knowledge of an event happening far away, or even one which has not yet taken place ; seeing and describing objects at a distance, or reading the thoughts of another person.

It is not difficult to understand the suspicion with which serious-minded persons receive these strange stories, and the unpleasant impression naturally made upon them when they see these facts distorted and turned to profitable account by certain persons with more or less questionable motives.

It must also be added that when a man of intelligence and good faith wishes to get to the bottom of matters and devotes himself to serious inquiry, conducted without prejudice, he very often simply ends by discovering fraud ; all the marvels disappear, and all that remains is very easily explained. It even happens sometimes that, when seeking for authentic proofs of an alleged fact, he finds it reduced to nothing, or that it never existed except in the imagination of some practical joker or of a reporter who was short of news.

The result of all this is that these facts lose their interest for all except the simple-minded who love marvels and believe that these things are marvellous, and the small number who turn them to profitable account. Scientists and serious-minded persons grow tired of finding at every step facts badly observed and of very doubtful authority, so that they thrust them aside with disdain and refuse even to discuss them.

Others, after having heard the accounts, entirely deny all the facts, saying that there is no truth in them, because they cannot be explained according to the theories of official science, and no demonstration, according to the usual methods of the known sciences, can be obtained that is even moderately satisfactory.

This prejudiced rejection is in no way scientific. There are well-attested facts, absolutely authentic, but which we cannot comprehend and which we do not know how to explain in the present state of our knowledge. Is that a reason for denying them? Experience has shown us that we may be able to explain to-morrow that which to-day is still a mystery. Twenty-five years ago science knew nothing of hypnotism, and obstinately refused to study it. Many denied *in toto* all these phenomena, of which the public spoke in a whisper, and when sometimes a fact became surrounded with undeniable evidence, they rejected it on the ground of trickery.

We ought only to regard as scientifically impossible that which is absurd, that is to say, contrary to mathematical or geometrical truths, the only ones which are immutable. Even opposition to a physical law should not suffice to make us deny a fact. Physical laws may be momentarily suspended or have their effect destroyed by other laws; whether we know those other laws or whether we do not. In the first case, we are able, up to a certain point, to explain the fact, that is to say, to connect it with a law and anticipate the circumstances under which it will be produced. In the second case we observe the phenomenon and its varying conditions, sometimes without being able to appreciate its importance, and, in any case, without being able to explain it.

Be that as it may, the phenomena which present an apparent opposition to a physical law do not thereby destroy the law in itself. We only need to recognise that the fact in question does not come under the operation of this law, but that it is ruled by another law of superior power, both laws remaining true on the whole and under the normal conditions of their application.

Let us take an example: the law of gravitation, by virtue of which all bodies, when left to themselves, fall or travel towards the centre of the earth, is indisputable. And yet, we may see any day a balloon, left to itself, rise in the air, away from the centre of the earth. Is not this an apparent contradiction? The balloon is subject to a double law: first, to the law of gravitation, which tends to make it fall to the ground; but, secondly, to the law of Archimedes, which, by causing it to lose an amount of its weight equal to that of the volume of air which it displaces, impels it to the higher regions of the atmosphere. Two forces are thus in opposition, the greater of which preponderates over the less.

The same law of gravitation would cause a piece of steel to fall to the ground: if, however, it is suitably placed beneath a magnet, it can be made to remain suspended in the air. Has the law of gravitation been destroyed thereby, or are we warranted in denying the reality of the phenomenon? Obviously, no.

What is here said of physical laws is equally true of physiological laws: we must therefore deny only what is absurd.

This is not a reason for accepting too readily, as real, phenomena which depart from known laws; on the contrary, we must proceed with great circumspection and require indisputable proofs as to their authenticity. When the facts are fully verified, they must be classed by analogy and grouped together in as large numbers as possible; then examined to see if they can be compared with other similar analogous facts which are better understood.

The study of psychical phenomena seems to us to present all the greater interest, because, up to the present, with the exception of a very small number, they have not been subjected to sufficiently serious observation and truly scientific analysis.

Serious-minded persons, and, particularly, men of science, have taken far too little interest, up to now, in these phenomena. The scientific attitude, in regard to facts of this character, can only be either to study them conscientiously or to preserve an open mind in regard to them.

If a man should say: "I only occupy myself with astronomy or botany, I have not the time to study psychical phenomena, I do not know anything about them and cannot adjudicate upon them"; there is nothing to be said against this: such an attitude is serious and correct—it does not depart from the scientific spirit.

But it must be recognised that the language of the majority of men, and even of scientists, is quite different from this. They despise psychical phenomena, not because they cannot study them, but because they do not believe in their existence, and declare them impossible, without having studied or even seriously examined them.

Now this negation, à priori, is altogether contrary to the scientific spirit. It is just as unreasonable as would be the complete acceptance, without verification or examination, of facts which had not been proved.

The methodical study of these phenomena is, on the contrary, forced upon scientists, because it is impossible for them to ignore them, and, to be in a position to judge them, they must submit them to a rigorous investigation and analyse them with scientific method.

The verification of psychical phenomena is extremely difficult, but it is not impossible. A number of serious spiritists, and even men of science of the first rank, are already engaged in collecting and studying them.

It was in England, first of all, that the study of these phenomena, known by the name of psychical, commenced. In 1867, the Dialectical Society of London formed a committee of thirty-three members to study and experiment on them. Later, from 1871 to 1874, Sir William Crookes made a number of laboratory experiments, which he subjected to a rigorous scientific control by means of registering apparatus.

Later still, there was founded in London the Society for Psychical Research, among whose members are a number of very distinguished persons.

Finally, in France, Dr. Dariex founded the *Annales*

des Sciences Psychiques, intended to record observations
and experiments which offered serious and scientific
guarantees of authenticity.

Shortly afterwards *La Société Universelle d'Études
Psychiques* was founded in France, which, under the
patronage and with the collaboration of savants of the
highest repute and world-wide standing, established a
union between all the scientific groups which devoted
themselves to observation and experiment as to these
phenomena, in order to centralise the results of all their
labours, and thus to be able to compare and class them
methodically.

Professor Charles Richet, member of the Academy of
Medicine and Honorary President of the *Société Universelle d'Études Psychiques,* has exactly expressed what
ought to be thought of these studies by every man of
science, in the following lines, which are taken from an
important article published in *The Annals of Psychical
Science :—*

" Undoubtedly the experimental sciences of physics,
chemistry, and physiology, are quite as positive as mathematics; but there is this difference between them, that
they do not involve a negation. They furnish us with
facts; but they can never prove that another fact non-
contradictory is impossible.

" For instance, oxygen combines with hydrogen to form
water. This is a fact which no other fact can upset; but it
is quite admissible that oxygen, which seems at present to
be a simple body, may some day be resolved into other
simple bodies. It is very possible, it is even probable,
that our theories concerning the exact nature of the
chemical phenomenon of combination will be completely
overthrown. But that will not matter at all. It will not
be less absolutely true that, under present conditions, the
gas which we call oxygen when combined with a different
gas, the gas we call hydrogen, produces a liquid body,
which is water.

" But in the proposition I have just put forth there
is a phrase which is fundamental. *Under present con-*

ditions oxygen combines with hydrogen; but conditions might exist in which the combination would be no longer possible.

"For instance, let us suppose that there is an extremely feeble pressure, other gases massed together, a very low temperature—it is quite conceivable in these circumstances that a combination between oxygen and hydrogen would become impossible. So that it would be inexcusable for a chemist to refuse to examine experiments in which it might be alleged that, *in certain conditions*, it would be impossible for oxygen to combine with hydrogen.

"Hence when we say that oxygen combines with hydrogen, we are not proving the negative side of the question, for under changed conditions it might happen that the combination could not be effected. The important point would be to discover these new conditions, which differ from the conditions already known, already described and determined. An unknown force may always modify a phenomenon, so that the negation of an experimental possibility would lead to the following absurd consequence: No force, known or unknown, can suspend or accelerate the combination of oxygen with hydrogen.

"Let us take another example. It has been professed, and is still professed, that bodies which are not the seat of any chemical change do not produce heat. This appears to be a universally classical, absolute, and positive law, one of the immovable bases of general physics. Now, the discovery of radium has destroyed the absolute generality of the fact, since radium, without any appreciable chemical change, emits perpetually considerable quantities of heat.

"This phenomenon does not contradict antecedent experiments. It is a new phenomenon, that is all. And the scientist who refuses to examine facts because they are new, because they present an appearance of contradiction to classical facts, would be rather a poor specimen of a man.

"Nevertheless, when, *à priori*, Spiritism is attacked,

it is, in reality, for no other reason than that of its new-
ness. ⟨There is nothing to be found in the facts of Spiritism
which formally contradicts data established by science.⟩

"Let us select for consideration the most extraordinary
among the innumerable facts alleged by spiritists; for
example, an apparition, the materialisation of a being. A
classical illustration of this is that of Katie King, observed
by Sir William Crookes.

"Certainly, this is a strange phenomenon, extraordinary and improbable. It is difficult to find language
which adequately expresses the astounding character of
this phenomenon : the apparition of a phantom, a being
who has weight, circulation, intelligence and will; the
medium being present at the same time as this new
being;—the *medium* preserving her weight, circulation,
intelligence and will. But, unheard of as may be the
existence of this phantom, it is not absurd; it does not
contradict established science. Can any one adduce an
experiment which proves that a human form cannot
appear ?

"It is the same with *raps* or intelligible knockings on
inert objects; with thought-transference or lucidity; and
with movements of objects at a distance. The negation
of these facts has not been made by science, and, indeed,
it cannot be made.

"I absolutely refuse to admit the validity of that
simplifying argument : 'It is impossible, because common-
sense tells us it is impossible.' Why impossible ? Who
has fixed the limit of what is possible and what is not
possible ? Let this consideration be carefully weighed;
all the conquests of science and of industry were formerly
looked upon as impossibilities.

. . . .

"We live indeed under the illusion of time : those
idola temporis against which Bacon protested. We are so
made that the future seems to us as though it ought
to resemble the present; and this is a psychological law
governing our mentality. The navigator who is under
shelter in some little haven protected against the waves

and winds, finds it difficult to realise, in spite of experience, that beyond the headland which closes in the bay, the sea is let loose and tossed about by the wind in its fury. In the same way, we men of 1904, we cannot persuade ourselves that in 2004, and, more certainly, in 3004—a future which defics the anticipations of our most audacious speculations—the scientific data will be absolutely different from those of the present. We have not the courage to tell ourselves that not a particle will remain standing of those theories which we look upon to-day as conclusive. Nevertheless the demolition of all our scientific scaffolding, so laboriously constructed, is not a probability : it is a certainty.

.   .   .   .

" The history of the past makes me very confident concerning the marvels of the future. The immense future lies before us. It is possible that some day science may pause ; that, after the prodigious and rapid extension which we are now witnessing with too little astonishment, she may pause in her conquests. But that moment has not yet arrived ; for, in spite of her triumphant appearance, our science is, after all, but the study of phenomena, and she has not yet got to the root of things.

" We need not go any further than this, namely, that in certain conditions, certain phenomena are produced. Hence come what we call laws : in reality, laws are only facts generalised. Let a magnet be turned rapidly round an electric wire and currents will be produced which will cause the production of sparks between the two extremities of the wire. We know this much ; and we have been able to determine some of the effects of these currents, the best conditions to produce them, the relation between speed and rotation, the diameter of the wires, the number of revolutions, &c. &c. But have we gained a more intimate comprehension of the nature of the phenomenon itself because we have been able to determine the conditions under which that phenomenon is produced ? It is as if we were to suppose that we have adequately understood the laws of the development of living beings, because we know empirically that the egg of a fecundated hen kept in an incubator for forty days produces a chicken.

" We behold facts and their results; we are able to determine their conditions; this is well, but it is only a first step towards the knowledge of things themselves; for, if we desire to go further and *understand* — *i.e.* understand the *raison d'être*, the efficient cause, the intimate mechanism, *à fortiori* the primary cause—we must own that of these we know nothing.

" Even scientists, who, rising above appearances, look upon all the phenomena of this material world as vibrations of one and the same force, vibrations differing in form and speed, capable of becoming at one time light, at another heat, attraction, electricity, even these have not advanced much further towards the solution of great problems, for a vibration is still only a phenomenon. Vibrations in the ether produce light, but why ? Why should the combination of carbon with oxygen produce an undulatory vibration in the ether which is luminous ? It is impossible to name any phenomenon whatsoever—however well it may be described as to its form—which is accessible as to its cause ; and it will continue to be so, if not always, at least for a long time to come, for an adequate and completely satisfactory notion of any one phenomenon, in its ultimate causes, would entail the satisfactory notion of all other phenomena.

" The universe would be known in its integrity, if a single point in the universe, the mirror of the mighty All, were absolutely and completely known.

" Therefore, since it must be frankly acknowledged that we only witness phenomena, we have no right to make our fallacious theories a reason for assigning limits to science. Very strange, very wonderful, seemingly very improbable phenomena may yet appear, which, when once established, will not astonish us more than we are now astonished at all that science has taught us during the last century. It is assumed that the phenomena which we now accept without surprise, do not excite our astonishment because they are understood. But this is not the case. If they do not surprise us, it is not because they are understood, it is because they are familiar; for if that which is not understood ought to surprise us, we should be surprised at everything—the fall of a stone thrown into the air, the acorn which becomes an oak, mercury which expands when it is heated, iron attracted by a magnet, phosphorus which burns when it is rubbed. These are all so many mysteries, which too often we pass by without pausing to consider, for a mystery which is seen daily soon ceases, because of our intellectual triviality, to appear mysterious.

" There is then nothing unscientific in the admission that at a moment of intellectual evolution of Humanity, other forces may be generated. Why should they not be ? One or other alternative is true, either we do already know all the forces of nature, or we do not know them all. There is no way out of this dilemma. The first alternative, that we know all the forces of nature, is so absurd that the mere mention of it is sufficient to show how foolish it is : it is evident that our feeble intelligence, endowed with five senses of limited range, does not penetrate into all the forces of nature (the force of the magnet, for instance). Hence, necessarily and undoubtedly, there are forces which escape us. Therefore, the future may reveal these to us (not all, but some of them).

.　　.　　.　　.　　.　　.　　.

" It is certain, indeed, that we can foresee nothing concerning that vast future; but we can nevertheless assert that the science of to-day is but a slight matter, and that the revolutions and evolutions which it will experience in a hundred thousand years will far exceed the most daring anticipations. The truths—those surprising, amazing, unforeseen truths—which our descendants will discover, are even now all round about us, staring us in the eyes, so to speak, and yet we do not see them.

" But it is not enough to say that we do not *see* them ; we do not *wish* to see them ; for as soon as an unexpected and unfamiliar fact appears, we try to fit it into the framework of the commonplaces of acquired knowledge,

and we are indignant that any one should dare to
experiment further."

It is strange to notice that men of the most sober
minds in regard to all other matters usually approach
the study of psychical phenomena with an obvious
prejudice and foregone conclusion which tends to falsify
their judgment. It seems that when they study these
phenomena their object is not to obtain enlighten-
ment and ascertain the truth, but to combat them as
though they had an interest in proving that they do not
exist. (They rightly call for the opinion of scientific men,
but should a scientist of universally recognised authority
and whose testimony they themselves have appealed to
tell them that he has assured himself of the reality of
psychical phenomena, he seems, *ipso facto*, to have lost
all credit in their eyes, and they no longer put faith
in his word.) They accept the observations which a celebrated astronomer may make on the stars; but if he says
that he has closely observed and verified some of these
phenomena, which, I do not know for what reason, are
opposed to their pre-conceived ideas, they say that he is
the victim of hallucination, or assert that he has been
deceived.

They believe in experiments made in a laboratory by
a physiologist of universally recognised scientific attainments, and admit, just as though they had themselves
seen it, all that he describes under the field of his microscope. But, let the same physiologist tell them that he
has seen in a room a few square yards in extent, phenomena which they have not seen for themselves, and they
claim that he has been duped by a coachman hidden in
the room, whom he was not able to discover after a stringent examination. In fact, if similar arguments had not
really been brought forward, we should not dare seriously
to state them, so greatly do they exceed the limits of
common sense.

With regard to those who wish to devote themselves
to the study of psychical phenomena, while recognising

the necessity of submitting these phenomena to a methodical and strictly scientific investigation, they should take into consideration that each science has its peculiar method, and that each science uses, for the study of its own phenomena, different instruments, specially adapted to the nature of the phenomena which are to be observed and the conditions in which they present themselves. Would it not be absurd to observe the stars with a microscope and examine microbes with a telescope? What should we say of one who tried to study the course of the stars with a balance and the method of successive weighings? And yet, among those who wish to devote themselves to the study of these psychical phenomena, there are many who make claims which are not less unreasonable than these.

Psychical phenomena are of a very special character, and account must be taken of this character in any serious and profitable study of them.

The first work ought to be that of methodical classification, commencing at the most simple and rising progressively to the most complex, comparing together, as far as possible, those which seem to be mutually dependent.

We shall then see what experimental method ought to be adopted. Doubtless, in many instances, we may be able to make use of processes and instruments which we have employed for other purposes; photography and weighing machines ought certainly to render some service; but it is very probable that it will be necessary to design new instruments, such as the sthenometer, specially adapted to the nature and conditions of the new phenomena which form the subject of research.

CHAPTER II

EXTERNALISATION OF SENSIBILITY

EXTERNALISATION of sensibility is a phenomenon which lies on the confines between hypnotic and psychical phenomena.

When I made my first experiments in hypnotism I observed, on several occasions, a new and strange phenomenon which impressed me all the more because, up to then, it had never been reported by any of the authors who, about that time, were commencing the scientific study of the various phenomena of hypnosis. In a treatise on Hypnology, which I published in 1892, I referred to this phenomenon in the chapter on Hypnotic Sleep in the following words:—

"I ought to describe here a phenomenon which has scarcely been noticed by writers. This phenomenon may, however, be of some importance in the practice of hypnotism. It is exhibited by means of a point, preferably of metal, such as the blade of a pair of scissors or a compass needle; but any other object, slightly sharpened, such as a pencil, a piece of wood or whalebone cut to a point give similar results, though somewhat less defined.

"In these conditions the phenomenon is produced, even in a waking somnambulistic condition, in certain subjects, but it is most intense in hypnotic sleep.

"If we hold one of these instruments between the fingers, as a pen is held for writing, and direct the point between the eyes of the person who is being experimented upon, the latter perceives, exactly at the point aimed at by the instrument, a well-defined sensation of tingling and weight. When this first sensation has been obtained, by allowing the instrument to remain motionless for a few seconds, a short distance from the skin, we may keep it always at the same distance, and move it slowly in various directions, so as to present it successively to various points on the face, and even of the body, of very sensitive persons. The subject, whose eyes have been closed from the commencement of the experiment, will be able to follow exactly the course travelled by the point, and, at any moment, indicate precisely the point opposite to which the instrument has stopped.

"The distance at which this sensation may be perceived, as well as the range of the sensitive surface, varies with the nervous sensibility of the person experimented upon, and it is a good means of quickly ascertaining to what degree a person may be hypnotised. I found that the sensitive distance varied on an average from one to ten centimetres, so that with the majority of easily hypnotisable persons, this result could be obtained by presenting the point at a distance of about one centimetre from the skin.

"I found that this special sensibility increases along with the hypnotic sensibility, and, like that, can be developed by training."

This phenomenon, which I designated, at that time, by the name of sensibility at a distance has, of late years, been closely studied by M. de Rochas and described by him under the name of Externalisation of Sensibility, a much better description.

"As soon as we magnetise a subject," says Colonel Albert de Rochas, "his sensibility disappears at the surface of the skin. This is an old-established fact, but what was not known was that this sensibility is externalised; there is formed around the body of the subject, as soon as this state of rapport commences, a sensitive layer, a few centimetres from the skin. If the magnetiser, or any other person, pinches, pricks, or strokes the subject's skin, he feels nothing; but, if the magnetiser performs the same operations on the sensitive layer, the subject experiences corresponding sensations. Further, as the profundity of the hypnosis increases, a series of similar layers is formed, almost equidistant, the sensibility of which decreases proportionately to their distance from the body."

To sum up, as we have seen, this phenomenon of externalisation of sensibility consists in this, that at the same time that anæsthesia is produced by the hypnotic state, the sensibility, which has disappeared from the surface of the skin, is not lost, but is transferred to points exterior to the subject.

This phenomenon would be remarkable enough, as we have described it, but it is rendered even more striking and much more extraordinary by the more precise experiments we are about to relate. In these experiments the sensibility of the subject no longer remained vaguely distributed over a layer of air, more or less near to the skin of the subject, but could be directed at will and fixed on various objects. We were thus enabled, by varying the nature, form, and position of these objects, or by moving them further from the subject, to produce much more conclusive experiments which were calculated to meet all objections. In these, we find that a well-defined body, absolutely distinct and independent of the subject's body, becomes charged with its sensibility, in such a way that the subject will feel, clearly and distinctly, everything which impresses this body, exactly as though these impressions were directly received upon his own body in its normal condition.

The subject who volunteered for these experiments is very easily hypnotisable. The first time I hypnotised him, I obtained at once the lethargic state, then, by the usual process, it was easy for me to make him pass into the cataleptic condition, and, in this phase of hypnosis, I obtained fascination, an indication of very great suggestibility. From catalepsy, I quickly brought him back again to lethargy, and then made him pass into somnambulism. My subject very quickly arrived at the third degree of somnambulism, in which state he was insensible to all excitations from without; but he was in direct communication with me; he heard and answered me if I ordered him to do so. He was essentially sugges-

tionable and executed unconsciously and involuntarily
the suggestions I made; he even carried out post-
hypnotic suggestions; in a word, his personality disappeared completely: finally, he became amnesic on
awaking.

Such being the state of the subject, I first of all satisfied myself that he was completely insensible by sharply
pricking the skin at various parts of the body with a pin.
I ascertained that he was everywhere in a state of complete anæsthesia. I then placed a glass filled with water
between his hands, whilst a person standing behind him
held his hands closely over his eyes. I then pricked the
surface of the water in the glass with a pin, and immediately the subject, by the expression on his countenance and an involuntary movement, showed that he
experienced pain. I then asked what he felt, and he
replied: "You pricked my left hand." I then applied the
point of the pin to the outside of the glass, not touching
the water: the subject experienced no sensation. I again
plunged the pin into the water, without touching the
glass in any way, and immediately the subject repeated:
"You have pricked my left hand." The experiment was
repeated several times: each time I pricked the glass he
felt nothing, but, when I pricked the water it contained,
he instantly felt the pricking and finally said, with some
impatience: "You are hurting me; you are pricking me."

I will simply remark, with regard to this experiment,
that when I prick the glass I put my pin very forcibly
against the outside, the subject might therefore feel a
certain pressure on his hands, a sensation of contact; if
there had been auto-suggestion, it would certainly have
shown itself at that moment, and yet he felt nothing.
When I pricked the surface of the water, on the contrary,
I was careful not to touch the glass with my fingers; no
mechanical pressure was transmitted, and yet he then
clearly felt the pricking.

I ought to add that the first time I made this experiment with this subject, I informed neither the subject nor
those present what I intended doing, and for a very good

B

reason—because I did not know myself. The idea of attempting the externalisation of sensibility only came to me when I saw the subject arrive so easily at the highest degree of somnambulism, and I put my idea into execution without saying anything.

In another experiment, after having placed the subject in the same somnambulistic state, and having, at first, as before, placed between his hands a glass of water in which I had externalised his sensibility, I took the glass and held it myself a short distance in front of the subject, but without any contact with him : he experienced the pricking in the same way, but it seemed to me that the impression was a little less strong. The glass of water was then placed on a table in front of the subject and the results were the same.

At this same sitting, I made a new experiment. Instead of pricking the surface of the water with a pin, I slowly pressed the extremities of my thumb and index-finger into the water, and quickly brought them together. The subject, as before, said that he felt pain, but with this difference, that when interrogated as to what he experienced, he immediately replied: "You are pinching me" and not "You are pricking me," as on the other occasions.

Several times over I pricked and pinched the water alternately; it did not once happen that the subject was deceived. He said: "You are pricking me" each time I placed the pin in the water, and "You are pinching me" each time I pinched the water with my fingers.

I tried charging other substances than water with the sensibility of the subject. First I took a small glass plate, which I covered with velvet. As before, the subject was put into a somnambulistic and anæsthetic condition, and the prepared plate was placed between his hands; he experienced just as clearly the prickings made in the velvet covering.

Cardboard did not give very appreciable results. At all events, under the circumstances in which I experimented, it did not seem to me to be so easily charged with the sensibility of the subject.

Wood was more favourable for the experiment. Some small boards, placed for a few moments in contact with the subject's body, were charged with his sensibility in such a manner that, after they were removed from him, he felt the prickings which were made in the wood.

I also experimented with a ball of putty, to which I had vaguely given the contour of the subject, at the same time fixing it on a glass plate. I sensitised the putty by bringing it near the subject's body, and made him hold the glass plate between his hands. After a few moments, on my holding the glass plate myself a short distance from the subject, he felt, sometimes in his head, sometimes in his body, sometimes in his limbs, prickings which were made in the portions of the putty representing the different parts of his body. Then, on my cutting off some of the subject's hairs while he was asleep, and putting them in the part of the putty representing his head, he strongly protested when they were pulled, saying that his hair was being pulled out.

In order to take account of the manner in which the sensation came to the subject, and of the rapidity with which it was perceived, I instituted the following experiment.

The subject was placed in a state of somnambulism, the glass of water put between his hands and charged with his sensibility, as in the first experiments. I then noticed that he instantly felt the pricking sensation when I plunged the pin in the water. One of my assistants in these experiments, M. Leuliette, kept his eyes fixed attentively on a chronometer, whilst the two other assistants signalled to him the precise moment when I pricked the surface of the water with the pin, and when the subject's face showed an expression of pain. There was no appreciable lapse of time between the two actions. I then gave the glass of water to an assistant, who held it in his left hand, and held the subject's left hand in his right. It was found that a fraction of a second elapsed between the time when I pricked the surface of the water with a pin, and the moment when the subject's face showed pain. On making a chain of two and then of three persons, holding each other's hands between the glass of water and the subject, I noticed an increasing slowness of the sensation. On employing five persons I obtained a delay of nearly two seconds between the moment when the pin touched the surface of the water, and that when the expression on the subject's face showed that he felt the sensation.

I now come to an experiment even more curious than those which I have narrated. The subject, being put to sleep, and brought, as usual, into a somnambulistic condition so that the whole of the cutaneous surface was completely insensible, I placed before him another person, awake and in a normal condition, who took hold of the subject's hands in such a way that his right hand held the subject's left, and his left the subject's right. Matters having been thus arranged, I caused, by suggestion, the sensibility of the subject to pass into the person in front of him; that is to say, I suggested to the subject that he should no longer feel anything himself, but that he should feel everything that was done to the person in front.

I then pricked with a pin the right leg of the person who was awake; the subject immediately said to me: "You are pricking my left leg." It was, in point of fact, the leg which was opposite to the subject's left leg. I pricked the waking person in the left arm, and the sleeping subject said: "You are pricking my right arm." I pricked the waking person on the ear, and the subject said: "You are pricking me on the head." I then observed that under the influence of the pricking the waking person made an involuntary movement which the subject asleep felt through the contact of hands—a muscular movement which informed him of the moment when the pricking was made. Admitting this hypothesis for a moment, how does it explain the fact that the subject distinguished between the pricking made on the right arm or the left leg, and that made on the right leg or the left arm, or on the head?

But there is a much more simple method of nullifying the objection that might be deduced from the unconscious movements of the waking person being communicated to the person asleep, that is, by cutting off all communication between the two subjects. That is what I did in the following experiments. After having caused the sensibility of the subject in the somnambulistic state to pass to the waking subject, the hands of the sleeper were released. The two subjects were thus completely separated; there was no material contact between them. I then pricked the limbs of the waking person and the subject felt the prickings in his corresponding limbs, that is to say, the limbs opposite to his own, the right side corresponding with the left side, as well as prickings in the head. If I pinched a limb instead of pricking it, the subject quickly recognised the difference, saying : " You are pinching me," instead of " You are pricking me," as he had done on the other occasions.

I will mention in the last place an experiment which was also very interesting. After bringing my subject into a somnambulistic condition, I placed him before a wall and so arranged the lights that his shadow was projected directly on to it. I suggested to him that his sensibility should be entirely transferred to his shadow, that is, that he himself would feel everything that was done to the form projected on the wall. I then pricked the wall at different points around the shadow. He did not move and experienced no sensation. I then pricked the shadow itself; the subject immediately made an abrupt movement and complained strongly. I commenced again at various points outside the shadow : the subject felt absolutely nothing ; but, whenever the shadow was touched, the sensation seemed to be more acute than in the majority of the other experiments. The subject complained of his head when I pricked the head of the shadow, and felt pain in the arm or leg when I pricked the shadow on the wall ; and when, at one time, I passed my hand over the wall where the shadow's head was, he said : " You are scratching me."

The experiments which I have just related suggest
some interesting considerations. In the first place, the
externalisation of sensibility to the degree which I have
described is a very rare phenomenon, whether it be
because it is only witnessed in a hypnotic state which
few subjects are capable of reaching, or, more especially,
because it constitutes one of those special faculties still
very little known, which are more or less developed in
certain subjects, but which only attain a very high degree
in a small number of cases. I have no hesitation in pre-
ferring this latter hypothesis; in fact, the subjects I
observed presented this phenomenon in the third and
even the second degree of somnambulism. Now, these
hypnotic phenomena, without being frequent, are met
with from time to time, though this was the first time I
had met with this externalisation of sensibility during
the many years I had devoted myself to research.

I ought to remark, in the second place, that these
phenomena are not always presented with the same
intensity. Each time I have operated with this subject,
I have always obtained the externalisation of sensibility,
but sometimes his sensations were vague and lacked dis-
tinctness, whether because he was not in so good a condition before the hypnosis and sleep was not so well
developed, or because some external circumstances might
have interfered with the experiments. Thus, in certain
cases of pricking, he clearly experienced a pain, but was
not able to define its nature. He said : " You are hurting
me," but he could not distinguish whether he was being
pricked or pinched.

In other cases, he could easily distinguish the kind of
sensation and the nature of the pain, but could not locate
it in the region corresponding with the part touched on
the object or person. Thus, in one of the experimental
séances, the sensation, which was none the less very clear,
was constantly felt on the left hand. In other experiments, the subject felt the prickings and the impressions
made on the object charged with his sensibility, always
in the head. In other circumstances he succeeded in

locating the sensations to a certain extent, but still somewhat imperfectly. Thus, he ascribed to the head all that
was done to the head and the upper part of the body of
the other subject, and to the body all that was done to his
trunk and limbs. I have also noticed that, in certain
cases when the sensations were vague and not well located,
if I awakened the subject and hypnotised him again, I
obtained very clear sensations with very remarkable precision of localisation.

In certain cases, on asserting to the subject by suggestion, that his sensibility had left him and had been
transferred to an object or person, we secured very clear
phenomena. It is, of course, to be understood that this
suggestion was only made before commencing the experiments, and we were careful that at the time of carrying
out the experiments the subject should not be forewarned
as to the various movements effected.

How then can we explain these phenomena of externalisation of sensibility? I will say at once that I have
witnessed the phenomenon, and have had it confirmed by
several witnesses; but I have not, up to now, found any
satisfactory explanation. I only wish to reply here to
certain objections or interpretations which some might be
tempted to give, and which must be rejected.

First of all, I think it is useless to discuss that of
fraud; those who have witnessed my experiments, and
the conditions in which they were carried out, can have
no doubt as to this.

The unconscious connivance of the subject is a more
serious objection. We know that subjects in somnambulism possess an extreme keenness of all the senses; the
subject might see through the eyelids; he might be aware,
through the sense of hearing, of all that is taking place
and react unconsciously or be influenced by auto-suggestion. The objection of unconscious connivance, and that
of auto-suggestion on the subject's part may be treated as
one, and the arguments which I will give reply equally to
both.

1. I will recall that in the first experiment I made

the subject could not know what I was going to do, because I did not know myself. I had no idea of attempting externalisation of sensibility with him until after he was in a somnambulistic condition.

2. When the glass of water was no longer between his hands, but was placed *behind* him, he felt the pricking and yet he could see nothing. Nor could he hear anything because the act of plunging the pin into the water did not make more noise than any other movement, which had no effect upon him.

3. When the subject held the glass of water between his hands, if I pricked the glass itself, he certainly experienced a sensation of contact. If there had been autosuggestion, it is then that it would have been developed. But nothing of the sort took place, he felt nothing; but, if I pricked the water without touching the glass, that is to say, without his experiencing the slightest direct sensation, he gave evidence that he felt the pricking.

I shall not dwell at length upon the objection made a little while ago before the Society of Hypnology by M. Mavroukakis. Our colleague showed to the Society a hypnotised person, holding a glass of water between his hands, and, while pricking the glass of water, he said to him : " I am pricking your head, your arm, or your leg." The subject evidently experienced all the sensations which were thus suggested to him. No one who had ever witnessed experiments in externalisation of sensibility could have thought that these proceedings resembled them. No one has ever denied that it is possible to suggest to a hypnotised subject a pricking, burning, or any other sensation, at any particular point. Here, the glass of water added nothing, and this experiment only demonstrated verbal suggestion, which is known to every one.

In externalisation of sensibility, on the contrary, we take all the necessary precautions that the subject shall have no foreknowledge in any way of the time or manner of pricking the object charged with his sensibility. We are careful to perform similar manipulations on surrounding objects, or on objects similar to those to which we have transferred his sensibility. This was demonstrated in our experiments with the glass, where the glass only was pricked; and yet the subject, *without foreknowledge*, clearly showed that he experienced impressions made on the object charged with his sensibility and that he did not experience them when made around or on other objects.

Another explanation seemed to me for some time to be more plausible, and yet I have had to abandon it because of certain experiments I made. This explanation consisted in supposing that the operator, who practised the pricking on the sensitised object, unconsciously made a mental suggestion, which was received and understood by the hypnotised subject. This hypothesis would account for the fact that the subject experienced and distinguished the different kinds of sensations—prickings, burnings, pinchings, &c., and that he localised them in various parts of his body when these sensations were experienced by another subject placed in front of him; and, even in this case, the mental suggestion might just as well come from the subject operated upon as from the operator.

This hypothesis was shown to be inadequate when I witnessed in certain specified cases a regular and progressive retardation of the sensation in the hypnotised subject. Whether the glass of water was held by the subject himself, or by one of three, four, or five persons in communication with the subject, the sensation ought to be equally rapidly perceived by him if the hypothesis of mental suggestion is true : it should be instantaneous in each case, and there should not be the regular retardation which we witnessed in certain circumstances.

By another experiment I tried to eliminate all possibility of thought transference.

In an adjoining room I had prepared two bottles, filled with warm and cold water respectively. A piece of string was attached to each of these bottles, so that the experimenter could lift and hold them, without knowing which contained the warm and which the cold water.

The two bottles thus prepared were brought in a box, and no one about the subject knew which was warm and which cold.

I then took each of the bottles in turn by the string, not knowing their temperature, and brought them within about a foot of the subject. Without hesitation he declared that he experienced a sensation of heat, then of cold, and always attributed the sensation of heat to the hot bottle, and that of cold to the other. All the persons verified the fact that he was not mistaken, and that he identified at a distance the warm bottle and the cold bottle.

The temperature of the warm bottle was not sufficiently high for it to be distinguished at this distance, and the two bottles being identical, no one could transmit any idea to the subject.

One of our colleagues made the following observation :—

" Every living body may be, in certain circumstances, a more or less active source of electricity. When we bring near the subject any pointed object held in the hand, such as a needle or pin, or even when the operator simply brings his finger near, an electrical discharge is produced, which causes the subject to give evidence of a sensation by hypnotic hyperæsthesia, and would explain the effect produced by this current, too feeble to be perceived by any one else."

We accept all the hypotheses, and desire to examine and study seriously all that are presented to us. In order to verify this one, we took a semi-circular metallic plate, which we placed by the side of the subject, in communication with the earth, without direct communication between the subject and the metallic plate. If the hypothesis of an electrical current were true, the electricity discharged by the point or by the fingers ought, owing to the presence of the metallic plate, to be lost in the earth and the subject would feel nothing. After interposing the plate, we brought the points or fingers near to the subject in exactly the same manner as before. The phenomenon was produced through the plate, and the subject experienced the same sensations as in the previous experiments made without any interposition. We therefore eliminate the hypothesis of a sensation due to an electrical current discharged by the operator.

In the course of these experiments a new and absolutely unexpected phenomenon presented itself.

The subject, after awaking, was always absolutely ignorant and unconscious of what had taken place while he was asleep, consistently with the law governing the state of memory in the hypnotic condition in which he was placed. It should be noted that the subject, having absolute confidence in us, did not know the kind of experiments we were making during his sleep; and we were careful after he awoke not to speak before him of the observations which had been made.

But, on several occasions, the day after the experiments, the subject told me that he had dreamt or felt in the night, when asleep, that he was being pricked or pinched, or that his hair was being pulled, all corresponding exactly with the experiments made during the previous day. One day even it happened that I had left the laboratory for a few moments to allow some colleagues to make certain experiments without any participation on my part. During this time one of them, wishing to try contact at a greater distance, flourished a cane around the subject. The following day, the subject told me that, during the night, he felt blows on the head with a stick.

We sought for the explanation of this phenomenon. It could not be the remembrance of what had been done during the hypnotic condition, which reappeared during the subject's sleep. In fact, we know by the laws of memory in hypnotic states, that for the subject to be able to recall to memory what has taken place in his hypnotic condition, he must again be plunged into a similar condition. Now, his sleep at night would not be a condition analogous to that in which we were making the experiments, because, after awaking from his hypnotic state, we know that he had lost the memory of all that had happened; if he had passed into a similar state during the night, he would also have lost, on awaking, the memory of what he had felt whilst in that state, and would not therefore have been able to tell us.

However, another observation made in the course of the same experiments put us on the track of what we believe to be the true explanation of this phenomenon.

When there was produced in the subject a sensation of pricking or pinching, by an action at a distance, if we left him quiet, we often noticed that a few moments after the first movement, the subject brought his hand to the sensitive spot, as though he still felt a painful sensation. If we had made numerous prickings, pinchings, &c., at different parts of the body, and then observed the subject, without having made a negative suggestion, we saw him turn, stroke the different parts of the body with his hands, and, if the excitations were very numerous and violent, writhe and moan as if he was still suffering, and simultaneously in all the parts affected.

The error must not be committed of taking these phenomena either for auto-suggestions or as indications of simulation on the subject's part. In fact, on the one hand, auto-suggestions, which sometimes come when the subject is not in deep sleep, or at the beginning of the hypnosis, do not occur in the circumstances or manner we have indicated ; and, on the other hand, the symptoms of the deep hypnotic state persist and can be reproduced at this moment.

We concluded that an excitation produced at a distance, in a subject whose sensibility has been externalised, leaves a persistent painful trace. We do not know the nature of the sensation thus experienced by the subject. It may probably be more vague than those which are perceived directly in the waking state. We do know that the subject habitually distinguishes between certain kinds of sensations, such as prickings, pinchings, heat, &c.

In the second place, and this is one of the principal conclusions of these last experiments, these excitations leave a persistent trace, as painful and definite as the sensation itself. We may compare them with a blow which leaves a sensible contusion, or with a mosquito sting which leaves an irritation behind : if later, the rubbing of a garment or contact with an object excites the sensitive part, the pain reappears very much as when it was first caused.

We may remark also that in these actions which we exercise at a distance on the subject, we act on a plane which is not clearly defined. The different points from which we can excite the sensibility of the subject, form, if I may so express it, a virtual plane situated in space. The result is that the excitation we produce is, in spite of us and unknown to us, now stronger, now weaker, which explains the differences in the intensity and clearness of the sensations perceived by the subject.

CHAPTER III

SPONTANEOUS PHENOMENA—MULTIPLE PERSONALITY
AND ABNORMAL CONSCIOUSNESS—ABNORMAL FACUL-
TIES IN HYPNOTIC SUBJECTS

WE observe occasionally, in certain special subjects, abnormal phenomena which present themselves spontaneously. These phenomena are, in some cases, the manifestation of abnormal knowledge, unconsciously to the subject, of the class we have seen produced in certain dreams; at other times, they seem to be connected with transmission of thought. Again, the facts of multiple personality seem to be connected with this class of phenomena. To give an idea of these multiple personalities I will give a résumé of the well-known case of Félida X.

Félida was born in Bordeaux in 1841, of healthy parents. She was intelligent and well-educated, and in later life had charge of a grocer's shop. When fourteen years of age, after puberty, her health was disturbed, her temper became gloomy, and she had her first fits, which came on every five or six days. They are thus described by Dr. Azam, who was called in to attend her:—

Félida X. is seated with some needlework on her knees; suddenly, without any warning, and, after a pain in the temples, more violent than usual, her head falls on to her chest, her hands stop working and fall inert beside her body, she sleeps, or appears to sleep, but it is a special kind of sleep, because neither noise nor excitation, pinchings nor prickings, will awaken her; further, this kind of deep, sudden sleep lasts two or three minutes; formerly it lasted much longer.

After this time, Félida awakes, but she is no longer

in the same intellectual state as before she went to sleep. Everything seems to be different. She raises her head, opens her eyes, smilingly greets the new-comers; her face brightens and is mirthful; she says but little, and she continues, humming all the time, the needlework she had previously begun. She rises, walks quickly, and scarcely complains of the thousand pains from which a few minutes previously she had suffered; she attends to the household duties, goes out, walks about the town, makes visits, sets about some kind of work, her manners and gaiety those of a young healthy girl of her own age. Her character is completely changed; from being sad she has become gay; and her vivacity borders on boisterousness, her imagination is almost over-excited; she shows emotion, pleasurable or the reverse, at the least thing; from being completely indifferent to all that happens, she has become sensitive in the highest degree.

When in this state she remembers perfectly all that has happened previously, when in similar conditions, as well as in her normal state. I should add that she has always maintained that the state, whatever it may be, in which she is when she is spoken to, is her normal state, which she calls the right one in contradistinction to the other, which she calls a convulsion.

In this condition, as in the other, her intellectual and moral faculties, though quite different, are undoubtedly complete; there is no delirious notion, no false appreciation, no hallucination. I might even say, that in this second state, in this "condition," all her faculties appear more highly developed and efficient. This second condition, in which pain is not felt, is much superior to the other; particularly in the important fact already noted, that while it lasts Félida knows what has happened, not only during all the previous attacks, but also during her normal condition, whilst normally she knows nothing that has happened during her attacks.

After a period which, in 1858, lasted three or four hours nearly every day, Félida's gaiety suddenly disappears, her head falls into the state of torpor previously described.

After three or four minutes she opens her eyes and returns to her normal condition.

The change is scarcely perceptible, because she continues her work with almost intense eagerness; most frequently it is some sewing commenced during the previous period. It is strange to her (since her somnambulistic condition is forgotten on awaking), and it becomes an effort of imagination for her to understand it. Nevertheless she goes on with it as well as she can, lamenting her unfortunate condition. Her relatives, who are used to this state, help her to understand.

A few minutes previously she had been singing some ballad; when asked to sing it again she was entirely ignorant of what was meant; when spoken to concerning a visit she had just received, she did not remember that she had seen any one. I think I ought to define the extent of this forgetfulness; it only refers to what has passed while she is in the second condition: no general ideas previously acquired are affected; she can read, write, count, cut out, sew, and do many other things perfectly which she could do before her illness, or which she has learned during previous normal periods.

If I had any doubts as to the complete separation of these two existences, they would have been dispelled by what I am about to relate. A young man of about eighteen or twenty years of age had known Félida since her childhood and used to come to the house. A great affection existed between them, and they were engaged to be married.

One day Félida, who was more sad than usual, said to me, with tears in her eyes, that her illness was becoming worse, her body was growing larger, and she felt sick every morning; in a word, she made me believe that she was *enceinte*. From the disturbed looks of those around my suspicions were confirmed. In fact, in the attack which shortly followed, Félida said to me before the same people: "I know perfectly well what I have said; you must have understood me; I tell you plainly I believe I am pregnant." In this second condition her pregnancy did not disturb her, and she was as lively as usual.

Having become *enceinte* during her second condition, she was ignorant of it during her normal state, and only knew of it when in her other similar condition; but this ignorance could not last; a neighbour, before whom she had expressed herself very clearly, and who was unduly sceptical, believed that Félida was acting a part, and brutally repeated to her the confidences she had made during the attack. The discovery affected the girl so much that she had hysterical convulsions, and I had to remain in attendance on her for three hours.

Félida shortly afterwards married the young man, and from 1859 to 1876 ten children were born, but only two of them lived. The periods of attack, or second condition, which, in 1859, only lasted for about one-tenth of her existence, gradually increased in duration until they became equal to her normal state, and then became further extended until they occupied almost the whole of her existence.

It has several times happened that she has gone to sleep at night in her normal condition and awakened in the morning in the second one, without either she or her husband being conscious of the change, which, therefore, took place during sleep. This transition has, moreover, become almost imperceptible by its rapidity, even in the waking state, which makes the situation very sad, because of the constant gaps produced in her memory, and the disturbances in her business and family relationships.

Abnormal knowledge, some examples of which will be given, is comparable with certain facts observed in the dream condition. Nevertheless, in the cases here reported, it will be noticed that the facts were not observed while the subject was in a sleep, but, as may be assumed from the circumstances, in a kind of spontaneous hypnotic condition.

The following examples are taken from Aksakof's work :—

"For some time" (reports Mr. John Young) "my wife

was under the influence of German spirits : she spoke and sang in German for several evenings in succession.

"No one in our circle understood this language. Desiring to assure myself of the fact, I invited a German doctor, Herr Tuler, to come and give me his opinion. He came twice and conversed with the medium in German for more than an hour on each occasion. His astonishment was great, but his joy at being able to speak in his mother-tongue was greater. In addition to German, my wife has spoken in Italian, a language of which she is equally ignorant." [1]

Judge Edmonds reports the case of his daughter, who only knew English or French, speaking in Hindustani, Spanish, Polish, Greek, and Italian, when in a trance condition. One day, he relates, his daughter maintained a long conversation with a Greek in his native language. " At the time the emotion of M. Evangelides (the Greek) was so great that it drew the attention of those present : we asked him the reason, but he avoided making any reply. It was only at the end of the séance that he told us that, previously, he had not witnessed any spiritistic manifestations, and that, in the course of the conversation, he had made various experiments in order to ascertain the nature of this class of phenomena. These experiments consisted of broaching various subjects through my daughter, concerning which she certainly could possess no knowledge, and, in frequently changing the theme, passing abruptly from matters of a private character to political, philosophical, and physiological questions. In reply to our interrogations he assured us that the medium understood the Greek language and spoke it correctly." [2]

Aksakof cites another remarkable example of knowledge not learned : that of a child "who played a piece without ever having learned music," as testified by Mr. N. Tallmadge, formerly senator and governor of Wisconsin, father of the medium.

The following is his statement :—

" In the month of June, 1853, on my return from New

[1] Aksakof, *Spiritism and Animism.*   [2] *Ibid.*, p. 358.

York, where I had observed several spiritistic manifestations, I went to a writing medium, who lived near me, and received a message advising me to organise a private circle in my own house, and predicting that a medium would be found who would surpass all my expectation.

" I expressed a desire to know the name of this medium, and was told it would be my daughter. ' Which?' I asked; ' because I have four.' ' Emily,' was the reply. Then I was enjoined to place Emily at the piano when the séances were organised. Emily was my youngest daughter, thirteen years of age. I ought to mention that she did not know much music, and had never played any air whatever. . . . I soon succeeded in organising this circle. I gave Emily a sheet of paper and a pencil. Her hand traced some straight lines which formed a stave. Then she put in the notes and added the signs. This done, she dropped the pencil and tapped the table as though touching the keys of an instrument. I then remembered that I was to place her at the piano. After a moment's hesitation she complied with my request, and sat down at the piano with the assurance of an accomplished artist.

" She attacked the keyboard resolutely, and executed Beethoven's Grand Valse in a manner which would have done honour to a good musician. Then she played several other known airs. She then played an unknown air, at the same time singing the improvised words corresponding with it."[1]

To these spontaneous phenomena we will add some facts, which, it is true, belong rather to the domain of hypnotism. We shall examine them here in order to show the relations which exist between facts of a hypnotic character and certain psychical phenomena.

The cases we have given are those in which a hypnotic or suggestive action is manifested at a distance, without the subject being able to perceive, by the aid of the normal senses, the influence exercised upon him. There is therefore here also the manifestation in the hypnotised subject of a new perceptive faculty, which does

[1] Aksakof, *Spiritism and Animism*, p. 370.

not exist in the normal state, and which is independent of the sensory organs, through which he is ordinarily in relation with the external world.

The first case refers to two experiments in inducing sleep at a distance, which were published some years ago in the *Annales des Sciences Psychiques*.

In September 1892 Mr. X. and his family were spending a holiday in the small town of Amélie-les-Bains.

There had been much talk during the year among the visitors, of the séances given at the Casino by a young man of the district, who called himself Dockman. Mr. X. attended through curiosity. The medium, who was about twenty years of age, dark and spare of figure, and evidently very nervous, had, it appears, three years previously, served as subject to a naval doctor, and these experiments had caused him to take up the vocation of thought-reader. Every one knows this class of performance, where one of the audience endeavours, more or less successfully, to transmit his will to the medium, without words or gesture, and even without contact, by a simple mental effort.

The penetration of the young mountaineer appeared to him to be frequently defective, and the medium himself confessed to him that he tried to guess by all sorts of indications the intentions of the thought-transmitter. "You ought," said Mr. X., laughing, "to go into trance so as to recover your former lucidity: if you feel inclined I am quite willing to render you this service."

Dockman appeared surprised and somewhat offended by this proposition. "It is I who send people to sleep," he said; "I am no longer put to sleep myself."

However, a few days later, probably to humour the mayor of the town, who seemed desirous of being present at a hypnotic séance, Dockman consented. Accordingly, one evening about six o'clock, before a circle of four or five persons, Mr. X. took hold of his thumbs and looked steadily at his eyes: at the end of a few minutes he fell asleep, if we may so call the comatose or cataleptic state into which he appeared to be plunged. His whole body was stiffened, his jaws contracted, and, with great difficulty, brief responses to questions were obtained. The awakening took place very slowly. A second sleep presented the same characteristics, except that the subject was more quickly awakened. Briefly, the subject did not seem very interesting, and Mr. X. did not see that much could be got out of him.

The following day, according to custom, Mr. X. went to the Casino about mid-day to have some coffee and be present at a rehearsal of a piece which was to be played that evening. The small theatre where the actors sang their vague ritornellos occupied the end of a garden, shaded by large trees; there were seats and tables for customers; and, overlooking the theatre and the garden, was a long terrace to which the habitués came every day to play cards.

Mr. X. seated himself on the terrace, and, while sipping his coffee, he looked down on the scene beneath him. Dockman was sitting in the garden with a friend, who was reading a newspaper; he presently almost turned his back and began to roll a cigarette. X. did not know how, but the idea came to him to try the experiment here described, and, with all the force of his will, he immediately put it into execution. Concentrating his mind entirely on this one thought, he looked steadfastly in Dockman's direction, and commanded him to stop all movements and to go to sleep. Dockman did not appear to perceive that X. was looking at him, but his actions quickly slackened, and his eyes became fixed. The unfinished cigarette remained in his hands, he suddenly dropped his eyelids, and became motionless as a statue. His friend raised his head, perceived his condition, questioned him, but obtained no response. A singer, seated at a neighbouring table, became frightened and screamed aloud. Mr. X. hastened and went down, and, in a few moments, by breathing quickly on his eyes, awoke his improvised subject, who did not even seem to know what had happened to him.

Mr. X. had made this experiment on the bare chance, not at all counting on success, and was himself astonished

at the result. On the following day he had the opportunity of repeating it. He reached the Casino about
half-past one. On this occasion Dockman was sitting on
the terrace by himself, at a table, writing a letter, bent
nearly double, his nose almost resting on the blotting-pad.
Mr. X.'s table was five or six yards away ; between them
was a party of four, playing cards. Mr. X. again concentrated himself with a nervous tension, which caused
him to vibrate from head to foot, and, while looking
quietly at Dockman, commanded him with all his power
to cease writing and go to sleep. The effect was less
rapid than before. It might be said that the subject
struggled against his will. After one or two minutes, he
gave visible signs of a thrilling sensation ; his pen remained suspended, as if he sought in vain for words : he
made a gesture with his hand as though throwing off an
obsessing influence ; then he tore up the letter he had
commenced and began to write another ; but his pen
soon remained fixed on the paper, and he went to sleep
in that position. X. went close up to him, with several
others who had stopped their games ; his whole body
was contracted and hard as a piece of wood ; they tried
unsuccessfully to bend one of his arms ; the stiffness was
only removed by means of passes ; the waking was accomplished by blowing on his eyes. When he had recovered
the use of his senses, Dockman begged Mr. X. not to
repeat these experiments ; he complained of having been
much fatigued by the former one. He affirmed, moreover, that he had gone to sleep on these two occasions
without having had the slightest suspicion that this
abrupt sleep had been caused by X. or by any one else.

It may, it is true, be claimed that in these two cases
the subject perceived, without knowing it, the person who
had already hypnotised him, and that he had then gone
to sleep by a phenomenon of auto-suggestion. We cannot,
from the data given, produce any absolute proof to the contrary. Nevertheless, we may ask ourselves why the subject did not go to sleep on several other occasions when
he was in the presence of the same experimenter. Why

should auto-suggestion be produced on these two occasions only on which the experimenter suggested sleep?

In the following case, taken from *États Profonds de l'Hypnose*, by Colonel de Rochas, we have a suggestion made at a distance after the subject had been brought back to the normal condition. And here the conditions of the experiment are such that they allow all possibility of auto-suggestion to be entirely eliminated.

"One evening," says Colonel de Rochas, "after a long séance, in which Madame X., already mentioned, had been magnetised by me and had given proofs of extraordinary sensitiveness, the idea came to me, on returning to my rooms, situated several miles away from her hotel, to give her the order to bring to me at eleven o'clock the following day a large book which I had lent her that day. I devoted all my energies to this order, which I repeated several times in a loud voice, supposing that, at this time, Madame X. would be asleep, or, at least, in calm and favourable isolation. I saw nothing of her on the following day, which did not astonish me; but, on the day after, I was greatly surprised when a servant brought me the book which Madame X. had certainly not had time to read. I hastened to her and said: 'My book then has not interested you, since you return it so quickly.' 'Quite the reverse,' she replied, 'but since eleven o'clock yesterday I have had the idea that you wished to have it, and I should have brought it myself had I not been so busy.'"

The following case is rather an example of thought-reading, for it will be noticed that the transmitter acted involuntarily and unconsciously. The fact is reported in the publications of the Angers Society of Medicine by Dr. Quintard. I give a summary of the report.

Ludovic X. is a child less than seven years of age, lively, gay, strong, in excellent health, and free from all nervous taint. His parents also show nothing suspicious from the neuro-pathological point of view. At the age of five, however, the child seemed to follow in the steps of the celebrated Inaudi. His mother, at this time, wishing to teach him the multiplication table, was surprised

to find that he could repeat it as well as she could!
Soon the child, taking to it as a sport, came to be able
to multiply large numbers in his head.

At the present time, one has only to read to him a
problem taken at hazard from a collection, and he, at
once, gives the solution. Take this, for example: "If
you put 25 francs 50 centimes in my pocket, I should
then have three times as much as I now have, less
5 francs 40 centimes. How much have I?" The problem
had scarcely been stated when the child, without even
taking time to think, replied correctly: "15 francs
45 centimes." At the end of the book, amongst the
more difficult problems, we find this one: "The radius
of the earth is equal to 6,366 kilometres. Find the distance to the sun, knowing that it is equal to 24,000
times the earth's radius. Express this distance in
leagues." The bantling, in his childish treble, gave, again
without hesitation, this solution, which is that in the
work: "38,196,000 leagues." The child's father, having
other things on his mind, did not, at first, pay much
attention to the performances of his son. At last, however, he gave heed to them, and, as his profession makes
him somewhat observant, he soon noticed that: (1) The
child scarcely listened, sometimes not at all, to the reading of the problem; (2) his mother, whose presence is
necessary for the success of the experiment, must always
have, before her eyes or in her mind, the required solution. From this he deduced that the boy did not make
any calculation, but guessed it, or, more correctly,
practised thought-reading on his mother; and he at
once decided to assure himself of this. Consequently,
he asked Madame X. to open a dictionary and ask her
son what page she had before her; the boy immediately
replied: "It is page 456," which was correct. This experiment was repeated ten times, each time with correct
results.

A phrase is written in a note-book, and, however long
it may be, it is sufficient, if it passes before the mother's
eye, for the boy to repeat the phrase word for word,

even though asked to do so by a stranger. It is not even necessary for the phrase, number, or word to be placed on paper; it is sufficient for it to be quite clear in the mother's mind for the son to perform the mental reading. But the child's triumph is in society games. He will tell, one after another, all the cards in the pack.

Dr. Quintard then discusses suggestion as an explanatory hypothesis.

"For it to be suggestion in the case before us, it must be proved that the mother has a certain psychical concentration, a certain degree of will-power indispensable to the success of the experiment. But the thought-reading is accomplished, most frequently, against her will. There is, in fact, a dark side to the picture. When the child reached the age to learn to read in earnest, his mother, who had devoted herself to this task, noticed, to her sorrow, that her son made no progress under her instruction. Guessing everything, he exercised neither judgment nor memory." Another physician, Dr. Tesson, examined the child and confirmed Dr. Quintard's observations before the Angers Society of Medicine.

In spontaneous somnambulism, we observe, in some subjects, phenomena which seem to belong, not to lucidity, but to a special faculty which gives them knowledge they do not possess in the waking state. This faculty is particularly developed, it seems, with regard to a fact which strongly impresses the subject, or in which he is specially interested.

The two following cases are quoted by Colonel de Rochas in his work *États Profonds de l'Hypnose*.

"Sergeant B. of the 113th Regiment, with whom I had made several experiments relative to polarity, was subject to fits of natural somnambulism, which occurred, on the average, every eight or ten days. The attack generally announced itself during the day by a great desire for sleep; and, at night, B. went to sleep as soon as he was in bed. After about two hours, he would rise, dress, go and seat himself at his table, and then, speaking quite aloud, he would frequently relate what was happening at that moment to persons connected with him; there were some piquant, but very annoying, revelations, because his room-mate was always there to receive them.

"A theft took place in the regiment; during the night the sergeant-major's purse was taken out of the pocket of his trousers, which were placed on a chair near his bed. Four or five nights afterwards, B., who had heard a good deal of talk about the affair, had his fit of somnambulism at the usual hour; but, instead of going to the table, he went out of the room, followed by his comrade, who was anxious to know what he was going to do. He went direct to the sergeant-major's room, looked at the trousers, smelled the floor, and, with bent head and open nostrils, like a dog following a scent, he went along the corridors, down the stairs, across the court, stopping sometimes to lie down on the ground and sniff, grumbling that he could scarcely sense any more; finally, after some turns towards the corners of the buildings where the imaginary thief that he was following seemed to have watched to see if any one was there, he went along a corridor, up a flight of stairs, and straight to the bed of a soldier he did not know at all, and in whose room he had never set foot. There, after a few seconds spent in examination, he said, 'Too late,' and returned to bed. On the following day the story was spread abroad. The soldier thus indicated had a bad reputation; he was arrested and an inquiry was held, in the course of which, astonished at the precision with which his movements were described, he said unguardedly: 'Who then followed me?' But this proof was not held sufficient and he was released, though every one was convinced of his guilt.

"Two years later at Grenoble a still more curious incident occurred, in that the seeker and the thief were probably the same person. A hundred franc note had been stolen, part of a much larger sum, from a drawer in an office in which a clerk had worked who served as one of my subjects.

"All his colleagues accused him, but being loth to believe him guilty, I sought to vindicate him by trying to make him find the real thief. Three days after the event I put him to sleep, and into as deep a hypnotic condition as possible. I then led him up to the drawer; I made him touch the bag, on which he recognised a contact, which he immediately followed with closed eyes, feeling the floor and the walls with his hands. He then led me up to the door of his room in the same house, but drew himself back, crying and whining, 'It was not I! It was not I!' Then he resumed the trace, descended a servant's staircase, crossed diagonally an inner court, where I observed some traces of footprints in the earth of a small garden, opened the locked double doors of a coach-house by raising the bar, and was preparing to proceed into the street when I stopped him.

"Interrogated as to the time at which the theft took place, he cried in terror: 'I see it! I see it!' and added, with tears, that it was at eleven o'clock on Sunday evening. It was discovered on Monday morning. I then took him again to the drawer, and gave him several things belonging to the employees. He felt these objects one after the other, then the bag which had contained the note, and declared that it was not the same contact; but, if the object given him belonged to himself, he quickly withdrew his hands, as if they were burnt, sobbing and protesting his innocence."

Some days afterwards a second experiment was made with the same results. Later, through other clues, convincing evidence of this young man's guilt was obtained, and he was dismissed. Although this case cannot be quoted as a certain proof, any more than the preceding, it gives not less interesting indications as to this sort of instinct, analogous to that which sets the hunting dog blindly on the track of game, and of the persistence in sleep of resolutions made in the waking state.

These different phenomena, whether spontaneous or connected with hypnotic states, serve to demonstrate to us, in their simplest form, certain psychical faculties, the development of which we shall study later; they also enable us to take account of the intimate relations which exist between certain hypnotic states and psychical phenomena.

CHAPTER IV

ABNORMAL DREAMS

WE shall proceed to consider the dream as an auto-suggestion, or a suggestion which is carried out by virtue of a
second condition occurring in the course of normal sleep.

This definition, which brings the dream within the
category of general hypnotic phenomena, and, particularly, into that of the phenomena of suggestion, is the
only one capable of giving us satisfaction by its exact
adaptation, not only to normal dreams, but also to the
numerous and various classes of super-normal dreams.

To say, in fact, that the dream is the psychical activity peculiar to sleep, and to connect the dream with the
phenomena of imagination, is no longer sufficient.

In fact, this is not a definition of the dream, because it
does not in any way explain what a dream really is; moreover, this definition has the serious defect of only being
applicable to a very limited class of dreams.

When we closely study the different categories of
dreams, we cannot help recognising all the characteristics
of a hypnotic phenomenon, and I will add that only
hypnotic phenomena can furnish the explanation of the
more complicated dreams. Finally, certain categories of
dreams undoubtedly belong to the highest class of hypnotic phenomena, in which are manifested the supernormal faculties of lucidity and premonition, which border
on psychical phenomena.

The origin of the suggestion which gives birth to the
dream may be very varied, the simplest being that which
comes through the sensory organs. These are the most
common kind of dreams with many people.

Pain is also frequently an origin of suggestion which

produces the dream. But those dreams do not go beyond the phenomenon of simple suggestion.

We observe also in dreams all the phenomena which may be met with in even the most profound hypnotic states. The first phenomena we see developed in the dream are thought transmission and mental suggestion. The first category of dreams, in which we see these abnormal faculties developed, is that of double dreams.

Mrs. Crowe, in her interesting work, *The Night Side of Nature*, quotes the following case of double dreaming :—

" I will relate a dream that occurred to two ladies, a mother and daughter, the latter of whom related it to me. They were sleeping in the same bed at Cheltenham, when the mother, Mrs. C., dreamt that her brother-in-law, then in Ireland, had sent for her, that she entered his room, and saw him in bed, apparently dying. He requested her to kiss him, but owing to his livid appearance, she shrank from doing so, and awoke with the horror of the scene upon her. The daughter awoke at the same moment, saying, ' Oh, I have had such a frightful dream ! ' ' Oh, so have I,' returned the mother ; ' I have been dreaming of my brother-in-law.' ' My dream was about him too,' replied Miss C. ' I thought I was sitting in the drawing-room, and that he came in wearing a shroud, trimmed with black ribbons, and approaching me he said, ' My dear niece, your mother has refused to kiss me, but I am sure you will not be so unkind.'

" As these ladies were not in the habit of regular correspondence with their relative, they knew that the earliest intelligence likely to reach them, if he were actually dead, would be by means of the Irish papers ; and they waited anxiously for the following Wednesday, which was the day these journals were received in Cheltenham. When that morning arrived, Miss C. hastened at an early hour to the reading-room, and there she learnt what the dreams had led them to expect : their friend was dead ; and they afterwards ascertained that his decease had taken place on that very night.

" They moreover observed that neither of them had

been speaking or thinking of this gentleman for some time previous to the occurrence of the dreams; nor had they any reason whatever for uneasiness with regard to him. It is a remarkable peculiarity in this case, that the dream of the daughter appears to be a continuation of that of the mother. In the one he is seen alive, in the other the shroud and black ribbons seem to indicate that he is dead, and he complains of the refusal to give him a farewell kiss."

We have placed this class of dreams here, because, in our opinion, they may be regarded as due to suggestion transmitted from one sleeper to another. This suggestion may take place through the sensory organs, as when one of the sleepers speaks or cries out aloud, evidencing his state of mind and inspiring the second sleeper with the ideas which form the source of suggestion. But the suggestion may also be mental, or arise from simple thought-transference, the two sleepers being in medium-istic conditions which permit of the one being the trans-mitting agent and the other the recipient.

That a dream can be suggested is not astonishing, but the suggested dream is sometimes only an impulse given to the subject. Then, the latter may go in his dream much further than the suggestion made, and see things of which the transmitter of the suggestion may know nothing, and which may have no existence in the subject's normal consciousness.

It is certain that a subject, whose whole attention is fixed by the phenomenon of dreaming on a topic which particularly interests him, such as the sickness from which he suffers and the means of alleviating it, may, for ex-ample, perceive in a much more precise manner than in the normal state, both the nature of his illness and the means of curing it. This is a phenomenon of abnormal knowledge, due to the dream, which I frequently employ with success on my hypnotic subjects.

The following case, which happened twelve years ago, is one of the first observed; it is given by Dr. du Prel in his *Experimental Psychology*.

"Associated with me were some friends, members of the Munich Society of Scientific Psychology, and I commenced this experiment on May 29, 1889. One of them, B.P., kindly offered himself as subject: another, D.G., as 'suggestioner.' The first named had received a bullet shot wound in the shoulder at Sedan and did not have the free use of his arm, which caused him great pain. He was placed in a hypnotic condition in a few minutes, a condition which was manifested by the automatic action of the cataleptic arm. Then on being questioned as to his wound and what would relieve his pain, he spoke briefly of morphia (an unsuitable means nevertheless) and of cold baths for the arm, which could only give him relief for about half-an-hour. There was no resemblance in this to the correct language of a medical somnambulist. Dr. G. then gave him these post-hypnotic instructions.

" 'You will dream to-night, you will recall the many and great sufferings your wound has already caused you ; you will call this to mind with so much force that your thoughts will be entirely occupied with finding a remedy for your pain. And I tell you that you will find one. You will learn in dream how to cure your malady completely. This remedy or curative method will so impress itself upon your memory that you will remember it perfectly when you awake to-morrow morning, and you will still remember it when you see Dr. du Prel, to whom you will relate your dream in all its details. What I have said to you, will and must happen.'

"Then he ordered him, as was always done, to awake free from pain, cheerful, and without fatigue.

"We then left B.P. to rest for a little time, after which he awoke quite easily. He had forgotten all that had happened, and we avoided all allusion to it. When I went to see him in the course of the following day, he thought that I had called respecting the affairs of the Society. I began to speak of the hypnotic séance of the day before, and he complained saying that it had not been successful. However, he had not had any pain after the séance, which was all the more astonishing as the weather was stormy.

But when he went to bed his pains became so acute that he had done nothing but turn over in bed, and was not able to get to sleep until three o'clock in the morning. Then he had an extraordinary dream. He heard a voice speaking, reproaching him for being negligent, and not using anything to relieve him of his pain; he must commence, he was told, by cold washings. Then, the voice continued, he must put on compresses of magnetised water, covered with india-rubber, and keep them on till they were completely dry: this would relieve, and, perhaps, put an end to his pain.

"The dream appeared to him so strange that he had told it to his wife the same morning.

"The latter confirmed the statement of her husband. I then explained to B.P. that the dream was the post-hypnotic accomplishment of the order which had been given him the previous day, and advised him to try the remedy he had dreamed. This was done, his wife magnetising the water for the compresses.

"I received a letter from her two months later, on July 24th; the improvement was perceptible, the pain had almost entirely disappeared, excepting during the very hot days, or when his office work was excessive or exhausting: on many days he had been quite free from pain. The treatment would be continued: she had even hypnotised her husband, and given him the suggestion of a second medical dream. He had, in fact, had a dream in which he was told that his sufferings would increase during the coming hot weather, which would necessitate a bath of magnetised water for his arm, and a compress. This dream was, however, somewhat confused, and not so clear and precise as the first, which she attributed to her lesser force of will.

"The patient wrote to me four months afterwards, that he was satisfied with his condition, but was compelled to continue the compresses to prevent the pain from returning. Two months later he told me that he was free from all pain, even though he had left off the bandages.

"This lasted for a whole year. The pain returned

later, the compresses having been discontinued for many months, and the summer of 1890 having been particularly stormy."

Here is another very peculiar dream in which the author was perfectly convinced that he had suggested a dream to himself; but, at the same time, he had the perception of a real fact which he could not previously have known.

This incident is narrated in the Report of the Dialectical Society of London, and was given by Mr. Cromwell Varley, F.R.S., the electrician for the Atlantic Cable Company.

"I had to catch the steamer" (says Mr. Varley) "that went early the next morning and was fearful of not waking in time, but I employed a plan which had often proved successful before, viz., that of willing strongly that I should wake at the proper time. Morning came and I saw myself in bed fast asleep; I tried to wake myself but could not. After a while I found myself hunting about for some means of more power, when I saw a yard in which was a large stack of timber and two men approaching; they ascended the stack of timber and lifted a heavy plank. It occurred to me to make my body dream that there was a bombshell thrown in front of me which was fizzing at the touch-hole, and when the men threw the plank down I made my body dream that the bomb had burst and cut open my face. It woke me, but with a clear recollection of the two actions—one, the intelligent mind acting upon the brain in the body, which could be made to believe any ridiculous impression that the former produced by willpower. I did not allow a second to elapse before I leapt out of bed, opened the window, and there were the yard, the timber, and the two men, just as my spirit had seen them. I had no previous knowledge at all of the locality; it was dark the previous evening when I entered the town, and I did not even know there was a yard there at all. It was evident I had seen these things while my body lay asleep. I could not see the timber until the window had been opened."

I will quote another example of suggested dream. In

this case it will be seen that on the occasion of the suggestive dream, a real phenomenon of lucidity was developed.

This narrative is reported by Dr. du Prel in his *Experimental Psychology*.

"I asked M. Notzing of Munich" (he writes), "our hypnotiser in the experiments carried out with Mdlle. Lina, to make this experiment: to give to Mdlle. Lina, when hypnotised, the post-hypnotic command, to dream of a certain person on the following night, to place herself *en rapport* with her, not to forget the dream, and to relate it on the following day.

"This post-hypnotic order therefore implied a transcendental psychological function in the domain of imagination, the accomplishment of which was postponed until the time of normal sleep. I had some reason to believe that the experiment would be successful, because hallucinations can be produced even in the waking state by post-hypnotic commands. A dream being fundamentally nothing but a succession of hallucinations, it is clear that a post-hypnotic hallucination may be referred also to the time of normal sleep, and be produced even more easily in that condition.

"But, as personal confidence ought not to play any part in scientific experiments, and the development of the experiment alone ought to bring conviction, I left the choice of a person who should be the subject of the dream to the experimenters, because malevolent sceptics might have objected that I had planned the thing with Lina.

"Those, therefore, who made this experiment caused the command to be given to Lina to dream on the following night of M. F. L. Lina had never seen him, and knew nothing of the place where he lived. This post-hypnotic order therefore implied a hallucination necessitating for its production a transcendental faculty—clairvoyance.

"The experiment succeeded completely. Lina was invited for the following afternoon to the house of one of the experimenters; she came and related, as an astonishing and inexplicable thing, that she had dreamed all night of

M. F. L. She described exactly his personality, giving various details as to his manner of talking, his dress, &c. She had seen him resting in an armchair in front of a villa, she spoke of the view that could be seen from the roof of the house over a lake, of a neighbouring wood, of the presence of a black St. Bernard dog, &c. All this might, it is true, have been in the imagination of the experimenters; and, if it be insisted upon, I admit that the hypothesis of thought-transmission is possible. But Lina also said—what none of the experimenters knew— that there were some young dogs in the villa, which was confirmed later on. She then stated that M. F. L. had under his care a lady whom she described: this description did not correspond at all with his wife, but with a friend of the family to whom it was recognised as applying.

"Lina's dream evidently did not correspond with what was taking place at the time, because M. F. L. did not stay outside the house during the night and the inhabitants of the villa were asleep: therefore, for the production of this dream, there must have been vision at a distance of time, either in the past, or in the future.

"This power of Lina's to see at a distance of time has moreover been observed several times, and there exist in connection with this phenomenon some notes drawn up and signed, *ante eventum*, naturally."

The preceding examples are sufficient to prove that we ought not to admit as correct the following statement by M. Bergson:—

"In sleep, properly so called, in the sleep which affects the whole of our body, it is recollections and always recollections, which form the web of our dreams."

Where can any trace of remembrances be found in the incidents we have quoted, which is capable of explaining all the circumstances of these dreams? Memory is no longer a sufficient explanation to account for the abnormal knowledge which is manifested.

Some years ago, M. Letourneau published in the *Bulletins et Mémoires de la Société d'anthropologie de*

Paris a singular theory as to certain dreams under the title of *Ancestral Dreams*.

The author set forth in the following terms the theory of ancestral dreams.

"Certain events, external or psychic, which have made a deep impression on a person, may be so deeply engraved upon his brain as to result in a molecular orientation, so lasting that it may be transmitted to some of his descendants, in the same way as character, aptitudes, mental maladies, &c. It is then no longer a question of infantile reminiscences, but of ancestral recollections, capable of being revived. From that will proceed, not only the fortuitous recognition of places which a person has never seen, but, moreover, a whole category of peculiar dreams, admirably co-ordinated, in which we witness as at a panorama, adventures which cannot be remembrances, because they have not the least connection with our individual life.

"As an example of this I only know the very curious dream made public some years ago by Abercromby, and which has often been quoted in works dealing with mental pathology. It relates to a Scotch property owner, who was on the point of being ruined by being sued for accumulated arrears of a tithe payable to a noble family. The person upon whom the claim was made was convinced that the tithe in question had been redeemed by his father a long time previously, but he was not able to furnish the proof. But, in a dream, the father, who had been dead for several years, appeared to his son and told him all the circumstances in connection with the payment which he had made in the presence of a solicitor, whose name he gave him, and who had preserved the papers relating to the transaction. But this lawyer, then a very old man, had completely forgotten the matter in question. The interested party, however, brought it back to his memory by reminding him of some incidents in connection with the changing of a Portuguese gold piece of which he had been informed in his dream. In consequence, the necessary papers were found, produced, and the lawsuit won."

M. Letourneau thus concludes :—

"It is therefore quite admissible that the detailed recollection of facts and events that have strongly impressed a person, leave on his brain an indelible imprint, hereditarily transmissible to his descendants, and which can be re-vivified in them during dream, when the temporary eclipse of the individuality leaves the consciousness with a free field for all latent traces of ancestral origin. This psychic basement of the consciousness may even have concealed in it other visual images than those revealed by dreams.

"We may refer to similar origins the change of character, sometimes so complete,which often occurs at the moment of death, as well as the facts hitherto unexplained, of ' infant prodigies,' even certain deliria or certain kinds of insanity.

"All these singular and inexplicable facts may be summed up in a general proposition which Maudsley has thus formulated : ' All that the ancestors of a man have felt, thought, and done, though the man himself may have known nothing of them, certainly influence everything that he will be disposed to feel, think, and do.'

"This man has inherited convolutions which are ready to resume, at certain epochs of his life, the same kind of activity that they performed in his ancestor."

In itself there is certainly nothing inadmissible in this hypothesis, but there is nothing to prove its reality ; it is, therefore, only based on pure hypothesis, the view of a very ingenious mind, it is true, but it rests upon nothing.

Even though it might hold good for some dreams, it would be a poor explanation for some of the abnormal dreams which we are here studying.

If this theory can be applied to certain dreams, in which the subject has a true perception of certain places or objects, of which he had no personal knowledge but which existed in the past just as the subject saw them in dream : on the other hand, this theory is no more capable than that of memory of explaining dreams combined with lucidity in the present or in the future, when this phenomenon of lucidity refers to accidental facts, present or future (which did not previously exist), as the subject dreamed them. This class of dreams is very numerous and very important; it includes not only the dreams which we have just described, but also those which we shall study later on in which lucidity is fully developed.

Before going further I wish to mention here a class of dreams, in which we find the subject manifesting, in a condition of sleep, knowledge that he did not possess in the waking state. This knowledge may, in truth, exist in his sub-consciousness, but it assumes quite an abnormal development owing to the condition in which the subject is at the time.

The following account is contributed by a correspondent to the *Sphinx* in the issue of January 1895 :—

"In 1881 I was in the first class of the School at Wolfenbüttel. The professor of mathematics set us some problems from time to time, the solution of which was left to us.

"Although I had a certain capacity for mathematics, the problem one day seemed to me impossible of solution. No matter in what way I began it, I found myself confronted with the same difficulty. On the eve of the day for handing in the solution, I impatiently threw pen and paper on the table, went and lay down and immediately fell asleep. I cannot now say how long I had been thus lying down, but real sleep soon passed and the following vision began to unfold itself.

"There came a thick and heavy cloud before my eyes which seemed to become clearer by degrees. I soon thought I was in a larger room, and in a few moments I saw that it was the first class room in the school. I turned round astonished and wished to leave it, but I noticed to my great alarm, that my feet were as though fastened to the floor, and it appeared to me certain that I was passing through some enigmatical experience.

"I began to ponder and to look for some means of deliverance from this magical bond: without knowing why, I took hold of my legs, which were rigid, with my right hand, but stood upright again immediately on distinctly seeing something dark pass before my eyes. I asked myself what this could be.

"I looked and saw a dark nucleus in the thick cloud of a moment ago, which since then had condensed and seemed to be only about three yards away from me.

"My eyes were fixed upon it for some time, until, finally, weary of my embarrassing position, I began to cudgel my brains how to put an end to it. These reflections were, however, unnecessary as I suddenly found I could move my legs. My joy was great! I had my liberty again! I ran quickly to the door, but there an unspeakable horror came over me: I had lost my right hand! I was seized with a deep despair, thinking of my parents who for so many years had deprived themselves in order that I might pursue my studies.

"Disheartened, I drew back from the door, asking myself if I could, in these circumstances, return home or not. While this was going on, I had drawn closer to the window, hoping to be able to call some one to my help: in this movement I brushed up against the black-board, and I noticed that the cloud had now begun to concentrate itself on the top left-hand corner of the board.

"Not seeing any one at the window I came back to look at this extraordinary cloud on the black-board, and at that moment it opened and showed a man's hand with outlines at first indistinct, but becoming gradually clearer. I stared hard at it and saw that it was my own hand, and I attentively followed its movements, which were all the more distinct as the daylight had returned in the interval.

"The lines formed themselves distinctly one after another, and I could see how, out of this apparent chaos, there was sketched an analytical presentation of my mathematical problem. Then the hand was again lowered, and drew the geometrical construction of the problem. Immediately afterwards it went up higher and began to write, setting out the calculation letter by letter and line by line : in a word, it gave the mathematical proof that the geometrical construction corresponded with the analysis, and thus the problem was solved.

" The designs, letters, and figures were set forth in lines of fire, and were deeply impressed upon my memory.

" After setting down the last point, the hand disappeared from the black-board with lightning speed and I felt a sharp pain in my arm : my hand was again joined to it. I uttered a cry of pain, and awoke, but, to my great surprise, in an altogether different place.

" My head seemed to be as heavy as lead, but I realised that I had seen the solution of the problem in this dream. I immediately went into my room, took pen and paper, and wrote down what I had seen: then I lay down and slept peacefully for several hours. On awaking nothing seemed clear to me, and everything was like a dream.

" But how can I describe my astonishment when my parents asked me why I had got up in the night and come into their room, and why I had not replied to them !

" I was so little certain of anything that I should have protested if I had not seen, at the same moment, on the piano, as a certain proof, the mathematical calculation. I did not even look at it, for what could there be that was rational in this lucubration of slumber ? The whole adventure began to amuse me, and I laughed heartily at it; but this laugh quickly stopped, because what I thought I had written in the intoxication of sleep was absolutely correct, and you may imagine how joyfully I set out for the school."

This class of dreams proves the justice of the theory I have put forward, which makes of the dream an auto-suggestion or a suggestion, and brings it within the category of hypnotic phenomena. If you will compare the preceding fact with the observation I have made in my *Traité de l'hypnotisme expérimental et thérapeutique*, in the chapter on suggestion, page 70, you will see that by hypnotic suggestion I have made a student solve an algebraical problem, the solution of which he could not find when in a waking state. The connection between these two facts is evident: the one took place in hypnotic sleep, under the influence of suggestion; the other in spontaneous sleep, under the influence of dream.

There is still another class of dream in which the faculty of lucidity appears to be completely developed. In these cases we likewise observe that the lucidity presents the same characteristics as somnambulistic lucidity. We have at first the cases in which the lucidity of the dream harmonises with existing things, but of which the subject can have no knowledge by normal means.

In these first cases, we see that the subject perceives in dream things which directly concern him, but are not of a tragic character, such as danger of a serious accident or of something that threatens his life.

The first case is taken from the *Journal of the Society for Psychical Research* for October 1889.

"On reaching Morley's Hotel at five o'clock on Tuesday, January 29th, 1889," says the writer (Mrs. A. M. Bickford Smith), "I missed a gold brooch, which I supposed I had left in a fitting-room at Swan and Edgar's. I sent there at once, but was very disappointed to hear that after a diligent search they could not find the brooch. I was much vexed, and worried about the brooch, and that night dreamed that I should find it shut up in a number of the *Queen* newspaper that had been on the table, and in my dream I saw the very page where it would be. I had noticed one of the plates on the page. Directly after breakfast I went to Swan and Edgar's and asked to see the papers, at the same time telling the young ladies about the dream, and where I had seen the brooch. The papers had been moved from that room, but were found, and to the astonishment of the young ladies, I said, 'This is the one that contains my brooch,' and there at the very page I expected I found it."

"We received a substantially similar account from Mrs. Bickford Smith's brother-in-law, Mr. H. A. Smith, who was a witness of the trouble taken to find the brooch, both at the hotel, and by sending to Swan and Edgar's, on the previous evening."

It will be noticed that Mrs. Bickford Smith did not herself make the first search. If she had returned to Swan and Edgar's before the dream it is possible that the

sight of the papers on the table would have revived some
memories of the sight of the brooch between the leaves
of the *Queen.* In spite of this we can regard the case
as a phenomenon of the sub-conscious mind. It is none
the less interesting because of the precision of the dream.

The following account is given by Mr. Myers in the
Proceedings of the Society for Psychical Research. The
story was told by a lady to Professor Royce of Harvard.

" A number of years ago I was invited to visit a friend
who lived at a large and beautiful country-seat on the
Hudson. Shortly after my arrival I started, with a
number of other guests, to make a tour of the very
extensive grounds. We walked for an hour or more,
and very thoroughly explored the place. Upon my
return to the house I discovered that I had lost a gold
cuff-stud, that I valued for association's sake. I merely
remembered that I wore it when we started out, and did
not think of or notice it again until my return, when it
was missing. As it was quite dark, it seemed useless
to search for it, especially as it was the season of autumn
and the ground was covered with dead leaves. That
night I dreamed that I saw a withered grape-vine clinging
to a wall, with a pile of dead leaves at the root. Underneath the leaves, in my dream, I distinctly saw my stud
gleaming. The following morning I asked the friends
with whom I had been walking the previous afternoon
if *they* remembered seeing any such wall and vine, as I
did not. They replied that they could not recall anything answering the description. I did not tell them why
I asked, as I felt somewhat ashamed of the dream, but
during the morning I made some excuse to go out in
the grounds alone. I walked hither and thither, and
after a long time I suddenly came upon the wall and vine
exactly as they looked in my dream. I had not the
slightest recollection of seeing them or passing by them
on the previous day. The dead leaves at the root were
lying heaped up, as in my dream. I approached cautiously,
feeling rather uncomfortable and decidedly silly, and
pushed them aside. I had scattered a large number of

the leaves when a gleam of gold struck my eye, and there lay the stud, exactly as in my dream."

Here is another case in which the importance of the vision perceived in dream was much greater, because it might have resulted in an accident; but it will be noticed that the particular object to which the dream referred was not specially present in the subject's mind immediately before the dream, as was the case in the preceding instance. This case is related by Col. Reynolds of Cheltenham, an excellent witness.

"About the year 1870 I was in charge of a length of roadway, together with the bridges large and small that carried it. Sometimes there were floods which endangered the bridges, and I was therefore always on the look-out to prevent serious damage which would have impeded the traffic. At the same time this had been my daily life for so long that no anxiety remained in my mind about it. I regarded my duties as merely routine work. I was in a fairly good state of health. One night I dreamt in a most vivid manner that I saw an exact picture of a certain small bridge. All the surroundings were complete, and left no doubt as to which bridge it was. A voice at the same moment said to me: 'Go and look at that bridge.' This was said distinctly three times. In the morning the dream still persisted in my mind, and so impressed me that I rode off at once about six miles to the bridge. Nothing was to be seen out of the ordinary. The small stream was, however, coming down in flood. On walking into the water I found to my astonishment that the foundations of the bridge had been entirely undermined and washed away. It was a marvel that it was still standing. Of course, the work necessary to preserve the bridge was done. There is no doubt that but for the dream the bridge would have fallen, as there was no reason whatever to attract my attention specially to this bridge. Though small, the bridge was an important one, as its situation was peculiar. The picture that was dreamt was so strong that it is even now fixed in my mind as plainly almost as it was then."

We now come to the study of premonitory dreams, that is to say, dreams which exhibit the faculty of lucidity in the future.

We will, by way of transition, quote a case in which the fact dreamed of is subsequent to the dream, but the idea of it probably existed before the dream. This case can therefore be regarded either as a case of lucidity as regards the present or of lucidity in reference to the future.

The narrative is taken from Mrs. Crowe's *Night Side of Nature*.

A gentleman engaged in business in the South of Scotland, dreams that on entering his office in the morning, he sees seated on a certain stool a person formerly in his service as clerk, of whom he had neither heard nor thought for some time. He inquires the motive of the visit, and is told that since such and such circumstances had brought the stranger to that part of the country, he could not forbear visiting his old quarters, expressing, at the same time, a wish to spend a few days in his former occupation, &c. &c. The gentleman being struck with the vividness of the illusion relates his dream at breakfast, and, to his surprise, on going to his office, there sits the man, and the dialogue that ensues is precisely that of the dream.

In the premonitory dreams which follow a grave danger threatens a person, and the dream is a warning which enables the danger to be avoided. In short, the dream is not realised, but the circumstances are such that we can presume that the event dreamed of would actually have happened if the subjects had not had the warning which enabled them to modify their plans. These records are also taken from Mrs. Crowe's well-known work :—

A butcher named Bone, residing at Holytown, dreamt, a few years since, that he was stopped at a particular spot on his way to market, whither he was going on the following day to purchase cattle, by two men in blue clothes, who cut his throat. He told the dream to his wife, who laughed at him, but as it was repeated two or three times, and she saw that he was really alarmed, she advised him to join somebody who was going along the same road. He accordingly listened till he heard a cart passing his door, and then went out and joined the man, telling him the reason for so doing. When they came to the spot, there actually stood the two men in blue clothes, who, seeing he was not alone, took to their heels and ran.

Now, although the dream was here probably the means of saving Bone's life, there is no reason to suppose this a case of what is called supernatural intervention. The phenomenon would be sufficiently accounted for by the admission of the hypothesis I have suggested, namely, that he was aware of the impending danger in his sleep, and had been able, from some cause unknown to us, to carry the recollection into his waking state.

The following case presents this peculiar feature, that the dream happens, not to the person threatened by danger, but to some one else.

The danger was again avoided by the precautions which were taken through the dream; as to the reality of the danger avoided and the exactitude of the dream, they are still better proved in this instance than in the former one.

" A circumstance of a similar kind to the above occurred in a well-known family in Scotland, the Rutherfords of E——.

" A lady dreamt that her aunt, who resided at some distance, was murdered by a black servant. Impressed with the vividness of the vision, she could not resist going to the house of her relation, when the man she had dreamt of, whom I think she had never before seen, opened the door to her. Upon this, she induced a gentleman to watch in the adjoining room during the night; and, towards morning, hearing a foot upon the stairs, he opened the door, and discovered the black servant carrying up a coal-scuttle full of coals, for the purpose, as he said, of lighting his mistress's fire. As this motive did not seem very probable, the coals were examined and a knife found hidden amongst them, with which, he afterwards con-sessed, he intended to have murdered his mistress, provided she made any resistance to a design he had formed, of robbing her of a large sum of money, which he was aware she had that day received."

The two following cases also refer to dreams premonitory of danger, but the fact foreshadowed by the dream is exactly realised.

"A professional gentleman, whose name would be a warrant for the truth of whatever he relates, told me the following circumstance regarding himself. He was, not very long since, at the sea-side with his family, and amongst the rest, he had with him one of his sons, a boy about twelve years of age, who was in the habit of bathing daily, his father accompanying him to the water-side. This practice had continued during the whole of their visit, and no idea of danger or accident had ever occurred to anybody. On the day preceding the one appointed for their departure, Mr. H., the gentleman in question, felt himself, after breakfast, surprised by an unusual drowsiness, which he vainly struggled to overcome, and at length fell asleep in his chair. He then dreamt that he was attending his son to the beach as usual, when he suddenly saw the boy drowning, and himself rushed into the water, dressed as he was, and brought him ashore. Though he was quite conscious of the dream when he awoke, he attached no importance to it; he considered it merely a dream, and nothing more; and when, some hours afterwards, the boy came into the room and said, 'Now, father, it's time to go; this will be the last bathe;' his morning's vision did not even recur to him. They walked down to the sea as usual, and the boy went into the water, whilst the father stood composedly watching him from the beach, when suddenly the child lost his footing, a wave having caught him, and the danger of his being carried away was so imminent, that without even waiting to take off his greatcoat, boots, or hat, Mr. H. rushed into the water, and was only just in time to save his son."

The second case is quoted by the same author.

"Mr. D., of Cumberland, when a youth, came to Edinburgh, for the purpose of attending college, and was placed under the care of his uncle and aunt, Major and Mrs. Griffiths, who then resided in the castle. When the fine weather came, the young man was in the habit of making frequent excursions with others of his own age and pursuits; and one afternoon he mentioned that they had formed a fishing party, and had bespoken a boat for the ensuing day. No objections were made to this plan; but in the middle of the night, Mrs. Griffiths screamed out, 'The boat is sinking! Oh, save them!' Her husband said, he supposed she had been thinking of the fishing party; but she declared she had never thought about it at all, and soon fell asleep again. But before long she awoke a second time, crying out that she 'saw the boat sinking! It must have been the remains of the impression made by the other dream,' she suggested to her husband, 'for I have no uneasiness whatever about the fishing party;' but on going to sleep once more, her husband was again disturbed by her cries: 'They are gone!' she said; 'the boat has sunk!' She now really became alarmed, and without waiting for morning she threw on her dressing-gown and went to Mr. D., who was still in bed, and whom with much difficulty she persuaded to relinquish his proposed excursion. He consequently sent his servant to Leith with an excuse, and the party embarked without him. The day was extremely fine when they put to sea; but some hours afterwards a storm arose, in which the boat foundered; nor did any one of the number survive to tell the tale."

In the examples which we have just considered the subject saw in a dream the vision of the event which was afterwards realised. Here is a further instance, also from the same author, of a slightly different character.

"One of the most remarkable instances of warning that has come to my knowledge is that of Mr. M. of Kingsborough. This gentleman, being on a voyage to America, dreamt one night that a little old man came into his cabin and said, 'Get up! Your life is in danger!' Upon which Mr. M. awoke; but considering it only to be a dream, he soon composed himself to sleep again. The dream, however, if such it were, recurred, and the old man urged him still more strongly to get up directly; but he still persuaded himself it was only a dream; and after listening a few minutes, and hearing nothing to alarm him, he turned round, and addressed himself once more to sleep. But now the old man appeared again, and angrily bade him rise instantly, and take his gun and ammunition with him, for he had not a moment to lose. The injunction was so distinct that Mr. M. felt he could no longer resist it ; so he hastily dressed himself, took his gun, and ascended to the deck where he had scarcely arrived, when the ship struck on a rock, which he and several others contrived to reach. The place, however, was uninhabited, and but for his gun, they would never have been able to provide themselves with food till a vessel arrived to their relief."

In this instance there is a premonition, through the dream, of an undefined danger. The dream plainly indicates to the subject that a danger threatens him, but he is not shown the scene which is to be enacted.

Another peculiar feature is to be noticed in this dream : the vision, seen in dream, gives the order to the subject to take his gun and ammunition. The event proved in the end that it was entirely to the subject's interest to obey that order. This thought of taking arms was not, under the circumstances, the natural corollary of the presentiment of a danger. There seems, therefore, to be in this dream something more than a premonition due to a single presentiment.

There are also dreams which really present the character of lucidity, although the scene perceived by the dreamer is not realised. The features of the scene are sufficient to make known to him a fact that is true: the intervention of the subject, mainly on account of the vision seen in dream, turns aside the danger which menaced him.

" A very remarkable instance of this kind of dreaming occurred a few years since to Mr. A. F., an eminent Scotch advocate, whilst staying in the neighbourhood of Loch Fyne, who dreamt one night that he saw a number of people in the street following a man to the scaffold. He perceived the features of the criminal in the cart distinctly, and, for some reason or other, which he could not account for, felt an extraordinary interest in his fate, insomuch that he joined the throng, and accompanied him to the place that was to terminate his earthly career. This interest was the more unaccountable as the man had an exceedingly unprepossessing countenance, but it was, nevertheless, so vivid, as to induce the dreamer to ascend the scaffold and address him with a view to enable him to escape the impending catastrophe. Suddenly, however, whilst he was talking to him, the whole scene dissolved, and the sleeper awoke. Being a good deal struck with the life-like reality of the vision, and the impression made on his mind by the features of this man, he related the circumstance to his friends at breakfast, adding that he should know him anywhere, if he saw him. A few jests being made on the subject, the thing was forgotten.

"On the afternoon of the same day, the advocate was informed that two men wanted to speak to him, and on going into the hall he was struck with amazement at perceiving that one of them was the hero of his dream! 'We are accused of murder,' said they, 'and we wish to consult you. Three of us went out last night in a boat, an accident has happened, our comrade is drowned, and they want to make us accountable for him.' The advocate then put some interrogations to them, and the result produced in his mind by their answers was a conviction of their guilt. Probably the recollection of his dream rendered the effect of this conviction more palpable, for, one addressing the other, said in Gaelic, 'We have come to the wrong man; he is against us.'

"'There is a higher power than I against you,' returned the gentleman, 'and the only advice I can give you is, if you are guilty, fly immediately.' Upon this they went away, and the next thing he heard was that they were taken into custody on suspicion of the murder.

"The account of the affair given was, that the three had gone out together on the preceding evening, and that in the morning the body of one of them had been found on the shore, with a cut across his forehead. The father and friends of the victim had waited on the

E

banks of the lake till the boat came in, and then demanded their companion, of whom, however, they professed themselves unable to give any account. Upon this the old man led them to his cottage for the purpose of showing them the body of his son. One entered, and, at the sight of it, burst into a passion of tears, the other refused to step over the threshold, saying his business called him immediately home, and went sulkily away. This last was the man seen in the dream.

" After a fortnight's incarceration the former of these was liberated, and he then declared to the advocate his intention of bringing an action for damages for false imprisonment. He was advised not to do it. 'Leave well alone,' said the lawyer ; 'and if you'll take my advice make off while you can.' The man, however, refused to fly : he declared that he really did not know what had occasioned the death of his comrade. The latter had been at one end of the boat and he at the other ; when he looked round he was gone, but whether he had fallen overboard and cut his head as he fell, or whether he had been struck and pushed into the water, he did not know. The advocate finally became satisfied of the man's innocence ; but the authorities thinking it absurd to try one and not the other, again laid hands on him, and it fell to Mr. A. F. to be the defender of both. The difficulty was not to separate their cases in his pleading, for however morally convinced of the different ground on which they stood, his duty, professionally, was to obtain the acquittal of both, in which he finally succeeded as regarding the charge of murder. They were therefore sentenced to two years' imprisonment, and so far as the dream is concerned here ends the story. There remains, however, a curious sequel to it.

" A few years afterwards, the same gentleman being in a boat on Loch Fyne, in company with Sir T. O. L., happened to be mentioning these curious circumstances, when one of the boatsmen said, that he 'knew well about those two men ; and that a very strange thing had occurred in regard to one of them.' This one, on inquiry, proved to be the subject of the dream ; and the strange thing was this ; on being liberated, he had quitted that part of the country, and in process of time had gone to Greenock, and thence embarked in a vessel for Cork. But the vessel seemed fated never to reach its destination, one misfortune happened after another, till at length the sailors said, ' This won't do ; there must be a murderer on board with us.'

" As is usual where such belief exists we draw three times by lot, and this man was designed three times. Consequently, he was put on shore and the vessel went on its way without him. What became of him is not known.

" It should be noted that in this dream the persons concerned in the matter were absolutely unknown to the subject ; however, the circumstances which followed are so precise that there can be no doubt as to the reality of the impression aroused by the dream."

We then see that the whole of this series of abnormal dreams which I have here quoted exhibit all the phases of hypnotic phenomena which harmonise with auto-suggestion, suggestion, thought-transmission, and finally with lucidity exercised, whether in regard to the present or to the future.

There is consequently a complete gradation which exhibits in a progressive form a phenomenon which seems to be allied to hypnotic phenomena from the most simple to the most complicated examples.

CHAPTER V

PHENOMENA OBSERVED AMONG THE ORIENTALS

WE know that a certain number of phenomena, which seem to approximate to those which we are here studying, are very frequently observed in Oriental countries by travellers who have reported these incidents.

A certain number of these facts have been well authenticated, and the personality of those who have reported them enables us to regard them as genuine. In order to render our study complete, we shall here quote some which we have selected from among those which have been most carefully observed.

Dr. Nobin Chander Paul, assistant army surgeon in India, published, a few years ago, a theoretical and practical treatise on Yoga. In this treatise, which was published in the *Lotus*, we find the following information relative to the hypnotic condition.

"The Mystical Hindus (Yogis) live in underground retreats (Guha); they abstain from salt in their food and are extremely particular as regards milk, which is their principal nourishment; they are night-birds, and remain indoors during the day; their movements are slow and their manners lethargic. They take two postures called Padmâsana and Sidhâsana, with a view to breathing as seldom as possible. They fear rapid changes and inclemencies of temperature. When the Yogis are able to hold themselves for two hours in the two motionless postures of which we have just spoken, they begin to practise Prânâyama, a phase of voluntary trance characterised by much perspiration, trembling throughout the whole of the body, and a feeling of lightness in the animal economy. They then practise Pratyáhara, a phase of auto-magnetism, during which the sensory functions are suspended.

"Then they practise Dhârana, during which phase the sensibility and voluntary movement entirely cease, while the body can remain in any posture that may be willed. It is said that the mind is quiescent during this phase of voluntary trance.

"After having attained to the degree of Dhârana, the cataleptic state, the Yogis aspire to what they call Hyârana, a phase of auto-magnetism, during which they claim to be surrounded by the bright light or supernal electricity called Anontajyoti (two Sanskrit words which mean eternal or universally penetrating light), which they say belongs to the Cosmic Consciousness. In the state of Dhyâna the Yogis are said to be clairvoyant. The Dhyâna of the Yogis is the Trya Avastha of the Vedantists, the ecstasy of doctors, the self-contemplation of the German magnetisers, and the clairvoyance of the French philosophers. The condition of Samâdhi is the last phase of auto-trance. In this state the Yogis, like the bats, the hedgehog, the hamster, and the dormouse, acquire the power of dispensing with food and drink.

"There have been, during the last fifteen years, three cases of Samâdhi, or human hibernation. The first case occurred at Calcutta, the second at Jesselmere, and the third in the Punjab. I was an eye-witness of the first case. There are two kinds of Samâdhi, called Samprajñâta and Asamprajñâta. Colonel Townshend, who could arrest the movement of his heart and of his arteries at will, and die or expire at pleasure, and then revive, was an example of Samprajñâta Samâdhi. The Yogis of Jesselmere, of the Punjab and of Calcutta, who entered upon a condition similar to death by swallowing their tongue, and could not take up their life again at will, were examples of Asamprajñâta Samâdhi; they could only be resuscitated with the assistance of other people, who drew back the tongue from the larynx, and replaced it in its normal position."

Colonel Townshend could, to all appearance, die whenever he pleased; his heart ceased to beat, there was no perceptible respiration, and his whole frame became cold

and rigid as death itself, the features being shrunk and
colourless, and the eyes glazed and ghastly. He would
continue in this state for several hours, and then suddenly
come to life again, but the revival does not appear to
have been the result of an effort of will, or rather, we are
not informed whether it was so or not. Neither are we
told whether he brought any recollections back with him,
nor how this strange faculty was first developed or discovered—all very important points and well worthy of
investigation.

I find from the account of Dr. Cheyne, who attended
him, that Colonel Townshend himself said that he could
" die or expire when he pleased; and yet by an effort
he could come to life again." He performed the experiment in the presence of three medical men, one of whom
kept his hand on his heart, another held his wrist, and
the third placed a looking-glass before his lips, and
they found that all traces of respiration and pulsation
gradually ceased, insomuch that, after consulting about his
condition for some time, they were leaving the room, persuaded that he was really dead, when signs of life appeared,
and he slowly revived. He did not die whilst repeating
the experiment, as has been sometimes asserted.

With respect to the Dervish or Fakir, an account of
whose singular faculty was, I believe, first presented to the
public in the Calcutta papers, about nine or ten years ago :
he had then frequently exhibited it for the satisfaction of
the natives, but subsequently he was put to proof by some
of the European officers and residents. Captain Wade,
political agent at Loodhiana, was present when he was
disinterred, ten months after he had been buried by
General Ventura, in presence of the Maharajah and many
of his principal Sirdars.

It appears that the man previously prepared himself
by some processes which, he stated, temporarily annihilate
the power of digestion, so that milk received into the
stomach undergoes no change. He next forced all the
breath in his body into his brain, which became very
hot, upon which the lungs collapsed, and the heart ceased

to beat. He then stopped up with wax every aperture of
the body through which air could enter, except the mouth,
but the tongue was so turned back as to close the gullet,
upon which a state of insensibility ensued. He was then
stripped and put into a linen bag, and on the occasion in
question, this bag was sealed with Runjeet Sing's own seal.
He was then placed in a deal box, which was also locked
and sealed, and the box being buried in a vault, the earth
was thrown over it and trodden down, after which a crop
of barley was sown on the spot and sentries placed to
watch it. The Maharajah, however, was so sceptical that,
in spite of all these precautions, he had him twice, in the
course of the ten months, dug up and examined, and each
time he was found to be exactly in the same state as when
they shut him up.

When he was disinterred, the first step towards his
recovery was to turn back his tongue, which was found quite
stiff, and required for some time to be retained in its
proper position by the finger ; warm water was poured upon
him, and his eyes and lips moistened with ghee, or oil.
His recovery was much more rapid than might be expected,
and he was soon able to recognise the bystanders and converse. He stated that during his state of trance his dreams
were ravishing, and that it was very painful to be awakened,
but I do not know that he has ever disclosed any of his
experiences. His only apprehension seems to be, lest
he should be attacked by insects, to avoid which accident
the box is slung to the ceiling. The interval seems to
be passed in a complete state of hibernation ; and when
he is taken up no pulse is perceptible, and his eyes are
glazed like those of a corpse.

Here is another fact which recalls the experiments
of certain mediums. The account was published by Dr.
Pascal in the *Annales des Sciences Psychiques.*

"It was at Benares on October 26th, 1898. A rich
vaishya, universally known and respected in the town,
Govinda Das, desirous of proving once more his gratitude
towards the Theosophical Society, which had given a great
impulse to what the newspapers of the country call 'The

Hindu Renaissance,' asked the High Priest attached to the Maharajah's palace if he would be willing to show to the members of the society, then assembled in their annual convention, the phenomenon of the mastery of fire.

"A rectangular trench nearly 9 yards long and 2 yards wide, and about 30 inches deep, had been excavated in a corner of the large garden of the villa, ' Gopal Lal Orderly Bazar,' the seat of the convention. Fifteen tall trunks of trees were burned in it from two o'clock in the afternoon, and threw off a tremendous heat around the spot. Towards half-past seven in the evening the large live embers were scattered by breaking them with enormous long bamboos, and they made an even bed of flaming embers. This bed was 5 yards in length, 2 yards wide, and at least 8 inches in thickness.

"At eight o'clock all was ready. A crowd of about two thousand people surrounded the hole, for the rumour of the phenomenon had been spread abroad and the invasion of the garden could not be prevented. A certain number of invited guests, of whom the writer was one, were placed on a hillock about three yards from the excavation, and could see without difficulty all that took place.

"Suddenly the crowd became agitated, cries were heard, and a small procession advanced, preceded by a Hindu dressed in white, wearing a turban and brandishing a kind of baton of command, somewhat similar to that of our drum-majors. Two thurifers followed, each carrying a small basket, surrounded by a row of small red and green flags, with a strong flame coming from the centre; they were accompanied by torch-bearers. Two men were particularly noticeable as they threw themselves convulsively about in the middle of the cortège and uttered cries like persons possessed.

"Eventually there came a shrine with glass sides, carried by six individuals: inside could be seen three images, some plates with inscriptions, two cross swords, placed vertically in the middle of the back face, and various other small objects which we could not identify. The

Brahmin came last in the procession, which stopped a few yards from the brazier. The priest took up a position on the left, sat down and commenced the incantations which were to produce the phenomenon, but the noise made by the crowd prevented us from hearing the words.

"The master of ceremonies, who was in front of the brazier, moved about and pronounced at regular intervals some brief syllables, to which the procession briskly responded with certain unknown words.

"The two fanatics continued their contortions and cried out as though they were being put to death. Then one of the swords from the shrine was given to each and some cocoa-nuts were thrown on to the ground : they threw themselves madly on to these, according to the ceremonial, breaking them with blows of the sword. The procession went twice round the furnace, and several times the fire was sprinkled with consecrated water. Finally one of the broken cocoa-nuts was thrown on to the fire; it was the signal. The more excited of the fanatics rushed on to the brazier, brandishing his sword and uttering terrible cries : he rapidly crossed the excavation, quickly followed by his comrade, and they passed and re-passed in a terribly agitated state. One of them—the first—became dangerous; he was disarmed with difficulty, and held by four men. Some of the spectators had already rushed in turn on to the fire — about fifty in all—and crossed it many times ; among them were men of the lower classes, children, and some Hindus of superior education.

"Some ran quickly : one stopped for a moment in the middle of the brazier, plunging his hand into the embers, seizing a handful, and taking them to the other side of the hole. Another came out with a flaming cinder as large as a small pullet's egg, sticking to the lower part of his leg, and talked to some of the spectators for eight or ten seconds without inconvenience : he was then told of it and pulled it off. The children particularly were delighted ; they passed and repassed through the fire, and boastfully showed that their little feet were not injured by it. Finally the procession went back again, and the Brahmin left the place. Some persons continued to cross the furnace, but this soon came to an end, because they said that after the priest and the shrine leave, the charm quickly ceases and the fire resumes its dominion. A number of natives then filled with live cinders the vessels they had brought, and proceeded to cook their food over a fire they regarded as sacred. We went down to the edge of the fire to judge as to its heat. It was difficult to endure it: we were obliged to turn away our faces and to withdraw. Some ladies, on the hillock, felt such heat on their faces that they had to screen them with their handkerchiefs.

" We had now to commence the inquiry and to examine the results. It was impossible to secure much information, because the majority of the experimenters had already mingled with the crowd. We examined, however, the soles of the feet of Govinda Das's brother, a well-educated man, a B.A. of Allahabad University. We had seen him cross the brazier twice, the first time rapidly, the second time more slowly. The soles of his feet were supple, and the skin, which was carefully inspected, was intact. But the crowd gradually withdrew, and we could not get any further information. We returned to the place the following morning at eight o'clock. The coals were reduced to very warm cinders, the radiation from them being clearly perceived at more than two yards from the excavation, and about ten natives were warming themselves. The night had been cold. We then went to the villa Gopal Lal. Amongst the delegates from the various branches of the Theosophical Society were some who had crossed the fire. They were well-educated men, very intelligent, and of good faith. The soles of their feet were delicate, like those of all the Hindus who wore shoes. One of them (an M.A. of Calcutta University) was absolutely unharmed, as well as another (a B.A. of Allahabad University).

" Four others came forward, who had crossed the fire after the Brahmin had left.

" The first showed at the centre of the sole a surface of about a third of an inch square burnt slightly brown, and the first layer of the skin was gone : the second and third showed greater burning, but still superficial, about as large as the nail of the little finger ; one was burned on on the inner part of the left big toe, the other on the sole the foot : the fourth, who was the last of the crowd to go on to the brazier, waited two or three minutes after the procession had left before coming forward : he had crossed it five or six times very slowly. Under the ends of the toes of one of his feet could be seen some small blisters, showing burns about a sixth of a square inch in extent, as though some small blistering plasters had been applied. The other foot showed nothing. The skin of the soles is tender. These burns were healed on the following day. We omitted to say that all those who crossed the excavation had naked feet. The sensation experienced on crossing the brazier, according to the statement of those we questioned, was similar to that felt when walking on fine and moderately warm sand.

" One of the experimenters stated that the sensation of heat was stronger in front of the fire than in the centre. The effect of the warm air on the respiration was, he said, not marked, but the length of time taken in crossing was not sufficient for him to judge.

" On the following day the Brahmin said to Govinda Das that the control of the fire had not been so complete as usual, because the images in the shrine had been touched by some Mohammedans and some persons in the crowd. A bystander who had previously crossed the fire, on a similar occasion, under the direction of the same priest, made the evening before, and spontaneously, the declaration that the sensation of heat to the sole of the feet was noticeably greater than on his first experiment, which tended to confirm the statement of the operator, and which explained, perhaps, why the most conclusive part of the ceremony was omitted, to the great dissatisfaction of the crowd accustomed to see it carried out. This part of the performance consisted in a peculiar combat, on the brazier, between the two men armed with swords.

"The second ceremony took place about December 7th of the same year in the park of the palace of Maharajah Tagore, who was then at his country-house at Benares. A Frenchman, the son of Dr. Javal of Paris, was present.

"We have nothing to say with regard to the ceremonial, which was in all points similar to that already described: the excavation was of similar dimensions to the first, and the bed of live coals was almost of the same thickness. Some hundreds of persons of all ranks and ages crossed it; at first five belonging to the Maharajah's court: they walked in the ordinary way, the others more quickly. They were not burned. When the crowd ceased to move about we went to the edge of the excavation, with the intention of putting our hands amongst the coals, to witness for ourselves the reality of the phenomenon. Cries rose from all parts: an interpreter came to tell us that the Brahmin had left the place some ten or fifteen minutes, and that the fire had resumed its power. The Maharajah came forward, and offered us, if we desired to cross the brazier, to have the ceremony performed again. We accepted, and, a few minutes afterwards, were informed that everything was ready. We then took off our shoes and stockings and went into the brazier. The first two steps gave us the impression of a burning on the soles of the feet: the other five merely gave us the sensation of an intense heat. We crossed at a gentle trot, making at least two steps a second.

"Immediately afterwards we examined our feet: there was a slight burn on the sole of the right foot, as large as the nail of the little finger, and two others of the same size on the sole of the left foot: the brown places denoting them were transformed on the following day into small blisters, which did not for an instant prevent us from walking, and which healed in a few days. Several Hindus, who crossed with us, were as lightly burnt.

"We then learned that the operation had been performed, not by the Brahmin, who had left the place some time before, but by his principal assistant, and that full control of the fire had not been obtained.

" We admit, as far as we are concerned, that if the fire was not completely subdued, its activity was extraordinarily reduced, because, had there not been a considerable counteracting influence, we should have been seriously injured: this point appeared to us indisputable.

"A third opportunity of being present at the same ceremony was offered us at Benares in February 1908, in the court of the Temple, to which the priest, of whom we have spoken, was attached.

"Everything happened as on the previous occasions: we think it well, however, to mention one interesting fact.

"Three Hindus, who had struck against each other while crossing, fell into the brazier.

"It took them a few seconds to get up and come out. Not one of them was burned, although the fire had had direct contact with a large portion of the body (legs and arms): their clothing was saved, and it was composed of very light, vaporous, and highly inflammable material.

" This phenomenon is of frequent occurrence in India. An annual festival is specially held for this purpose in the temple of Dharmuraja at Mulapel. It had just been held, about October 20th, at Nagpur, during our stay at Benares, fire-grates being employed, which allowed a wide range to the flames.

"Several highly esteemed and well educated Hindus, well known to us, related to us that they had been present on various occasions at these ceremonies, when the fire-grates were from ten to fifteen yards long.

"One of them, M. A. H. of Allahabad University, saw the priest whose exploits we have related walk with impunity with slow steps in a brazier ten yards long: another could cross a fire a dozen times consecutively. On the south-west coast similar ceremonies frequently take place, in the course of which priests of a lower order sacrifice a goat, and hold it with impunity on the brazier for an hour: these facts have been confirmed to us by an inhabitant of the country, a man whose word cannot be doubted, and who has witnessed it many times.

" In Europe the trial by fire successfully undergone by

sorcerers was for many centuries regarded as a proof of possession, and these unfortunate beings were put to death: no one thought that a demon, with the powers that are attributed to him, could, if he had a will, rescue his followers not only from the action of fire, but from any kind of death: but logic was not the dominant feature of that epoch. In the stories of possession and of convulsionaries we find numerous examples of immunity from fire.

"In our own days the mediums Eglinton, Home, and many others have been able to take live coals in their hands and hold them there for some time without being burned. These phenomena are therefore not new. Those at which we were present are sufficient proof to us of the existence of a power capable of subduing to a considerable degree the destructive energy of fire.

"It was not extinguished, but it did not burn. We consider that a furnace, similar to that which we have seen, could not be crossed with the naked feet, in the conditions stated, without serious burnings resulting each time."

CHAPTER VI

PHENOMENA OF LUCIDITY, MOTRICITY, AND PROJECTION OF THE DOUBLE OBSERVED IN FAKIRS OR ORIENTAL SORCERERS

THE following phenomena are of the same character as those observed with mediums. We find in them phenomena of motricity or of externalisation of force, phenomena of lucidity, and the phenomenon of the projection of the double.

The following is ˙an account given by M. Jacolliot of experiments made in his presence by two fakirs.

M. Jacolliot was, in 1866, Imperial Agent at Pondichery, and has written on Ancient and Modern India,[1] and tells us first of a fakir named Salvanadin.

The fakir squatted down on the pavement, and placed his seven-knotted stick between his legs.

Salvanadin asked to have brought to him seven small flower-pots full of earth, seven thin sticks of wood, each about a yard long, and seven leaves taken from any tree, no matter what.

When these objects had been brought, *without touching them himself*, he had them placed in a horizontal line, about two yards from his outstretched arms, and instructed a servant to place one stick of wood in each pot of earth, and to put on to each stick a tree leaf with a hole in the middle. All the leaves dropped down the sticks, acting as covers to the pots.

The fakir raised his joined hands above his head, and pronounced the following invocation in the Tamil language :—

---

[1] *Occult Science in India and among the Ancients.* By Louis Jacolliot, Chief Justice of Chandenagur (French East Indies). London : William Rider & Son, Limited, 8 Paternoster Row, E.C.

" May all the powers that watch over the intelligent
principle of life and over the principle of matter protect
me from the wrath of evil spirits, and may the immortal
Spirit shield me from the vengeance of Yama."

He then stretched out his hands in the direction of
the flower-pots and stood in a sort of ecstasy. Suddenly
a light wind, coming no one knew whence, stirred the
leaves, and blew Jacolliot's hair across his face several times,
while the curtains of the verandah were undisturbed.

After about a quarter of an hour the fig leaves began
to move slowly upward along the sticks, then as slowly
descended. Jacolliot, who was greatly excited, saw that
there was no visible means of communication, passing and
repassing several times between the fakir and the sticks
while the leaves still rose and descended.

He examined everything, removing the leaves from
the sticks and the sticks from the pots, and emptied the
earth on to the pavement. He then ordered seven goblets
to be brought from the kitchen, and earth and fresh leaves
from the garden. He cut a bamboo cane into seven pieces,
and arranged them himself in the same way as had been
done previously, placing everything at a distance of four
yards from the fakir, who made no movement. Five
minutes afterwards the fakir merely extended his arms,
and the leaves again began to rise up the sticks.

Then, having bored seven holes in a plank, he placed
the seven bamboo sticks in them, and the same phenomena
occurred as before.

He repeated the experiment in twenty different ways,
but always with the same result. The fakir asked : " Is
there not some question you wish to put to the invisible
spirits before they go ? "

Jacolliot, not expecting such a question, asked how he
could communicate.

" Ask anything you please and the leaves will remain
still if the spirits have nothing to say, or will rise should
the contrary be the case."

Jacolliot then threw into a bag a number of brass
letters and figures, and thought of a friend who had been

dead for twenty years: he drew the letters out of the sack one by one, and watched the leaves.

After fourteen letters or figures had been drawn, the letter A appeared, the leaves then began to move, rose to the top of the stick, and fell back again. It was the first letter of the name. When the bag was empty, he put the letters in again, continued, and obtained, letter by letter and figure by figure, the following words:—

"*Albain Brunier died at Bourg-en-Bresse (Ain), January 3rd, 1856.*"

This was correct.

The same fakir made one scale of a balance fall with a peacock's feather when it had a weight of 176 pounds on the opposite scale. A wreath of flowers fluttered about in the air by a mere imposition of hands. Musical sounds were heard in the air, and a shadowy hand drew luminous figures in space.

The French judge was never once able to detect trickery.

This took place at Pondichery. But another fakir, even more extraordinary, visited him at Benares. This was Covindasamy, who came from Trivanderam with the bones of a rich Malabar merchant, who had desired that his ashes should be thrown into the Ganges, the sacred river of the Hindus.

Covindasamy lodged in a cottage on the banks of the Ganges, and Jacolliot received him at his house, on a terrace which overlooked the sacred river, and was protected from the sun by an awning of woven grass fibres.

In the middle of the terrace was a fountain, the water of which fell in a fine shower into a marble basin.

Jacolliot asked Covindasamy if he preferred one place rather than another.

"Just as you please," he replied. They therefore remained on the terrace in broad daylight.

The fakir assuming a squatting position, extended his two hands towards a large bronze vase filled with water; within five minutes the vase commenced to rock to and fro upon its base, and approached the fakir gently and with a regular motion.

F

Some metallic sounds came from the vase, as though it had been struck with a steel rod—a noise similar to that made by hail falling on a zinc roof.

Jacolliot asked that he might direct the operation, and the fakir consented.

The vase advanced or retreated at his wish: sometimes the knocks changed into a continuous roll like a drum: sometimes they came with the regularity of a clock striking the hours: and again the sounds came regularly every ten seconds by the watch.

A musical-box was brought by a servant; it played a tune, and the knocks on the bronze vase accompanied the tune of *Robin des Bois* with the regularity of the baton of the conductor of an orchestra.

The tune was changed, and the box played a march from *Le Prophète*, and the blows moderated their pace to keep time with the slower measure.

There was no other witness besides Jacolliot. The vase when empty could hardly be moved by two men.

The fakir rested his two fingers on the edge of the vase, which soon rocked to and fro in regular time, and the water remained stationary in the vase: three times the vase rose seven or eight inches from the ground, and fell back gently without perceptible shock.

Covindasamy rose, went towards the vase, and placed his hands over the surface of the water without touching it: he remained thus motionless for an hour.

The water began to be gently agitated, as though a light wind ruffled the surface; a rose leaf, thrown into the water, drifted to the opposite edge.

The motion of the waves became more violent, as though the water were in a state of intense ebullition. It soon rose higher than the fakir's hands, and the waves rose to a height of two feet above the surface.

The fakir withdrew his hands, and the agitation abated: he replaced them, and the water again passed into a state of ebullition.

He placed a pencil on the water, and made it move like a compass-needle by the motion of his hand at a distance; then he gently placed his forefinger on the centre of the pencil, and it slowly descended to the bottom of the vase while his hand remained on the surface.

Leaning on the judge's cane the fakir gradually rose to a height of two feet from the ground, with his legs crossed in Oriental fashion.

Jacolliot, astonished, tried for a long time to discover how Covindasamy could thus break the laws of statics; the stick gave him no visible support, and there was no apparent contact between it and his body except through his right hand resting on the knob.

He then took a small wooden table made of teak between his thumb and forefinger, and placed it in the middle of the terrace, asking the fakir to fix it there so that it could not be moved.

Covindasamy placed his hands over it for a quarter of hour and said :—

" The Spirits are here, and nobody can remove this table without their permission."

Jacolliot incredulously took hold of the table, thinking he could lift it, but it remained fixed to the ground; he redoubled his efforts, the table top came off in his hands : he took hold of the legs, but the result was the same.

A flute played without being touched; a toy from Nuremberg, a small windmill, turned without any visible motor.

Before the departure of the fakir, who wished to return to Trivanderam, the French judge obtained two more séances, one in the daytime and the other at night.

At the first the Hindu brought a small bag of fine sand and poured it out over a surface of nearly twenty square inches on the ground : he asked Jacolliot to sit opposite to him with paper and pencil.

The fakir placed a penholder on the sand.

" When you see this penholder stand upright on the sand, trace on your paper any figures you please; you will see an exact copy of them in the sand."

This is exactly what happened.

Jacolliot traced some strange figures, and the penholder imitated them; he stopped, and the penholder did the same.

"Can you think of a Sanskrit word?"

He thought of *Purusha*, the celestial generator, and the word was written on the sand.

"Think of a sentence."

"Vishnu sleeps on the mount." The sentence was written.

Jacolliot asked for the 243rd *sloka* of the fourth book of Manu.

The following was given: "The man who makes virtue the object of all his actions, and whose transgressions have been wiped out by pious acts and sacrifices, reaches the celestial mansions, radiant with light and clothed in the spiritual form."

Jacolliot placed his hand on a small closed book, the Rig-Veda, and said: "What is the first word of the fifth line of the 21st page?"

The answer came, "Devadatta—given by God." This was correct.

"Put a mental question," said the fakir. I did so. "Vasundard—the earth," was the reply.

Jacolliot had asked: "Who is our common mother?"

At the end of the terrace he saw a Hindu in a garden drawing water from a well and pouring it through a conduit to a bathing room. Covindasamy stretched out his hand, and the well rope ceased to move. The Hindu began to chant all the magical incantations he knew, but the words died away in his throat. The fakir withdrew his hand, the well rope moved, and the Hindu's voice returned.

Concentrated and absorbed, before leaving, the fakir made Jacolliot hear some harmonious airs, like those heard rising from the valley by huntsmen in the mountains; then Covindasamy rose about a foot from the ground and finally took his leave.

Such are the facts relating to these Indian mediums as they are recorded in a large volume by M. Jacolliot. We could quote a much larger number, seen by Père Hué, a missionary, who lived for a long time in Thibet.

We will now instance some observations of the phenomenon of lucidity.

This power, as we are told by Dr. Pascal, is very strongly developed in the Hindus, the Redskins, the Druses, Kurds, Laplanders, Tartars, and a large number of other remnants of disappearing or degenerate races. There exists among some of these races a real mental telegraphy which closely connects them in times of danger. At the time of the Indian Mutiny the news of the outbreak arrived in the Indian bazaars long before the official telegraphic dispatches.

Napoleon Ney (in *Mussulman Societies*) relates that in 1883 M. de Lesseps explored the *chotts* of Tunisia. During his stay at Sfax, he read to an assembly of prominent natives a letter from Abd-el-Kader, who recommended them to regard favourably the application and project of Colonel Rondaire. On the evening of the same day he embarked for Gabes, where he arrived the following morning. In the evening he was at the village of Menzel, where the native chief congratulated him on the letter from the Emir, adding that the good news had reached them from Sfax during the day. Now from Sfax to Gabes by road is seven days' journey, and it was impossible for the chief to receive the news by water, the way M. de Lesseps had taken.

The *Missouri Republican* published, a few years since, a curious article on mental telegraphy among the Redskins : the manner in which they communicated with each other, the writer said, would remain a mystery which would never be revealed. The only thing established is that such communications are sent and received between persons far apart. After inquiry it has always been established that the communications were perfectly correct.

There is also universal agreement as to the fact itself, and no one can deny the existence of this power of mental communication at a distance—a power which seems to be confined to certain individuals of the tribe. This fact was proved several times during the war between the English and these tribes in 1789.

With regard to the mysterious sect of the Druses, in Lebanon, the secret of their telegraphy is marvellously preserved: they are thus kept in touch with all external matters that interest them.

Here is an interesting example reported by Mr. Scrugham. He was engaged as civil engineer in the construction of a line of railway in the interior of India. They came upon a rock which it was necessary to pierce, and, in expectation of this, they had ordered a battery of tripod perforators, worked by steam. But these perforators were late in arriving, and Mr. S. one day asked one of his assistants if he had any news of them from Calcutta, some thousands of miles distant. He replied in the negative, and did not even know if the steamer had arrived at Calcutta. During that time one of the Hindus, whom the Government had placed at the disposal of the engineer, came forward: he had received an excellent education and spoke English fluently. He told Mr. S. that the steamer had arrived at Calcutta, and that the perforators had been landed on the quay: " But," he added, " there is a part missing; what funny engines they are, with their three feet!"

They showed him a photograph of these perforators, and he pointed out to them the essential part which was missing in all of them. Mr. S. then telegraphed to Calcutta, and he learned that the perforators had been unpacked and that one necessary portion was missing from each one. The work was thus interrupted for some time. Mr. S. then called the Hindu and asked him where the missing pieces were. He replied that they had never been disembarked; they were at the bottom of the hold, hidden under a load of heavy packages destined for another port. The telegraph was again set to work, and the missing parts were found in the hold exactly as the Hindu had said. Some days afterwards the perforators arrived without accident and were set to work.

The singular phenomenon of projection of the double, which we shall now quote, is related by a missionary who was a witness of it in Africa.

A certain Ugema Uzago, who was at the time chief of the Jabikou tribe and a celebrated fetish-man, had an extraordinary power over the natives, because he cured the illnesses from which they suffered, found them the means of making fortunes as well as of recognising their enemies, a pleasing euphemism, which, in the minds of these people, signified that they would soon get rid of them.

This Ugema was a friend of the missionary, or, at least, having often sought assistance of the reverend father, it pleased him to pass as such, and, frequently in the evening, he came to converse with him on his affairs—and to ask for some tobacco.

One evening he told the missionary that the Master, whom they all feared, had invited all his disciples to assemble on the following evening on the Yemvi plateau.

"I shall therefore not be able to come here," added Ugema.

"But how," exclaimed the priest, "can you meet on the Yemvi plateau? It is four long days' walk. You will never get there."

Ugema rose up proudly:—

"Come with me to-morrow evening," he replied; "you will see that we know how to manage things, we black magicians."

The missionary took care not to miss so excellent an opportunity of witnessing the skill of the celebrated sorcerer, and the following evening at six o'clock, before nightfall, he had joined him.

"I am going to commence immediately the preparations for my departure," Ugema said to him. "As soon as I have finished, on your life, do not interfere with me, that would certainly be death for you, and also for me."

"I solemnly promised him," wrote the missionary, "not to say a word, nor to disturb him in his incantations by any gesture, or cry, or anything. I would be as mute as the trunk of a dead tree."

"But," I said to him again, "pardon, one word only. You are going, are you not, to the plateau at Yemvi, to the old deserted village."

" Yes, I have already told you that."

" Well, I have a commission to give you; will you do me a service."

" Very willingly."

" On your way, at the foot of the mountain, you pass through the village of Ushong, do you not ? "

" Certainly."

" You know the contractor there who purchases india-rubber ? "

" Esaba, is it not ? "

" Yes, that is right."

(I ought to say that Esaba, the black merchant of this village, is a Christian, with the baptismal name of Vincent, who, in case of need, teaches a little catechism, baptizes the dying, instructs children, and is moreover most devoted to us. When we are at his village it is always he who gives us hospitality and renders us a thousand services.)

" Well, on passing his door, would you tell him that I particularly wish to see him, if he could come immediately and at the same time bring me the cartridges which I left in my small tin case with him. He can leave everything else. The cartridges only : that is understood, is it not ? "

" Your commission shall be executed. Esaba will receive your message this very evening, and to-morrow will set out. Now, not a word."

In face of such assurance, it will be understood how my astonishment increased and how desirous I was to see the end of this affair, a singular one at the very least. How would Ugema go to the feast ? Four days' walk in a few minutes. And then, as I have just said, I had an easy means of control through Esaba. To carry out this part of his mission would entail a three days' journey, and then he would not be able to lose any time on the way.

However, Ugema and myself went into the fetish-man's hut. A fire, on to which some aromatic herbs and some strong-smelling wood had been abundantly thrown, burned in the centre, and the clear and brilliant flames illuminated the whole place. I seated myself in a corner. Already, singing a strange air and an impressive melody, Ugema had taken off his usual clothing: one by one, he reclothed himself in his fetish garments, stopping at each to commence a new song with a slow and strange rhythm, a kind of intonation, in which the voice was suddenly raised, and immediately fell again; often a chant of prayer or of adoration, more frequently an appeal to the spirits, the spirits of the woods, the forests, the waters, and of the dead.

At the same time Ugema slowly circled around the fire, timing each movement and constantly accelerating the rhythm. The fetish garments were put on. For a long time yet Ugema turned around the fire, up to the moment when the brands were consumed and only threw flickering glimmers across the room : a few sooty flames, insufficient to dissipate the surrounding obscurity. Suddenly Ugema stopped ; a strident imperative whistling was heard from the roof. I raised my head ; a supple form glided rustling across into the room ; a black serpent of the most dangerous kind spread himself out on the floor, raised his head towards me with an irritated air, moving his forked tongue with extreme rapidity, rose up, looked at me in a doubtful manner, swayed himself again, then sprang on to the sorcerer, embracing and enfolding him. Ugema unmoved took a phial, emptied a reddish coloured liquid with a strong garlic odour over his hands, rubbing successively his whole body, commencing at the feet; in the serpent I had already recognised his familiar animal, his Elangela, the executor of his death-sentences: the black serpent detached itself from his waist and coiled itself round his neck, swaying and waving itself around his head, following the rhythm of the dance, and the melody sung.

Without the fetish-man making a gesture or sign to stop me or pronouncing a word in prohibition, I lighted a torch which enabled me to see all the details of the scene.

The fire threw scarcely any more flickerings: one flame remained, then all was extinguished. Ugema stretched himself out on the bed : a peculiar acrid smell filled the room, I had tremendous difficulty in resisting the torpor which seemed to come over me altogether. I approached Ugema : the serpent had disappeared, the fetish-man slept soundly, but a very peculiar sleep, the sleep of death, without a movement, a cataleptic sleep : I raised his eyelids, the eye was white and glassy, making no movement when the flame of the torch was held before it. I stood in front of him, raised his arm, which fell back inert and rigid, with a corpse-like stiffness : I raised the leg with the same result, I pressed a pin into the flesh : there was no muscular contraction ; at the parting of the lips there was a slight whitish foam ; the movements of the head were imperceptible : Ugema slept.

All the night I watched him, I remained at his side : nothing seemed to show any sign of life. Not a gesture or movement.

Not until morning, towards eight o'clock, did Ugema begin to move slightly ; I watched him curiously : life returned by degrees, the movements, at first spasmodic, ceased : Ugema raised himself up from the wooden couch on which he was stretched out, looked at me in a stupefied manner as though to ask what I was doing there, when consciousness returned to him.

" Ah ! " he said to me, " how tired I am."

" Well ! and this famous journey ; you see that you have not been able to take it."

" What, I have not been able to take it ! What do you say ? "

" Were you last night on the plateau at Yemvi ? "

" Certainly ! Oh, it would not do to disobey the Master's command."

" And what have you done ? "

Ugema replied : " There were very many of us, we enjoyed ourselves greatly."

It was impossible to gather anything from that.

" And did you carry out my commission ? Did you tell Esaba ? "

" Certainly."

"You spoke to him last night?"

"I spoke to him last night."

"But I have not moved from this room; you were on the bed. I have watched over you through the night."

"No, *I* was not on the bed: my *body* was there; but what is my body? My *self* was not there: *I* was on the mountain at Yemvi."

Not wishing, for the moment, to insist further, I stopped the conversation and shortly afterwards made my way to the Mission, wondering and asking myself what could be thought of it all; was it dream, phantasm, illusion, or reality?

Three days afterwards, Esaba came to the Mission.

"Father," he said to me, "here are the cartridges for which you asked me the other day through Ugema. What else do you want me for?"

It was very easy for me to find something.

"At what time did Ugema arrive?"

"In the evening, about nine o'clock, three days ago, as I have said."

(This was exactly the time when Ugema fell into the cataleptic sleep.)

"Did you see him?"

"Oh, no! you know well that we blacks are afraid of night phantoms. Ugema knocked at my door, and he spoke to me outside, but I did not see him."

"Ah, well, and that is all."

Without doubt, Ugema had been present at the sorcerer's feast: without any doubt his *ego* had in a few moments performed a journey of several hours: without any doubt his *ego*, his double, had acted, spoken, heard.

These observations, it will be seen, have been made with great care. The author, in making his assertions as to the condition of the subject, has proved that he was not present as a purely passive spectator and cannot be accused of illusion or exaggeration. We regard the record as being of great value.

CHAPTER VII

POLTERGEIST PHENOMENA

It is sometimes observed that certain of the phenomena which we have studied in mediums appear also to manifest themselves spontaneously.

Most frequently there is no apparent cause for the phenomena of this class that suddenly manifest themselves in a house, in the midst of a family, and which seem sometimes to attach themselves by preference to one room or to one group of persons. The phenomena are, most frequently, very strange, and they last for a certain time in spite of all that the witnesses can do to stop them.

Then, some fine day, they cease as abruptly as they commenced and everything goes along once more as usual.

It is easy to assure oneself that these phenomena are precisely of the same character as those produced through mediums. We observe, in fact, in these cases, all the phenomena which we have studied as mediumistic, from the most simple up to the most complex.

The first phenomenon generally observed consists of noises which are heard spontaneously : these are knocks which are apparently struck on the walls or on the furniture, creakings and rubbings of various kinds, sounds of footsteps, whistlings and various cries, and sometimes very loud noises.

It is clear that the only noises and phenomena which interest us at present are those which occur out of reach of any human being, and which cannot be ascribed to any trickery.

At the same time as the noises, we find movements of objects taking place without contact. Pieces of furniture are moved about, sometimes overturned, even in rooms where no one is present and sometimes when they are locked up. Articles are thrown this way and that, in the presence of several people : often fragile objects are thrown to the ground and broken.

In the third place we find *apports;* that is to say, objects which were not previously in the apartment are spontaneously brought into it, and seem to fall from the ceiling. Objects are thus transported from one room to another, without the doors or the windows having been opened, and without any one being able to ascertain how they came into the room.

Lastly, but in very rare instances, the phenomenon of materialisation is found to occur ; that is to say, various forms make their appearance having most frequently the aspect of phantoms.

As will be seen, the majority of the phenomena which are obtained in experiments with mediums happen successively : nevertheless, we may remark that spontaneous phenomena present certain special characteristics, which we shall now consider.

Incoherence. What first strikes us, when we observe these phenomena, is their absurdity. Bells are set ringing, lights are extinguished, articles are removed from their places and taken into others where they have no right to be. For example, cooking utensils are carried on to beds, boots and shoes are placed on mantelpieces, while the ornaments on the latter are set down on the floor. Articles arranged in cupboards are thrown into disorder and mixed up confusedly with other things.

Violence is another of the characteristics of these spontaneous phenomena. The sounds are usually loud, the room or the house seems to be shaken ; sometimes it is thought that there has been an earthquake. When objects are thrown, it is usually with force. It seems that the force manifested in these movements is always much greater than is necessary to obtain the effect produced.

There is here a considerable difference between the movements obtained by the experimental externalisation of the force of the medium. In the experiments the medium makes efforts to attain a definite object; the force employed is strictly limited to the anticipated effect. Often the movement is produced slowly, and as though by successive efforts.

The roughness of the spontaneous force is one of its peculiar traits. The furniture is not moved gently as happens in experiments with a medium, but is thrown with force instead of being carried about, and often the articles are broken. Sometimes it even seems that this force is exercised with a malevolent intention, for the purpose of causing damage.

Clumsiness also seems to be a characteristic of the force thus brought into play. When an object is transported from one point to another, it knocks against or overturns others on its way. Other articles fall to the ground before arriving at the place to which they were apparently intended to be transported. Ornaments on mantelpieces or tables are thrown down or broken.

In experiments with mediums, on the contrary, the movements are effected with surprising gentleness and tact. The most fragile objects on a whatnot are brought on to the floor without accident; glasses filled with liquid are carried over the hands of the spectators to the middle of the table, the table is raised and not a drop of the liquid is spilled. It seems that this force, which is the same in both cases, is disorderly, without rule or restraint in the spontaneous manifestations; while in experimental phenomena it is most frequently precise, well regulated, and dexterous.

In all cases of this particular kind of haunting it should be noted that they are always associated with the presence of a medium.

This medium is in the house or belongs to the family where the phenomena are produced, or to the neighbourhood.

The medium is usually a young boy or girl, sometimes a child, but most frequently a girl.

We observe also that the phenomena are greater in intensity when produced in the immediate vicinity of the medium, and that her presence seems necessary for the production of the phenomena. When the medium is far removed from the house or the family in which these manifestations are produced, the phenomena cease.

Sometimes the phenomena are produced in the place to which the medium has moved; but most frequently they cease altogether.

The following account of manifestations of this character was published in the *Annales des Sciences Psychiques* as an extract from the *Western Gazette*, January 11, 1895 :—

"The little village of Durweston, situate about three miles from Blandford, has been for some weeks past the scene of considerable excitement in consequence of the supposition that one of its cottages is haunted. The cottage in question is one of a double tenement, situate at Norton—a spot isolated from the rest of the village, some considerable distance from the highway, and on the outskirts of a wood. The cottages are owned by Viscount Portman; his keeper (named Newman) occupies one, and the other until recently has been in the occupation of a widow (named Mrs. Best), her daughter, and two little orphan girls, who were boarded out to Mrs. Best by the Honourable Mrs. Pitt, of Steepleton. It is in the latter house that these occurrences, which have caused such a scare in the village, took place. More than a month since Mrs. Best—who, it may here be stated, is a most respectable woman, of a quiet, inoffensive disposition, and on good terms with her neighbours and the village generally —became puzzled by faint knocking and scratching in various parts of the house, and could account for the same in no possible way. As days passed there was a repetition of these strange noises, which gradually increased in loudness, until they could be heard by the keeper Newman in his own house. About a fortnight since, these sounds—which the village blacksmith described as then being as heavy as sledge-hammer blows—were succeeded by still more startling events, for, according to Mrs. Best's version, stones came violently through the bedroom windows, smashing the panes, and then returned through

the windows. The neighbours instituted a thorough
search of the surroundings to see if there was any one
hiding who was playing a joke upon the woman, but
there was not the slightest trace of a human being, nor
of footsteps."

In the latter part of January Mr. Westlake proceeded
to Durweston and took down the statements of some of
the principal witnesses—about twenty in all.

The disturbances, it appears, began on December 13,
1894. On the 18th December Mr. Newman witnessed
some of the phenomena.

The following is an extract from Mr. Westlake's notes
of an account given to him by Mr. Newman on the 23rd
January 1895:—

"On Tuesday (December 18th), between 10 and 11 A.M.,
Mrs. Best sent for me, and told me that Annie (the elder
girl, about thirteen years of age) had seen a boot come out
of the garden plot and strike the back door, leaving a
muddy mark. I went into Mrs. Best's, and I saw a bead
strike the window; and then soon after, a big blue bead
struck the window and broke it, and fell back. Then
a little toy whistle struck the window, but did not break
it. Then I sat down in the chair, and said: "You're a
coward, you're a coward; why don't you throw money?"
I was looking at the door opening into the garden; it was
wide open, leaving a space of 15 inches between it and
the inner wall, when I saw coming from behind the door
a quantity of little shells. They came round the door
from a height of about 5 feet. They came one at a time,
at intervals varying from half a minute to a minute. They
came very slowly, and when they hit me I could hardly
feel them. With the shells came two thimbles. They
came so slowly, that in the ordinary way they would have
dropped long before they reached me. They came from
a point, some, I think, a trifle higher, and some no higher,
than my head. Both the thimbles struck my hat. Some
missed my head and went just past, and fell down slanting-
wise (not as if suddenly dropped). Those that struck me
fell straight down.

" The two children were all the time in the same room with me.

" Then right from behind me a slate-pencil came as if from the copper. The pencil was about 2½ inches long, and went slowly on a slant to a bowl on the floor in the pantry ; and another piece went in the same direction just over the bowl, and fell into a pot of dirty water.

" Then a hasp, like the hasp of a glove, was dropped into my lap from a point above the level of my head.

" I never saw any of the things begin to move. I saw some of them just after they had started. The time was somewhere between 10 and 11 A.M.—a nice clear day; I don't remember whether there was sunlight.

" A boot then came in from outside the door. It came in moving along a foot above the ground, and pitched down. The boot had been lying right in front of the door, where it had previously fallen. This boot came towards me, and fell down just at my side. Mrs. Best took it and threw it out —it was an old dirty boot from off the garden plot (it was a woman's boot). I think the boot moved about as slowly as the other things, but cannot quite remember. It finally fell softly.

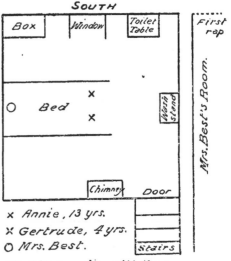

" After the boot was thrown out into the garden, I went out and put my foot on it, and said, " I defy anything to move this boot." Just as I stepped off, it rose up behind me and knocked my hat off; there was no one behind me. The boot and the hat fell down together.

G

" A few days later the two children, with their foster-mother, Mrs. Best—a woman, it should be said, of about sixty years—went to stay in Mr. Newman's cottage for some days. Whilst they were there the Rector of Durweston, the Rev. W. M. Anderson, came to witness the phenomena. On his first visit (Friday, the 4th January 1895) nothing took place. On Thursday, January 10th, he went again, accompanied by Mr. Sheppard, the schoolmaster. Mrs. Best took the two children upstairs and put them to bed, herself lying down in the bed with them. The chart on p. 97 shows the disposition of the furniture.

" Loud rappings were heard, apparently on the walls in different parts of the room. Mr. Sheppard went outside the house to see that no one was playing tricks from outside, whilst the Rector remained within, the noises still continuing. Subjoined is an extract from Mr. Anderson's account, written on the 25th January 1895, of the events of that evening :—

" I put my ear and hand to the wall, but could not detect any vibration ; but when resting my hand on the rail at the bottom of the bed, I could distinctly feel a vibration varying according to the loudness of the knocking. It is, perhaps, needless to say that I searched the room and the house, also Mrs. Best's house from top to bottom. Occasionally there was a noise on the wall, as if some one were scratching with their nails. This scratching also appeared to be produced on the mattress of the bed, although I am sure it was not produced by any of the three occupants of the bed, as I could see their hands, and watched them very closely all the time.

" There was a lighted lamp, a small hand-lamp giving a good light, on the washstand the whole time. When the rapping first began, I noticed that it frequently ceased when I came into the room, but after a short time it made no difference, and was loud and continuous when every inmate of the house was in the room. About 2.15 A.M. it was suggested by some one, I believe Mr. Sheppard, that the 'agency' should be asked whether it would write any communication on a slate ; the number of raps requested for an affirmative were given. There was no slate in the Newmans' house, but Mrs. Best told us where we should find one in her house. Newman, Mr. Sheppard, and myself went into her house, found the slate and a piece of pencil, and returned. In reply to several questions as to where the slate was to be placed, the number of knocks asked for was given for the window-sill (inside, of course), the sill being some nine or ten inches wide. I may mention that every conceivable place in the room was suggested one after the other, but the right number of raps was not given, but a short, sharp knock, which seemed always to be given for a negative. We almost gave up at this point, until, as an afterthought, I suggested the window-sill, which was at once accepted. The next question was as to who was to remain in the room, and according to the knocks every one was to leave, except the two children and Mrs. Best; the light was also to be removed. The sign to be given when the writing was finished was four raps. We all retired down the stairs, which are about ten in number, and straight. I remained at the bottom of the stairs, with the bedroom door wide open; it was very dark at the time. Some fifteen seconds elapsed, and amid perfect silence we all heard the pencil scratching on the slate. Mrs. Best gave a suppressed groan, which I could distinctly hear. Four sharp raps were given almost simultaneously with the dropping of the pencil on the slate, and Mrs. Best gave a loud, screaming call, 'Come!' I was in the room instantly; the whole thing taking less time than it would take to read this description. The light showed some unmeaning scratches on the slate. We asked for something legible, which was promised in the usual way. It was with the greatest difficulty that we could persuade Mrs. Best to remain in the room a second time, but we prevailed on her to do so; I promised to remain on the stairs. The second time a flourish (something like this) was on the slate—

" Only the curves were beautifully drawn, with firm, bold lines, such as no child could produce. The same proceedings took place a third time, when

$$\underset{\text{MONY}}{\overset{\text{M}}{\mid}}$$

was found on the slate, and the fourth time

$$\underset{\text{O}}{\overset{\text{O}}{\text{GARDEN}}} \quad \left(\underset{\text{O}}{\overset{\text{O}}{\text{jardin}}}\right)$$

Every time I was nearer to the bedroom door, which was wide open and opposite the window. The last two or three times I was so close that I could almost hear Mrs. Best breathe, the silence being death-like. The slightest movement by any one in the bed would have been detected by me in a moment, and I am absolutely certain that the writing could not have been done by any one in the room without my knowing it. On one occasion the pencil rolled off on to the floor, and was broken in two pieces.

" Mrs. Best cannot write ; the younger child cannot, she was asleep; Annie Cleave can. I told Mrs. Best that I was myself convinced that no one had moved in the bed much less left it, but I said people would say this had been the case. She said she was prepared to take a solemn oath that none of them had moved or left the bed, which was some four feet or more from the window.

" We could get no more replies in the way of raps, and nothing more was heard that night. Mr. Sheppard and I left at ten minutes to three.

" I should like to say a word about the characters of those who have witnessed and heard these abnormal phenomena. With one exception (Spinney) they are all known to me personally, and the veracity and honesty of them all is beyond question. Mrs. Best is an earnest Christian woman, who bears perhaps the highest character in the village.

" Later the children were taken to another house in the village, where raps and other noises were heard ; and were finally separated, the elder child, Annie, being removed to another village, Iwerne Minster, to the house of a single woman. There the disturbance still continued: noises were heard, generally on the outer walls of the house ; a big stone was flung on the roof of the porch ; and snow-drops were dug up out of the garden and flung about. On March 7th, Miss W. H. Mason, Local Government Board Inspector of Boarded-out Children, came down and took the child Annie to stay in her flat in London for a week. No disturbance worth recording took place during her stay in London."

Miss Mason had the child examined by a doctor, who pronounced her of a markedly consumptive tendency, and apparently hysterical. A sister two years older than herself has died of consumption. According to another witness, Annie, during the earlier disturbances, saw a queer animal with green head and green eyes and a big bushy tail, sitting up and pulling her doll to pieces with its paws. Gertie, the younger girl, she added, saw the same apparition when Annie called her.

CHAPTER VIII

HAUNTED HOUSES

THE following case of a haunted house is of special interest, as it was observed by Professor Lombroso, whom no one would suspect of an excess of credulity, or of being a victim to suggestions resulting from his surroundings. This case, therefore, presents guarantees of authenticity.

The Turin newspaper *La Stampa*, in its issue of November 19, 1900, mentioned some extraordinary phenomena which were occurring in a wine and spirit shop at No. 6, Via Bava, Turin.

For those unacquainted with the topography of Turin, it may not be amiss to say that the Via Bava is in the suburb of Vanchiga, and commences at the Piazza Vittorio-Emmanuele I. On the day mentioned *La Stampa* was brought to my notice.

Whilst I was casting a rapid glance over this paper I was struck by this pompous title, "The Spirit Devastators of the Via Bava." Naturally, without taking up the time to read this lengthy account, and fearing that I should arrive too late (because in these cases one cannot arrive too quickly), I quickly got into everybody's carriage—the tram-car—which took me in twenty minutes to the scene of action. Alas! too late! However, if the entertainment itself was over there were at least the spectators, who could themselves, in turn, serve as entertainers.

In the street a crowd of persons of all classes were struggling for entrance into the wine-shop; and in the shop itself a veritable swarm of drinkers were seated at the tables, and occupying themselves, between glasses, by composing epigrams about the spirits who to-day were dumb; others were trying to push their way through with their elbows, in order to make inquiries of everybody; to hear something related, to see, to touch, to examine, commencing with the bottles and the saucepans, even to the chairs, which, it is said, were broken, and several of which were transported from one place to another.

At the far end of the shop, at the counter, through a cloud of smoke and dust, we could distinguish a tall, corpulent, red-faced man (the landlord), who was turning and bending to right and left, holding in one hand a bottle of wine and receiving in the other his customers' money, in the midst of a tempest of voices, cries, commands, and protestations from all directions. Sometimes the price of the wine drunk by one customer, who had taken advantage of the crowd to slip away unseen, would be demanded from another; the anger of the master fell upon the waiter, a boy of thirteen years of age, who would have needed a hundred eyes and a hundred arms to have met the wants of everybody, and—most important thing of all —to make them pay.

In a word, it was impossible in the midst of such a Noah's Ark to take account of anything. It was with great difficulty that I succeeded in getting a few words with the master and mistress of the house. I interrogated one or two other persons and then went out.

I returned the same evening, without obtaining any better result. A still denser crowd barred the way, and the wine-shop was that evening closed by order of the police to prevent disturbance.

The report was spread at the same time that the phenomena had not been renewed. For some time I found it impossible to go into the matter, and when eventually I returned to the Via Bava all was completely restored to order and I was compelled to content myself with obtaining the evidence which I give here.

If it was not possible to see anything I could, however, make some reflections, and this is the reason why I have prefaced my account with this long rambling statement.

Why had so many people been set in motion by the simple title of a newspaper article?

Did they expect to discover the trick? I ought to state that I found in the place not only some idle and common people, and students, but also some people who are usually called serious-minded, and who had come there not to make a noise and laugh at credulous people, but with the simple desire to see, and impelled by the example of others.

I hope that this may be a good sign—that is to say, that this denotes the slow but continuous infiltration among the masses of beliefs formerly regarded as erroneous.

I will now give the facts in the following order. First, I will state in an objective manner the simple outline of the facts: with the warning, however, that they come from the tales of witnesses of very diverse values, and that they should only be accepted for what they are worth.

Then I will transcribe the written declarations which I have obtained from several witnesses, reserving to myself the criticism of the facts and testimony in accordance with my personal judgment.

The Facts

In order to make the phenomena more comprehensible it will, perhaps, be useful to describe the place where they occurred. I have stated that it was in a wine and spirit shop, No. 6, Via Bava, known as the Bottigheria Cinzano. I will here give the plan.

A. The first room, for the use of customers.
   1. Entrance door which opens on to the Via Bava.
   2. Window.
B. Second room, devoted to the same purpose as the former.
   3. Door opening on to a corridor which communicates with the hall of the house.
   4. Window looking on to the court.
   5. Opening covered by a simple cloth curtain, through which one passes to a small room C, which serves

as a kitchen and living room for the people of the house. This room is lighted by a window (6), and communicates with a garret (used as a bedroom) by means of a small staircase. The persons inhabiting this place were the landlord named Fumero, his wife, and a lad of thirteen years employed as waiter.

The beginning of the phenomena dates back to the early days of November. M. Raynero, the proprietor of the Annonciata Baths, situated at 51, Via del Po, was a friend of the Fumero family, and was informed at the commencement of November of the phenomena which had for some time past been occurring in that house. A cat seemed to be taken with strange mad attacks; it jumped as though possessed, and threw down the bottles.

The food which had been placed in the kitchen cupboard in the evening disappeared during the night,and so on.

But, on November 16th, the phenomena commenced which caused a stir in the whole district. On the morning of that day only the woman and the boy were in the shop. They both stated that first of all a vessel containing some liquor, which was on the kitchen table, overturned of its own accord; then other vessels were thrown down and broken, and then began a mad dance, in which the furniture, saucepans, and all kinds of things took part. Some were dented, others broken, and others disappeared.

Fumero's wife fainted away through fright, the neighbours ran in and telegraphed to her husband, who was away from Turin, and he returned that evening. All through the day, in the presence of several people, tables chairs, and utensils danced. Some garments were thrown down from the upper to the lower chamber and damaged. They were taken back to their place, and they were again thrown down with still greater violence by an invisible hand which seemed to make sport of the general fright.

The phenomena continued in the same way on the 17th and the following days with a few moments of respite.

In the meantime other things occurred in addition to those already mentioned, but outside the house.

M. Fumero had several cellars in the basement, and one of these was under the room B, and was only used for storing bottles. It was ascertained that when any one went into this cellar, and even in the absence of persons the bottles, empty or full, were broken, always by the work of the same unknown agents.

It was stated that a priest, who had been asked to bless the place, immediately took flight, because he obtained results exactly the opposite to what he had expected. The police came in their turn, but they were powerless; many even maintained that the guards and their superior officers served as involuntary targets for the projectiles thrown by the unknown hand.

Be that as it may, it appears that the police gave a hint to poor Fumero, that these things must cease, by love or by force. Fumero understood and complied, being already greatly annoyed by the material and moral damage he had suffered. Thus when Cesar Lombroso went to the shop on November 21st, he was told (without knowledge as to who he was) that Professor Lombroso had been and that everything had ceased. Lombroso then revealed his identity, and, going down into the cellar, was able to verify the phenomena of which we shall speak later.

On November 22nd, Mme. Fumero, acting on advice, went to Nole Canavèse, her native place. She remained there three days, during which time nothing unusual occurred, either at Via Bava or at Nole. On her return to Turin, the phenomena reappeared in an altered form, but substantially the same.

On November 26th, Mme. Fumero went away again, but this time the phenomena continued.

It was at this time that the migration of the shoes took place, as related in the attestation of M. Raynero. The wife returned to Turin and the phenomena ceased at the end of November—that is to say, only when, after it was seen that they were not due merely to the presence of Mme. Fumero, it was decided to discharge the waiter. He went to another shop in the same street, but nothing out of the ordinary happened, and so the matter ended.

EVIDENCE COLLECTED

Negative Evidence.—This was furnished by the police, by several Turin newspapers, by all those who had seen nothing; and, finally, by the curé of the parish of l'Annonciata (Via del Po), who remained for two hours in the place and not only saw nothing abnormal, but was convinced that there was nothing but joking and deception in the whole affair.

Positive Evidence.—There were numerous positive testimonies; therefore I have only collected the most important ones, or those which seemed to me to be most worthy of confidence.

Attestation of the Proprietors of the Wine-shop and of two Customers

" We declare that we were present several times at the Bottigheria Cinzano, 6, Via Bava, during the month of November 1900, when some strange occurrences occurred, such as the spontaneous movements of objects, breaking of bottles, &c., which we could not attribute to any practical joking or fraud whatever.

" In virtue of which we sign :

" BARTHOLOMEO FUMERO, Proprietor of the Bottigheria Cinzano.

" ANTOINETTE FUMERO, wife of the above.

" CARLO DEGOSTINI, Maker of Macaroni, 7, Via Pescator.

" FELICE HOPPETTI, Carpenter, 5, Via Bava.

"TURIN, *December* 15, 1900."

The following declaration was written by myself in the presence of the witness, in accordance with his own narrative.

Attestation of Raynero

" I, the undersigned, proprietor of the Baths of the l'Annonciata, at 51, Via del Po, attest upon my honour that what is here said is in conformity with the truth and the absolute conviction I have formed as to the real existence of the inexplicable facts which happened during the month of November in the Bottigheria Cinzano at 6, Via Bava. The following are two facts to which I can best testify—

1. "On November 27th, I was in the front room (A) of the wine-shop in company with M. Fumero, whose wife had gone to Nole. I was seated at a table (a) with another person. The waiter was in the back room (B) engaged in washing bottles, in a corner where I could clearly see him all the time. Suddenly two shoes, which came from the kitchen, fell at my feet. I instantly hastened to the kitchen, followed by M. Fumero, to catch the joker—if there was one—in the act. I mounted the staircase which led to the garret, but could find no one there; I was then convinced that the shoes came of themselves to my feet. Previously the shoes must have been in their usual place. I saw them while they were still in the air. The waiter, during the phenomenon, had not moved from the spot where he had previously been.

2. "I was in the cellar with M. Merini, Accountant, and while I held a lighted candle in my hand, I saw some full bottles thrown over and broken. Immediately after M. Merini had remarked that the fermentation of the wine might be the cause of the disturbance, some empty bottles began to break. Certainly no one had anything to do with the breaking of these articles.

"These two facts, more than anything else, led me to the belief that the phenomena which occurred in the refreshment room could not be due to any fraud, either on the part of Fumero's wife or of the waiter, or, indeed, of anybody else.

"I must therefore recede from the opinion that I first expressed when Mme. Fumero told me of the mad antics of the cat, the disappearance of food, &c., that she and the waiter were doubtless subject to some malady which induced them to commit these acts in secrecy.

"CHRISTOFLE RAYNERO.

"TURIN, *December* 22, 1900."

I also drew up the following declaration of M. Merini, the Accountant, who was not able himself to find time for that purpose. It may, however, be considered as exactly agreeing with his opinions, and as giving each of his statements its proper value.

Attestation of the Accountant, M. Merini

" I learnt about the phenomena of Via Bava through the newspapers of other towns some days after they first happened. I went immediately to the Bottigheria Cinzano, 6, Via Bava.

" It was an afternoon between November 19th and 25th. I was unwilling to believe the facts which were reported, but I was nevertheless inclined to accept them if I could be present at some absolutely clear manifestation. I arrived at the spot at a time when, according to the persons present, the manifestations were in full swing. Those whom I questioned related many marvellous things, among which I noted evident exaggeration of details, and some contradictions; then, learning that manifestations had taken place in the cellar, before any one was there, I expressed a desire to go there myself.

" There (in the cellar), in company with several other persons, I saw bottles break without apparent and reasonable cause. I wished to remain alone, the better to verify the phenomenon. The other persons having assented to this proposal, I shut myself up in the cellar, while all the rest withdrew to the end of the passage, from which the staircase leads to the upper floor. I began by assuring myself, with the aid of a candle, that I was really alone. This examination was easy, thanks to the smallness of the cellar, and the difficulty that there would have been in hiding behind the few utensils which were in it. Along the walls, lengthwise of the cellar, there was a series of strong beams supported at each end by posts. The planks resting on these beams were completely covered with bottles, empty and full. I also observed that the window looking out on the courtyard, which formerly served to light the cellar, was at that time obstructed by a plank.

"I then saw several empty and full bottles break of themselves before my eyes. I placed a ladder near the spot where they broke most frequently, and mounted to the top rung. I took an empty bottle which had been broken shortly before, and of which only the lower half remained; I separated it from the others, placing it at some distance from where it had previously been, namely, on the top of one of the posts which supported the shelves. After a few minutes the bottle broke again and flew into splinters. This is one of the facts which I can certify most precisely.

"On examining attentively the manner in which the bottles broke, I was able to make out that the fracture was preceded by the special cracking noise peculiar to breaking glass. I had already observed that the empty bottles broke in this way, from which it was evident that the explosion could not be due to the pressure of gas produced by fermentation, which besides was very improbable.

"To give an idea of the noise made by the bottles in breaking, and of the way in which they crumbled to pieces, I will add that it might be compared to the breaking of those drops of glass which fly into powder when they are scratched, and which are known as Prince Rupert's Drops.

"As to the mysterious cause of these phenomena, I confess that, although I had no reason to be afraid, I always experienced in their presence a certain feeling of astonishment and fear, for which I can give no reason; except that I recognised that the cause of these phenomena was an intelligent one and uncontrollable by any person's will. In other words, if I were convinced that spirits existed, I should truly have to say that they were the invisible authors of this uproar. I state this explicitly, because I confess that before seeing such things I was far from believing that they could produce such an effect on me.

"I declare on my word of honour that the foregoing

is the truth, and that I am sure that I was not the victim of illusion or fraud.

"PIETRO MERINI, *Accountant.*

"TURIN, 9, VIA PIETRO MICCA,
"*January* 9, 1901."

Phenomena observed by Professor Lombroso

"I went into the cellar, at first in complete darkness, and heard a noise of broken glasses, and bottles rolled at my feet. The bottles were ranged in six compartments one above another. In the middle was a rough table on which I had six lighted candles placed, supposing that the spirit phenomena would cease in the bright light. But, on the contrary, I saw three empty bottles, standing on the ground, roll as though pushed by a finger, and break near the table. To obviate any possible trick, I felt and carefully examined by the light of a candle all the full bottles which were on the racks, and assured myself that there was no cord or string which could explain their movements.

"After a few minutes first two, then four, then two other bottles on the second and third racks detached themselves and fell to the ground, not suddenly, but as though carried by some one; and after their descent, rather than fall, six of them broke on the wet floor, already soaked with wine; only two remained whole. Then at the moment of leaving the cellar, just as I was going out, I heard another bottle break."

Criticism of Evidence

In case any reader should find the following pages scarcely in harmony with the title of this section, I would ask him to reflect on the difficulty experienced, in this case, in collecting the facts and recording them in such a way as to leave no doubt as to their authenticity, so that some conclusion can be drawn from them.

If you go to the shop in the Via Bava, you will hear

related by one, and then another, a thousand different incidents, and it will seem to you that there can be no doubt as to their authenticity.

But take the pains to question them, insisting on such and such a point, and you will immediately perceive that nearly all your interlocutors contradict themselves on points they had previously affirmed, or do not agree with some one who was present at the same events, and you will be persuaded that all was merely a trick or a hallucination.

If that astonishes you, I may tell you that nothing on the contrary is more natural.

In fact, it is sufficient to reflect that if we cannot regard as always exempt from error even those who are endowed with the scientific training which is indispensable in such cases, and who are well acquainted with the difficulties (which cannot always be foreseen) presented by the verification of mediumistic phenomena, it will be much worse still for those who, while possessing scientific aptitudes, do not possess the experience which is gained by studying various mediums.

From that it follows that many studious and learned persons have fallen into gross errors.

To mention only one of these, I will refer to the supposed imposture of all the mediums from 1848 up till to-day. Thus any amateur investigator of spiritism, who possesses perhaps a name honourably known in other branches, can allow himself to joke about experiments of Crookes—to quote the name of a known experimenter—because on reading his account he found he could make such or such an objection ; or because, having decided to hold a séance, he observed that the materialised form of Katie King resembled that of the medium, a thing which could not happen if Katie King was a person having a separate existence, &c. &c.

This is the sort of confusion of ideas which is produced by incompetent men. It seems to me like a surgeon performing a delicate operation on a sick person after having studied human anatomy only in the text-books.

But a truce to digressions. Therefore, if those who ought to show themselves competent, permit themselves to form certain judgments, what can a poor joiner or wine-seller, both almost without education, tell you that is serious or worthy of belief?

There is, however, one thing which has some value if regarded with a certain breadth of view. If, for example, the four witnesses whose names appear at the foot of the first attestation find it difficult to agree among themselves, in describing such or such a fact, in such a way as to leave no doubt as to its truth, they are not therefore fools; far from that. If they have had little education, they have had experience as men who have seen life, and we cannot refuse to place a certain amount of confidence in them when they tell us decisively and with an enthusiastic conviction: " I have seen." And the same may be said of many other persons who repeat the same refrain: " I have seen."

And that is why those who, from the circumstances in which they were placed, ought to have been better able than the others to state the facts precisely as they happened, are those who, on the contrary, have given the least precise account, and hence the vagueness of the first attestation.

The second, signed by Raynero, is more extended, and states precisely two important facts—the throwing of shoes by an unknown hand, and the spontaneous breaking of the bottles in the cellar; moreover, his manner of telling the story inspires more confidence, because he allows himself to be less carried away than the others into exaggeration of the facts, while relating them with earnest conviction. I do not, however, consider that we can blindly accept his evidence on one point—that which deals with the conclusions which he draws from the facts; that is to say, the non-participation of the wife and waiter in the phenomena, these two persons being the only ones on whom suspicion rested. My suggestion is, however, that if this participation did occur, it was entirely sub-conscious. Further on I shall give some other reasons in support of this view. For the present, it is sufficient to say that,

H

although there are indications which cause us to suspect that the phenomena are not really supernormal, we must logically exclude all thoughts of ordinary trickery.

Having expressed these doubts on Raynero's conclusions, I will now discuss the facts which led Raynero to such a conclusion.

Any one who carefully reads the description of the telekinetic phenomena, which consisted in the throwing of the shoes, with the plan of the place before him, cannot fail to observe that the explanation given by Raynero is insufficient to prove that there was not fraud on the part of the waiter.

Urged by a doubt of this character after Raynero had signed his declaration, I proposed to go with him to the place in order to thoroughly clear up certain points. This was done immediately. We shall now see with what caution such evidence ought to be received.

I therefore ascertained—and Raynero also agreed—that in the place where he was seated (A) at the moment when the shoes fell, it would have been difficult for him to see if the waiter, engaged in his work in the other room (B), had disappeared for a moment to throw the articles, which, with unconscious premeditation, he must previously have taken from their usual place. Even from the point in question Raynero could not completely see the waiter, and no one thought of putting him under surveillance; moreover, after the event took place there was no suggestion that it might be due to fraud, so that it could not even be ascertained if, immediately after the phenomenon occurred, the waiter was calmly engaged in his work or not.

In these circumstances my opinion is that we can no longer speak of certifying such a phenomenon.

When I had put these observations to him, Raynero began to hesitate, then to doubt if the phenomenon had really occurred, as I had done myself. But, after having considered a little, he reverted to his first opinion, and observed that he had seen the shoes when they were still in the air, and that, according to the course they took, it could be inferred that they had been thrown from a point near the top of the staircase. It consequently seemed to him that the waiter could not have accomplished this feat without being seen and without making some noise, because, owing to his small stature, he would have had to go nearly up to the middle of the staircase. I am willing to accept this correction by Raynero, although it is difficult, even admitting that such details remained impressed on the memory, to get rid of doubts as to the accuracy of the observation, seeing that at the time no one expected any such phenomenon.

I think I should also add, as a scrupulous narrator, a detail as to the circumstances in which the phenomenon was produced. At my request Raynero told me again that the window of the garret (above the kitchen, C) was then open. It seemed to me hardly probable, if not impossible, that some one could hide in the garret and then get away through the window. I found it to be equally unthinkable that the shoes were thrown from the court through the window in such a way as to pass through the garret and fall at Raynero's feet. We can therefore, without much fear of being mistaken, set aside these hypotheses.

Having examined the circumstances, we have to pronounce and decide whether the phenomenon in question is to be attributed to fraud on the part of the waiter, or if it must be considered as a true supernormal phenomenon.

I consider that, owing to the conditions of the phenomenon being imperfectly verified, although there exists a certain probability that they were produced by supernormal means, it is best to abstain from a definite judgment.

After all this discussion, and after so prolonged an examination, some may ask themselves why, if the phenomenon appears to be doubtful and due to fraud, I have made so specious an argument, based on a sub-conscious fraud of the waiter, instead of on a real and conscious deception.

These questions demand a few words in reply. In the first place, I have tried to show why one could not accept entirely the evidence of an individual who, among several whom I questioned, might, it seemed to me, inspire confidence by the exact manner in which he reported the facts; then to make the readers understand that these facts ought to be rigorously attested in order to be taken into consideration.

Under such circumstances it is necessary to be cautious, seeing that, in this matter, we are still generally too ignorant to be able to pass over in silence certain details which seem *a priori* to be useless.

It is necessary above all to show discretion in the question of "sub-conscious" or "automatic" fraud, to which I must return, because it is denied or ignored by a very large number of people, but on this I shall only enlarge as far as is necessary to justify what I have said above.

May I then be permitted·to call to mind that at the time of the experiments, now historical, made at Milan, through Eusapia Paladino—experiments in which a number of persons, well known throughout the whole of Europe, took part, and which marked a milestone in the progress of these ideas in the orthodox camp—an individual (now dead) claimed to reveal how Eusapia Paladino produced these phenomena.

The publicity given to this discovery caused many persons to confuse together the phenomena which could not in any way be attributed to fraud, with others, with regard to which this accusation could be brought, and to go so far as to charge with the greatest stupidity ten or twelve persons who, fortunately, were not mere nobodies.

Later on, in fact, it was discovered what constituted Eusapia Paladino's frauds and their "automatic" or "subconscious" nature. Up to the present time, it should be said that such "sub-conscious" frauds have been but little studied in mediums, because those who have been interested in these mediumistic phenomena either accept everything, or attribute everything to common fraud, whereas this latter is much rarer than we suppose in our excessive pride, which causes a person of ordinary cunning to fancy himself shrewder than every one else. For my part I declare, from my own experience, that I consider that "sub-conscious simulation," both in physical phenomena and in the so-called communications from beyond the tomb, is very frequently, if not always, bound up with authentic phenomena.

I should then have considered it quite natural, and in the order of things, if along with the authentic phenomena of the Via Bava there had been observed " unconscious automatisms " of which I speak ; and, for more than one reason, I even incline to the belief that such was the case.

As to the evidence of the Accountant, M. Merini, I state at once that there is little to say : the fact which he relates is expressed with such precision of detail that there is almost nothing to object to it. Further, in conversing with him, I am convinced that his mind is well balanced, his judgment calm and sure, his conviction firm and complete. Not only has he never manifested any repugnance to the publication of his name ; but he even wishes that I should say here that he is ready to repeat to any one who desires to hear it what he has related to me.

This last feature sufficiently characterises the individual.

Finally, I have no need to comment on the declaration of Professor Lombroso, because no one would refuse to credit his statements.

Notes and Conclusions

I hope it has been made clear to the reader who has impartially followed us up to this point that supernormal phenomena really took place in the Via Bava.

Some one, however, will say : " Who was the medium that produced all these extraordinary things ? " And, in fact, it is admitted that these phenomena are always due to the presence of certain persons gifted with special aptitudes.

But I do not know how to reply to such an apparently simple question. Was it the waiter that was the medium? Or the wife? Or both? Several séances have, however, been held in the same cellar in the Via Bava, with the same persons, without obtaining any result to be compared with the other phenomena.

I should be inclined to believe that there was a *mediumistic contagion.* I could not, however, affirm this.

Be that as it may, why did these phenomena break out suddenly, and why did they disappear in the same manner? We have not been able to find out the real reason.

I believe, however, that it is not surprising that the wife and the waiter, although both mediums, did not produce anything outside of a determined sphere. Perhaps they were special mediums, "occasional mediums," so to speak, of whom we find numerous examples. And thus it was that at the end of November the phenomena ceased altogether, and were no longer produced, even in the new place to which the waiter went after leaving the Bottigheria Cinzano.

It will not be unacceptable to the reader, I hope, if I add a few words about the Fumeros and their waiter.

Bartolomeo Fumero is a man of about fifty years of age. He is square-shouldered, and has the red face usually found in drinkers. He is of an impulsive nature, falling easily into exaggeration when talking. (Thus, doubtless, he exaggerated the damage he had suffered.) In other respects his neighbours regarded him as a very honest man, incapable of injuring any one.

His wife, when I saw her for the first time (on the occasion of the phenomena), seemed to be ill. Now she is well, but she is still pale and delicate. She was not willing to admit to me that she had ever been subject to any hallucinations whatever. Professor Lombroso, on the contrary, in his statement, makes an allusion to these hallucinations. She is clever, knows how to write and keep accounts. She underwent an operation for hystero-ovariotomy a year ago.

The waiter is not of full height, and is of moderate intelligence. There is apparently nothing else to remark concerning him. With regard to fraud, I recall an observation made by a workman who was one day present at a spontaneous breaking of bottles. He saw, or thought he saw, that this breaking of bottles was always preceded by a sudden movement of the waiter. The workman explained that by saying that *the waiter threw out the force*. We record the observation; even such a phenomenon is not new, since it has already been observed with other mediums—for instance, with the very well-known Neapolitan medium, of whom we have already spoken with regard to sub-conscious fraud. I shall return to this question of *apparent* fraud in connection with the observations made with other mediums.

Let us, then, sum up. Via Bava was the scene of perfectly authentic phenomena of a supernormal character; also of less well-defined phenomena, obscurely connected with the first.

We have, in fact, spoken of hallucinations, of subconscious frauds, and even—as if this were not sufficient to complicate all verification of the facts—of a case of undoubted appearance of fraud in the automatic movements of the waiter preceding some of the phenomena.

We can easily understand why such uncertainty is prejudicial to the effect which these phenomena ought to produce on public opinion. Only, if the question is so far from clear, this is due mainly to the indifference with which the majority of scientific men regard this class of studies. As to the majority of the public, they take advantage of these uncertainties to create confusion and to throw doubt even upon what is now absolutely proved; that is to say, that in Spiritism, Mediumship, Occultism—call it what you will—there exist facts opposed to the general idea which we have formed as to the laws governing the physical world.

CHAPTER IX

TELEPATHY

Telepathic warnings without Hallucinations or Visions—Telepathic warnings with Hallucination—Telepathic warnings with Vision

WE shall define telepathy as *the knowledge which a subject (called the percipient) receives of a fact concerning another subject, whom we call the agent, and which takes place at a distance, outside the range of the normal senses,* and without this fact being able to come to his knowledge by the normal operation of his senses or by any known means.

It seems, however, that, in the majority of cases, the phenomenon of telepathy is due to the operation of the faculty of lucidity possessed by the percipient, and that, consequently, we may connect telepathy with the more common phenomenon of lucidity, of which it only forms a special case.

However, there are some instances which are classed in the category of telepathic facts, in which there seems to be something intervening which is foreign to the phenomenon of lucidity.

First, there are cases in which a hallucination without vision, occurring to one or several percipients, coincides with a fact which interests them and has taken place at a distance from them, but does not communicate to them the knowledge of this fact. It is true that, in these cases, we can say that the percipient has a vague, general perception of an accident, and these cases may be considered as a phenomenon of rudimentary lucidity not fully developed.

But there are, besides, cases in which a telepathic vision leaves undeniable objective traces of such a character that we can no longer class this vision in the category of hallucinatory visions.

These cases are only a combination of several psychical phenomena, and we know with what facility and frequency these various phenomena are mixed together and superposed one on another. We may, therefore, here consider that a new phenomenon has to be added to that of lucidity.

In order to obtain a scientific classification of the phenomena of telepathy we have to consider on the one hand the transmitting agent; and on the other, the percipient.

With regard to the agent, we find that in the majority of cases it is at the moment of the approach of death that the telepathic communication is made. In cases where the agent is living, most frequently he is the victim of an accident, suffering from intense emotion and considerable anguish. Also there are some very rare instances in which the agent has himself a knowledge of the telepathic vision which he produces. Finally, in some of these last-named cases, not only is the agent conscious of the vision produced, but it is voluntary and produced by an effort which he himself makes to appear to the percipient. With regard to the percipient, we have first of all to consider whether he is in the waking or in the sleeping state at the moment when he receives the telepathic communication.

In the second place, we have to consider the manner in which he receives this communication. In the waking state we find simple premonitions, without hallucination or vision, and, in one case, premonition manifested through automatic writing.

In other cases we find telepathic communications, with hallucination without vision, in which the hallucinations may extend to several persons, but the communication has a vague and incomplete character. Finally, we shall find, on the part of the percipient telepathic communications with vision, this vision either consisting in the simple appearance of the picture of the agent; or presenting more complex character, and making known to the percipient some very circumstantial details as to the fact or the accident that has befallen the agent. These visions sometimes present themselves with the very peculiar characteristic of being seen by other persons at the same time as the recipient to whom they are sent.

Here is a case in which we find, in the waking state, a premonition of the danger incurred by some young men in an accident. This premonition occurred, as we shall see, without vision and without hallucination. The communication otherwise is vague, and, while certainly making known that a danger had been run, it did not designate its character. One particular point to note in this case is that the communication came, not to the person most nearly related to the subject who had encountered the danger, but to a stranger who served as intermediary to communicate it to the person concerned.

This account is taken from the *Annales des Sciences Psychiques* :—

"On April 30, 1889," says Madame X., " I was present at Benediction at the Convent of the Sœurs de la Sagesse on the occasion of the feast of the Blessed Father de Montfort. At the moment of Benediction the good mother, whose praying - stool was separated from my chair by a grating, turned abruptly towards me (she had to turn three quarters round) and said to me : ' Madame, I am going to pray to our good father (the Blessed de Montfort) for your young people, that he will protect them ; he loves all young people ; you pray also for them.' This seemed to me very strange, because it was at the moment of Benediction when every one was wrapped in contemplation, and the good sisters generally were as still as statues. Sister Saint A. had never seemed to take any interest in my children, whom she scarcely knew, and her manner and attitude were generally so reserved, so calm, and the expression on her face at this moment was so singular that all present were strongly inclined to laugh, and it was passed from chair to chair that the good mother was going mad. They did not remember ever having seen her turn away from her prayers to address such words to her neighbours.

"After the ceremony I returned home, and there I was told that my two sons had nearly been run over in a carriage accident, and that only a quarter of an hour before. Both of them had been violently thrown out of a gig, and under a cart. The horse stopped short just at the moment when the wheel was about to pass over one of them. The younger had a broken arm, the elder only sustained some bruises."

The same evening Madame X. told her husband the good mother's presentiment; he remembers the fact and confirms it.

Here I leave Madame X., senior, to tell the story; she was a woman of very clear mind, but, like her daughter, very credulous as to interventions from beyond the tomb.

"'On the evening of the accident, as we wished to make our acknowledgments to Father de Montfort, I went to the convent to have some candles burnt in the chapel. I found the nuns all 'in the air' (sic), and the good mother in tears. They had learned of the event, and were in the choir blessing the name of the saint. The good mother came to me and said: 'During Benediction, I felt a blow at the heart (sic); I thought of your children, and looked for their mother to tell her to pray for them.'

"It is certain that the good mother turned towards Madame X. at the moment of Benediction to exhort her to recommend her children to the care of Father de Montfort, which appeared somewhat extraordinary, and it was not a habit of the elderly nun, as many persons remarked and still remember. It is certain that at the same hour, and as far as it is possible to say, within the same quarter of an hour, Madame X.'s children were in great danger."

Extract from a letter from Madame X. to Dr. Emery

"JONZAC, *January* 9, 1891.

"The account of the accident has been often told to me, and quite recently again during the New Year holidays by the three actors, my two sons J. and R., and my nephew E.; they were then aged respectively eighteen, fourteen, and seventeen years. They were therefore perfectly able to understand the gravity of the occurrence, and no one was in a better position to tell the story.

"On April 29, 1889, they all three set out for a ride in a gig. On their returning to the town, their light carriage, carelessly driven, collided with a large cart filled with stone which was going in the same direction as they were. They were violently thrown out. J. and E. suffered from contusions and bruises; R. found himself lying under the wheel of the cart; he did not faint, and he felt himself absolutely lost. As he has often repeated since, he 'had death in front of him.' His brother J. rushed to the wheel and tried to stop it with his hands.

"Was it his effort, although too feeble, or was it simply the movement of the driver, on hearing the noise? The wheel stopped just after breaking R.'s arm. Another step of the horse, or a further movement due to the impetus gained, and I should never have seen my son again. All the witnesses of this scene, and they were numerous, because people were coming from the five o'clock train, thought that he was completely crushed; some regarded it as a miracle, others as extraordinary, that greater damage had not been done.

"During this time I was at the well-known service in the chapel of the sisters of La Sagesse. My place was against the railing, almost behind that of the Superior, Madame H. But at the moment of Benediction the good mother rose, turned round, and looking at me said: 'Madame X., I am going to pray to our good Father for your boys; he will protect them, he loves all young people, you must pray also.' This seemed to me to be very strange, and I must admit even made me laugh, because the good mother, with whom, it is true, I am on very good terms, scarcely knew my children; they had never been to see her; she could scarcely have known that it was their holiday time. My mother, who was by my side, was also surprised and asked, 'What did the good mother want with you?' I told her that I did not know what had come to her. Several of the ladies present asked me the same question as we left the chapel.

"After the ceremony I went to make a visit, when some one came to look for me to tell me of the accident.

"As to the coincidence of time there is no doubt whatever. I have told you that when R. was under the cart, people were coming from the 4.55 train : he fell down in front of the Auberge Bobrie; if you calculate, it must have been 5.15. Vespers commenced at 4.30—three quarters of an hour would be taken up in chanting the psalms, anthems, and canticles before the Benediction; that is the time always taken. We were so impressed that my mother returned immediately to the convent to ask them to burn a candle in front of the saint's statue. She found the nuns in tears. They had just been told of what had happened, and were clustering round the good mother, who said that she had felt a blow at her heart and had immediately thought of the young X.'s. She was an elderly, saintly, and very simple woman.

The following case comes from Dr. Liébeault.

Here again there was neither hallucination nor vision ; the communication was made by means of automatic writing.

" This incident happened in a French family from New Orleans, who had been living for some time at Nancy in order to settle up a business matter. I had made the acquaintance of this family, because the head of it, M. G., had brought his niece, Mlle. B., to me that I might treat her by hypnotism. She had become slightly anæmic and was suffering from extreme nervousness, which she had contracted at Coblenz, in a school where she had been teacher. I was easily able to put her into a somnambulistic condition, and she was cured in two sittings. Since the production of this state of sleep had demonstrated to the family and to Mlle. B. that she could easily become a medium (Mme. G. was a spiritist medium), this young lady practised the invocation of spirits, in which she sincerely believed, by the assistance of the pen, and at the end of two months she became a remarkable writing medium.

"I have seen her with my own eyes rapidly write several pages of what she called messages, in well-chosen terms, without erasure, and at the same time engage in conversation with persons around her. The curious thing was that she never had any knowledge of what she was writing. 'Therefore,' she said, 'it can only be a spirit that directs my hand; it is not I.'

"One day, I think it was February 7, 1868, about eight o'clock in the morning, when the table was being laid for breakfast, she felt a desire, something that impelled her to write (that is what she called a trance), and she immediately ran to her large note-book, in which she traced in a feverish manner, with the pencil, some indecipherable characters. She again drew the same characters on the following pages, and when at last the excitement of her mind cooled down, it could be read that a person, named Margaret, had announced her death.

"It was immediately supposed that a young lady of this name, who was her friend, and had been a teacher in the same school at Coblenz, had died. All the family, including Mlle. B., immediately came to me, and we decided to find out the same day if the death had really taken place. Mlle. B. wrote to a young English lady, one of her friends, who was also a teacher at the boarding-school in question, making some excuse, as she did not wish to make the real motive known. By return of post we received a reply in English, from which they copied for me the essential part, which I found in my writing-case about a fortnight ago. It expressed the astonishment of this young English lady at receiving Mlle. B.'s letter, which she had not expected so soon, seeing that the special reason for writing was not apparent. But, at the same time, the English friend hastened to announce to our medium that their common friend Margaret had died on February 7th, about eight o'clock in the morning. Moreover, a small square piece of paper was inserted in the letter; it was a notification of the death. It is needless to tell you that I verified the envelope containing the letter, and that it appeared to me to have really come from Coblenz. Only I have since regretted that I did not, in the interests of science, ask the family to go with me to the telegraph office to make sure that they had not received a telegram during the morning of February 7th. Science ought not to have any bashfulness; truth has no fear of being seen. I have only a moral proof of the truth of the fact, that is, the honour of the family G., which always seemed to me to be above suspicion."

The two following cases are of hallucination without vision. They are quoted by M. Flammarion in his work and are supplied by General Parmentier, who states that the two facts occurred in his family.

"Several persons had met for a luncheon party given at Andlau in Alsace. After waiting awhile for the master of the house, who had gone out hunting, they sat down to the table without him, his wife saying it could not be long before he came in. They began breakfast very merrily, expecting every minute to see the over-zealous votary of St. Hubert appear. But time went on. Every one was astonished at the length of the delay, when suddenly, though the day was calm and the heavens blue, the window of the dining-room, which was wide open, was shut violently with a great noise, and opened wide again immediately. The guests were astonished that this could have happened without overturning a decanter of water which was standing on a table close to the window, and that the decanter remained undisturbed. Those who had seen it and heard the noise could not understand anything of what had occurred. 'Some misfortune has just happened!' cried the lady of the house, rising from the table in affright. The luncheon came to an end. Three-quarters of an hour later the dead body of the sportsman was brought in on a stretcher. He had re-received a charge of shot full in his heart. He died immediately, having only time to exclaim: 'My wife! my poor children!'"

In this case, we are justified in placing in the category of hallucinations the phenomenon perceived by the witnesses. In point of fact, it follows from their statement that the window could not be closed without overturning the decanter, and this remained unmoved. It therefore seems to have been simple perception of a loud noise that the witnesses, probably by auditive analogy, had attributed to the closing of the window. The account seems to leave it to be supposed that some of the witnesses had also seen the window closed; but in addition to the fact that the visual phenomenon is not sufficiently proved, it can be completely explained by a secondary hallucination, caused by the noise heard in the direction of the window.

The fact of the decanter being undamaged cannot leave us in doubt as to the hallucinatory character of the phenomenon observed, or, at the very least, as to the error of interpretation of the noise heard.

A circumstance which also ought to be noted is that the phenomenon was perceived not only by the subject directly interested, the wife of the agent, probably in communication with him, but also by other persons present, who seem to have observed the phenomenon in the same manner.

I ought to add that the telepathic phenomenon in this case impressed the percipient with the idea that a misfortune was about to happen, but it does not seem to have communicated clear perception of what had really happened. It is therefore only an instance of incomplete or attenuated lucidity.

We place in the same category the following case, which we extract from the same source:—

"It occurred at Schlestadt, in the Department of the Bas-Rhin, on a warm summer night. The door of communication between the bedroom and the salon had been left open, and in the salon two windows were kept wide open by chairs whose backs touched them. The father and mother of M. Parmentier were asleep.

"Suddenly Madame Parmentier was awakened by her bed being sharply shaken up and down. She was astonished and somewhat alarmed; she woke her husband, and told him what had occurred.

"Suddenly a second shock took place, this time very violent. General Parmentier's father thought it was an earthquake, though earthquakes are very rare in Alsace. He got up, lighted a candle, and seeing nothing unusual went to bed again. But immediately afterwards the bed was again shaken violently and a great noise was heard in the adjoining salon, as though the windows were violently closed and all their panes broken. The earthquake seemed to continue worse than ever. M. and Mme. Parmentier got out of bed and went to examine what mischief had been done in the salon; they found nothing. The windows were still wide open; the chairs had not moved; the night was calm; the sky clear and full of stars. There had been neither earthquake nor windstorm—the noise and commotion had been fictitious. M. and Mme. Parmentier lived on the first floor; on the second floor, below them, lived an elderly woman whose wardrobe creaked abominably every time she opened or shut the door. This disagreeable creak had been heard among the noises, and they had asked each other what could induce the old lady to be opening and shutting her wardrobe door at that hour. When they found that nothing had been disturbed in the salon, that the windows were still open and the furniture unmoved, Mme. Parmentier grew frightened. She began to think that something had happened to her friends, to her father and mother, whom, on her recent marriage, she had left shortly before at Strasbourg, and who were all, as she thought, in perfect health.

"But she soon afterwards heard that her old governess, whom she had not seen since her marriage, and who had gone back to her family in Vienna, had died that same night, and that before she died she had several times expressed regret that she had been separated from her dear pupil, for whom she had a warm attachment.

"When next day Mme. Parmentier asked her neighbour on the ground floor if she had opened her creaking

I

cupboard in the middle of the night, if she had been shaken in her bed, and if she had heard unusual noises the answer was 'No,' and she added that, being an old woman, she was a poor sleeper, and if anything unusual had occurred she would certainly have noticed it."

Here are two cases which resemble each other sufficiently, while differing from other telepathic phenomena, for us to place them in a category by themselves.

Let us then examine them, and try to explain them the one by the other.

First of all, we notice that the noise heard did not proceed from the cause to which the percipients at first attributed it—that is to say, the abrupt closing of the windows. We have the proof of this—in the first instance, by the decanter which remained intact; in the second instance, by the chairs which were placed in front of the window, and which were found in their places after the phenomenon.

But this evidence is not sufficient for us to demonstrate that the phenomenon was purely hallucinatory. In point of fact, a real noise might very well have been produced outside, have been heard through the open windows, and by reason of the similarity of sound and direction have been attributed to the closing of these windows.

We might be able to admit this hypothesis in the first instance, where the noise was heard by every one present in the dining-room. But, in the second case, the hypothesis is inadmissible, because the noise was loud enough to have wakened an aged person, only sleeping lightly in a room immediately underneath. Further, it may be pointed out that in the second case the creaking of a cupboard was heard, when it was ascertained that the door had not been opened.

We are therefore led to recognise the purely subjective character of these two phenomena.

We shall call this category that of telepathic communications with hallucination but without vision.

One further observation must be made as to these two

cases; it is that the hallucination, although collective, only becomes a telepathic warning for the percipient for whom the communication was intended. In the first case, it was only the wife of the huntsman who had the perception of the accident that had happened to her husband, and she expressed it by crying out, " Some misfortune has just happened !" In the second case, M. Parmentier attributed what he saw and heard to an earthquake, when Mme. Parmentier believed that some misfortune had happened to her people. She was mistaken in her interpretation with regard to the person to whom she attributed it, but it was really she who was in the thoughts of her dying governess.

The warning is therefore vague and the communication incomplete.

We now come to some cases in which the telepathic warning is more definite. The percipient has no longer the vague perception of an accident or of the death of a person whom he cannot designate, but the fact is rendered more precise by the appearance of the person who has died.

In the first case, it is true we have not the certain indication that there was a vision, but the whole of the story enables us to conclude that it was by means of a dream that Mme. X. learned of the death of her father.

The story has been published in the *Annales des Sciences Psychiques.*

" In the month of November 1870, I was at Madrid with my family—that is to say, my father, mother, brother, and sister. My brother was three years old, my sister eight, while I was thirteen years of age. We three children slept in a bedroom adjoining our parents' bedroom, and separated from it by a glass door left half open.

" At two o'clock in the morning my mother woke up with a start and crying. She rose and came to our room and awakened us all saying : ' Pray for your grandfather (my father) who has died !' Now at that time, our grandfather was in Paris, which was besieged by the German Army : we only received news once a fortnight, and that irregularly, by balloon despatches. My grandfather was suffering from an internal complaint. We knew that he was ill, but not that his condition was serious. But I remember perfectly that, without apparent motive, our mother came to us in the middle of the night to awaken us. I believe that it was the only time that such a thing happened. My father tried to tranquillise my mother, who wished to put us into mourning the next day. At the request of my father she did not do so; nevertheless she made all preparations for going into mourning, and told everybody: 'My father is dead.'

"About a month afterwards we had the confirmation of her dream; we learnt that my grandfather had died rather suddenly during the night which preceded the dream. I am unfortunately not able to give more details, because I was very young. My grandmother, father, and mother have all died since that time, and, besides, the papers were burned during the second siege of Paris. But I think that I can say that my grandfather's death preceded my mother's dream by a few hours—and a few hours only."

In the above case the vision of the image of the agent is very clearly described; it was this vision that made known the death to the percipient, but without giving any particular details of it.

In the following case, the transmitter appeared to the receiver and told him that he had just died. The receiver stated that he had the vision before waking, but since the incident occurred during the night, we cannot be quite sure that it was not a dream.

"On February 4, 1888,[1] M. Montégoût rose in the morning to make his visit of inspection in the Colony. When he returned at lunch-time his wife said to him: 'La Mothe-Pradelle is dead!'

"At first surprised at this abrupt news, his fears were quickly removed when Mme. Montégoût told him the following story: She had waked up in the night, and, on opening her eyes, she saw before her La Mothe-Pradelle,

---

[1] *Annales des Sciences Psychiques.*

who pressed her hand and said to her: 'I have just died: adieu.'

"On hearing this M. Montégoût chaffed his wife a good deal and told her that she had dreamed all that.

"She, for her part, declared that she was not asleep when she saw the apparition.

"One or two days afterwards I went to dine with M. Montégoût, who related to his guests how he had chaffed Mme. Montégoût.

"But the director of the Colony said that he believed in the reality of the apparition and, consequently, in the death of the deputy.

"The discussion was lively, and ended with the bet of a dinner.

"Six or eight weeks later there came to the Colony a number of the *Indépendant de Bergerac*, announcing that M. de La Mothe-Pradelle, Deputy of Dordogne, had died on the night of February 3rd or 4th, 1888."

We now come to some cases in which it happens that the percipient has had, in a waking state, a vision of the agent.

A regiment, not very long since stationed at New Orleans, had a temporary mess-room erected, at one end of which was a door for the officers; and, at the other, a door and a space railed off for the messman. One day two of the officers were playing at chess, or draughts, one sitting with his face towards the centre of the room, the other with his back to it. "Bless me! why, surely that is your brother!" exclaimed the former to the latter, who looked eagerly round, his brother being then, as he believed, in England. By this time the figure, having passed the spot where the officers were sitting, presented only his back to them. "No," replied the second, "that is not my brother's regiment; that's the uniform of the Rifle Brigade. By heavens! it is my brother, though," he added, starting up and eagerly pursuing the stranger, who at that moment turned his head and looked at him, and then, somehow, strangely disappeared amongst the people standing at the messman's end of the room. Supposing he had gone out that way, the brother pursued him, but he was not to be found; neither had the messman, nor anybody there, observed him. The young man died at that time in England, having just exchanged into the Rifle Brigade.

In the following case also the image of the agent appears to the percipient, but this picture has a particular characteristic expression, which leaves no doubt in the percipient's mind as to the reality of the fatal event.

"On February 21, 1879," [1] writes the communicator of the narrative, "I was invited to dinner with my friends M. and Mme. B. On going into the drawing-room I noticed the absence of one of the usual guests, M. d'E., whom I nearly always met at their table. I remarked upon this and Mme. B. told me that d'E., who was in the employ of an important bank, was doubtless very busy at that moment, because he had not been seen for two days. Nothing more was said with regard to d'E. The repast went off very merrily, and Mme. B. did not show the least sign of preoccupation. During dinner we planned to spend the evening at the theatre.

"At dessert Mme. B. rose in order to go and dress in her room, the door of which leading into the dining-room remained half open.

"B. and I remained at the table smoking our cigars, when, after a few moments, we heard a terrible cry. Thinking that an accident had happened, we rushed into the room and found Mme. B. seated and apparently ill.

"She recovered by degrees, and then told us the following story: 'After leaving you, I dressed myself for going out, and was about to tie my hat-strings, when suddenly I saw in this glass d'E. coming in at the door. He had his hat on, and looked pale and sad; without turning round I said to him: Well, d'E., here you are—sit down; and as he did not reply I turned round and could see nothing. Being frightened I called out as you heard.' B., in order to reassure his wife, began to chaff her, regarding the apparition as a nervous hallucination, and said that d'E.

[1] *Annales des Sciences Psychiques.*

would be much flattered at learning how much he was in her thoughts; then, as Mme. B. was still trembling, in order to stop her emotion we proposed to start out at once, saying that we should miss the 'curtain-raiser.'

"'I did not think of d'E. for a single moment,' Mme. B. told us, 'since M. Fournier asked me the reason for his absence. I am not nervous, and I have never had any hallucination. I am sure there is something extraordinary about it, and as for myself, I do not wish to go out before having news of d'E. I beg of you to go to his house as the only way to reassure me.'

"I advised B. to accede to his wife's request, and we both set out for d'E.'s house, which was only a very short distance away. As we walked we joked a good deal on Mme. B.'s fears.

"On reaching the house we asked the concierge if d'E. was at home. 'Yes, sir, he has not come down to-day.' D'E. lived in small bachelor's chambers; he kept no servant. We went up to his room and rang several times without getting any reply. We then rang louder, and knocked as hard as we could, but without better success. B., who was disturbed in spite of himself, said to me: 'This is absurd. The concierge was mistaken; he has gone out. Let us go down.' But the concierge said that he was quite certain that d'E. had not gone out.

"Really frightened, we went upstairs again with him, and again tried to obtain an entrance; then, not hearing any movement in the room, we sent for a locksmith. We forced the door and found the dead body of d'E., still warm, lying on his bed, pierced with two revolver shots.

"The doctor, whom we immediately fetched, found that d'E. had first tried to commit suicide by swallowing a phial of laudanum, and finding that this did not act sufficiently quickly, he fired two revolver shots into his heart. Although I am not able to state the time exactly, it was, however, almost absolutely coincident with the so-called hallucination of Mme. B. On his mantelpiece he had left a letter addressed to M. and Mme. B. announcing his determination, a letter showing particular affection for Mme. B."

CHAPTER X

Telepathic Vision of a Scene—Voluntary Telepathic Apparition

THE following are two cases in which the agent was not dead, but had met with an accident. The percipient was in a semi-waking condition, in which he saw not only the image of the agent, but also had a vision of certain details of the accident that had happened to him.

In the first case [1] the percipient, Mrs. B., seems to have clearly seen the whole of the accident. She wrote with regard to it :—

"*May* 9, 1883.

"This happened in January last, on a Tuesday. I was about to set out on one of my usual visits to Southampton. I had received a letter from a friend in the morning, who told me that he was going hunting that day, but that he would write to me on the following day, so that I should find his letter on my return. When in the train, being tired, I put my book down and closed my eyes, and immediately the following scene came before me : in the hunting-field two horsemen were preparing to jump over a low wall; my friend's horse took the jump, was not able to clear the wall, and fell on to his head, throwing his rider under him. The whole scene vanished. I was wide awake all the time. My friend was a good horseman, and there was no reason why such an accident should happen to him. Immediately on arriving at Southampton I wrote to him, telling him simply that I knew he had met with a fall, and that I hoped he was not seriously injured.

"On my return on Wednesday very late at night, not finding the promised letter, I wrote him a few lines, saying

---

[1] *Annales des Sciences Psychiques.*

that I hoped to hear some news on the following day with regard to his fall. On the same evening that I returned I told two people what I had seen, and I had even spoken of it to some friends with whom I dined on the Tuesday evening after my arrival, and they all laughed at me. On Thursday morning I received a letter from my friend. He told me that he had had a fall when trying to jump over a low stone wall, that the horse had not cleared it and had fallen on his head, and that he himself had not been greatly injured, and had remounted the horse a little later on. When he wrote he had not then received any of my letters, because my letter of Tuesday would not arrive in Scotland until Thursday morning, and that of Wednesday not until Friday. When he received my letters he declared that I must have been asleep. Nothing of the kind had ever happened to me before, or has happened since. It all seemed to me very natural, and did not alarm me in the least."

Mrs. B. replied to the questions I addressed to her as follows:—

" My friend, who is a stubborn Scotchman, refuses to say a word more on this matter. All I know is that there were two horsemen, who were riding towards the same place."

She said that her vision took place about three o'clock in the afternoon, and that she learned from her friend that the accident took place "after lunch." She did not for a moment think that a disaster had happened, and she was sure that her friend was not much hurt. She could not say whether her eyes were closed or open, but she was sure that she had never had an impression of a similar character.

In this case the proof of telepathy or of second-sight— the older and better-known expression—seems to have been established by the concurrence of events.

Mrs. B., on arriving at Southampton, wrote to her friend (whom we will call Mr. X.), and told him that "she knew he had met with a fall from his horse, and that she hoped he was not much hurt." The same evening she related her vision to the friends with whom she dined, who all laughed at her.

On Wednesday evening, on her return very late at night, not finding the expected letter at home, she wrote to Mr. X., and told him that she hoped to have news of his fall on the following day; further, she told two persons what she had seen. She eventually received the promised letter on Thursday morning, which had crossed her two letters, and which described the accident just as she had seen it. The production of these letters, with their respective envelopes showing the post-mark, would have established the fact that Mrs. B. could not have known that Mr. X. had had a fall, since it was materially impossible for her to have been informed of it, as her vision took place at a time very near to the time of the accident: it would have proved that the letters had really crossed, and that they could not have reached their destination soon enough to influence either Mrs. B. or her friend.

In the second case (mentioned in Myers' *Human Personality*) the percipient did not see the whole of the scene of the accident, but he perceived in the vision from the transmitter the exact particulars of the wound that he had received.

On the evening of February 10, 1894, Mr. Kearne was sitting in his room expecting the return of two friends. After allowing half-an-hour beyond their usual time of arrival he began to get uneasy, but arguing to himself that there was no occasion for alarm, he took an interesting book and became absorbed in it, his mind being perfectly quiet. After some twenty minutes he says: "Suddenly, without a moment's warning, my whole being seemed roused to the highest state of tension or alertness, and I was aware, with an intensity not easily imagined by those who have never experienced it, that another being or presence was not only in the room but close to me. I put my book down, and although my excitement was great, I felt quite collected and not conscious of any sense of fear. Without changing my position, and looking straight at the fire, I knew somehow that my friend A. H. was standing at my left elbow, but so far behind me as to be hidden by the arm-chair in which I was leaning back."

On moving his eyes slightly Mr. Kearne distinguished the lower portion of one leg, and recognised the grey-blue trousers often worn by his friend. The stuff appeared semi-transparent, reminding him of tobacco smoke in its consistency, but he did not wish to see more, and gazed at the fire in front of him. After an appreciable time, probably some seconds, although it seemed much longer, he distinctly saw, about four feet away from him, and almost immediately behind his chair, the figure of his friend, the face very pale, the head slightly thrown back, the eyes shut, and on one side of the throat, just under the jaw, a wound with blood on it. The figure remained motionless, with the arms close to the side, and Mr. Kearne looked steadily at it. Then all at once he roused himself and turned deliberately round, when the figure vanished; he then realised that he had seen the figure behind him—an impossible feat physically. Being accustomed to psychical phenomena, Mr. Kearne carefully noted the time of the apparition, 10.50 P.M. He thought that an accident must have happened to his friend. At 11.35 a cab stopped at the door, and his friend arrived : he had been, as a matter of fact, the victim of an accident which had caused a wound identical with that which Mr. Kearne had telepathically seen. On leaving the station Mr. A. H. had gone into a restaurant to have some supper. He complained of the heat, and went out into the street to get some fresh air. He suddenly felt his senses leave him, and fell heavily forward, striking his jaw on the edge of the curb. It was apparently during this faintness that he had telepathically affected his friend Mr. Kearne.

I will now quote two instances in which the agent was dead : the percipient saw in a dream the whole of the scene accompanying the death, with an extraordinary precision as to small details, which makes these two cases very remarkable.

The first was mentioned in *L'Echo du merveilleux* in 1906, and was narrated by Lieut.-Colonel Etienne Peroz.

"It was at the station of Niagassola in the Soudan, where, for several months, along with my little garrison and the population of the village protected by the fort, I had been besieged by the army of Samory. One must have read the description of a siege in the darkest hours of the Middle Ages to be able to imagine the horrible distress in which all these soldiers, old men, women, and children, lived for close on six months. Famine, pestilence, and smallpox were among the evils let loose, and they thinned the population alarmingly.

"Two-thirds of the adult population, three-fourths of the children, more than four thousand of the inhabitants died during those terrible days.

"Two thousand emaciated figures were still guarding the walls when the siege was raised.

"Our garrison had also suffered considerable mortality. Out of twenty-two non-commissioned officers and privates, gunners or foot-soldiers, at the end of the siege, only five were left. Of my faithful black sharp-shooters, one-fourth had disappeared. But I forget my story—a curious instance of telepathy. These sorrowful reminiscences are, after all, the cause of this digression. Well, a few months before I left France, I had seen embark on the expedition for China directed by Admiral Courbet, of glorious memory, a comrade for whom I had sincere affection. Lieutenant Zaph had served under your command, and therefore, like myself, you have appreciated his good will, energy, and courage. It was with real anguish of heart that I had parted from him, as though I should never see him again. But time had passed and I confess that my life of dangers somewhat obscured the memory of him, when one night, at Niagassola, I saw Zaph, wounded and dying—sorrowful moments of which I can see again all the details and circumstances.

"A band of Chinese Black-Flags passed close to a

hoarding, engaged with a company of marine infantry. I heard the fusillade and looked on, between two clouds of powder smoke, at the terrible hand-to-hand combat, when I saw Zaph, his sword in one hand, his revolver in the other, encouraging his men; then, before my eyes, he fell struck by several shots. I leaned over his body, the face of which was covered with blood, and with his last look he seemed to bid me adieu. I was so struck with this dream that on opening my eyes I went to the table and seizing my pen I made a note in the margin of my diary of the *Siege,* of the dream I had had, with the hour and date.

"We had been cut off from communication with the rest of the world for eighty days and we lived thus isolated for three months longer.

"When we were eventually released, and news from France could reach us, and when I had read through the voluminous packet of letters from my family and my friends, I looked through the newspapers, when a number of the *Tablettes des Deux-Charentes,* a naval paper, apprised me of the death of my comrade Zaph, in China, on the same date and in the exact circumstances that I had dreamed.

"It is a problem which I shall not attempt to solve, but this coincidence impressed me for a long time. Was it his spirit that came to me at the moment of his death? Was my double projected and transported close to him? Unfathomable mystery!"

The second case is equally precise in its details and presents this further peculiarity that the percipient had never seen the agent. We are unable to admit here that the thoughts of the agent were carried, at the moment of death, to the percipient.

We shall find similar cases of knowledge of events reaching persons who were complete strangers to the matter, in the phenomena of typtology.

The writer of this narrative is the wife of a merchant, a Quaker, and very trustworthy. Some years ago she told us of the event with more details, while it was still fresh in her memory. Her husband can guarantee that she told him these facts at the very moment: he can also bear witness to the strange effect which the dream had upon his wife's mind for some time afterwards.

"*From* Mrs. GREEN *to* Miss RICHARDSON

"NEWRY, 21*st First Month*, 1885.

"DEAR FRIEND,—In compliance with thy request, I give thee the particulars of my dream.

"I saw two respectably dressed females driving alone in a vehicle like a mineral-water cart. Their horse stopped at a water to drink; but as there was no footing he lost his balance, and in trying to recover it he plunged right in. With the shock, the women stood up and shouted for help, and their hats rose off their heads, and as all were going down I turned away crying, and saying, 'Was there no one at all to help them?' upon which I awoke, and my husband asked me what was the matter. I related the above dream to him, and he asked me if I knew them. I said I did not, and thought I had never seen either of them. The impression of the dream and the trouble it brought was over me all day. I remarked to my son it was the anniversary of his birthday and my own also—the 10th of First Month, and this is why I remember the date.

"The following third month I got a letter and newspaper from my brother in Australia, named Allen, letting me know the sad trouble which had befallen him in the loss, by drowning, of one of his daughters and her companion. Thou wilt see by the description given of it in the paper how the event corresponded with my dream. My niece was born in Australia, and I never saw her.

"Please return the paper at thy convenience. Considering that our night is their day, I must have been in sympathy with the sufferers at the time of the accident, on the 10th of First Month, 1878."

It is referred to in two separate places in the newspaper.

From the " Inglewood Advertiser."

"FRIDAY EVENING, *January* 11, 1878.

" A dreadful accident occurred in the neighbourhood of Wedderburn on Wednesday last, resulting in the death of two women named Lehey and Allen. It appears that the deceased were driving into Wedderburn in a spring-cart from the direction of Kinypanial, when they attempted to water their horse at a dam on the boundary of Torpichen Station. The dam was 10 or 12 feet deep in one spot, and into this deep hole they must have inadvertently driven; for Mr. W. M'Kechnie, manager of Torpichen Station, upon going to the dam some hours afterwards, discovered the spring-cart and horse under the water, and two women's hats floating on the surface. The dam was searched, and the bodies of the two women, clasped in each other's arms, recovered."

Extract from Evidence given at the Inquest.

Joseph John Allen, farmer, deposed: " I identify one of the bodies as that of my sister. I saw her about 11 A.M. yesterday. The horse had broken away, and I caught it for her. Mrs. Lehey and my sister met me when I caught the horse. They then took the horse and went to Mr. Clarke's. I did not see them afterwards alive."

William M'Kechnie deposed: " About 4 P.M. yesterday I was riding by the dam when I observed the legs of a horse and the chest above the water."

Mr. Green confirms as follows :—

"NEWRY, 15*th Second Month*, 1885.

" DEAR FRIEND EDITH RICHARDSON,—In reference to the dream that my wife had of seeing two women thrown out of a spring-cart by their horse stopping to drink out of the deep water, I remember she was greatly distressed about it, and seemed to feel great sympathy for them. It occurred on the night of the 9th of January.

" The reason I can remember the date so well is that the 10th was the anniversary of my wife and our son's birthday. As the day advanced she seemed to get worse, and I advised her to go out for a drive; when she returned she told me she was no better, and also said she had told the driver not to go near water, lest some accident should happen, as she had such a dreadful dream the night before, at the same time telling him the nature of it. As my wife's niece did not live with her father, he was not told of it until the next morning, which would be our evening of the 10th, and which we think accounted for the increased trouble she felt in sympathy with him.

" THOS. GREEN."

I shall place the following case in the same category: the details of the vision are also very complete; and this case only differs from the preceding in the fact that the agent was not dead.

The family of M. N. consisted of himself, his wife, daughter, and son; the latter had been recently promoted to the grade of midshipman, and had spent the summer at Pavlovsk, in the neighbourhood of St. Petersburg.

From their earliest years the brother and sister had an affection for one another which almost amounted to adoration.

While there the young midshipman received orders to go for a month's sea voyage, and his relatives accompanied him to the port where he had to embark. At the moment of parting, turning towards his sister, he said to her : " Do not forget me : you are called Vera (which means 'faith '), and we are saved by faith : think of me and all will be well."

" Have confidence," replied the young girl. " I shall think of you very often ; but do not run any risks by going too far on the sea, it is so terrible ! "

" Come, come, you sailor people, with your presentiments and superstitions," said her father laughing, in order to drive away the sorrow of their parting; " you will make me laugh at you."

The weeks passed. Letters frequently came from the young sailor, and at home they became more calm and reassured the nearer the day approached for the return of the traveller.

The weather up to then had been very fine and favourable; suddenly it changed: the sky became cloudy, and the rain came.

One day was particularly bad: during the morning the rain fell in torrents, and the wind blew violently. Vera was very nervous and agitated all day, anxious on her brother's account, wondering where he was and how he was going on. Towards the evening she became quite ill, and her parents induced her to lie down.

At ten o'clock all was quiet in the house: the storm had spent its fury. Suddenly a terrible cry, which had nothing human about it, came from the young girl's room. Everybody hastened to her, and they found Vera in violent hysterics. She was in convulsions for a long time, and it was only with difficulty that they could calm her to some extent.

In reply to the questions that were put to her, Vera said that she'had had a terrible vision.

" I do not seem to have gone to sleep at all, although I saw something terrible. At first everything seemed enveloped in a frightful gloom: the tempest increased around me, and the thunder deafened me with its noise. By the light of a flash of lightning I saw the sea agitated and covered with foam. Suddenly it was illuminated for a moment by a red light, and I saw my brother struggling against the waves. Then the darkness returned; after a little time a second flash of lightning broke through the clouds, and by its light I saw my brother lying on a rock with his head covered with blood—the horror and fright awakened me."

On the evening of the following day M. N. received a telegram as follows :—

" Alive and well; thanks to Vérotschka. Shall arrive in a few days. Your son, N."

As may be imagined, M. N. was greatly astonished, but

K

at the same time pleased to receive the telegram, although it appeared incomprehensible. The enigma would soon be solved.

The following day on reading his newspaper M. N. found a detailed report of the shipwreck of the vessel on which his son was serving. He immediately proceeded to Kronstadt, where he found his son alive but suffering from a serious wound on the head.

On the day of the shipwreck the vessel was close to the Aland Islands. The wind rose and became more and more violent, and all the sailors said that a tempest was blowing up.

At eight o'clock in the evening the young midshipman finished his watch and went into his cabin to refresh himself with a cup of tea, after which, putting on some warmer clothing, he went up on deck to look at the tempest. It was, in fact, terrible. The vessel, which could no longer contend against the waves, had to be abandoned to the current.

More than once young N. thought of his people at his father's house and, in thought, asked his sister to pray for him that he might be rescued, along with the crew, from an almost inevitable death.

In the midst of the hurricane he suddenly heard a terrible noise; the unfortunate vessel had gone on to the rocks. The shock was so violent that all on deck were thrown down and the midshipman N. overboard. After rising to the surface he tried to keep up and make towards the vessel in the hope of receiving help.

The wind brought him the order: "All hands on deck."

A red light pierced the darkness and he heard a gun fired.

Soon N. became aware that it was impossible for him to get to the ship, the waves mounted so high that he was powerless to swim across them.

In thought he put himself into the hands of the Almighty, and keeping himself above water as well as he could, he let himself be carried along. Suddenly he saw coming closer to him something like a thin bright mist, which gradually took a human form, and in the white apparition he recognised his sister Vera, who smiled to him and held out her arm as though to point out a certain spot. The brother followed the phantom of his sister. He did not remember how long he took or where he swam to : suddenly he felt a sharp pain in his head and lost consciousness.

On the following morning some fishermen found him lying unconscious on a sand-bank with a deep wound in his head.

The sand-bank was ten leagues away from the place of the shipwreck. A boat was sent out to assist and they found the vessel still on the water, but abandoned by the crew who, not trusting themselves to a lifeboat, had fallen a prey to the sea.   M. MAKAREVSKAJA.

I now come to a series of very remarkable cases.

We observe that a much more active part is here taken by the agents in the telepathic communication, for they are, in these cases, conscious of the vision which they produce in the recipients.

In the first case, the phenomenon is further complicated by the fact that the vision is perceived by two different persons.

In October 1883 [1] Mr. Wilmot was on the sea between Liverpool and New York. A tempest raged for eight days ; but on the night following the eighth day the sea became a little calmer. For the first time since his departure Mr. Wilmot was able to enjoy a refreshing sleep. Towards the morning he had the following dream : his wife, whom he had left in the United States, came to the door of his cabin clad in her nightdress. She seemed to see that he was not the only occupant of the room, hesitated a little, then went forward to her husband, stooped down and kissed him, and, after gently caressing him for a few moments, withdrew. Mr. Tait, his fellow-passenger, occupied a berth which was almost directly over his. On awaking Mr. Wilmot saw Mr. Tait, leaning on his elbow in

[1] Myers' *Human Personality.*

bed, looking fixedly at him. He said: "You're a pretty
fellow to have a lady come and visit you in this way."
After the explanations which followed it seemed evident
to Mr. Wilmot that Mr. Tait when awake had seen in an
hallucination—was it an hallucination?—the same details
as he had in dream. The strangeness of the fact did not
stop there. When Mr. Wilmot landed one of the first
questions his wife put to him was: "Did you receive a
visit from me a week ago Tuesday?"

"A visit from you!" he said; "I was on the sea a
thousand miles away."

"I know," she replied; "nevertheless it seemed to me
that I visited you."

And then Mrs. Wilmot stated that the bad weather
had caused her much anxiety. On the night in question
she slept very little: towards four o'clock in the morning
it seemed to her that she went to look for her husband.
She crossed the wide and stormy sea, came at length to
a steamship, whose side she went up and then descended
into her husband's cabin.

"There were two berths," she said, "yours and one over-
head farther back. A man was in that one and he looked
right at me. For a moment I was afraid to go in; then I
went to your bed, stooped down and kissed you, and then
went away."

In the following cases not only is the agent conscious
of the telepathic phenomenon that he produces, but by an
effort of the will he makes himself visible to the percipient
chosen by him. These cases of experimental telepathy
are very rare; but they present the greatest interest.

The subjoined example of experimental telepathy is
narrated by M. B., and is taken from *Phantasms of the
Living*.

"On a certain Sunday evening in November 1881,
having been reading of the great power which the human
will is capable of exercising, I determined with the whole
force of my being that I would be present in spirit in the
front bedroom on the second floor of a house situated at

22 Hogarth Road, Kensington, in which room slept two ladies of my acquaintance, Miss L. S. V. and Miss E. C. V., aged respectively 25 and 11 years. I was living at this time at 23 Kildare Gardens, a distance of three miles from Hogarth Road. I did not mention in any way my intention of trying this experiment to either of the above ladies, for the simple reason that it was only on retiring to rest upon this Sunday night that I made up my mind to do so. The time at which I was determined I would be there was one o'clock in the morning, and I also had a strong intention of making my presence perceptible.

" On the following Thursday I went to see the ladies in question, and in the course of the conversation (without any allusion to the subject on my part) the elder one told me that on the previous Sunday night she had been terrified by perceiving me standing by her bedside, and that she screamed when the apparition advanced towards her and awoke her little sister, who saw me also.

" I asked her if she was awake at the time, and she replied ' most decidedly ' in the affirmative, and upon my inquiring the time of the occurrence, she replied, ' About one o'clock in the morning.'

" This lady at my request wrote down a statement of the event and signed it.

" This was the first occasion upon which I tried an experiment of this kind, and its particular success startled me very much. It was not only my will that I had strongly exerted. I had also made an effort of a special nature which it is impossible for me to describe. I was conscious of a mysterious influence pervading my body."

The signatures of the two young ladies are appended to this document.

The second case has been taken from the *Annales des Sciences Psychiques*.

The case is that of Mme. Russell of Belgaum (India), wife of Mr. H. R. Russell, Inspector of Schools in the Presidency of Bombay.

"*June* 8, 1886.

" In accordance with the wish you have expressed I write the following facts as well as I can recall them. I was living in Scotland, my mother and sisters being in Germany. I lived with a friend who was very dear to me, and I usually went to Germany every year to see my relatives. It so happened that I could not go to my family, as was my custom, for two years, when suddenly I decided to go and see my relatives. They knew nothing of my intention. I had never gone at the beginning of spring, and there was not time to advise them by letter. I would not send a telegram for fear of frightening my mother. The thought came to me to will with all my might to appear to one or other of my sisters, but in such a manner that they might know of my intended arrival. I thought of it with all the intensity possible for a few minutes only, desiring with all power to be seen by one of them (I myself experienced a vision in which I seemed to be partly transported into their midst). I did not concentrate my thoughts for more than ten minutes, I think. I left Leith by steamer, one Saturday evening, at the end of April 1859. I desired to appear at the house about six o'clock in the evening on the same Saturday. I arrived at the house about six o'clock on the following Tuesday morning. I went into the house without being seen, because the hall was being cleaned and the entrance door was open. I went into the room. One of my sisters had her back turned to the door. She turned round when she heard the door open, and on seeing me gazed fixedly at me, became deadly pale, and let fall what she had been holding in her hand. I had said nothing. Then I spoke and said: 'It is I. Why are you so frightened?' She then replied: 'I thought I was seeing you as Stinckin (another of my sisters) saw you on Saturday.'

" In reply to my questions, she told me that on Saturday evening, about six o'clock, my sister distinctly saw me come into the room, where she was standing beside the door, open the door of another room where my mother was, and close the door behind me. She darted forward after what she believed to be me, called me by my name, and was quite stupefied when she did not see me with my mother. My mother could not understand my sister's excitement. They looked everywhere for me, but naturally could not find me. My mother was very much upset; she thought I might be dying.

" My sister who had seen me (that is to say, my apparition) had gone out on the morning of my arrival. I sat down on the steps to see what would be her experience when she returned and saw me in the flesh. When she looked at me sitting quite still she called me and nearly fainted. My sister had never seen anything supernormal, either before or since; and I have not renewed these experiments since, and I shall not do so any more, because the sister who first saw me, when I was really in the house, fell seriously ill as the result of the shock which she experienced.

It is necessary to make some remarks on the subject of these telepathic phenomena, which we have tried to class in a methodical manner.

We must observe first of all that this classification is not final. Though we have taken as a general basis the state of the agent and the manner in which the communication reaches the percipient, it necessarily happens that some cases cannot be placed as they should be with regard to both agent and percipient at the same time.

This provisional classification will nevertheless be useful to enable us to study the phenomenon in a more methodical manner.

Considerations relating to the Agent

In the majority of cases we have seen that the agent is at the point of death at the moment when the telepathic communication takes place.

The researches which have been made have nearly always shown an almost perfect coincidence between the time of the death of the agent and the telepathic communication.

In the less numerous cases in which the telepathic communication seems to have taken place after death, we can in all probability attribute this fact to a delay in its reception.

In other cases, the agent has not died, but has met with a serious accident, and, most frequently, this accident is accompanied by loss of consciousness.

This loss of consciousness may be regarded as a momentary death, and the state of the subject at this time is probably the same as it would be at the approach of death.

In some much rarer cases, the subject is simply in a state of sleep; and, finally, when there is voluntary telepathic communication, the subject is in a very special condition of concentration of mind.

The state of sleep, accompanied by a persistent preoccupation with the same subject, in the same way as voluntary mental concentration, is of such a nature as to produce a special condition, which we may regard as analogous to some hypnotic states.

Normal sleep can be easily transformed, as we have seen, into a hypnotic condition; with spontaneous somnambulists it often occurs as the result of violent crises or lively emotions.

It therefore seems that in the persons who become the agents of a telepathic communication, the conditions requisite for the production of a hypnotic state are often present. It is not therefore unreasonable to think that it is by reason of a hypnotic condition of this character that the agent acquires the new faculties that are manifested in the telepathic communication.

Considerations relating to the Percipient

Let us first of all look at the conditions in the case of the percipient.

In a number of cases the percipient is asleep, but we shall observe that this does not apply to one-half of the cases.

In other cases we find a condition of semi-sleep. We may even include among these the cases in which the condition of the subject is not perfectly defined, but where the circumstances permit us to believe that he was disposed to fall into unconscious somnolence.

In some circumstances the subject in a waking state is impelled to place himself in a state of superficial somnambulism by auto-hypnotism. This happens in the examples of automatic writing.

Finally, the subject is in a waking state, but, as the result of chance conditions, he is motionless before a brilliant object which seems to fascinate him. The subject is looking in a glass, or, perhaps, is at a table before a glass, a decanter, &c.

The subject is in a waking state, but is dreamy, preoccupied; his attention is fixed on one thought only, and most frequently this thought, or the object of his pre-occupation, is no other than the agent from whom he is about to receive a telepathic communication.

These conditions are certainly of a character to act upon the psychical body of the percipient, and to bring it into a condition of special receptivity. Remembering at the same time what we have seen in hypnology and the particular conditions which we are examining, we shall not go too far in saying that these conditions are of such a character as to place the percipient in a state of superficial somnambulism or of passive mediumship.

Let us then see in what way the reception of a telepathic communication comes to the percipient.

First of all it may be a purely mental impression, such as is produced in experimental thought-transmission. This is the case in simple premonition and presentiment. They are simple telepathic warnings without hallucination or vision.

In the second place, there may be hallucination without vision. Most frequently it is an auditive hallucination; the noise of a hurricane, of windows or doors being violently closed, of glasses or other articles being broken, of knocks made on doors or walls, of steps on the floor, or there may be a motor hallucination, the subject feels a movement or a shaking of the bed or the chair in which he is. It must be noted that this hallucination may be collective, we can even say that it frequently is so, but the hallucination has only a telepathic significance for the percipient concerned; other people, who perceive it simultaneously, attribute it to some commonplace cause which is afterwards found not to be the real one.

Lastly, the telepathic communication may be received in the form of a vision, and this vision can be subdivided into several categories :—

The simple vision of the image of the agent.

The vision of the agent with some details of his condition on the image itself—pallor, sorrow, wounds.

The vision of the agent along with a more or less detailed vision of the scene and circumstances of the accident.

The vision is perceived by several persons.

The vision leaves objective traces of its passage.

Considerations on the Relations or the Rapport between Agent and Percipient

Generally speaking, there exists a great intimacy between the two subjects, often the links of parentage or friendship; it is rarely that the two subjects are unconnected with each other.

We may assume, as a deduction from the relations existing between them, that, most frequently, the agent thinks of the percipient at the time of the communication, and with all the greater intensity since he is in an abnormal state, a state of anguish in which all his thoughts are momentarily concentrated on a single object, namely, the percipient.

The percipient by reason of his intimacy with the agent, and often because of the conditions in which he knows the latter is, often turns his thoughts towards him. The agent is the object of one of his principal preoccupations, and one can even say that, if he is not always present in his memory, a latent and sub-conscious part of his mind is constantly directed towards him.

The result of these conditions is that, in cases of this kind, the two subjects are often in conditions analogous to those in which experimenters voluntarily place themselves for thought-transmission.

There now remains, outside of these conditions, the case in which the telepathic phenomenon is observed between two subjects who are unknown to each other, or only very slightly connected.

In such cases one must invoke another mechanism, and here the phenomenon of lucidity is dominant.

The percipient, owing to a state of lucidity, sees what is happening around the agent, towards whom his faculty of lucidity is directed by an intermediary subject more or less closely related. That is so, in the instances where the percipient witnesses the scene at the moment of its accomplishment.

In cases where the percipient witnesses the fact or the accident subsequently to the time when it takes place, we may assume that, on account of his being in a special state, he is in such a receptive condition that he can receive the impression of a thought, previously sent forth by the agent. This thought has up to that time remained latent in the same way as it is still latent for all subjects who are not in a state of receptivity at the exact time when the thought is emitted.

We shall find similar cases in the phenomena of typtology.

CHAPTER XI

CRYSTAL-GAZING

General Study and Experiments

CRYSTAL-GAZING is an experimental procedure which produces a number of interesting phenomena, among which we may, perhaps, include manifestations of the faculty of lucidity.

The same might be said of audition in the shell, or clairaudience, an experience which only differs from the former because it brings the sense of hearing into play instead of the sense of sight.

Crystal-gazing is a very common practice, particularly in England; it is, moreover, as we shall see, very easy to accomplish.

The experiment consists principally in placing a mirror or glass ball, more or less brilliant, in front of the subject, who gazes attentively at it and distinguishes, after a time, more or less definite pictures.

Nature of the Object or Mirror employed

The practice is a very ancient one, and is met with in all countries; the objects employed have therefore been very varied.

At first, mirrors of every kind, particularly metallic, were employed; these mirrors were either concave or convex—sometimes spherical.

Sometimes any hollow vessel is used, into which liquid is poured, which then serves as the reflecting surface. Most frequently, a glass or bottle filled with water is used.

In some countries, especially in England, crystal balls, perfectly spherical, are specially manufactured for this purpose, which have given to this experiment the name of " Crystal-gazing."

For the crystal ball may be substituted an empty glass globe, which is filled with pure water and inverted, so as to present a spherical surface to the gazer.

I generally use the crystal ball; but, for special occasions, when I wish to secure particular results with certain subjects, I use a mirror consisting of a glass plate, covered on the under surface with a black or white coating, according to circumstances.

We shall see, in the chapter devoted to the method of experimenting, the position in which the subject should be placed.

If the experiment is to give any result, he will first see the mirror assume a different tinge. It then seems to become turbid, forming red or blue clouds, which whirl like smoke, and, finally, pictures are formed.

Formation of Pictures

The pictures are sometimes of a uniform tone, similar to a photograph; at other times they are coloured, and present the natural tints.

Some pictures are fixed and motionless, like a painting; others are constantly changing, and show the persons animated, as in a cinematograph.

The first pictures are often simple—a portrait, bust, plant, animal, or house. Then they become most complicated—a complete moving scene, as in a theatre; a room, a street, a public thoroughfare filled with various people, who walk about, come in and go out, just as in real life.

The subject thinks that he is present at the scene as a spectator, and so makes remarks and observations; but, in other cases, he thinks he is living in the midst of the scene which unfolds itself before him, and the illusion is so strong that he makes gestures, holds out his hands to greet something which he sees, replies to the persons who appear to be present, &c.

Nature of the Pictures

The subject may see :—

1. An object which has lately attracted his attention.

2. A scene relative to something which has just occupied his thoughts.

3. The representation of an unconscious memory.

4. Pictures of which he had been conscious but had forgotten, and which only exist in his sub-conscious memory.

5. Purely fancy pictures, which correspond to nothing real.

6. Pictures of which he was never conscious, but which exist in his sub-consciousness.

7. Visions verbally suggested in a previous hypnotic condition.

8. Visions suggested verbally by those around, whether he is conscious of it or not, at the moment of the experiment and in the auto-hypnotic condition in which he has placed himself.

9. Visions due to a conscious transmission of thought from some one present.

10. Visions due to an unconscious transmission of thought from some one present.

11. Visions due to a conscious telepathic influence from an absent person.

12. Visions due to an unconscious telepathic influence from an absent person.

13. Visions of something at a distance, unknown to the subject, but known to some one present: that is conscious or unconscious thought-reading.

14. Visions of something happening at a distance, unknown to the subject and every one else present: this is a phenomenon of lucidity.

15. Visions of something in the past, unknown to the subject, but known to some one present.

16. Visions of something in the past, unknown to the subject and every one else present.

17. Visions of something in the future, which may be foreseen by the subject.

18. Visions of something in the future, which cannot be foreseen by the subject, but can be foreseen by some one present.

19. Visions of something in the future, which cannot be foreseen, either by the subject or any one present.

It will be noticed that, in a certain number of cases which we shall quote, several methods of perception often appear successively or are combined. Thus, it is not uncommon for the subject to perceive first of all pictures due to unconscious memories or to his imagination, and, afterwards, things coming from mental communications.

In cases in which the phenomenon of lucidity makes its appearance, it is not uncommon for the subject to be placed on the track by perception of the thoughts of some one present.

From the numerous experiments in crystal-gazing which have been made in England by Miss Angus and published in the *Annales des Sciences Psychiques*, we extract the following, which will give a fairly complete idea of these experiments.

Miss Angus' Experiments

1. A lady one day asked me to see a friend of whom she was thinking. Almost immediately, I called out: "Here is an old, old lady, who looks at me with a triumphant smile on her face. She has a prominent nose and a nut-cracker chin. Her face is quite wrinkled, especially about the eyes, as if she was always smiling. She wears a small white shawl with a black border. But she cannot be old, as her hair is quite brown! However, her face looks as though it were very old." The picture then disappeared, and the lady said I had given a perfect description of her friend's mother instead of the friend, and that it was a joke in the family that the mother must dye her hair to have it so brown, and that she was eighty-two years of age. This lady asked me if the vision was

clear enough to enable me to recognise a resemblance to her son's photograph. The following day she placed several photographs in front of me, and, in a moment, without the slightest hesitation, I pointed out one which bore a striking resemblance to my vision.

2. One afternoon I was with a young lady whom I had never seen or heard spoken of before. She asked me if she could look in my crystal ; when she was doing so it occurred to me to glance over her shoulder, and I saw a boat tossing about in a very rough sea, although land was still in sight. Everything vanished, and, suddenly, a small house appeared with five or six steps (I forget the number which I then counted) leading up to the door. An old man was sitting on the second step reading a newspaper. In front of the house there was an open field covered with thick tufts of grass, in which some lambs, or rather some very small sheep, were grazing.

When the second scene had disappeared, the young lady told me that I had given a very clear description of the place in the Shetland Isles where she and her mother were about to spend a few weeks.

3. At a recent experiment in crystal-gazing I succeeded, for the first time, in making another person see what I saw in the crystal. Miss Rose came to see me one afternoon, and asked me to look in the crystal for her. I did so, and immediately called out: "Oh! there is a bed with a man lying in it, who seems to be very ill (I saw that he was dead, but restrained myself from saying so), and here is a woman in black who stays beside the bed." I did not recognise the man as being any one whom I knew, and told her to look for herself. Almost immediately she cried out: "Oh! I see the bed too! But, oh! take it back, the man is dead!" She had received a great shock, and said that she would never look in it again. Soon, however, her curiosity made her look once more, and then the scene again appeared, and very slowly from a cloudy object at the side of the bed the lady in black emerged very distinctly. She then described some per-

sons who were in the room, and said that they were carrying away something which was completely draped in black. When she had seen that she pushed away the crystal and refused to look at it again. She returned on Sunday (this happened on Friday) with her cousin, and we teased her about her fear of the crystal, so that she said she would look in it once more. She took the crystal, but immediately threw it aside, saying, "No, I will not look at it, because the bed with that fearful man is still in it."

On their return home, they learned that the cousin's father-in-law had died that afternoon; but to prove that he had not been in our thoughts, although we all knew that he was not well, no one had suggested that it was he: his name had not been mentioned in connection with this vision.

4. A short time after I had become the happy owner of a crystal, I undertook to convert certain very hardened sceptics, and I will briefly relate my experiments with two or three of them.

One was a Mr. B., who was so thoroughly determined to catch me at fault that he gave out that he was thinking of a friend whom it would not be possible for me to describe.

I had only met Mr. B. the previous day, and I knew nothing, so to speak, concerning him or his personal friends.

I took the crystal, which was immediately covered with a fog, out of which a group of persons gradually emerged, but too indistinctly to enable me to recognise any one, until suddenly a man came up at a gallop. I remember that I said: "I cannot explain what he is like, but he is clothed in a very singular manner, with something so bright that the sun which is shining on him dazzles me completely, and I cannot describe him!" Then, as he came nearer, I called out: "But he is a soldier in glittering armour; only he is not an officer—he is only a soldier." Two friends who were in the room said that Mr. B.'s emotion was intense, and my attention

L

was diverted from the crystal when I heard him say: "It is astonishing: it is perfectly true! I was thinking of a boy, the son of a crofter, in whom I am particularly interested, and who is a soldier in London, which will explain the group of persons around him in the street!"

5. Another case was more interesting, because I entered in some way or another into the thoughts of a lady, whilst another lady did her best to influence me.

Miss D., one of my friends at Brighton, had a singular magnetic power, and thought she was absolutely sure of success with me and the crystal.

Another lady, Miss H., who was present, laughed at all this, particularly when Miss D. insisted on holding my hand with one of hers and placing her other hand on my forehead! Miss H., with a disdainful air, took a book, and, going to the other end of the room, left us to our folly.

I very quickly felt myself becoming excited, a thing which had never occurred before when I looked in the crystal. I saw a group of people, and I felt a sort of strange impression that I was among them, and we seemed to be waiting for something. Presently a young horseman passed, in racing costume; his horse went by at a canter, and he smiled and nodded to those whom he knew in the group, and we then lost sight of him.

In a moment we all seemed to feel that something had happened, and I became very anxious to see something that was just beyond the range of my vision. Soon, however, two or three men approached and carried him past me, and again I experienced an intense anxiety to know whether he was only dangerously wounded or if he had really lost his life. All this happened in a few moments, but these were long enough to leave me in such agitation that I could not realise it was only a crystal vision.

During this time Miss H. had put her book on one side and came to us quite impressed. She told me that I had given a perfect description of a scene at some races in Scotland, at which she had been present a week or two previously—a scene which had many times been in her thoughts, but of which she had never told me, since we were strangers to each other. She also told me that I had exactly described her own feelings at that time, and that I had reproduced it all with the utmost clearness.

The other lady was rather disappointed that, after having so strongly concentrated her thoughts, I should be influenced, not by her, but by another person who had laughed at the whole affair.

This anecdote was related to me, a few days after it happened, by Miss Angus. Her version was that she saw a gentleman rider going to the post and nodding to his friends. Then she saw him carried on a stretcher through the group. She seemed, she said, to be actually present, and to feel, in some way, agitated. The fact of the accident was eventually told me in Scotland by another lady, a stranger to all these persons.

CHAPTER XII

CRYSTAL-GAZING (*continued*)

Experiments of La Société Universelle d'Études Psychiques

La Société Universelle d'Études Psychiques has interested itself in these experiments and commissioned a certain number of sectional groups to pursue the study. We will give an account of some of their experiments.

One of the Society's groups met one Sunday afternoon for the purpose of conducting some experiments. The group consisted of Dr. Joire, M. Douchez, M. Leroy, Mlle. J., Mlle. D.

Mlle. D. had never been hypnotised and had never been present at any experiment of this character, but was willing to serve as the subject. I put her into a light sleep—the first degree of somnambulism. I then awakened her, and we agreed to try an experiment in crystal-gazing.

Mlle. D. was then placed with her back to the window, with the crystal ball in front of her on a table covered with a black cloth.

Thinking to induce at the outset a simple hallucinatory vision, I said to her: " You will see in the crystal the picture (I said ' portrait ') of Mr. D."

I then told her to describe exactly to us what she saw and we would leave her to speak.

The picture became clearer by degrees. Mlle. D. told us she could see a very small photograph surrounded by a circle of gold; it was a lady's brooch. The photograph was that of Mr. D. The subject very clearly distinguished this jewel in a white box; there was something under the brooch which she could not clearly distinguish; this small box was enclosed in a larger box, where there were four gilt pins with real pearl heads. Close by, she described a case for correspondence cards, all on a shelf of a hanging wall-cupboard. (Then followed a description of the character and the situation of the furniture in the room.)

Those are the details which Mlle. D. gave us of the very, clear picture which she saw in the crystal. The hallucination lasted about twenty minutes.

Mr. D. was the only person present who knew of the existence of the brooch and the room described; but he did not know the situation of the brooch and the objects around it.

On the following day he went to the house of the owner of the brooch, who lived in a town about thirty-seven miles distant, to ascertain how much of the vision was real. The following are the results of his inquiry :—

The brooch was really in a cardboard box on the shelf of a cupboard, and at the bottom of the box was some pink cotton-wool (which the subject could not distinguish). The box containing the brooch was placed in a larger box containing the four gilt pins with white pearl heads. Also, on the same shelf, he found the box of correspondence cards. But the description of the furniture, which came at the end, was not quite correct. I do not regard this case as sufficient to constitute a case of lucidity, the experiment having been an impromptu one, and the conditions not having been prepared in advance. Nevertheless, I give it as an interesting example of crystal-gazing, and especially to induce investigators to take up these experiments, so easy to try, and which may sometimes give results worthy of attention.

SOCIÉTÉ UNIVERSELLE D'ÉTUDES PSYCHIQUES, LILLE
SECTION

*Report of Experiments given at the Annual General
Meeting by Dr. Joire, President of the Society*

A celebrated physician once said, "There are no diseases; there are only sick people." This statement, always true, has been many times repeated by those who have had medical experience other than in theory or in the laboratories. This fundamental truth in medicine could, perhaps, be profitably transported to the domain of psychical studies. That is to say, we should not seek to reproduce, at hazard, and with any chance subject, the phenomena which we desire to observe. But there are mediums who ought to be studied—that is to say, we ought to take them as they present themselves, each with his own peculiar powers, and observe through them the phenomena they are able to produce. That is the foundation of the scientific method which we ought to apply to the study of psychical phenomena, any other order of procedure being irrational and anti-scientific.

In this way we shall some day be able, when we hear of a medium presenting externalisation of force, to show M. Gustav le Bon the phenomenon of levitation, for which he has promised a reward to the subject; but not, of course, as he seemed to suppose, by establishing a kind of competition between all mediums taken at random, which would be a scientific absurdity.

These experiments which I now describe belong to the domain of lucidity and premonition. They present this peculiar characteristic, that in their production I have employed the phenomenon of clairvoyance combined with that of clairaudience.

These experiments were made with a medium whom we discovered through some interesting phenomena which she had given elsewhere, and of which we had received details.

Prima Nitija is a medium who, in regard to the phenomena obtained through her, excels all other mediums hitherto known. She is, in fact, able to produce experiments which can be submitted to scientific control, which is not usually the case with other mediums when left to themselves.

First of all, some spontaneous phenomena put me on the track of this subject's special faculty. One of them is of sufficient interest to be quoted.

One day Nitija, while at my house, in a condition of deep somnambulism, began to speak, and the following conversation took place between us:—

"Oh, how tired I am," said Prima.

"What has made you tired? What have you done?"

"The long walk which I have just taken has tired me."

"Where have you come from? Where have you been?"

"I came from R., and that is a long way; my legs ache. I am very tired."

Now R., mentioned by the subject, is a neighbouring town about seven miles away. I knew very well that she had not been there, either on that day or on the previous one; there had been no question of such a journey, because she never went there; that morning she had only been on some errands in the town.

Shortly afterwards, without attaching any importance to her words, I awoke Prima. I noticed that she still showed signs of fatigue, and, without having any recollection of the conversation which had taken place while she was asleep, she said to me again:

"I do not know why, but I am fearfully tired—one would think I had walked all day long."

"It is nothing," I said to her. "You went on several errands this morning, that has made you tired, but it will soon pass away."

The following day I again met Prima, who greeted me with the words:

"Yesterday, when I was with you, I missed a visit from an uncle whom I had not seen for a very long time, and who came to see me just at the time I was with you."

" Ah ! what did he come to see you for ? "

" He came to ask me if I would go to the fair at R. with him."

Had Prima Nitija, then, had, during her somnambulistic sleep, knowledge of what what was happening at the time at her house, and had this suggested her dream ?

Put on the track by this observation, I endeavoured to try the powers of my subject by means of the crystal. I therefore one day made her sit down in front of the crystal, and requested her to tell me exactly what she saw.

After a very short time she told me that she could see a room which she described in detail.

In this room she saw a lady in walking costume, with her hat on, ready to go out.

In the same room was a gentleman, with his hat in his hand, apparently waiting for the lady.

The medium recognised this lady as Mme. X., and, by the description which she gave, there was no possible doubt. "But," said Prima, "this lady seems to be very much put out; she has lost something which she has been looking for everywhere, and she cannot start until she has found it."

She saw her open a cupboard and look on all the shelves and feel with her hand on the top shelf.

She seemed satisfied, for she had found what she wanted—a key which she held for a moment and then put in her pocket.

She closed the cupboard, and then started to go out.

Mme. X., interrogated on the following day, was greatly surprised when she was told of her search for the key. She admitted the accuracy of all the details given above, but she was angry at the mention of the person who was with her, and asked why she had thus been spied upon.

In another experiment I again placed the subject before the crystal, and indicating a member of the Society who was present, I said to her: "You will see Mr. X. in the crystal, and find out where he has been this morning."

After a few moments Prima described a room with bare walls, and furnished only with some chairs and a table, covered with books and papers.

She recognised Mr. X. in the room, standing talking with two other people. One of them went up to the table, took some of the papers, looked at them, and returned to the two others.

All three talked with animation, she said; they gesticulated, showed each other the papers they held in their hands, and apparently they were not in agreement.

One of the three had his back constantly turned to her; he was rather stout. "But," remarked Prima, "there seems to be something strange which makes his neck large, perhaps a big cravat which makes his neck look thick."

Mr. X. then told us that that morning he had kept an appointment with two other people, in an office answering to the description given by Prima. There had been an animated discussion over a matter which had not been settled.

He explained that the third person, whose back only the subject had seen, was a man who wore an English cap, placed far back on his head, and coming down almost to his neck, and this, in fact, seen from the back, would give the impression that he had a very thick neck.

This last feature is noticeable; the subject saw something which she could not understand.

She did not describe an object seen in imagination, but proved to us by the description given that she did not know what it was that she saw. She described to us the object which she perceived, but the witness alone recognised what it was, and he had to explain it to us in order to show that the description was really correct.

In another experiment I tried to combine clairaudience with clairvoyance. I gave Prima Nitija a tin box, telling her to hold it to her ear, and that she would hear, as at a telephone, the voices of the people she would see in the crystal.

Before commencing the experiment I put her to sleep,

and gave her the suggestion that she would see in the crystal something which she would do on the following Sunday, it being then Friday.

When Prima was awakened, I placed the crystal before her and, at the same time, gave her the box through which to listen. She heard at first vague and confused noises, as at the telephone, in which she could distinguish nothing. She then repeated various phrases which she heard distinctly:

"Tell him that you would like to travel."

A man's voice: "You ought to go; you need a change."

"Why do you not come?"

Some women's voices, talking to each other, prevented her from hearing.

A woman's voice: "What a pretty house! Where is your eldest son?"

At this moment she was unable to hear anything more, but she described a picture which appeared in the crystal.

She saw at first a house with a *porte-cochère*. She looked through a hall, with a door on the right by which she entered a room which she described.

She stated, between times, that she did not recognise this house. The room which she now saw was a dining-room.

She saw a sideboard, various ornaments on the mantel-piece, and, in the chimney-corner, suspended against the wall, was a "tear-off" calendar.

Before going farther into the description of the room, wishing to assure myself whether the suggestion I had made to her was taking effect, I insisted that she should look and tell me the date on the calendar.

She at once read the figure 17. I asked her to read the day of the week. She looked carefully and finally read: Sunday. I at once ascertained that the following Sunday would, in fact, be the 17th.

I permitted her to continue her description of what was in the room.

A round table, around which she could distinguish, on one side, two, and, on the other, three people.

In the corner, to the right of the entrance door, Prima saw an object placed on the ground. She could not well distinguish this object, but described it as being cylindrical in shape with longitudinal stripes; it had the form and appearance of a drum, she said.

The table was laid, and coffee was being taken.

One of the persons seated at the table she recognised as a relative of her own, whom she had not seen for more than a year; facing her was his wife, two of their children, and one other person.

Finally, she saw a person coming into the room, and recognised herself. Several persons rose from the table, but the man remained seated; Prima approached him, and, at the same time, she heard the following dialogue:

"Well, this is good news! You are no longer ill!"

"I have never been."

"But we were told so."

"Not at all."

Various noises then prevented her hearing.

Then, again, she caught different phrases of a dialogue, in which she could not well understand what was said by the man's voice.

"Why do you stop there?"

"You are not happy."

"If you will listen to me, you will be happy."

At this moment several people went out; there only remained her relative, his wife, and Prima.

The man said again: "What are you in want of?"

"Nothing much," replied Prima.

A confused discussion ensued, after which this final phrase was pronounced by a man's voice:

"Would you like to take a journey with me?"

Prima was herself greatly puzzled at the result of this experiment, because she had not for a long time seen the relative whom she recognised in the crystal; she knew that he had since changed his residence, and she wondered whether she would find his new house, which was unknown to her, like the picture shown to her in the crystal.

On the Monday she told me of the visit which she had made on the Sunday.

I note, in passing, that the subject seemed to have completely forgotten the phrases which she had heard, and which I carefully noted down at the time of the experiment. So that, though she described very well all that she had seen, I had to interrogate her closely in order to make her repeat the conversation.

She was, first of all, struck by the exterior aspect of the house, as being exactly like the vision in the crystal. The principal door, the hall, the door of the apartment on the right were just the same.

She herself, on entering, said: "What a pretty house!"

The interior arrangement of the room was also exactly as she had described it to me: the sideboard, the mantelpiece with its ornaments, the calendar, the table, and in the corner, to the right of the door, not a drum, but one of those small Moorish stools, which in the shadow, with its carved sides, would have a cylindrical appearance, and show longitudinal lines which would give it a strong resemblance to a drum.

Here again, as in the previous experiment, we can ascertain that it was not the thought of the object which presented itself to the mind of the subject and caused her to create the picture she described. But she seems to have originally seen a picture which she did not recognise, and her description of it, even in its inaccurate particulars, showed that it did not arouse in the subject's mind the thought of the real object.

In these particular instances, therefore, the picture seen in the crystal did not arise either from a sub-conscious recollection or from a thought, more or less conscious, which gave rise to an hallucination.

The people at the table were really just as they had been seen.

Her relative was dozing, and did not at first rise with the others to receive his visitor.

The conversation turned at first on the health of the

visitor, and the phrases I have recorded were repeated word for word.

Not seeing the eldest child with the others, Prima herself asked: " Where is your eldest child ? "

Then the man asked Prima if she was happy where she was, and while they were thus talking the other people rose from the table.

Just here a remarkable incident took place. A parrot, of whose existence Prima was ignorant, chattered and screeched and made such a deafening noise as to drown the voices of the talkers. It was this noise, indistinctly heard, which she had first compared with children crying and then with women quarrelling.

Finally, her relative asked Prima if, by way of relaxation, she would not like to accompany him on a journey he was going to take.

All that had been seen and heard by the subject on the Friday was realised exactly on the Sunday.

I should add that although the visit to this relative, whom she had not seen for about a year, might have been in the subject's mind at the time of the experiment, the details which she gave were quite unexpected, and could not be a sub-conscious recollection. In fact, she had never before been in that house.

All these facts were ultimately checked and verified by strict inquiry, which enabled us to testify that Prima had neither dreamed nor imagined, nor could she have known beforehand the events she saw in the crystal on the Friday, which were recorded at the time, and which came to pass on the following Sunday with the utmost precision.

I must also draw attention to the singular character of the mental audition. As will be seen from the account of the experiment and the real experience, the phrases were heard without order or coherence, but all of them were repeated in the course of the conversation, and fitted naturally into their places.

We may therefore say, with regard to this mental audition, what I have said concerning certain of the pictures seen in the crystal.

It was not an original idea of the subject's own which created an hallucination and caused her to follow an imaginary conversation relating to the preconceived idea. On the contrary, the subject, in some way or other, perceived some phrases and snatches of conversation which she repeated, but without understanding their sense, and they were so incomplete that they had no intelligible signification. For all that, however, they were finally found to adapt themselves exactly and naturally to the reality.

CHAPTER XIII

MENTAL AUDITION

UNDER the name of mental audition, clairaudience, or hearing in the shell, we describe some experiments which, considered as psychical phenomena, are exactly of the same character as crystal-gazing. The only difference is that they bring the sense of hearing into play instead of the sense of sight.

The subject generally makes use of a sea-shell, in which is heard the murmur of aerial waves, which circulate in the interior convolutions. The shell is placed to the ear, and the subject, after waiting a short time, hears voices, as in a telephone receiver. We have often replaced the shell by a metal box, which produced the same effect.

We give, first of all, a case of mental audition without apparatus, which was published in the *Blackburn Times* and the *Review of Reviews*.

Mr. Wolstenholme states that some years ago, when the following incident occurred, he was living at 4 and 6 Preston New Road, Blackburn; after explaining the business which had called him to Preston, he continued:

" At this time I had a pony called ' Fanny,' and as she did not get much exercise, I decided to drive her to Preston, a distance of nine miles. In the morning, I harnessed her in a passage at the back of my house. On each side was a wall, about eight feet high; on one side it was the parting wall between the back parts of the adjoining houses, and on the other the wall faced a large timber-yard. I was quite ready for my journey, and went into the house again to get a rug and whip. On returning with these and standing in the trap, arranging the rugs, &c., I heard a man's voice quite close to my ears, saying, ' Take some string in your pocket.' I at once turned round to see who had spoken, when, to my surprise, there was no one in the passage or near at hand.

"There is a cab-rank in the street, at the end of the passage, and, thinking it was one of the cabmen who had spoken, I got out of the trap and went to the end of the passage to see who it was. There was not a single cab on the rank, and the only person I could see was a lady who was seventy or eighty yards away on the other side of the street.

"There was no apparent reason why I should take any string in my pocket. I went back into the house and related the incident to my wife. 'Ah, well!' she said, 'take the string, it is not very heavy.' And I took several yards.

"I reached Preston without accident, went to the Dog Hotel, and left Fanny in charge of the landlord. After the meeting we returned to the hotel to have some tea, and at twenty minutes to nine I set out on my return journey. It was a very dark night, but I had good lamps. Fanny trotted along at a good pace, and all was going well, when suddenly she stopped, and whether I whipped or coaxed her she would not move a step forward, but backed the trap against the hedge by the side of the road.

"I jumped out and hurried to the horse's head to see what was the matter. I at once saw that one of the traces was broken inside the piece of metal which fastened it to the collar. The defect, which was hidden by the metal, had escaped my notice, and I was quite unaware that there was any defect in the harness.

"I took off the collar, and at once saw the utility of the string I had put in my pocket. I mended the collar temporarily, so that Fanny was able to take me back home. Without the string I must have left the trap on the road and walked six miles on foot.

"Who warned me? I do not know. All I know is that a voice sounded close to me, not more than a foot away, and that it was a man's voice. The nearest person I could see was a lady, and she was seventy or eighty yards away."

We have narrated this incident, although it was spontaneous, because it refers to the same phenomenon that we are now studying.

Mr. Myers, in his work on *Human Personality*, quotes the following experiments by Miss X. on hearing in the shell.

The following are the exact words of Miss X. :

" Nature has endowed me with an exquisitely fine and sensitive ear, which has developed during three years' scientific musical education, and it was with a certain amount of confidence that I took a smooth-lipped porcelain shell, large enough to hold in the palm of my hand, and, placing it close to my ear, awaited results.

" At first I heard the monotonous sound of the sea which all children know, but after a few minutes' concentrated attention my ear became accustomed to the sound, which became, so to speak, the undertone of the more articulate sounds which followed.

" I found the experiment more fatiguing than that of the crystal, and this time I did not continue it. I never prolonged the experiment beyond six or eight minutes.

" After twenty experiments I summed up the results as follows :

" 1. Eleven times I heard human voices. They followed rapidly during only one experiment, and may be divided into two groups.

" (*a*) Those more or less recognisable, sometimes coming separately, and sometimes rising like a Tower of Babel, with the effect of a large assembly. It was probably the memories of something I had heard, although of a kind which did not come to my knowledge in the ordinary manner. Sometimes I heard distinctly the exact repetitions of some conversations in which I had taken part, or, still more frequently, what I had overheard.

" For example, after a dinner, the shell would repeat the conversations of my neighbour on my right, rather than that of the person on my left, with whom I was conversing. There was, in this instance, I believe, an analogy

M

with crystal-gazing. The crystal more frequently shows what is unconsciously rather than consciously observed.

"(b) Voices which I did not recognise and which were of such a character that I could not distinguish them, and which gave me information or advice which my conscious self was capable—although, perhaps, with effort—of giving, such as a quotation from poetry or prose, a number, an address, advice to write a letter or send a parcel.

"2. Nine times I heard musical sounds, and I am certain that out of these nine times the shell positively assisted my memory five times. I was able to distinguish, and follow without difficulty—as I could generally in a concert-hall—first one part, then another, of a chorus or orchestra alternately, and to change at will, as I am rarely able to do, without the score, even by a conscious effort, a few hours after hearing a symphony or a concert.

"It is well to point out that the shell happily does not merely reproduce street noises or the unpleasant roarings of street urchins and barrel-organs. Is not this because, as in crystal-gazing, fatigue or irritation, which may, perhaps, be a source of danger in itself, suffices to prevent the success of the experiment?

"All this, however, might be attributed, in different degrees, to expectation, and, to this extent, was disappointing. However, on June 3rd a slight incident occurred which I found encouraging.

"I had been out-of-doors for two hours and had let myself in with my latch-key; I had particularly noticed that no letters or cards had arrived, and I had spoken to no one before coming into the room where my friend A. was sitting reading. It was close upon lunch-time and I took the shell to pass the time. As I had observed with regard to crystal visions, a definite fact is quickly constructed and comes to the surface at once, and the shell did not lose a second in greeting me with the clear murmur 'Endsleigh Street,' to which I could attach no meaning. Then A., raising her head, told me that our friend, Q. H., had called and had been waiting an hour for me. 'Has he come from Oxford for the day?' I asked, 'or is he staying near here?' (as he usually did). 'No,' said A, 'he has taken a room in Endsleigh Street.'

"As far as I can remember, I had never been in this street in my life, and this name was not connected with any remembrance.

"It is difficult to suppose that the coincidence was purely accidental.

"A few days later, I was still more encouraged. On June 11th, a Saturday, Mr. G. A. Smith spent some time with us, making some experiments in thought-transference, which succeeded very well and greatly interested me. Mr. Smith left the house shortly after seven o'clock. After dinner I took the shell which had played a part— not a very successful one—in our experiments.

"This, according to my notes, is exactly what occurred.

X. *to* G. A. S.

"June 11, 1892. *Saturday evening,* 8.30.

"Why, whilst the shell was repeating exactly what you said about your excursions on the rocks at Ramsgate, should it stop all of a sudden and ask, still with your voice, 'Are you then a vegetarian?' Perhaps the last time you dined you refused meat? Tell me if you were responsible for this impertinence."

G. A. S. *to* X.

" June 13*th.*

"Certainly, the shell spoke the truth. As you know, I left you after seven o'clock. After about a quarter of an hour's walk, I suddenly met Mr. M. I was thinking of our experiments and fear I did not follow his conversation very well, but he alluded to some dishes at a vegetarian restaurant, I do not know where, and then, being immediately interested in the question as to whether he was a champion of the vegetarian cause, I interrupted him with the question: 'Are you then a vegetarian?' I think these are the exact words I used. He will surely recall them, and I must ask him."

G. A. S. *to* X.

"*June 23rd.*

"I have thought over to-day where I was on June 11th, on leaving you when I met Mr. M. It took me exactly eleven minutes. If it was a quarter past seven when I left you, it was probably half-past seven, or a few minutes later, when I put the question to Mr. M.

"Mr M. was not at home, and although asked to reply at once, he only wrote on June 22nd the following to Mr. Smith (without relating the exact details of the preceding conversation): 'The principal thing is that you asked me, I am sure, on the occasion of which you speak, when I praised the café in Oxford Street, if I was a vegetarian. That is the heart of the question, and it is well established.' "

Even the triviality and grotesqueness of the incident give rise to reflection, apart from its connection with shell-audition, which, however, supplies us with a curious example of arriving at unexpected knowledge through its means.

Since that time I have made notes of about fifty new experiments, but those I have mentioned may be regarded as typical of all. Half-a-dozen, at most, cannot be counted, as proving telepathy; twenty, perhaps, may be classed as the emergence of recollections which would never otherwise have come to light again, and another dozen may be regarded as the result of expectancy. All the rest consisted of musical sounds, some of which were purely due to imagination. The others were of a very definite character, so much so that I succeeded in reproducing them on the piano or writing them down at the same moment, but they did not differ at all from what I could improvise in the ordinary way.

Twice only have I heard connected rational phrases, of which, at the time, I could not see the connection, either with recollections or things imagined; but in these two cases I eventually discovered their origin, the one in a book and the other on the fourth page of a letter which I had thought finished on the third page, but the fourth page of which I think I must have read, when taking it out of the envelope, and forgotten.

CHAPTER XIV

CRYSTAL VISIONS COMBINED WITH LUCIDITY

THIS chapter will be devoted to two cases of crystal vision, in which the faculty of lucidity appeared in a most interesting manner, and the authenticity of which is completely verified. The first case is taken from *Les Annales des Sciences Psychiques*.

"At the commencement of the spring of 1885 (writes the correspondent of this journal) I was living at Colabo with my husband, a major in the Royal Artillery stationed at that place, about two miles from Bombay. I had been studying for some time Gregory's *Animal Magnetism*, a subject in which I was particularly interested. I had several times made various fairly successful experiments on some of my servants—mostly Indians. I had great influence over my children's ayah, a half-caste. I frequently caused her to look in a large glass of water, which I had previously magnetised, and thus learned news of my distant friends.

"This girl was neither common nor ignorant—she was, on the contrary, well brought up, having received a good education in a Protestant school at Belgaum. She spoke and wrote English almost as correctly as myself. She told me many things which I found to be correct, and others which I have not yet been able to verify.

"The Royal Artillery, of which my husband was in command, was encamped with other European troops at Colabo. On the day of Lord Reay's arrival at Bombay there came an order for the troops to go to Apollo Bunder, the place of landing, with all the officers in full regimentals. We were still at lunch when my husband told his orderly to make ready his uniform, but the man came back shortly, confused and stammering out:

"'Sahib, I cannot find the belt.'

"'Do not be so silly, you must be blind,' replied the major, rising up impatiently and going to his dressing-room.

"But from the sounds which reached me, it appeared that the sword-belt could not be found, and that my husband was furiously accusing each of his servants. Cries of 'Not me, Sahib; I very good man; I not thief' filled the air. The cries, shoutings, and noises grew perfectly deafening. My husband came into the dining-room and said :

"'Well, here is a capital opportunity to test Ruth's clairvoyance. Call her and tell her to find my belt.'

"I called for Ruth, who came in pale and trembling, thinking that we were going to accuse her of the theft.

"I reassured her, and explained what we wanted of her ; but she asked me to excuse her, alleging that the other servants would never forgive her if the thief was discovered through her. I calmed her fears, and promised that I would reveal to nobody, not even to my husband, the name of the thief, if it was shown to her in the water. I alone would know it, and would even pardon the theft if the stolen object was restored.

"After filling a large goblet with water I made the passes over it, and told Ruth to taste it.

"'It is very bitter,' she said. 'If Mem Sahib would magnetise me I think I could see.'

"It is perhaps well to add that Ruth always found a taste of bitterness in magnetised water. I often placed side by side two glasses filled with water, of which only one had been magnetised. Ruth tasted both, and then told which of the two had been magnetised, declaring that it had a bitter taste, and she never made a mistake. I once procured a very powerful magnet, thinking that it would doubtless have more effect than my hand; but Ruth refused to look in the water, declaring that she saw flames, which sprang up as though they would burn her face. It seemed impossible to deceive her; she recognised every time what she called the 'condemned glass.'

"Returning to our story, after this long digression, which, however, seemed necessary, Ruth was bending over her glass of water.

"'Well,' I said, 'can you see anything ?'

"'No, Mem Sahib, nothing.'

"'Look for the thief,' I commanded firmly, and I again made passes over her neck and head, but without result; she persisted in saying that she could see nothing. I began to think that she was trifling with me, and that she had deceived me.

"A new idea occurred to me:

"'Ruth, try to see the major the last time he wore his full-dress belt.'

"A long silence ensued, then she said:

"'I see the Sahib, he is dressing; he puts on his uniform, now his belt. Now he is off! There he is in the saddle, and he starts.'

"'Do not leave him for a second,' I said, with renewed firmness.

"'Ah! but he goes so fast, and I am tired,' she replied, out of breath.

"'Come on! Come on!'

"'Sahib is with other Sahibs; there are many soldiers and a large crowd. It is a large Tomasha; some great person who is going. They are quite near the water.'

"'Now rest yourself, but do not lose sight of the major.'

"After a moment's silence she added:

"'The Sahib goes into a large house by the side of the water. He goes into a dressing-room, changes his uniform, places it in a small zinc trunk with the exception of the belt, which is left hanging on a coat-rack.'

"'The Yacht Club,' cried my husband. 'Patillo (to his orderly), send some one immediately to see if the belt is still there.'

"'I should much like to know,' resumed my husband, 'if I really left it there. The last time I wore it was the day Lord Ripon left for England.'

"'We shall soon know,' I replied triumphantly, because

there was no doubt in my mind that the belt would be found there.

"A short while afterwards the messenger came running back, and the great tumult which I heard around him convinced me, before seeing him, that my predictions were correct; he ran nimbly up the stairs, carrying the belt over his head; he had found it on a coat-rack in the dressing-room, as Ruth had indicated.

"This young woman could not have had any idea where the sword-belt was; she had only been in my service for a short time, and had entered it long after the departure of Lord Ripon.

"In the spring of the same year I was greatly interested in a grand polo tournament, which was to be held at Meerut. One of my friends at that time was to take part in it, and although a good horseman, and an excellent player, he had had frequent accidents when on horseback, which caused me some anxiety on his account. Once more I had recourse to Ruth. We shut ourselves up together in my room, and I began to magnetise a glass of water; but this time she asked for a piece of brown paper to be placed underneath, declaring that she could then see much more distinctly. She placed her hands around the glass, in order to soften the light.

"'Go to Meerut.'

"After a wait of at least ten minutes she said, 'I am there.'

"'Look for Sahib,' I said, mentioning the name of my friend.

"'I see a tall, dark, thin man, with a small black moustache, and large terrible eyes.'

"'Follow him and tell me what happens to him.'

"'He is going on all right, but the other side is winning. 'Ah!' she cried, with compassion, 'there is a gentleman who has been bitten on the leg by a horse. He is suffering much.'

"'And my friend?' I inquired anxiously.

"'No, no, not the friend of Mem Sahib; that is a fair gentleman with red face and very light hair.'

"'Ask his name,' I said to her, fixing my eyes on her, and exercising all the force of my will.

"'But I cannot,' she replied hesitatingly.

"'Do as I tell you,' I replied firmly.

"'I will ask his servant, if you can make me see him.'

"I tried with all my power, but absolutely without any result.

"'Hush! I hear his name; it is Captain X.'

"I jumped for joy: she had never seen the man she mentioned, nor even heard him spoken of. I am quite sure of this, whereas she might, perhaps, have recognised my friend from his photograph. But, in truth, I had never thought of Captain X. since we had left the place where my husband's battery had formerly been encamped.

"It is more than five years since these events occurred, and I do not recollect which side won the match, whether it was my friend's or not, but I very well remember what I have here stated.

"When my husband returned that evening I asked him if he had heard any news of the tournament.

"'No,' he replied; 'we shall not be able to hear before to-morrow.'

"'Well, but I can give you some. Ruth tells me that Captain X., of the 17th Lancers, has been bitten on the leg; Z. is all right, but she believes that his friends are beaten.'

"'We shall see to-morrow morning if Ruth is right again,' said my husband, laughing. He related at the officers' mess what he called my 'telegram through the glass of water,' and I believe they had a good laugh over my credulity. Nevertheless, the message received on the following day confirmed Ruth's story in all points.

"Some time afterwards we received a visit from a friend of my husband, the chief magistrate of the district of Assigurgh. My husband told him of the strange power which Ruth possessed; it then occurred to him to ask my permission to see if she could recover some valuables which he had lost.

"'I ought to tell you first of all,' he said, 'that I am absolutely sceptical and it will require very strong proofs to convince me.'

"I felt humiliated, because if this young woman was a humbug, I was her dupe, or something worse. I sent for Ruth, who was quite as indignant as I was, and refused point-blank to do what was expected of her. I insisted, trying to make her understand that it would redound to the credit of both of us, so at last she consented, though with rather bad grace.

"After the preliminaries, I transmitted the questions from the major to her:

"'Go to Assigurgh and describe my bedroom.'

"Ruth described the room very correctly, as the magistrate was willing to admit.

"'Now tell me what I have lost.'

"'I see a casket, not very large. It is of zinc, and contains money and a roll of paper.'

"'You are right! cried the major astonished. 'Now tell me where this casket is at present.'

"'It is in a small room. Must I open it?'

"'Yes, and tell me what is inside.'

"She stopped for a moment.

"'There are only some papers, Sahib; the money is gone.'

"'Describe to me the man who has taken the money.'

"'He is not there; the room is empty.'

"'Look for him.'

"'He is in Sahib's room. He is a short, dark man, with a pleasing face, dressed in white, with a scarlet and gold turban. He has a scar on his left hand.'

"'Thunder! It is my butler; just the man I suspected,' cried the major.

"Some days after Major X. had returned to Assigurgh he wrote to me that he had found the casket in the house, or rather in his servant's room, but the papers were no longer there; the box was empty.

"I concluded that Ruth had seen the casket before the papers had been taken out. I have often noticed that she had no particular conception of time in regard to the events, although she very well described the facts of the moment.

"Another time I lost a piece of pink satin embroidered with gold, and it could not be found anywhere. I did not suspect any of my servants, believing them to be devoted, and all, with one exception, had been for a long time in my employ. I did not believe this man to be guilty, because I was convinced that he never went into my room. However, Ruth declared that he was the thief, and he gave me back the missing article; but on learning how I had made the discovery he spread abroad the rumour that I was a sorceress."

The following account was published in the *Annals of Psychical Science* for May 1905, over the signature of Dr. Edmond Waller.

"Two summers ago my father ordered from London an object known under the name of a Crystal-gazing Ball. He and his family left Paris on a visit to our country-seat before the object arrived.

"A few days afterwards, on a Saturday, I received the package from London, and took it the same evening to my parents in the country. Immediately after dinner all of us—father, mother, sister, friends, and even domestics—tried to see what the glass ball could show us; the only result was tired eyes, we could see nothing. On the evening of the following day one of the servants, a faithful old woman who had been in our service for years, as soon as she looked into the crystal (we had resumed our experiments of the preceding night) turned very pale; we asked her what she saw. 'A coffin!' she replied. A few weeks afterwards her brother, a young fellow of twenty-three years of age, died of typhoid fever. For several evenings in succession we tried the crystal, but with the exception of the above incident we saw absolutely nothing; finally the crystal was put away in a corner and neglected by every one.

"A few months later, I went one day to see my parents in Paris. I felt suddenly a strong desire to try again with the crystal, and I asked my mother to allow me to take it away with me. The next evening for forty-five minutes I conscientiously tried, but could see absolutely nothing. I worked—if I may use that word—with the crystal for nearly three weeks, without any better success. I lost my enthusiasm, or rather I became tired of my repeated failures, and I put the object, which had given me so little satisfaction, in the bottom of a drawer, with the fixed determination never again to tire my eyes and waste my time with such an uninteresting article.

"However, one afternoon a few months later a curious morbid sensation seized me. I went home much earlier than usual in hopes that a good night's rest might restore me to my normal state of mind. I went to bed, but it was impossible to sleep; and, moreover, I could not help thinking of the crystal. After several hours of insomnia I got up, and somewhat hesitatingly I opened the drawer in which the crystal lay. I took it out and put it on the table in the dining-room; I sat down in front of it, and scarcely had I put my hands on the table and raised my eyes, when I saw one of my friends in the crystal. Only her bust appeared; the likeness was striking, and yet on the face there was something which I saw in that crystal which I had never seen on my friend's face. It was not so much the features which were different, it was something more profound; I will not enlarge on this point, but will leave the reader to draw his own deductions. This experience left me sad and happy at the same time; happy, because I had at last seen something in the crystal; sad, because of that curious expression on my friend's face.

"For the sake of the relation it bears to this history, I ought to say that the young woman who happens to be its heroine had been for me, but a few years previously, a young girl for whom I had felt more than simple admiration. She was one who commanded universal respect by reason of the atmosphere which surrounded her. She was for me what a woman ought to be in the finest sense of the word. I used to see her and her mother frequently. We were suddenly separated, to my great grief. We corresponded with one another for a few months; but little by little—I ought to confess it was my own fault—our correspondence became rarer, and finally ceased altogether.

"Two years had gone by when one day I heard of the marriage of my friend; she was now Mrs. D. She and her husband came to Paris on their honeymoon. Mrs. D. brought her husband to see me; he was one of those men whom one often sees among English officers, a fine athlete—a big, impulsive, generous-hearted man. From the very first moment a great—a very great—friendship sprang up between that man and myself. I often saw the young couple together, but I saw D. more often still.

"Unfortunately, my friend was obliged to leave with his regiment, which was ordered to the Transvaal. As one of his wife's oldest friends, and possessing the greatest confidence in me, D. asked me if, during his absence, I would watch over his wife—the being he loved more than all else on earth. This was an indescribable joy to me— first of all, to be able to protect this young woman against the insolences of life in a great city, a life for which she was unfit, for she was morally too beautiful to be able to see the hideousness of the masses surrounding her; secondly, it was a proof of the confidence her husband had in me. Most unfortunately I was unable to fulfil my promise of protection, for soon after her husband's departure Mrs. D. was obliged to accompany her mother to America. I wrote to her three times, but received no answer to my letters. It was the crystal which served to bring us into touch with one another again. And now, having given these few, I think, necessary details concerning my two friends, I will return to the evening following the one when I saw my friend's face in the crystal.

"I felt extremely fatigued that day, and again went home very early. Notwithstanding my fatigue, I took up the crystal and gazed into it for a quarter of an hour, but without the smallest result. My eyes were positively in a state of congestion, when at last I threw myself on my bed and quickly dropped off to sleep. In a few hours I awoke, surprised to find myself in that position. I got up, sat down in front of the crystal, and instantly I saw the silhouette of my friend side by side with that of a man; the latter was less distinct than my friend, they were both surrounded by trees and people. I closed my eyes for a second, opened them and looked again into the crystal; this time I distinctly saw Mrs. D. and the man who was with her—a man whom I had never seen before—as well as the paddock of the race-course at Longchamps, with all the customary surroundings of this race-course during a meeting.

" Although at that time I often went to races, my many social duties made it extremely difficult for me to be present at the race-meeting to take place on the Sunday following the evening in question, and, most certainly, if it had not been for the crystal I should never have postponed several important engagements in order to go to the races that Sunday. I was unable to be present at the first two races ; but one of my uncles had a horse running in the third, and for various reasons I was rather interested in this trial.

" I arrived at the gate of the weighing yard just as the bell rang announcing the start. I rushed to the winning-post, thinking little of the crystal which was the cause of my presence at the course, and still less of the visions I had seen in it.

" As I came up to the stand, a little to the left of the president's box, how great was my stupefaction to see (1) Mrs. D. and (2) to recognise beside her, for the second time in my life, and for the first time in flesh and blood, the man of my crystal ! I saw absolutely nothing of the race. After my first movement of astonishment, in spite of all the *covenances*, I drew near to Mrs. D. and the individual accompanying her ; but I had been seen, and they both avoided me in so marked a manner that I dared not insist.

" I took a chair and sat down. I felt suddenly cold all

over—I saw nothing, heard nothing; it was only several minutes later that one of my friends, with a formidable slap on the shoulder, succeeded in arousing me out of the state of lethargy into which I had fallen. Believing I was ill, and telling me I was positively livid, he tried to insist upon my leaving the race-course and taking me home. But a profound fascination held me to the spot, and like a hound on the track, I followed the two individuals of my crystal.

"Thoroughly upset, when the meeting was over I took a cab and drove to the hotel where Mrs. D., her husband, and her mother generally stayed when in Paris. I left a letter imploring my friend to grant me an interview as soon as possible. For a reply she sent me a short note, in which she told me I would see her soon, underlining the words, *you don't know all*.

"For seven months I did everything in my power to obtain an interview with her. Finally I was told at the hotel that Mrs. D. had gone to the south of France.

"Meanwhile I had continued my experiments with the crystal, though more or less intermittently. Several times I saw in it Mrs. D., her husband, the individual whom I had seen with her at Longchamps, war-scenes in the Transvaal, but there was nothing very precise in my visions.

"Seven days later I heard of Mrs. D.'s departure to the Riviera; I saw the following vision in the crystal: Mrs. D. accompanied by a man—not the one of whom I have been speaking, but a totally different individual. I saw them take a cab, and the following scene unrolled itself in the clearest fashion before my eyes, just as though I were sitting in an orchestral stall at a theatre.

"The streets were dirty; the cab was an ordinary one, and went in the direction of, and stopped in front of, a well-known restaurant close to the Opera. The two occupants got out of the cab, entered the restaurant, walked down a long corridor, went upstairs, turned to the left, and were shown into a private room by a head waiter. I saw everything, furniture and other utensils, very clearly.

"The man who accompanied Mrs. D. left her alone in the room, and followed the waiter; then it was that I had a sensation of speaking with Mrs. D., as though I were really present with her. Simultaneously with this sensation the scene disappeared, and there was nothing before me save the crystal ball.

"Two days afterwards I had a great surprise. Whilst I was attending to a patient the domestic came into the room and handed me a card. It was D., who I thought was still in the Transvaal. He was in a hurry, and could not wait to see me; he fixed a rendezvous for afternoon-tea in a shop in the Rue Caumartin.

"It was with a certain emotion that I went to the spot agreed upon. My friend was alone. While shaking hands he told me he had been wounded and sent home. He said he had refrained from telegraphing in order to give us a surprise, and he thanked me at the same time for the proof of friendship I had given him in taking such a brotherly interest in his wife. A more disagreeable sensation than mine at that moment it would be impossible to imagine, with my friend's big, honest eyes fixed upon me, feeling myself grow paler beneath his regard, and unable to utter a word! What would he imagine? The situation was not rendered any pleasanter by Mrs. D.'s sudden appearance on the scene. She came hurriedly towards us, shook me warmly by the hand, and made me understand by her looks that she wanted me to tell little, and that little falsehood.

"At that moment a double reasoning rose within me: Ought I to consider the day at Longchamps as black as I had painted it? And as for the scene in the private room, could not a crystal have lied? and was it not only my pessimistic nature which had made me see evil where none existed? If such were the case, my strict duty was to think no longer of my past fancies and suspicions, and especially to refrain from speaking of them to D. On the other hand, I could not understand Mrs. D.'s conduct, and without knowing why, I could not help believing what the crystal had suggested to me; it was with the greatest difficulty that I was able to pass the following half-hour with D. and his wife without making any allusion to the crystal.

"Our conversation was, in fact, very confused and disjointed; there was something disagreeable in the air, so to speak.

"I arranged to meet D. again the next day and to dine with him and his wife; but when the moment came, I felt in such an ill humour that, fearing my gloomy countenance might mar the evening, I begged my friends to excuse me. I went home early in a state of excessive and unaccountable excitement. Instead of dining I took my crystal, sat down in front of it and gazed into it. For several minutes I saw nothing, then all at once and very clearly I saw Mrs. D. with the same individual who, in the previous vision, had accompanied her to the restaurant. For the second time the crystal made me a spectator of the scene in the private room, with this difference: I remained until Mrs. D. and her restaurant friend left the building; I saw the man lead the woman to a private carriage, and without hearing a word, unable to explain how the phenomenon was produced, I understood that he fixed a rendezvous with Mrs. D. at a spot which was unknown to me, and that he would return on Wednesday at the same hour and at the same restaurant. I understood that the order had been given for the same room to be kept for them. Everything was so clear, that I had not the slightest doubt but that I was gazing at a reality—for several minutes I was thoroughly convinced of it.

"At four o'clock on the following afternoon D. came to see me. Almost at once the conversation turned upon delicate ground—his wife. Was it the expression of my face, my manner of acting, which made him suspicious? I cannot say, but, suddenly and abruptly, my friend demanded a concise and precise account of my state of mind concerning himself and his wife. Without stopping to think, and convinced somehow that I had to tell him of my feeling, I explained all to him.

N

" Bitter words followed, and it was only out of respect for the spot we were at that we refrained from committing violent acts—acts which we should certainly have regretted. I loved the man more than ever, I was jealous of his stubbornness and, for his own sake, I now determined not to permit him to live any longer in his fool's paradise.

" As for his wife, I could not help feeling a great pity for her, and doing all in my power to prevent her from falling any lower. I implored my friend to watch very closely the people with whom she came in contact. After a few more or less flattering epithets—which might be summed up very simply in his looking upon me as a fool—D. made me promise to go to the theatre with him and afterwards to sup in the very same private room where, according to the crystal, his wife was to be.

"I accepted without any hesitation, convinced that my friend was right, that all would be for the best, and that henceforth my little glass ball would but serve as a letter-weight and nothing more. I had not felt so happy for a long time.

" We were punctual at our rendezvous; we passed a most agreeable evening, criticising rather the crystal and my mild folly than the spectacle at which we were present. We went straight from the theatre to the restaurant, where the crystal was going to be definitely, once and for all, condemned as a liar of liars.

" We arrived at the restaurant at twenty minutes past twelve. The room which my friend had reserved resembled very little the room I had seen in the crystal. We were overflowing with good humour and light-heartedness; we sat down to supper and cast far out of our minds every thought of the crystal and its manifestations. We spoke of things which had nothing whatever in common with the cause of our tête-à-tête in that private room.

" Half-an-hour passed by, when all at once, without any reason, what seemed like a hallucination to my friend and myself seized hold of me; my gaiety disappeared, and I could scarcely articulate a single word. A few minutes passed in this way, when suddenly my friend and I recognised the voice of Mrs. D. I knew not what to think, much less what to say. D. rushed out of the room like a madman.

" I followed him as quickly as I could, but not quickly enough to prevent a catastrophe. D. sprang upon the individual who had been so faithfully reproduced by the crystal, and only released his hold of him at the door of the restaurant. The man was in a sorry state; he disappeared immediately—probably to avoid any further scandal.

" Almost without saying a word to each other, D. and I separated. He went to his hotel; and I, acting on his wish, looked after his wife.

" The consequence of this drama was the separation of the husband and wife, and for me the loss of the man for whom I had such a deep friendship. Quite recently and indirectly I learned that Mrs. D. was confined in an asylum."

CHAPTER XV

TYPTOLOGY

Nature and Description of the Phenomenon

WE shall now study the experiments known under the name of Typtology, experiments which sometimes give rise to exceedingly interesting phenomena. Experiments in typtology are carried out in the following manner:

Several persons seat themselves around a table, which is generally a small three-legged loo-table. They place their hands lightly on the edge and wait to see what happens.

If it is desired to obtain any interesting result, the experimenters ought to regard the matter seriously, abstaining from talking, laughing, or joking.

Each sitter should avoid pressing his hands too heavily on the table, so as to make it tip over in front of him; the hands ought to rest lightly on the table, not seeking to impart to it any voluntary movement, but, at the same time, not opposing any oscillations, however slight, which may be felt, and to follow it as passively as possible in all its movements.

What then happens? Generally, after a period of waiting, long or short, the table is felt to shake slightly under the fingers; it inclines slowly towards one side, whilst the opposite foot is raised. This movement is more or less marked, then the table reverts to its normal upright position on all three feet.

Usually, after this first movement, a second, then a third of the same character are quickly produced; finally, similar movements succeed each other more or less regularly, consisting in the raising of one of the feet of the table, which then falls back on to the floor, causing a slight sound, and now commences the experiment in typtology, properly so called.

One of the experimenters asks questions, and it is agreed that the movements of the table shall be taken as replies, according to the number of raps given by the foot that is raised. One rap signifies "yes"; two raps "no"; for other words the letters of the alphabet are indicated by the number of raps given: one rap for *a*, two raps for *b*, three raps for *c*, &c.

Each word being spelled in this manner, we proceed by questions and answers, and a conversation may be carried on.

What happens in reality ? The movements of the table are most frequently determined by the unconscious movements of the whole of the experimenters; very often, it must be confessed, the replies are quite commonplace and correspond to what the experimenters know.

In these cases it has been found, for example, that if a certain reply to a question is anticipated, it will always be given accordingly. If, when the first letter of a word or a name is rapped, a person calls out a word commencing with this letter, this word, to the exclusion of every other, is spelled out. In the second place, the replies are always given in accordance with the ideas of the people around the table; they are the reflections of their thoughts, their inclinations, and their preferences.

But there is also another form, which is of far greater interest. Among the persons at the table there may be a sensitive who, unconsciously, directs all the movements of the table; the others then only follow the movement due to the impulse thus given.

This sensitive may then give replies which only exist in his sub-conscious mind, and of which, in consequence, his normal consciousness is absolutely ignorant. In this case, the phenomena become much more interesting; because we know how much more extended the sub-consciousness is than the normal consciousness, how much knowledge it possesses which astonishes us, what a multiplicity of facts it contains. Very often some of the more surprising phenomena are due to the revelation of sub-conscious knowledge, the origin of which we search for in vain unless some fortuitous circumstance puts us on the track and shows us how it may have penetrated into the subject's mind.

But more than this, the subject may possess peculiar abnormal faculties, and, without anticipating here what may be the nature of these special faculties, the subject then becomes what is called a " medium."

One of the special faculties which the subject may possess is that of lucidity. We have studied this in a previous chapter, and we have seen that typtology is the usual method, the favourite means by which the faculty of lucidity is manifested ; but, by others, this lucidity is manifested indifferently by all methods, of which typto-logy is only one. That is why, in many cases, we find typtology mingled with automatic writing, hallucinatory vision, &c., and these different processes succeed and complete each other, so as to give rise to a more definite communication, which is the complete manifestation of the subject's faculty of lucidity.

We may here note that the majority of experiments in typtology emanate from circles which attribute to them a spirit origin. In the authentic accounts which we shall here quote we shall keep to the exact expressions used by their authors, while only assigning to them a documentary value.

Among the facts related in typtological communica-tions, which cannot be attributed to the sub-consciousness of the subject, the following very curious one is quoted by Professor Max Seiling in *Psychische Studien* for Decem-ber 1907.

It is a remarkable story of an elderly lady, who was induced in a most singular manner to interest herself in another person. In a spiritistic séance with a friend (in December 1906) a deceased relative manifested and stated that Richard Wagner (for whom this lady had a great admiration) desired that she should interest herself in a young tenor named E. (the full name being given). To all the questions addressed to the spirit on this subject only one reply was given, that the singer was at Erfurt, and that he had been discovered in a chimney. This lady, who lived a long way from Erfurt, and knew neither the town nor any one there, procured first of all the address of a musical society there and inquired if a singer of this name was known; she was told that the person in question was tenor at the opera-house of the town. Armed with this knowledge, the lady resolved to write to the singer and ask him to visit her. He only accepted the invitation after the third letter, because he did not know how to reconcile the pressing invitation with the reticence shown in the letters. When, in telling the story of his career, he stated that he had been a chimney repairer and that his voice was discovered when he was singing a song during his work, the two ladies looked at him with surprise; the enigma of the chimney was solved in the most simple manner. It was clear that the protection of the old lady would be very useful to him in regard to his future, and, as he had a Wagnerian voice, the communication supposed to emanate from Wagner had a basis of reality.

The following is a case which we reproduce from *Light*. We know that séances of the character described were frequently held at General X.'s house, and we therefore believe the following account to be correct. The General's wife writes:—

"During the year 1895 my husband, General X., was in garrison at T. We decided, by way of amusement, to attempt some séances, with the assistance of several officers and two ladies.

"We hardly knew how to set to work, although, by a strange concourse of circumstances, we all knew something of magnetism. Three of the gentlemen, under my influence, served as mediums. Captain J., an artillery officer, obtained the most marvellous physical manifestations. We all soon became serious investigators, and during nineteen séances we were fortunate in witnessing important spiritistic phenomena.

"In October 1885 General X., at his own request, was appointed to A. For several days we were in great confusion, owing to the packing and removal. My husband, all his things being in disorder, thought that a wardrobe, which would be the last thing to be removed, would be a safe and convenient place in which to leave an old green portfolio, which contained some shares representing a large sum, as well as 6000 francs in bank-notes, which he had set aside for the expenses of the journey. Unfortunately, having a key of my wardrobe, he completely forgot to tell me that he had placed the portfolio there, and thought that in hiding it behind a pile of skirts he had taken sufficient precautions. Two or three days afterwards, wishing to settle some accounts, he looked in the wardrobe, and found neither the portfolio nor its contents. He was very much upset by this discovery, and sent for a police officer. We searched all over the house, and all its inhabitants became upset and very unhappy. Nothing was found, and as the search was fruitless, General X. proposed to hold a séance on the subject. As our house was denuded of furniture, we asked Major H. and his wife (who were to follow us to A. later on) to let us hold it in their rooms. Both were members of our circle; unfortunately, three other investigators were absent, and so it was only a very small company that met that evening in Mrs. H.'s drawing-room. The members present were General X. and myself, Major and Mrs. H., Captain T. (medium), Lieutenant George L., and a second, and very important, medium, my former lady's-maid, Augustine.

"The story of this medium is as follows:

"She had been in my service for four years. By chance, I discovered her marvellous magnetic and mediumistic power; but my doctor advised me to send her away, because her presence took away all my strength. Having heard of the loss we had sustained, and knowing that three members of the circle were absent, she modestly offered to join us, and we had much pleasure in accepting. The séance commenced about half-past eight. We were all seated around a large circular table, and, the lights being extinguished, we joined hands in silence. After a few minutes the table began to tremble and to move as though there had been an earthquake. It then rocked violently from side to side, and began to rap on the floor.

"My husband asked: 'Who is there?' and the reply was: 'Mrs. X.'s guide.'

"'Will you help us?'

"'Yes. What do you want?'

"'We wish to know if we can find our portfolio?'

"'It is not lost.'

"'What has become of it?'

"'Taken, stolen.'

"'By whom?'

"'Three thieves; lady's-maid, coachman, and seamstress.'

"'How did they do it?'

"'The day before yesterday, Mrs. X. asked her maid to put some handkerchiefs in her wardrobe; Mrs. X. was dressing, but the door of the wardrobe hid the maid from view. She found it, slipped it under her apron, and hastened to the linen room, where the seamstress was mending the linen. They came to an understanding. When she went home in the evening, the seamstress took the portfolio with her and entrusted it to her lover.'

"'How did the coachman become mixed up in it?'

"'Your maid is a widow with four children, and though ten years older than Louis, she is greatly in love with him. They are engaged. She thought that money would compensate for her years, and that the theft would bind him to her, so that she told him all and made him her accomplice. Tell them that you know all: turn them out of doors.'

"'Good! But how shall we get back the money?'

"'This evening! This evening! Louis, the coachman, who is a soldier, remembers what the police officer said aloud: Where a civilian would get off with five years' penal servitude, a poor soldier gets ten. The thieves are now at daggers drawn.'

" Here Captain T. jumped up and cried out:

" ' Stop ! Stop ! I see them.'

" We all asked : ' Where ? Who ? '

" The table rapped out : ' Let him speak.'

" The captain continued with emotion :

" ' I see Mrs. X.'s bedroom. It is brilliantly lighted. There are three people there : two women and a man. They are looking all about the room. They are quarrelling. They are very angry. Oh ! They have it with them. The man is frightened. What are they doing? They are turning the sheets and counterpanes upside down. Then they put them back again in their places. Now they go to the windows close to the wardrobe.'

" Augustine called out excitedly :

" ' I see that. I see Mrs. X.'s bedroom. Oh, but you are mistaken, sir. There are four people in the room, two men and two women. Go out ! Go out ! What are you doing in Mrs. X.'s bedroom? Oh look ! They have brought one of those Austrian black cane chairs from the General's dressing-room. They are dragging it up to the wardrobe. What are they going to put on the top of the wardrobe ? Take away that chair.'

" The table replied :

" ' They want to put it in a place where you can find it. They know that you are our friends. They know that you are consulting us. No doubt they know all about your séances.'

" Captain T., in a bewildered manner, said :

" ' Let me get hold of the villains. I will strike them.'

" Here the valiant captain seized a stick lying near to him, and, leaning on the table, brandished it in the air in a savage manner, the other members of the group surreptitiously lighting some matches, looked on in silence.

" Captain : ' They are leaving the room.'

" Augustine : ' Oh ! They are going out one after the other, in single file, through the little door which leads into the General's dressing-room. All is dark. We cannot see anything more.'

.

"Table: 'Don't be afraid. It is on the top shelf of the cupboard.'

"General: 'What cupboard?'

"Table: 'Go to the house.'

"All: 'Yes. Let us all go with you. Let us start.'

"Table: 'No! The General and Mrs. X. only; no one else. You can all go to-morrow morning as early as you like. Let General and Mrs. X. start quickly. The maid will meet them and ask for news. Tell her all is right, but we shall know nothing before to-morrow. Then lock your doors and search for the portfolio.'

"'Where?'

"'It is on the top shelf of the cupboard. Good night! Good night!'

"Then the table was raised almost up to the ceiling, slowly descended, inclined before each member separately, and then became again a common, simple, solid and senseless piece of furniture.

"We insisted, but it was impossible to obtain a single word more. We returned home in a very nervous and restless condition. As soon as we were alone, with the doors locked and bolted, we examined the bed. Yes, it seemed somewhat disordered and as if some strange fingers had touched it, but beside the wardrobe, instead of one of the pretty white Venetian chairs, which formed part of the furniture of my room, there stood there, forgotten, the identical Austrian black cane chair, which the two mediums had seen at the séance. I jumped upon it. There was nothing on the top of the wardrobe; nothing inside it; nothing in or on the bed. Somewhat frightened, we went out, one after the other, through the little door which led into my husband's dressing-room, and there a chair was missing. In the dressing-room was a large cupboard let into the wall, according to the custom of the eighteenth century, in which my husband kept his hats, gloves, ties, and handkerchiefs. The police had searched it from top to bottom, and on going out some hours before, the General had taken from it his gloves and a handkerchief.

"I sprang at this cupboard, opened wide the massive

door, and there, on the top shelf, resting on some ties, was the object of our search.

"We opened it. Nothing had been taken: nothing at at all, not even the six thousand francs, the identity of which could never have been established, because they were bank-notes, and it goes without saying that we did not know the numbers of these notes.

"I have purposely abridged the account of this memorable séance, the two examples of clairvoyance being naturally the most interesting fact.

"MRS. (GENERAL) X."

It will be noticed in this case that the phenomenon of lucidity with hallucinatory vision is mixed up with the phenomenon of typtology—this is frequently the case: direct lucidity and automatic writing often supplement the typtological communications, a fact which shows that we have a warrant for ranging these different cases in the general category of phenomena of lucidity.

CHAPTER XVI

TYPTOLOGY (*continued*)

EXPERIMENTS

I GIVE several cases, the authenticity of which is guaranteed by Dr. Vidal, who has also given me particulars of other experiments of the same kind which he has himself witnessed. I have restricted myself to the following, which are the most important and sufficiently demonstrative.

Table—Case of M. Rouillon

I resume here the unique experiments, in the course of which we witnessed facts which, however unlikely and, at present, hardly explicable, are none the less perfectly true. One evening, in September 1893, when at a "table-turning" séance, the idea came to me to ask the table to give by the method of raps denoting the letters of the alphabet, the name of the saint corresponding to a given day. The name was unknown to every one present, and there was no calendar at hand. The table rapped out, "Monica." On proceeding to verify, this was found to be correct. Another experiment of the same kind was successful at this séance; after that and on the following days, we obtained nothing. Nevertheless, I had been struck by the replies rapped out on the table, and I often thought of them.

Towards the end of October 1893, I discussed this question with M. Vidal, principal of the college at Limoges. He was incredulous, and replied, "Until I have seen I will not believe." It was agreed that we should arrange to hold a séance, which took place at the College, in the room of M. Loze, bursar. The good faith of the persons present is beyond doubt, and, moreover, I have obtained numerous similar results at home with my two children, Alice and Hélène, aged ten and thirteen years.

Here is the report of our experiments, according to full notes taken at the time.

Séance held October 28, 1893

M. Vidal, his sons Étienne and Marcel, MM. Loze and Rouillon, were seated round the table. They "formed a chain" with their hands placed on the edge of the table.

After about thirty-five minutes movements began to occur. I asked the name given on the calendar for June 12th. We were all of us ignorant of this (as was always the case at our séances). The calendar was on a table-desk, three feet from us, resting against the only lamp which lighted the room, and thus acted as a screen for us; this calendar showed six months on each side: at the time of the question the side showing the first six months was turned towards the lamp, and none of us could see it. The reply came, "Trinity." We looked and found this to be correct.

I withdrew from the circle. The four remaining sitters each placed one hand on the table, and did not form a chain.

Question. What is the name for January 2nd ?

Answer. Basil (correct).

Q. What is the name for September 2nd ?

A. Firmin.

"I looked at the calendar, which was placed so that the month of September was in the dark. The answer was inaccurate. M. Loze remarked that Firmin is in the month of September, that it is written in large letters, and that there is a "2" in the date (25th). We replaced the calendar with the side showing the second half year towards the light.

M. Vidal asked, "What is the name on December 5th ?"

A. "Sabas."

This name was quite unknown to any of us. We were astonished, and thought it was a failure, simply a chance combination of letters. We looked at the calendar, and found Sabas at the date indicated.

At the conclusion of the séance all present signed the report establishing the reality of these facts.

Séance of October 30, 1893

Held in M. Loze's room at the College. There were seated round the table: Messrs. Étienne Vidal, Loze, Martin, tutor at the College, and Duris, tutor.

The conditions were the same as at the previous séance, no one either in the room or around the table knowing the answers to the following questions which were put by M. Vidal, who seemed to have the greatest influence over the table.

Q. What is the name on January 14th?
A. Hilary (correct).
Q. What is the name on February 21st?
A. Pepin (correct).
Q. What is the name on January 28th?
A. Charlemagne (correct).
Q. What is the name on December 27th?
A. Innocents.

There was here an error of one day. The name "Innocents" occurs on December 28th.

Q. What is the name on May 16th?
A. Cyriac.

This was an error of months. Cyriac's name occurs on March 16th.

Q. What is the name on May 26th?
A. Clet.

Another error of months. The name Clet is on April 26th.

The following is still more curious.

Abdon was told us as the name for July 30th.

This name did not occur on the calendar, either at this date or any other. But in the evening, when in the bursar's office, I saw a calendar hanging up on the wall, and found on July 30th the word "Abdon." Similar things have happened several times in the course of my experiments with my two children. To find the name denoted by the table we have sometimes had to consult a dictionary or another calendar. The name dictated through the table always agreed with the date fixed by us.

Séance held January 3, 1894

Held at my house. There were no strangers present. My daughter Alice (aged ten) and myself were alone at the table, and were the only people in the room. I shuffled, like a pack of cards, the thirty-one sheets for January 1894, which I had taken off a loose-leaf calendar, the printed side turned downwards away from our sight. Alice carried the packet to a distance. She looked straight into my eyes while putting down the packet after turning it over quickly. We were both ignorant of what was printed on the top leaf. We then placed our hands on the edge of the table (proceeding exactly in the same way on each occasion). We asked for the number on the sheet of which the printed side was uppermost, but hidden from our sight by some object, or else out of the line of vision.

Out of twenty-six answers twenty were correct.

2. I tore off the 365 days from the calendar, proceeding as stated above, all being mixed—months as well as days. The packet was again carried to a distance. We did not know the word on the sheet; no one could see it.

We asked through the table for the name of the saint on the leaf turned up. Four questions produced four accurate replies, giving the following names:—

> Agatha,
> Catherine,
> Just,
> Sosthenes.

My children and myself have often repeated similar experiments with equal success, during a period of twelve days, after which these phenomena became gradually fewer, until they ceased altogether. We have often tried new experiments since, but have not obtained anything.

My two little daughters are very healthy, gentle, and timid in character. They have never been hypnotised or magnetised, and are not at all somnambulistic.

Here are two curious experiments, of a truly fantastical character, dating from the same period.

One evening I asked my elder daughter to place the tips of her fingers of one hand only in the middle of a thick top of a solid walnut dining-table, weighing at least fifty-five pounds. The room was not lighted, but the window, the shutters not being closed, gave sufficient light to enable us to distinguish objects. I myself placed my hands on the edge of the table, but avoided exerting the slightest pressure. My child and myself were alone.

I said, " If there is here an intelligent force, will it manifest itself by raising the table three times ? " Immediately to my great astonishment the table was raised on two legs to a height of from six to eight inches, and three times fell back with a noise. The experiment was three times repeated with equal success.

I finally said, " Turn the table upside down." The table was immediately raised, inclined as though easily lifted by a strong hand, and fell heavily with its edge on the floor.

I remember that during this experiment I recommended my daughter to pay attention to the movements of the table, so that she should not get hurt. I should add that my child, even if she had the will, is very delicate and quite unable to produce movements of such violence, and I could see in the semi-darkness along her body the line of her unoccupied arm.

The following experiment was made on January 13, 1894, in M. Loze's room at the College. I quote from a letter which I sent on January 21st to Professor Richet, which contains an exact account of it.

" We made some new experiments in psychic force a week ago. I have kept in mind one prominent fact which,

O

after several days' deliberation, I have decided to communicate to you.

"There were round the table Messrs. E. Vidal, Loze, and myself. Without any preliminary question the table dictated :

 " 'Jeanne Eymery.'

 " 'Are you dead ?'

 " 'Yes.'

 " 'Where ?'

 " 'Barnabé.'

 " 'What caused your death ?'

 " 'Murdered.'

 " 'By whom ?'

 " 'My husband.'

 " 'When ?'

 " 'January 10, 1894.'

 " 'Was your husband arrested ?'

 " 'Yes.'

 " 'Where is he ?'

 " 'Périgueux Prison.'

"We regarded this as a joke, and expressed our astonishment at the rôle of the unconsciousness which is capable of forging stones out of nothing, and did not even try to verify these strange lucubrations.

"That evening at supper M. Vidal asked his son :

 " 'Well, did you get anything ?'

"M. E. Vidal laughingly replied :

 " 'Oh, nothing. We had a visit from some one named Jeanne Eymery, who was murdered by her husband,' &c.

"Mme. Vidal exclaimed :

 " 'But that was in to-day's *Petite Gironde.*'

"M. E. Vidal was astonished when he read the full account in the newspaper, and went in search of M. Loze and acquainted him with this strange discovery.

"I send you the newspaper in question.

"Your first idea will no doubt be that some one had read or learned in some way the facts so strangely reported. This was not so, and our three signatures are appended as testimony to our joint assertion."

From information which I wrote for to the Governor of Trélissac, to which Barnabé is attached, as well as that from the Secretary of Jeanne Eymery's native commune, it appears that her only Christian names were Marie and Françoise. But it was stated that her husband's name was Jean Eymery, and that a wife often called herself also by the same name as her husband. It is true that "Jeanne" is not "Jean," but we may have added the letter "E" which commences the surname to the Christian name Jean, which would give it the pronunciation of Jeanne, but with one letter short in the spelling of the word. There was thus no contradiction on any point between the communication through the table and the facts in the newspaper.

On Christmas eve, 1893, M. Loze, bursar at Limoges College, invited his friend, M. Étienne Vidal, to come into his room and have a glass of white wine. It was about ten o'clock. A large wood fire was burning in the fireplace, before which was placed the small table which held a bottle and a plate. M. Vidal had his forearm, and M. Loze his elbow, on the top of the small table. The conversation turned on quite other things than experimental psychism.

Suddenly M. Vidal felt the table rising, once, then twice, and with such force that they only just had time to clear it.

" Hold, hold," said M. Vidal; "it seems as if it wanted to speak. Wait a minute."

They placed their hands on the table and asked:

" Who is there ? "

" Demi-Siphon."

"Dead or living ? "

" Dead."

" Ah ! it is a woman. What were you ? "

" *Danseuse.*"

"Where ? "

" Moulin-Rouge."

" What caused your death ? "

" Accident."

" What accident ? "

" Rupture of the perinæum through over-straining."

" Will you give us an interesting séance ? "

Then there occurred some exceedingly curious phenomena, but of a special character which can scarcely be narrated here; and, finally, the table rapped out, " Slates."

Some time before M. Loze had produced two slates with thick wooden frames, which he had fastened together by two copper screws. These were unscrewed and the slates separated. M. Loze cleaned them with a wet sponge, and put them to dry in front of the fire in full light. Then he went to look in a drawer for a fragment of pencil, and placed it between the two slates. M. Vidal again examined them on both sides before the lamp and in the presence of M. Loze, who also examined them carefully, placed one over the other, and fastened the screws. They were placed flat on the table without contact with the hands.

The table rapped as though impatient. They asked what was wanted.

" Move the lamp away."

M. Loze carried the lamp to a recess about two paces away, from which light still came; the fire also gave a fairly bright light. They could easily have seen the time by a watch. During this time M. Loze had not lost sight of the slates which remained on the table, and were not touched by M. Vidal. He said :

" Write something, and when you have finished rap once."

The table remained still for a moment, then gave two raps, which according to the code signified " No."

" Is there something which is not right ? "

" Yes."

" What ? "

" Hands."

" You want the hands placed on the slates ? "

" Yes."

This was done, and after a moment one rap was heard.

" Is it finished ? "

" Yes."

The lamp was brought back, and the slates were unscrewed by M. Vidal, and on one of them were some very clear marks, like interlaced figures of eight.

Encouraged by this result M. Vidal, without rubbing anything out, screwed up the slates again and replaced them on the table. The lamp was removed. They asked for something more definite. The table did not move. They heard the pencil moving, and one rap was struck. By the light of the lamp M. Vidal unscrewed the slates, and on one of them saw some characters which he could not at first make out.

Interrogated, the table replied : " Reversed."

M. Vidal then recognised an " L," and M. Loze, in turn, an initial which he sometimes used when signing his name. Without looking at the slate he took a thin piece of paper and traced the initial in question ; then placing it upside down by the light of the lamp he recognised the similarity with the drawing on the slate. When the latter was taken to the looking-glass M. Loze's signature became clearly recognisable.

Without effacing anything, the slates were again screwed up, and the table was asked to write, " as every one did."

They heard the noise of the pencil and one rap came. The slates were opened by M. Loze, and on one of them was written in very clear characters : " Demi-Siphon."

The slates were again fastened by M. Loze, who asked :

" In one word, one only, applicable only to yourself, what was your mode of life ? "

They again heard the noise of the pencil, and again came the single rap.

The slates were opened, and on one of them was legibly written the word, " *Vadrouille.*" The writing was remarkably clear and firm.

Some further questions were then put to the table, which suddenly stopped and refused to move.

Neither M. Vidal nor M. Loze had ever heard of Demi-Siphon, and the name and details were absolutely unknown and were an enigma to them.

On the following day, on relating their experience to some of their colleagues, they learned that some days previously the newspaper *Le Temps* had announced the death of a Moulin-Rouge *danseuse*, who was known by the nickname of " Demi-Siphon." M. Vidal told me recently that he did not know whether the stated cause of death (rupture of the perinæum) had been found correct. But I think I remember that the information received about that time confirmed this statement also. During the whole of the evening on which this séance was held M. Vidal and M. Loze were alone in the room.

CHAPTER XVII

AUTOMATIC WRITING AND LUCIDITY

I SHALL quote in this chapter a case in which lucidity was manifested through automatic writing, a procedure analogous to typtology.

We shall also see that phenomena of externalisation of force first manifested themselves with the medium. As I have, however, already remarked, these different phenomena are often mixed, or succeed each other in the same séances.

AUTOMATIC WRITING

In 1881 I was at the Military College at Florence, where I was spending my first year; I was then fifteen years of age.

In November of that year, after the death of my eldest sister, my mother had begun to study Spiritism, but I was quite ignorant of this fact. On account of the great sorrow which this death had caused the family, I was taken away from the College. One day, having gone to my mother to ask her permission to drive the horses to Cascines—I was then much taken up with horses—she asked me to stay with her for a moment, and to place my hands on a small table in front of her.

I have since learned that my mother, who was not at all mediumistic, often tried about this period, when she was alone, but could obtain no response.

On seeing me, the idea came to her to try with me, without informing me what she was doing. I sat down, astonished and annoyed at her request, placed my hands on the table, and then asked her why she made me do such a thing.

My mother replied:

"It is a physical experiment I am trying. Wait a little."

At the end of a very few moments I heard some very strange noises which came from the interior of the table—very distinct creakings and noises. I was almost frightened, and I saw that my mother was greatly moved. She said to me: "Keep still, I will explain to you presently what this is," and, to keep up my patience, she tried to make me believe that the heat of my hands caused the table to creak. The table rose and moved about and we followed it up to a bureau, in the centre of which was a piece of green cloth. The table touched the bureau, and my mother said out loud, to my great astonishment, as though not speaking to me: "Can you rap three times in the centre of the bureau under the green cloth?" She had not finished the sentence before three knocks sounded just under the square of cloth.

My surprise was so great that my mother gave me the explanation of the phenomenon, which I simply accepted as everything is accepted at that age. Just at this moment a gentleman, one of our friends, entered, and the phenomenon was immediately repeated before him; it was again repeated when my father came in.

I tried this class of mediumship for several weeks; afterwards automatic writing developed in me, and we gave up the table and all those physical experiments which may be of great interest to scientists, but not to those who seek in these phenomena the proof of the survival of the soul. My mother wished to have proof of the survival of her daughter, and we thought we had got it. I have written automatically things which my sister when ill had said to my mother, at the country house where her illness came on, while I was at Florence at the Military College, which I did not leave until after the death of my sister.

Other proofs came to support this, and this phenomenon had a special character, in that more than a hundred and fifty personalities of whom I had no knowledge whatever manifested, so to speak, through my handwriting, and each time they presented themselves again, it was always with the same style, the same language, of the same period, and with the same moral character. Automatically, and without knowing or understanding what I had written, I have rapidly traced with the pencil, in the Italian language of the thirteenth century, mystical visions which have been admired by our best writers; philosophical and highly moral dialogues have resulted from the numerous requests made by the spectators; many of these replies were in modern language; a large number of the remainder were in the ancient dialect, debased Latin, which was the common tongue of the thirteenth century. In these dialogues were developed by degrees Buddhistic theories and the quietism of Madame Guyon.

Neither my mother nor myself, nor any one else present, knew one word of these things or doctrines.

I have received writings relating to the town of Badi in Umbria and its neighbourhood; small villages, almost unknown, were mentioned. Names of ancient Italian families, now extinct, have been mentioned in relation to anecdotes unknown to us, but which always had an air of truth. We have often verified the accuracy of these names in the archives of Florence and Siena. These anecdotes, these names of persons, towns, and villages, never came pointlessly, but always as the result of some previous conversation in which I had taken no part. I was always like a passive instrument, unconscious, somewhat like a telephone, but never in trance.

Disagreeable occurrences sometimes happened in connection with my unconscious writing. I will relate one that was particularly unpleasant.

My father, in 1883, painted the portrait of Mrs. B. M. (I do not give the name in full, because the story in question might be distressing to her), an American lady, well known because of her position, high intelligence, and philanthropy.

When she sat for her portrait the conversation turned upon Spiritism, and she learned that I was what is called a writing medium. She asked my father to allow her to be present at a séance; this greatly embarrassed him, because he knew that my mother strongly objected to admitting any stranger to our meetings, which were no longer experiments, but a time for meditation and private consolation for herself. My mother, in fact, asked my father to decline a visit from this lady, but the latter insisted so strongly and pressingly that he was absolutely compelled to satisfy her.

My mother asked a friend, a lady who spoke English very well, to be kind enough to act as interpreter, and we met one evening at our house to try to evoke Mrs. B. M.'s husband who had been dead for several years.

Whilst sitting for her portrait Mrs. B. M. had told my father of the great sorrow her husband's death had caused her, the care she had taken in carrying out his last wishes and his smallest desires, both with regard to the education of the children and in administering his estate, and she expressed her satisfaction at having thus carried out her duty towards the memory of her husband.

That was all we knew of the family with which we were not acquainted before Mrs. B. M. came to my father's studio. In the evening previous to the séance with this lady, my mother had asked me to think (that is what we say instead of " evoke," as many others say, and it is more-over, correct, because it is almost always sufficient for me to think in order to secure the personality requested) of one of her uncles, who, she believed, could help her in this difficulty, to obtain something which would satisfy this newcomer to our séances; it was like a preparatory séance, in order to avoid a complete failure, but we could only obtain indefinite promises.

The following evening Mrs. B. M. came to my mother's drawing-room at nine o'clock precisely.

Mme. P., the interpreter, was present, as well as my father and his friend, a lawyer, M. C. I was sitting at a table, pencil in hand, and with some blank paper in front of me. After a very few minutes my pencil wrote the following words in French:—

"Il y a une inimitié, que je ne puis comprendre, entre Madame et feu son mari." ("There is an enmity, which I cannot understand, between Madame and her late husband.")

My mother, convinced as she was, like all of us, of the perfect harmony of this family, was disturbed at these words, pretended not to understand, in order to avoid repeating this phrase, and again asked if it was possible to enter into communication with Mrs. B. M.'s husband. And the pencil inexorably repeated the phrase:

"Il y a une inimitié, que je ne puis comprendre, entre Madame et feu son mari."

Mme. P. told us that Mrs. B. M. wished to know at all costs what had been written, and the phrase was translated by her into English.

None of us will ever forget the profound emotion which was experienced at seeing Mrs. B. M. stand up, and, looking very pale, cry out:

"What! still!"

It was truly a striking event.

She then explained in English in a few words to Mme. P. that there had been very serious disagreements between her and her husband, but that she believed death had effaced all resentment in him towards her, since she had on her part forgiven him, and had executed his last wishes with the utmost faithfulness.

My mother then insisted on knowing if it would not be possible to have another more favourable communication.

My pencil traces this strange sentence:

"Impossible; he is in Negroland."

We were certainly quite mystified by this rebuff, and my mother wished at any cost to interrupt, being much perturbed at having to say such a foolish thing to this lady. But M. C. insisted, wishing to possess the key to this enigma, and asked:

"Why do you say he is in Negroland?"

And the pencil wrote:

"He has a mission to try and bring about the abolition of slavery."

" Why has he such a mission ? "

" Because he is a negro."

My mother, very discouraged and losing all interest in the séance on receiving this unacceptable explanation, so offensive to this lady, took up the piece of paper quickly, thinking that she was not seen, crumpled it in her hands, and threw it on the floor.

But Mrs. B. M. had seen it, and cried out:

" Madame, you have no right to do that. What is written on it is for me."

And she demanded the piece of paper which was given to her. Then she straightened it out and Mme. P. read what was written.

She immediately rose, appearing greatly moved, wished us " Good evening " and left.

We were much astonished and grieved at the impression this lady had received. My mother kept saying :

" It is the first time we have been thus mystified, because the last sentence is an ill-timed joke, but the first was very true and moved Mrs. B. M. greatly."

The following morning my father had a sitting with this lady. He returned home for luncheon, laughing heartily, and said to my mother at the top of his voice: " He was a negro ! He was a negro ! "

We could not understand it. Then he told us that Mrs. B. M. had related her story to him at length, and said that after her marriage her family had discovered that her husband was of Indian origin—that is to say, a man of colour. It could scarcely be seen, but it was a very great mésalliance for an American. Thence the origin of this enmity which lasted for life, but which Mrs. B. M. believed had ended with death, because, she said, she had carried out all her husband's wishes.

Other writings, obtained by automatic writing, are much more interesting than those I have quoted, but unfortunately they are in Italian, and the greater part in ancient Italian of the twelfth century, and I am not able to translate them.

CHAPTER XVIII

TYPTOLOGY AND LUCIDITY

Experiments of the Société d'Études Psychiques at Nancy

WE will devote this chapter exclusively to a series of experiments which were made by the Société d'Études Psychiques at Nancy, under the direction of M. X., a member of this Society.

These experiments were conducted and verified under scientific conditions which cause them to be of great value. In order to preserve them in their integrity we leave them as the author has given them in the original document published in the Bulletin of the Société d'Études Psychiques de Nancy.

"In the group to which I belong we have indulged in the pastime of interviewing invisible beings by means of the table and writing; and we have obtained surprising results which nine times out of ten have been verified. I give attestations which will leave no doubt in the minds of those who can admit that the experimenters, whom I assert to be honourable persons, were acting in good faith.

The method we employed was very simple. We made a choice among the invisible personalities who were willing to reply to us. We left out those who appeared to us not to be serious, conscientious, or sincere. To the others we put plain questions, the replies to which could be verified.

We did with them as we should have done with living persons. We did not ask them to foretell the future, which must be almost as difficult for them as for us. We did not ask for forecasts about races, or the winning number in a lottery, or if the ministry would go out of office before the end of the year. But we asked them for details as to their past, the salient facts of their earth life, and the names of people whom they had known.

Some hesitated to give us these details: others only replied to part of our questions. But some of them gave the information asked for, and I will communicate their replies. I will then give the proof that these replies are in accord with the facts.

I will commence with the strangest of these communications. I do not wish to conceal the fact that at first it appeared very improbable. It is a real legendary tale.

There were five of us at the table: M. and Mlle. G., both engaged in tuition; Mlle. C., a perfectly serious and respectable person; the medium, very young, connected with the people of the house, and myself. I know all these persons and can guarantee their perfect good faith.

BERTOLF DE GHISTELLES

After a few moments the table moved, giving abrupt raps, following each other two by two, and the psychic force was manifested. I asked the name of the invisible being that was causing the table to move, using the alphabet as usual. It replied that its name was Bertolf. This unusual name interested us, and the following is the dialogue which ensued.

Question. Bertolf must be a Christian name. Have you any other name?

Answer. Bertolf de Ghistelles.

Q. Were you French?

A. Flemish.

Q. Will you tell us the name of the locality where you lived?

A. Dunkerque.

Q. Have you been a long time in the Beyond?

A. Yes.

Q. In what year did you die?

A. In 1081.

Q. What were you?

A. Husband of a Saint.

Q. Do you mean that your wife is honoured as a saint, that she has been canonised?

A. Yes.

Q. What was her name?

A. Godeleine de Wierfroy.   Can she forgive me?

Q. You did her harm?

A. Yes.

Q. You killed her perhaps?

A. I had her strangled.

Q. Why?

A. Through jealousy, impelled by my unworthy mother.

Q. Have you seen her again?

A. Lady Mary has hidden her under her mantle.

Q. Have you found any members of her family?

A. Heinfried and his wife Ogine, her father and mother.   They have forgiven me.

Q. Is the festival of your wife celebrated anywhere?

A. Yes.

Q. On what date?

A. July 6th.   Her sweet name signifies Friend of God.

(Some one present remarked that "God" in Flemish must signify *Dieu,* and asked if *leine* meant "friend.")

The table replied, "Lief, friend."

Q. What do you mean?

A. In Flemish, Godluf.

Q. Did you die in a tragic manner?

A. No, in a monastery.   I remained there nine years.

Q. To do penance?

A. Yes, the Holy Father told me to repent.

Q. Who was Pope?

A. Urban.

Q. Who reigned in France in your lifetime?

A. Robert, Henri, Philippe.

Q. Did you have for suzerain a Count of Flanders?

A. Yes.

Q. What was he called?

A. Guiscard.

Q. Are you happy ?

A. (Feebly) Yes.

Q. Have you suffered ?

A. For long centuries.

Q. What is the name of the monastery where you lived ?

A. Vinoca.

Q. Was your wife born in France ?

A. No.

Q. In what Province ?

A. Le Boulonnais.

None of us had even heard of Bertolf or Godeleine. We consulted the calendars, but could not find any saint of this name.

Eventually the idea occurred to me to consult the encyclopædia *Larousse,* not in the hope of finding the name of Bertolf, but in order to assure myself that the sovereigns he had mentioned had really reigned at the times stated, and I was just coming to the name of Guiscard when I stumbled across the following article:—

"Godelive, Godelieve, or Godeleine of Ghistelles (saint), born near Boulogne in 1040, died at Ghistelles in 1070. She married Berthold, Lord of Ghistelles, near Bruges, who, after having subjected her to odious treatment, had her strangled and thrown down a well.

"Berthold became a monk—impressed, it is said, by the miraculous cures effected by the water from this well, around which a Benedictine abbey was built which was afterwards transferred to Bruges.

"Godelive is specially honoured at Bruges on July 6th."

I will not conceal the objection that may be made. It will be said: "One of the persons present had read this story somewhere and remembered it when putting his hands on the table. Then, by unconscious pressure, he directed the movements of the table and replied to your questions without knowing."

My reply would be: "For that it would be necessary for the person to be in a state of somnambulism, which was not the case with any of us. But I prefer to leave this objection on one side for a moment and pass on to another case. The refutation will come better presently in conjunction with other cases. Here is another instance.

GARCIA MORENO

The circle was almost the same as for the previous communication. The spirit said his name was Garcia Moreno, and he was born at Guyaquil (South America).

Question. What was your profession?

Answer. President.

Q. President of what?

A. The Republic of Ecuador.

Q. At what age did you die?

A. 53 years, Friday, August 6, 1875.   Dio ni muere!

Q. Why those words?

A. I spoke them as I fell.   I died a Christian.

Q. Will you be kind enough to translate them, because we do not know Spanish?

A. They mean "God does not die."

Q. Of what illness did you die?

A. (by violent raps) Assassinated by Rayo and his accomplices in front of the Government palace at Quito.

Q. What weapon was used?

A. The machete.

Q. What is the machete?

A. A Mexican knife.

Q. Are you happy?

A. I have caused the death of some men.

Q. For what reason?

A. To repress a conspiracy.

Q. Do you regret it?

A. Yes.

Q. Who was the instigator of the conspiracy you repressed?

A. General Maldanato.

Q. Were you alone when you were assassinated by Rayo?

A. Yes.

P

Q. Is there anything you can tell us which will prove to us that you were Garcia Moreno ?

A. If you wish I will narrate a combat to you.

Q. Willingly. Only it will perhaps take 'a long time by means of the table. Will you write this narrative ?

A. Yes.

Q. In Spanish ?

A. No.

Q. You know French sufficiently ?

A. I have stayed in Paris.

(We handed a pencil to the medium and by mechanical writing we obtained the following account.)

"This naval combat, of which I was the hero, is one of the most pleasant recollections of my existence. After a treaty had been signed advantageous to my country, I was attacked on returning from a political expedition with a few companions. The vessel having been sunk, we took possession of an English vessel. On the refusal of the captain we proposed to shoot him, and make a winding sheet of his flag, but he . . . quickly gave in and with . . . cannon I sunk the ironclad *Guya.* I took possession of Bernadino and of the schooner. I was the victor."

The words replaced by dots are indecipherable in the text, but, in general, the writing is clear, firm, and energetic.

We were curious enough to inquire from another spirit concerning this Moreno, who had manifested for the first time in our séances, and we spoke to one who frequently came to us. This spirit replied as follows, still by means of the pencil, but in an entirely different handwriting.

"I know this person, who is undoubtedly very intellectual. Thanks to him his country valiantly maintained a coalition which was terminated by an honourable treaty. He is very learned, and is endowed with indomitable energy—in short, he is no ordinary man ; one can admire and extol his high qualities. But, unhappily, these are accompanied by an extreme passion for domination, which degenerates into cruelty. He has been charged with several political crimes.

"Further, he is the champion of the Church, and his religious ideas have pushed his tendencies to extremes."

Briefly, the result of these communications was that Garcia Moreno was a man of merit, very fanatical in his nature; that he was born at Guyaquil, had been President of the Republic of Ecuador, was assassinated on August 6, 1875, at the age of fifty-three, by a man named Rayo, assisted by several accomplices, after having shed blood in repressing a conspiracy.

Now I opened *Larousse* again, and this is what I read :—

"Moreno (Gabriel Garcia), President of Ecuador, assassinated at Quito in 1875. Exiled in his youth, he went to Paris and London, where he studied, returned to Ecuador, took up the profession of chemist, married the daughter of General Flores and became chief of the conservatives at Quito. President of the Republic from 1861 to 1865, and again from 1869 to 1875, he was scheming to become president again when he was assassinated.

"He was an able administrator, and carried out very important public works and restored the finances. An ardent Catholic, he gave the Church sovereign authority and sent the Pope a million francs; excited the mistrust of the neighbouring states, was beaten by Morquera, President of New Grenada, entered into conflict with Peru and, having to cope with several liberal insurrections, displayed an arbitrary exercise of authority and excessive severity in repressing them."

It will perhaps be thought that *Larousse* played a very great part in these verifications, and the sitters may be supposed to have been familiar with it. That is a mistake: none of them had ever opened *Larousse*, myself excepted, and I am certain that I had never seen these biographical notices previous to my researches.

Besides, it will be noticed that the information given by the spirit calling himself Garcia Moreno is different on more than one point, and more complete. In *Larousse* there is no mention of Rayo, or of the machete, the name of a weapon which was unknown to us until then.

Be that as it may, it will be seen that *Larousse* was not the only source from which we drew in order to verify the revelations which were made in our séances.

On Sunday, October 7, 1906, M. Thomas, our devoted and scrupulous secretary, was present at one of these manifestations. The following is an account of what took place in his presence.

HENRY CHARLES MONTAGNE

The spirit in reply to our questions gave his name as Henry Charles Montagne, who died ten years previously at Nha-Trang (Annam), and had lived in Paris. I sum up his communication in the following form, in order not to fatigue the reader by the repetition of questions which are almost always the same.

This spirit said: "I am buried at Père-Lachaise. I was clerk to the Residency at Tonkin. My father was very well known in the literary world. His name was Edouard Montagne, and he occupied an important position in the Société des Gens de Lettres. I have a great veneration for him."

We asked Henry Montagne to whom we could apply for confirmation of these statements. He replied: "Ask my father's colleagues, the greater number of whom were present at my funeral, which took place on November 26, 1896. I died on the previous July 9th. You can inquire particularly of Daniel Riche."

He then gave these details:—

"I was thirty-one years of age. I died in a tragic manner on the anniversary of my birth, mortally wounded by a tiger in carrying out an order I had received."

All the names mentioned in this communication were unknown to us, with the exception of that of M. Daniel Riche and M. Edouard Montagne, whom I alone had known by reputation. My first care was to look in the dictionary for the name of Nha-Trang. It proved to be the name of a place in Annam, not of a locality, but of a province.

I then wrote to Paris to obtain information—not to M. Daniel Riche, whose address I did not know, but to the office of the Société des Gens de Lettres, and received the following reply:—

"PARIS, *October* 15, 1906.

"DEAR SIR AND COLLEAGUE,—Yes, Henry Montagne was the son of a former delegate of the Société des Gens de Lettres, Edouard Montagne, the immediate predecessor of M. de L. He was killed by a tiger at Nha-Trang (Annam), on July 9, 1896. His body was brought to Paris on September 26th, and was buried on the 28th at Père-Lachaise, in the family vault, &c."

Then came the signature of a well-known member of the society. That is all very well, it may be said again, but these three accounts mention some sensational incidents. M. Henry Montagne's death must have caused a certain stir ten years ago, and some one of you may have preserved the recollection, without knowing it, in a corner of his memory. I would simply draw attention to the precision of the dates. This unconscious memory would have to be very faithful! There is only one difference. The spirit said "November 26th" where my correspondent wrote "September 26th."

In any case, if I have so far only quoted sensational facts I have grouped them together designedly. I will quote others which are less sensational, then I will come to those which are quite free from sensation.

HENRI THOMAS

In a séance which took place last May, a psychic personality manifested at the table by very feeble raps. We entered into conversation; I give here the questions and the replies:—

Question. What do you want of us?

Answer. To converse.

Q. Then will you tell us who you are? Your name?

A. Henri Thomas.

Q. Have you been dead for long?

A. Two years and a half.

Q. How old were you?

A. Twenty years.

Q. Do you know of what illness?

A. Accident.

Q. What is the name of the place where you lived?

A. Gondrecourt.

Q. Were you born at Gondrecourt?

A. No. At Demange-aux-Eaux.

Q. Had you a profession?

A. Yes; teacher.

The remainder of the conversation is of no particular interest.

I wrote to the schoolmaster at Gondrecourt, asking him if he had had a colleague or an assistant of the name of Henri Thomas, and in what way he had died. He replied at first by a very vague letter, which showed his discretion, and by which it appeared he did not see the necessity for giving me the information. I communicated this letter to M. Thomas, the namesake of the deceased, who wrote again, this time as secretary of the Société d'Études Psychiques. The following is a copy of the reply, which has been added to my collection. I merely omit the preliminary sentences.

"Thomas (Henri) was born at Demange-aux-Eaux (Meuse) on October 10, 1883. He entered the Normal School at Commercy on October 1, 1899, and left on July 20, 1902, with the higher certificate. On October 1st of that year he took the position of probationary teacher at Gondrecourt, about four miles away from his family. He was a very good, kind master, somewhat timid, conscientious, and of very good conduct. On Thursday, November 26, 1903, at 7 P.M., he placed himself in front of a train on the line from Bar to Neufchâteau. We learned of his tragic death on the following day. All who knew him were profoundly astonished by it.

(Signed) "L., *Director of the School at Gondrecourt.*"

Here, again, there was a difference—only one. At Gondrecourt they were convinced that he had committed suicide: the spirit said "accident." Apart from that the two accounts were identical.

Before going further, I ought to relate another of these impressive manifestations. Afterwards I will pass on to more simple narratives.

MAURICE BOUCHE

One evening a spirit came and said that his name was Maurice Bouche, and that he was very unhappy. His first words were :—

"Children, follow the advice of your parents."

I ought to say that we had some very young people present. He went on to say some very excellent things in melancholy tones. At the end we asked him where, when, and how he died. But before going further, I asked whether any one in this gathering had heard of Maurice Bouche (the reply was in the negative). The fact therefore was not well known, so that no objection could be raised afterwards. Be that as it may, none of the persons present knew him.

Well, the following is the spirit's reply :—

"I died three years ago, at Lille, on the scaffold."

Not knowing to whom to apply for confirmation of this statement, I put some inquiries to a gentleman who had lived at Lille. He told me that Maurice Bouche was a young man of good family, who was ruined through bad company. Falling lower and lower, he ended by joining some robbers. One day he was arrested for complicity in the assassination of an old lady of property, and was, in fact, executed at Lille about three years previously.

Certainly, if we accept the theory of latent memory, I admit that this might apply to this last manifestation. But it has never been explained, to my mind, why these recollections should remain completely dormant for three, ten, or even twenty and thirty years, and be suddenly awakened because we were seated in a circle with our

hands on the table. Neither does it further explain why
they take on the mode of speech of a personality, and why
they should tell us point-blank things that were quite
unexpected: we cannot even say that they "can do everything but talk," according to the old saying which is
applied to intelligent dumb animals. They can talk;
they only lack the material body. If the intelligences
thus manifesting were only recollections momentarily
effaced, it would assuredly be a very strange mnemo-
technical phenomenon, as strange as spiritism itself.

THE WEAVER VIRY

But this hypothesis does not appear to hold good in
view of other revelations which I have kept until the last.
Let us listen to this typtological conversation with the
spirit of a brave boy who was neither assassinated nor
executed, who had no history, and of whom, however, we
have discovered certain traces.

Question. What was your name?
Answer. Viry.
Q. What was your profession?
A. Weaver.
Q. In what country did you live?
A. Vosges.
Q. Were you a workman in a spinning factory?
A. No; a weaver.
Q. In what part of Vosges did you live?
A. Gerbépol.
Q. That is where you were born?
A. Gérardmer.
Q. In what year did you die?
A. In 1877, on November 26th.
Q. What age were you?
A. Twenty years.
Q. Did you die as the result of an accident?
A. Congestion.
Q. In your bed?
A. No, outside, at the Grande-Source.

Q. You were ill previously ?

A. No; drunk.

Q. You were in the habit of drinking ?

A. No.

Q. To what do you attribute this congestion *?*

A. Cold.

Q. Why do you come here to-day ?

A. To converse.

Q. Do you know us ?

A. No.

At the end of this séance the following letter was sent to the Mayor of Gerbépol :—

" SIR,—I should be glad if you would tell me if a man named Viry, who lived, I am told, in your locality and who died about the year 1877, has left any relatives in the country, and if anything is remembered about him.

" In order to facilitate your inquiries I may add that Viry was a weaver, and would be from twenty to twenty-five years old."

The following is the reply received from the Mayor of Gerbépol :—

" SIR,—In reply to your letter of the 15th inst., I have the honour to inform you that there is not in our town any relative or connection of young Viry, weaver, born at Gérardmer, who died at Gerbépol on November 26, 1877, aged nearly twenty years.

" His family came from Gérardmer, and only lived here for a few months. A sister of this young man was married to a man named G. H. of Gerbépol, who at present lives at Saint-Dié. She died some time since, leaving, I believe, four children, of whose present address I am ignorant.

" This young man was found dead in the snow.

(Signed)   " E. C., *Mayor of Gerbépol.*"

The majority of the persons present were not born in 1877; it would therefore have been difficult for them to have read the newspapers, supposing that the Nancy newspapers, which had few correspondents at that time, had mentioned the sudden death of a poor Vosges mountaineer.

However, as there are many who are always ready to believe in chances and coincidences more extraordinary even than the spiritualistic explanation, I will admit that an old number of a newspaper, dated from November 1877, might have fallen after thirty years into the medium's hands, that she had conscientiously read it, and that the facts and dates had been carefully stored in her memory in order to be brought up at the opportune moment.

But then how will they explain the following manifestation, which put our circle into communication with the spirit of an old lady, in very humble and obscure circumstances, who died peacefully in her bed in a village of the Ardennes, of which we did not even know the name ? The following is the account of two conversations we had with this spirit, whose language denotes much intelligence and elevation of feeling.

Madame Duchêne

First Séance (June 7th)

The spirit declared her name to be Mme. Duchêne, retired teacher, who died at the age of seventy-eight years at Vendresse (Ardennes). We could, she said, write to the Mayor of Vendresse, who would confirm these details.

Second Séance (June 12th)

Question. Who were you ?
Answer. Mme. Duchêne.
Q. Where were you teacher ?
A. In the Marne.
Q. What town ?
A. Not necessary.

Q. Why do you not reply to that question?

A. I have told you all that is necessary.

Q. You have said that you died at Vendresse (Ardennes) at the age of seventy-eight years.

A. That is sufficient.

Q. How long since?

A. Two years and a half.

Q. Of what illness?

A. Old age.

Q. You authorise us to write to the Mayor?

A. I wish it.

Q. Why do you wish it?

A. In order to prove the truth of what I have told you.

Q. Could you not give us other proofs also?

A. I must observe certain limits.

Q. By whom are these limits fixed?

A. Higher spirits.

Q. Plural or singular?

A. Plural.

Q. When you were living did you believe in immortality?

A. No.

Q. And now?

A. I am forced to believe it.

Q. You were doubtless astonished on finding yourself in the Beyond.

A. Yes.

Q. What was your experience after death?

A. At first I seemed as though stunned.

Q.· How long did this amazement last?

A. Some weeks.

Q. When you could take cognisance of your situation, what did you feel?

A. A sensation of deliverance.

Q. You are happy?

A. Yes.

Q. Have you found those whom you have lost?

A. Yes.

Q. All ?

A. Yes.

As a result of this communication I hastened to write to the Mayor of Vendresse. He replied to me as follows :—

"VENDRESSE, *June* 16, 1906.

"SIR,—In reply to your inquiry, I have the honour to inform you that Mme. Duchêne, widow, *née* Bretagne, died at Vendresse on September 7, 1903, and that she bequeathed all her fortune to M. L., formerly schoolmaster. "BONNIN, *Mayor.*"

You will see from this reply that the Mayor did not suspect my reason for writing to him. He, no doubt, took me to be a claimant for what Mme. Duchêne had left.

Be that as it may, it is explicit, and I see no other explanation possible for this revelation, so clearly confirmed, than the spiritualistic one.

I must remark in passing that the higher spirits are the most sparing of personal details as regards themselves, that is, as to their life on earth. It would seem as though they felt scruples in making our researches too easy. I merely state this without going into the cause of the scruple ; that would take me too far. However, the information Mme. Duchêne consented to give us was sufficient for us to identify her.

LOUIS NAUDE

I have now, I believe, given seven verified manifestations. Not wishing to abuse your patience, I will mention the rest more briefly. They are, however, quite as interesting in their results. The eighth was very short.

Question. Who were you ?

Answer. Louis Naude.

Q. What was your profession ?

A. Postman.

Q. In what locality.

A. Lardoize.

Q. What Department?

The reply was somewhat confused. We distinguished the letters *a r d*. Some believed that the spirit meant Ardèche, and others Gard. But as we expected another spirit we rapidly passed over this detail and asked¡ where Louis Naude died. He replied:—

A. In the Rhône. My body was removed to Arles.

Q. Was that long since?

A. Three years.

I waited some time before seeking to verify this communication, which appeared somewhat trivial. On consulting the *Dictionnaire des communes* I found in Ardèche a place named Ardoix, and in the Gard a hamlet named Lardoize, attached to the town of Laudun. I decided to write to both. The Mayor of Ardoix had never heard of a postman named Louis Naude, but the following reply came from the Mayor of Laudun, who was also Mayor of Lardoize.

"LAUDUN, *September* 6, 1906.

"SIR,—In reply to your favour of August 27 last concerning Louis Naude, formerly in the service of the P-L-M, I have the honour to inform you that since his departure in March 1903 I have had no definite information concerning him.

"Mme. Louis Naude has, since then, left the locality; however, I have been able to procure her present address and transmit it to you below.

"For the Mayor
(Signed) "SOGNIER, *Secretary*."

I did not think it my duty to write to Mme. Naude, not wishing to push my researches to the point of indiscretion; for this reason I do not mention her address. It was sufficient to know that Louis Naude had really existed; that he was a postman, and that he had lived in a place called Lardoize. What the wandering and invisible personality that was manifested to us had said, had been confirmed by the Mayor of Laudun.

Jean de Boutary

The ninth communication is a very curious one. The spirit gave the name of Jean de Boutary, and said he had lived under the Regency. His language was that of a young nobleman, rather dissipated, of light character and somewhat sceptical.

We asked him what was his principal occupation.

He replied : " I went into high society."

" Whom did you know ? Will you be good enough to mention a name ? "

" Cardinal Dubois."

" And whom did you know among the people ? "

" Among the people I only knew pretty girls."

We asked Jean de Boutary where he was born. He replied that he was born at Montauban, and that he divided his time between that town and Paris.

" Have you any descendants ? " we asked him.

He replied in the affirmative. " But," he said, " they do not bear my name exactly. They are called Dubois de Boutary."

" And where do they live ? "

" At Montech (Tarn-et-Garonne)."

No member of the circle had heard mention of Montech. We consulted a book and found that this place really existed, that it was situated in the Department of Tarn-et-Garonne. I wrote to the Mayor of Montech, and some days afterwards I received the following reply, with the heading of the Mayor's office :—

" Sir,—There are at Montech two families named Boutary, one Lafon-Boutary, and the other Dubois de Boutary.

" I believe that the Lafon-Boutary family came from Montauban, but that of M. Dubois de Boutary must, if I am not deceived, originally belong to Montech.

" These two families have representatives in the town, and you can write to them.

" For the Mayor,"
(Signature illegible).

I did not deem it necessary to trouble these two families; this letter was sufficient confirmation of the information given by Jean de Boutary. Here again is a communication which cannot be explained by mnemonics, or by latent memory.

But this was not the most extraordinary. That emanated from a spirit named Simonne. I must make you acquainted with Simonne.

Simmonne de Lewitz

The personality that took this name must have been that of a young girl who died at fifteen years of age a hundred years ago. She is intelligent, talkative, exceedingly curious, and seemed to be familiar with the use of sharp language.

She said she belonged to a family of Lewitz, which had emigrated during the Revolution, and that she had been brought up with an aunt in Brussels. She stated, moreover, that she had been very badly brought up, in the company of servants, who had taught her to swear. The one she preferred was Pierre, the gardener, whom she had met in the Beyond.

Simonne was never willing to give us any information that would help to establish her identity: one of her defects is her self-will and her disturbance of the séances with her jokes, which are often annoying. The following are the accounts of the most interesting séances which she gave us.

Séance of June 15th.

Question. Since you are not willing to say anything concerning yourself to-day, tell us of Pierre. What was his family ?

Answer. Batoix.

Q. Had he any children ?

A. Yes, five.

Q. What were their names ?

A. (Simonne gave several names, Jean being among them.)

Q. Has Jean also left any children ?

A. I think so ; I will tell you that to-morrow.

Q. Why not to-day ?

A. That is my business.

Following Séance

Q. You can tell us if Jean, son of Pierre Batoix, has left any children ?

A. Yes.

Q. Has he at present any descendants ?

A. I believe so.

Q. Then there are still some Batoix ?

A. No; they are called Louvet. Their mother married a Louvet.

Q. Do you authorise me to write to this Louvet, to know if you have not deceived me ?

A. He will not reply.

Q. Why ?

A. He is dead.

Q. I believe that you are making game of me.

A. Not at all. His wife still lives.

Q. And is she called Mme. Louvet ?

A. No doubt. What would you have her called ?

Q. Has she any children ?

A. Yes.

Q. How many ?

A. Twelve.

Q. Simonne, I believe more and more that you are making game of me.

A. If you do not believe me, write to the Mayor.

Q. Then tell me the name of the town.

A. Acquin.

Q. I do not know any place of that name.

A. Write nevertheless.

Q. In that case tell me the name of the post-town.

A. Lumbres.

Q. These are strange names you have given me. If I write to the Mayor of Acquin, *viâ* Lumbres, do you think that I shall get a reply?

A. I know nothing myself; I am not his secretary. But write all the same.

The following day I looked up a directory, and, much to my surprise, I found the name of Acquin as a town, with Lumbres (Pas-de-Calais) as the post-town. I wrote to the Mayor of Acquin and received the following reply:—

"ACQUIN, *June* 28, 1906.

"SIR,—The widow Louvet has always lived in Acquin. Several of her numerous children are in situations, but she has still eight, all young, to support. She is well worthy of interest, especially considering that her health is very precarious. MASSON, *Mayor.*"

After that the theory of latent memory seems to me a very poor one, and I could break off my narratives here.

But while I am dealing with Simonne, permit me to quote the following:—

ELISABETH DE LEWITZ

Simonne had spoken of us, it appears, to all the members of her family that she had found in the Beyond. She had in particular a sister named Elisabeth de Lewitz, who lived much longer than our little friend. She had flourished, so she said, in the times of Louis Philippe, and this noble lady, urged by curiosity, did not disdain to be present at one of our séances. These communications between the spirits and living persons seemed almost as extraordinary to her as they did to us. She asked us several questions, and replied to ours. In return for this interview we asked her to tell us if there remained any descendants of her family, of whom Simonne, more careless, had not been able to tell us.

Elisabeth de Lewitz hesitated a little, then replied in the affirmative. But she added: "I do not know if I ought to tell you their name."

"Why?"

"They are not nobles."

"No matter for that," I replied. "We are not noble either. Tell us their name therefore."

The table remained for a moment with one foot in the air, then rapped out the following letters:—

"Affra."

"And where does this family of Affra live?"

"At Perpignan," replied the spirit.

"What street? What number?"

"Rue Neuve, number 8."

We did not know at all if there was such a street in Perpignan, and the name of Affra seemed to us a very strange one. As a matter of duty, I wrote at once to the Mayor of Perpignan to inquire if a family named Affra had lodged at this address. I give the reply as it came from the Mayor's secretary.

"PERPIGNAN, *August* 30, 1906.

"SIR,—I have the honour to inform you in reply to your letter of the 27th inst., that there is living at Perpignan a family of the name of Affre, not Affra. M. Affre is a Notary at Perpignan, Rue Neuve, 8.

"For the Mayor,
"*Delegate Municipal Councillor*,"
(Signature illegible).

You will see that there is only a mistake in one letter, and this mistake is easily explained. In the typtological alphabet the letter *a* is expressed by one rap only, like the word "yes." Often after one letter has been given we ask, "Is that all?" and the table replies "Yes." It is probable that after the letter *r* in the name of Affre we put this question. The table having replied "Yes," we probably took this "yes" for an *a*. But this mistake is quite insignificant, because Affra and Affre are much alike, especially so near to the Spanish frontier.

Here, therefore, are ten psychical communications confirmed by proofs. There are many others I could relate. Among these last named are communications from quite remarkable people, which contain definite information as to the Beyond, the psychical life, the part played by fluids, &c. This information is all the more interesting for us who think we know those who give it. But that is beyond my limits, and I must stop there for the moment, leaving you to draw your own conclusions.

For my own part, I will only say that if any one can furnish me, as an explanation of these phenomena, with any theory more acceptable than the spiritualistic one, I shall be glad to hear of it. But with regard to the objections of the materialists and dogmatists, I notice that they only offer hypotheses as explanations, and between hypotheses and verified facts I choose the facts, surprising as they may appear.

Augustin Cauchy

Six persons were at the table. Scarcely anything had been obtained for about three-quarters of an hour, except from some vulgar entities, whose language was often trivial or disconnected. Suddenly the knocking changed, and raps became clearer and more uniform, and the following conversation ensued, by means of the alphabet.

Question. Who are you?

Answer. Augustin.

Q. That is a Christian name. Can you tell us your surname?

A. Cauchy.

Q. You will forgive us for putting some categorical questions. We want to know who are the spirits that reply to our call.

A. That is right.

Q. Can you complete your name by some information that will help us to establish your identity?

A. *Beatus qui intelligit super egenum et pauperem.*

Q. That is a maxim ?

A. It is the epitaph engraved on my tomb.

Q. Can you translate it for us ?

A. "Blessed is he who understands the poor and has pity on the unfortunate."

Q. That is the epitaph of a good man. But your tomb, where is that ?

A. In the Sceaux cemetery, on the road shaded by chestnut trees which leads to the slope of Plessy-Piquet.

Q. Have you been dead very long ?

A. Fifty years.

Q. Can you give me the exact date of your decease ?

A. Yes, May 17, 1857.

Q. What was your profession ?

A. During my career I had many vicissitudes.

Q. You had, however, one favourite occupation ?

A. Science.

Q. You were perhaps professor ?

A. I was.

Q. Where ?

A. At the Sorbonne.

Q. Have you left any works ?

A. Yes.

Q. I should be very grateful if you would give the title.

A. Mémoires.

Q. You had a number of pupils ?

A. Yes.

Q. Some of them must have attained to prominent positions. Can you tell us their names ?

A. I cannot.

Q. Why ?

A. It would be transgressing our laws.

Q. What laws ?

A. The laws regulating spirits.

Q. Then tell us what are those laws and who has decreed them ?

A. Our Divine Master.

Q. You are a religious spirit ?

A. I have never been ashamed to live as a Christian.

Q. I do not think the Gospel contains the law you say. There are therefore some special laws for spirits ?

A. Yes.

Q. You state that you have lived as a Christian. What do you mean by that ?

A. I have always endeavoured to follow faithfully the divine precepts. Science does not exclude faith. Look at Newton, Pascal, Descartes : did these valiant defenders of the faith of our fathers neglect science ?

Q. What do you understand by faith ? Is it faith in a future life, in eternal justice, or in a collection of dogmas ?

A. The faith as it is taught us by the Gospel, that sublime book.

Q. Do you not find that the Gospel contains principally moral precepts rather than the obligation to believe in dogmas which have since become narrowed down ?

A. It is those precepts which form the base of our religion.

Q. Have not some useless and very complicated things been constructed on this base ?

A. Why that observation ?

Q. Because the details of narrow or puerile practices have caused their fundamental bases to be lost sight of.

A. A clear conscience sees farther than practices.

Q. I see that you are a believer. How do you reconcile your present situation with your beliefs ?

A. Explain.

Q. Are you in one of these places which the Church recognises after death—heaven, purgatory, or hell ?

A. But I am in heaven.

Q. Do you mean that you are in the state of mind that corresponds to heaven, or that you are really in heaven ?

A. In heaven.

Q. Then you have seen God ?

A. Yes.

Q. Can you describe Him ?

A. Description is impossible. I was dazzled by the Almighty Power of the Creator.

Q. Who told you that this dazzling spectacle which you cannot define contained God?

A. I have seen Him, I tell you. I have seen Christ illuminating the heavens with the splendours of his glory, the divine word in His humanity.

Q. You may have seen a fluidic personage in a luminous atmosphere, but how did you recognise Christ?

A. How could I fail to recognise Him? He is my Saviour, who became as we were.

Q. If you are in heaven, how is it you can be at the same time on earth? How is it you are here?

A. To spread these teachings. God has given us power to work with men.

It will be seen that the personality calling himself Augustin Cauchy was clearly characterised. He is a very orthodox believer who sacrifices none of his religious principles, and whose aim is to reconcile them with the teachings of science and the facts which he asserts that he has witnessed in the Beyond.

I made some inquiries as to this savant. It was not difficult to find traces of him, and what I have since read about him agrees with the foregoing.

Cauchy was an ardent legitimist, who refused to take the oath to the Government of July and the Second Empire, and who was compelled on two occasions to leave the chair of the Sorbonne and teach in a foreign country. It was certainly possible for one or other of the persons present to have learned some biographical details of this subject. But what is difficult of explanation, since none of them had ever lived in Paris or visited the cemetery at Sceaux, is the communication relative to the epitaph. Now, this information was correct. I have, in fact, written to the keeper of the cemetery at Sceaux, and the following are the particulars he was good enough to send me :—

"SCEAUX, *November* 9, 1906.

"Sir,—In reply to your letter of the 3rd inst., I have the honour to inform you that I have made a search in the cemetery for the Cauchy tomb, which fortunately I found, and I have copied the following epitaph engraved on the tombstone, and which reads :—

AUGUSTIN-LOUIS
BARON CAUCHY
DIED AT SCEAUX MAY 23, 1857
BEATUS QUI INTELLIGIT
SUPER EGENUM ET PAUPEREM

"This abandoned grave is in a deplorable state, covered over by weeds; it was necessary to clean it in order that I might send you the information asked for.

(Signed)   "VINCENT, *Keeper of the Cemetery at Sceaux,* 174 *Rue Houdan, Sceaux (Seine)*."

This honest keeper added that the cleaning necessary to decipher the inscription took him about an hour. It had therefore been for a long time illegible to visitors, and we may ask how the Latin text and the translation could have come, unconsciously or otherwise, to the knowledge of any member of our circle.

CHAPTER XIX

TYPTOLOGY AND LUCIDITY—*(continued)*

CASE OF DR. PETERSEN

THE following case is published by M. Anastay, President of the Marseilles Society for Psychical Studies, in the Bulletin of that Society.

The importance of this investigation will not fail to be perceived, both because of the care with which M. Anastay has arranged the documents which are absolutely authentic in this case, and because of the verification resulting from an official inquiry made by the authorities, and which included the evidence and the medico-legal report on which the finding of the judicial authorities was based.

THE CASE OF THE DISAPPEARANCE OF DR. PETERSEN.

In the course of December 1904 the *Almanach de la Savoie* for 1905 (an almanack which appears to give special prominence to the sensational and tragic occurrences in the district) published the following information :—

A Disappearance

" We were informed about October 20th of the disappearance of a young doctor of medicine, M. Munch Peterson, of the Fredericks Hospital, Copenhagen, and son of a professor of medicine in that city.

"Dr. Harold Munch Petersen came to Aix-les-Bains with a circular ticket *viâ* Germany and Switzerland, and from there should have gone to Paris by way of Lyons. A post-card sent from Culos to his sister on October 3rd, stated that he was leaving for Aix. Since then his family, to whom he often wrote, have not received any news.

"At Aix his card was found at the Grand Cercle, where he had sent it with a request for an invitation, but his name was not found either on the police register or in the list of visitors. He had a letter for Dr. Cazalis, who had not seen him. The prefecture of police has searched in vain for him in Paris. It seems that he must have left Aix almost immediately after his arrival, since he did not put up at any hotel. The family offer a reward of three hundred francs to any one who would give the police any information which would enable them to trace him.

"His portrait is given herewith (the almanack published the portrait of Dr. Petersen), and his description is as follows:—

"Dr. Harold Munch Petersen, 33 years of age: short; fair hair; blue eyes; rather pale; slight fair moustache; speaking French imperfectly.

"M. Gauthier, Commissioner of Police, has made inquiries showing that Dr. Petersen arrived at Aix, and his identity has been established.

"On the morning of October 5th, before going out on his bicycle to make an excursion in the neighbourhood, the doctor ordered eggs and tea for breakfast, saying that he would not return until the evening.

"Since then he has not returned, and it is feared that he may have met with an accident on one of the surrounding mountains."

The news soon spread, and public opinion, which had recently been disturbed by the murder at the Villa Solms, was much divided, some inclining to believe it was an accident, others a crime; some stories made the victim die on a mountain, others in the Lac du Bourget; others again favoured the suggestion of suicide. At bottom no one knew anything as to the cause of this mysterious disappearance, not even the authorities, who, pressed by the Prefect, who himself received orders from the Ministry, at the instigation of the Danish Legation, were worn out with the efforts they had made in every direction.

The devoted Commissioner of Police, M. Gauthier, whose zeal and perspicacity were beyond all praise, after having cleverly traced Dr. Petersen at Aix-les-Bains, and learned that before leaving the hotel where he had stayed he had expressed the intention of going to the Mont-du-Chat, which lies to the west of Aix-les-Bains, and is one of the most dangerous mountains of the district, had immediately sent the gendarmes and foresters in this direction, as well as to "La Chambotte," a mountain 2730 feet high which overlooks the eastern side of the lake. This clue appeared all the more important because one of Dr. Petersen's brothers, a doctor of law and professor at the University of Copenhagen, while taking an automobile trip round the lake, had collected what seemed to be evidence in favour of this hypothesis. Several innkeepers at Bourget and Bordeau stated, in fact, that on October 5th they had seen a traveller on a bicycle who was very like the photograph shown to them.

Inquiries had also been made at Mont-Revard, a favourite point for excursions, situated to the east of Aix-les-Bains, but without any appreciable result. The banks of the lake had also been explored, but the fishermen, whose working season it was, declared that if there had been a dead body near the bank, in shallow water their nets would have brought it up.

At this juncture the Commissioner, M. Gauthier, who had had the matter in charge for some days, received a visit from the Justice of the Peace at Aix-les-Bains, M. B., who handed him the following anonymous letter which he had just received:—

"Aix-les-Bains, *October* 26, 1904.

"To the Justice of the Peace.

"Permit me to bring to your knowledge the following communication just received, and to remain anonymous for the present.

"If by this means the body is discovered, I will make myself known by producing a copy of this letter.

" The doctor died on a perpendicular precipice of the Revard, under an overhanging rock near a house which is used as a shelter for sheep when overtaken by storms.

" A point which will be very useful for discovering the body is to look for traces of blood on all the stones around the place in which it lies."

After examining this paper, it was wisely agreed to take note of its contents without, however, placing exaggerated confidence in it, and the same evening it was communicated to the brigadier of gendarmerie, who promised to send his men again the next day to the slopes of the Revard.

This was done, and the summit of the mountain was specially examined. Several châlets were found which corresponded to the description, but all efforts were fruitless. As winter was coming on, and all the mountain paths would soon be covered with snow, the search was given up until the following season.

M. B. was not long in discovering by chance that the author of this anonymous letter was a lady then on a visit to Aix, Mme. Vuagniaux, a convinced spiritist, the wife of M. Vuagniaux, a talented artist, and both of them paid us a visit at Marseilles in January 1905, with a very warm recommendation from the president of the Geneva Society for Psychical Studies, Mme. Rosen-Dufaure, who introduced M. and Mme. Vuagniaux to us as highly reputable persons enjoying general respect and esteem. In fact, they impressed us as being worthy and serious-minded people. We hastened to introduce Mme. Vuagniaux to some ladies of the Marseilles Society for Psychical Studies, and it was not long before they began experimenting with the tables.

Mme. Vuagniaux did not speak of what had happened at Aix-les-Bains, although she said that she had several times felt inclined to do so, and the winter passed without other incident.

We now return to the " communication," for such it was, as ingenuously stated in the letter to the magistrate at Aix-les-Bains. Mme. Vuagniaux, being concerned, like all the other inhabitants of the town, as to the fate of Dr. Petersen, had remarked one day to those around her that the spirits, who knew many things, ought to enlighten her as to the fate of the unfortunate doctor.

At an evening meeting with her friends, Mme. B. and Mlle. B., they made the table " talk," and without these ladies asking anything, as is frequently the practice with spiritists, they obtained by typtology the following communication :—

" The doctor died in a cave with perpendicular sides at Revard. You can give the information or find him yourselves.

" You should see the Commissioner, and tell him that you know that the doctor died on the Revard in a rock cavity on a precipice close to a house which serves as a shelter for the flocks of sheep when they are overtaken by rain. A very important point for discovering the body is to look for a trace of blood on all the stones surrounding the spot where he fell."

Communication received October 26, 1904, signed Marie Vuagniaux, Mme. L. B., Mlle. M. B.

M. Vuagniaux was engaged in painting in an adjoining room when he was called to be witness of this commuication. He sent us the following attestation :—

" The President of the Psychical Society of Marseilles.

" I certify that when engaged in the room adjoining that where the séance was held, I was called and witnessed the communication No. 1 just as it has been sent to you.

(Signed) " C. VUAGNIAUX."

" AIX-LES-BAINS, *August* 12, 1905."

Mme. Vuagniaux was much surprised at this manifestation. The following day, while alone, she was impressed to ask the spirits for further details, and she obtained the following by intuitive mediumistic writing :—

" The doctor, in order to climb the Revard, passed by Roche du Roi and Mouxy ; in the last place he was seen by some persons. His body is at the bottom of a ravine, a little distance from the sheepfold. He fell twice, first of all at the foot of a perpendicular wall, then lower down into a chasm under an overhanging rock.

"That is all; there is nothing to alter. If God wills he will be found. There is a house which is near the road; the gendarmes will inquire. He was seen to pass there; he was on foot."

Finally, a third communication said :—

"My dear child, it is your usual guide speaking to you. I see you wish to know if I can confirm the information which has been given you. I can. The doctor is dead; his spirit is still in trouble. He will be found from the information given. I can add this—you must look at the foot of a wall which overhangs a precipice; he fell there first of all, then into a chasm. We shall do our best to help. It was well on in the evening—about six o'clock —when he fell. He was seen, when passing Mouxy, by several people. Adieu, my child. YOUR GUIDE."

M. Vuagniaux was called to witness these fresh communications, and the following is the attestation he added to the preceding :—

"I declare that I took cognisance, at the time they were received, of the communications Nos. 2 and 3 received by my wife through mediumistic writing the day following, and the day but one after No. 1 was given by raps at a séance. C. VUAGNIAUX."

In the course of the winter Mme. Vuagniaux obtained some communications which confirmed the explanations given, and advised her to continue the search. In April she and her husband returned to Aix-les-Bains, but the Revard was covered with snow and enveloped in mist. On May 5th, after a special séance, it was decided that the following week, if the weather permitted, M. V., assisted by a member of the Alpine Club, should recommence the search.

It was then that the following information appeared in the newspapers, which spread with lightning rapidity and at once stopped the generous intention of M. and Mme Vuagniaux.

Discovery of a Body

Mysterious Disappearance—Search Seven Months after.
Gruesome Find

"AIX-LES-BAINS, *May* 10th.

"On October 3rd last, Dr. Harold Munch Petersen of Copenhagen, aged thirty-three years, came to Aix-les-Bains to stay a few days.

"On the morning of the 4th Dr. Petersen asked the proprietor of the hotel for information as to the excursions which could be made in that district. During the day he visited the town, and at this date the registers of the Grand Cercle show that he visited that establishment. In the evening the doctor dined at the hotel, and went to bed at an early hour. At five o'clock in the morning Dr. Petersen rose, and, after taking a light breakfast, he went for a bicycle ride. Since then he has not been seen.

"The Danish doctor's family, much surprised at receiving no news of him for several days, sent one of his brothers and a friend to make inquiries.

"On October 15th they arrived in Paris, and went to the Danish Legation, which immediately asked the police department to make inquiries as to this mysterious disappearance. The doctor's movements were traced, and it was ascertained that he had gone to Aix-les-Bains. The brother and friend immediately took the first train for Savoy.

"On their arrival at Aix-les-Bains active search was made under the direction of the Commissioner of Police by the Aix-les-Bains gendarmeric, the brigades of the district, and the forest-keepers. All search was fruitless until Tuesday evening, May 9th, when Antoine Jacquin, farmer at Mouxy, on going into a coppice on Mont Revard, discovered a dead body entirely eaten by birds of prey. Only the calves, which were covered with leggings, were intact. M. Antoine Jacquin at once informed the Commissioner of Police of his discovery. Some papers found at the place where the body was discovered leave no doubt that the body is that of Dr. Harold Petersen."

The disappearance of Dr. Petersen and the negative result of the search caused great excitement among the townspeople. Many conjectures were made as to this disappearance, which seemed somewhat mysterious after the dark memories of the tragedy of the Villa Solms. The inhabitants of Bourget and Bourdeau stated that on October 5th they had seen the Danish doctor on a bicycle returning to Col-du-Chat. Their statements must have been erroneous, because chance led to the discovery of the body of the unfortunate doctor in exactly the opposite direction. To obtain further information we went to the place where the body was discovered, in company with M. Jacquin and M. Exertier, formerly Mayor of Mouxy, and M. Blanc. We arrived at the spot after a walk of three hours. M. Antoine Jacquin gave us an account of the discovery in the following terms :—

" I own a property situated on the western slope of Mont Revard, about 4500 feet above the sea-level, called the *Bois Noir*, but better known as the *Gorge des Chérassons*.

" This property is on a steep slope ; at the top there is a rock thirty feet high, formed of two vertical portions of equal dimensions, separated by a small platform. This rock, which cannot be climbed, is consequently a barrier to the ascent of the Revard.

" The Alpine Club path which leads to the top of the Revard on the west side passes nearly two hundred yards below my land.

" I only come to this place once in three or four years on account of the difficulty of getting to it. It takes two hours of difficult walking, and the ground is almost valueless, with only a few fir trees on it.

" On the afternoon of May 9th, I went up to my property, the *Gorge des Chérassons.* About one hundred and fifty yards from the base of the rock I have mentioned I found some fragments of grey clothing. Greatly surprised I went higher, and at various points I saw other pieces of the same material. About forty yards from the base of the rock I came across a dead body, or rather a skeleton, seated and bent forward.

"I saw other pieces of material close to the body. Higher up I found a small knife, a watch, and, further on, the chain. About twenty yards from the base of the rock I discovered the remains of a shirt, a circular railway ticket, and a wallet containing some foreign bank-notes.

"Lower down, about a hundred yards away from the body, I found a black leather purse, containing a ten-franc and a five-franc piece, and some foreign coins of small value. I also found an eye-glass.

"*This body could only have been discovered by me. Every two or three years I go up to this place, which is my property. It is absolutely deserted and dangerous; no tourist or huntsman ever ventures to make the ascent.*

The Hypothesis

"It is supposed that Dr. Petersen was making the climb to the top of Mont Revard, and that afterwards he had taken the Alpine Club road to return on foot to Aix-les-Bains by an arid path on which, at a distance of nearly a mile, there is a châlet; below this there are two very difficult passes, overhung by two peaked rocks about four yards high.

"It is supposed that Dr. Petersen lost his footing and fell on to the first rock, when he would be thrown on to the second, and then would fall into M. Jacquin's wood.

The Presumptions

"The circumstances in which the body was discovered lead to the supposition that Dr. Petersen was the victim of an accident.

"But an anonymous letter, if we can believe certain statements, addressed to the magistrate when the press reported this disappearance in October last, gave precise information as to it, with particulars as to the place where Dr. Petersen had met his death.

" A judicial inquiry will be held as to this painful death. The remains of Dr. Petersen have been left on the scene of the accident, awaiting removal by the authorities."

The Chambéry magistrates then ordered the Commissioner of Police of Aix-les-Bains to go to the site on the Revard with a doctor, in order to ascertain if the death was due to accident, or to crime, or suicide, and to open a searching inquiry to ascertain if there was cause for suspicion against any one. The result of the inquiry was given in the following terms in the *Progrès de Lyon* of May 13, 1905 :—

Disappearance of Dr. Petersen—Removal of the Body

" Contrary to our expectations, the Chambéry magistrates did not go to the place where Dr. Petersen met his death, it having been established that the death was due to a mountaineering accident.

" Yesterday morning at six o'clock M. Gauthier, Commissioner of Police ; Dr. Guyenot, official doctor ; Favre, sergeant-major ; Martin, gendarme ; Blanc Lanote, Brigadier of Police ; and Gauthier, junior, took the cog-wheel railway for Mount Revard. After a walk of three hours the party arrived at the *Bois Noir*.

" After a rest, the body was placed in a sheet, and a stretcher was improvised out of some fir tree branches.

" After many difficulties the party arrived at Aix-les-Bains : the body was transferred to the hospital mortuary, and the doctor held a post-mortem examination. No fracture of the skull was discovered. The ribs of the left side were completely broken. It is supposed that Dr. Petersen left Mont Revard on foot in order to return to Aix-les-Bains, taking the Alpine Club path. At about 130 yards from the châlets the path divides into two.

" Instead of continuing to follow the Alpine Club path, the doctor took the other path, which leads to the edge of a rock. Here he must have slipped and fallen, rolling over two peaked rocks.

"According to Dr. Guyenot, death was not instantaneous. The Danish doctor regained consciousness for a few moments, and was able to drag himself to the foot of the rock where he was found and seat himself there."

Thus ended, for the few witnesses who had followed the affair in all its details, the strange coincidence between an accident which remained for a long time unknown and a revelation produced in the course of a judicial inquiry with regard to it.

Our readers know that this revelation stated that: (1) Dr. Petersen died on Mont Revard; (2) this death was due to a mountaineering accident; (3) as to this accident, numerous details were given which were really true, such as the vicinity of a châlet, the double fall on perpendicular rocks, the survival of the victim, &c., but they also know that some slight mistakes were also made.

Before examining these circumstances more closely, and drawing from them such deductions as seem to be permissible, we will here finish the descriptive part of our narrative, by saying that the mortal remains of the unfortunate Danish doctor repose peacefully in the cemetery at Aix-les-Bains; in the picturesque words of the sympathetic Commissioner, M. Gauthier, "close to the spurs of the Alpine chain which inexorable fate had marked for the termination of his too short career."

We will now examine the circumstances of the Alpine tragedy which was the subject of the preceding narrative, to see what we may learn from it to the advantage of psychical science.

Let us say first of all that if the discovery of the dead body had followed close upon the statement of Mme. Vuagniaux, the dramatic interest would doubtless have been increased. But ought we therefore to say, from the scientific point of view, that the importance of the resemblances between the information revealed, and those supplied by the subsequent inquiry, has been diminished?

No, because the non-discovery of the dead body was not due to any defect in the search, which was, as we have seen, extensive and conscientious; nor yet to lack of precision in the particulars revealed; because the main characteristics of the place indicated seem to have been given in the "communications." In reality, the non-discovery of the body was due to a special circumstance: the marked inaccessibility of the place where Dr. Petersen's body was lying, and which was found to be a neglected corner of the Revard.

In point of fact the witness Jacquin declared in his interview with the *Progrès de Lyon* that "the inhabitants of Mouxy are not very enthusiastic about going into their woods, for they are very dangerous places to get at," and, in a private letter, that "the searches of the gendarmerie may have been very thorough, but to get to this dangerous spot one must know the way, and run considerable risk." Dr. Guyenot was not less explicit in saying that this spot "is difficult of access and extremely dangerous."

What is of importance to us, therefore, is not to know whether or not the body was discovered after the revelation, but whether special and striking agreements are found between the communication and the fact, and what is their origin.

First of all, in order to see things from a slightly higher standpoint, is there sufficient agreement to claim our attention and justify a study such as we submit to the consideration of our readers? Yes, because one of the most enlightened witnesses, not to be suspected of partiality, the Commissioner of Police, M. Gauthier, when questioned by us as to the effect produced upon him by these agreements, was good enough to give us the following detailed account of the impression made upon him at the time of the recognition of the body, and which has not yet been effaced. The reader will find in it that warmth and vitality which characterises the narration of actual experiences.

Speaking of the time when the party mentioned by the editor of the Lyons newspaper had arrived at the top of the Revard, and had then to discover the place where the body of Dr. Petersen had fallen and to ascertain the causes of his fall, M. Gauthier said:—

" The keeper knew the situation of the Jacquin property. He was to lead us by some rocks which had been mentioned, which bordered the upper edge of the property. We wended our way from the station towards the south part of the plateau, about a mile and a half from this station : we passed by five small buildings a little way apart from one another. The one served as a cheese dairy during the summer ; a second, during bad weather, sheltered the flocks. Had the sibyl spoken truly in her letter addressed to the magistrate ? Here is the building which serves as a shelter for sheep. Where is the cave ? I look and search in vain. We come to a deep and steep gorge. We continue our perilous descent. The keeper comes to the top of the rocks, at the bottom of which is the sloping property of M. Jacquin. We walk silently and thoughtfully, when suddenly the keeper cries out:

"' Doctor, come forward I pray you, but carefully ; your shoes are not iron shod, and in spite of your stick you may slip and tumble into the chasm.'

"' Take hold of a branch of the bush by your side.'

"' That is it ! Do not go any farther ; bend over and look.'

"' What a strange sight ! There is the rock with vertical walls from the top of which the doctor probably fell.'

"' Oh, what a strange thing ! I see a cave which I had not known ; it is hidden under the Revard. And to think that for nearly thirty years I have traversed the dangerous parts of this mountain.'

" At these words Dr. Guyenot turned, and our eyes met.

" The rock with vertical walls (the anonymous letter said, ' perpendicular precipice '), the cave seen for the first time by the keeper (but it was the cave described by the sibyl !).

" With great difficulty, the doctor came towards me. We exchanged impressions ; we were struck with astonishment.

"'All this is right,' I said, 'the shed for the sheep, the perpendicular precipice, the cavo. Is it really under the rocks with vertical walls, in this cave, that the dead body of Dr. Harold Munch Petersen lies?'

"We had not long to wait for the reply to my question.

"In fact the forest keeper, by means of a horn, sent forth a rousing call. The mountaineers, the gendarmes, the secretary and the Brigadier of Police (who had taken two hours and a half to come from the station at Pugny to the top of the *Bois Noir*) replied by shouts. They saw us, again ascended, and were soon not far from us, by the side of the dead body, about forty yards from the rock beside which we were standing.

"The particulars given to the magistrate by the lady were accurate."

Commissioner Gauthier demonstrated in his report that Dr. Petersen had gone towards the summit of Mont Revard by the Alpine Club path; he had breakfasted there, and had descended again by the same way; "when near the pond he had taken a false direction, by going along the path to the right which leads to the chasm," and he ended with the conclusion that "it was certainly a mountain accident that caused the death of Dr. Harold Munch Petersen; and it cannot be attributed to any other cause."

On the other hand, the legal doctor stated to his companions that "Dr. Petersen survived the accident for several hours, but it is impossible to specify the exact time which elapsed before he died."

The principal features of the revelation appear, therefore, to combine in proving its veridical character, and it remains for us to consider the possible hypotheses in explanation of this remarkable case, after having examined as closely as possible the details we already know.

It was possible to suppose that Dr. Petersen had died by falling from a rock, and the revelation might in all strictness only be the effect of a coincidence, but the veridical details furnished by the famous "communication" seem to us to exclude, by their number and particular character, this rather simple hypothesis.

It mentions first of all a " perpendicular precipice," which is correct; then a " cave," which ought to play an important part in the recognition of the spot, since this term is repeated three times in the original communications. Now this important detail is confirmed, since a natural cave existed in the immediate neighbourhood of the double-staged rock on which the doctor fell. We see by the plan (Plate II.) that the opening of this cave which drew the attention of the keeper and others was about fifteen yards from this double-staged rock. But if we consider the form of this cave we find that it is more closely and truly *over* the dead body, since " if a line was drawn towards the east, from the top of a perpendicular raised from the place of the body, it would come, if not to the southern extremity of the cave, at least quite close to this extremity." This cave, which serves as a refuge for badgers, has an opening of nearly a yard wide, a yard and a half high, projecting about two yards, and seems to hang in space: it becomes larger towards the south, where the double-stage rock is, until it attains a depth of seven or eight yards, thus constituting " a large chamber, so that if a man fell into this cave he would not be able to get out."

Dr. Petersen might, according to M. Gauthier, who gave this opinion simply as a hypothesis, have fallen from a rock which overhangs this cave and come to the spot where he was found, which would make the " communication" more literal on this point; but we are bound to accept the version generally accepted by the mountaineers who have seen the place, and by Dr. Guyenot, who believed that Dr. Petersen had fallen from the adjoining double-staged rock (Plate II., Fig. 2). Be that as it may, the doctor's body was found neither in nor under this cave, but below it. There was therefore a slight inadequacy of terms in this description, but not a marked incorrectness.

With regard to the second point in the letter sent to the authorities, the sheepfold, there was no mistake in

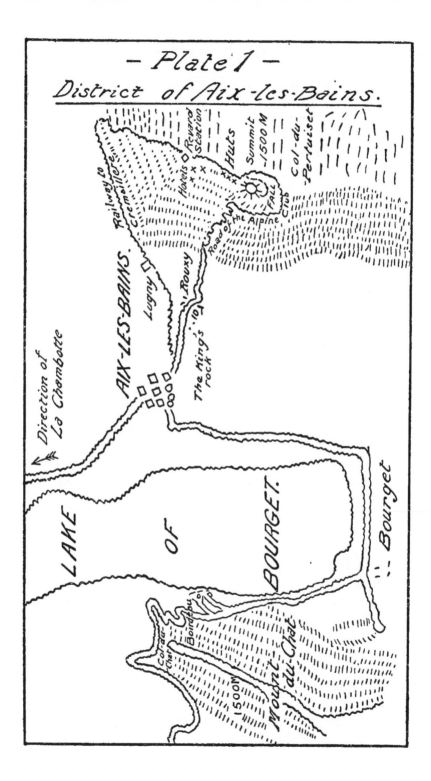

– Plate 1 –
District of Aix-les-Bains.

this either. The sheepfold existed, and was, according to the witnesses, from four to five hundred yards from the spot. Every one knows how, on mountains as on the sea, distances are relative, and we think that the description in the communication can be considered fairly correct, and that is certainly the impression which the narrative related above seems to have made upon the excellent M. Gauthier.

We pass to other details a little less important, because they are reported in two documents which have not been officially authenticated.

The spots of blood may have had their importance while the event was still recent, but not after the rain or snow had swept away the traces.

If Dr. Petersen passed on foot by the Roche du Roi and Mouxy, no one has been able to testify to it, except a woman of Mouxy, who declared that some one who passed without a bicycle and bearing a resemblance to Dr. Petersen, stated that he was going to the Revard, on the day of the accident. The fact, which is almost established, that the doctor did not use his bicycle, seems to give some support to this statement.

The assertion that Dr. Petersen fell twice, at the foot of a perpendicular wall, then under a cave, repeated again in other words ("look at the foot of a wall which overhangs a precipice; he fell there first of all, then into a chasm"), although badly expressed, since it may, strictly speaking, be applied to a fall from the rock which overhangs the cave, is nevertheless striking enough, because it appears to us to apply better to the official hypothesis, which made the doctor fall from the double-staged rock forming the end of the gully *des Chérassons* to the right of the cave.

Finally we come to the time of the fall, which, as it seems to be erroneous, has the effect of a slight blemish on a pretty face. We might infer from it that the doctor, overtaken by the night, was venturing too incautiously, and that is perhaps the unconscious thought that was suggested to Mme. Vuagniaux at a moment when, putting

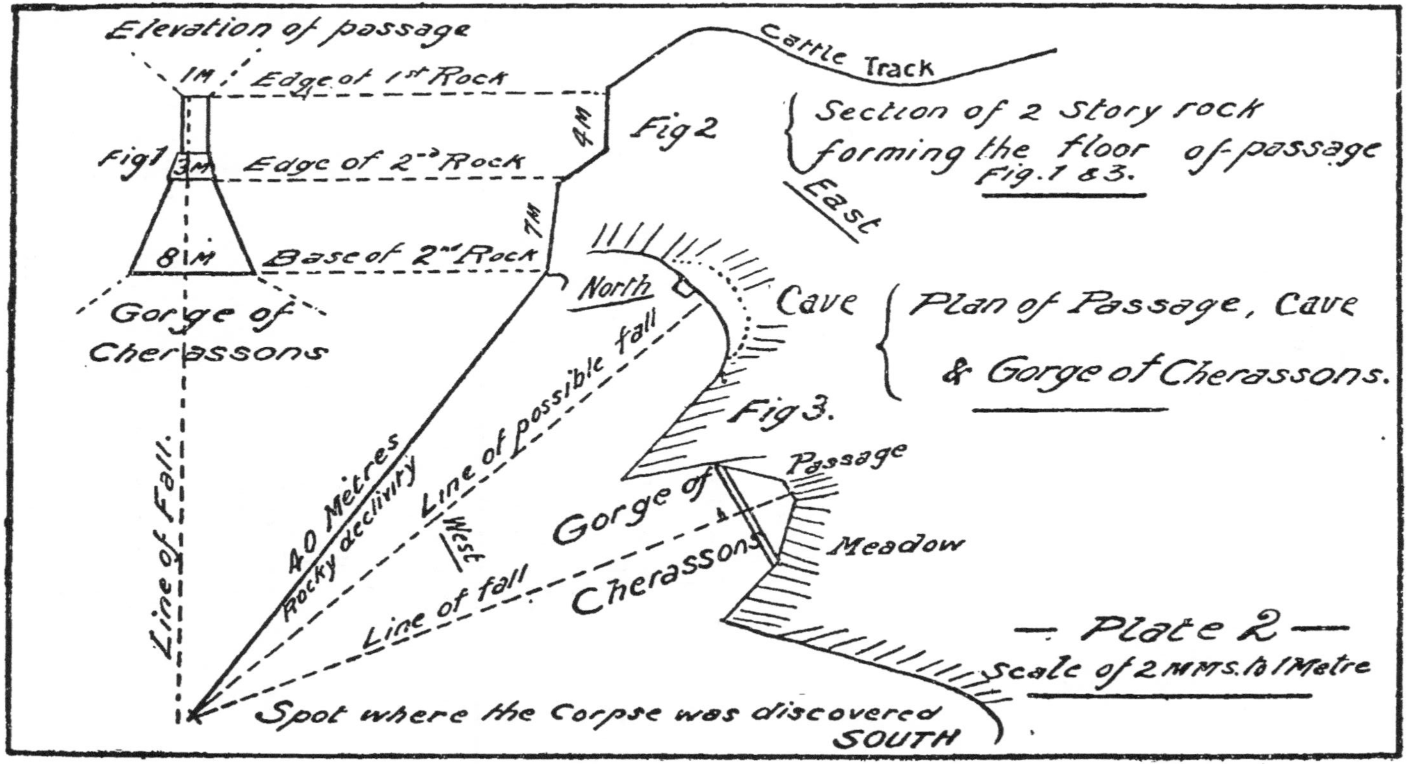

Elevation of passage

Cattle Track

Fig 2

Section of 2 Story rock
forming the floor of passage
Fig. 1 & 3.

East

Cave { Plan of Passage, Cave
& Gorge of Cherassons.

Fig 3.

Passage

Meadow

— Plate 2 —
Scale of 2 mms. to 1 Metre

Edge of 1st Rock

1M.

Edge of 2nd Rock

3M

4M

Base of 2nd Rock

7M

North

Fall

Line of possible

Gorge of Cherassons

West

Line of fall

SOUTH

No Mercey's
Rocky declivity

Spot where the Corpse was discovered

Gorge of Cherassons

Fig 1

8 M

Line of Fall.

some mental questions to herself, as we have seen was her custom, she no doubt offered her own explanation.

We consider it as proved that the fall took place at the time when the watch stopped, that is to say, at 3.54.

This constitutes the sole error, though only a slight one, which we have to notice, if we do not take into account that which results from the declaration that "the body will be found from this information," which is weakened by a preceding declaration that the body will be recovered "if God wills it."

In summing up the impressions produced by the relations established between the event and the revelations which followed it, we will say that in this case, as in nearly all those which are reported in mediumistic séances, we find that mixture of truth and falsehood or error, which always gives a slight vagueness to the whole, and throws our mind into incessantly recurring perplexities. But if the proportion of truth and falsehood varies in each case, here the true seems to greatly predominate over the false. If we may be permitted a comparison, we would say that the communications of Mme. Vuagniaux produce almost the effect of messages which might be transmitted by means of the telephone from a person who had seen the place and the scene, who had only a limited time allowed, say half a minute for each communication; this would prevent him from choosing his terms, and would make him sometimes go rather wide of what he meant to say.

We come now to the hypotheses which might be proposed in explanation of this case.

The simplest that presents itself to the mind is that of *an unconscious knowledge of the intentions of Dr. Petersen, combined with that of the places which might have been known to be dangerous by one of the witnesses of the scene.*

We have seen that the doctor had asked for particulars at the hotel as to the excursions to be made, and that he had, on the day before the accident, left his card at the Grand Cercle, where he might have spoken of his plans. One of the witnesses who was present at the spiritistic séance might therefore, while sitting at a table in a café, or while walking in a public garden, have heard, without being aware of it, a remark made by some one near him.

First of all, the inquiry that we have made is rather unfavourable to this idea. In the absence of the President of the Cercle, who had resigned, the assistant manager, M. R., has been good enough to inform us that " no one at the Cercle could furnish any information as to Dr. Petersen, who had passed absolutely unnoticed among the crowd of habitués of the establishment." Further, M. G., Controller of the Cercle, who recorded the name of the visitor, has declared that the doctor, " who spoke French with difficulty, did not say a word as to his intention of going to the Revard, and, moreover, did not speak of anything whatever." At the hotel where the doctor was staying I had still less success. The manager gave the following reply to our question whether the doctor had given any indications whatever as to his projected excursions :—

" AIX-LES-BAINS, *August* 6, 1905.

" SIR,—In reply to your letter of the 4th inst., I have the honour to tell you that on leaving my house the doctor said to my daughter, who had told him of several walks that he could take, that he was going on his bicycle to the *Col du Chat;* that is how the police were misled in their search, because no one would have suspected that the doctor had gone to the Revard, a mountain on which there were no carriage roads. E. V."

In order to reply to the objection that some one of those present might have known of the dangerous parts of Mont Revard, we ought to say that neither M. nor Mme. Vuagniaux, nor Mlle. B., had ever climbed this mountain. Mme. B. had only been there once, ten years previously, with her husband and a relative; she recollected having passed through some vineyards, then along some paths which were not dangerous, and she retained only a pleasant memory of this excursion, on account of the marvellous view which she had enjoyed from the summit.

Moreover, all the preceding indications, one of which represents the Jacquin property as an isolated spot, " absolutely deserted and dangerous, where no tourist or huntsman would risk making the ascent," ought to demonstrate, *a fortiori*, that the spot is impracticable for a woman. Finally, the most characteristic declarations were made when Mme. Vuagniaux was alone.

Since the hypothesis of sub-consciousness must be set aside, we have to consider that of telepathy.

The doctor, before dying, might, by the power of his thought, have impressed some strata, more or less deep, of the sub-consciousness of persons who, in a waking or sleeping state (and in the latter case by dreams forgotten on awakening), may have preserved this impression in a latent state, and in the form of pictures more or less animated, to be brought to light at a favourable moment.

What may perhaps give a semblance of force to this supposition is that Dr. Petersen was in an excellent condition for telepathy, according to the generally accepted rules: he was young, overtaken in full vigour by a terrible and desperate state of mind, far from all assistance, his agony lasting, according to the legal doctor, perhaps for "several hours." But, on the other hand, why should this mental force go in search of persons quite unknown to him ? How can it be explained that an influence deposited in the sub-consciousness of a person had to wait twenty-one days before manifestation, and is there any proof of a parallel phenomenon ? All our ideas as to telepathy are of quite recent origin, and this supposition, which we are unable in our special case to support by any proof, cannot detain us longer.

We pass to the hypothesis, perhaps more acceptable, of telesthesia.

One of those present may have projected his sub-consciousness, and seen, by means still unknown to official science (clairvoyance or lucidity of somnambulism and the semi-hypnotic states), the events which he translated into the form of a spirit communication.

Magnetisers hold that things sometimes happen as though this hypothesis were a reality, but first of all their experiments have been made with subjects put to sleep, and not in a waking state, as was the case with our spiritists; and then, has it really been demonstrated that a somnambulist has the power to " see " into the past and into the future? These facts are rare and uncertain; they shine out in each psychic as a fugitive light which soon goes out—sometimes it is revived, only to be finally extinguished; so that, in the present state of science, we cannot see what to reply to any one who should say : " You claim that lucidity is an autonomous phenomenon and has nothing in common with spiritism: Well, for my part, I claim that spiritism alone exists, and that in the cases where you think you observe lucidity it is a 'spirit' that is the cause of it." We even find that a number of minor considerations come to the help of this spiritist opinion and support it by their influence; but that is not our aim, and we accord no greater value here to the spiritist hypothesis than to the preceding one, being guided by the scientific spirit which prevents us from advancing further than our position will allow us. We are desirous, above all else, of guarding against premature and hazardous theories, and, in especial, against the very human tendency to push unprovable hypotheses to extremes, and to set one up against the other too dogmatically.

Every one will be free here to interpret the facts according to his liking and preference. Some will, for example, say that a " spirit " who was interested in Dr. Petersen would not fail to leave on one side the rocks and other details of the scene, and to tell us of his watch and other personal articles, valuable as means of recognition; of the position of the body, still more characteristic, &c. Others will reply that the "spirit" did not wish to give signs of identity, but only to afford the opportunity for finding the body, for the sake of the family. We are not condemning these endeavours to arrive at some tenable hypothesis; but we should pass beyond our limits if we allowed ourselves to be led on to draw conclusions more extended than our premisses warrant.

E. ANASTAY.

CHAPTER XX

TYPTOLOGY

Analysis of the Phenomena

THE phenomena observed by means of typtology are certainly so strange that the mind retains them, half questioning their actuality, and cannot help seeking for an explanation of them.

The imagination easily comes into play, if we allow it a free course, and the most varied theories arise, all of which by different methods seem capable of giving us the interpretation of a certain number of facts.

For our part, on the contrary, we shall endeavour to eliminate the rôle of imagination, and to examine these facts by applying to them the method of scientific analysis which we follow when we study any phenomenon of this kind. We shall therefore pass from the more simple to the more complex, from the known to the unknown: seeing, first of all, if we cannot find in other facts better studied and experimentally demonstrated an explanation which we can apply to these peculiar phenomena.

First of all, it seems to us a mistake to seek one single interpretation for facts which, although resembling each other in many points, may arise from causes different in nature.

Consequently we may admit that an interpretation which will exactly apply to a certain number of cases, leaves the field free for other interpretations which apply better to other cases.

Among the phenomena, which result from a faculty peculiar to certain subjects, which will help us in the interpretation of a large number of cases of typtology, we place thought-transference in the first rank.

Let us see, in the first place, if we can scientifically accept thought-transference, and whether it is admitted that a subject can perceive a thought that is not revealed by any external sign. More generally still, the question here put can be at once stated in a more complete and precise manner. Is it possible for a direct mental communication to pass from one living person to another ?

This possibility no longer appears to us to be in doubt. In fact, the numerous experiments of M. Boirac and Colonel de Rochas, as well as our own, seem to have irrefutably demonstrated that the human mind can, without any physical communication, exercise a direct influence on another human being.

We even recognise that this influence can be exercised by two different methods: by mental suggestion and by transmission of thought. These two methods must be kept absolutely distinct from each other, as we shall show, and we shall have occasion to invoke them successively in order to explain the various phenomena.

Mental suggestion [1] is the action which the mind or the will of the individual exercises on the body of another living person. It is not, therefore, properly speaking, a communication from mind to mind ; it is the influence of the mind on the organs of another subject. If A., for example, acts by mental suggestion on B., he can put his muscles into play, make his limbs perform movements or acts more or less complicated. But B. does not know to what these movements will lead. He does not know beforehand what he is going to do ; he is like a puppet, of which the strings are pulled by A.

Thought-transference, on the other hand, is the influence directly exerted by the mind of one subject on the mind of another. There is here a real communication from mind to mind. If, therefore, A. transmits to B. the thought of an action, B.'s mind first of all perceives the thought of this act, and secondly, his organs carry it out. The phenomenon may be more or less complicated by

---

[1] See the *Treatise on Hypnotism* by the same author.

other circumstances; but it is always the mind which is the transmitter, and another mind which is the receiver.

Before applying thought-transference as an explanation of typtological phenomena, it is necessary to draw attention to some laws of thought-transference, which experiment and observation have already enabled us to recognise:—

(a) Thought-transference requires, in the percipient, a special faculty, which may be developed by training, or may be due to momentary exaltation.

(b) It requires in the agent an aptitude which may be acquired, but which can be diminished or augmented by various conditions.

(c) All agents cannot act indifferently on any percipient; there must be a special relation, a certain harmony, original or acquired, between the two subjects.

(d) In addition to this general disposition the percipient must be, at the time when the phenomenon is to be produced, in a special condition, which, for us, is a species of hypnotic state, which we have called the state of passive mediumship.

(e) In this condition the percipient is easily able to vibrate in unison with the agent to whom he is accustomed —that is to say, to be capable of receiving his thought.

(f) It may also happen that he is accidentally, or by reason of various circumstances, vibrating in harmony with another agent, more or less distant, and who may even be quite unknown to him.

(g) The percipient may be prevented from receiving the thought, because of circumstances that are opposed to the hypnotic state of which we speak, or because of the influence of other persons who, consciously or not, act on him by mental suggestion to prevent him from receiving the thought transmitted.

(h) It is not necessary for the agent to be conscious of the act of the transmission of thought.

(i) The percipient, provided that he possesses the faculty of lucidity, can read a thought which only exists in the sub-consciousness of the agent.

S

(*j*) The percipient may also be unconscious of the act of thought-transmission which operates through his instrumentality, and he may give expression to the thought unconsciously in an indirect manner.

(*k*) The act of transmission and the act of reception are not necessarily simultaneous ; a longer or shorter time may elapse between the moment when the transmitter sends forth the thought and the moment when the receiver perceives it.

To sum up, we see that the essential principle of thought-transference may resolve itself into this : an agent and a recipient independent of each other, and who may act unconsciously ; the reception may not take place until some time after the act of transmission.

These few laws, which all who have studied thought-transference will accept, enable us to interpret many phenomena.

Let us, therefore, examine in succession, and according to a regular plan, the various phenomena which may occur, commencing with the simpler ones and coming progressively to the more complex examples.

(*a*) The medium makes a statement which he believes to be unknown to him, and which is certainly unknown to all present, but inquiries reveal that the fact may have come to the sub-consciousness of the subject ; whether by sight, by written documents which he may have accidentally seen, or by hearing—he might have heard the fact mentioned without paying any attention to it.

In this case there is a simple passing into the consciousness of something existing in the sub-consciousness. The phenomenon seems very simple, but it is necessary to notice it, because it frequently occurs, and we do not always recognise it when it is not subjected to careful inquiry.

(*b*) In another case the medium speaks of something which he does not know, but which is known to some person present. This is simple thought-transmission.

(*c*) The medium says something that he does not know, which is not in the conscious thoughts of any of those present, but which may have come, more or less accident-

ally, to the knowledge of one of them, who may therefore ·
have it in his sub-consciousness. In this case there is
thought-reading on the part of the percipient, the trans-
mitting agent being unconscious of it.

(*d*) The medium makes something known which is
quite unknown to himself and all present, but known to
some one else more or less distant. Here we have thought-
transmission from a distance, which, according to circumstances, may be either conscious or sub-conscious on the
part of the agent, but which is generally sub-conscious on
the part of the percipient.

We now come to the case which seems the most
difficult to explain: the medium speaks of things of which
every known person is ignorant. We may even admit that
it can be proved that the things were only known to a
deceased person.

We ought to divide these cases into two categories.

In the first, it is a question of a hidden object, of a
letter or something written—in a word, of an object or
material sign, the existence of which no one knows, and
which is outside the range of the subject's normal senses.
Lucidity is sufficient to explain these cases. We know, in
fact, that lucidity is a faculty possessed by certain subjects, by which they perceive the existence of objects
which are not within the range of their normal senses.
This faculty enables them to discover an object, to follow
a person, or to read a letter at a distance, as is proved,
amongst others, by the experiments carried out by M.
Ferroul, M. Bruynel, and myself.

In the second category we place the cases in which the
medium states things which are only known to a deceased
person, and of which there does not exist any material or
written trace.

It seems very unlikely that cases of this nature should
present themselves with certainty, but we desire to admit
all the hypotheses. What can most easily happen is that
the case does not present the usual conditions in which
lucidity is manifested, and thus the researcher may be led
to another interpretation.

We may again find this interpretation in a phenomenon of thought-transmission, in which the deceased person is the agent and the medium the percipient. This transmission of thought may again be exercised a long time after the death of the agent. We have seen, in fact, in the laws of the transmission of thought (see last law k), that the act of the transmission and the act of the reception of thought are not necessarily simultaneous; there may be a lapse of time, longer or shorter, between the moment at which the agent sends forth the thought and the moment when the percipient receives it.

This circumstance ought not to astonish us. We are accustomed, in fact, to recognise that the vibrations which produce sound are transmitted so slowly that we become aware of the delay at a comparatively short distance. With luminous rays the propagation is much more rapid, and we must base our calculations on infinitely greater distances. We know, however, that the luminous rays coming from certain stars take a considerable time, many years even, to reach us. More than that, we know again that certain stars, of which we now see the luminous rays, have quite disappeared from the place where we think we see them. These luminous vibrations are therefore latent, and require, in order to be perceived, that our eye should take the position which it ought to have in order to receive them, as if the source of emission were still in existence—that is to say, that our eye must be in a certain state of receptivity. What is there surprising, then, if these vibrations, emitted by a living organism, also remain latent until a percipient vibrates in unison with them— that is to say, is in a state of receptivity capable of perceiving them ?

This is a simple hypothesis, if you will, but rational enough, presenting striking analogies with other and better-known phenomena, and which enables us to interpret one of the facts which appear the most difficult of analysis among those presented by mediums.

We desire to state precisely that this does not cause us to reject any other hypothesis whatever, but we consider the one which we have stated as being among the most admissible in the actual state of the experiments as known to us.

A certain number of facts also lead us to regard thought in a different manner from the conception generally held.

According to this hypothesis, thought is not a purely abstract phenomenon. All thought created by the mind has a characteristic entity which is indestructible, or, at least, which leaves an imperishable trace. This entity is, on the mental plane, a picture representing the thought— a picture henceforth ineffaceable. Imperceptible to every mind in the normal condition, this picture only becomes accessible to certain subjects possessing peculiar faculties, chief among which is the faculty of lucidity.

The perception of thoughts, on the mental plane, requires that the subject should be in a peculiar condition, different from the normal, like that which is necessary for them to exercise their faculty of lucidity.

This hypothesis—a purely working hypothesis, if you will—adapts itself admirably to what we know of the faculty of lucidity. It gives us a very plausible interpretation of the phenomena of typtology which are the most difficult to explain, and, moreover, it also gives us the explanation of telepathic facts which are out of the ordinary, and which appear to us to be otherwise inexplicable.

In other classes of facts—for example, the photographing of the picture of the thing thought of—we have, so to speak, along with the explanation of the phenomenon, a proof of the well-foundedness of this hypothesis, since thought creates a picture which, without being perceptible to our senses, is able to impress the photographic plate.

In some phenomena of externalisation of force, when the force acts in an intelligent manner, and in materialisations, it is still this mental thought image which is strengthened by the accumulation of the thoughts of a group of persons, condensed by the medium. This mental image receives its form by the mental effort of all present, and therefore it corresponds to the whole of the ideas which predominate among the group; but only certain mediums are able to give it a sufficient cohesion for it to be perceived by one or more of our normal senses. Most frequently it is the sense of sight or hearing that is first affected, so that we have visions, apparitions, and abnormal noises. Then in other cases, with mediums possessing higher faculties, the mental picture is materialised further, in such a way as to exercise an impression of contact either on persons or on objects; finally, in the cases of still higher phenomena, by means of material elements, borrowed either from the medium or the spectators or from the surrounding matter, some of the materialised pictures leave a part of this new material form remaining as permanent features of their passing, even after the medium has returned to his normal condition and ceased to exercise his mediumistic faculties.

This hypothesis can, we think, be applied to the interpretation of certain cases, and it will be useful for us in understanding some of the phenomena, particularly if we do not fall into the error of trying to generalise at all costs.

Other interpretations, again, can be adapted to different cases, and I must repeat here that I do not reject, *a priori*, any hypothesis. I am therefore not afraid to say that I am quite disposed to admit the spiritistic hypothesis in cases where other theories, already verified by other experiments, are shown to be insufficient, and where the spiritistic hypothesis supplies a better explanation of the phenomena.

We have not, in fact, any repugnance to admitting that a spirit, separated from any physical body, can enter into communication with us. It is rather those who will not recognise the possibility of the existence of entities independent of the body who are the dupes of a singular illusion.

Our bodies only possess five senses, by means of which we are in communication with the external world. It results from this that we have become accustomed to refer

everything to the exercise of these senses. We judge all
the objects that surround us according to the impressions
they produce on our different sense-organs; but that is
only a limitation arising from our nature, and we should
show ourselves very narrow-minded if we claimed to deny
the existence of everything that does not fall within the
range of our senses.

In a different and more restricted order of things, what
discussions have we not seen arise, for example, on the
possibility of life on planets other than our own? Some
learned men have denied this possibility, basing their
arguments on the evidence they have been able to secure
on the subject of these stars, such as their temperature,
absence of water, absence of respirable atmosphere, &c.
All these objections were based on the fact that it would
be impossible for beings *like ourselves*, endowed with a
physiological nature similar to that of the beings who
live on the earth, to live under different conditions. If we
consider things from this point of view, it is very evident
that no man like ourselves could live outside of the
physiological conditions for which our organs are constituted. But is that a serious reason for affirming that life
cannot exist there? Are our minds so narrow that we
cannot conceive of beings constituted differently from
ourselves.

Our senses are only narrow windows, through which
our mind can regard a very limited portion of the immense
reality. Let us suppose a man shut up in a cabin having
only one small opening through which he could see outside. Through this opening he sees all that comes within
the radius of his vision—light, a small patch of the sky,
trees, plants, &c. But what should we say of that man if
he tried to maintain that nothing existed beyond what he
could see? What should we think of him if he stated that
nothing existed, either to right or left of his cabin, beyond
what he could see through his little peep-hole?

The position of man in the universe is identical with
that of this prisoner: he has been so much accustomed
from his birth to judge everything by the impressions

that he receives through the organs of his senses that it
requires an effort for him to rise to the conception of anything different; nevertheless, it would be the most absurd
thing of all for him to believe that he could know everything, and that nothing existed beyond what he could
comprehend.

CHAPTER XXI

LUCIDITY

Nature and Extent of the Phenomena

LUCIDITY is a faculty by means of which a subject has knowledge of things not within the range of the normal senses.

Only certain subjects possess this faculty, and it may then be developed by practice and methodical training; but I do not think it would be possible for a subject to acquire it who did not naturally possess the elementary germ.

In the case of subjects who possess this faculty it is well to train it; because this faculty, like all others, can diminish, and may even be lost, if it is not cultivated.

The faculty of lucidity, in the case of those who possess it, is not permanently exercised, but requires for manifestation a special condition other than the normal.

Condition of the Subject in whom Lucidity is Manifested

In a general manner we may say that the subject in whom lucidity is manifested is always, at the moment of the occurrence of the phenomenon, in a hypnotic condition; but we can divide these hypnotic states, in which lucidity is manifested, into three classes :—

1. The subject may be apparently in a waking state, and may seem to be still in his normal condition.

This happens with subjects in whom lucidity is manifested in the course of conversation, for example.

It is also the case with subjects in whom lucidity is manifested in the course of a chiromantic examination.

At other times, though more rarely, lucidity is manifested in the course of any occupation whatever; the subject begins spontaneously to talk, and reveals what he has perceived by lucidity.

In all these cases, to which might be added several others of the same character, the subject may appear to unpractised eyes to be in a normal, waking condition. But an observer accustomed to the study of hypnotic phenomena would have no trouble in noticing at a certain time a peculiar fixing of the eyes, a vague look, and a sluggishness or peculiar automatism in certain movements, indicating the passing to that state which some authors have called somnambulistic waking, and which we have placed among the first degrees of the somnambulistic condition, because we have demonstrated that this is no longer a waking condition.[1]

This somnambulistic condition of the first degree into which the subject enters, apparently quite spontaneously, disperses just as spontaneously, so that the subject appears not to have left the waking condition in which he then again finds himself.

2. The subject is in a condition of light hypnosis, induced by artificial means.

This is what we observe in crystal vision. We have already studied this question, and have seen that the experiment of crystal-gazing very frequently gives place to the manifestation of the phenomenon of lucidity. It is the same with audition in the sea-shell.

In both cases the expectant attention, accompanied by the fixed gaze on a brilliant object in the crystal vision, and by the monotonous and continuous murmuring of the sea-shell, in the second instance, is of just such a nature as to induce this hypnotic condition.

Although most frequently there may be nothing of this nature in persons who profess to have clairvoyant

[1] See the author's *Treatise on Experimental and Therapeutic Hypnotism.*

power, we know that this phenomenon may sometimes be observed in them in a very real manner.

The following cases ought to be included in the present category; for coffee grounds, the egg, the glass, or the mirror play absolutely the same part as the crystal ball, both that of inducing the hypnotic condition necessary for the manifestation of the faculty of lucidity, and that of causing the various rays which come from the object employed to be transformed into visual hallucination.

We shall also include in this category the phenomena of lucidity which are manifested by means of typtology or automatic writing. The medium, who is the subject possessing the faculty of lucidity, is placed in the hypnotic condition by the fixity of attention and gaze.

We considered some instances of lucidity through typtology in a special chapter, when we studied experiments in typtology, which offered still other phenomena than lucidity.

3. The subject is in a condition of deep somnambulism.

Two cases may here be mentioned: that when the somnambulism is spontaneous, and that when it is induced.

With regard to spontaneous somnambulism, the subject passes into this condition during sleep; he is seen to be restless, as in a dream; he is heard to speak, and the phenomenon of lucidity is manifested in this somnambulistic dream.

The most frequent and the most interesting cases are those in which lucidity is manifested in a condition of induced somnambulism.

This is the case with hypnotic subjects more or less trained, in whom the hypnotiser has discovered the existence of this faculty of lucidity.

He places them, in the ordinary manner, which we have studied in the *Treatise on Hypnotism,* in a condition of deep somnambulism, and in that condition they may exercise, in the most varied and extensive manner, the faculty of lucidity.

OBJECTS OF LUCID PERCEPTION

Lucidity considered in its Object

The objects perceived by the faculty of lucidity may be very varied, and perhaps also varying in simplicity or complexity.

The most simple object may be something material, which the subject perceives as it is and describes in all its detail, whether he previously knew the thing itself or something similar, or whether the object is quite unknown to him and he never had any previous notion of any similar object. In that case he describes the object as it really exists and as he perceives it; but he knows nothing of the place where it is or of its surroundings, and he knows nothing of the use to which it has been put, nor what will eventually become of it.

Lucidity may have a person—either living or deceased—for its object.

The subject will describe this person as he perceives him, and this perception, in the case of true lucidity, corresponds to a reality. But it should be observed that this reality may not be that of the present moment; the subject then perceives the individual correctly, but at a time more or less remote. If it is a deceased person, he perceives him at an epoch of his life, determined by certain circumstances which we shall consider later.

If the individual is living he may see him at some previous epoch, or at the same moment when he describes him, or at some future time, more or less distant.

Be that as it may, the subject describes first the external aspect of the person—his clothing, his attitude, his features; and he will describe with such exactitude of detail that those present who know the individual will have no hesitation in recognising him.

The subject, again, may not confine himself to the external aspect of the person he perceives; but lucidity may enable him to discover the traits of his character, his qualities and defects, his tendencies and habits; he may give a moral description of the person, as correct as the physical portrait, and make an analysis which will astonish even those who know him most intimately.

The perception of the subject in the state of lucidity may not be limited to a thing or a person, but may extend to a whole scene.

The subject will then describe the surroundings in which he sees various people moving. He will give exact details of the place in which they are, of the relations between the different persons, and of the small objects around them, as though he were on the spot.

The perception of the subject instead of extending to the description of a scene may bear more particularly on one fact. It is then the circumstances of this fact which will form the object of particular details which the subject will give, and he may give these details with as great precision as when he was describing a material thing or a person. We can, in these cases, ascertain through him the way in which a thing happened with an exactitude greater than that of the combined testimony of personal witnesses. For the subject perceives and describes the fact as he would have described it at the moment when it took place, whilst the evidence of personal witnesses would have been subject to the influence of the different impressions which the various witnesses would have received and the possible defects of their memory.

We will consider also the application of the lucidity of the subject to an action, as being somewhat different from that exercised on a fact.

A fact is the result of one or of several actions; but action may be considered as a movement more prolonged in space and time than a fact.

Now, the lucidity of a subject may have for its object the perception of a complete action. The subject will then perceive the person or persons who take part in this action; he will recognise them and describe them with exactitude; he will follow them step by step in the different phases of the action which they set out to accomplish. The subject can describe to you the preparation of the act; he will know the projects which preceded it; he will describe the preparations; he will follow the principal actor, or the one to which he is attached, as he moves about from place to place in the preparation and accomplishment of this act; and, finally, the perception of the subject may be prolonged through all the effects and consequences of the principal action.

The application of lucidity to an action is therefore one of the most extensive and interesting which can be met with.

Finally, when we rise to an order of things more immaterial, and, perhaps, still more astonishing, lucidity may have for its object thought itself. We have seen that the subject may give the description and the moral portrait of a person; it is certain that he can also perceive his thought. This phenomenon, surprising though it may be, is yet one of the most frequent that is witnessed when one carefully observes a subject who possesses the faculty of lucidity.

How far Lucidity may Extend

As regards its extent, lucidity is manifested in time and space.

In time, lucidity extends to the past, the present, and the future.

In space, lucidity manifests itself on objects which are in the same place, on surrounding objects, and on distant objects.

The manifestation of lucidity in time and space gives rise to certain very important considerations on which we ought to dwell for a short time.

It is difficult, in the first place, to imagine lucidity as being exercised in the past, present, and future. But we can simplify this formula of lucidity in time; because if we consider the matter attentively, we shall see that we have only to concern ourselves with the past and the future.

The present, in fact, does not exist; it is an imaginary conception, like a geometrical point or line.

Take one of the most simple acts, the perception of a sound by your ear or of an image by your eye.

Up to the moment when the sound arrives at your auditory nerve, up to the moment when the visual ray strikes your retina, this phenomenon of audition or of vision is in the future; but at the same moment that it is produced it no longer exists, it is in the past.

And you cannot raise the objection of a prolonged sensation, a durable sound or a permanent vision; the sensation which is prolonged is, in fact, only the succession of identical impressions, repeated in a more or less rapid manner, but always transitory, and they are in the past immediately they have ceased to be in the future.

The past is therefore only the succession of things in the future which have already taken place in the past; and the past leads us on to the future by a chain of phenomena which does not present any discontinuity.

It is necessary to understand also that lucidity is nothing else than a phenomenon of thought. Now, time and space have no existence for thought. You read a newspaper which tells you what is taking place in the antipodes. Your thought is immediately transported to that country, and, at the very moment when you are reading, without making any further effort, you perceive as easily what is passing in the antipodes as you know what is taking place where you are.

You read the story of the conquest of the Gauls by Julius Cæsar, and the facts of those remote times are presented to your thought with as much ease and just as clearly as the facts of the previous day, the account of which you read in your newspaper.

Dreams are again an example of the ease with which thought is transported, without effort, in time and space. You dream of past or future things with the same apparent reality, you find yourself transported in dream to far-distant countries, just as to places very close at hand; and you feel, you act, you completely live, in those times and in those various places, without effort and with the same impression of reality.

We must not forget the analogy that exists between dream and the phenomenon of lucidity. We shall, therefore, be no longer astonished that lucidity, being essentially a phenomenon of thought, can be exercised indifferently in time and space.

There is one objection, which is very frequently made, with regard to the manifestation of lucidity in time. This objection refers rather to a philosophical difficulty than a practical impossibility, yet we ought to examine it none the less carefully; it concerns free will and the exercise of the human will.

How can we admit, we are told, that a lucid subject can tell us what is to happen in the future, since man, by his free will and the exercise of his choice, can accomplish or not such or such act; that act, therefore, cannot be foreseen, and, further, it may modify other events.

We have no wish to deny in any way the free will of man, nor the possibility that he, by his free determination, can modify certain events. All the discussion on this point rests on a false interpretation that is ordinarily made of the prevision to which the faculty of lucidity has given rise.

A prevision is not a fatality; and because a subject possesses the faculty of lucidity, and tells you that such event ought to happen, according to all the logical consequences of probability, of which you yourself have not the perception because you do not possess the faculty of lucidity; it does not therefore follow that this fact will necessarily happen.

No one can deny that there is a natural concatenation in the succession of facts, which are normally dependent one upon another. This dependence results from the very nature of the facts, and logic enables us to see their connection.

If I see you making preparations for departure and getting your trunks ready, I can conclude, by simple logic, that you are going to undertake a journey. This foreknowledge, which is almost certain to be realised, does not in any way modify your free action, because it is by the determination of your own will that you set out on the journey.

But if, from more precise information, I know that a contrary order will reach you, which will prevent your departure, I can then tell you that you will not undertake this voyage, although you have still the intention and the will to make it, and you do not yourself know that your determination, always free and voluntary, will be modified by events.

We have as an example some very simple facts, which everybody can forecast without possessing the faculty of lucidity, but in the case of somewhat more complex facts, the mechanism is still the same. The difference which characterises lucidity is simply this : that the subject, who possesses the faculty of lucidity, has the perception of causes which you cannot know in the normal state ; and, further, thanks to this same state of lucidity, he can forecast, with a logic infinitely more exact and certain, the effects of the causes which he perceives.

It remains none the less true that a superior force may always oppose a known force, and that your will can modify some events. But let us not forget that the lucid subject has also the perception of the quality of your will, whether it is feeble, strong, or changeable ; of your character and inclinations ; of your interests and the influences which are exerted on you ; we have seen that he can even perceive exceptional facts capable of acting upon your determination. In how many cases, then, can you assert that your free action will turn against all these factors, and cause you to decide contrary to logic and reason ?

There is no occasion to be astonished beyond measure at this possibility that the subject in a state of lucidity can perceive things unknown and unperceived by all persons in a normal condition. The mere fact of the hypnotic state places the subject beyond the reach of all distractions, all external influences, and concentrates his thoughts exclusively on the object of his researches and

T

vision. If you add to all this the knowledge he may have, by the same lucidity, of the character, inclinations, even the thoughts of the persons connected with the object of his clairvoyance, we can conclude that he is in an undoubtedly superior condition to judge and appreciate things with all possible correctness and to deduce with unfailing logic the consequences of all he perceives.

The Subject's Mode of Perception

Perception is gained in different ways, depending first of all on the object of the lucidity, and sometimes also on the special disposition of the subject; finally, in certain special cases, on the artificial procedure (crystal ball, shell, &c.) which may be employed to induce the manifestation of lucidity.

Most frequently the perception is referred by the subject to the ordinary action of his physical senses. Thus the subject, when describing what he perceives, usually says: "I see such and such a thing," "I perceive such a detail." If you press him a little, he will say: "Wait until I look, I cannot see very well," &c. If, in a scene, different people speak together, he will tell you: "I am listening, I do not hear very well; they make a noise which prevents me from hearing." You will find also that the subject can tell a man's voice from a woman's voice: he distinguishes different inflexions of voice: you will see him sometimes give a start at an unexpected sound.

It is, however, certain that the senses of the subject are not impressed in a normal manner, something takes place analogous to what happens in hypnotic suggestion, when we suggest to a subject to hear voices, to listen to music, to look at a picture, to taste some food.

Let us remember that the subject then experiences all the sensations corresponding to these different senses, and, further, will present all the physiological consequences which would be produced if an external action really impressed the sense organs; these we shall witness, as we have demonstrated :[1] modifications of the eye, the secretion of tears, of saliva, &c.

We have, moreover, in dreams, and particularly in lucid dreams, an example of the manner in which the subject perceives in this phenomenon of lucidity. In dreams the subject seems to act through all his senses; he sees, he hears, he feels, and yet all his impressions are the result of a simple mental perception. It is the same in the phenomenon of lucidity.

In other very singular cases, the subject does not perceive by sensory impression; he does not see and he cannot see, in spite of the efforts which he sometimes makes, the details of the facts of which he is mentally informed. But he has the perception of the impression which this fact would produce upon another person. It seems, in these instances, that what he originally experiences is the perception of an emotion of vexation, joy, disappointment, weariness or pleasure experienced by the person with whom he is *en rapport.* He then tries to discover the cause which produces this emotional impression, but he only knows it in a vague manner; he can give some indications, but he cannot define it exactly.

All this tends to demonstrate to us that lucidity is really a thought phenomenon; and, in many cases, it is for the most part a phenomenon of thought-reading or of thought-transmission.

The phenomenon of lucidity, like other psychical phenomena, as we shall see further on, helps to bring us to this deduction, that thought is not a simple transitory phenomenon as has hitherto been believed.

Thought gives birth to an image or an entity, of a nature which we cannot define, which is not entirely fanciful, but has a real and permanent existence. This is demonstrated by the fact that thought can be transmitted across space, from one mind to another; also by another fact, that thought is able to impress a photo-

[1] See the Author's *Treatise on Experimental and Therapeutic Hypnotism.*

graphic plate with the form of an image; finally, by the phenomena of force, imprints and materialisations, in all probability most frequently produced by the accumulation of an immaterial thought force, due to the power of a special faculty of a subject whom we call a medium.

CHAPTER XXII

LUCIDITY IN SPONTANEOUS SOMNAMBULISM

I GIVE here an instance of lucidity in spontaneous somnambulism. Although occurring at a somewhat distant date, this case presents all desirable guarantees of authenticity. In fact, it is recorded in judicial proceedings which have recorded and authenticated the account. The situation of the subject, who was in prison, and the special surveillance to which she was subjected, give us a sure guarantee that she could receive no knowledge of the facts except through the faculty of lucidity. The judicial documents also give us an absolute guarantee as to the date at which the subject related what she had perceived in a somnambulistic condition.

This fact, therefore, is of great importance, and it is impossible to raise any serious objection in regard to it.

We find the account in Mrs. Crowe's work, *The Night Side of Nature*.

"A circumstance fully as remarkable as any recorded, occurred at Odessa, in the year 1842. An old blind man, named Michel, had, for many years, been accustomed to get his living by seating himself every morning on a beam in one of the timber yards, with a wooden bowl at his feet, into which the passengers cast their alms. This long-continued practice had made him well known to the inhabitants, and as he was believed to have been formerly a soldier, his blindness was attributed to the numerous wounds he had received in battle. For his own part he spoke little, and never contradicted this opinion.

"One night Michel, by some accident, fell in with a little girl ten years old, named Powleska, who was friendless, and on the verge of perishing with cold and hunger. The old man took her home and adopted her, and, from that time, instead of sitting in the timber yards, he went about the streets in her company, asking alms at the doors of the houses. The child called him *father*, and they were extremely happy together. But when they had pursued this mode of life for about five years a misfortune befell them. A theft having been committed in a house which they had visited in the morning, Powleska was suspected and arrested, and the blind man was left alone once more. But instead of resuming his former habits, he now disappeared altogether, and as this circumstance caused the suspicion to extend to him, the girl was brought before the magistrate to be interrogated with regard to his probable place of concealment.

"'Do you know where Michel is?' inquired the magistrate.

"'He is dead,' replied she, shedding a torrent of tears.

"As the girl had been shut up for three days, without any means of obtaining information from without, this answer, together with her unfeigned distress, naturally excited considerable surprise.

"'Who told you he was dead?' they inquired.

"'Nobody.'

"'Then how can you know it?'

"'I saw him killed?'

"'But you have not been out of the prison.'

"'But I saw it nevertheless.'

"'But how was that possible? Explain what you mean.'

"'I cannot. All I can say is, that I saw him killed.'

"'When was he killed, and how?'

"'It was the night I was arrested.'

"'That cannot be; he was alive when you were seized.'

"'Yes, he was; he was killed an hour after that. They stabbed him with a knife.'

"'Where were you then?'

"'I can't tell, but I saw it.'

"'The confidence with which the girl asserted what

seemed to her hearers impossible and absurd, disposed
them to imagine that she was either really insane, or
pretending to be so; so leaving Michel aside, they proceeded to interrogate her about the robbery, asking her
if she was guilty.

"'Oh no,' she answered.

"'Then how came the property to be found about
you?'

"'I don't know; I saw nothing but the murder.'

"'But there are no grounds for supposing Michel is
dead; his body has not been found.'

"'It is in the aqueduct.'

"'And do you know who slew him?'

"'Yes, it is a woman. Michel was walking very slowly,
after I was taken from him. A woman came behind him
with a large kitchen-knife; but he heard her, and turned
round; and then the woman flung a piece of grey stuff
over his head, and struck him repeatedly with the knife;
the grey stuff was much stained with the blood. Michel
fell at the eighth blow, and the woman dragged the body
to the aqueduct and let it fall in without ever lifting the
stuff which stuck to his face.'

"As it was easy to verify these latter assertions, they
despatched people to the spot; and there the body was
found with the piece of stuff over his head, exactly as she
had described. But when they asked her how she knew
all this, she could only answer, 'I don't know.'

"'But you know who killed him?'

"'Not exactly; it is the same woman that put out his
eyes; but perhaps he will tell me her name to-night; and
if he does, I will tell it to you.'

"'Whom do you mean by *he?*'

"'Why, Michel, to be sure!'

"During the whole of the following night, without
allowing her to suspect their intention, they watched her;
and it was observed that she never lay down, but sat upon
the bed in a sort of lethargic slumber. Her body was
quite motionless, except at intervals, when this repose was
interrupted by violent nervous shocks, which pervaded

her whole frame. On the ensuing day, the moment she was brought before the judge, she declared that she was now able to tell them the name of the assassin.

"'But stay,' said the magistrate; 'did Michel never tell you, when he was alive, how he lost his sight?'

"'No; but the morning before I was arrested, he promised me to do so; and that was the cause of his death.'

"'How could that be?'

"'Last night Michel came to me, and he pointed to the man hidden behind the scaffolding on which he and I had been sitting. He showed me the man listening to us, when he said, 'I'll tell you all about that to-night;' and then the man——'

"'Do you know the name of this man?'

"'It is *Luck;* he went afterwards to a broad street that leads down to the harbour, and he entered the third house on the right——'

"'What is the name of the street?'

"'I don't know; but the house is one story lower than the adjoining ones. Luck told Catherine what he had heard, and she proposed to him to assassinate Michel; but he refused, saying, 'It is bad enough to have burnt out his eyes fifteen years before whilst he was asleep at your door, and to have kidnapped him into the country.' Then I went in to ask charity, and Catherine put a piece of plate into my pocket, that I might be arrested; then she hid herself behind the aqueduct to wait for Michel, and she killed him.'

"'But since you say all this, why did you keep the plate? Why didn't you warn Michel?'

"'But I didn't see it then. Michel showed it to me last night.'

"'But what should induce Catherine to do this?'

"'Michel was her husband, and she had forsaken him to come to Odessa and marry again. One night, fifteen years ago, she saw Michel, who had come to seek her. She slipped hastily into her house, and Michel, who thought she had not seen him, lay down at her door to watch; but he fell asleep, and then Luck burnt out his eyes, and carried him to a distance.'

"'And is it Michel who has told you this?'

"'Yes; he came, very pale and covered with blood; and he took me by the hand and showed me all this with his fingers.'

"Upon this, Luck and Catherine were arrested; and it was ascertained that she had actually been married to Michel in the year 1819, at Kherson. They at first denied the accusation, but Powleska insisted, and they subsequently confessed the crime. When they communicated the circumstances of the confession to Powleska, she said: 'I was told it last night.'

"This affair naturally excited great interest, and people all round the neighbourhood hastened into the city to learn the sentence."

"Who shall venture to assert," says Dr. Ennemoser, "that this communing with the dead in sleep is merely a subjective phenomenon, and that the presence of these apparitions is a pure illusion?"

I wish to remark that I place this fact in the category of phenomena of lucidity, because it clearly indicates that the subject has this mental perception, in a special condition: a phenomenon which, as a whole, we designate under the name of lucidity; but I do not wish to prejudge in any way the origin of this perception or the manner in which it is produced, which, moreover, may very probably not be the same in all cases.

CHAPTER XXIII

LUCIDITY IN A STATE OF LIGHT SOMNAMBULISM ARTIFICIALLY INDUCED

WE have now to examine a succession of phenomena of lucidity observed in persons who make a profession of this faculty. We shall see that these facts in which are mingled lucidity in the present, past, and future, are remarkable for their correctness.

These facts come within the category which we have described under the title of lucidity in a state of somnambulism induced by artificial means. We believe, in fact, that the looking at the hand, the observation of coffee grounds, and all such similar proceedings, are simply means that the subject usually employs which result, as their principal effect, in placing him in a special condition whereby the faculty of lucidity is manifested.

The account of the first case was drawn up by Dr. Liébeault, and quoted in Dr. Gyel's work. The authority of Dr. Liébeault lends every guarantee of authenticity to the facts which he relates.

Observations of Dr. Liébeault

M. S. de Ch—— came to consult me this afternoon at four o'clock on account of a nervous condition, which was, however, in no way serious. M. de Ch—— was greatly preoccupied in mind with reference to a pending lawsuit, and also with regard to the following events. On December 26, 1879, he was walking along one of the streets in Paris, when he saw written over a door " Mme. Lenormand, Necromancer." Led by curiosity he went into the house, and was taken into a dimly lighted room. He waited there for Mme. Lenormand, who came almost immediately and asked him to sit down at a table. This lady then went out, came back, seated herself opposite to him, looked into the palm of one of his hands and said: "You will lose your father within a year from to-day. You will become a soldier at once (he was then nineteen years of age), but you will not be a soldier for long. You will marry young, two children will be born to you, and you will die when you are twenty-six." This astounding prophecy which M. de Ch—— told to some of his friends and relations he did not first regard as serious; but his father died on December 27, 1880, after a short illness, just a year after the interview with the palmist; and this event somewhat cooled his incredulity. And when he became a soldier for seven months only, married shortly afterwards, became the father of two children, and was then just on the point of reaching his twenty-sixth year, he became distracted with fear, and thought that he had but a few days to live. It was then that he came to me. On the same and the following days, I tried to put M. de Ch—— into a deep sleep, in order to dispel the dark obsession engraven on his mind—that of his approaching death, which he imagined would occur on February 4th, the anniversary of his birth, although Mme. Lenormand had not stated the exact date.

I could not put this young man into even the slightest sleep, owing to his great agitation.

However, as it was necessary to take away the conviction that he was about to die, a dangerous one (because often convictions of this character are accomplished to the letter through auto-suggestion), I changed my plan and proposed to consult one of my somnambulists, an old man of seventy years of age known as the prophet, because on being put to sleep by me he had accurately foretold the precise date when he would be cured of articular rheumatism of four years' standing, and even the very time when his daughter would be cured, this last cure being due to the assertion impressed upon her by her father, that she would recover her health at a given time. M. de Ch—— at once agreed to my proposition and kept the appointment which I made with him. On entering into rapport with this somnambulist his first words were, " When shall I die ? "

The experienced sleeper, suspecting this young man's trouble, replied, after making him wait awhile—

" You will die in forty-one years from now."

The effect of these words was marvellous. The consultant immediately became merry, open-hearted, and full of hope, and when February 4th had passed, the day which he so greatly feared, he believed himself safe.

I did not think anything more of this until at the beginning of October I received a funeral card, informing me that my unfortunate client had passed away on September 30, 1885, in his twenty-seventh year, that is to say, at the age of twenty-six, as Mme. Lenormand had predicted.

The following case, which is of the same character, is taken from the *Annales des Sciences Psychiques :*—

" The following strange but veridical facts were related to me by Mme. B. during the winter of 1869 ; she lived at La Bouille, a small village on the banks of the Seine, near Rouen. At this time Mme. B. was twenty-three years of age, was still unmarried, and lived with her family in a house on the quay at La Bouille.

" One day when they were having atrocious weather with torrents of rain and snow, an old lady, soaking wet, came and asked for hospitality. She had come by boat from Rouen to La Bouille, and wanted to take the coach to the top of the hill in a few hours. While waiting the old lady said that she was going in the direction of Havre, that she was a cartomante, and asked Mme. B.'s mother if she would like her to predict her daughter's future. Both accepted with pleasure. Then the cartomante (who was also a clairvoyante) looked long into the hand of the young girl, and asked the mother for some coffee grounds, which she arranged in a certain way. Having looked carefully into these grounds, and concluded her observations, she made the following predictions to the young girl, which were fulfilled to the very letter.

" First of all she said to her :

" ' At the present moment you are in love with a young man who lives far from here, you expect him to-day, and this is the place reserved for him.' She pointed out the place at the table on which eight covers were laid, and there was nothing to mark this place more than any other. 'This young man will not come—his father has locked him in; he escaped through the window at the risk of breaking his neck, and his father, an arbitrary and violent man, overtook him, and has forbidden him, under very great threats, ever to see you again. He will marry later and be very unhappy.'

" Some time afterwards, through a friend of this young man, the family learned that all that the cartomante had said was true, and it was exactly as she had related. The young man never came again, and on the urgent instance of his father married a rich young woman with whom he lived very unhappily, and finally they were separated.

" But strangest of all was the prediction which followed.

" ' As to the future,' continued the cartomante, ' you will shortly leave La Bouille, then in the place to which you will go, not far from Blois, you will meet a young man who will ask you to marry him ; but as he is much younger than you, several persons will oppose this marriage. This young man will draw a bad number in the conscription, but he will not serve, as he will be discharged. You will be very happy with this young man, but he will die young.'

" The whole of this prediction was realised to the letter. Mme. B., then Mlle. M., went to live in the neighbourhood of Blois; she one day met M. B., who was seven years younger than herself; he asked her to marry him, and in spite of the opposition of the two families, who pointed out the great difference in their ages, they were married.

" The following year M. B., who was then only twenty-one years of age, drew number four, one of the worst numbers in the conscription, but he was discharged and did not serve as a soldier. Twelve years afterwards he died of consumption at the age of thirty-three. As will be seen, the whole prediction came true point by point. Perhaps the cartomante even saw that the young man would die of consumption, but, seeing that the future of the two was inevitably fixed, did not wish to pain the young woman.

"We can, perhaps, suppose that, struck by this prediction, the young girl had been caused by suggestion to accomplish this predicted destiny ; but this hypothesis, which certain sceptics would advance, is destroyed by the fact that M. B. and Mlle. M. were greatly struck by each other, and fell in love at first sight. Both of them, then poor, had to overcome the strenuous opposition of both their families, and married in spite of everything. Mme. B. was very happy in her married life, but we can understand her fears and her sorrow when the doctors told her that her husband was consumptive. Fortunately for his peace of mind, his wife had never uttered one word as to these predictions."

Here, finally, is a case which is even more interesting than the preceding ones, because the lucid subject gave many more details, which were all verified. One important fact which will not fail to be noticed is that certain details were so completely opposed to the ideas of the persons who were in the company of the lucid subject, that, while testifying to the absolute correctness of other points, they could not help believing for a long time that the subject had made a mistake in regard to the particulars in question. The accuracy of these details, however, was demonstrated later by a judicial inquiry, which remains as undeniable proof of their authenticity.

M. L. D. Ervieux has related in the *Annales des Sciences Psychiques* the following case of extraordinary clairvoyance :—

"Some may still remember the form of the old block of buildings which stood between the Rue Washington and the Rue Bel-Respiro, in the Champs-Élysées in Paris. Instead of the immense building lighted by electricity, there were then two houses; the one was partially destroyed by fire and was abandoned by the tenants and owners ; the other stood back from the road, across a courtyard, separated from the street by railings. It was always let to temporary residents. All the suites of rooms were furnished, the rents were very high, and they could only be taken by rich people.

"In the autumn of 1883 Lady A. had taken the entresol and first-floor in this house. Her family was large, and she kept several servants. Although she had several carriages and coachmen, it very rarely happened that all the members of the family were absent at the same time.

"However, one day in September or October, 1883 (the exact date can be ascertained at the police office in Rue Berryer), the house was left solely in the charge of the servants for half-an-hour.

"On that day I dined with Lady A. Everything when I arrived was in its normal state—at least it appeared to be so—and it was the same when I left between eleven o'clock and midnight.

"Lady A., in spite of her great fortune, was a methodical woman, and very active, only allowing herself a few hours of sleep. Every evening, when her guests had left, she made up her accounts.

"Her astonishment and consternation were great when she found that evening that the sum of 3500 or 3600 francs was missing from the inner pocket of an immense travelling-bag, in which she was in the habit of keeping her jewels and money.

"The lock, however, had not been forced; only the edge of the bag seemed to have been somewhat separated. Yet Lady A. was certain that about two o'clock in the afternoon, in the presence of her maid, she had opened her bag, paid a bill, and put back the money in the usual place. In her trouble she did what every one else would doubtless have done in similar circumstances, she rang for her maid, who did not know anything of the matter, but who had time to tell the servants of the theft that had been committed. So that the thief or thieves, if they were among the servants, could put the stolen money in a place of safety.

"On the morning of the following day the police, who had been informed of the matter, came to Lady A.'s house. They examined the family and servants, the cupboards, the shelves, all the furniture, in fact.

"Naturally they found nothing.

"The superintendent, having concluded his fruitless search, conversed for a moment with Lady A. He asked her what were her impressions as to the manner in which the theft had been carried out, which of her servants were least trustworthy, in order that he might, with more certainty, carry out his investigations.

"Lady A., in enumerating her servants, asked the superintendent to exclude from his suspicions the second valet, a young man of nineteen or twenty years of age, of good appearance, very respectful, well used to her service, who had earned the nickname of 'Le Petit,' not on account of his stature, for he was rather tall, but from a sentiment of kindly familiarity resulting from his good qualities. As to the butler and the lady's-maid—more particularly attached to the personal service of Lady A. than any of the others —the mistress abandoned them to the worst suspicions of the police. It was decided, nevertheless, acting on the advice of the superintendent, that Lady A., in spite of her desire to send them away at once, should keep those two servants at least a fortnight longer, in order to make it easier for the detectives to follow their movements.

"The morning was almost entirely spent in these formalities without any result, when, about eleven o'clock, Lady A. sent her youngest daughter's governess to my house to tell me what had happened, and to ask me to accompany this lady to a clairvoyante whose gift of lucidity I had some days previously alluded to.

"I did not myself know this clairvoyante, but a female relative had told me of a consultation she had had with her, when she greatly astonished her with a prediction of the future.

"I did not even know where this prodigy lived, so

I went first of all with Mlle. C. to find out her address in order that we might go there immediately.

"Her house was behind the church of Our Lady of Loretto. Her staircase was in the courtyard, and a small placard indicated the floor on which she lived.

"The interior was more than modest. She herself opened the door. She showed us into a green drawing-room, like that of any small dentist, except for a magnificent engraving after Raphael, 'God Dispersing Chaos,' and a painting referring to some legend of the Kabbala.

"As there were two of us she wished to separate us; but we made her understand that as we were both on the same errand we only wished for one consultation. She may have taken us for relatives; she only asked us if the thing about which we came concerned one of us more than the other.

"I indicated Mlle. C. She, of course, living with Lady A., was most concerned with the theft.

"Mme. E., our clairvoyante, brought a bowl filled with coffee grounds and asked Mlle. C. to blow upon it three times, after which the grounds were turned into another bowl, the first being placed over the second in order that the contents might partly pass into the new vessel, the first bowl only retaining on the inside some more or less solid particles of the powdered coffee, which formed, when free from the liquid, certain strange designs which had no significance for us, but in which the pythoness seemed to read,

"During this occult preparation, in order to occupy us. Mme. E. had spread out her cards and commenced.

"'Ah! but it is a theft, and a theft committed by some one in the house, and not by some one coming in surreptitiously, &c.'

"This promised well. We admitted that this statement was true. As to the thief, he unfortunately was unknown to us.

"'Wait,' Mme. E. said to us, 'I want now to see the details in the coffee grounds, which must have settled.'

"She took hold of the upturned bowl, into which Mlle. C. again blew three times, and then took her eyeglass.

U

"Then, as though she had been present on the spot, she described to us Lady A.'s house, bit by bit, without being mistaken as to a bedroom or a drawing-room. She saw pass before her, as in a magic-lantern, seven servants, whose sex and duty she told us exactly. Then going again into Lady A.'s room she saw a wardrobe which seemed to her very strange.

"'It has,' she declared to us with astonishment, 'a cupboard in the centre with a glass door, and on each side of this main cupboard there are two others without glass, and all this is . . . Oh! why is this cupboard never closed? And yet it always has money in it, which is . . . in . . . what a strange thing! . . . it opens like a purse, in the form of a pouch . . . not like a trunk. . . . Ah! I have it! . . . it is a travelling-bag . . . what an idea to put money there! and particularly how imprudent to leave this cupboard open!'

"'The thieves know the bag well . . . they did not force the lock. They brought a large tool in order to press apart the two sides, then with the aid of a chisel or pliers they took out the money, which was in bank-notes. . . . They contented themselves with that, because they did not know that at the bottom there were some very fine jewels and a sum in gold. Still, how clever they were!'

"We had let her talk. All that this woman had said astonished us in the accuracy of its details, even the smallest.

"With the exception of this last revelation concerning the jewels and the sum of money, of which we knew nothing, but which might have been in the place indicated by the clairvoyante, all was correct. She was fatigued and stopped. We were desirous of knowing more.

"We asked her, we beseeched her, to tell us which of the servants had committed the theft, since she had told us that it was one of them.

"She declared that it was impossible to tell without

placing herself within the reach of the French law, which would not allow a thief to be recognised as such without proofs, simply by the employment of occult means.

"Upon being pressed, however, she assured us that Lady A.'s money would never be recovered: this was very probable, since the theft would never be brought home to the thief, and then, what was more astonishing, she said that two years later he would 'suffer capital punishment.'

"After several futile attempts, it was clear that we could not draw anything further from Mme. E.

"We therefore went away, regretting that among all these perfectly correct statements one slight error should have crept in.

"Every time that she looked in the coffee grounds she had said that she had seen 'Le Petit' close to horses.

"We assured her that he had never served as footman, being always engaged on indoor work, and the footmen lived with the coachmen; Mme. E. stubbornly persisted in saying this. The more we contradicted her, the more she affirmed it.

"We ended by abandoning this mere trifle, which, however, displeased us as a blot in a perfect picture, because this consultation had been surprising in its accuracy.

"When we got to Lady A.'s house we opened the famous bag, and there, as Mme. E. had told us, the jewels and gold were found intact. We could hardly believe our eyes. When I told the story of the result of our consultation to Lady A., I was glad that Mlle. C. had accompanied me. I should never have attempted to quote all the details so precisely as given by the clairvoyante of the Rue Notre-Dame-de-Lorette. I only repeated them later, because there were two persons to hear them.

"At the end of a fortnight Lady A. discharged her butler and lady's-maid. 'Le Petit,' without giving reason, left Lady A.'s service three or four weeks later. The money was never recovered, and a year later Lady A. set out for Egypt. Two years after this event Lady A.

received from the Seine Court of Justice a summons to go to Paris as witness.

"The author of the theft at her house had been found. It had been ascertained that 'Le Petit' with all his good qualities was none other than Marchandon, the murderer of Mme. Cornet.

"As is known, he suffered the capital penalty, as the clairvoyante of the Rue Notre-Dame-de-Lorette had stated, and during the proceedings it was ascertained that 'Le Petit' had in the Champs-Élysées, quite close to Lady A.'s residence, a brother who was a coachman in a large house.

"'Le Petit'—or Marchandon, as he really was—spent all his spare time with his brother, as he was very fond of horses. This was therefore the reason why Mme. E. had persisted, in spite of our contradictions, in saying that she continually saw "Le Petit domestique' in the presence of horses.

"She had again seen true in this small detail which was revealed in the course of the trial."

CHAPTER XXIV

LUCIDITY IN DEEP SOMNAMBULISM

WE come now to the more demonstrative and complex phenomena of experimental lucidity: lucidity in induced somnambulism.

The cases we shall quote are furnished by various experimenters, and accompanied by verification of the reality of the facts perceived by the subjects, and by proofs of the authenticity, which ought to render them convincing.

The majority of authors who have thoroughly and earnestly studied hypnotic phenomena have, moreover, nearly always observed at certain times similar cases of lucidity.

"I have seen repeated in my presence," says Dr. Azam in *Hypnotisme et double conscience*, "the strange things related of spontaneous somnambulism. I have seen very accurate writing done with a thick book interposed between the face and the paper; I have seen a very fine needle threaded in the same position, the subject walking about a room with the eyes tightly closed and bandaged; all without any other real guide than the resistance of the air, and perfect precision of movement, guided by the hyperesthetic muscular sense."

As an example of vision without the help of the eyes, I will first record the following experiment of Dr. Gibier, related in his work *Analyses des choses*. (The subject was hypnotised, and a cotton pad placed on each eye covered by a large thick napkin tied behind the head.) "I took from my bookcase the first book which came to hand, opened it at random above the subject's head, held the printed text within an inch of the hair of the young

woman who was hypno-magnetised, and commanded her
to read the first line of the page to her left. After a
moment's pause, she said: 'Ah, yes, I see—wait.' Then
she continued: 'Identity again leads to unity, because if
the mind . . .' I turned the book over and found that
the first line, less two words, had been correctly seen and
read. If I caused a third person to write a word, or some
name, on the floor, with a piece of chalk taken from an
adjoining room, the same young woman, with her eyes
bandaged, would read the word written, without any
mistake, as soon as she had her feet on it. She was led
backwards on to the written word, and she had her head
stretched forward somewhat, which enabled those present
to testify that it was impossible for her, even if she had
been awake, to see under the bandage."

M. Jules Cacheu has published in the *Annales des
Sciences Psychiques* the following account by Mme.
Testand, of incidents which occurred in her presence:—

"At that time when much attention was paid by the
public to magnetism, table-turning, and occult sciences,
M. Cuisinier de Lisle thought of trying his own magnetic
power on a young servant, Theresa, about eighteen years
of age, then in his employ, who was quite willing to
serve as the subject of his attempt. The experiment was
wonderfully successful.

"M. de Lisle went to work in the following manner:

"Sitting in front of Theresa, he grasped her two
thumbs firmly in each of his hands and gazed fixedly at
her. The young girl went off to sleep, closing her eyes
tightly, but a little time elapsed before she had a clear
vision and could reply to questions put to her. 'Can
you see?' asked the operator. 'Not' yet.' A little later
she said, 'Yes, I begin to see.' At last she said, 'Now
I can see very well.'

"Then in spite of the fact that all the doors and
windows of the room were closed, she told the names of
all the people who came into or went out of the house.
'Here is M. —— coming in; there is Mme. —— going out.'

"One day, being in a magnetic sleep with her eyes closed, the servant Antonio, also in M. de Lisle's employ, came quietly behind her and 'made a face' at her; she immediately turned round and did the same at him, to the great astonishment of the spectators, who could not understand or imagine that she had eyes in her back, or that she could see behind her.

"Most of the time it was not even necessary for M. de Lisle to give her verbal orders: he had only to think of what he wished her to do, and she immediately carried out all that was in his thoughts. Thus, when the young girl was in the kitchen and M. de Lisle at table in the dining-room, she would suddenly come in with a plate in her hand, because her master, without speaking a word, had willed that she should bring him one.

"Every morning, about four or five o'clock, M. de Lisle would go out to his duty on his ship, anchored about a mile and a half from the shore, and would leave about ten o'clock to go home to Castignan for lunch. The young woman would announce the time of his arrival to within a minute. She would say to Mme. de Lisle: 'Madame, it is time to lay the cloth for lunch, I see Monsieur coming down the ship's ladder; he is getting into his boat, he will be here in twenty minutes.' This never failed to happen as she had said.

"But the following is the most extraordinary and remarkable fact, which happened in the presence of Mme. Testand-Marchain, who can absolutely affirm the truth of it, as of all that has been related.

"M. de Lisle had as lodger in his house, merely out of charity and without any payment, a former schoolmaster named Lorgeril, then employed at the Toulon arsenal. One day this Lorgeril thought of marrying a person living in the town of Hyères, four or five leagues from Toulon, and asked permission to go and pay his addresses to her, and, if successful, to arrange the terms of marriage.

"After he had gone, M. de Lisle thought of finding out through his servant Theresa, by putting her to sleep, what Lorgeril did during his journey, and how his matri-

monial projects turned out. He therefore put Theresa
to sleep.

"We must say at this point that if M. de Lisle knew
the town of Hyères he was totally unaware in which street
and house Lorgeril's *fiancée* lived, and as for Theresa, she
did not know the town or even the way to get there.

"When she was asleep and in a state of vision he said
to her, 'I want you to go to Hyères.'"

"She replied, 'But, sir, how can I? I do not even
know the way.'

"'I wish you to go there, try. Have you found it?'

"'Yes, sir.'

"'Well, walk.'

"'I am walking; but it is a long way, a very long way,
and I am not nearly there.'

"'Are you there?'

"'Yes, sir, I have arrived. I see a place where there
are many palm-trees.'

"'Very good. Now look for the house where
Lorgeril is.'

"'Ah, sir, I do not know where it is.'

"'Look for it.'

"'Yes, sir, here is the street. How steep it is; what a
hill to climb!'

"'Are you there?'

"'Yes, sir, I am at the door of the house, but I dare
not go in.'

"'I wish you to go in, enter!'

"'Ah, sir, there are a lot of stairs before coming to the
room.'

"'Are you there?'

"'Yes, sir.'

"'Ah, well! Now knock, so that they may open to
you.'

"At this time she was close to the mantelpiece. She
made a motion as though knocking, but her hand stopped
just before reaching the marble, without touching it.

"'Have you entered?'

"'Yes, sir. I see Lorgeril very well and the person

in question, they are together; but they do not seem to
be coming to an understanding, and I do not think the
marriage will take place."

"Just at this moment M. de Lisle, without saying
a word to the clairvoyant, formulated, only in his head,
this somewhat indiscreet thought, 'Will he stay at the
house all night?' 'Oh no, sir, quite sure, certainly not,'
she replied immediately.

"'What do you see in the room?'

"'I see them getting up from the table; they have
finished eating.'

"'What have they eaten?'

"'I do not know, sir, the table is cleared.'

"'That does not matter, look carefully; there must be
something left on the plates.'

"'They have eaten some ragout of lamb, also some
orange salad.'

"'I also see on the mantelpiece of the room three
oranges which Lorgeril has bought, and which he will
bring to Toulon to-morrow to give to your three children.
Lorgeril will leave there to-morrow, and will reach here
at four o'clock in the afternoon.'

"'It is not likely,' said M. de Lisle to the clairvoyant,
'that if Lorgeril is to reach here to-morrow it should be
at four o'clock in the afternoon, because he has work in
the port, and in order to go to his work he would have
to arrive here in the morning.'

"'No, sir, no; I tell you that he will get here at four
o'clock to-morrow afternoon.'

"The following day, as the young woman had predicted,
as four o'clock struck Lorgeril returned. M. de Lisle, who
was waiting for him, said to him as he entered the garden:

"'Well, my poor Lorgeril, so your love affair has
turned out badly. That is a pity; you were, however,
well looked after—ragout of lamb, orange salad . . .'

"Lorgeril opened his eyes wide in astonishment. 'Sir,
sir—how, how . . .'

"Finally, M. de Lisle raised his wonderment to the
highest pitch by saying to him, "Come, Lorgeril, put

your hand in your pocket and give me those three oranges you have bought for the children.'

"Lorgeril then threw the three oranges on the sandy path of the garden, fled precipitately to his own room, quite frightened, saying, 'Ah, Monsieur de Lisle, you have dealings with the devil.'"

We now come to a case of lucidity, immediately verified by means of the telephone. This method of verification, when it is possible, is absolutely irrefutable; it leaves no room, in fact, for any mistake of memory; nor can the objection be raised that the subject could have obtained any knowledge of the facts described between the time of their occurrence and that of the experiment, seeing that the subject can be made to describe the facts at the time they occur and can be kept in sight while they are being verified.

This experiment is related in the *Annales des Sciences Psychiques.*

CASE OF LUCIDITY

Controlled by Telephone

In 1892, at the beginning of the winter, I was at the house of a manufacturer whom I will call M. A., and who then lived on the Quai de la Tournelle at Paris. M. A. did not believe in the lucidity of somnambulists, whom he generally described as "humbugs," without having, however, ever taken the pains to study them, even superficially. That day, in consequence of a conversation at which I had not been present, two young men, known to M. A., brought into his office a woman of twenty or twenty-five years of age, the mistress of one of their friends, a pharmaceutical student, from whom they had concealed this freak.

This woman, whose name I do not remember having heard, had a rather insignificant face, an appearance of regular rather than robust health, with a rather tired look, and common, unintelligent features. She had no society habits, and seemed at once confused and vain of the attention which was paid her—in short, an ignorant peasant and, apparently, anything but cunning. She did not seem hysterical, and I did not hear she was subject to any nervous trouble.

The two young men who had brought her explained that they wanted her to give a proof of lucidity; but no experiment had been prepared, and, moreover, M. A. was ignorant that she was coming that day, because the somnambulist had been obliged to wait until her lover was absent before leaving her room.

After taking off her cloak, she sat down and asked for a glass of water, which she drank in one draught; then gazing at the gas lamp which was burning in front of her, on the table, she went to sleep in a few moments. Then she asked—and her speech was somewhat indistinct at first—that we would put in her hands an object belonging to the person it was desired to follow. M. A. gave her a letter written by one M. L.; the somnambulist felt it carefully, smelt it several times and said, "Yes, this is from a gentleman who often comes here; he has an office in this neighbourhood, but he does not live there. I do not know where he lives. He is very tall, he wears an official decoration, he is careful of his appearance, and when no one is looking at him he arranges his beard with a small comb which he always carries in his pocket. And then he dyes his hair and beard. He looks about forty years of age, but he is fifty at least."

The first part of this vision tallied exactly with what we all knew of M. L., but the revelation of his finical ways seemed so slightly in harmony with the sober character of the man that we could not help making energetic gestures of dissent, to which M. A., who knew M. L. much better than ourselves, replied by making us a sign that the somnambulist was right. He then asked what M. L. had done during the day; she followed him in his rounds among contractors, public offices, &c., and it was possible, on the following day, to corroborate a part of these assertions, which were admitted to be correct, in spite of the silence of M. L., who was greatly offended with this "foolish joking."

After a few minutes' rest, the somnambulist being still asleep, M. A. gave her a letter from one of his correspondents, M. Mousson, of whom the somnambulist gave an exact description.

"Where does this gentleman live?" M. A. asked.

"That is rather difficult. I see clearly that it is in Paris, in a place where there are many people and many carriages, but you ought to help me a little."

"Look in the neighbourhood of the Bourse."

"Ah! I am there. It is Place de la Bourse, at such a number, on such a floor."

This was correct.

"What is this gentleman doing at this moment?"

"He is writing a letter. I think it is in English, because it is going to London."

"What does he say in this letter. Read it."

"He is explaining why there has been a delay with a commission that has been given him, but that it is not his fault, and he will send the desired reply the day after to-morrow."

Thereupon M. A. went out of his office into an adjoining room, where there was a telephone, and asked to be put into communication with M. Mousson; it was impossible to hear in one room what was said in the other.

During this time the somnambulist continued: "Now he is reading over his letter; he gets up and takes a book which he moistens (a letter copying book) while speaking to a little boy who has come into the room. . . . Ah! he has stopped! . . . Hallo! he is talking into a little box which is on the table (the telephone transmitter). Oh! but what is the matter? he looks quite astonished, poor man. It seems as though something unfortunate has happened to him."

(At this moment M. A. was telephoning to M. Mousson: "You have just written a letter in English to London asking them to excuse you for an involuntary delay. Is that true?" "Yes, but how do you know?" "It is a somnambulistic experiment; I will explain it to you. Now have the kindness to do exactly what I tell you.")

"Ah!" resumed the clairvoyant, "now he looks a little more relieved. He listens in a little round thing which he holds to his ear (the receiver). . . . But what is he doing? What a funny machine. Now he has finished his conversation; he hangs the little round thing on the box. But he still seems much perplexed."

(At this moment M. A. came back into his office.)

"He has taken his hat, he is going out: he comes back and takes some papers from the table: he goes out and locks the door: he is going down the staircase: he has stopped on the landing: he seems absorbed in thought: he continues to descend: he is outside: he has stopped again and is looking at his papers. He seems as if he did not know what to do. . . . He turns to the left: no, he comes back to the right: he goes down the street on the right (the Rue Vivienne): he goes almost to the edge of the pavement (at the corner of the Rue Feydeau): he stops again: he looks all round him: he has come back: he goes up the stairs and back into his rooms."

All that the somnambulist had said was the exact description of the actions accomplished by M. Mousson, according to the somewhat complicated instructions as M. A. had transmitted to him by telephone.

In this moment the séance was almost void, or, at least, without interest, the somnambulist being fatigued and the spectators overwhelming her with questions without method or patience. Shortly, the young woman evinced a desire to awaken; one of the number breathed on her eyes; she drank two more glasses of water and left. Since then I have never heard of her, and I did not know who she was.

Added to this is an attestation by M. Côte, engineer, who was present at the experiment at M. A.'s house. I have lost sight of the latter, and I do not think that his evidence could be of great use, because of his unscientific and even less methodical mind. M. L. would never confess that the somnambulist was right in saying that he dyed his hair; moreover, he is a staunch Catholic, who could only see the action of the devil in these phenomena.

The two young men who accompanied the somnambulist are pleasant, gay fellows, who must long ago have lost all recollection of this séance, and I should not know, moreover, where to find them. With regard to M. Mousson, who has been good enough to authorise me to publish his name, I have submitted the present account to him, as well as to M. Côte. He admitted it to be correct, as did also a lady who was in his office at the time of the experiment; he even promised me to write out a separate account, but in spite of several letters and fruitless visits, I have not been able to obtain any reply from him; whether it be that his numerous engagements have prevented him from carrying out his promise, or whether M. L., to whom he must have spoken of it, has dissuaded him, which is perhaps more probable.

PHENOMENA OF LUCIDITY OBSERVED BY M. LÉOPOLD DAUVIL IN THE HYPNOTIC EXPERIMENTS PUBLISHED BY HIM.[1]

At an evening party given by the English Consul, one Saturday in October 1884, I found all the distinguished society of Saint-Denis assembled, and if this book is read by some West Indians who were present at this gathering, they will see that I have reported the facts in all their true simplicity.

Among the numerous subjects (forty-two), which I had hypnotised, I chose four of the best, those from whom Colonel de Rochas, to whom I had related the facts, could have asked all that hypnosis has produced in the way of degrees, from calm, inert, unintelligent sleep, up to the externalisation of sensibility in all its forms, and even to the separation of body and spirit, as will be proved by the notes which I have copied exactly.

These four subjects were M.M. Cossé et Drau, naval writers; Mlle. Loubelle, now the wife of a general; and M. Radigné, naval officer, of great intelligence and know-

[1] *Écho du Merveilleux*, 1908.

ledge. We were at the house of Consul and Lady St. John, in the midst of over a hundred spectators, among whom were M. Beaucastel, head physician, and all his medical staff.

I sent Cossé to sleep, and produced on him the whole range of Charcot's experiments. Dr. Beaucastel asked me to produce catalepsy, which was done without difficulty. Then I obtained a quiet awakening, which I had never done before. "My friend," I said to the subject, "I want you to return to consciousness." I then made him stand up, by means of a few passes extending from the head to the feet. "Now, tell us yourself what I ought to do to awaken you calmly and take away all fatigue from your body."

Cossé took my left hand, passed it over his head, from the occiput to the base of the cerebellum, then over all the circumvolutions, after which, turning half-way round, he added, as he had never done before, knowing probably nothing of medicine or anatomy: "Ask one of the doctors to put his finger between the fourth and fifth vertebræ, and at that place you will project a jet of fluid."

I did this and Cossé opened his eyes smiling, and showing by the movements of his back, neck, and head that he had an evident feeling of comfort.

The Consul's wife asked, "Can you request this gentleman to go to a distance, to London or Berlin or Paris, and describe something that he sees there?"

"We will try, Madame."

In order to put these four subjects to sleep I simply looked at them and put a finger on their forehead; they were hypnotised, their eyes remained opened but fixed and haggard, the body limp, the spirit free. Cossé being asleep and seated in an arm-chair, a lady asked him if he knew Bordeaux.

"No."

"Can you go there?"

"Yes."

The doctor continued questions, for I left the subject completely independent.

"My friend," he said to him, "we are getting out at Bordeaux station. Can you see it?"

"Yes, it is a fine new station."

"Right. It is the Gare Saint-Jean; you can see it clearly?"

"Quite."

"We have come to the platform,"

"I am there; I see a splendid bridge."

"We are on the Cours de l'Intendance."

"I am there."

I then asked to take my subject again.

"You say you see what the doctor asked you to see?"

"Quite well."

"Well, then, tell us what you see now."

His large eyes wide open, his body remaining motionless, Cossé seemed to look to right and left, as into space.

"I see," he said, "some beautiful houses, to the left a large café, some marble tables, plenty of people sitting down, customers, doubtless, and musicians. Oh! what beautiful lamps, what brilliant light, like moons" (doubtless the Jablochkoff lamps).

"And to the right, behind you, what do you see?"

"A large monumental building all lighted up."

"Yes, it is the Grand Theatre."

And the subject gave an exact description of it, with its portico raised on six or eight steps, and its lines of gas-jets.

"All that does not surprise me," said a young doctor; "the subject is reading in the brain of the magnetiser."

"As he read in mine then," said the head doctor, "and you venture to say it does not surprise you? to me it is marvellous, sir."

"But," said a pharmacist, M. Cornuel, "we can secure a proof of the subject's independence of mind. Did he not say that the Bordeaux theatre is lighted up?"

"Yes," said Cossé, still asleep; "yes, at this moment many people are going up the steps."

"Well," continued the young pharmacist, "tell us what piece is being played and we shall be convinced."

Then a strange thing happened; the subject rose

abruptly, came from the arm-chair, crossed the drawing-room, made as though he was climbing up some steps, raising one leg after the other, and stooping down towards a picture.

"What are you looking at?" I asked him.

"A placard."

"What placard?"

"The one which is in this frame, under this wire-work."

"Then tell us what you see."

"A yellow placard. Wait."

And 3000 leagues from the Bordeaux theatre this young man read in the midst of perfect silence: "Grand Theatre, Bordeaux, this evening, Saturday, October 20th (or 24th), 1884, first performance of 'Aïda,' music by Verdi."

Certainly, that was not impressed on the brain of any of those present. But the marvel was confirmed when, fifteen days afterwards, on the arrival of a mail-boat from France, one of the doctors, who was from Bordeaux, opened the *Journal de la Gironde*, which he had received, and we noticed that, on the date of the English Consul's party, Verdi's "Aïda" was performed at the Bordeaux theatre.

I leave readers to make their own reflections on this subject. For my part I am content to affirm the fact, which appears marvellous to me every time I recall it.

My second subject was Mlle. Louise Loubelle, a tall and beautiful young girl, fair, with sea-green eyes, thought-ful brow, rather taciturn, of nervous temperament, im-pressionable, perhaps slightly inclined to hysteria, but showing no sign of it during the four months that I had hypnotised her. She magnetised herself by the Braid system with her ring, after a lady's diamond ear-ring had one evening put her in a hypnotic condition.

I shall mention in connection with her an instance of great magnetic flight which occurred in the house of Colonel Morsali, the chief of the gendarmerie, at one of his charming private gatherings.

Mlle. Louise, being in a sleeping condition, with her

x

eyes very wide open and staring, Mme. Ledin, wife of a general commissioner, asked if the subject could go to her home at Albi and bring news of her father.

Mlle. Loubelle, who had never left the shores of her distant island, replied, "With pleasure," and whether by her own thoughts or by the brain of the questioner, she saw herself at Albi on a square which she described quite accurately, although it was dusk. She arrived at the house indicated, seeming to stop and look at its simple architecture, which she described, then made as though she was going up two steps, and pulled the bell handle horizontally. This gesture surprised Mme. Ledin, who had never expected this remarkable particular. Why had not the sleeper's hand pressed the button, or pulled a string, or simply knocked ? The door was undoubtedly opened to the invisible visitor, who said :

"There is a servant about fifty years of age, with a yellow silk handkerchief on her head, her hair is grey. I go in; there is a door to the left, a door to the right, a short corridor with a staircase at the end. The door to the right is half-way opened ; I see a gentleman with white hair, sitting down, and bent over a small white earthen-ware stove. Your sister, madame—it can only be your sister, because she is so much like you—is beside your father. She is fair and pretty like yourself."

"Enough ! enough !" cried Mme. Ledin, with tears in her eyes. "Thank you ! I believe. It is my father, it is my sister, with our old Bridget. I am very happy, but I do not wish to know any more."

The second part of this séance is not less interesting than the first. An officer, a native of Albi, like Mme. Ledin, and hitherto incredulous through prejudice, also wished to interrogate Mlle. Loubelle, whom I awakened in the same manner as Cossé had instructed me for himself, and which always ensured a calm return to the waking state without fatigue. I made light passes on the fore-head, the base of the skull, the vertebræ of the neck and the spine, and the subject awoke smiling, as though coming out of a pleasant dream.

After a quarter of an hour's rest I asked her to go to sleep again. She gazed at a beautiful topaz stone which she wore on her left hand, went off to sleep again, and asked Commandant Héral:

"What do you desire?"

"That you should go with me round this square (still at Albi) and tell me what you particularly notice."

"I own I do not see very clearly; however, I seem to distinguish there at the end of the square on the right, raised up a little on a high pedestal, something like the outline of a statue thrown against a dark sky, but I do not see well. Oh! that is funny; there is a man carrying some fire at the end of a long pole. He is coming to light the lamps."

This fact calls for explanation, because it is characteristic. It was then at the island of Reunion, 10.20 P.M., but the longitude east of Albi being 52° 50′ gives a difference of 3 hours 53 minutes; that is to say, that when it was 10.20 at St. Denis, it would only be about 6.27 at Albi, when it would be time, in September, to think of lighting the street lamps.

Who now, among the numerous witnesses in this tropical drawing-room, would have thought of this difference of longitude, of the sun's delay which the clairvoyant so clearly indicated? Then the gas lighted up the square at Albi, and doubtless the statue which had attracted the attention of our new Isis became more clearly visible. She went on:

"This figure seems to me to be that of an officer," she said. "Has he not his left hand on his sword? His hair is as though tied up. His costume is of the time of Louis XV. or Louis XVI. His right hand holds an open map. Is he an engineer, a sailor? But a rather high railing hides the lower part of the body, and then, between the statue and the railing, and concealing the pedestal from me, I see some curious objects like chains, small cannon."

"Bravo! bravo!" cried the Albigensian commandant; "I had quite forgotten those details; it is perfectly correct."

"And you will remember, my dear commandant," I said to him, "that never having been myself to Albi, I cannot suggest the replies to the subject."

"Well," added the commandant, "if Mademoiselle can read the name that is on the pedestal I will own myself conquered and convinced."

"Will you then read this name," I said to the clairvoyante, "if you can."

"It is very high up," she said, opening her eyes exceedingly wide. "It is long to read; there are many words written."

"The name, the name only," I said, impressing her mind.

"Wait! It is, it is—" and spelling she said, "L-a—La—R-o-u-s-e—La Rouse."

I went close to her, a thought having sprung up in my brain.

"I think," I said to her, "that some object, a chain, or a bar of the railing, prevented you from reading the whole name," and taking the young woman's head in my hand I displaced it slightly. "La Pérouse!" she cried out, in the midst of a thunder of applause from the astonished spectators.

I must add that these recollections, thanks to my old notes, were in no way effaced from my memory, when in 1896, before going with some cyclists to make a tour from Pau to Tarbes and Auch, I had a strong desire to go to Albi, and putting my wish into execution, I went over sixty miles out of my way to see for myself what I had glimpsed twelve years previously through the eyes of my subject, and I had the pleasure of recognising by a side of the square at Albi the little house of Mme. Ledin's father, and, right at the end, the statue of the celebrated navigator La Pérouse, as it had been described 3000 leagues away from France, by a young sleeping Creole.

We will relate now a series of experiments which are due to Dr. Ferroul, of Narbonne. The authority of Dr. Ferroul, the shrewdness and scientific exactitude which

he brings to bear on all his experiments, render them of
especial value.   Further, he has taken pains to have them
verified and attested by a large number of witnesses, thus
furnishing undeniable proof of authenticity.

EXPERIMENTS OF DR. FERROUL ON LUCIDITY [1]

Anna B. was born at Narbonne, and has never left
this locality ; she may now be about twenty-six years of
age.   She is an ironer, and suffers much from debility ;
her face is pleasant, but she is exceedingly pale and thin.
Three years ago Dr. Ferroul was extremely sceptical with
regard to all the phenomena recorded in the *Annales des
Sciences Psychiques.*   He was one day called to attend
Anna B., who had had a nervous attack in the street.
Solely as the result of some words uttered in an autho-
ritative tone, Anna immediately got up and returned to
her normal condition.   Dr. Ferroul then thought of trying
some hypnotic experiments with her ; he therefore had
her come to his house, and was not slow in perceiving
that she had some strange psychic faculties.

When placed in the magnetic sleep, she spontaneously
made known to him certain of his own acts which she
could not have previously been aware of, and without being
guided to these declarations.   Dr. Ferroul was therefore
led to make various progressive experiments, and I will
relate some cases I have from Dr. Ferroul himself, and
which made a great noise in the town, and could be authenticated by various witnesses.

We regret that the many engagements of Dr. Ferroul
did not leave him time to make a further series of
methodical experiments, in presence of a circle which
would have drawn up an official report of verification.
Dr. Ferroul, who is of a very active temperament and of
a positive character, has always declared that he wished
to proceed capriciously, at random, according to the
inspiration of the moment, and did not wish to read or

---

[1] From the *Annales des Sciences Psychiques.*

learn anything about previous investigation on these subjects.

Although this system may appear regrettable from the point of view of scientific analysis, and to prove the facts for distant readers, we must recognise in view of the results of investigations made by a number of experimenters, that psychical phenomena do not lend themselves well to the experimental method of physical phenomena, which invariably brings about a constraint, an obstacle, which causes the phenomenon to be abortive, or imperfectly realised.

Moreover, the temperament of the person who sets the subject to work counts for much in obtaining the phenomena. Thus Dr. Ferroul, alone, obtained with Anna the results which we will describe; other physicians who have sent Anna to sleep have only obtained with her the ordinary hypnotic phenomena, and have disturbed for some time the faculties of lucidity. There is therefore between Dr. Ferroul and Anna some psychical relation particularly favourable to the development of these strange faculties: the one as a powerful positive motive power, the other as negative agent.

Dr. Ferroul was not long in perceiving that Anna could see distant scenes, taking place at the very moment when she was in the somnambulistic condition. Then he also soon found that she could perceive facts which happened several days before. In that condition Anna was completely independent of time and space.

In the induced sleep she always spoke in a low tone; she resisted sometimes, complaining, and, if Dr. Ferroul insisted, she had nervous attacks which prevented him from going on with the experiment. Besides, she generally had the demeanour and language of a child.

1. Case of Le Boulon

This case occurred in June 1894 when Dr. Ferroul was expecting two persons who were to come by train from Boulon, a place about fifty-four miles from Narbonne.

These persons did not come, and not receiving any news explaining the cause of the delay, Dr. Ferroul went to Anna, put her in the somnambulistic state and ordered her to proceed to Le Boulon. He gave her the necessary directions, as he knew the place, but Anna had never been there.

"I am there," she said, describing it, "but I see no one."

"Go into the house."

"I am there. Ah! good gracious! What has happened! Madame is on the bed, hurt in the shoulder and the back, but she is not bleeding. There, the carriage was upset, the coachman fell on one side, but he is not hurt."

Anna then said that the doctor was dressing the hurts, and was asking for a longer bandage than the one he held in his hand, and other details. (I have read all those details in Dr. Ferroul's notebook.) Immediately afterwards Dr. Ferroul sent a telegram to Le Boulon: "Is it true that you have had a carriage accident?"

The following morning he received a letter from his friend (which I have read). This friend began by expressing astonishment that Dr. Ferroul should know of the accident; the particulars given in the letter agreed with those given by the somnambulist.

2. *Case of a Person who had Disappeared*

In June 1894 the *Dépêche de Toulouse* and the Narbonne newspapers gave particulars of a young girl who had disappeared, whom we will designate by the letter D.

She was servant to M. Fabre's father-in-law.

She was last seen by M. Fabre, a chemist at Narbonne and deputy-mayor, on Sunday, June 24th, at half-past nine in the evening. She left his house to return to her master's.

The last named returned home at ten o'clock, found the door open, and the servant's apron on the drawing-room table, but the servant had disappeared.

They searched for her until late, but in vain; on the

following day, Monday, they made further inquiries which proved useless, and being greatly disturbed they communicated with the newspapers, which gave a description of her in their issues of Tuesday morning.

On Tuesday evening M. Fabre asked Dr. Ferroul to try Anna's lucidity on the case.

Dr. Ferroul said that probably it would not be successful because there was no trace; neither he nor Anna knew the servant, but on the chance of success he tried the experiment.

Anna having been sent to sleep, Dr. Ferroul said to her:

"Go back to half-past nine on Sunday evening at M. Fabre's house in the Rue de la République; you will find there a young servant about sixteen years of age, of such and such a description.

"I see her," said Anna.

"Well, follow her and tell me what became of her."

The somnambulist declared that D. returned to the house which she described; that she went into her room and made her toilet. She described the room, and stated that in the corner there was a trunk with some dirty linen inside which smelt.

She spoke of an individual who came and had some conversation with D., persuaded her to go downstairs, and led her into a coach-house in front of the house; that, meanwhile, M. and Mme. Potet arrived, and surprised at seeing the house open, began to make a search. The girl D. and her companion heard all that took place, and did not dare to go out.

The man, seeing that she could not go back, told her to go with him, and that he would find her another place.

At Dr. Ferroul's request she described the individual, but could not give his name, which D. had not pronounced.

D. raised some objections because of the difficulty she would have in bringing away her things. The man said he would see to that.

Anna then said :

"They have gone; they are on the Quai de la Charité.
D. said to the man :

"You see high up there that small lighted window, that is the room belonging to Marie, Fabre's servant."

"Have you said anything to Marie?"

"No."

"But," said Anna, "they went down some very funny streets. I have never seen those streets. Ah! there they are going into a house—a woman receives them. He tells her she is his mother, but she is not his mother—she is a go-between."

Other details followed, then Anna said :

"Ah! they are getting up, they go to the station. She takes a ticket for Béziers; she goes along first, second, third platform; she gets in the train, she arrives at Béziers. Ah! I cannot see any more of her, there are so many people. I have lost her."

Not being able to gather anything more, Dr. Ferroul transmitted these notes to M. Fabre, who went to find his father-in-law. They went into D.'s room and found, in fact, that there was some dirty linen in a trunk; but they were unable to elucidate anything, and Tuesday passed without news of D.

The following evening, Wednesday, M. Fabre's servant had gone to post a letter and saw D. in the company of a woman. D. tried to hide herself as best she could. When questioned she could not escape from Marie's reproaches. She then replied that she had just come from Béziers, where she had been to look for a situation. Marie quickly went to inform M. Fabre, who sent a police officer to the house of the woman with whom Marie had seen D., but D. had gone away again. Two days afterwards the agent discovered her in a hotel and he took her to the mayor's office, where the deputy-mayor questioned her. D. ended by confessing that an individual had induced her to go away, and gave his name. M. Fabre shut D. up in a cell and sent for the individual in question, whose description corresponded exactly with the information given by Anna Brieu.

When questioned he at first denied everything. M. Fabre told him that D. had confessed all, and showing a bold front began the account of the facts as given through the somnambulist. Seeing that the young man was losing his assurance, the deputy-mayor went on and related what had happened on the Quai de la Charité. The man then became confused, and seeing he was on a good track M. Fabre went on.

Then the young man confessed the truth, and said:

"Yes, it is true! But I did not know that she was under age. In any case she tells a lie when she says that I took her to a woman's house; there was no woman in this affair. I took her to a certain hotel; it was the waiter who gave us the key of a room. I left the hotel at three o'clock in the morning, and I do not know what became of her."

M. Fabre put the individual back and again questioned D.

"But," he added, "I know also what you did at Béziers, but I wish you to tell me, and if you do not tell the truth, beware."

"Well," she said, "all Monday I looked for a place at Béziers; I did not find one. In the evening I went back to the station to take the train, but I missed it. At the station I met a boatman whom I knew at Narbonne, and who took me to his mother's house to sleep."

This, therefore, explained the strange gap in Anna's declaration, who had mixed up the incidents at Béziers with those of Narbonne, and had only mentioned one individual when there were two concerned. The streets which the somnambulist did not recognise as belonging to Narbonne were probably the streets of Béziers.

Therefore on Tuesday evening Anna was able to perceive incidents that occurred on the nights of Monday to Tuesday, and Tuesday to Wednesday. One may therefore ask if matter in general does not possess the same property as the cerebral substance of preserving impressions, namely, the traces of luminous and sonorous vibrations. The fluidic sensorium, or astral body of the subject extending to a distance, would cause matter to vibrate, just as it causes the substance of the brain to vibrate, and the impressions received are given back again.

Matter would then give back its impressions as though it were an additional brain, and would constitute for the subject a sort of temporary and supplemental brain.

But it will be urged against this hypothesis that matter has received a crowd of impressions, and it will be asked why there should be given to Anna Brieu the acts, gestures, and words of D. and her friend, rather than any other scene. We reply that the same objection exists with regard to the faculties of the brain, and, moreover, the selection is perfectly made. If I desire to recall the town of Marseilles, it is that town and no other that presents itself to me. Without being able to explain how this clear distinction is made between the picture of Marseilles previously received and that of any other town, we can conceive that, by reason of the same law, the initial idea that put Anna on the track of a given series of facts caused this series of events and no other to be developed. Even the gaps which were discovered in the perception of the somnambulist support this hypothesis, because we find the same omissions in the ordinary working of the memory. We mix up facts, or sometimes supervise them, and it may happen that in the picture of a town evoked by the will we erroneously place a street or a monument belonging to another town. It is these anomalies which often result in the contradictory evidence of different witnesses of the same scene.

A. GOUPIL.

The undersigned certify to the accuracy of the facts reported above, relating to the disappearance of the girl M. D. and to the information supplied by the somnambulist Anna Brieu.

(Signed) P. FABRE, *deputy-mayor.*

L. WEILL, *merchant.*

F. NÈGRE, *journalist on the* " Petit Paris-Narbonne," *employed in the mayor's office.*

March 17, 1896.

3. *Case of the Sub-prefecture*

This happened in July 1894, at the time of the reactionary laws. As chief of the Socialist party, Dr. Ferroul was in conflict with the Government party.

One day the mayor's secretary came to inform Dr. Ferroul that a detective had arrived from Carcassonne to take the chief commissioner at the mayor's office and bring him before the sub-prefect.

Dr. Ferroul thought of making use of Anna's faculties. He sent for her, put her to sleep, and sent her to the sub-prefecture.

" I am there," she said.

" Where are you ? "

" In the courtyard."

" You ought not to be in the courtyard. Find me the sub-prefect."

" There he is ! He is in his office with three people— the chief, another man who has come from a distance, and a man with a white beard whom I do not know."

" How do they name him ? "

" Ah ! they do not name him. Do you know, Dr. Ferroul, what that man thinks ? "

(In this condition Anna Brieu expresses herself like a child.)

" What does he think ? "

" He thinks : ' What am I doing here ? They will compromise me with their police affairs. I am going.' Ah ! the detective from Carcassonne takes out a letter and gives it to the sub-prefect. He tells him that it is an anonymous letter that has been sent him. Wait; he is talking about you to the sub-prefect."

" What does he say ? "

" He says : ' As to Ferroul, I will take away all his rights; I will only leave him what I cannot take away of his mayoral duties.' Ah ! the detective from Carcassonne hands him a list, and says that it is a list of people to be watched.

" What is there on this list ? "

The somnambulist mentioned three names, then added :

" Ah ! he has put it in his pocket; I cannot see any more. Two detectives have come in, Chaubet and Tirefort; they give them an order—they have gone; the gentleman with the white beard is going also."

" Follow him," said Dr. Ferroul, " and try to find out who he is."

" Ah, he goes into such a house; they tell him that monsieur is not there, but they do not call him by any name. He goes to another house, the servant opens to him and calls him M. X."

In his newspaper, *La République sociale* of July 22, 1894, Dr. Ferroul spoke of this meeting at the office of the sub-prefect and quoted the words used in regard to himself by the sub-prefect, but without saying in what way he had obtained the information.

The sub-prefect in great agitation sent for the chief commissioner. Dr. Ferroul was warned and again made use of the somnambulist, who gave him certain information, and amongst it the following :

" Ah ! the commissioner thinks you have obtained the information through me, but he does not dare say so."

(The case of the servant that disappeared had been spread abroad, and was doubtless the cause of this mental reflection of the commissioner.)

However, the sub-prefect and the commissioner, imputing some indiscretion to Chaubet and Tirefort, asked Dr. Ferroul to dismiss the two detectives. Dr. Ferroul refused. They then made a report to the prefect against the two agents, one was dismissed and the other suspended.

In his following issue Dr. Ferroul protested, and mentioned the list and the letter in blue pencil.

The conviction of the commissioner resulted from the fact that the two detectives were not present when the detective passed the list and the anonymous letter to the sub-prefect, which was pointed out to the commissioner when the *République sociale* mentioned these documents.

" It is therefore you," they said to the commissioner,

" who has informed the mayor what you said at the sub-
prefect's office."

Two or three days afterwards, Dr. David, a physician at
Narbonne, was in a carriage with the commissioner, going
to the suburbs to make a medico-legal examination.
Adroitly leading the conversation up to hypnotic phenomena, the commissioner asked Dr. David if he thought
it possible a sleeping subject could go and witness the acts
and gestures of persons at a distance."

" Quite," replied Dr. David, " but for that there must
be a preliminary training and a specially gifted subject."

" Well, there are no means of making the sub-prefect
believe that ; he says it is all humbug."

" In order to settle it, shut yourself up with the
sub-prefect at an appointed time ; if Dr. Ferroul tells
you exactly what you have said, the sub-prefect will be
satisfied."

" Bless me, no ! He would say that I had divulged
it, and I should be discharged."

" On the day that you were alone with the sub-prefect
did you not think that it was through Anna that Ferroul
had these particulars ? "

" Upon my word, yes ? But I did not dare to say so
for fear the sub-prefect would laugh at me."

Another Case of Lucidity obtained with Anna B.
in 1894

Two groups, over five hundred yards apart, had arranged
to experiment at the same time.

Dr. Ferroul, Dr. David, and Anna B. were in one room,
and the persons in the other were to act in any way they
pleased.

A simple pass over her eyes was sufficient to put Anna
into the state of lucid somnambulism. She always spoke
in a low voice, with a confident air, and emphasised what
she said by putting her finger on her nose.

In this experiment she preserved, as in an ordinary
dream, the perception of distance. Dr. Ferroul having

given her the order to go to the other group, she imagined that she was going thither on foot with him and said:

"Do not go so quickly; I cannot follow you."

She then described the persons assembled there, some of whom were unknown to her, and Doctors Ferroul and David. She gave their names when she heard them named by the other persons.

Here is one part of her statements:

"They say that that is not possible."

"Yet, let us try," said M. B.

"What shall we do?" said M. H.

"Play some innocent games," Mme. H. said.

"Ah! they put little K. in the midst of them; they bandage her eyes (here she gave a description of the game).

"No matter," says M. B., "we look like a lot of —— gathered here."

"Oh! oh!" says M. H.; "there are ladies present, &c."

Dr. Ferroul took a note of all that the subject said, and when the experiment was over he put the report into an envelope and sent it immediately to the persons assembled; the account was found correct in every detail.

Letter Lost and Read by Lucidity

Dr. Ferroul had not received a letter to which a reply was urgently requested.

He instructed Anna B. to go to the house of the person who had written the letter and who lived in a distant town, and to go back so many days in order to come to the time at which the letter was written, and to find out what had become of it. Anna said she saw this person taking the letter to post and put it in the letter-box. Dr. Ferroul told her to follow the letter.

But having retained the idea of comparative dimensions, she resisted and said:

"Me! go into that little hole? Never."

Seeing that she was going to cry, Dr. Ferroul awakened

her, then put her to sleep again and recommenced, but telling her to read the letter while it was being written.

Anna read it, and Dr. Ferroul replied as though he had received the letter. His reply and the particulars afterwards received agreed absolutely with what the sensitive had said.

M. X., a friend of Dr. Ferroul, had gone to Poitiers a few days before. Dr. Ferroul wished to try, by way of experiment, to find out when he would return. In thought he transported Anna to the station at Poitiers.

Anna, who knew M. X., spoke of seeing him on his arrival at the station, and said that he took a carriage.

"Ah, well," said Dr. F., "get in with him."

"But he will see me."

"No, do not be frightened, I am a sorcerer, and he will not see you."

The somnambulist passed from one point to another of the events as they occurred, just as takes place in an ordinary dream. She observed first of all the name of the street and the number of the house to which M. X. went; then she said that he was introduced to some people whom he called M. and Mme. M., whom Dr. F. did not know at all.

The somnambulist then spoke of a luncheon, in the course of which M. X. said that he did not care for the wine they gave him until it had been five or six years in bottle; then she spoke of other incidents.

Suddenly she said: "Oh, do you know, he thinks that he must send a telegram announcing his return at seven o'clock the day after to-morrow."

"But on what day does he think that?"

"I do not know."

"Is there not a calendar there?"

"Ah, yes, I see one on the wall; but what date is it to-day?"

"The fourth," said M. F.

"Then they have forgotten to tear off three leaves, because it is marked first, I see."

City of Paris, October 1st, menu of the day, such and such dishes.

Dr. Ferroul telegraphed on the chance to the address given by the somnambulist, asking that they would send him the calendar in the dining-room without touching it, and he would return it the next day.

He received the calendar, which bore the date of October 1st, as Anna had declared. M. X. arrived by train at seven o'clock in the morning, and said that all that the somnambulist had stated was correct.

Reading through an Opaque Sealed Packet

On November 19, 1894, Dr. Ferroul succeeded with his subject Anna in a very remarkable experiment of reading through an opaque packet, through which a normal person, endowed with good sight, could not read by transparence. This packet consisted of:—

1. An opaque green outer envelope;
2. A second envelope of English paper enclosed in the first;
3. Two sheets of cross-ruled paper, enclosing
4. Another sheet on which two verses were written.

Thus there were two envelopes and two sheets of paper to pass through before coming to the sheet containing the inscription to be read.

The outside envelope was sealed with five seals on the back; a supplementary seal was placed on the front of the envelope, just opposite to one of the corner seals on the back.

A hole had been made in the envelope, at the place where the two seals were to come, in order that the wax, penetrating through this hole, might fasten the second envelope inside the first and not allow it to be withdrawn without tearing. Three little dots, hardly perceptible, had been marked with a pen on the outside envelope by M. Goupil, who had carefully measured the distances between them. M. Goupil had also made a drawing of the seals, carefully indicating their outlines and the black spots with which they were covered, in order to be quite certain of being able to recognise them and make sure that they were his own seals.

The inside envelope bore in the corners the letters *a*, *b*, *c*, *d*, traced with a pencil (the *b* seen upside down might be mistaken for a 2); it bore also two dots at a measured distance apart. The *a* was enclosed between the two seals opposite one another, and which passed through the first envelope. It was perhaps because of this that the somnambulist did not see this letter, which was hidden on both sides by the wax.

The packet was entrusted to Dr. Ferroul, who was entirely ignorant of its contents, in order that he might cause it to be read by his subject when in a state of somnambulism. When he had made the experiment he returned with the packet and a sheet of paper on which he had written down the information given by the subject.

After a very careful examination the packet was recognised as being quite intact.

Dr. Ferroul then handed to M. Fabre the sheet of paper giving the following particulars :—

" White English paper envelope *d*, 2, *c*.

" Square-ruled, another paper inside.

" The man has made two verses; he is not making game of me.

> " Votre parti certainement
> Se tue par l'assainissement."

(This sheet also bore the following note by Dr. Ferroul:)

" On awaking her she told me that she had dreamed it and had told it to some one. This person has come and attested this."

This sheet having been examined and read by the eight witnesses of this experiment, M. Goupil handed the packet to M. Aldy, lawyer, that he might open it, and that the witnesses might at once ascertain what was the result. As shown by the official report prepared at the time, the success of the experiment was complete. The very concise note added by Dr. Ferroul to the description of the packet by the subject needs to be made more complete.

After the somnambulist had declared what was in the packet, Dr. Ferroul awakened her and told her what she had said.

"Oh," said she, "I dreamed it three days ago, and I said to X. that I would read you a packet in which there were two verses ending in *ment,* but all that I remembered was that the last word was *assainissement.*"

Dr. Ferroul then called the person in question, who asserted that Anna had really said this.

Official Report

NARBONNE, *November* 19, 1894.

The undersigned, assembled at the Café de la Bourse at half-past eight this evening, certify as follows :—

Dr. Ferroul having declared to us that he would prove the lucidity of Mlle. A. with regard to a sealed packet provided by M. Goupil, first asked M. Goupil to certify that his packet remained intact.

Dr. Ferroul then handed to M. Fabre, restaurant-keeper, the writing in pencil herewith enclosed, containing the statements by Mlle. A.

" White envelope, English paper, *d,* 2, *c.*

" A sheet of paper cross-ruled.

" Another sheet of paper inside.

"The man makes two verses; he is not making fun of me.

" Votre parti certainement
Se tue par l'assainissement."

After the witnesses had examined the pencil writing drawn up by Dr. Ferroul according to the dictation of his subject, M. Goupil handed to M. Aldy, principal deputy-mayor and lawyer, the sealed envelope in order that he might open it himself; the second envelope was slightly torn at the corner where the two seals were, and the witnesses found that everything was in conformity with the statements made by the subject.

Made at Narbonne, November 19, 1894.

> HUBERT FABRE.
> MURAT, *municipal councillor.*
> DR. FERROUL, *mayor.*
> ALDY, *lawyer.*
> PIGLOWSY, *landowner.*
> F. NÈGRE, *journalist.*
> MAYMOU, *restaurant-keeper.*
> GOUPIL, *engineer.*

We ought to remark that this experiment took place in November 1894—that is to say, more than a year before Röntgen's discovery was known. Radiography is therefore here out of the question, and in spite of the fact that it enables expert operators to photograph and therefore read writing enclosed in an opaque packet, it in no way diminishes the value of this experiment, which seems to have been carried out under the best conditions.

CHAPTER XXV

LUCIDITY IN THE FUTURE

A PHENOMENON STUDIED BY THE SOCIETY OF SCIENTIFIC PSYCHOLOGY AT MUNICH

WE shall devote this chapter to the study of a case of lucidity in the future, which has been scientifically ascertained and verified by the Society of Scientific Psychology at Munich. The following is the report of the President of this Society.

Karl du Prel left to the Society of Scientific Psychology at Munich a document which has been legally transmitted to me as President of this Society. It was contained in a packet of which the superscription, seals, &c., are minutely described further on.

In 1892 du Prel deposited this document in the hands of M. Wenglein, notary and councillor to the court at Munich, who did not wish to open it himself, although he was authorised to do so, under certain conditions, as will be seen later. I, in my turn, left it in the office of M. Pündter, successor to M. Wenglein, who had died in the meantime. I went to the painter Hubert Frosch, whose name was inscribed on the packet as holding full powers from Baron du Prel to decide, after his death, the date for opening the document; I wished to obtain from him certain explanations as to the matter, of which I was quite ignorant, and to come to an agreement with him, in any case, as to the date of opening. M. Frosch told me that it related to some very remarkable predictions made at Jerusalem in 1885, and which had been verified in a surprising manner in almost every detail. A great part of those predictions having been realised in 1891, he found occasion, through others, to inform Baron du Prel of this affair, and the latter drew up a statement, on his information, in order to verify such of the predicted facts as had not yet been realised. Mme. Frosch confirmed to me the repeated surprises which her husband had experienced, on finding the events prophesied realised one after another; she gave me the details of these events, which chiefly concerned the deceased painter Bruno Piglhein and his relations with Karl Frosch, all corresponding perfectly with the account given by her husband. This lady had had special reason for fixing in her memory all that her husband had so impressively related to her, after his return from the East, about these curious prophecies; for she herself played a part in them which is not indicated in the documentary account made known later. According to her husband, the prophet had predicted that she also would become a painter, would earn high distinction, and give lessons in painting.

M. Frosch had protested in vain against this prediction, asserting that such a thing would never happen. At the time when this prophecy was given M. Frosch might have been right; but as time went on and brought its vicissitudes it nevertheless was destined to be realised. Mme. Frosch became a painter of flowers of some repute, under the pseudonym of Maria Nyl, and did not lack either honours or pupils. The opening of the document was finally fixed for November 30, 1899, at half-past ten in the morning, at the office of the notary M. Pündter. The following is the text of the notarial memorandum relative to the opening of the document:—

NOTARY'S STATEMENT

This day, November 30, 1899, there appeared before me, Dr. Franz Pündter, royal notary at Munich, at my office, the undermentioned gentlemen:—

1. Ritter Eugen von Stieler, painter, of Munich.
2. Karl Hubert Frosch, painter, of Munich.
3. Karl Albert Baur, painter, of Munich.
4. Ludwig Deinhard, author, of Munich.

5. Martin Grief, author, of Munich.

6. Dr. Walter Bormann, author, of Munich.

These gentlemen requested me to state by notarial document as follows:—

Dr. Walter Bormann, in the first place, deposited a document signed by Dr. August Ullrich, Director of the High School for Girls at Nuremberg, and dated the 25th of this month, conferring upon him full power to replace him at the opening of du Prel's document by the accredited notary, and the right to act in his place as might be necessary.

The same gentleman handed to the notary a packet sealed with five private seals and bearing on its front the following superscription : "Property of the Society of Scientific Psychology at Munich. This document is to be opened at a time determined by me. In case of my decease, M. Karl Frosch will fix the time. It is to be opened in the presence of the persons whose seals are affixed to the back of the packet. Munich, January 14, 1892. Karl du Prel."

On the back of the packet are affixed five different seals, each with a signature, as follows :—

1. January 21, 1892, Karl Albert Baur, Hessesstrasse 1A.

2. Deinhard, February 12, 1892, Georgenstrasse 13, II.

3. Paul du Prel, Herrenstrasse 13.

4. February 3, 1892, Eugen von Stieler, Fürstenstrasse 16, II.

5. Dr. A. Ullrich, Schlossstrasse 6A, I.

The gentlemen present mentioned at the commencement of this document first assured themselves that the packet handed in by Dr. Bormann was intact in every part, and, in particular, that the seals were intact; then these same gentlemen, especially those who had signed the packet on the back—that is to say, Karl Albert Baur, Ludwig Deinhard and Eugen von Stieler, as well as Dr. Bormann, empowered by Dr. August Ullrich—requested me to open the said packet in the presence of the persons

assembled, the signatories of the packet having recognised
as valid the authority given by Dr. August Ullrich of
Nuremberg to Dr. Bormann, and Baron Carl du Prel, one
of the signatories to the envelope having been declared to
have died on August 5th of this year. In conformity
with the invitation given me, I opened the envelope given
me in the presence of the persons above mentioned and
drew therefrom a sheet of large-sized letter paper, having
writing on all four sides, the writing commencing as
follows:—Statement: "Munich, December 27, 1891. To-
day at four o'clock in the afternoon the following gentlemen came to me," and ending with the words: "Perhaps
again the seer purposely remains obscure and passed over
in silence the clear and distinct vision that he may have
had on this point.   CARL DU PREL.
                              K. FROSCH, *Painter.*"

This document was read before the gentlemen present,
word for word, by me, the notary, in the exercise of my
duty, in accordance with their wish; then it was returned
with the envelope to Dr. Bormann. Dr. Bormann claimed
a copy of the preceding attestation, and added that in
his capacity of President of the Society of Scientific Psychology of Munich he was qualified, as well as M. Deinhard, a member of the Executive Committee of that
Society, their claims being officially recognised, to sign
this copy. A minute to this effect was adopted and duly
signed. Before signing, Dr. Bormann again handed to the
notary the document mentioned in the preceding attestation and invited him to add to the present statement a
certified copy of the document, and to file it among the
other papers. This statement was read, adopted, and
signed.
     Eugen von Stieler.
     Karl H. Frosch.
     Karl Albert Bauer.
     Ludwig Deinhard, member of the Executive Committee
          of the Society of Scientific Psychology.
     Martin Grief.

Dr. Walter Bormann, President of the Society of Scientific Psychology.

Dr. Pündter, royal notary.

The following is the purport of the document in question, with the omission of some unimportant passages, which are left out because some persons now living are there designated, and which, moreover, contain some unrealised predictions concerning the artist Frosch.

KARL DU PREL'S DOCUMENTS

Munich, December 27, 1891. To-day at four o'clock in the afternoon, MM. Martin Grief, author; Ernest Müller, artist; and Karl Frosch, artist, came to me. Karl Frosch related to me as follows:—

In April 1885, I was at Jerusalem in company with the artist Bruno Piglhein and his wife, as well as the artists Joseph Krieger and René Reinike. We lodged at the German hospice. We were one day introduced to an elderly gentleman, said to be a professor at Edinburgh and an orientalist, named . . . the name is omitted in the document, because at the time of drawing it up M. Karl Frosch had forgotten it; he was afterwards easily able to ascertain the name at the hospice. It was Robert Laing, born in Scotland, but not a professor at Edinburgh, as is wrongly stated here. He was then a Fellow of Corpus Christi College, Oxford, and perhaps the same person as a member of the Society of Psychical Research, R. Laing, at present Professor at the Boys' High School at Christchurch, New Zealand; he joined us at our table. He often spoke of strange things—saying, for example, to M. Reinike, that he had known him in a previous existence and conversed on things relating to the transmigration of souls, so that we regarded him with astonishment, and could not help thinking that he was slightly deranged. One day, after the meal—I remember very well all the circumstances of this colloquy—he said to me: "Ah, well, gentlemen, your work—a panorama of Jerusalem which we had painted conjointly—your work interests me, and I am determined to consult the future as to your destiny, and what will happen to you all. "You two," he said, pointing to Piglhein and myself, "will become mortal enemies through your work." This statement made us both laugh, but he continued:

"And you, this affair will be your loss."

"Mine!" I cried.

"Not yours," he replied, "but this gentleman's." And he pointed to Piglhein.

"And what will his loss be!" I asked. I expected it would be a fall of Piglhein from his artist's trestle or something similar.

But my interlocutor added: "The painting will be finished; but something will happen in connection with this matter, with this painting, and that will be your loss, Monsieur Piglhein."

Piglhein laughed and said: "Really, you are a pleasant companion."

His wife also laughed, and wished to know at what time this event would come to pass.

"Will the picture be finished?" I asked.

"Yes," he replied; "but the event will happen some years hence."

Mme. Piglhein laughing, said that after some years, twenty or thirty perhaps, her husband would surely die.

"No," he replied, "if I speak of some years it means five or ten years. It may be ten years, but it will not be longer, because I have seen it too distinctly, and when I see a thing clearly it happens within about ten years."

"And what will happen to me?" I asked.

"You will paint the picture three or four times and nothing unpleasant will happen to you."

"But why shall we become mortal enemies?" I asked.

"Because of this painting," he replied. "You will have to see many countries on account of this business. I have seen the sea and a boat, and that indicates a long voyage. You will find yourself on this boat with two painters. I have seen that very distinctly. The sight of these two painters struck me; they are wearing peculiar cloaks and fur-lined caps such as I have never seen before either in England or at Jerusalem. You seem to have suffered much from sea-sickness; you are really looking ill. You will take one of your panoramas to England, perhaps because of a proposition that will be made to you. I see that distinctly. I see St. Paul's Cathedral in London with its great dome. From this time you will have a lawsuit because of this picture; this suit will originate in London. There will be proceedings, and action will also be taken against you in Germany."

"What will be the result?"

"Nothing; the suits will have no results."

"What more will happen to me?"

"Nothing but good."

"How many times shall I paint the picture?" then asked M. Reinike.

"You will not even take part in its completion."

"But I wish to take part in it; that is the purpose of my journey to Jerusalem."

"What of that! You will not take part in this painting."

At this moment Krieger, who had been absent up to now, came into the room. I related to him what had been said, and urged him to also ask for a prediction for himself. At first he refused, because he was obliged to go out again, but he presently asked:

"Shall I marry?"

"Yes, but it will not be a happy marriage. It will not be long before you are divorced."

The seer urged us to write down all that he had said. He might have said many more things, he said, but he did not wish to continue since we were not willing to believe even what he had already said.

"Have you heard of second-sight?" he asked me.

"I have heard it said that it is common in Scotland."

"Well, I am gifted with this second-sight," remarked the seer.

I ought to add that the seer wore on his finger a ring which had been given to him by a Brahmin to whom he had rendered a service. When he desired information on any subject he had only to look at this ring, and then he saw a picture forming before him, like a dream. When it was a town, he saw it from above, over the country. Before we parted he again repeated to me once more that the words he had already used, " This affair will be your loss," did not apply to both of us, Piglhein and myself, but only to Piglhein. That was a matter of course, he observed, since otherwise what he had prophesied could not come true.

" In the five years that are to come," he added, " you will suffer much unpleasantness."

" However, I am pleased with Munich," I replied, " and I have no intention of leaving that city."

" So many unpleasant things will happen that Munich will cease to be so congenial to you. But after that you will be happier. Your life will be quiet, and you will reach a good age."

Among the events predicted, the following have since come to pass. I really made long journeys in connection with this picture, particularly to America. My colleagues, two German artists, who came from America over this matter, and invited me to make this voyage, had made for them in Munich a kind of shepherd cloaks with capes, like the peasants of the good old times used to wear, furnished with large metal clasps, almost as big as plates. They made a sensation everywhere, and also on board ship. I was really sea-sick on the voyage, and was ill for six days.

The artist Reinike did not, in fact, work on the picture. I painted it four times. One of the copies came from America to London under my name, but against my wish and desire. In connection with this a lawsuit was commenced at London. The picture was confiscated because M. Halder (who was the owner of it) had already let out the picture to an English contractor, who, by virtue of this fact, issued proceedings against the American company. I was also prosecuted at the Munich court for infringement. But as the seer had said, it came to nothing. The day before the trial, when I was at dinner, I received a letter from my lawyer, Dr. Vimmer, telling me that the trial would not take place, because the plaintiff had abandoned the suit at the last moment. He therefore had to bear the heavy cost of the proceedings.

Piglhein and myself were set at variance on this occasion. As to the artist Krieger, he has married since then, but has entered an action for divorce against his wife. (On this point see the statement below made by M. Krieger. Shortly afterwards the divorce was granted, as Mr. Laing had predicted.)

I will also add that the statement of the seer concerning Piglhein's loss must not be understood in a pecuniary sense. It is sufficient to recall the question that Mme. Piglhein put on this point (as has been given above, with the seer's reply).

As in the course of these later years a great part of the prophecies in question have been realised, contrary to our expectation, I went, on the proposition of M. Martin Grief, in company with the gentlemen named above, to Dr. Carl du Prel who—in order to establish documentary evidence in favour of the reality of second-sight, in the event of the remainder of the prophecies being realised— wrote out the present statement, the accuracy of which I certify by my signature, with this reservation, that having reported the facts from memory I cannot guarantee the literal exactness of the conversations held.

K. FROSCH, *Artist.*

Addition made by Dr. Carl du Prel

That part of the prophecy which concerns M. Piglhein is couched in abstract terms, whilst the second-sight visions are always concrete.

I conclude from this that this part of the prophecy has another source than the others, and may not be realised; perhaps again the seer purposely remains obscure and passed over in silence the clear and distinct vision that he may have had on this point. CARL DU PREL.

The document ends here. After the statement was drawn up in December 1891, and the packet had been secured with seals affixed by four persons besides Dr. du Prel, and the document deposited with the notary in 1892, the following facts occurred :—

During the night of April 27th to 28th, 1892, a fire at Vienna destroyed in a moment this picture of Jerusalem with the crucifixion of Christ, which had entailed so much labour, executed with the richest resources of art, so universally known and admired, and which Piglhein had executed with the assistance of the artists Karl Frosch and Josef Krieger. Bruno Piglhein braced himself against this stroke of fortune and conceived the idea of painting the picture again, of reproducing it more beautifully than ever, thus setting destiny at defiance. This desire was not realised, and the poor artist died of heart-disease at Munich on July 15, 1894. (He was born at Hamburg on February 19, 1848.)

But is it permissible to say that there was an agreement between these events and the prophecy of Robert Laing? After the death of Piglhein in 1894, Carl du Prel did not open the document, whether it was because his engagements had caused him to forget its existence, or whether he had not thought that these subsequent events formed a realisation of the prophecy. This was not the way in which the artist Frosch looked upon it; as he told me, after the destruction of the picture as well as on the death of Piglhein, which happened nine years after the prophecy, therefore *within the approximate limit of ten years which was fixed*, he vividly recalled the seer and wished to know if du Prel had opened the document in order to set before the world the realisation of this prophecy. Meeting Baron du Prel in the street one day he felt impelled, he said, to speak to him and remind him of the facts; but he did nothing. It is greatly to be regretted that the prophecies were not committed to writing in 1885, as Robert Laing had asked. If what was written by du Prel, according to the statements of M. Frosch at the end of 1894, is compared with the events which afterwards occurred, it cannot be said that there is an absolute realisation of the prophecy, although there is an almost complete agreement between the statement and the facts. M. Frosch thought that the destruction of the picture was mentioned in the statement of the predictions, and he formally declared this to me before the document was opened on November 30th. As the document after being opened did not bear out his statement, he declared he was convinced he had told the Baron of this fact, and that no doubt du Prel had omitted to insert it in the statement, and that he himself, on reading it through too quickly, had failed to notice the omission, as well as some other slight errors.

In a matter of verification of prophecies it is evident that the literal accuracy is necessary, and that all delay in drawing them up, by which their freshness is lost, is a misfortune. When the hearers of a prophecy fail to write down immediately what they have heard and await its realisation in order to pass judgment on it, two possibilities are presented to strict criticism :—

1. As the more or less enigmatical and hidden allusions concerning a prophesied fact can only be cleared up after its realisation, the true meaning of the prophecy is only revealed at that moment, and the words which relate to it also only come to the memory at the time when their explanation appears clearly and distinctly.

2. Imagination may, as the realisations are perceived, pervert the remembrance unwittingly and unconsciously, and give to the original prophecy, by altering it, however slightly, a form which makes it harmonise exactly with the event, as soon as the latter presents some points of agreement with the sense of the prophecy. It is scarcely possible that the artist Frosch did speak to the Baron du Prel of the predicted destruction of the picture, because, if such had been the case, du Prel would probably not have used the indefinite expressions contained in the document: " The painting will be finished ; but something will happen in connection with this matter, with this painting, and that will be your loss, Monsieur Piglhein."

It would rather seem that the exact words of the prophet were not remembered by Frosch, which would not be astonishing after an interval of six years and a half, and that for this reason he had given to the prophecy this indefinite form, which did not completely miss its true meaning even if it did not fully express it. Moreover, M. Frosch in all sincerity declared himself, at the end of the document, that he could not guarantee the literal accuracy of the conversations which took place. If Laing had predicted the destruction of the picture, such a prophecy, some would think, would have impressed a painter destined to take so important a part in its construction too vividly for him to have forgotten it.

This objection is not without weight; but it is not final, because all of us, as years go by, gain this psychological experience, that even facts and events which have acted most powerfully on our mind and heart disappear from our memory, until the moment perhaps when some powerful stimulus awakens these emotions which were apparently effaced and brings them again to life.

Thus we find that the recollection may be effaced of psychical facts much more important than more or less imaginary predictions. If in reality, at the moment of the drawing up of the document, the prediction of the destruction of the picture was no longer present to M. Frosch's memory, nothing is more natural than that it should be revived in his mind after the fire. From that the thought that he had informed du Prel of this prophecy is only a step. Be that as it may, here is the declaration of M. Karl Frosch as it was drawn up by me in his presence.

"M. Karl Hubert Frosch, artist, of Munich, affirms that he clearly recollects that Mr. Laing told him of the destruction of the picture, and that the account which he gave to Baron du Prel made mention of this fact. He adds that he, moreover, asked Mr. Laing in what way the picture would be destroyed, to which he replied that he had a vision of it but had forgotten this detail.

"The prophet spoke German well, as can also be

attested by M. Boyer, the proprietor of the hospice at Jerusalem. KARL H. FROSCH."

"MUNICH, *December* 6, 1899."

The shrewd remark added to the document by du Prel concerning the abstract nature of the greater part of predictions of this character would not apply here, in case the seer had forgotten the vision, as M. Frosch says in his declaration, and had only announced the fact of the destruction. The artist Josef Krieger has also personally given his testimony, in the same way as M. Frosch, according to the recollections which remained with him :—

"The artist Joseph Krieger affirms the following with regard to the prophecies made at Jerusalem in 1885, in his presence, by the Scotchman, Robert Laing. The destruction of the panorama and the death of Piglhein were prophesied to occur within a period of ten years. Further, M. Krieger recollects that, according to the statement of the prophet, Piglhein would only paint the picture once whilst M. Frosch would paint it several times. He also recollects the elegant gesture Piglhein made by touching the front of his head, indicating that this gentleman was not in his right mind. He likewise understood that Reinike, according to the prophet, would not collaborate in the work. Finally, he confirms the prediction made with regard to himself, concerning his marriage, which was precisely realised.

"He related that Mr. Laing wore a ring at which it was his habit to look when he wished to obtain visions.

"M. Krieger again met the prophet two years afterwards, when travelling in Norway. He passed him in a carriage and was recognised by him, but no words were exchanged.

"M. Krieger did not hear it stated that MM. Frosch and Piglhein would become mortal enemies, and that there would be a lawsuit, because he was obliged to be absent on an urgent matter at the time when this was said. JOSEF KRIEGER."

"MUNICH, *December* 6, 1899."

Z

Mme. Nyl Frosch affirms that, according to the statements which her husband made to her, in the first place
the seer had formally prophesied that both the picture
and Piglhein would perish. Moreover, what could be the
fact "in relation to this matter, to this picture," which was
to bring about the loss of Piglhein? Besides the lawsuit
and the destruction of the picture itself, it is difficult to
imagine other possibilities. Moreover, another lawsuit of
several years' duration followed the burning of the panorama, because the Austrian insurance company, the Phœnix,
refused to pay the sum fixed, which amounted to 150,000
marks. They ended by paying; making only a small
deduction. We do not know whether in reference to this
Piglhein had any difficulties with the owner of the picture.

The confirmation of the prediction relative to the
destruction of the panorama would have had a very
special importance as regards the exact verification of
Laing's prophecies, because the death of Piglhein, within
the interval of ten years fixed by the seer, is of no great
value, since many persons die in a similar lapse of time.
At all events, it is of importance as far as it does not
contradict the prediction; therefore it does not annul it,
without, however, verifying it.

That this sudden destruction of his great picture must
have deeply affected the artist, who was already suffering
from heart-disease, and might accelerate his death, is not
an improbable hypothesis. It is almost certain, from the
psychological experience which we have as to the artistic
temperament. This is confirmed by Captain Halder, the
former proprietor of the panorama, who wrote me from
Burghausen, near Salzach.

"The loss of this, his largest work, deeply affected him.
When I sent to his studio (Landwehrstrasse, 23), on the
morning of the 28th, the unfortunate telegram, immediately before my departure for Vienna, he embraced me,
and we both wept like two children. Then he said to me:
'The wooden pavilion at 42 Goethestrasse is still standing;
send immediately to stop its demolition; we will paint
a new Calvary, and it will be better than the last one.'

He wanted to do it for 80,000 marks (he had received 150,000 marks for the first picture). I made them stop the demolition at once, and went to Vienna, then to my partner, M. Notoff, at Dresden. I begged him to contract for the new picture, but he firmly refused."

The strong desire that Piglhein had to recommence his work proved of itself what a blow this destruction of his work had been to him. We must add to this the influence of the irritating lawsuit before the destruction of the picture, and which was equally "in relation to this matter, to this picture," as stated in the document. It is possible that the seer may have used this exact expression to indicate the lawsuit in question, and that he had also predicted the destruction of the work.

I also thought it my duty to seek for the evidence of the two other persons living at Munich, whose presence at Laing's prophecies is indicated in the document.

(Professor) Piglhein's wife, whom I visited in company of Dr. Fealk Schupp, Vice-president of the Society of Scientific Psychology of Munich, could not remember either the prophecy or the prophet; but she was of opinion that since MM. Frosch and Krieger guaranteed the reality of the fact, she had no reason to doubt its accuracy. She was certain that if any one had spoken to her husband in her presence of his approaching death, he being very excitable by reason of his heart complaint, she would have laughed heartily in order to efface this unpleasant impression. The very remarkable thing is that Mme. Piglhein is specially mentioned twice in the document as laughing at the doleful words of the prophet, which is in favour of the sincerity of her present statement as well as that of the document.

The artist René Reinike could not remember the prophecies, but he remembered Robert Laing very well. He stated that, young as he was, these singular events would not have had the slightest attraction for him, and that the observations of Robert Laing, who wished to assign to him, amongst other things, a previous existence among the Arabs, had simply seemed absurd to him.

In order to give greater force and evidence to the preceding events, and to offer fresh proofs of the good memory of the artists Frosch and Krieger, I asked these gentlemen to write me a description of Robert Laing, and the place where the prophecy was made. M. Karl Frosch very willingly consented. As to the appearance of the seer, he wrote with great sincerity: "I only recall that he was of medium height, with greyish hair, with a sharp look, and as he walked he bent his body slightly forward."

As M. Frosch was specially engaged upon decorative painting, he was able, with a sure hand, to draw a sketch of the dining-room, of antique aspect, with a wide and high-vaulted roof, of the hospice, which was once one of the residences of the Templars.

The artist Krieger, although he was quite willing to accede to my request, has not yet been able to do so, as he was suddenly called away to a distance.

Lastly, I wrote to Mr. Laing at Christchurch, New Zealand, asking him to give me his evidence should he be the same person as Robert Laing. I told him nothing as to the events which had occurred and to which the prophecies related, nor as to the tenor of these prophecies; I merely asked him to let me know what he still remembered of the predictions he had made. Although seers quickly forget the visions they have had, it is permissible to think that Robert Laing would at least have partly preserved the recollection, if not of his visions at that time, at least of the statements he had made to those concerned. As soon as I receive a reply I shall at once publish it.

For the *explanation* of this prevision of the future, we may profitably consult the profound considerations on this subject in the second volume of du Prel's work on the *Discovery of the Soul* (Leipzig, 1885). With regard to the part the Brahmin's ring played in the visions, we may consider that to be purely auto-suggestive. The above-mentioned case does not unfortunately present the absolute evidential guarantees required for a purely critical examination. Nevertheless, the knowledge and the discussion of the events that are reported seem to us calculated to awaken the interest which the study of so delicate a problem as prophecy deserves, and we may learn from it that all statements in reference to such matters ought to be drawn up at the proper time and with scrupulous accuracy.   Dr. W. Bormann.[1]

After having studied this very curious and well attested case of lucidity, wishing to have some more precise information as to the personality of the subject himself, and hoping to obtain from him some new experiences, I asked one of the English correspondents of the Société Universelle d'Études Psychiques to find Robert Laing and put me into communication with him. The following are the particulars I received of this person who is endowed with so strange a faculty :—

R. L. is a most curious person. He is sixty-two years of age, and a bachelor. He was shut up for some years as a madman, and willingly speaks of what he saw and the tricks he played while he was in the asylum.

He has changed his name, has travelled considerably ; has resided for a number of years in the East, lived amongst the Brahmins, the Moravian Brothers, in monasteries, in German universities, in the Latin quarter, &c. He attaches great importance to numbers, letters, forms, and colours : where we simply speak of a coincidence, he sees an allegory.

He has read much of Rabbinical and Jewish writings. He has not only the head of the Wandering Jew—bald head and long white beard—but also, he states that he has Jewish blood in his veins. He claims to have had, at certain times in his life, the recollection, the clear vision of his previous incarnations, except, he says, for one link which is missing in the seventeenth century. He also believes that he profits by the experience and knowledge he gained during his previous existences.

He possesses a very fine collection of rings, seals, mysterious emblems, monograms, &c.

[1] Extract from *Psych. Studien*, April and May 1900.

When he drinks wine he puts an enormous ring at the bottom of his glass.

This gentleman, who has read all the mystics, has a horror of prearranged and scientifically conducted experiments. He therefore refuses, as he says he has always done with Myers and others, to furnish material proofs of the Beyond and of the mysterious powers which have sometimes acted in him, and which he declares he cannot explain, although he has left a confession which is not to be opened until twenty years after his death.

Passive expectancy is his usual attitude, and he has no wish to act with a view to forcing his powers or the forces latent in him : when he *feels* himself in intimate communion with the universal mind, he *sees* himself an instrument, a witness of the Unknown. All that he has ever been able to do in the way of reading the past, predicting the future, &c., belongs to the domain of spiritualism and not of science. He speaks of finding himself on another plane of inquiry and perception, almost in another condition of existence, with which scientific methods have nothing to do, and in fact it is only by the voice of his intuitions that he claims to walk towards the truth, the ultimate reality.

Such is the person whose expressions I have respected. He seems to have a strange mixture of Oriental, Jewish, primitive, animistic, and rationalistic Christian opinions and doctrines.

You, like myself, will regret that I have not been able to obtain from him any decisive experience.

V. LEULIETTE,
Corresponding Member of the Société Universelle
d'Études Psychiques.

Our correspondent's report is very complete, as will be seen, and gives a very clear idea of this strange personality. It is, after all, mysticism which dominates, whether it be all sincere or mixed with a certain stage effect, as is quite possible.

The most regrettable fact is that we are not able to

produce any new experiments in conditions we could ourselves arrange. But we have other subjects possessing
this faculty of lucidity in regard to the future, with whom
we propose to arrange some methodical experiments. This
question is therefore left for study, and we may expect
definite results from strictly scientific experiments.

CHAPTER XXVI

PHOTOGRAPHY OF THE INVISIBLE OR OF THOUGHT

In a study such as we are making it is impossible not to notice the photographs of thought. Is thought capable in any manner whatever of impressing a photographic plate?

This question has already been debated and a certain number of experiments made. Unfortunately, nearly all these experiments left something to be desired on some point, so that it must be said that, at the present time, we have no sufficiently certain scientific documents on this question. The reader must please to remember that we still make great reservations as to this phenomenon, and we leave to the authors, whom we mention in this chapter, all the responsibility for the facts they put forward. Numerous experiments are still in progress, and the near future may witness the transformation into certainty of that which is now only hypothetical.

Let no one be astonished, in the first place, at the difficulty experienced in definitely describing this point either negatively or affirmatively. We have already made a number of experiments which have given no result, and we have not been able to draw any conclusion from them.

We know well that certain scientific inquirers have endeavoured to verify for themselves levitation phenomena, for example; and that not being able to get them produced in their presence have immediately come to the conclusion and stated that these phenomena do not exist, that in short they are impossible. It has not been our custom to reason in this manner; therefore, if we have not what some persons would consider the advantage of affirming or denying so rapidly, we shall not suffer in the future from the denials which serve to prove the imprudence of these hasty and dogmatic conclusions.

We also know very well that if it is possible for thought to impress a photographic plate and imprint a picture on it, we are entirely ignorant of the conditions necessary for this to happen; and, to specify some of the possible conditions that we can imagine, we do not know whether or not the plate ought to be placed in a camera, as is done when photographing an ordinary object. We do not know whether, instead of the dark camera, which enables us in ordinary photography to receive the images on the plate, there is not some quite different apparatus which would enable it to receive the pictures emitted by our thoughts.

But let us suppose the most simple case, that is to say, that an image invisible to our retina, projected by thought into space, can, by means of an ordinary apparatus, impress a photographic plate. We do not yet know how to focus this picture, or what exposure to give.

Let us suppose that an excellent apparatus and some good photographic plates are placed in the hands of a man who has never seen a photograph taken, and who is entirely ignorant how to illuminate the object to be photographed, how it can be brought to a focus, how to develop, &c.; with time and patience he will probably be able some day to take good photographs, because it is in this way that the photographic art has been created; but before that he must certainly try a multitude of experiments, in which he will have fogged plates, plates without an impression, &c. And in the course of these experiments, if he sees some photograph obtained by a better operator, he will not have the right to deny its authenticity and to say that it is impossible to photograph, but he will only be able to say with truth that he does not yet know how to set about it.

On going a little further into the numerous details which constitute the art of photography, and supposing it possible to photograph thought, we know nothing as to the preparation of the plates, which may be very different from ordinary plates, or as to the chemicals to be employed, &c.

It would be puerile to object that, if we need special and new apparatus, processes, and chemicals, it would no longer be photography.

Radiography is not true photography; and how long a time has elapsed since the origin of photography before the means were found for photographing through opaque bodies. Every one knows that we may set up the most perfect photographic apparatus, or arrange the most sensitive plates in front of a wooden box in any manner we please, but we shall never be able to photograph the objects enclosed in it if we have not an X-ray apparatus. Who, therefore, can state that there does not exist some process capable of imprinting on a sensitive plate pictures which are invisible to our retina? There is nothing absurd in this, and those who do not wish to apply themselves to it cannot, without making themselves supremely ridiculous, blame or deride others for such researches.

This being so, let us see what photographs of thought have been obtained according to the experiments which have been made up to now.

In a recent essay Colonel de Rochas quoted from a lecture given on this subject by Mr. J. Traill Taylor; we will give some extracts from this document.

Mr. Taylor was a man very well known on the other side of the channel, both as a savant and a photographer; he was the author of several works dealing with the physical and chemical knowledge necessary for the rational practice of his art; he was a member of the Council of the Photographic Society of Great Britain, and editor of the *British Journal of Photography*. It was after some séances which were held in April and May 1892 in Glasgow with a well-known medium, Mr. David Duguid, in which photographs were obtained of objects not visible to the spectators, that Frederic Myers, the eminent author of *Human Personality*, asked Mr. Taylor to try to reproduce these extraordinary phenomena in London with Mr. Duguid, taking the necessary precautions to avoid all cause of error, voluntary or involuntary.

" The presence of smoke " (wrote Mr. Taylor) " may be considered as implying the existence of flame. Spirit photography, so called, has of late been asserting its existence in such a manner as to warrant competent men making an investigation, conducted under stringent test conditions, into the circumstances under which such photographs are produced and exposing the fraud, should it prove to be such, instead of pooh-poohing it as insensate because we do not understand how it can be otherwise—a position that scarcely commends itself as intelligent or philosophical. If in what follows I call it spirit photography instead of psychic photography, it is only in deference to a nomenclature that extensively prevails, and not as offering a surmise from any knowledge of my own as to what is matter and what spirit, or the distinction between mind, spirit, and matter, for in truth I do not know. I approach the subject merely as a photographer.

" Before I proceed, a few words on the origin of spirit photography may not be out of place. In March 1861, W. H. Mumler, the principal engraver in the employ of Bigelow Bros. & Kennard, the leading jewellers of Boston, when whiling away an idle hour as an amateur photographer, had a form other than that of any one present developed on his collodion plate. He surmised that it arose from an image having been previously on the plate, and its having been imperfectly cleaned off. Subjected to a more thorough cleaning, the form again appeared more strongly marked than before, and he could offer no other explanation than the one given. It got noised abroad through the press that a spirit had been photographed, and although Mumler strove to suppress the misrepresentation, as he regarded it, yet he eventually succumbed to popular demand, and took two hours a day from his regular work, devoting them to photography This he had to extend to the whole of each day, entirely discarding his regular profession. Many men of eminence sat to him, most of whom he did not know at the time. He seems to have encouraged his sitters in the adoption of such test conditions as they deemed satisfactory. The figures that usually appeared on the plate with the sitters were, if I rightly infer, those on whom the sitters' minds had been set. That eminent portrait photographer, Mr. Wm. Black, of Boston, so well known all over the world as the inventor of the acid nitrate bath, undertook to investigate the *bona fides* of Mumler's methods. Through a friend who had just previously sat and obtained a figure, Black offered fifty dollars if Mumler would operate in his presence and obtain a picture. Invited to come, the acute Black critically examined camera, plate, dipper, and bath, and had his eye on the plate from the moment its preparation began until it was sensitised and locked in the dark slide, removing it himself from the camera and carrying it into the dark room, where, on development, a figure of a man was seen leaning on B.'s shoulder. Black was thunderstruck, and got away the negative, no charge whatever having been made. Mumler now claimed publicly to be a spirit-portrait photographer, and as such he eventually opened a studio in New York, having previously satisfied Silver, Gurney, and other photographers as to the genuineness of his claims, never hesitating to operate in their galleries if required, and with their apparatus and chemicals. Mumler was arrested in New York; whether on the ground of witchcraft or of endeavouring to obtain money under false pretences, I am at present uncertain, but his trial was the sensation of the day, and numerous witnesses were examined. He was honourably acquitted.

"In this country, a number of amateur photographers have investigated this subject with more or less success. These include some F.R.S.'s, scientists, artists, and others. I question whether any have so persistently done so as the late Mr. John Beattie, of Clifton, and his friend Dr. Thompson. Mr. Beattie was a skilled professional photographer of the highest eminence who, some time prior to his death, had adopted the views of the spiritualistic school. The figures he obtained on his plates were much blurred in outline, some being misty in the extreme. I possess some two or three dozen of these, taken by, or in the presence of, Mr. Beattie, whose intelligence, honesty, and powers of observation no one would venture to doubt. Many such photographs are claimed to have been produced by Hudson, a professional photographer, formerly of the Holloway Road, and I submit for examination a work by the late Miss Houghton, containing fifty-four of Hudson's spirit photographs.

" There are many ways by which, assuming the genuineness of only one of all spirit photographs hitherto produced, the spurious article may be made even better than any alleged real ones I have yet seen. A plate secretly impressed previous or subsequent to being placed in the camera fulfils the condition; so does one at the back of which is placed a phosphorescent tablet in the dark slide. Pressure on the surface, such as that of a Woodbury relief film, also causes an image susceptible of development; in short, trickery in a whole variety of forms may, and has been, impressed into the service.

" The higher department of fluorescence may with success be employed. Here is something to which believers in the visibility of spirit forms to a camera are quite welcome. At the time, and à propos of the Mulmer trial in New York, I wrote that a good many absurd things have been said pro and con on the subject; but a writer in the latter category, who asserted that anything that is visible to the eye of the camera, and thus capable of being depicted by photography, must therefore necessarily be visible to the human eye, was surely ignorant of that important branch of physics popularly known as fluorescence. Many things are capable of being photographed which to the physical eye are utterly invisible. Why, for that matter, a room (visually dark) may be full of the ultra-violet rays of the spectrum, and a photograph may be taken in that dark light. Objects in a room so lighted would be plainly visible to the lens of the camera—at any rate, they could be reproduced on the sensitive plate, while, at the same time, not an atom of luminousness could be perceived in the room by any person possessing ordinary or normal vision. Hence the photographing of an invisible image, whether it be of a spirit or a lump of matter, is not scientifically impossible. If it reflect only the ultra-violet rays of the spectrum it will be easily photographed, although quite invisible to the sharpest eye.

"Again, Cromwell F. Varley, F.R.S., well known as one of the most eminent of electricians, says (*Electricity*, June 1871), when passing a current of electricity through a vacuum tube, the results of which were indicated by touches of light about the poles :—In one instance, although the experiment was carried on in a dark room, this light was so feeble that it could not be seen, and the operators doubted if the current were passing. But photography was at work, and in thirty minutes a very good picture was produced of what had taken place. This, he says, is a remarkable fact; indeed, it borders on the wonderful, that a phenomenon invisible to the human eye should have been, so to speak, seen by the photographic lens, and a record of it kept by chemical agency. It is highly suggestive, and we may anticipate that it will be turned to good account by practical philosophers.

"Some very striking phenomena in photographing the invisible may be produced by the agency of fluorescence. Figures depicted upon a background by one or other of certain substances I shall presently name, although invisible to the eye, may become visible to the camera. Of these the best known, although not the most effective, is bisulphate of quinine. Such a solution, although to the eye it is colourless like water, is to the camera as black as ink. Fill three phials respectively with water, quinine, and common writing-ink, and you have two whites and one black, but photograph them, and you have two blacks and one white. The camera has reduced the transparent quinine solution to the colour of the ink. Those of you who may care to experiment in this direction, please take notice that the quinine must be acidulated with sulphuric acid, and that hydrochloric acid, even a small trace, will destroy this property.

Among other substances that are fluorescent, or that change the refrangibility of rays of light, are mineral uranite, certain salts of uranium, canary glass, alcoholic solution of chlorophyll, aesculine, tincture of stramonium seeds, and of turmeric. There are others known to be still better, but my experiments in this direction are yet too incomplete to warrant my even indicating them.

"Let me for a moment enter the realm of speculation, and assume that there are really spirits invisible to the eye, but visible to the camera and to certain persons called seers or clairvoyants only. Might we not suggest that there is some fluorescent compound in the eyes of such persons not present in those whose eyes are normal, and that it is to this they owe their seeing powers? Some of you may probably be aware that Dr. Bence Jones and other philosophers have actually established the fact of such fluorescent substances being found in some eyes. May not this throw some light upon the recognised fact of certain animals being able to see in the dark?

"When the subject of fluorescence is more thoroughly investigated (it is a discovery of Sir D. Brewster, who was followed by Herschel and Professor Stokes, and is as yet but of yesterday), we may hope for a vast accession to our knowledge of subjects as yet very slightly understood.

"At the Bradford meeting of the British Association for the Advancement of Science, in 1873, Dr. Gladstone, F.R.S., demonstrated before the Mathematical and Physical Section what I have said respecting invisible drawings on white cards having produced bold and clear photographs when no eye could see the drawings themselves. I myself brought back to London these photographs, and, for ought I know, may have them still."

It will be seen that Mr. Taylor is well informed as to the way in which photographs can be faked. This forms in our eyes a certain guarantee with regard to the experiments he has himself made, since he could detect simulation better than any one else. Mr. Taylor continues:—

"For several years I have experienced a strong desire to ascertain by personal investigation the amount of truth in the ever-recurring allegation that figures other than those visually present in the room appeared on a sensitive plate. The difficulty was to get hold of a suitable person known as a sensitive or 'medium.' What a medium is, or how physically or mentally constituted to be different from other mortals, I am unable to say. He or she may not be a photographer, but must be present on each occasion of trial. Some may be mediums without their being aware of it. Like the chemical principle known as catalysis, they merely act by their presence. Such a one is Mr. D. of Glasgow, in whose presence psychic photographs have long been alleged to be obtained. He was lately in London on a visit, and a mutual friend got him to consent to extend his stay in order that I might try to get a psychic photograph under test conditions. To this he willingly agreed. My conditions were exceedingly simple, were courteously expressed to the host, and entirely acquiesced in. They were, that I for the nonce would assume them all to be tricksters, and, to guard against fraud, should use my own camera and unopened packages of dry plates purchased from dealers of repute, and that I should be excused from allowing a plate to go out of my own hand till after development, unless I felt otherwise disposed; but that, as I was to treat them as under suspicion, so must they treat me, and that every act I performed must be in presence of two witnesses, nay, that I would set a watch upon my own camera in the guise of a duplicate one of the same focus—in other words, I would use a binocular stereoscopic camera and dictate all the conditions of operation. All this I was told was what they very strongly wished me to do, as they desired to know the truth and that only. There were present, during one or other of the evenings when the trials were made, representatives of various schools of thought, including a clergyman of the Church of England; a practitioner of the healing art who is a Fellow of two learned societies; a gentleman who graduated in the Hall of Science in the days of the late Charles Bradlaugh; two extremely hard-headed Glasgow merchants, gentlemen of commercial eminence and probity; our host, his wife, the medium, and myself. Dr. G. was the first sitter, and, for a reason known to myself, I used a monocular camera. I myself took the plate out of a packet just previously ripped up under the surveillance of my two detectives. I placed the slide in my pocket, and exposed it by magnesium ribbon which I held in my own hand, keeping one eye, as it were, on the sitter and the other on the camera. There was no background. I myself took the plate from the dark slide, and under the eyes of the two detectives placed it in the developing dish. Between the camera and the sitter a female figure was developed, rather in a more pronounced form than that of the sitter. The lens was a portrait one of short focus; the figure being somewhat in front of the sitter was proportionately larger in dimensions, and was that of a lady. I did not recognise her or any of the other figures I obtained as being like any one I knew.

"Many experiments of like nature followed; on some plates were abnormal appearances, on others none. All this time Mr. D., the medium, during the exposure of the plates, was quite inactive. After one trial, which had proved successful, I asked him how he felt and what he had been thinking of during the exposure. He replied that his thoughts had been mainly concentrated upon his chances of securing a corner-seat in a smoking-carriage that night from Euston to Glasgow.

"If the precautions I took during all of the several experiments, such as those recorded, are by any of you thought to have been imperfect or incomplete, I pray of you to point them out. In some of them I relaxed my conditions to the extent of getting one of those present to lift out from the dark slide the exposed plate and transfer it to the developing dish held by myself, or to lift a plate from the manufacturer's package into the dark slide held in my own hand, this being done under my own eye, which was upon it all the time; but this did not seem to interfere with the general working of the experiments.

"The psychic figures behaved badly. Some were in

2 A

focus, others not so; some were lighted from the right, while the sitter was so from the left; some were comely, as the dame I shall show on the screen, others not so; some monopolised the major portion of the plate, quite obliterating the material sitters; others were as if an atrociously badly vignetted portrait, or one cut oval out of a photograph by a can-opener, or equally badly clipped out, were held up behind the sitter. But here is the point—not one of these figures which came out so strongly in the negative was visible in any form or shape to me during the time of exposure in the camera, and I vouch in the strongest manner for the fact that no one whatever had an opportunity of tampering with any plate anterior to its being placed in the dark slide or immediately preceding development. Pictorially they are vile, but how came they there?

"Now, all this time I imagine you are wondering how the stereoscopic camera was behaving itself *as such*. It is due to the psychic entities to say that whatever was produced on one half of the stereoscopic plates was reproduced on the other, alike good or bad in definition. But on a careful examination of one which was rather better than another, I deduce this fact, that the impressing of the spirit form was not consentaneous with that of the sitter. This I consider an important discovery. I carefully examined one in the stereoscope, and found that, while the two sitters were stereoscopic *per se*, the psychic figure was absolutely flat. I also found that the psychic figure was at least a millimetre higher up in one than the other. Now, as both had been simultaneously exposed, it follows to demonstration that although both were correctly placed vertically in relation to the particular sitter behind whom the figure appeared, and not so horizontally, this figure had not only *not* been impressed on the plate simultaneously with the two gentlemen forming the group, but had not been formed by the lens at all, and that therefore the psychic image might be produced without a camera. I think this is a fair deduction. But still the question presents itself, How came these figures there? I again assert that the plates were not tampered with by either myself or any one present. Are they crystallisations of thought? Have lens and light really nothing to do with their formation? The whole subject was mysterious enough on the hypothesis of an invisible spirit, whether a thought projection or an actual spirit, being really there in the vicinity of the sitter, but it is now a thousand times more so."

Let us remark first of all that there are two entirely different kinds of photographs which experimenters have called thought-photographs. The first only shows spots, lines, whirling clouds, more or less formless; the other, on the contrary, represents an object of a definite form.

The first scarcely interests us at all, because it does not come within the compass of what we are studying here. Nevertheless, in order to be complete, we ought to say a few words, leaving the authors we shall quote to bear the full responsibility of their statements.

It is said that photographs have been obtained of the effluvia emanating from a magnetic bar, and even pictures of the aureoles surrounding fingers placed on a sensitive plate in the developing bath; also aureoles surrounding freshly cut leaves.

In these cases there may be produced some kind of magnetic effluvia, which leave a trace on the plate. This would, however, have nothing to do with thought-photography.

But even on this supposition there would still be causes of error to eliminate. In the case, for example, of impressions of fingers, can it not be supposed that the heat from the fingers, or the chemical action of the skin, which always gives off a perspiration, imperceptible though it may be, would be capable of acting on the developing bath, or on the plate itself, and that what we see may be only the traces of chemical decomposition?

The following is the report of some experiments made by M. Albert Jounet, a very competent experimenter whose prudence and scientific spirit in research are well known to us.

Effluvia of the Gaze

"First of all I tried (by the process employed by Dr. Luys) to obtain the photograph of the effluvia from the eye on a sensitive dry plate, impressed as in ordinary photography before being immersed in the developer. Several attempts were unsuccessful, because the plate was held too close to my face. The heat and the effluvia produced enormous white spots on the plate. I then placed a sensitive plate in a photographic apparatus, from which, on the advice of M. Ferrari, photographer, I had removed the lens. I placed the left eye in the opening left by the removal of the lens, and I gazed at the plate for half-an-hour.

This hole was only large enough to admit the eye and a very little of the arch of the eyebrow and the socket. The plate was in the dark slide of the apparatus, about four inches from the eye. The whole experiment was made in the completely darkened laboratory; my head and the apparatus were further enveloped in a black cloth. On development the print showed some marks as though made with a paint-brush, radiating around the point where I thought my gaze was fixed, and in addition a rather large spot on one of the small sides of the plate, corresponding, in my opinion, with the direction of the nose and nostrils.

The plate being about four inches from the eye, it seemed difficult to ascribe the markings to the heat from the socket, which would have been carried off by the metallic edges of the hole. Moreover, I do not see how heat could make such singular paint-brush marks; it would have given a more uniform aureole. Finally, it would be impossible to ascribe them to lines of force produced in the bath, since the experiment was made on a dry plate.

Effluvia from the Hand influenced by Thought

I made some experiments with the hand, the plate being immersed at the time in the developer. Here we can invoke heat or lines of force. But why should a plate, impressed, while I was thinking of a pagan article read that morning and at the same time of God, only the middle finger being placed on the plate, have produced soft lines in the form of a river, ending in the remains of waves, peppered with black spots, the whole symbolising a sort of bust?

Why should another plate, impressed during a mental prayer to the Virgin and to the Blessed Albert the Great, have produced very long lines rising from the fingers like long jets of water, a phenomenon which I have not found on any plate impressed in the course of purely physical experiments without any religious idea?

Photographic Experiment on the Relation between Human and Terrestrial Polarity

From the purely physical point of view I have tried to discover by photography if Reichenbach's theory was true, whether the left side of a man and the south pole of the earth, and similarly the right side of a man and the north pole of the earth, were of opposite and attractive polarity.

I therefore placed my left hand on a plate immersed in the bath, the tips of the fingers directed towards the south, then as a counter-proof, the fingers of the right hand on another plate, the tips of the fingers directed towards the south. Now the traces of effluvia were wider and more extended in a southerly direction than on the second, which tended to confirm Reichenbach's theory— a theory which, moreover, is substantiated by the experiments of M. Durville.

I also placed the fingers of the right hand on a third plate, pointing the fingers towards the north, and the fingers of the left hand on a fourth, pointing them towards the north. On the third plate the effluvia were wider and more extended in a northerly direction than on the fourth.

According to my experiment it therefore seems that Reichenbach and Durville are right, that the south of the earth attracts and develops the effluvia of the right hand. But it is necessary for other researchers to repeat my experiment on this subject in order to confirm and establish it definitely.

We might also investigate photographically what are the relations between the right side of man and the east, west, zenith, and nadir; between the left side of man and these same directions; between the head, feet, back, and chest; the south, north, east, west, zenith, nadir, &c. Here is a field for investigation—the relations photographically demonstrated between human polarity and terrestrial and cosmic polarity.

Another experimenter, Commandant Darget of Tours, has also specially studied this phenomenon. The following is the account he gives of certain of his experiments :—

"I have already spoken (he writes) of the projection of a section of the brain of a calf, which had been slaughtered, on a photographic plate, which a butcher, in my presence, had held on its head.

"This phenomenon made me think that a newly cut plant which had been left for two or three days to die and exhale its vitality on to a plate might produce similar effects.

"My expectation was not in vain; it was even surpassed, the physiological effects of the loss of life in the plant being shown with a surprising intensity. On April 30th I took from the hands of one of my children a small fern which had been cut half-an-hour previously from our garden, and which had been placed in a book in order to flatten it. I took it to my dark room, and opening a box of Lumière plates I placed the fern on one of the plates; then I closed the box again. Two days afterwards I took the plate and developed it in the ordinary way in a bath of hydro-quinone. I was not surprised, but greatly pleased to see a picture of my fern appear. But what was my wonderment when I saw on the first print that each leaflet had thrown a shadow of its own, extending more than two millimetres away from it.

"Then I saw that this shadow was divided into zones. I then saw clearly that this shadow was only the continuation of the perisprit of the astral body of the plant, and that the zones were spasmodic convulsions, the successive contractions of the vitality as it left the organism.

"The phenomenon had been threefold :—

"1. Exact portrait of the plant.

"2. Effluvia thrown from each leaflet.

"3. Zones of contraction during its suffering.

"I then took the same plant, this time devoid of life, and placed it under a plate in the same manner, leaving this also two days. I developed it at the end of this time and obtained nothing, not the slightest imprint. This did not astonish me, the life having entirely left it during the first experiment.

"Therefore, when I propose to place a plate on the heart and head of a man who is believed to be dead, and who might be in danger of being buried alive, I believe that I am right. Traces of life, if any, will show themselves. Doubtless also we shall finish by finding plates more in accord with the vital fluid than the ordinary plates now in use."

Commandant Darget wished by another experiment to eliminate the action of the stored-up light.

"This stored-up light," he said, "the effects of which I believe to be greatly exaggerated, did not give me any results, although I made experiments in order to have it at its maximum.

"In fact, having exposed to the sun for two hours a five-centime copper piece and a five-franc silver piece, I put them on a plate for several hours, and the plate when developed showed nothing.

"I then took a leaf of the same fern that had been in the sun from six to eleven o'clock in the morning, and put it on a plate as on the first occasion. I did not get the least trace.

"When you tell me that animals do not die in the same way, and that I shall not always obtain the same results, you are quite right, and I might try ten times to obtain the photograph of a section of the brain of a slaughtered calf, and yet I might not obtain, as it happened for the first time on the proofs of which I have spoken, the design of the convolutions and anfractuosities of this organ with the same intensity and accuracy.

"Nevertheless, I think I can assert that with the present photographic plate, independent of any that may be discovered more sensitive to the vital fluid, physiological science can be enriched by new and unsuspected truths.

"One word more on the so-called *stored-up* light.

"On February 10th last I met M. Peigné, a photographer at Tours, who asked me to come into his laboratory, in order to see if the magnetic fluid could really be graphically shown.

"1. Two plates put in the same basin gave colours under my fingers in the same period of time. M. Peigné's plate had green and yellow borders outside the fingers, and carmine, red with large blue spots under the fingers. Further, some long effluvia, radiating from each of his fingers, extended almost to the edge of a 9×12 ctm. ($3\frac{1}{2} \times 4\frac{3}{4}$ in.) plate.

"This is what I call the fluid of the magnetisers. With regard to myself I had good colour, but not any effluvia.

"2. Two dry plates, with two five-franc pieces taken from M. Peigné's purse, gave, in his case, their circumference and some letters of the inscription. In my case the circle only.

"It follows that his magnetism was more powerful than mine.

"But it must be acknowledged that if the two pieces had been exposed to the sun for some hours they would have imprinted neither their circumference nor the letters, any more than in the experiment related at the commencement."

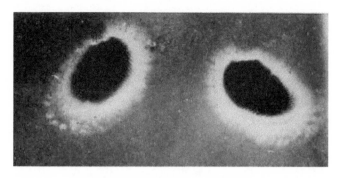

Fig. 5.—Radiation from two thumbs of Commandant Darget.

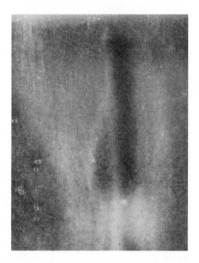

Fig. 6.—Thought-photograph (first bottle). Obtained by Commandant Darget when thinking intensely of a bottle which he had just been looking at.

Fig. 7.—Thought-photograph (second bottle). Obtained by Commandant Darget.

The second category of thought-photographs is still more interesting. Here certain pictures appear sometimes with such clearness that it is difficult to attribute them to chance.

Unfortunately the experiments are not yet sufficiently conclusive for us to be able to say that their existence is scientifically demonstrated.

In France, a man whose rectitude can be doubted by none, Commandant Darget, states that he has obtained some, which we reproduce in order to convey some idea to those who have no knowledge of them.

The following is the manner in which the author himself says he obtained them:—

There are first of all two photographs representing a bottle.

"They were taken, like that of the cane," writes Commandant Darget, "gelatine side downwards, the fingers touching the plate on the glass side, in order to project the fluid and the thought constructing the fluid, putting it in place, so to speak, and making the *Mens agitat molem;* to effect this a strong exertion of will-power was needed. M. A., through whose mediumship one of the photographs was obtained, told me that he did not wish to try again because of the headache from which he suffered after these experiments."

The following is Commandant Darget's own account of the manner in which he obtained the photographs of the bottle.

"On May 27, 1896, M. A. showed me in *L'Illustration* of May 23rd a finger with some fluidic flames obtained by Dr. Le Bon in the developing bath when touching the gelatine. He invited me that very evening to try the same experiment. I did so, and obtained a large radiation around my five fingers.

"Then M. A. said to me that if one could represent an object, the phenomenon would become remarkable. Here I must enter into some details.

"M. A. had just poured me out a glass of old brandy; I had kept the bottle before my eyes for half-an-hour. I had expressed my intention of tasting it again, saying jokingly, that this would give me more fluid. Then I put a plate in the bath, which I touched on the glass side and not on the gelatine side. I thought first of all of a table; my thought glided on to the image of a chair, which also vanished, giving place to the image of the bottle from which I had drunk. It must be observed that I had a similar bottle containing the developer before my eyes, and I saw it, by means of the red light, in the dark room.

"The picture which came on the plate when developed is shown herewith. It is certain that the outline of a bottle can be distinguished; it is so clear that it cannot be attributed to a shadow or to a chance fogging.

"M. A. having pointed out that in order to thoroughly prove the reality of this phenomenon, it would be necessary to obtain a second bottle, we agreed to try.

"He did not omit to make me drink of the same old brandy; for my part, I looked for a long time at the bottle.

"Having gone into the dark room, I tried the same process as in the preceding experiment, placing my fingers on the glass side of the plate in the bath. When the plate was fixed and washed we looked for the picture of the bottle and found it."

Commandant Darget also obtained some very curious photographs, amongst others that of a walking-stick.

This is what he says himself:—

"The photograph of the walking-stick was obtained at Vouziers eleven years ago. It was a stick with a handle which I generally used. I had put it on my desk where I made my photographs that evening, after closing the windows and taking out my red lantern.

"With regard to the eagle, it was produced in this way. Mme. Darget was in my office, lying on my sofa, about ten o'clock in the evening. I said to her: 'I am going to put out the lamp and to try (as I have already done sometimes) to take a fluidic print over my forehead. I will hand you a plate for you to do it as well.'

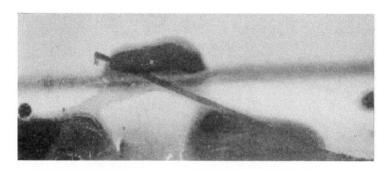

FIG. 8.—Thought-photograph. The walking-stick. Obtained by Commandant Darget.

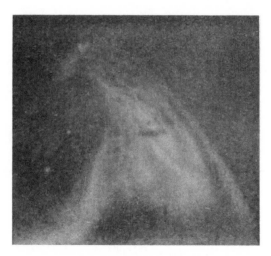

FIG. 9.—Dream-photograph. Eagle. Obtained by Commandant Darget.

"I therefore handed her a plate, which she held with both her hands about an inch in front of her forehead. A short time afterwards, it might be about ten minutes, she said to me : 'I think I have been asleep; I am very tired, I am going to lie down.' And, feeling her way in the darkness, she handed me the plate.

"I then went to develop it, and was surprised to see this astonishing figure of an eagle. I have called it ' a dream-photograph,' although my wife does not remember having dreamed of a bird or anything else while she held the plate.

These various experiments which we have desired to make known to the reader are, as may be seen, still quite incomplete. They indicate, however, a path which it would be well to follow, because it seems to be rich in discoveries of great importance.

We have recently made this question a subject of study in the various groups of the Société Universelle d'Études Psychiques, and experiments are at present in progress, the results of which we cannot yet give.

We shall now see what are the principal points that ought to be observed if we wish to experiment on these phenomena, and if our experiments are to possess scientific value.

First of all, we must avoid everything which might produce on the plates any trace that might lead us into error. We must avoid all accidental fogging arising from imperfect closing of the apparatus containing the plate, or from a badly constructed dark room.

The experimenter should only operate with plates purchased by himself, and taken from a box which he had himself opened at the time of the experiment.

The experimenter ought only to use instruments and materials belonging to him, well known to him, and verified immediately before the experiment.

The experimenter ought to have before his mind all the possible processes of trickery, and particularly those described by Mr. Taylor; he ought himself to prepare the background and all the accessory objects which might be taken in the photograph. In each experiment he ought to compare the results obtained with other trial plates which are placed in the bath without having been exposed.

All these conditions fulfilled, here are some experiments which can be made :—

Method of M. Jounet: In the dark room, place the sensitive plate at the bottom of a rectangular box, one of the slides of which remains open. While holding the eyes against this opening look at the plate, as though looking in a stereoscope, and think of an object of very simple form, of which it is desired to see the picture imprinted on the plate.

According to the procedure of Commandant Darget, take an object of very simple form, gaze attentively at it for a few moments in order to engrave it firmly on the mind ; then go into the dark room and make the three following experiments :—

1. Place a photographic plate with the glass side against the forehead for a quarter of an hour, mentally picturing the object decided upon, and strongly desiring to make an impression on the plate.

2. Place the hand on a plate (or hold the plate in the hand) for a quarter of an hour, operating as before.

3. Put the plate into a developing bath, placing the fingers of one hand on the edge of the plate for ten minutes. There should always be the desire to imprint on the plate the picture of the object which is very strongly thought of.

After each operation develop the plate at the same time as another (check) plate.

It is well to isolate oneself as much as possible, and to be free from all disturbing influences during the course of the experiments, which ought to be made with very sensitive plates.

I particularly advise the following new methods, in which the co-operation of the medium is made use of :—

1. The medium being in a spontaneous condition of

waiting, a light hypnotic condition, or completely hypnotised, suggest to him the desire to impress the picture of an
object on a plate, which should be placed on a table under
his hand, the hand touching the glass side.

2. Suggest to the medium that he can see the picture
on a plate held in front of him in the dark room.

3. In the light focus a photographic apparatus on a
white background. Then suggest to the medium to make
the object appear on this screen, and when he says he sees
it clearly take an instantaneous photograph.

Try the same experiment again with a black background.

Always expose check-plates before the medium enters.

4. In the dark room focus the apparatus on a white
background, then darken the room. Suggest to the
medium to make the desired picture appear on this background and to see it. When he sees it, uncover the lens
and give a prolonged exposure, as long as the picture
remains visible to the subject.

The same operation with a black background and
check-plates as in the preceding experiment.

In all these experiments the subject should be continuously held by an experimenter, so that he is known
to be completely motionless throughout the experiment,
outside the range of the apparatus.

I would also advise, as in the experiments on motricity, to surround the medium with a group of experimenters, who all, at the same time as the medium, should
have present in their thoughts the picture they desire to
appear, and like him have their gaze fixed on the white
or black background with the desire to make the picture
appear.

By thus experimenting in a careful and methodical
manner we may hope, when we meet with favourable
conditions, to succeed in photographing pictures invisible
to our retina, if such a thing is possible, as certain
experiments quoted in this chapter lead us to suppose.

CHAPTER XXVII

REPORTS OF THE LONDON AND MILAN COMMITTEES ON PSYCHICAL PHENOMENA

WE come now to a class of phenomena different from the preceding: these are the phenomena in which externalisation of force is manifested.

As the phenomena which we are now about to examine are much more difficult of belief than all the others, we will first of all give some extracts from the reports of two scientific committees, which devoted themselves to a very strict study of them in a spirit of rigorous scientific investigation.

The authority of the persons forming these committees is such that no one can doubt the results of their inquiry, and the conclusions to which they came.

It will be noticed that these two Committees were composed of men whose names and qualifications stand equally high as guarantees of authenticity and sincerity. Moreover, they worked in two different countries and at different times; it would therefore be absurd to reject their evidence, under the pretext that they had all been led into error in the same way.

SOME EXTRACTS FROM THE REPORTS OF THE COMMITTEE OF THE DIALECTICAL SOCIETY OF LONDON

The Dialectical Society of London, which was founded in 1867, under the presidency of Sir John Lubbock, and comprised the principal English savants, resolved on January 6, 1869 :—

"That the Council be requested to appoint a Committee, in conformity with Bye-law VII., to investigate

the phenomena alleged to be Spiritual Manifestations,
and to report thereon."

On January 26, 1869, the Committee was nominated
and consisted of the following:—

H. G. Atkinson, Esq., F.G.S.
G. Wheatley Bennett, Esq.
J. S. Bergheim, Esq., C.E.
Chas. Bradlaugh, Esq.
G. Fenton Cameron, Esq., M.D.
George Cary, Esq. B.A.
E. W. Cox, Esq., Serjeant-at-Law.
Rev. C. Maurice Davies, D.D.
D. H. Dyte, Esq., M.R.C.S.
Mrs. D. H. Dyte.
James Edmunds, Esq., M.D.
Mrs. Edmunds.
James Gannon, Esq.
Grattan Geary, Esq.
William B. Gower, Esq.
Robert Hannah, Esq.
Jenner Gale Hillier, Esq.

Mrs. J. H. Hillier.
Henry Jeffery, Esq.
H. D. Jencken, Esq.,-Barrister-at-Law.
Albert Kisch, Esq., M.R.C.S.
J. H. Levy, Esq.
Joseph Maurice, Esq.
Isaac L. Meyers, Esq.
B. M. Moss, Esq.
Robert Quelch, Esq., C.E.
Thomas Reed, Esq.
Russell Roberts, Esq., Ph.D.
W. H. Swepstone, Esq., Solicitor.
William Volckman, Esq.
Alfred R. Wallace, Esq., F.R.G.S.
Josiah Webber, Esq.
Horace S. Yeomans, Esq.

Report of the Committee

GENTLEMEN,—The Committee appointed by you to investigate the phenomena alleged to be Spiritual Manifestations, report thereon as follows:—

Your Committee have held fifteen meetings, at which
they received evidence from thirty-three persons, who
described phenomena which, they stated, had occurred
within their own personal experience.

Your Committee have received written statements relating to the phenomena from thirty-one persons.

Your Committee invited the attendance and requested
the co-operation and advice of scientific men who had
publicly expressed opinions, favourable or adverse, to the
genuineness of the phenomena.

Your Committee also specially invited the attendance

of persons who had publicly ascribed the phenomena to imposture or delusion.

Your Committee, however, while successful in procuring the evidence of believers in the phenomena and in their supernatural origin, almost wholly failed to obtain evidence from those who attributed them to fraud or delusion.

As it appeared to your Committee to be of the greatest importance that they should investigate the phenomena in question by personal experiment and test, they resolved themselves into sub-committees as the best means of doing so.

Six sub-committees were accordingly formed.

All of these have sent in reports, from which it appears that a large majority of the members of your Committee have become actual witnesses to several phases of the phenomena without the aid or presence of any professional medium, although the greater part of them commenced their investigations in an avowedly sceptical spirit.

These reports, hereto subjoined, substantially corroborate each other, and would appear to establish the following propositions:—

1. That sounds of a very varied character, apparently proceeding from articles of furniture, the floor and walls of the room—the vibrations accompanying which sounds are often distinctly perceptible to the touch—occur, without being produced by muscular action or mechanical contrivance.

2. That movements of heavy bodies take place without mechanical contrivance of any kind or adequate exertion of muscular force by the persons present, and frequently without contact or connection with any person.

3. That these sounds and movements often occur at the times and in the manner asked for by persons present, and by means of a simple code of signals answer questions and spell out coherent communications.

4. That the answers and communications thus obtained are, for the most part, of a commonplace character; but facts are sometimes correctly given which are only shown to one of the persons present.

5. That the circumstances under which the phenomena occur are variable, the most prominent fact being, that the presence of certain persons seems necessary to their occurrence, and that of others generally adverse; but this difference does not appear to depend upon any belief or disbelief concerning the phenomena.

6. That, nevertheless, the occurrence of the phenomena is not insured by the presence or absence of such persons respectively.

Reports of the Experimental Sub-committees

Since their appointment on the 16th of February 1869, your Sub-committee have held forty meetings for the purpose of experiment and test.

All of these meetings were held at the private residences of members of the Committee, purposely to preclude the possibility of prearranged mechanism or contrivance.

The furniture of the room in which the experiments were conducted was on every occasion its accustomed furniture.

The tables were in all cases heavy dining-tables, requiring a strong effort to move them. The smallest of them was 5 ft. 9 in. long and 4 ft. wide, and the largest 9 ft. 3 in. long and 4½ ft. wide, and of proportionate weight.

The rooms, tables, and furniture generally were repeatedly subjected to careful examination before, during, and after the experiments, to ascertain that no concealed machinery, instrument, or other contrivance existed by means of which the sounds or movements hereinafter mentioned could be caused.

The experiments were conducted in the light of gas, except on the few occasions specially noted in the minutes.

Your Committee have avoided the employment of professional or paid mediums, the mediumship being that of members of your Sub-committee, persons of good social position and of unimpeachable integrity, having no

2 B

pecuniary object to serve, and nothing to gain by deception.

Your Committee have held some meetings without the presence of a medium (it being understood that throughout this report the word "medium" is used simply to designate an individual without whose presence the phenomena described either do not occur at all, or with greatly diminished force and frequency), purposely to try if they could produce, by any efforts, effects similar to those witnessed when a medium was present. By no endeavours were they enabled to produce anything at all resembling the manifestations which took place in the presence of a medium.

Every test that the combined intelligence of your Committee could devise has been tried with patience and perseverance. The experiments were conducted under a great variety of conditions, and ingenuity has been exerted in devising plans by which your Committee might verify their observations and preclude the possibility of imposture or of delusion.

Your Committee have confined their report to facts witnessed by them in their collective capacity, which facts were palpable to the senses, and their reality capable of demonstrative proof.

Of the members of your Sub-committee about four-fifths entered upon the investigation wholly sceptical as to the reality of the alleged phenomena, firmly believing them to be the result either of imposture or of delusion or of involuntary evidence, under conditions that precluded the possibility of either of these solutions and after trial and test many times repeated, that the most sceptical of your Sub-committee were slowly and reluctantly convinced that the phenomena exhibited in the course of their protracted inquiry were veritable facts.

The result of their long-continued and carefully conducted experiments, after trial by every detective test they could devise, has been to establish conclusively :—

First. That under certain bodily or mental conditions of one or more of the persons present, a force is exhibited sufficient to set in motion heavy substances without the employment of any muscular force, without contact or material connection of any kind between such substances and the body of any person present.

Second. That this force can cause sounds to proceed, distinctly audible to all present, from solid substances not in contact with, nor having any visible or material connection with, the body of any person present, and which sounds are proved to proceed from such substances by the vibrations which are distinctly felt when they are touched.

Third. That this force is frequently directed by intelligence.

At thirty-four out of the forty meetings of your Committee some of these phenomena occurred.

A description of one experiment, and the manner of conducting it, will best show the care and caution with which your Committee have pursued their investigation.

So long as there was contact, or even the possibility of contact, by the hands or feet, or even by the clothes of any person in the room, with the substance moved or sounded, there could be no perfect assurance that the motions and sounds were not produced by the person so in contact. The following experiment was therefore tried.

On an occasion when eleven members of your Sub-committee had been sitting round one of the dining-tables above described for forty minutes, and various motions and sounds had occurred, they, by way of test, turned the backs of their chairs to the table, and about nine inches from it. They all then knelt upon their chairs, placing their arms upon the backs thereof. In this position their feet were, of course, turned away from the table, and by no possibility could be placed under it or touch the floor. The hands of each person were extended over the table at about four inches from the surface. Contact, therefore, with any part of the table could not take place without detection.

In less than a minute the table, untouched, moved four times; at first about five inches to one side, then about twelve inches to the opposite side, and then, in like manner, four inches and six inches respectively.

The hands of all present were next placed on the back of their chairs, and about a foot from the table, which again moved, as before, five times, over spaces varying from four to six inches. Then all the chairs were removed twelve inches from the table, and each person knelt on his chair as before—this time, however, folding his hands behind his back, his body being thus about eighteen inches from the table, and having the back of the chair between himself and the table. The table again moved four times, in various directions. In the course of this conclusive experiment, and in less than half-an-hour, the table thus moved, without contact or possibility of contact with any person present, thirteen times, the movements being in different directions, and some of them according to the request of various members of your Sub-committee.

The table was then carefully examined, turned upside down and taken to pieces, but nothing was discovered to account for the phenomena. The experiment was conducted throughout in the full light of gas above the table.

Altogether, your Sub-committee have witnessed upwards of fifty similar motions without contact on eight different evenings, in the houses of members of your Sub-committee, the most careful tests being applied on each occasion.

In all similar experiments the possibility of mechanical or other contrivance was further negatived by the fact that the movements were in various directions, now to one side, then to the other; now up the room, now down the room—motions that would have required the co-operation of many hands or feet; and these, from the great size and weight of the tables, could not have been so used without the visible exercise of muscular force. Every hand and foot was plainly to be seen, and could not have been moved without instant detection.

Delusion was out of the question. The motions were

in various directions, and were witnessed simultaneously by all present. They were matters of measurement, and not of opinion or fancy.

And they occurred so often, under so many and such various conditions, with such safeguards against error or deception, and with such invariable results, as to satisfy the members of your Sub-committee by whom the experiments were tried, wholly sceptical as most of them were when they entered upon the investigation, that there is a force capable of moving heavy bodies without material contact, and which force is in some unknown manner dependent upon the presence of human beings.

Your Sub-committee have not, collectively, obtained any evidence as to the nature and source of this force, but simply as to the fact of its existence.

There appears to your Committee to be no ground for the popular belief that the presence of sceptics interferes in any manner with the production or action of the force.

In conclusion, your Committee express their unanimous opinion that the one important physical fact thus proved to exist, that motion may be produced in solid bodies without material contact, by some hitherto unrecognised force operating within an undefined distance from the human organism, and beyond the range of muscular action, should be subjected to further scientific examination, with a view to ascertain its true source and power.

REPORT OF THE MILAN COMMISSION FOR THE INVESTIGATION OF PSYCHICAL PHENOMENA

Taking into consideration the evidence of Professor Lombroso on the subject of mediumistic phenomena produced through Mme. Eusapia Paladino, the undersigned met at Milan for the purpose of holding a series of séances with her with the object of verifying the phenomena, by submitting her to experiments and to observations as rigorous as possible. Seventeen séances in all were held in M. Finzi's rooms at Via del Monte di Pietà, between 9 P.M. and midnight.

The medium, who was invited to the séances by M. Aksakof, was introduced by Chevalier Chiaia, who was only present at a third of the séances, and his attendance was almost entirely confined to the earlier and less important ones.

In view of the stir made in the press by the announcement of these séances, and the varied opinions expressed with regard to Mme. Eusapia and Chevalier Chiaia, we think it our duty to publish without delay this short report of all our observations and experiments.

Before entering upon the subject we must at once remark that the results obtained did not always correspond with our expectation. Not but what we had a large quantity of facts, apparently or really important or marvellous ; but, in the majority of cases, we were unable to apply the rules of the experimental art which, in other fields of observation, are regarded as necessary in order to arrive at sure and indisputable results.

The most important of these rules is to change, one after the other, the methods of experiment, so as to ascertain the real cause, or, at least, the true conditions of all the facts. Now it is exactly from this aspect that our experiments seem to us to be at present wanting in completeness.

It is quite true that the medium, in order to prove her good faith, often spontaneously proposed to change some particular feature of one or the other of the experiments, and several times took the initiative in these variations. But this was often only with regard to matters apparently immaterial from our point of view. The variations, on the contrary, which seemed to us to be necessary to place beyond doubt the true character of the results, were not accepted as possible by the medium ; or, if they were carried out, in the majority of instances only made the experiment of no effect, or at least led to obscure results.

We do not believe that we have the right to explain these facts by the injurious suppositions which many still find the most simple, and of which the newspapers have made themselves the champions. We believe that the phenomena are of unknown nature, and we admit that we do not know the conditions necessary for their production. To attempt to fix the conditions on our own account would be as extravagant as to pretend to repeat Torricelli's barometer with a tube closed at the bottom, or to make electro-static experiments in an extremely humid atmosphere; or, again, to produce a photograph by exposing a sensitive plate to broad daylight before placing it in the camera. But while admitting all this, which no reasonable man can doubt, it is none the less true that the obvious impossibility of varying the experiments according to our fancy has singularly decreased the value and interest of the results obtained, by taking from them in several instances that rigour of demonstration which we have a right to demand in facts of this character, or rather, at which they ought to aim.

For this reason, out of the innumerable experiments carried out, we omit or only cursorily mention those which seem to us inconclusive, and with regard to which various conclusions might easily be drawn by different experimenters.

We shall note, however, in considerable detail, the circumstances in which, in spite of the obstacle we have mentioned, they seem to us to have attained a sufficient degree of probability.

I

Phenomena observed in the Light

1. Mechanical movements unexplainable by contact of the hands alone.

(*a*) *Lateral raising of the table under the medium's hands when seated at one end of the shorter sides (ends).*— We used for this experiment a deal table made expressly for the purpose by M. Finzi, 3 ft. 8 ins. long, 28 ins. wide, and 32 ins. high, weighing nearly eighteen pounds. Among the various methods by which responses were given by the table, it was impossible not to observe the blows frequently produced by two of the feet, raised at the same time under the hands of the medium, without being preceded by any lateral movement of the table, with force and rapidity and several times in succession, as though the table was fixed to the medium's hands, and these movements were, moreover, more remarkable since the medium was always seated at one of the ends of the table, and we never ceased to hold her hands and feet. These phenomena were also produced when, for greater ease of observation, we left the medium alone at the table, her two hands placed completely on the top of the table and her sleeves turned up almost to the elbow.

We remained standing around it, and the space over and under it was well lighted. In these conditions the table raised itself at an angle of from thirty to forty degrees and remained thus for some minutes, while the medium held her arms extended and struck her feet against each other. On pressing with the hand on the side raised, we felt a considerable elastic resistance.

(*b*) *Measure of the force applied for the lateral rising of the table.*—For this experiment the table was suspended by one of its short sides from a dynamometer held by a cord, which was fixed to a small beam resting on two cupboards. In these conditions the end of the table was raised nearly six inches, and the dynamometer registered over seven and a half pounds.

The medium was seated at the same end of the table, with her hands completely placed on the table to right and left of the cord connected with the dynamometer. Our hands formed a chain above the table without pressure, in such a way that they could in any case have only tended to increase the pressure on the table. On the contrary, we asked that the pressure should be diminished, and soon the table rose on the side where the dynamometer was. M. Gerosa, who followed the indications of the apparatus, called out this diminution represented by the successive figures: 3, 2, 1, 0 kilogrammes; then the table was raised so far that the dynamometer rested horizontally on the table.

Then we changed the conditions by placing our hands under the table, the medium particularly placing hers, not only under the table, by which means she could have reached the cross-bar and thus pulled the table down, but under the cross-piece itself which connected the table legs, touching it with the back of her hand instead of the palm. Thus all the hands could only have diminished the traction on the dynamometer. On the desire that this traction should be immediately increased, M. Gerosa said that the figures showed an increase from 3 kgr. 5, up to 5 kgr. 6 (from $7\frac{1}{4}$ to $12\frac{1}{4}$ lbs.).

During all these experiments each of the medium's feet rested on the feet of her neighbours to right and left.

(c) *Complete raising of the table.*—It was natural to conclude that, if the table, by an apparent contradiction of the laws of gravitation, could be partially raised it could also be completely raised. This, in fact, did take place; and this raising, one of the most frequent phenomena with Eusapia, lent itself to a satisfactory examination.

It is generally produced under the following conditions: the persons seated round the table place their hands on it and form a chain; each hand of the medium is held by the nearest hand of each of her next neighbours; each of her feet rests under one of their feet, and they also press their knees against hers; she usually sits at one of the smaller ends, the least favourable position for a mechanical raising. After a few minutes the table makes a movement to the side, rises either to right or left, and finally rises altogether with its four feet horizontally in the air, generally to a height of four to eight inches, but, in exceptional instances, to twenty-four or twenty-eight inches; then it falls back on to all four feet simultaneously.

It often remains in the air for several seconds and while there makes certain undulatory movements, during which the four feet of the table can be examined. During the raising the medium's right hand, as well as her neighbour's, often leaves the table and they remain suspended

in the air above it.   During the experiment the medium's
face becomes convulsed, her hands contracted, she groans
and seems to suffer, as is generally the case when phenomena are produced.

In order to observe the fact better we gradually
eliminated the persons round the table, for we found
that a chain of several persons was not at all necessary
either for this phenomenon or for others, and eventually
we only had one person at the table, with the medium on
his left.   This person placed his foot on Eusapia's two feet
and one hand on her knees, and held the medium's left
hand in his other hand, the medium's right hand being
placed on the table, in sight of all, or else the medium
held it in the air during the raising.

As the table remained in the air for several seconds it
was possible to obtain several photographs of the phenomenon, a thing which had not previously been done.
Three photographic cameras were placed in different parts
of the room, and a magnesium flash was given at a suitable moment.   We obtained in all twenty-one photographs, some of which were excellent—thus on one of
them we saw Professor Richet, who held one hand, the
knees and one foot of the medium, while Professor
Lombroso held the other hand, and the table rose
horizontally; as could be seen by the space between the
extremity of each foot and the extremity of the corresponding shadow.

In all the previous experiments we principally turned
our attention to carefully inspecting the position of the
medium's hands and feet, and in this respect we think
we can say that they were quite above suspicion.

However, we cannot pass over in silence one fact, to
which we paid no attention until the evening of October 5th, but which probably must have occurred in
previous experiments.   It was found that the four
feet of the table could not be regarded as completely
isolated during the raising, because one of them at least
was in contact with the lower edge of the medium's
skirt.

On that evening, a little before the raising, we saw Eusapia's skirt blown out on the left side until it touched the foot of the table.

One of us was deputed to prevent this contact and the table was not raised as at other times, and it only occurred when the observer intentionally permitted this contact to take place, as shown in the photographs taken of this experiment, and also in those where the foot in question is visible to some extent at its lower end. It was noticed that at the same time the medium had her hand resting on the upper part of the table and on the same side, so that this foot was under the medium's influence in the lower part by means of the skirt and in the upper part by means of her hand.

We could not verify in any way the degree of pressure exerted at this moment on the table by the medium's hand, and we could not ascertain, owing to the brevity of the raising, what counterbalancing influence on the table was exerted by contact with the skirt.

In order to avoid this contact we proposed that the raising should occur while the medium and her co-operators were standing, but this was not successful. We then tried placing the medium on one of the longer sides of the table, but the medium objected to this, saying that it was impossible. We are therefore forced to state that we did not succeed in obtaining a complete raising of the table with the four feet absolutely free of all contact, and there are reasons for fearing that a similar objection exists in the movements of the two feet which took place on the medium's side.

In what way could the contact of a light material with one foot of the table at its lower end assist the raising? This we are unable to say. The hypothesis that the robe could conceal a solid support skilfully introduced to support momentarily the foot of the table, can scarcely be accepted.

In fact, to support the whole table on only one foot by means of the action which could be produced by one hand on the upper part of the table, would demand that the hand should exert on the table a very strong pressure such as we do not think Eusapia would be capable of exerting, even for three or four seconds.

We have convinced ourselves of this by making the experiment ourselves with the same table.

The only raisings of the table that would be free from this uncertainty would be those in which the two feet furthest from the medium were raised; but this very frequent kind of raising is too easy to produce by a slight pressure of the medium's hand on the side where she is placed, and is not of the slightest value as proof. The same remark applies to the lateral movements, on the two feet placed to right and left of the medium, which she could easily produce by the simple pressure of one hand only.

(d) *Variations of the pressure exercised by the whole body of the medium seated in a weighing-machine.*— The experiment was very interesting but also very difficult, because we know that every voluntary or other movement of the medium on the plate of the scale will cause oscillations of this plate, and consequently of the lever.

In order to make the experiment conclusive, the lever must remain a few seconds in its new position in order to allow of the weight being measured by moving the counterpoise. We made the attempt with this hope. The medium, seated on a chair, was placed on a balance, and we found her weight to be 136 lbs. After some oscillations there was a very pronounced depression of the lever for some seconds, which permitted M. Gerosa, who was at the lever, to measure the weight immediately; it was 114 lbs., or a decrease of 22 lbs.

On our expressing the desire to obtain the reverse result, the end of the lever was soon raised and showed an increase of 22 lbs. This experiment was repeated several times and at five different séances; once there were no results, but the last time a registering apparatus enabled us to obtain two curves of the phenomenon.

We tried ourselves to produce similar depressions and

only succeeded when we stood upright on the plate, and then leaning over first to one side and then to the other with very extensive movements, such as we had never seen the medium make, and which her position in the chair would not have permitted. While recognising that the experiment could not be declared absolutely satisfactory, we completed it by that which will be described in section 3.

In this experiment of the balance some of us think that its success probably depended upon contact of the medium's gown with the floor on which the balance directly rested. This was verified by an observer specially appointed on the evening of October 9th. When the medium was on the balance, the one who was charged with the supervision of her feet soon saw the lower end of her gown stretch out, so as to hang below the platform of the machine. When this was objected to the levitation did not take place, but when we allowed Eusapia's gown to touch the floor there were constant and evident levitations, denoted by great variations in the indications on the dial, registering the variation of weight.

On another occasion we tried to obtain the levitation of the medium by placing her on a large drawing-board and the latter on the platform of the weighing-machine. The board prevented the dress from touching the floor, and the experiment was not successful.

Finally, on the evening of October 13th, another balance in the form of a steel-yard was prepared, the plate quite isolated from the floor—nearly a foot distant from it. As we particularly watched to avoid all chance contact between the plate and the floor, even by the edge of Eusapia's gown, the experiment failed. However, in these conditions we believed we obtained some results on October 18th, but this time the experiment was not conclusive; we were not sure whether a mantilla which Eusapia was wearing round her head and shoulders had touched the top of the scale during the continuous movement of the medium. We concluded that no levitation had been entirely successful when the medium was completely isolated from the floor.

2. Mechanical movements with indirect contact of the medium, in conditions that render mechanical action impossible.

(*a*) *Horizontal movement of the table, the medium having her hands placed on three balls or on four casters.* —For this experiment, as conclusive as it was difficult, the feet of the table were furnished with casters. A board, sixteen and a half inches long and twelve and a half inches wide, was placed on three wooden balls an inch and a half in diameter, and then placed on the table. The medium was asked to place her hands on the middle of this board, her sleeves were drawn back about her elbows; her neighbours placed their feet and knees against hers, the legs of the table being isolated in the angles formed by the legs of the medium and the controllers. In these conditions the table moved several times backwards and forwards, to right and to left and parallel to itself for a distance of four to five inches, while, during this time, the board, although it was on the balls, moved with the table as though forming a part of it.

In a second experiment of the same character the balls which, at the commencement of the phenomenon, easily escaped from underneath the board, were replaced by four easily moving casters attached by pivots to the four corners of the board, which gave greater stability to the apparatus without making the movements more difficult. The result was the same as in the preceding case.

(*b*) *Raising of the table with three balls or four casters, and a board interposed between the table and the hands of the medium.*—This phenomenon, already obtained in the first experiment, was repeated with the board on casters in the conditions already detailed. The table was completely raised on the side of the medium and under her hands, together with the board on balls or on casters, to a height of four to six inches without any displacement of the board, and fell back with it.

By means of this experiment we obtained indisputable proof that lateral and vertical movements of the table could be obtained independently of any effort of the medium's hands. In this case surveillance was only exercised on the medium's hands; the table had several people around it, and it was not easy to verify if there had been contact between the feet of the table and the medium's dress, which in other experiments seemed to be an essential condition of success. The same remark applies to the experiment reported a little later on under section 3.

In order to remove all reason for doubt, we had arranged a piece of cardboard cylindrically around the medium and her chair, so as to protect her from all external contact up to a height of two feet from the floor. The medium had scarcely seen it, when she declared that to keep her enclosed in that would take away all her power. Therefore we were compelled to abandon it. Once only was it used, but in such circumstances as made it almost superfluous.

3. Movements of objects at a distance without contact with any of the persons present.

(a) *Spontaneous movements of objects.*—These phenomena have been observed on several occasions during our séances; frequently a chair placed not far from the table, between the medium and one of her neighbours, began to move and sometimes approached the table. A remarkable instance occurred during the second séance, in full light: a heavy chair, which was not far from the table and behind the medium was displaced. M. Schiaparelli, who was close to the medium, rose and put it back into its place, but he had scarcely sat down again when the chair came towards him a second time.

(b) *Movements of the table without contact.*—It was desired to obtain this phenomenon by way of experiment. For that purpose the table was placed on casters. The medium's feet were controlled as stated in number 2, and all present formed the chain with their hands and those of the medium. When the table began to move, we all raised our hands without breaking the chain, and the table, being isolated, made several movements as in the second experiment. This experiment was repeated several times.

(c) *Movements of the arms of the rocking balance.*— This experiment was made for the first time in the séance of September 21st. After having made certain of the weight that the medium's body exercised on the balance while she remained seated, it was interesting to see if this experiment would be successful at a distance; for this purpose the balance was placed behind the medium's back as she was seated at the table, in such a way that the platform was about four inches from her chair. We first of all placed the edge of her dress in contact with the platform, and the lever then began to move. M. Brofferio stooped down on the ground and lifted up the edge with his hand, he found it was not quite straight and resumed his place; the movements continued with a fair degree of force. M. Aksakof placed himself behind the medium, completely isolated the platform from her gown, folded the latter under her chair, and by means of his hand assured himself that the space between the platform and the chair was quite free, as he at once informed us. While he was in this position the lever continued to move, and to beat against the cross-bar, as we both saw and heard. The same experiment was made a second time on September 26th, in the presence of Professor Richet. He immediately left his place by the side of the medium, and he assured himself by passing his hand in the air, and on the ground between the medium and the platform, that the space was free from all means of communication by a thread or any other artifice.

(d) *Blows and reproductions of sounds in the table.* —These blows are always produced during our séances in order to express "yes" or "no," sometimes they are strong and clear and seem to sound within the wood of the table; but, as we have remarked, the localisation of the sound is not an easy matter, and we were not able to try any experiment on this point, with the exception of rhythmic blows or various rubbings which we made on the table, and which seemed to be reproduced, though feebly, in the interior of the table.

II

PHENOMENA OBSERVED IN DARKNESS

The phenomena observed in complete darkness were produced while we were all seated around the table. The medium's hands and feet were held by her two neighbours. It invariably happened that there was not much delay in the production of the most varied and singular phenomena which we should have desired to observe in full light. The darkness evidently increased the facility of these manifestations, which we may class as under :—

1. Knocks on the table, undoubtedly stronger than those heard in full light under or in the table. A loud noise like that of a heavy blow of the fist or a slap on the table.

2. Blows and raps on the chairs of the medium's neighbours, sometimes so strong as to make the chair and the person turn round. Sometimes when the person rose his chair would be withdrawn.

3. Transporting of various objects on to the table, such as chairs and clothing and sometimes other things, carried several yards and weighing several pounds.

4. Transporting in the air of various objects, musical instruments, for example, percussions and sounds produced by these objects.

5. Transporting of the medium on to the table, with the chair on which she was seated.

6. Appearance of phosphorescent points of very short duration and of lights, particularly of luminous discs, which were often duplicated, for an equal though very short length of time.

7. Noise of two hands clapping together in the air.

8. Breath of air like a light wind limited to a small space.

9. Touchings produced by a mysterious hand, sometimes on parts of the body, sometimes on the naked flesh ;

2 c

and, in the last instance, we experienced precisely the same sensation of contact and of heat as would be produced by a human hand. Sometimes these touchings produced a corresponding sound.

10. Vision of one or two hands projected on a phosphorescent paper or on a feebly lighted window.

11. Various work executed by the hands; knots tied and untied, pencil - marks left on a sheet of paper or elsewhere. Imprints of these hands on a sheet of blackened paper.

12. Contact of our hands with a mysterious figure, which was certainly not that of the medium.

All those who deny the possibility of the phenomena try to explain these facts by supposing that the medium has the faculty of seeing in the complete darkness in which the experiments are made, and that, by a clever trick, she is able by moving about in the dark to make her two neighbours hold the same hand, leaving the other free for the production of the touchings. Those of us who had the opportunity of seeing Eusapia's hands are obliged to acknowledge that it was not easy to keep watch over them and be sure at all times where they were. At the time when some important phenomenon was about to be produced she would begin to move the whole of her body, twisting about and trying to free her hands, particularly the right, as though the contact annoyed her. In order to maintain their continuous supervision her neighbours were obliged to follow all the movements of the fugitive hand, during which operation it was not rare to lose the contact for several moments, just at the time where it was more desirable to be quite sure of it. It was then not easy to know whether the right or the left hand of the medium was being held.

For these reasons many of the very numerous manifestations observed in the darkness were regarded as insufficiently demonstrative in value although in reality probable; therefore we will pass them over, dwelling only on some cases concerning which there can be no doubt either as to the certainty of the control exercised or as to the manifest impossibility of their being the work of the medium.

(a) *Apports of different objects while the medium's hands were tied to those of her neighbour's.*—In order to assure ourselves that we were not the victims of an illusion, we attached the hands of the medium to those of her neighbours by means of a single cord about one-tenth of an inch in diameter, in such a manner that the four hands controlled each other. The length of the cord between the medium's hands was from eight to twelve inches, and between the medium's hands and those of her neighbour about four inches, only a small space being left so that the hands of those next to the medium could also hold the medium's hands during her convulsive movements.

The connection was made in the following manner. The string was wound tightly three times round each of the medium's wrists without leaving any play, so tight indeed as almost to hurt her, and then tied with two single knots. This was done so that if by any trick she could free her hand—the fact of its being wound round three times would at once prevent her from replacing her hand in the original manner.

A bell was placed on a chair to the right of the medium. The chain was formed, the medium's hands were held as usual, as well as her feet; the room was placed in darkness, the desire being expressed that the bell should immediately ring, after which we proposed to release the medium. Immediately we heard the chair turn over, describe a curve on the floor, go towards the table, and soon place itself upon it. The bell rang, and was then projected on to the table. The light was quickly turned up, and we saw that the knots were in perfect order. It is evident that the movement of the chair could not have been produced by means of the medium's hands during this experiment, which only lasted ten minutes altogether.

(b) *Imprints of fingers obtained on paper.*—In order to assure ourselves that we had really to do with a human hand, we fixed on the table, on the opposite side to the medium, a sheet of paper blackened with smoke, and expressed the desire that the hand should leave an imprint on it, that the hand of the medium should remain in its place, and the black should remain on our hands.

The medium's hands were held by those of MM. Schiaparelli and Du Prel. The chain was formed and the room darkened. We then heard a hand knock lightly on the table, and M. Du Prel immediately stated that his left hand, which was held by M. Finzi's right hand, had felt some fingers rubbing it.

Having turned up the light we found several imprints of fingers on the paper, and the back of M. Du Prel's hand was blackened, while the medium's hands on being immediately examined bore no trace of black. This experiment was repeated three times. As we insisted upon having a complete print, on a second sheet we obtained five fingers, and on a third the almost complete impression of a left hand. After that the back of M. Du Prel's hand was completely blackened and the medium's hands perfectly clean.

(c) *Appearance of hands on a slightly illuminated background.*—We placed on the table a card coated with a phosphorescent substance (sulphide of calcium), and other cards on chairs in different parts of the room. In these circumstances we clearly saw the outline of a hand placed on the card on the table, and on the background formed by the other cards we saw the shadow of a hand passing and repassing around us.

On the evening of September 21st, we saw on several occasions not only one but two hands at a time projected against the feeble light—a window closed only by curtains (it was night outside, but not absolute darkness).

These hands moved rapidly—not, however, too quickly for us to be able to distinguish the outline clearly. They were completely opaque, and were projected against the window as absolutely black outlines. It was not possible for the observers to come to a decision as to the arms to which these hands were attached, because only a small part of the arms near the wrists was seen in the feeble light from the window, from our point of observation.

These phenomena of the simultaneous appearance of the two hands are very significant, because they cannot be explained by the hypothesis of trickery on the part of the medium, who could not in any way free more than one hand, thanks to the surveillance of her neighbours. The same remark applies to the clapping of two hands in the air which was heard several times during the course of our experiments.

(d) *Raising of the medium on to the table.*—We place this raising among the most important and most significant facts. It was twice effected, on September 23rd and October 3rd. The medium, who was seated at one end of the table, while groaning loudly, was raised with her chair and placed with it on the table, seated in the same position, her hands being all the time held, and accompanied by her neighbours.

On the evening of September 28th the medium, while her two hands were held by Professors Richet and Lombroso, complained that hands were seizing her under her arms; then, in a state of trance, she said in the changed voice usual to that condition : " Now, I bring my medium on to the table."

At the end of two or three seconds the chair, with the medium who was seated on it, was not thrown but carefully raised and placed on the table, and Professors Richet and Lombroso are sure that they did not in any way assist this lifting by their own efforts. After having spoken, still in a trance condition, the medium announced her descent ; M. Finzi was substituted for Professor Lombroso, and the medium was set down on the ground with the same care and precision, MM. Richet and Finzi accompanying, but without assisting in any way, the movements of the hands and body, and questioning each other every moment as to the position of the hands.

Moreover, during the descent, they both felt several times a hand which touched them lightly on the head. On the evening of October 3rd, the same phenomenon was

repeated in very similar circumstances, MM. Du Prel and
Finzi being by the side of the medium.

(e) *Touchings.*—Some of these deserve to be particularly noted, because of a circumstance which may furnish
an interesting idea as to their possible origin; and first
of all we must notice the touchings which were felt by
persons outside the reach of the medium's hands.

Thus on the evening of October 6th, M. Gerosa, who was
three places away from the medium (about a yard and
a half, the medium being at one end of the table and
M. Gerosa at one of the corners next to the opposite end),
having raised his hand in order that it might be touched,
felt several times a hand which struck his as though to lower
it, and, as he persisted, he was struck with a trumpet, which
a short time previously had been sounding in the air.

In the second place, we must note certain delicate
touchings which no one could perform in the darkness
with the observed precision.

Twice (September 16th and 21st) M. Schiaparelli's
glasses were taken off and placed on the table in front of some
one else. These glasses were fixed to the eyes by means of
two springs, and considerable attention was necessary to
take them off, even if done in full light. They were,
however, taken off in complete darkness with so much
delicacy and quickness that the experimenter only knew
that he no longer felt the usual contact of the glasses
against his nose, temples, and ears, and he had to feel with
his hands in order to make sure that they were no longer
in their usual place.

Similar effects resulted from many other touchings
which were executed with great delicacy—for example
when one of the spectators felt his hair and beard stroked.

In all the innumerable manœuvres executed by the
mysterious hands, we never noticed any clumsiness or
shock, such as inevitably happens when one works in
the dark.

The darkness was, in the majority of cases (with one
or two exceptions already mentioned), as complete as possible, and it must be admitted that neither the medium

nor any one else could see, even vaguely or confusedly, the profiles of the persons seated around the table.

We may add, with regard to this, that heavy and bulky objects, such as chairs and pots full of clay, were placed on the table without ever touching any of the numerous hands placed on the table; and this was particularly difficult in the case of the chairs, which were so large as to occupy the greater part of the table. One chair was turned over forwards before being placed on the table, and placed lengthways without injuring anyone, in such a manner that it took up nearly the whole of the table.

(*f*) *Contacts with a human face.*—One of us, having expressed the desire to be kissed, felt in front of his mouth the rapid noise of a kiss, but it was not accompanied by the contact of lips; this happened on two occasions (September 21st and October 1st). On three different occasions one of those present touched a human face with hair and beard; the contact of the skin was absolutely like that of a living face, the hair was much more harsh and bristly than that of the medium, while the beard, on the contrary, appeared to be very fine (October 1st and 6th).

(*g*) *Sounds from the trumpet.*—On the evening of October 6th, we had placed a trumpet behind the medium and behind the curtain. Suddenly we heard several notes sounded behind our heads. Those who were by the side of the medium were able to assure themselves that the sound did not come from their direction. The trumpet was found to be transported to the table, on the side opposite to the medium.

(*h*) *Experiments of Zöllner on the penetration of a solid through another solid.*—We know the celebrated experiments by which the astronomer Zöllner tried to prove experimentally the existence of a fourth dimension of space, which, from his point of view, would have served as the base of an acceptable theory for many mediumistic phenomena.

Although we well knew that, according to a widespread

opinion, Zöllner was the victim of a very skilful hoax, we considered it very important to try a portion of his experiments with the assistance of Mme. Eusapia. If only one of them had succeeded, when undertaken with the necessary precautions, we should have been compensated with interest for all our trouble, and we should have received manifest proof of the reality of mediumistic facts, even in the eyes of the most obstinate opponents. We tried successively three of the experiments of Zöllner, viz. :—

1. The interlinking of two solid rings (wood or cardboard) previously separate.

2. The formation of a single knot in an endless cord.

3. The penetration of a solid object from the outside into the interior of a closed box, the key of which was carefully guarded.

None of these attempts were successful. It was the same with another experiment which would have been equally conclusive, that of taking a mould of the mysterious hand in melted paraffin.

Only one fact, which if it was certain could be considered as belonging to this category, was produced in the séance of September 21st, but unfortunately without our being previously informed; there was therefore lacking, when the phenomenon took place, that continued supervision which is more than necessary. One of us having at the commencement of the séance placed his overcoat on a chair, out of the reach of the medium, we saw, at the end of the séance, various articles brought on to a phosphorescent card placed on the table, which articles the owner of the overcoat immediately recognised as coming from an inside pocket of this garment; then the medium began to moan, complaining that something had been put round her neck and was strangling her.

When the light was turned up we found that the overcoat had been moved from its original place, but on giving our attention to the medium, who was distracted and in a bad temper, we saw that she had the coat in question on her back and that her two arms were in the sleeves.

Throughout the séance her hands and feet had been as usual under the control of her two neighbours.

We know how on such an occasion more than on any other, confidence in the production of such a remarkable phenomenon depends entirely on the certainty and continuity of the control of the two hands; but, as the phenomenon was quite unexpected, the attention of the medium's neighbours could not have been centred continually on exercising this supervision. These two experimenters declared that they did not believe that they had loosed hold of her hands; but not having (because of all the distractions caused by the phenomena produced) kept their attention fixed solely on this point, it must be admitted to be possible (but not probable) that they momentarily liberated the medium without knowing it.

Phenomena previously observed in darkness afterwards obtained in light with the medium in view.— It remained for us, in order to secure conclusive evidence, to try to obtain the important phenomena occurring in darkness without losing sight of the medium. Since darkness is, as it seems, so favourable for their manifestation, it is necessary to leave the darkness for the phenomena—keep the light for ourselves and the medium. In order to do that we proceeded as follows in the séance of October 6th: one portion of the room was separated from the other by means of a curtain, in order that it might remain in darkness, and the medium was placed seated on a chair before the opening of the curtain, with her back in the darkened part; her arms, hands, face, and feet were in the lighted part of the room.

Behind the curtain we placed a small chair with a bell, about half a yard or less from the medium, and on another chair, farther away, we placed a vase full of moist clay, perfectly level at the top. In the lighted part we formed a circle around the table which was placed in front of the medium. Her hands were all the time held by MM. Schiaparelli and Du Prel. The room was lighted by means of a lantern with red glasses, placed on another table. This was the first time that the medium was subjected to these conditions.

The phenomena soon commenced. By means of the light of a candle without red glass we saw the curtain swell out towards us; the medium's neighbours, holding their hands against the curtain, felt a resistance. The chair of one of them was violently drawn away, then five raps were given, which signified that less light was asked for.

Then we lit the red lantern, which we also partially shaded with a screen, but we shortly afterwards removed this, previously placing the lamp on our table in front of the medium. The edges of the opening of the curtain were fixed to the corners of the table, and, at the request of the medium, folded back over her head and fastened with pins; then something began to appear on the medium's head on several occasions. M. Aksakof rose, put his hand in the opening of the curtain over the medium's head, and immediately stated that fingers had several times touched him; then his hand was drawn through the curtain; finally, he felt that something was pushing away his hand—it was the small chair; he took hold of it, then the chair was taken from him again and fell on to the floor. All present put their hands in the opening, and felt the contact of hands. In the dark background of this opening, over the medium's head, blue lights appeared several times; M. Schiaparelli was vigorously touched through the curtain on the back and side. His head was covered and drawn into the dark part, while with his left hand he all the time retained hold of the medium's right, and with his right hand of M. Finzi's left.

In this position he felt himself touched by naked, warm fingers, saw lights describing curves in the air and illuminating a little the hand or the body to which they belonged. Then he resumed his place, and a hand began to appear at the opening without being withdrawn so quickly, and consequently was more distinctly seen. The medium not having yet seen this, raised her head to

look at it, and immediately the hand touched her face.
M. Du Prel, without loosing hold of the medium's hand,
put his head in the opening over the medium's head, and
immediately felt himself strongly touched in different
parts by several fingers. The head again showed itself
between the two heads.

M. Du Prel went back to his place, and M. Aksakof
held a pencil in the opening—the hand took hold of the
pencil and did not let it fall ; then, shortly afterwards, it
was thrown through the opening on to the table.

A closed fist once appeared on the medium's head ;
then, afterwards, the open hand slowly came into view,
with the fingers held apart.

It is impossible to count the number of times that this
hand appeared and was touched by one of us : it is sufficient to say that doubt was no longer possible. It was
certainly a human and living hand which we saw and
touched, while at the same time the bust and arms of the
medium remained visible and her hands were held by her
two neighbours. At the end of the séance M. Du Prel was
the first to pass into the darkened part, and told us that
there was an impression in the clay—in fact, we found
that this was put out of shape by a deep scratching of
five fingers belonging to a right hand (which explains the
fact that a portion of clay had been thrown on to the
table, through the opening of the curtain towards the end
of the séance), a permanent proof that we had not been
hallucinated.

These facts were repeated several times, under the
same or a slightly different form, on the evenings of
October 9th, 13th, 15th, 17th, and 18th. The position of
the mysterious hand often did not allow us to suppose that
it belonged to the medium ; however, for greater certainty,
on the evening of the 15th we attached a rubber-band to
her left hand, wrapping it round each of the fingers
separately. This enabled us at any moment to distinguish
which of the two hands was in charge of her neighbours.

Apparitions again took place on the 15th, and finally
on the 18th (although with less intensity), under the

rigorous control, solemnly attested by them, of MM. Richet and Schiaparelli; both gave special attention to this part of our experiments. These conditions were this time, as always, somewhat difficult to realise, because the medium continually moved her hands, and instead of holding them on the table in front of us, held them down on her knees.

Conclusion

Thus, therefore, all the marvellous phenomena which we observed in complete or almost complete darkness (chairs, with the persons seated on them, forcibly drawn back, touchings of hands, lights, imprints of fingers, &c.) have also been obtained without losing sight of the medium, even for a moment. In that respect the séance of October 6th was for us certain and absolute evidence of the correctness of our former observations in the dark. It was an incontestable proof that, in order to explain the phenomena occurring in complete darkness, it is not absolutely necessary to suppose trickery on the part of the medium or illusion on our part; it was proof to us that these phenomena may result from a cause identical with that which produces them when the medium is visible, with sufficient light to verify her position and movements.

In publishing this short and incomplete report of our experiments, it is also our duty to say that our convictions are as follows:—

1. That, in the circumstances given, none of the phenomena obtained in more or less intense light could have been produced by the aid of any artifice whatever.

2. That the same opinion may be affirmed in a large measure with regard to the phenomena obtained in complete darkness. For some of them we can well admit, strictly speaking, the possibility of imitating them by means of some adroit artifice on the part of the medium; nevertheless, according to what we have said, it is evident that this hypothesis would be not only improbable, but even useless in the present case, since, even admitting it,

the assembly of facts clearly proved would not be invalidated by it.

We recognise, however, that from the point of view of exact science our experiments leave much to be desired; they were undertaken without our knowing what we required, and the various apparatus that we used had to be prepared and improvised by MM. Finzi, Gerosa, and Ermacora.

Nevertheless, what we have seen and ascertained is sufficient to prove to us that these phenomena are well worthy the attention of scientists.

We consider it our duty to publicly express our gratitude and acknowledgments to M. D. Ericole Chiaia, who for many years with zeal and patience, and despite clamour and vilification, has followed the development of the mediumistic faculty of this remarkable subject, by calling the attention of students to her—having but one end in view, the triumph of an unpopular truth.

CHAPTER XXVIII

PHENOMENA OF MOTRICITY

STUDY AND EXPERIMENTS

WE now come to the phenomena of motricity, or of movement of objects without contact. This phenomenon is one of the most difficult of acceptance in the present condition of science.

It seems, in fact, that the phenomenon in question must be in opposition to the known laws of physics and mechanics. Let us observe first of all, however, that it presents no absurdity; that is to say, that it is not in contradiction to any of the laws which have been recognised as necessary, the geometrical or mathematical laws.

Physics at the present day is in direct opposition to the physics of a hundred years ago. There are many facts now recognised which our fathers would have described as impossible and contrary to the natural laws of physics, because they had not our knowledge of electricity or of photography.

If a hundred years ago a scientist had been invited to hear at Paris a lecture delivered in Berlin, he would have taken the proposer for a madman, or else he would have thought that he was making fun of him, and would not have gone a step out of his way to test what he would have declared beforehand to be absurd and impossible.

If it had been insisted upon, if a large number of persons apparently sincere had assured him that they had heard in Paris what had been said in Berlin, he would have replied : "Since sound only travels about 1115 feet a second, supposing that you have sufficiently acute hearing to hear in Paris words uttered in Berlin, you can calculate the time taken before these words could reach you; it is therefore impossible for you to hear in Paris a lecture at the very moment it is delivered in Berlin."

This is what our scientist would have said a hundred years ago on the basis of the known laws of physics. In our days there is not a pupil of the fourth standard who would be justified in being ignorant of the telephone.

This same scientist would have enclosed various objects in a locked wooden box, put the key in his pocket, and defied you to describe the objects enclosed in the box. He would have had no hesitation in offering a prize of a thousand francs to any one who could see such articles and describe them. And if after demanding certain conditions of darkness and light in order to apply a radioscope, you had then told him exactly what his trunk contained, he would not have hesitated to accuse you of having obtained the result by surreptitious methods, by opening the trunk with a false key, and he would have remained obstinate in his conviction that nothing could have enabled you to see through the trunk.

Let us suppose now that this scientist wished to put you to the proof, and had enclosed in his box a large hat, challenging you to say what it contained. With your radioscope you could easily tell him the number of pins on the hat, and describe to him their shape and exact position. He would then tell you that since you could see small pins through wood, you ought also to see equally well a big hat.

In all this would not the absurdity and unreasonable pretensions be on the part of the scientist?

When therefore we speak of setting objects in motion without contact, many scientists, who are no wiser than the scientist of the last century whom we have been postulating, tell us, "It is impossible—it is absurd." But that does not disturb us at all, and we continue our experiments and observations notwithstanding. We know well that within fifty years those who will be ridiculed, those who will be regarded as absurd, will be the very scientists of the present time who are unwilling—I do not say to admit, but to examine and study.

Things, however, are beginning to alter; a large
number of scientists are observing and studying instead
of denying.

First of all, several persons have said: mediums who
can set in motion large objects without contact are very
rare; show us therefore a small object only—a pencil,
a pen, an object as light as you please—that can be set in
motion without contact, and when you have shown us
that we will admit this mediumistic force.

In fact, if it is demonstrated that there exists a force
capable of being projected from the human body and of
putting any small object in motion without contact, we
only need to assume that the medium is a being endowed
with this force in a much higher degree in order to admit
that he can move much larger objects without contact.

As the result of much research, I have been able to
give this demonstration with an apparatus I have invented for that purpose, and which I have called the
"Sthenometer."

The sthenometer is an instrument I have made in order to
demonstrate the presence of a force emanating from the nervous
system, and to measure this force.

It is sufficient to bring the hand near to the apparatus, in order
to see the needle move in proportion to the force projected.

This force, which emanates from the human body, appears to
be the same as the force projected from mediums, which has
hitherto been so difficult to demonstrate and study.

A point of special interest to medical men is that this force is
found to be modified in various maladies of the nervous system.
The observation of these modifications will be of very great utility
for the diagnosis, prognosis, and treatment of these illnesses.

We read in the *Journal des Practiciens:* "M. Joire has
demonstrated that neither sound, heat, light, nor electricity can
explain this displacement of the needle, which always moves three
or four minutes after the hand is brought close to it.

"These experiments have been repeated by M. Joire before the
Société d' Hypnologie et de Psychologie, at Dr. Bérillon's Institut
Psycho-Physiologique, in M. Huchard's department at Necker.
The results were shown to be quite conclusive.

"Consequently, it is proved that there emanates from the human body something of which we are ignorant, and which is perhaps capable of producing luminous phenomena, and more certainly the displacement of a light body at a distance."

The following are the different observations we have been able to furnish with regard to this force by the use of the sthenometer.

When the hand is brought close to the apparatus with the fingers extended, opposite to the point of the needle and perpendicularly to its direction, we notice, after a few moments, a movement of the needle, generally towards the hand.

This movement takes place slowly, progressively, and in a very characteristic manner, different from the agitation of the needle produced by shaking the apparatus.

FIG. 10.

The movement of the needle is sufficiently considerable to dispel all possibility of illusion. It is not a displacement of a few degrees only, but is often observed to the extent of 20, 30, and 40 degrees.

If the displacement obtained with each hand successively is observed, we notice that that obtained with the right hand is normally greater than that obtained with the left hand.

The amplitude of the displacement of the needle varies with the individuals, and particularly with the condition of health.

We have noticed in some subjects, but in rare circumstances, a displacement of the needle in the opposite direction—that is to say, a repulsion.

The conclusions to be drawn from these experiments and observations are as follows :—

It is proved by means of the sthenometer that there emanates

2 D

from the living organism a special force, which is transmitted to a
distance, and appears to be specially dependent upon the nervous
system.

This force is modified and disturbed in various diseases of
the nervous system, and the observation of these disturbances
by means of the sthenometer is of great practical interest in the
treatment of these complaints.

It is therefore proved that there exists a force capable
of being projected from the human body and of setting
objects in motion without contact.

We will now study this force as exhibited by mediums.

I shall give in this chapter the summary of a number
of mediumistic phenomena obtained with children. The
author of this account has intimately known the family in
which the phenomena were produced, and all the persons
who were present at the experiments in which he himself
took part. This, therefore, gives it a very special interest.

Mr. Davis occupies an important position in the telegraph department. The mediumship of the children has
not, I believe, been since manifested.[1]

In the account which I shall give of these phenomena
which took place in a family circle at Rio-de-Janeiro, the
one difficulty is that of presenting the facts in such a
manner as to give the proper impression of their value.
Facts, isolated from the series to which they belong, may,
like quotations detached from their context, lead to errors.
Yet there are many things in cases such as the following
which are of too private a nature to be published. There
are names and circumstances relating to persons outside
the circle which for this reason cannot be mentioned; and
even as regards those with whom we are personally concerned there are, as will be easily understood, some things
too private to be repeated. I shall therefore confine myself to a description as exact as possible of the physical
phenomena.

Towards the middle of 1888 we received at Rio a
visit from the well-known Fleury Slade, who, after a stay

---

[1] See *Annales des Sciences Psychiques*, vol. iii., 1892, pp. 242, 302, 351.

of a few weeks without success, left us to go to Buenos Aires, and returned to Rio after six weeks' absence. He seemed then to be more fortunate in his séances, and although on this account I would prefer to abstain from speaking, even in passing, of a professional medium, it is only fair to attribute to him the great interest which psychical phenomena then aroused, and perhaps the appearance of a power which produced them. Mr. Davis, whose acquaintance I made when Slade came to us for the first time, was induced to form a circle at his own house. He occupied a small country house in a lonely place on the slope of a small hill overlooking the sea. But in November 1888 he removed to the foot of the hill, much nearer to the sea.

While Slade was at Buenos Aires, at least twenty-five weekly séances were held at Mr. Davis's house without the slightest result.

Eventually on August 14th some slight manifestations were obtained with fairly good proofs of identity, and as these rapidly increased in power and frequency, they kindly invited me to join the circle. The members who then composed it were Mr. and Mrs. Davis, their daughters C. and A., aged twelve and nine and a half years respectively, their maternal grandmother, and myself; we may also include Mr. X., a friend of Mr. Davis, but he did not come very regularly.

The strength of the proofs depends almost entirely upon the members of the circle, and upon their competence as observers and their reputation for honesty.

At the end of August and during the following months we had proof upon proof of the reality of the psychic force and of the strange intelligence which accompanied it. Heavy objects were put in motion, without conscious effort on our part, and sometimes without any kind of contact. What seemed to be direct writing appeared on the walls and in closed books, and we could obtain it on slates by carefully observing regularity in holding our séances. Knocks were very frequent and were of all kinds, from the slightest to the most violent. Impressions of fingers, and once that of a foot, were produced on the floor without normal cause.

Clairvoyance and, in a slight degree, clairaudience were developed : sometimes the contact and the grasp of hands which did not seem to belong to any of the spectators were felt, even by myself.

Very characteristic marks of individuality were maintained throughout the course of the manifestations, and, in some cases, it was clearly indicated that the intelligence at work could not be identified with the sub-conscious cerebration of the persons present.

These phenomena were at first both relevant and irrelevant. The instruments of their production were ordinary English children : this naturally aroused in them a certain pride, and in us the excitation of our faculties of observation and reasoning, our curiosity being greatly stimulated. After having increased in intensity, and given us reason to expect still more marvellous manifestations, the power ended by decreasing to such a degree that it was reduced to simple automatic writing. This synchronised with the change of residence ; but I think that the cause should be mainly attributed to the heat of an exceptionally bad summer.

When it again became cold the power reappeared, but it never again reached the degree attained in 1888, and on June 4, 1889, the departure of Mr. Davis's family for England put an end to the séances.

It ought to be stated that from commencement to finish there was nothing that could be truly ascribed to a morbid condition of the nervous system, either in the children or in the adult observers : none of those present were at any time in a state of consciousness differing in appearance from the normal state.

Warned by failures and disappointments in other cases, Mr. Davis and I decided to submit everything to a strict inquiry and to judge each phenomenon at its true value.

According to notes taken at the time, and my recollections corrected by those of other witnesses, I will now try to enter into details, and I will arrange the facts, not according to their succession in time, but according to the class to which they belong.

Movement of Heavy Bodies attributable to Psychic Force

At the first successful séance held on August 14th, at which Mr. and Mrs. Davis and their two children C. and A. were present, the table gave some raps, the hands of the members being, in accordance with custom, placed in a chain on the table. The letters indicated by the raps gave the name of a relative, Fanny Z., who had been dead for some time, and this name was persistently given, although the sitters believed that it was really Frances. Mme. Z., who was not in the room at the time, was asked to come, and she stated that the deceased had always been familiarly called Fanny, although her real name was Frances.

The sitters had been quite opposed to the name given by the table until the corroborative explanation was given by Mme. Z.

From this time the power, as I have already said, rapidly developed; there were spontaneous manifestations, or they would come when asked for at any hour of the day.

It was after this first appearance of phenomena that I was invited by Mr. Davis to take part in the séances. During tea the dining-room table, around which Mr. and Mrs. Davis and their five little daughters were seated, swayed right and left and rose on one side by sudden and very emphatic movements, which often indicated, according to the usual signs for yes or no, approbation or disapprobation of the statements made in conversation.

During this singular conduct of the table, the two elder daughters C. and A., from whom the power seemed principally to come, were quietly seated, one on each side of their mother, who was well placed for discovering any interference on their part. The same thing happened on other occasions in my presence, and, as Mr. Davis assured me, at the time the members of the family were present.

The table, in short, acted like a living, moving being endowed with human intelligence.

The tone adopted in conversation with these strange influences was rather jocular; and on one occasion, when I left the room after tea, the table ran after me as though it wished to call me back. C. was then the only other person present in the room, and, so far as I was able to see, she did not even touch the table, still less push it.

On another occasion, when we were around the table, it raised itself and fell down again slowly and deliberately, in a manner so entirely different from its usual method that we immediately supposed the presence of a new influence. The alphabet was recited and repeated, and we got the name of a lady who, in former years, had been a personal friend of Mme. Z. The others had only heard her spoken of. We then inquired her age, which I must not mention because her relatives, who are still living, would guess to whom it referred; but as to the number of years a mistake was made, against which the table immediately protested, correcting Mme. Z. as to the number of units, which I believe was five instead of four. Mme. Z. immediately admitted that her memory had played her false.

Other phenomena of a spontaneous character, or which were produced in accordance with our request, proved the presence of a psychic force even better than the inconvenient movements of the tea-table. The chair on which Amy, a child of thirteen months, was seated was moved backwards and forwards in a space of about ten or twelve inches between the table and the wall, and so abruptly that the chair, partly under the table, was in danger of falling over backwards.

The child, instead of being frightened, seemed to feel quite safe, and laughed, although we were sometimes very anxious. At our request the chair was raised again and the violence of the movements moderated. Mme. Z. was sitting on the right of the child, and A. on the left. In its movements the chair remained parallel with the table—that is to say, it did not move at all—as though it had been drawn forward and sideways by the foot of one of those sitting next to it, and generally it glided across and not lengthwise of the floor boards, which were uncarpeted, as is usual in Brazil. Being seated close to Amy I tried to move the chair, and I can say that, although my lower limbs are of more than average strength, I was only able to move it with great difficulty, and the result of my effort was to turn the chair half round. If, therefore, instead of having, as was the case, every reason to trust Mme. Z. and her little daughter, I had had the best reason for distrusting them, I should nevertheless, in the absence of all visible mechanism, have regarded this particular phenomenon as genuine.

Another incident worthy of record was connected with a little dog named Tury, who was as usual seated upon a chair away from the table and close to the wall. No one being near to him I jokingly challenged the visible influence to move the chair, so as to compel the dog to jump down. For about a minute nothing happened, then the dog left the chair, apparently by his own will. Two or three seconds passed after he had jumped down, and then the chair oscillated before us all. In the same manner a child's swing, which hung in a corner of the room, was at my request made to oscillate slightly but quite visibly, and this was observed by Mr. Davis and myself. There was, it is true, a window open behind it; but as we then carefully observed, there was no sensible breeze coming from that direction. The temperature of the house and that of the outside were very similar, and it was one of the very calm Brazilian nights.

An account of a phenomenon of levitation suggested to us another experiment with the tea-table. I asked C., who was seated a little farther away than I was, her little sister D. being between us, to place her hand on the back of my chair; this she did, seeming to touch the chair very slightly. The chair began to sway to right and left, and continued the movement even when I raised my feet from the floor. This indicated the application of a great force, and was amply sufficient to prove the action of a physical force, if not to raise me entirely from the floor. During all this C. remained seated and motionless, and it was evident that she did not make the slightest effort.

The following evening Mr. X., who was very strong, took C.'s chair, while I remained on my own, and he tried to produce the same effect, in the same conditions. As a result his own chair slid on the floor while mine remained motionless. My weight, which has not changed much since then, is 207 pounds.

There were some other experiments with the tables, better carried out, during the regular séances at which I assiduously took part from that time.

Once a light table with three legs was turned upside down, and my hands as well as those of Mr. and Mrs. Davis and their two daughters were lightly placed on the legs. Care was taken to see that the legs were only lightly touched, and in these conditions the table sprang rapidly from the floor on to the knees of one of the sitters and then down on to the floor again, repeating this action with each of us in turn.

At the Thursday evening séances the table generally placed itself in the desired position when we had seated ourselves, either immediately before or after our hands had been placed on the surface. These movements, however, nearly always caused us surprise, and as we had in view the study of much more important phenomena, we did not submit them to a very strict examination.

An interesting case of apparent alteration of the weight of the table was observed by Mr. X. when C. was beside him. At his request, while he was moving it, it became alternately very light and very heavy, so although it was only an ordinary card-table, he more than once had to set it down on the floor again.

I will give here an account of an interesting phenomenon which happened previously with Slade, but which, in the case of a professional medium, might perhaps be attributed to conjuring. Having once been for a walk on the hill before entering Mr. Davis's house, I found on arriving that the children had just finished their lessons.

The thought came to me on seeing the slates and books on the table that I would try in A.'s presence to obtain the disappearance of a solid object, and when we were alone in the room, on my suggestion, we both took a slate on which a book had been placed, and held it under the table. The slate was forcibly turned over and the book fell to the ground. This was a failure. I then took a slate pencil of ordinary length which was on the table, placed it on the slate, and with the assistance of the little medium I again held the slate out of sight, in the shadow of the table ; after a moment we drew back the slate : the pencil had disappeared.

We looked for it on the floor under the table, but in vain. On putting the slate back in its place the pencil seemed to fall upon it. I tried again, in exactly the same conditions, and again the pencil disappeared. This time, besides looking everywhere for the pencil, I asked A. to shake her arms and called Mr. Davis, who was in the next room. I explained to him what had happened, and asked him to help us in our search. Some minutes passed before he found anything; then having put his hand between the cross-bars joining the legs of the table he found the pencil, which seemed to have been placed there by some one. At this point particularly the wood was smooth and the surface vertical, and the pencil could not have been driven into the hard wood of which the table was made. In addition, the experiment was quite new to the young girl, whom I myself watched in full light, and she could not have let go the slate for an appreciable time without my perceiving it, while, as to her other hand, I was holding that on the table.

CHAPTER XXIX

MOVEMENT OF OBJECTS WITHOUT CONTACT

EXPERIMENTS OF DR. DARIEX

AT the Psychological Congress in Paris in 1900 Dr. Dariex made a very important communication on some experiments in the movement of objects without contact, which took place at his house and were verified by a committee.

We will give this report in full, and it will be seen that all the observations were made in a thoroughly scientific manner.

Report of the Collective Experiments instituted for the verification of Movements of Objects without Contact.

We the undersigned :—

Dr. Barbillion, of the Faculty of Paris, formerly house-physician at the hospitals, residing at 16 Quai d'Orléans, Paris ;

Paul Besombes, civil engineer, living at 7 Rue Boutarel, Paris ;

Dr. Joanne Meneault, of the Faculty of Paris, formerly house-surgeon at the Marine Hospital at Berck-sur-Mer, residing at 51 Rue Monge, Paris ;

Louis Morin, pharmaceutical chemist, residing at 9 Rue du Pont-Louis-Philippe ;

Certify to the correctness of the following facts :—

Dr. Dariex, residing at No. 6 Rue du Bellay, Paris, having on several occasions, and particularly on January 24, 1889, believed that he had witnessed the production of some strange phenomena at night in his study, asked the above-named persons to verify the observations already made as to the existence of these phenomena.

According to Dr. Dariex, chairs have been found thrown down in his study, and that on several occasions when, through the precautions taken to avoid all trickery, it appeared impossible for any living person to have come into the room, the doors and windows of which had been methodically closed and sealed.

For ten days, from January 26th, to February 4th, the undersigned met regularly at Dr. Dariex's house at 8 o'clock in the evening and 8.30 in the morning—sometimes all were present, sometimes one or more were absent. Dr.

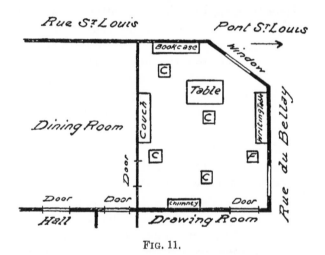

FIG. 11.

Barbillion and Dr. Dariex were not absent from a single meeting, and were present at the whole of the experiments.

Dr. Dariex's study is on the first-floor of the house at No. 6 in the Rue du Bellay, and is in the part of the flat which forms the corner of this street and that of Rue Saint-Louis-en-l'Ile.

It is lighted by two windows looking on to this street, and communication with the other rooms on the floor is by two doors : the one leading into the drawing-room and opening outwards, and the other leading into the dining-room and opening inwards.

The above plan shows the arrangement of the rooms.

The furniture in the study consisted of a bookcase, writing-desk, table, couch, easy-chair, and four chairs; there was no cupboard. After having scrupulously examined the windows and doors, as well as the various pieces of furniture, the walls and the floor, the undersigned are convinced that there was nothing that could cause the fall or displacement of any article of furniture or any object by the aid of mechanism, wires, or any other means; that it would be equally impossible for any one to hide in the study or to come into the room after the windows and doors had been closed and sealed. Under these circumstances, each evening at 8 o'clock the following precautions were carefully taken and the iron shutters were fastened and the windows closed, seals being placed on the casements close to the fastenings. The door opening into the drawing-room was locked from the study, the key being left in the keyhole and secured by a band of cloth sealed at both ends.

Seals were affixed to the door, and a band of cloth was fastened with sealing-wax to the door itself, and to the adjoining wall. Throughout the whole of our experiments this drawing-room door remained thus secured.

The only opening remaining was the door leading into the study from the dining-room. The chairs in the study were arranged in an order agreed upon, but not always exactly in the same place. Then the experimenters went out of the study into the dining-room, Dr. Dariex first, and each of them from the dining-room cast a glance round the study in order to finally assure himself that the chairs were upright and in their places.

Then Dr. Barbillion locked the door of the study and kept the key in his possession; seals were affixed and a band of cloth placed over the keyhole. Seven or eight impressions were made with a seal belonging to M. Morin, which he kept in his possession and took home with him. The form and arrangement of the seals were carefully noted.

These precautions were regularly and rigorously taken at 8 o'clock each evening, and we met again at 8.30 the following morning to remove the seals, the operation being always preceded by a minute examination of the seals and of the lock. The following is an account of what happened during the ten days of our observation:—

First night, Saturday, 26th January, to Sunday, 27th January—Nothing.

Second night, 27th–28th January—Nothing.

Third night, 28th–29th January — two chairs were overturned : the one, which was placed close to the bookcase, had fallen on to its left side ; the other, placed close to the arm-chair, was thrown on its back towards the window and the table.

Fourth night, 29th–30th January—Nothing.

Fifth night, 30th–31st January—Nothing.

Sixth night, 31st January–1st February—Nothing.

Seventh night, 1st–2nd February—Nothing.

Eighth night, 2nd–3rd February—Nothing.

Ninth night, 3rd–4th February—Nothing.

Tenth night, 4th–5th February — Two chairs were overturned : the one placed near the table was thrown on to its left side, towards the couch ; the other, placed near the arm-chair, had fallen on its back in the direction of the window.

In view of these facts, the precautions taken by us to prevent all trickery, and the care with which the seals were affixed and afterwards examined, we are convinced :—

1. *That no one could have remained in the study after we had come out of it ;*

2. *That no one could have gone into it during the night before we arrived the following morning.*

And we are led to the conclusion that during the night, on two occasions during the ten days, in a room completely closed and which no living person could have entered, chairs were thrown down contrary to our expectation and anticipation ; that this manifestation of an apparently mysterious force, produced outside of the usual conditions, does not appear to us to be in conformity with any ordinary explanation, and without wishing to prejudice in any way the precise character of this force and draw positive conclusions, we are inclined to think that the phenomena are of a psychic order, similar to those which have been described and verified by a number of observers. Dr. BARBILLION.

Dr. MENEAULT.

M. MORIN.

L. BESOMBES.

Dr. DARIEX.

All the signatures were authenticated by the Mayors of the Fourth Arrondissement and of Pont-de-Vaux (Ain), to which place Dr. Meneault shortly afterwards removed.

As stated in the report, sometimes all the experimenters were not present. As the experiments necessitated twenty regular appointments at fixed hours, it can be easily understood that at some time or another some one would fail to keep them ; but the experimenters were all present when the phenomena were found to have taken place. All verified the seals, found them intact, and before any one entered the study saw from the dining-room the overturned chairs. This is the reason why all have signed the official report without restriction. We all had, moreover, absolute confidence in each other, because we were all friends of long standing, and knew we were all incapable of deceiving one another.

I should have liked to have had a larger number of witnesses; but, at that time, few people in France dared to speak of psychical phenomena for fear of being taken for fools or hallucinated, and I myself, less experienced and less convinced than I am to-day of the necessity of daring to approach these investigations, openly shared to some extent the general faint-heartedness, and only talked of the matter with my friends; thus I only ventured to propose to my intimate acquaintances that they should come and verify what I had already observed. I did not know whether the phenomenon would be again produced, and I did not wish to expose myself to the vexation which would have resulted if I had convened a similar committee of persons who did not know me so well, and who knew nothing of psychical phenomena, of their inconstancy, their variability, and of the numerous obstacles in the way of such experiments.

From the 5th of February, my friends having declared that the verification was sufficient, and that it was useless to prolong it, I had my bed made every evening in the study, and slept there up to February 26th, at which date I was called into the country through a family bereavement. I heard nothing, and no chair was again overturned.

Was fraud possible? Could we have been played a trick by a very simple Breton servant, whom Professor Charles Richet knew, and whom he thought incapable of it, and whom I myself, during the nine years she was in my service, had never found out in any deception? Is it possible that this girl, who had certainly not had any experience or practice with seals could, on four occasions, have removed and replaced, without it being perceived, *at least six seals each time*, even to the irregularities and blisters of which we had taken note, which seals, when we wished to remove them, adhered to the cloth so firmly that the cloth itself tore; and of which my friends and myself could not succeed in removing and replacing even one, although we made several attempts, by all the methods and with all the instruments we could think of?

How many times we have discussed, particularly with Professor Charles Richet, in what way my servant could have deceived us! The hypothesis that she could have got into the room in spite of the seals and overturned the chairs has always been declared inadmissible by those who have examined it; that of iron wires introduced under the doors is not admissible, when we consider the arrangement of the room, the furniture, the position of the chairs, and the way in which they were thrown down; to suppose that they were overturned by a shaking of the house is inacceptable, because during the twelve years and a half that I have lived in the same flat no chair has been thrown down save during the time of these experiments. Could they have been overthrown by an animal that had come down the chimney and gone back the same way without being caught? This would be an absurd hypothesis; first of all, the metal curtain in front of the fireplace was completely lowered, and there was a grating in the fireplace behind the screen; then can it be imagined that this animal could descend in the night, through the narrow tube of a Parisian chimney, about eighteen yards in height, simply to amuse itself by overturning chairs and then returning by the same way as it had come? The only animal capable of doing this and of remaining unseen in the study, which we carefully examined before affixing the seals, would be a mouse. But a mouse is quite incapable of overturning chairs weighing eight pounds.

There remains one objection, and that is the following:—

" A certain time having elapsed between the affixing of the seals and the verification of the phenomena, a mould of the wax seals could have been taken with the view of executing a counterfeit seal, enabling a substitution to take place."

This objection is the most serious one, and might at first sight seem calculated to throw doubt; fortunately in the interests of truth it will not stand a careful examination of the facts.

As a matter of fact, the first time I had recourse to the guarantee afforded by the seals, during the private experiments I had made previous to the collective experiments, I affixed the seals, *without any one knowing my intention,* at eight o'clock in the evening.

Then, although the keys and the seal had not left my pocket, at ten minutes after midnight, that is, four hours later, I again found my seals quite intact and a chair had been thrown over in the study.

It was quite impossible in four hours, between eight o'clock and midnight, to procure a seal similar to mine. I could not therefore myself have been deceived in this manner. Could I have deceived the others?

This would also be impossible. As we said in the report, *the form and the arrangement of the seals were carefully noted.*

This is already a very important guarantee, because it is not easy to obtain regular seals in a vertical plane with melted wax; they were all of unequal thickness and of very varying outlines, so that out of fifty probably not two would be found so much alike as to be confused; but, in addition to this precaution, another was taken, towards the end, at my request: from a sheet of paper, on which one of us had rapidly written in rather large characters some sentences which completely covered it, we cut a strip, about six inches by three inches, which was necessary for the application of the seals. The following morning, this strip was compared with the rest of the sheet from which it had been cut, and which had been taken away at the same time as the key of the seal, and we convinced ourselves that the portions which had been cut out and the remaining pieces corresponded exactly. This precaution had been taken on February 4th; nevertheless, on the following morning we found two chairs thrown down.

Were these phenomena independent of the presence or of the vicinity of some person, some "medium," to use the stereotyped expression? I know nothing as to this, but I presume that if the presence of some one was necessary, if there was a medium there, it must have been my servant, whose health and nervous system were then very delicate. She had never been subject to spontaneous somnambulism, but a year ago I was led by the force of events to the conviction that she was hypnotisable. The reason for this was that some gastric-intestinal troubles, doubtless principally of nervous origin, had made their appearance; for nearly three weeks I used the proper medicaments, but they all failed or only gave indifferent results, and the patient became gradually weaker, until she got into such an extremely weak state that she was unable to stand upright. Her condition, which was serious and very alarming, seemed as though it could not last for any length of time.

The seriousness of the situation caused me to try therapeutic suggestion. Hypnotic sleep was very easily obtained. The first suggestion led to considerable improvement; the second accentuated this improvement; and after the third the cure was complete. It had taken four days.

Was it chance? Had the time for the cure come when I commenced the therapeutic suggestion? That is not probable, because several months later the same troubles returned, and medicines gave no better results than before, although they were taken exactly as I had prescribed, and generally in my presence. This time I did not wait so long before having recourse to therapeutic suggestion, and two suggestions brought about a complete and lasting cure.

Since that time I had made numerous experiments with the movements of objects without contact, and I have had the pleasure of finding that these experiments, even though they were not always convincing, and were sometimes even open to suspicion, often afforded sufficient guarantee in favour of the reality of the phenomenon, and corroborated what I had already been able to observe. These experiments have been published in the *Annales des Sciences Psychiques*.

Dr. DARIEX.

CHAPTER XXX

PHENOMENA OF LEVITATION

INVESTIGATIONS AND EXPERIMENTS

LEVITATION is a phenomenon which consists in the raising of an object without any contact with the medium or the sitters. The phenomenon of levitation sometimes operates on the medium himself. He is then found raised above the floor either alone or with the seat on which he was sitting. It is clear that in order thoroughly to verify the levitation of a medium, it is necessary, first of all, that he should not have any point of support on any person or object which would enable him to raise himself. In the second place, it is essential that the phenomenon should last so long that it cannot be attributed to a leap in the air.

Certain authors have discussed the mechanism of the phenomenon of levitation, and have asked if the medium loses weight, becomes lighter than the air, and is raised in the same way as a balloon, or if in this phenomenon we are to look for some force which operates on the medium and raises him.

Such discussion is entirely superficial—in fact, gravity, which holds all bodies on the surface of the earth, is nothing but a force applied to a body in a definite direction.

Levitation, whether of an object or a medium, necessitates the intervention of a different force, or of the resultant of several forces, which is applied to a body in opposition to the force of gravity and superior to it. Exactly the same thing happens when an object is set in motion without contact; it needs a force superior to the force of inertia of the object to be applied to it. Levitation must therefore also be connected with an external or projected force, which is applied to the medium or to the object levitated.

As the phenomena of levitation most frequently occur in the dark we seek means of controlling them, which permit of the verification of the phenomena and enable us to study them in various phases, while the medium is in the dark.

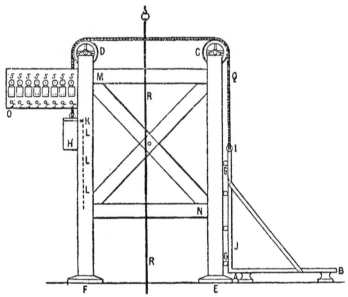

Fig. 12.—Dr. Joire's Apparatus for verifying the Phenomena of Levitation.

I have devised the above apparatus, which enables us :—

1. To verify the levitation at the time it takes place.

2. To measure exactly the height to which the medium is raised.

3. To ascertain for how long a time the medium remains at the various heights to which he is successively raised.

This apparatus is composed of wooden supports, E, F, held together by the cross-beams M, N.

A, B is a movable platform on which the chair and the feet of the medium rest.

This platform is fixed to a vertical bar I, J, which runs on rollers G, working in a rail in the upright E.

The platform is suspended by the rope Q, which is attached to the ring I, passes over the pulleys C, D, and at the other extremity is attached to the counterweight H, working in a groove in the upright F.

The counterweight is made a little heavier than the platform I and B, which bears the seat on which the medium sits. If we release the counterweight when the platform is empty, the latter will be drawn upwards.

When the medium is placed on the apparatus we release the counterweight, and the weight of the medium keeps the platform A, B in contact with the ground.

The counterweight H bears a copper needle K, which follows its movement and slides over copper contact-pieces L fixed along the upright F.

The needle K and the contact-pieces L are connected with a set of electric bells O, having different sounds, while under each bell there is an opening T, in which appears a number corresponding to the bell under which it is.

Let us now see how this apparatus works.

The front part, which includes the platform and the upright E, is placed inside the room where the experiment is made; the back part, which includes all the apparatus connected with the upright F, remains outside the room. The room is closed by a curtain, which I have indicated by the line R.

At the slightest levitation of the medium, when placed on the apparatus, the weight H descends, carrying the needle K with it.

The contact-pieces L have been so arranged that each corresponds to an elevation of the platform A, B through a space of 5 centimetres (2 inches).

The result of the working of the apparatus is:—

1. A person placed near the upright F can follow with his eye the movement of the needle, which corresponds exactly with the movement of the platform A, B, and consequently of the medium.

2. The persons surrounding the medium inside the room, which is in darkness, can equally follow this movement by hearing the ringing of the different bells, which sound in succession.

3. The time during which the ringing of the bell lasts indicates the time during which the medium remains at the height shown by the corresponding contact-piece.

4. By means of the figures which appear on the board we can definitely verify after the experiment the height to which the medium has been raised.

This very simple apparatus can be constructed anywhere, and may be of great service in verifying and registering in an exact mathematical manner the phenomenon of levitation.

A certain number of mediums have exhibited phenomena of levitation.

We will first of all give an account of levitation phenomena witnessed in some private experiments; and afterwards numerous cases of levitation observed with mediums well known through other phenomena.

M. Palazzi, of Naples, published in December 1893 the account of a séance in Rome at which he was present in company with a painter, M. Francesco Alégiani, in presence of M. Henri de Siemiradzki, Dr. Nicola Santangelo, physician of Venosa, Professors Ferri and Lorgi of the University of Rome, M. Hoffman, editor of the review *Lux*, M. Gorli, and several other men and women; in all about twenty persons, among whom were three mediums, the engineer Palmiani, and two students, MM. Arturo Ruggieri and Alberto Fontana. The last named was the most powerful medium.

Fourteen persons formed a chain round the table, which was lighted by a red lamp. M. Fontana was at one of the corners; his right hand was held by M. Gorli and his left by Dr. Santangelo who, on account of the corner of the table, was at the side, at right angles to that where the other two sat.

The table began to creak, to raise itself partially, then to raise itself completely a distance of 30 centimetres (1 foot) from the floor.

The room was then completely darkened, in accordance with the request made through the table by means of raps.

After a very short time, suddenly and without any warning, the three persons above mentioned were raised at the same time and carried on to the table, MM. Fontana and Gorli standing, Santangelo kneeling. This difference in position may be explained by the fact that the force in operation was not completely displayed in the case of Santangelo, who was not in the same line as Fontana; and it had to leave him kneeling, not being sufficiently powerful to raise him upright.

In any case there must have been a force capable of raising suddenly and instantaneously three persons, two of whom, MM. Gorli and Santangelo, were very heavy.

This phenomenon was duly authenticated by several persons, including Mme. Ferri and M. Siemiradzki. Meanwhile the medium was raised above the table, a phenomenon witnessed and verified by the majority of the sitters, not only by those who were close to the medium, but also by Mme. Ferri, M. Siemiradzki, and myself, who were on the opposite side of the table. We passed our hands several times flatwise underneath the medium's feet, between his feet and the table; he was raised about 10 centimetres (4 inches).

As there was perfect darkness it might be supposed that the two feet under which the hands were passed were not those of the medium, but that one belonged to the medium and the other to M. Gorli standing by his side; we therefore brought the red light and let it fall on the two controllers, and asked the force acting, which was said to be a spirit named Oscar, to reproduce the phenomenon while the medium remained on the table alone and held by controllers to right and left; this challenge was accepted.

The room was again placed in darkness, and the medium felt himself raised above the table.

We then verified very clearly that he was raised higher than on the first occasion, since a majority of the sitters could pass their hands under his feet, not only flatwise as previously, but with the hand upright on its edge.

When the levitation had been verified the medium came down on to the table again.

Then we asked the spirit to bring him down himself from the table; which was immediately done. During the time that the medium was gently descending he continued to implore us not to let go his hands.

A few moments after the medium was seated in his chair he was suddenly thrown full length under the table with such force that M. Gorli was dragged with him, and Dr. Santangelo was thrown down.

The feet of the medium and M. Gorli struck ours, and we were standing at the opposite end of the table.

We asked M. Gorli to set M. Fontana on his feet again, but after a few attempts he told us that M. Fontana was so heavy that he could not succeed in moving him.

Several other persons also tried in vain to raise the medium.

M. Gorli still remained beside the medium; we got him to stand upright, fearing that he was contributing to make M. Fontana heavy. The latter, still greatly frightened, urged MM. Gorli and Santangelo not to release his hands.

M. Siemiradzki, a tall and robust man, then tried to raise the medium, but he soon stated that M. Fontana "was nailed to the floor," and that he could not succeed in moving him.

Mme. Ferri also wished to try, but she met with the same negative result. Professor Ferri, who was sitting by my side, exclaimed in great surprise: "And yet my wife is stronger than a man."

We finally asked the spirit Oscar himself to raise the medium; he was put back on to his chair in the twinkling of an eye.

Dr. Santangelo has confirmed to me these facts of levitation obtained in the séances of December 8th and 15th, 1893, in a letter from which I have made the following extract:—

"In perfect darkness both in the first and in the second

séance, we verified the levitation of the medium Ruggieri, who was raised to a height of almost a yard above the level of the table, as I assured myself, a fact verified in the first séance by Mlle. Possidini, who was on my left, and in the second séance by Mme. Ferri.

" In the course of the evening, the medium, after having been raised in the air, was forcibly drawn under the table and compelled to remain motionless, lying on his back. Mme. Ferri, M. and Mme. Siemiradzki, and myself tried to move him at least one centimetre, but all in vain; he was as though made of lead and firmly welded to the floor.

"There is, however, more to relate. On the second evening an event occurred which strongly impressed me, and which still impresses me every time I repeat it. When the medium Ruggieri commenced to rise I held him firmly by the hand, but seeing myself drawn with such force as almost to lose my footing I held on to his arms, and thus I was raised in the air with my companion, who was on the other side of the medium. We were all three raised in the air to a height of at least three yards above the floor, since I distinctly touched with my feet the hanging lamp which was suspended from the centre of the ceiling.

" During the rapid descent, the light being turned on, I found myself kneeling on the table, almost in danger of breaking my neck, although nothing so unpleasant happened to me.

" Yes, I myself, at Rome, flew in the air without wings, and this I can attest before God and man, but, before I was, the three mediums Cecrehini, Ruggieri, and Boella were also raised into space until they almost touched the ceiling."

Here is also another example of the levitation of a medium under special test conditions.

Mr. Macnab, engineer, published in 1888 the results of his experiments in the *Lotus Rouge*, then under the management of M. Gaboriau. He refers to levitations as follows :—

" The medium M. F. is frequently raised into the air during the séances; but this happens more frequently to a friend of mine, M. C., a sculptor, who is also a medium. He told us that once he was raised along with his chair. In fact, we heard his voice as he changed his position. Note that he had thick shoes, though we did not hear the slightest footstep; eventually, when we turned on the light, he was found seated on the chair, which was on the bed. Another time, having accidentally lighted up while he was levitated on the music-stool, he fell heavily from a height of from fifty to sixty centimetres, so heavily that the foot of the stool was broken. Three engineers, MM. Labro, Th., and M., were witnesses.

"It seemed to me important to have more palpable proofs of this levitation and I devised the following arrangements: I spread out on the ground a square of very thin material which we call adrianople; it is a kind of calico dyed red. In the centre we placed a chair, and made M. C. sit on it; the other medium M. F. was not there. We each held a corner of the material, and as there were five of us, one of the corners was held by two people.

"I put out the light and almost immediately we felt the chair rise, remain some time in the air, and then gently descend. The material was not even stretched, and the least strain would have torn it.

"This experiment greatly frightened M. C. The persons present were M. R., M. C., two ladies, and myself.

"I do not think that any objection can be raised to this experiment of the levitation of a medium, verified by means of material stretched under the chair.

"He was already seated in the chair when we extinguished the light; the raising took place almost immediately. There were five of us around him, and it was impossible for him to descend and rise again without our knowledge.

"Levitation is not necessarily vertical, as many people think. For example, in the presence of M. de Rochas, the following fact occurred which I observe at almost every séance:—

"M. C. was sitting by my side, against the window,

when suddenly he was removed and placed against the piano, quite close to M. G. This was done so rapidly, that we heard, almost simultaneously, the noise which the chair made in rising and that which it made in coming down again; whilst in the air, it had turned half round, for M. C. had his back to the piano, whereas a moment previously he had it against the window.

" In one séance M. Montorgueil, and in another M. de Rochas, passed their hands under the medium's feet during his ascent and were able to assure themselves that he did not employ any of the ordinary processes of gymnastics."

CHAPTER XXXI

LEVITATION PHENOMENA OBSERVED WITH THE MEDIUM D. D. HOME

THE following is the description given by Mr. Frank Podmore of the ordinary séances with the medium Home:—

"The room was commonly illuminated by one or more candles, a single gas-burner, or a shaded lamp, so that, in comparison with the almost complete darkness insisted on by other mediums, it could honestly be described as well lighted.

"The manifestations would then usually begin with raps, followed shortly by a quivering movement of the table, which is described by one witness as like the vibration in the cabin of a small steamer when the engine begins to work; by another as resembling a 'ship in distress, with its timbers straining in a heavy sea'; and, in a finer flight of imagination, is characterised by another witness as 'literally trembling, as if every vein of the wood was a human nerve.' The table would then tilt up, move about, or 'float' suspended in the air; musical instruments would perform in the convenient obscurity afforded by its shelter; hands would be felt clasping the knees of the sitters and pulling portions of their dress; handkerchiefs, flowers, and other light articles, and even heavy bells, would be handed about the circle, under the table, by the same means.

"The performance would be interspersed with messages rapped out by the spirits, or delivered through the mouth of the entranced medium. At this point the sitting would commonly terminate. But if the conditions were judged favourable to the higher manifestations, the lights would be turned out, the fire screened, and the table drawn up to the window, the company sitting round three sides, leaving the side next the window vacant, with Home sitting at one end of the vacant space. Hands would then be seen, outlined against the faint light proceeding from the window, to rise over the vacant edge of the table, move about the papers lying on its surface, or give flowers to the sitters. Afterwards the medium would be levitated, that is to say, suspended in the air without material support."

We will now give an account of some extraordinary instances of levitation, at a séance at which Sir William Crookes was present. Home was transported from one room to the other, externally, through the windows, at a great height from the ground; there was not even a balcony or projection in the wall between the two windows.

" The apparatus prepared for testing the movements of the accordion consisted of a cage, formed of two wooden hoops, one foot ten inches and two feet diameter respectively, connected together by twelve narrow laths, each one foot ten inches long, so as to form a drum-shaped frame, open at the top and bottom ; round this, fifty yards of insulated copper wire were wound in twenty-four rounds, each being rather less than an inch from its neighbour. The horizontal strands of wire were then netted together firmly with string, so as to form meshes rather less than two inches long by one inch high. The height of this cage was such that it would just slip under my dining-table, but be too close to the top to allow of the hand being introduced into the interior, or to admit of a foot being pushed underneath it. In another room were two Grove's cells, wires being led from them into the dining-room for connection, if desirable, with the wires surrounding the cage.

" The accordion was a new one, having been purchased by myself for the purpose of these experiments at Wheatstone's in Conduit Street. Mr. Home had neither handled nor seen the instrument before the commencement of the test experiments.

"Mr. Home sat in a low easy-chair at the side of the table. In front of him and under the table was the aforesaid cage, one of his legs being on each side of it. I sat close to him on his left, and another observer sat close to him on his right, the rest of the party being seated at convenient distances round the table.

"For the greater part of the evening, particularly when anything of importance was proceeding, the observers on each side of Mr. Home kept their feet respectively on his feet, so as to be able to detect his slightest movement.

"The temperature of the room varied from 68 to 70 degrees Fahrenheit.

"Mr. Home took the accordion between the thumb and middle finger of one hand at the opposite end of the keys. To save repetition this will be subsequently called 'in the usual manner.'

"The bass key having been previously opened by myself, and the cage being drawn from under the table, so as just to allow the accordion to be pushed in with its keys downward, it was pushed back as close as Mr. Home's arm would permit, but without hiding his hand from those next to him. Very soon the accordion was seen by those on each side to be waving about in a somewhat curious manner; then sounds came from it, and finally, several notes were played in succession. Whilst this was going on my assistant went under the table, and reported that the accordion was expanding and contracting; at the same time it was seen that *the hand of Mr. Home by which it was held was quite still, his other hand resting on the table.*

"Presently the accordion was seen by those on either side of Mr. Home to move about, oscillating and going round and round the cage, and playing at the same time. Dr. A. B. now looked under the table, and said that Mr. Home's hand appeared quite still whilst the accordion was moving about emitting distinct sounds.

"Mr. Home, still holding the accordion in the usual manner in the cage, his feet being held by those next to him, and his other hand resting on the table, we heard distinct and separate notes sounded in succession, and *then a simple air was played.* As such a result could only have been produced by the various keys of the instrument being acted upon in harmonious succession, this was considered by those present to be a crucial experiment. But the sequel was still more striking, for Mr. Home then removed his hand altogether from the accordion, taking it quite out of the cage, and placed it in the hand of the person next to him. *The instrument then continued to play, no person touching it, and no hand being near it.*

"I was now desirous of trying what would be the effect of passing the battery current round the insulated wire of the cage, and my assistant accordingly made the connection with the wires from the two Grove's cells. Mr. Home again held the instrument inside the cage in the same manner as before, when it immediately sounded and moved about vigorously. But whether the electric current passing round the cage assisted the manifestation of force inside it, it is impossible to say.

"The accordion was now again taken without any visible touch from Mr. Home's hand, which he removed from it entirely and placed upon the table, where it was taken by the person next to him, and seen, as now were both his hands, by all present. I and two of the others present saw the accordion distinctly floating about inside the cage with no visible support. This was repeated a second time, after a short interval.

"Mr. Home presently re-inserted his hand in the cage, and again took hold of the accordion. It then commenced to play, at first chords and runs, and afterwards a well known sweet and plaintive melody, which was executed perfectly in a very beautiful manner. Whilst this tune was being played I grasped Mr. Home's arm below the elbow, and gently slid my hand down it until I touched the top of the accordion. He was not moving a muscle. *His other hand was on the table, visible to all, and his feet were under the feet of those next to him.*"

LEVITATIONS OF HOME

These levitations were witnessed by a large number of people, and notably by Sir William Crookes, who has given the following account in his work, *Researches in the Phenomena of Modern Spiritualism.*

" These levitations have occurred in my presence on four occasions in darkness. The test conditions under which they took place were quite satisfactory, so far as the judgment was concerned; but ocular demonstration of such a fact is so necessary to disturb our pre-formed opinions as to the naturally possible and impossible, that I will here only mention cases in which the deductions of reason were confirmed by the sense of sight.

" On one occasion I witnessed a chair, with a lady sitting on it, rise several inches from the ground. On another occasion, to avoid the suspicion of this being in some way performed by herself, the lady knelt on the chair in such a manner that its four feet were visible to us. It then rose about three inches, remained suspended for about ten seconds, and then slowly descended.

" At another time two children, on separate occasions, rose from the floor with their chairs, in full daylight, under (to me) most satisfactory conditions; for I was kneeling and keeping close watch upon the feet of the chair, observing distinctly that no one touched them.

" The most striking cases of levitation which I have witnessed have been with Mr. Home. On three separate occasions have I seen him raised completely from the floor of the room. Once sitting in an easy-chair, once kneeling on his chair, and once standing up. On each occasion I had full opportunity of watching the occurrence as it was taking place.

" There are at least a hundred recorded instances of Mr. Home's rising from the ground, in the presence of as many separate persons, and I have heard from the lips of the three witnesses to the most striking occurrences of this kind—the Earl of Dunraven, Lord Lindsay, and

Captain C. Wynne—their own most minute accounts of what took place. To reject the recorded evidence on this subject is to reject all human testimony whatever; for no fact in sacred or profane history is supported by a stronger array of proofs.

"The accumulated testimony establishing Mr. Home's levitations is overwhelming. It is greatly to be desired that some person, whose evidence would be accepted as conclusive by the scientific world—if, indeed, there lives a person whose testimony *in favour* of such phenomena would be taken—would seriously and patiently examine these alleged facts.

"Most of the eye-witnesses to these levitations are now living, and would, doubtless, be willing to give their evidence.

"The best cases of Home's levitations I witnessed were in my own house. On one occasion he went to a clear part of the room, and, after standing quietly for a minute, told us he was rising. I saw him slowly rise up with a continuous gliding movement, and remain about six inches off the ground for several seconds, when he slowly descended. On this occasion no one moved from their places. Less frequently the levitating power extended to those next to him. Once my wife was thus raised off the ground in her chair."

Sir William Crookes wrote to Home on April 12, 1871 :—

"You need not hesitate to quote me as one of your strongest supporters. Half-a-dozen séances of the kind held yesterday, with some qualified scientific men, would be sufficient to scientifically establish these truths, which would then become as incontestable as the facts of electricity."

The detailed account of the levitation which took place on December 16, 1868, in London, in a dark séance, in the presence of Lord Lindsay, Lord Adare, and Captain Wynne, was given to the Dialectical Society by Lord Lindsay in the following terms :—

"Home, who had gone into a trance, walked about uneasily ; he then went into the hall. While he was away,

2 F

I heard a whisper in my ear: 'He will go out of one window and in at another.'

"I was alarmed and shocked at the idea of so dangerous an experiment. I told the company what I had heard and we then waited for Home's return. We soon heard the window of the other room raised, and almost immediately we saw Home floating in the air outside our window. The moon was shining full into the room; my back was to the light, and I saw the shadow on the wall of the window-sill, and Home's feet about six inches above it. He remained in this position for a few seconds, then raised the window and glided into the room feet foremost and sat down.

"Lord Adare then went into the other room, and noticing that the window through which he had passed was only open about eighteen inches, he expressed his surprise that Home was able to pass through this opening.

"The medium, still entranced, then replied: 'I will show you.' Turning his back to the window, he inclined backwards and was projected horizontally, head first, the whole body completely rigid, and then he returned to the room. The window was seventy inches from the floor; the two windows were 7 feet 6 inches apart, and only one had a sill about a foot wide for flower-pots."

CHAPTER XXXII

LEVITATION PHENOMENA WITH EUSAPIA PALADINO

Levitations of Eusapia Paladino

1. *Levitations at Naples in* 1899.—Cavaliere Chiaia, at the Spiritist Congress in 1899, gave an account of the experiments he had made at Naples with Eusapia in the presence of Professor Don Manuel Otero Acevedo of Madrid and Signor Tassi of Perugia.

The medium was in trance, and the gas had been lowered at her request.

After a few minutes, during which time nothing was heard but the usual grinding of the medium's teeth while she was in a lethargic condition, Eusapia, instead of conversing, as she always does, in a very bad Neapolitan dialect, began to speak in pure Italian, asking the persons seated on either side of her to hold her hands and feet. Then, without hearing the least rubbing or any rapid movement of her body, or the slightest undulation of the table around which we all were, MM. Otero and Tassi, who were nearest to the medium, were the first to perceive an unexpected ascent, for they felt their arms gently raised, and not wishing to leave hold of the medium's hands they stood, so as to follow her in her levitation.

This splendid case of levitation is all the more worthy of attention, because it took place under the most rigorous control, and with the same apparent ease with which a pen could be lifted. What particularly surprised these gentlemen was to feel the two feet of the medium placed on the small surface of the table (32 inches by 24 inches), already partly covered by the hands of the four experimenters, without any of these hands being touched, although it took place in perfect darkness.

Although astounded by so extraordinary and unexpected an event, one of us asked John if it would be possible to raise the medium a little above the table, with feet together, in such a way as to enable us to witness the levitation better. At once, without discussing this exacting request, Eusapia was raised from four to six inches above the table, so that each of us could freely put his hand under the feet of the "magician" suspended in the air.

In relating this to you I do not know which feeling is stronger in me, whether it is satisfaction at having obtained so magnificent and marvellous a phenomenon, or whether it is the painful suspicion of being taken for a visionary, even by my most intimate friends.

Happily there were four of us, including the ever-suspicious Spaniard, and two believers well disposed to accept the evidence of facts.

When our magician came down from the table without our assistance, and with a dexterity no less marvellous than that employed in mounting it, we had other reasons for astonishment. We found the medium stretched out, her head and a small portion of her back supported on the top of the table, and the remainder of the body extended horizontally, straight as a bar, and without any support to the lower part, whilst her dress was adhering to her legs as if her clothing was fastened or stitched around her. Although produced in darkness, it is not necessary to repeat that this important fact was scrupulously supervised with the greatest possible care by all, and in such a manner as to make it as evident as though it had taken place in broad daylight.

Further, I have had the opportunity of witnessing something more extraordinary still. One evening I saw the medium stretched out rigid in the most complete cataleptic state, holding herself in a horizontal position, with only her head resting on the edge of the table for five minutes, with the gas lighted and in the presence of Professor de Cintiés, Dr. Capuano, the well-known writer, M. Frédéric Verdinois, and other persons.

Levitations at Warsaw in 1893 *and* 1894

Eusapia came to Warsaw at the end of 1893, and remained there during January 1894. She was examined by several persons, and became the subject of very warm controversy.

There were several cases of levitation rather badly described in the extract from the report given by the *Revue de l'Hypnotisme.* Here is a very clear one.

Once, relates M. Matazewski, I was a witness to the raising of the medium in the air in the middle of a room without any support. She was then in a state of trance, and was raised gradually, slowly, and lightly in the air (still in a standing position), and came down again to the floor as slowly and smoothly. It was as though some one had raised and lowered the medium. Eusapia remained suspended in the air long enough for us to freely pass our hands under her feet, to make perfectly sure that she was not touching the floor. She was raised to a height of several inches. The phenomenon was four times repeated.

Dr. Ochorowicz has thus spoken of the levitations in *L'Illustration* of Warsaw.

"Another most surprising and very rare fact (also obtained at the Congress at Milan) was the complete levitation of the very person of the medium, who, held throughout by the hands and feet, was raised from the ground and carried in a cataleptic condition along with her chair on to the table.

"'I will raise my medium in the air,' Eusapia said in very correct French (a language she does not know in her normal condition), and she was actually raised. Such was at least my impression during several seconds. By passing my hand under her boots I am able to testify that there was a space of from four to five inches between them and the table.

"On another occasion the medium was suddenly raised from the floor. She was standing, and Mme. Ochorowicz had time to pass her hand between Eusapia's feet and the floor. The levitation over, the medium, still in a semi-conscious condition, walked towards the table, and putting her hands on it tried to imitate very clumsily, or perhaps to produce, a fresh rising in the air. 'This peculiarity is worthy of note,' said M. de Siemiradzki, who was a witness, and it is to similar automatic movements, very easy to distinguish from real phenomena, that we ought, in many cases, to attribute the apparent fraud of which Eusapia is often accused."

Here is the report of a number of experiments in the levitation of Eusapia Paladino, given by Colonel de Rochas, who has himself taken part in them and has been able to control the phenomenon under the most favourable conditions.

Levitation at l'Agnélas

In September 1895 Eusapia came to France to my country-house, situated at l'Agnélas, near to Voiron (Isère) in order to be studied by a committee consisting of M. Sabatier, Dean of the Faculty of Sciences of Montpellier; Colonel de Rochas, administrator of the Polytechnic School; Count Arnaud de Grammont, Doctor of Science; Dr. Dariex, Doctor of Medicine, Director of the *Annales des Sciences Psychiques*; M. Maxwell, Deputy Procurator-General at Limoges; Baron de Watteville, a graduate in science and law.

There was a levitation in the séance of September 27th. The official report published by the committee thus describes the phenomenon :—

10.50.—MM. de Grammont, Sabatier, and de Rochas were successively touched on the head, shoulder, back, and arm. At this moment Dr. Dariex, who was tired, left the séance, Dr. Maxwell giving up his place on the left of Eusapia to Colonel de Rochas, and Count de Grammont leaving his place as control of Eusapia's legs and going to the right, replacing M. Sabatier; M. Ed. de Rochas held the left hand and Count de Grammont the right hand of Eusapia.

Eusapia asked that the table might be moved away from the window and brought into the middle of the drawing-room. The hands were controlled as stated above ; her right foot rested on the left foot of Count de Grammont, and her left on the right foot of Colonel de Rochas.

Eusapia on several occasions said, "Altare, altare," meaning "Rise, rise," indicating that she wished to try to rise. She made Count de Grammont and M. Ed. de Rochas, who held her two hands, repeat the movement of accompanying her hands in the air, but without any traction or noticeable resistance. After a few minutes, and in almost perfect darkness, in which our outlines could scarcely be distinguished, Eusapia, without supporting herself on the hands of the controllers, who simply followed hers, or on the feet of the same observers on which hers rested, appeared to Count de Grammont, who held her right hand, to be raised whilst seated, with a continuous and rather rapid movement, not by a bound or appreciable jump, but somewhat as though going up in a lift. The chair was raised with her, and Eusapia's feet came almost as high as the table. The observers rose at the same time in order to follow the movement.

From this moment she escaped from the control of the two observers, her hands being released. M. Sabatier, who was at the right of Count de Grammont, tried to ascertain by touch, in the darkness, whether Eusapia, when she was being raised, placed her knee on the table as a lever, but he could not be certain of anything. Count de Grammont and Colonel de Rochas stated that Eusapia had been raised with her chair nearly to the height of the table, without exerting any pressure on them and without supporting herself on their hands or their feet.

The surprise caused confusion and perceptible relaxation of the control. The only thing ascertained was that Eusapia was standing on the table along with her chair.

She tried to rise again vertically ; M. Sabatier quickly passed his hand under the soles of Eusapia's feet and found that her heels were raised above the table, but that Eusapia was supporting herself on the extremities of her feet and toes, as though standing on tiptoe.

Eusapia then collapsed; her neighbours received her in their arms and seated her on the ground.

We ought to add that one of the persons who was quite close to the table almost completely fainted away, not from emotion, but through weakness, saying that he felt drained of strength as the result of Eusapia's efforts.

Some years ago Eusapia gave a series of experiments at Genoa, which were scientifically controlled by Professor Porro. We shall only give here that portion of Professor Porro's account which refers to the phenomenon of levitation.

So far as he was concerned, Professor Porro, at the commencement of his experiments, openly declared that he was neither materialist nor spiritualist; he was not ready to accept *a priori* either the negations of the psycho-physiologists or the beliefs of the spiritists.

However, Professor Porro remarked that he knew pretty nearly what to expect in Eusapia's séances, because of the reports he had read in the papers and the reviews, but more especially in the two very important works of Colonel de Rochas and Dr. Vesani-Scozzi.

He added that the nine persons who were present with him at the two séances represented the most diverse shades of opinion on the subject, from the most convinced spiritists to the most incorrigible sceptics. Moreover, his task was not to write an official report, approved by all the experimenters, but merely to report faithfully his own impressions.

Professor Porro did not omit to give a detailed description of the premises of the Minerva Club, where the first séances were held. The premises consisted of an ante-room, three other rooms, and the hall in which the experiments took place.

This room measured seventeen feet each way. On the south-west side were two windows, the one provided with an iron grating and the other with outside wooden blinds.

The windows remained closed during the séances; the opening of each window was separated from the remainder of the room by heavy red curtains, to which were attached large black cloths. Bands of the same material were fastened against the window-panes, so as to prevent all passage of light and all communication with the street.

Every evening, before commencing the experiments, the entrance doors were closed, and the various rooms which composed the small flat carefully inspected. Then the doors on the north-west, which gave access to the other rooms, were closed, and there was left open only that on the north-east, leading into the ante-room, in a corner of which a candle was kept burning.

This light was sufficient to allow the phenomena which took place on the table and on the curtains to be indistinctly seen, when, in accordance with the instructions given by means of raps on the table, the gas and the electric light (white and red) had to be extinguished in the hall where the experiments were held.

During the séances the hands of the medium were always held by those nearest to her on the right and left; these, in turn, formed a chain with the three other experimenters. The five persons of the circle who, awaiting their turn, did not form part of the chain, were at the other end of the hall, in a locked enclosure erected for the purpose.

In the official account of the first séance Professor Porro said that he had not seen certain lights which some of his companions said they had seen.

"But I have seen, and that clearly," he added, "the table, of unpolished pine wood, with four legs, a yard long and two feet wide, rise several times from the floor and remain suspended in the air, without any contact with visible objects, a foot or two above the floor, for the space of two, three, or even four seconds.

"This phenomenon was repeated *in full light*, without the hands of the medium or of the five persons who formed the chain around the table touching it in any way; Eusapia's hands were supervised by her neighbours, who also controlled her legs and feet, in such a way that no part of her body could exert the least pressure to raise or keep in the air so heavy a piece of furniture."

In another experiment Professor Porro took an instantaneous photograph by magnesium light, which clearly shows the levitation of the table. (See Fig. 13.)

The hands of the experimenters as well as those of the medium are placed on the table. We can clearly distinguish both feet of the medium, and we can see that her left foot is held by that of the control on the left. No one could raise the objection of a collective hallucination after seeing this photograph.

In another séance Professor Porro thus describes the levitation of the medium :—

" The trance was very deep and more painful than usual.

" Suddenly the medium raised both her hands, grasped by mine and those of No. 5 (Professor Morselli), and while uttering moanings, cries, and exhortations, she was quickly raised with her chair, until both her two feet and the two front feet of the chair were set down on the front of the table.

" It was a moment of great anxiety. The levitation was accomplished without any shock, rapidly, but without any sudden jerks.

" In other words, if one wished by an effort of supreme scepticism, to imagine an artifice capable of producing the same result, one would have to think rather of a traction from above, by means of a cord and a pulley, than of a push from below.

" But these two hypotheses will neither of them stand the most elementary examination of the facts.

" Nor is this all. Eusapia was again raised, with her chair, from the upper part of the table, so that No. 11 on the one side and myself on the other were able to pass our hands under the feet of the medium as well as under those of the chair.

Fig. 13.—Instantaneous photograph, showing levitation of a table.

" Moreover, the fact that the two back feet of the chair remained beyond the table, without any visible means of support, made the results of this levitation still more irreconcilable with the supposition that Eusapia was raised by means of a leap which she had taken, dragging the chair with her.

" Eusapia came down again without any jerk, by degrees, held all the time by her hands by No. 5 and myself; the chair, which rose a little higher, turned over and placed itself on my head, from which position it spontaneously returned to the floor."

In another séance levitations of an object were manifested *in full light*.

"Scarcely was the electric light extinguished," said Professor Porro, " than we noticed an automatic movement of the chair on which had been placed a plaster block, while Eusapia's hands and feet were carefully controlled by myself and No. 3. At all events, as if in order to forestall the objection that the phenomena occurred in darkness, the table asked typtologically for light and the experimenters lighted the electric lamp.

" Immediately all present saw the chair on which was the plaster block, which was anything but light, moved between myself and the medium, without being able to comprehend what caused the movement.

"Mme. Paladino placed my extended hand on the back of the chair and put her left hand on it; when our hands were raised, the chair was also raised without contact to a height of about six inches.

" The phenomenon was repeated several times, also with the intervention of the hand of No. 5, under conditions of light and of control which left nothing to be desired."

CHAPTER XXXIII

MATERIALISATIONS OR PHANTOMS

GENERAL INVESTIGATIONS

In the facts which we are about to examine two new phenomena will make their appearance: those, namely, of materialisation and of dematerialisation.

These two phenomena which appear very difficult to explain, have been observed in a rigorous and scientific manner by witnesses of such authority and scientific standing, that they can no longer be regarded as doubtful. They appear to indicate modifications of material elements under the influence of the medium.

From the first general view of cases of this nature which have been observed and verified we are able to draw the following conclusions:—

1. The medium can produce effects which seem to be caused by a solid material body, which manifests itself only to the sense of touch, or by the material traces which it leaves on other bodies. We have in many cases attributed these phenomena to an externalisation of force from the medium.

As examples, we have the experiment with Eusapia Paladino reported by Dr. Allain, in the course of the séances which were held at the Société Universelle d'Études Psychiques at Paris; the imprints and moulds produced by Eusapia and other mediums, &c.

2. The medium produces the apparition of a visible and tangible material form. This takes the form of some part of the human body, head, hand, arm, &c.

These members have not generally the same appearance as the corresponding portions of the medium's body.

3. The medium produces the formation of a material

form representing a considerable portion of the human body: bust or incompletely formed body.

4. In certain cases it has been proved that the medium's body lost a part of its weight, in proportion as the materialisation became more complete.

It seems, therefore, in such cases that the materialised form borrows a portion of the material elements of the medium's body.

5. The medium produces the formation of a material form representing a complete body identical with the medium's body. These are the cases which are called Projection of the Double or Bi-location.

6. The medium produces the formation of a material form of human appearance, this body being absolutely dissimilar to the medium's body.

7. In this latter case, whatever may be the origin of the material element of which the body is constituted, its form seems to depend upon the dominating thought of the circle in which it is formed.

In America and England, where the evocation of the dead and reincarnations are believed in, the forms of deceased relatives are often seen to appear.

In France, where the most diverse views are held, all kinds of apparitions are seen, but always according to the dominant thought of the circle.

The apparition appears in a costume such as those present imagine ought to belong to the nationality or period to which it belongs.

The form of the apparition sometimes depends for its origin upon the medium, who suggests to the circle the idea of the form which is expected to be seen.

8. The apparition thus produced possesses certain attributes of a material body: it can touch the spectators, speak and enter into conversation with them, touch and transport objects.

9. The apparition can be photographed.

10. These apparitions or materialisations are intimately connected with the action of a medium, whose presence is necessary for the production of the phenomenon.

11. The materialisation is most frequently seen in the same place where the medium is; but, if the medium's presence is customary, it is not indispensable, and there are some cases in which an apparition is produced under the influence of a medium, but at some distance from the place in which he is.

These phenomena are connected with a force still almost unknown, and it is necessary to beware of following the lead of some, who are strongly inclined to the marvellous, and who, not daring to fathom their depths, insist on regarding them as supernatural interventions.

In all ages, the most serious-minded people who have taken the trouble to examine the facts have appreciated them at their true value. Saint Augustine in his *City of God* speaks of a case of projection of the double and of materialisation under the form of an animal, and gives some explanations which are worth recording.

"I shall never believe," he says, in explanation of the fact, "that demons have the art or ability, I do not say to change the spirit of a man, but even to give to his body the form and proportions of that of an animal.

"I would rather believe that in this man the element of imagination which is transformed into phantoms, assuming the infinitely varied aspect of external things under the influence of thoughts or dreams, and although incorporeal, taking on with marvellous celerity the representation of the body—I would rather believe, I say, that this element, when the senses are dulled or deadened, can, in some inexplicable manner, be presented to the senses of others in corporeal form.

"Thus, while this body lies somewhere, still alive, but with the senses more strongly bound than during sleep, the phantom of his imagination, incorporated so to speak under the form of some animal, appears to the senses of other people, and he sees himself as in dreams, carrying burdens under this form." (Book xviii., c. 23.)

It is evident, from the same work, that the theory here put forward by Saint Augustine, whose authority from the philosophical point of view no one has doubted, is applied in his mind, not only to cases of projection of the double or bi-location, but also to all cases of materialisation.

In fact, the case of which he speaks here is not one of the projection of the double, but a true case of materialisation, such as we still see, since it relates to the apparition of an animal form, therefore one quite dissimilar to that of the subject.

We might be led into error by the expression "the element of the imagination which is transformed into phantoms"—we might, I say, from this expression only, think that the author is referring simply to hallucinations. But his idea is much more extensive, and he is careful to develop and explain it in the next sentence, by saying: "The phantom of his imagination, incorporated so to speak under the form of some animal, appears to *the senses* of other people, and he sees himself, as in dreams, carrying burdens under this form."

There is, therefore, no doubt; he does not say "appears to the sight," but "appears to the senses"; meaning that the phantom not only strikes the sense of sight, but all the senses; and, further, this phantom is capable of action, since he says, "carrying burdens."

This explanation, therefore, has in view apparitions presenting all the characteristics which we have ascribed to the materialisation phenomena which we are considering.

On the other hand, one whose authority as a scientist is universally recognised, Sir Oliver Lodge, has expressed himself as follows regarding the action of mind upon matter :—

"The action of mind on matter, the reaction of matter on mind, are these, after all, commonplaces? In this case, where will the possibilities stop?

"Here is a room where a tragedy has taken place, where the human mind has been submitted to the most intense anguish. Are the traces of this agony still there, and are these traces perceptible to a mind in vibratory harmony with them or receptive? I affirm nothing, save that there is nothing here that is inconceivable. If that happens, the phenomenon may assume several forms: vague uneasiness, perhaps, or imaginary sounds, or indistinct visions, or again, perhaps, a dream or a picture of the event as it is represented. Be it understood that I do not consider these things as being so conclusively proved as other phenomena I have studied; but belief in such facts may be forced on us, and the imputation of superstition, when applied to them, is without justification. If they are true, they will take their place in a well-ordered universe by the side of others having affinity with them, but with the advantage of being better known.

"There are also the objects left behind. Is it admissible that an object of this kind, a lock of hair, an old garment, retains some characteristic of a dead person or some vestige of the personality? And what of a letter? A painting? We call the artist an old master. Certainly, much of the personality of the old master may be thus preserved. The emotion experienced on looking at a work is a sort of transmission of thought emanating from the deceased. A painting differs from a piece of music in that it is a sort of perpetual incarnation of himself. All can see it, some only can comprehend it. Music demands incarnation. It can be executed, as we say, and then appreciated, but only by a mind in unison with the author and able to think; therein resides, in the order of things, transmission of thought, but it is a delayed transmission of thought. This fact can be assimilated to telepathy, but to a telepathy not only acting at a distance in space, but at a distance in time. (As stated in an article in *Light* it would not be a question of technical telepathy, because here the phenomenon is produced by the usual ways and means; true telepathy always operates by unaccustomed ways and means.)

"Let us reflect on these great things and not be unduly sceptical with regard to the small ones. We should, certainly, always maintain an attitude of sound and critical investigation, and in this sense a certain degree of scepticism is not only legitimate but necessary. The class of scepticism I abhor is not that which seriously questions and submits everything to rigorous proofs, it is rather that which peremptorily affirms and dogmatically denies; but this is not true scepticism in the proper meaning of the word, because it rejects research and prohibits examination. It is too positive as regards the limits of knowledge and the exact point where superstition commences.

"Occult phenomena and dreams, phantoms, crystal visions, premonitions, clairvoyance—all are superstitions! Yes, but perhaps they are also in the domain of facts. As far as they impose on our credulity they are only trifles as compared with the things with which we are already familiar, even very familiar, in our foolish incapacity to understand them."

The different observations we have made on the subject of cases of materialisation confirm the hypothesis we have put forward above, in regard to the question of lucidity through typtology.

Thought, we say, is not a purely abstract phenomenon. All thought, created by the mind, has a real existence, indestructible, or, at least, which leaves an imperishable trace. This entity, or image representing thought, is not in the material plan which we know—that is to say, it does not generally come within the cognisance of our senses.

But let a subject be placed in an abnormal state, in which he possesses special receptivity, by means of communication different from that of his normal senses. This is the phenomenon of thought-transference. Let a subject possessing a special faculty be in an abnormal state in which this faculty can be freely exercised, and he is able, guided by some indication, imperceptible to our senses, to seek far and wide and perceive the mental images created by one or by several persons. Then we have the phenomenon of lucidity.

Let other subjects possess a special faculty which enables them to give to the image representing their thoughts an intensity which endows it with new properties, and this picture, still without appearing to our senses, will be capable of impressing a photographic plate and of

2 G

appearing before our eyes by this means. Here we find the explanation of thought photographs.

Let other subjects, perhaps still more rare, also possessing a special faculty, be able to combine the mental pictures emitted by a whole group of people, and, so to say, condense them, after the manner of an accumulator; then these mental pictures may be materialised more and more completely. They will, first of all, be capable of coming within the sense of sight of other persons; then they will be able to impress the other senses, and, eventually, they will assume all the properties of the material bodies, and we shall have materialisations of phantoms with the properties which we have set forth above.

It must be observed that these peculiar faculties which we attribute to the subjects who give rise to the various phenomena of which we speak, are perhaps not different faculties for each class of phenomena ; but they may easily be one and the same faculty, in varying degrees. Nothing up to now has enabled us to decide this point.

Our hypothesis, it will be seen, not only applies to the majority of the psychical phenomena we are studying, but it gives a very satisfactory and, at the same time, the most simple interpretation of them that has been enunciated up to the present time.

There is a case of projection of the double quoted by Aksakoff.[1] Emilie Sagée, thirty-two years of age, a Frenchwoman, fair, and of a nervous temperament, but healthy and intelligent, was, in 1845, a teacher at a boarding-school at Nuwelike in Livonia. During the eighteen months she was at this school the forty-two boarders and the professors state that her double was frequently projected, giving them the spectacle of two Emilie Sagées simultaneously visible, and each as distinctly seen as the other. One day when she was giving a lesson to thirteen of the young ladies, among whom was Mlle. de Guldenstubbe (the narrator of the story), and while, in order that they might better understand her explanation, she was writing the passage to be explained on the black-board, the pupils

[1] *Animism and Spiritism.*

were suddenly startled by seeing two Emilie Sagées, the one by the side of the other. They resembled each other exactly and made the same gestures. Some months passed and similar phenomena continually took place. There was seen from time to time, at dinner, the double of their teacher, standing behind her chair, imitating her movements as she ate, but with neither knife nor fork, nor eatables in her hands. However, it did not always happen that the double imitated the movements of the real person. Sometimes when she rose from the chair the double would be seen to remain seated. One day the whole of the pupils were together in one room doing embroidery. They were all seated at the table and could easily see what was going on in the garden (the room was on the ground-floor with four large glass doors opening on to the garden). Whilst working they saw Mlle. Sagée engaged in gathering some flowers. At the upper end of the room was another mistress who was in charge of the pupils and was seated in a green morocco arm-chair. Presently this lady left the room and the arm-chair was empty.

But this was only for a short time, for the young ladies suddenly perceived in it the form of Mlle. Sagée. They immediately looked into the garden and saw her still occupied in gathering flowers, only her movements were slower and heavier, like those of a person overcome with sleep or exhausted with fatigue. They again looked at the arm-chair where the double was seated, silent and motionless, but with so real an appearance that if they had not seen Mlle. Sagée, they would have believed it was she herself.

These curious phenomena lasted with some variations for about eighteen months. They noticed that in proportion as the double became clearer and more consistent, the person herself became more rigid and enfeebled; and, conversely, in proportion to the disappearance of the double the corporeal body regained its strength. She herself was unconscious of what happened, and only knew about it from what she was told.

As the pupils' parents became uneasy on the matter

and withdrew their children, Mlle. Sagée was dismissed.
She then said that she had been discharged from eighteen
boarding-schools for the same reason.

She went to live with a relative who had several
children; the latter frequently saw the projection of her
double, and were in the habit of saying that they saw
" two Aunt Emilies."

An important observation was made in the course of a
séance with Eusapia Paladino at the Société Universelle
d'Études Psychiques in Paris by Dr. Allain, Vice-President of the Society.

" In the course of the séance, at the moment when the
most extraordinary and noisy phenomena were taking
place," writes Dr. Allain, " so extraordinary and noisy
indeed, that there seemed to me to be the greatest doubt
as to their genuineness, I put my left hand mechanically
on the curtain of the medium's cabinet, on the outside
that is to say, at the left-hand end of the front of the
cabinet. But what was my astonishment when I felt
forming under my fingers a sort of relief, giving a sensation such as might be produced by one of the cardboard
masks with which children play at carnival time, being
held against the curtain. Without losing a moment I
then plunged my right hand into the opening at the side
of the cabinet and made my two hands meet, one on each
side of the curtain. I found that during five, six, seven,
perhaps ten seconds, though my left hand continued to feel
this projection, my right hand could not, on the contrary,
find any corresponding cavity on the inside. And yet my
two hands were only separated by the curtain.

" Is it possible to suppose that at this moment Eusapia,
whether cheating or not, but in any case much occupied
with the phenomena produced, had found it possible to
produce her famous fluidic image ? I do not believe it, and
believe it the less because I was careful to state aloud what
I felt, and Eusapia appeared to be absolutely ignorant of
it, because she made no allusion to it either at the moment
when the thing happened, or afterwards in the numerous
séances which I had with her.

" We must also dismiss all idea of mental suggestion on my part, for I am personally far from being scientifically certain of the possibility of this suggestion, and, at the very moment when the incident above related took place, my mind was rather weary of the somewhat grotesque occurrences I had witnessed than desirous of producing others.

" Evidently there remains the possible hypothesis that I had been the victim of hallucination, but is this probable in a man who not only enjoys, and who always has enjoyed, excellent health, but who, moreover, as doctor and lawyer, has long studied, together with his master, Professor Garnier, at the Infirmary, the different hallucinations that are to be met with in mental pathology ? "

The following is an account of a séance in which the commencements of materialisation were seen to occur.

At the end of 1891, the American Society of Psychical Research, presided over by the Rev. M. Savage, of Boston, made various experiments, the most important of which is worthy of being quoted. The account of this séance was signed by the members present. The Society included such men as Dr. Heber Newton, Mr. A. Livermore, and a number of others well known in science and letters. Another clergyman, very well known in America, who is also a member of this Society, was present at the séance. He declared that he believed it impossible and ridiculous to explain these facts by the theories of fraud and illusion.

The medium was Mrs. Roberts of New York. The séance was held in a hall, usually public, at Osnet, Massachusetts. A large cage of iron wire resting on a wooden framework had been constructed. This cage was very strongly made by a competent workman. In the front of the cage was a door, which could be fastened with a padlock. This cage was placed along the wall of the room, which was on the second floor, and could only be entered by one door. Before the medium entered the cage her clothing had been examined by a lady, who declared that it was of dark colour (the importance of this detail will be seen). When the séance commenced about sixty people were present in the room, the members of the Society being in front, and among the number were some medical men, who came to observe the phenomena under such novel conditions. Mrs. Roberts, a short, slight woman, seemed pale and anxious, because the conditions were altogether unusual.

At eight o'clock Mrs. Roberts entered the cage, and immediately the committee, consisting of the Rev. M. Savage and a well-known doctor, closed the door with the padlock, and further tied a very stout thread on each side and at the centre of the door. This door was sealed with wax, on which a special seal was impressed. All this was done to prevent the medium coming out of the cage. Then the gas was lowered, and the séance commenced. More than thirty forms came out of the cabinet in which the medium was, and materialised in front of it in full view of the spectators, the phenomena lasting for an hour. The various forms which appeared were sometimes tall, sometimes short, and they were recognised by those to whom they addressed themselves. The materialisation of the various forms outside the cage was a most impressive sight. At first a white nebulous spot appeared on the floor in front of the cage; it grew larger by degrees, finally assuming the form of a human being clothed in white. The movements of the hands could be seen manipulating this white vapour, and gradually rendering it consistent. All of a sudden a completely developed human form showed itself to the spectators. Then, with an expression of radiant joy, the form made its way towards one of the persons present, and the words "Mother" or "Sister" were heard murmured quite softly; then the form returned, as though with regret, towards the medium and disappeared. Some forms of tall and strong men also appeared, and yet the medium was a small and thin woman, which, in this case, renders altogether improbable the supposition that the form was the double of the medium.

Mrs. Roberts suddenly appeared in front of the cage, and advanced slowly towards the astonished spectators. The gas was relit, and the cage examined by the members of the committee. The lock was still fastened, the threads and seals were intact, and yet the medium, who had seated herself in the cage before the committee, was now outside it.

CHAPTER XXXIV

MATERIALISATIONS

OBSERVATIONS OF SIR WILLIAM CROOKES

SIR WILLIAM CROOKES was the first man of science who dared to occupy himself publicly with the study of psychical phenomena. After experimenting for a long time with several mediums, he published a work in which, after having described his various experiments, he ventured to declare himself convinced of the reality of psychical phenomena.

At that time it needed great courage to pay attention to phenomena, which only aroused contempt and derision on the part of orthodox science. We give here some extracts from Sir William Crookes' observations which cannot be omitted from a study of psychical phenomena.

Sir William Crookes experimented for three years, from 1872 to 1874, with a young girl, fifteen years of age, Miss Cook, through whose mediumship a female form materialised, which called itself Katie King. The medium lived in the house, and was always with the experimenter's family, and the most minute precautions were taken against possible fraud.

The medium retired into a dark cabinet, which was separated by a curtain from the room in which the spectators were assembled. Katie King soon appeared, fully materialised, having all the appearance of a normal being. After a variable period she disappeared as she had come. She always seemed to come out of the cabinet, but sometimes disappeared in full view of the spectators.

The phenomena lasted for three years. Katie had announced at the commencement the date of their cessation

She was photographed on many occasions, and during the later manifestations at the same time as the medium.

Even from the first weeks Sir William Crookes was able to see the medium and apparition simultaneously, by means of a phosphorus lamp. On the invitation of Katie, he followed her into the cabinet.

"I went cautiously into the room," he says, "it being dark, and felt about for Miss Cook. I found her crouching on the floor. Kneeling down, I let air enter the lamp, and by its light I saw the young lady dressed in black velvet, as she had been in the early part of the evening, and to all appearance perfectly senseless; she did not move when I took her hand and held the light quite close to her face, but continued quietly breathing. Raising the lamp, I looked around and saw Katie standing close behind Miss Cook. She was robed in flowing white drapery, as we had seen her previously during the séance. Holding one of Miss Cook's hands in mine, and still kneeling, I passed the lamp up and down, so as to illuminate Katie's whole figure and satisfy myself thoroughly that I was really looking at the veritable Katie, whom I had clasped in my arms a few minutes before, and not at the phantasm of a disordered brain. She did not speak, but moved her head and smiled in recognition. Three separate times did I carefully examine Miss Cook crouching before me, to be sure that the hand I held was that of living woman, and three separate times did I turn the lamp to Katie and examine her with steadfast scrutiny.

"Later, the phenomena became more powerful, and it was a common thing for the seven or eight of us in the laboratory to see Miss Cook and Katie at the same time, under the full blaze of the electric light. The medium's head was muffled up in a shawl to prevent the light falling on her face."

The medium and Katie were very much alike, but there were certain points of difference which Crookes has carefully noted.

"Katie's neck was bare last night; the skin was perfectly smooth both to touch and sight, whilst on Miss

Cook's neck is a large blister. . . . Katie's ears are unpierced, whilst Miss Cook habitually wears earrings. Katie's complexion is very fair, while that of Miss Cook is very dark. Katie's fingers are much longer than Miss Cook's, and her face is also larger. In manners and ways of expression there are also many decided differences. Miss Cook's hair is so dark a brown as almost to appear black; a lock of Katie's, which is now before me, and which she allowed me to cut from her luxuriant tresses, having first traced it up to the scalp and satisfied myself that it actually grew there, is a rich golden auburn.

"One evening I timed Katie's pulse. It beat steadily at 75, whilst Miss Cook's pulse a little time after was going at its usual rate of 90. On applying my ear to Katie's chest I heard a heart beating rhythmically inside, and pulsating even more steadily than did Miss Cook's heart when she allowed me to try a similar experiment after the séance. Tested in the same way, Katie's lungs were found to be sounder than her medium's, for at the time I tried my experiment, Miss Cook was under medical treatment for a severe cough."

Certain people who wish to be regarded as strong-minded, and have themselves no scientific authority, nor any sound argument to oppose to the serious evidence given by recognised scientists, content themselves with purely and simply denying the statements, without producing any evidence in support of what they say, and think, perhaps, that such common and misplaced mockery will serve instead of argument.

One of these persons has thus expressed himself with regard to the experiments carried out by Sir William Crookes.

"I have convinced myself in London, without the slightest doubt, as to the puerile and gross frauds of the famous Florence Cook (now Mrs. Corner), who splendidly duped the distinguished William Crookes with the phantom of Katie King, who was no other than her own sister."

But the séances which Sir William Crookes had with Florence Cook took place, almost exclusively, in his own house, and in the presence of a select circle of observers invited by himself. They were carried on under conditions which rendered all complicity impossible, as may easily be seen by referring to his work, *Researches in the Phenomena of Spiritualism.* On page 109, he says:—

"During the last six months Miss Cook has been a frequent visitor at my house, remaining sometimes a week at a time. She brings nothing with her but a little handbag, not locked; during the day she is constantly in the presence of Mrs. Crookes, myself, or some other member of my family, and, not sleeping by herself, there is absolutely no opportunity for any preparation, even of a less elaborate character than would be required for enacting Katie King. . . . She has always submitted with the utmost willingness to every test that I have proposed."

Another fact which must not be lost sight of is that, as Sir William Crookes said: "Katie King is half a head taller than Miss Cook and looks a big woman in comparison with her"; and this can be seen from the photographs in which Miss Cook and Katie were taken simultaneously.

This fact clearly refutes the pretended discovery of M. Bois, for when these séances were held Florence Cook was a young woman, less than twenty years of age, and her sisters were too young to play the rôle of Katie, even if they had wished or had the opportunity to do so. Therefore, when a journalist says that he has "convinced himself" that Katie King was none other than Miss Cook's sister, we can only conclude that he was wrongly informed, seeing that the facts, for the accuracy of which we can vouch, are quite opposed to his statements.

It is really not worth while to try to refute such trivial arguments as these, which do not even rest on the slightest trace of evidence. To all appearance they arise from the well-known credulity of the incredulous.

Moreover, Sir William Crookes expresses himself as follows with regard to Miss Cook. I think no one need hesitate between the arguments of a scientist of such world-wide reputation as Sir William Crookes and the statements of a journalist.

"Every test that I have proposed she has at once agreed to submit to with the utmost willingness; she is open and straightforward in speech, and I have never seen anything approaching the slightest symptom of a wish to deceive. Indeed, I do not believe she could carry out a deception if she were to try, and if she did she would certainly be found out very quickly, for such a line of action is altogether foreign to her nature. And to imagine that an innocent schoolgirl of fifteen should be able to conceive and then successfully carry out for three years so gigantic an imposture as this, and in that time should submit to any test which might be imposed upon her, should bear the strictest scrutiny, should be willing to be searched at any time, either before or after the séance, and should meet with even better success in my own house than at that of her parents, knowing that she visited me with the express object of submitting to strict scientific tests—to imagine, I say, the Katie King of the last three years to be the result of imposture does more violence to one's reason and common sense than to believe her to be what she herself affirms."

As to the precautions taken to prevent all possible deception, the following is the statement of the distinguished physician, Dr. J. M. Gully, who was present at a large number of séances, and who has dispassionately and philosophically investigated these extraordinary phenomena.

"All those who have been present at the Crookes' séances know what careful precautions were taken in order that the medium's movements should be controlled.

"These precautions proved to me beyond doubt that the form that appeared was not that of Miss Cook, but had an altogether separate existence."

The following also is the statement of Mr. Cromwell Varley, F.R.S., the well-known electrical engineer, the originator of the trans-Atlantic cable.

"As I had been requested to investigate some materialisation phenomena, I agreed to do so with Miss Cook at some séances which were held at Mr. Livermore's house.

The medium was treated like a telegraphic cable, and an electric current was passed from her right wrist along her arms to her left wrist." That was done all the time, in order to secure exact data. Varley made use of a reflecting galvanometer and various other instruments. By this means the medium could not interrupt the current, even for a hundredth part of a second, without the fact becoming immediately known. "Despite all this," Mr. Varley says, "the half-materialised form of Katie appeared down to the waist only, the remainder of the body being missing or invisible. I held the hand of this strange being, and at the end of the séance Katie told me to go and awaken the medium. I found Miss Cook entranced (in a lethargic condition), as I had left her, and all the platinum wires intact. I then awakened Miss Cook."

A similar experiment was made by Varley in the presence of Sir William Crookes. A weak electric current was maintained throughout the séance. Sir William arranged wires in such a manner that if Miss Cook had moved, even unconsciously, she could not have passed beyond the curtains enclosing the cabinet in which the medium was seated. Despite all these precautions Katie came six or eight feet in front of the curtains; no wire was attached to her arms, and the electrical test was quite conclusive.

As an additional precaution Sir William Crookes asked Katie to plunge her hands into a chemical solution. But no special deflection of the galvanometer ensued. The opposite would have infallibly happened if Katie had had the wires on her, because the solution would have modified the current.

CHAPTER XXXV

STUDY OF THE MEDIUM SAMBOR

WE will examine in this chapter the remarkable phenomena obtained through a Russian medium. These observations have been published by M. Petrovo-Solovovo in the *Annales des Sciences Psychiques*.[1]

Sambor very willingly submitted to a rigorous control, and frequently asked for it. In the first place, it should be noted that his hands were controlled in a perfectly satisfactory manner; they were held—or, at least, they always seemed to be—in the strict sense of the word, which was not the case with other mediums—Eusapia, for example.[2] The chain of hands was almost always formed on the knees of the spectators and without contact with the table.

In the numerous cases which it fell to my lot to control, Sambor was never opposed to my holding his hand in the most careful and satisfactory manner, namely, by grasping with my five fingers the palm of his hand and his four fingers. It happened certainly that I was present at some séances where the chain of hands was sometimes placed on the table, which made the control more satisfactory; but this took place but rarely, for a short time only, and, I think, always at the request of some person other than the medium.

---

[1] I shall often have occasion to make use of this term *phenomena* in my account, and to avoid all mistake, I will hear say that it ought not to be taken to imply the authenticity of the facts described. In my mind it is equivalent to an expression such as the following: "Incidents which seem (or even are reputed) to proceed from an unknown cause." The same reservation applies to such words as trance, &c.

[2] Even if he detached his hand from that of his neighbour, he always did it in so distinct a manner as to leave no room for reasonable doubt.

The chain once formed, the hands of the medium were placed sometimes on the knees of their neighbours, sometimes on his own.   In the latter case the hypothesis of any action of his legs is eliminated.   When I was sitting next to Sambor, it most frequently happened that I put my foot or my leg against his, which was sufficient to neutralise any possible action on his part.[1]   Further, the medium frequently tapped with his feet during the séance, which thus enabled their position to be observed.

I repeat that Sambor was the first to ask for a rigorous control.   At Kieff, in some of the séances, he was submitted to some very extraordinary tests.   For my part, I confess that I am opposed to them.

I ask for a strict control of the hands, and a satisfactory control of the feet, the elimination of all manifestations capable of being produced by a movement of the head or by any instruments whatever.   Apart from this, I regard ligatures of any description as useless.

Sambor was much disposed to ask for light during the séances, and he often related in support of this request, some examples of striking manifestations obtained under such conditions.   Having had occasion to verify some of his statements, I believe *the greater part* of them to be accurate, and am quite ready to believe that light does not prejudice the phenomena of this medium in particularly favourable circumstances.   But the results of my personal experience are that there is very little opportunity of observing the phenomena in any light whatever, even in a very feeble one.

I therefore think that new observers who begin to make experiments with Sambor ought first of all to proceed in total darkness, and then allow a little light in the room if the results obtained in the dark are particularly striking.

---

[1] As to the objection which has been made to this by several who have experimented with Eusapia, and consider such control illusory: I admit this when the medium is a female; with a man it is very different, provided one pays attention to his movements.

I should add, however :—

(a) That we have had some satisfactory experiments with Sambor by placing him *in front of a curtain*, behind which there was consequently a dark corner, and

(b) That in the circle, in whose séances I generally took part last winter, there was once in my absence (and with the addition of several persons who had never before attended our séances) an astonishing séance with the same medium in semi-darkness.

Sambor is, or is supposed to be, in a trance condition when any phenomenon takes place. Some years ago this condition was often manifested by violent movements on his part, movements so violent that we could not always hold his hand; at other times he fell to the ground, &c. At the present time he remains much quieter.

Only once, at least in my experience, the voice of "the spirit" (we shall speak later in detail of this phenomenon) was heard while the medium was not yet asleep. He manifested considerable emotion, which seemed to be quite sincere, and appeared to be very much interested. At the same séance he said he had seen the face of a child (his control, according to the spiritistic expression, is supposed to be a little girl), and one of the persons present (a sensitive, it appeared) declared that he had seen the same thing.

I shall give some details of the different classes of phenomena presented by Sambor in the following order :—

(a) Movements of Objects without Contact, and Touchings.

(b) Luminous Apparitions.

(c) Raps, Levitations, Voices, &c.

(d) Direct Writing.

(e) Passing of Matter through Matter.

(f) Materialisations.

Movements of Objects without Contact

This phenomenon took place at every séance which did not give absolutely no results. Articles placed outside the circle were carried on to the table in the midst of the spectators and *vice versâ;* articles which had fallen to the ground were raised from the floor and placed also on the table, and I have very often witnessed similar phenomena.

My impartiality makes it my duty, however, to add that for the greater part my personal observations relating to this class of facts must be considered as indecisive. In fact, when movements of this class are produced in total darkness, the control of the hands only, and even of the feet, ought not to be regarded as eliminating all possibility of fraud. We ought also to be sure that the distance at the commencement separating the medium from the objects transported has not changed during the séance, and in such conditions it seemed to me rather difficult to be quite certain of this.

It is for these reasons that, in speaking of manifestations of this character with Sambor, I only dwell upon those which presented, so to speak, an exceptional character in some respect.

I will commence with the account of a séance where various movements of objects were witnessed in a faint light in similar conditions to those of the experiments with Eusapia Paladino; except that the control of Sambor's hands could not give rise to any doubt.

The séance in question was held on March 7th (19th) at the house of Colonel B., one of the most assiduous members of the circle in the séances of which I took part last winter.[1]

There were present Colonel B., M. P., M. Édouard R., M. Vsevolod S. (a well-known Russian writer), the medium, and myself. I will not describe the first part of the séance, which took place in almost complete darkness. By dint of patience we succeeded in obtaining some manifestations, more or less convincing. It was then

---

[1] The account was published by me in *Rebus* (M. Pribitkow, editor) of June 6th (18th), 1899, from notes made by me on the following day, or the day but one after the séance. I am quoting from *Rebus* in giving the present account.

decided to continue the séance in semi-darkness. A small lamp was placed on the ground in a corner of the room, and a large book was placed in front of it to shield the light still more, though it was already turned quite low, after which we arranged ourselves as shown on the plan.

Some unimportant details in the arrangement of the room where the séance took place are not reproduced on this plan.

From the first there was complete or almost complete darkness in the room. The door leading from the cabinet

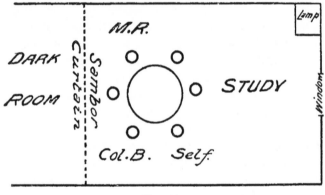

Fig. 14.

into the room was left open; to make up for this we lowered the curtains on both sides of the door and placed the medium in the middle.

The chain of hands was formed, as usual, on the knees of those present. The light, although very feeble, was still sufficient for us to see the head and hands of Sambor.

In these conditions various phenomena took place. First of all something white and very long was suddenly projected through the opening of the curtain on to Colonel B., my neighbour on the left, and myself; it was a small album of photographic views which had previously been in the room and had been opened in falling. When this part of the séance ended we saw another similar small album on the floor, half-way between the table in the middle of the room and the curtain, as though it had not had sufficient power to reach the medium.

Strictly speaking, it would be possible to assume that the medium had secretly possessed himself of this small album during one of the intervals of the séance, and had kept it in reserve up to that moment. This hypothesis seemed to me to be refuted by another phenomenon which was produced at this same séance. Once, while looking right in front of me, I saw an object, the nature of which I could not at first determine, come down on to the table between the medium and his left-hand neighbour, M. Édouard R. This movement was not very slow—nor yet very rapid—but an appreciable although very short time elapsed between the moment when I first saw this object, illuminated by the rays from the lamp, and that at which it touched the top of the table. It was a piece of wood; there was a small pile of them on the ground quite close at hand. This piece of wood passed close beside M. R.'s face, and he seemed quite surprised. It is clear that in this case at least the medium could have made no preparations for the production of the phenomenon.

One of the characteristic features of this séance was the touchings which several of us felt through the curtain. Bringing my left hand, which was joined with Colonel B.'s right hand, up to the curtain I distinctly felt a contact of fingers.[1]

But it was M. R. who was the special object of these touchings; once it was evidently attempted to draw him on to the other side of the curtain. They took hold of him under the arms, and pulled the flaps of his frock-coat—unfortunately he was afraid and unwilling to respond to this invitation. Colonel B. then rose and proposed to go behind the curtain in his place—but the phenomenon was not repeated.

It is distinctly noted in my account that during all the cases of contact enumerated above, the medium's hands were not only held but seen.

[1] This would be on a level with the medium's elbows.

I have not made a note of the cases in which Sambor's hands were covered by the curtain.

Sambor's hands, therefore, were not implicated; nor was his head either, for we could see it. It was impossible for me to determine the position of his feet; and this perhaps may be regarded as a matter for regret, though for my part it seems to me hardly probable that he could have picked up the piece of wood with his feet and made it pass quite close to M. Édouard R.'s face without the latter noticing it. That corner of the room was very dark at the time, and if I saw distinctly the piece of wood when it came on to the table, it was only owing to the rays from the lamp falling on it, without illuminating the space behind; but I do not think this circumstance detracts much from the value of the incident. In short, I had the impression at this séance that at the very least the phenomena of touchings, &c., were not due to the action of the feet.[1]

I pass on to another séance which was held in total darkness, but was of such a character that it was quite evident that the medium took no part in the phenomena.

The following account is according to a report published by me in *Rebus* :—

Séance held February 27th (March 11th), 1899, at the house of Dr. B. at St. Petersburg. I brought my friend M. G., Attaché at the Russian Legation at X., as he had

---

[1] I must say here that I was very careful in my article only to state things of which I was absolutely certain. It was quite possible, for example, that the feet of the medium were controlled in an absolutely satisfactory manner (by the feet of his neighbours) at the séance in question, but I was wrong in not assuring myself of this by questioning MM. R. and B. The same remark applies to the report as to the raising of the table described below. I believe, however, that at the séance of January 11, 1899, it may be considered very probable that at least one of the feet of the medium was accounted for. The reader must not assume from what is here said that I am not in favour of a rigorous control; quite the contrary, but when one is not directing the experiments it is not always possible to insist on all desirable conditions without being thought somewhat importunate.

(These last words certainly do not apply to the medium, who was the first to ask for a rigorous control, and I should be grieved if any one should take them in bad part.)

never been present at a spiritistic séance. There were also present Dr. and Mme. B——n, Mlle. Geibel, Mlle. K——n, M. A. Boujinski. At eleven o'clock my friend and colleague S——n came. Until he arrived nothing of any interest took place; but directly M. S——n was there, the phenomena assumed a remarkable character.

1. Notes were several times struck on a piano, placed at the other end of the room (which was very large) and on the side of the table (around which we were seated) furthest from the medium.

2. At the request of the medium when in a state of trance, and also at the request of the spectators, a glass of tea placed on the same piano during one of the intervals of the séance was brought across the room to the medium. We heard the spoon clink in the glass, and I heard Sambor drinking from this glass quite close to me (I was seated on his left).

3. I had the distinct sensation of some one making movements behind me. I felt several contacts of an indefinite character on the head; then at my request a palpably human hand, with quite distinct fingers, was placed on my face.

4. I had in one of the inside pockets of my frock-coat my wallet filled with papers, and a piece of string with the two ends sealed, which I had prepared in the hope of obtaining knots as Zöllner had done; on two occasions a hand (I had the very definite sensation of a forearm) felt in my pocket for these articles and took them out. I afterwards recovered the wallet and the string, but, alas! without a knot.

5. Sambor, still in trance, asked the spirit to open the door of the room a considerable distance behind him; the door was slowly half opened several times and we saw (the room at the side being partly illuminated), by the gleam of light which was formed, the outline of an arm which pushed the door; once I even thought I saw distinctly the outline of a head.[1]

---

[1] All these manifestations were produced in the same part of the séance. I have not described the others which occurred, either at the beginning or the end of the séance, and which were not so remarkable in character.

I declare in the most formal manner, and the reader will be disposed, I hope, to attach some value to this statement, in view of the reserves which I have several times had occasion to make, that none of these phenomena could be produced by the hands or the feet of the medium. I was quite certain as to his left foot and hand all the time. M. S——n was on the immediate right of Sambor, and he did not express any doubt as to his control of the medium; but that is not the essential point, because supposing even that the right hand or the right foot of Sambor were liberated (a very improbable hypothesis as regards the hand) that would not be sufficient to cause the notes of the piano to be played, or to bring the glass of tea, or to open the door.

All these phenomena could only have been produced by a person walking across the room with perfect freedom, and this would necessarily require the complicity of at least three members of the circle. I reject this hypothesis as categorically as the first. The only rational explanation would be to suppose the complicity of a person outside the circle and other than the medium. But there was no one in the place except the servants. It therefore could only have been the case that the medium had an understanding with one of them. It is, unfortunately, impossible to refute such a proposition absolutely. I will therefore content myself by remarking that it seems to me improbable.

I also had occasion later to broach this subject with Mme. B——n. She answered very decidedly in the negative.

I shall now say something with regard to a phenomenon, which I had the opportunity of observing several times at Sambor's séances, which was less extraordinary in character than the séance just described which I might call unique of its kind. It relates to the raising of tables, sometimes very heavy, which were transported outside the circle over the chain of hands.

I admit that for small tables the thing may be feasible, by means of the teeth; but when tables weighing thirty-four pounds and nearly a yard wide are concerned, this supposition seems to me very improbable. But a table of this weight and size was transported outside a circle at a séance held at my house on December 30, 1898 (January 11, 1899), a séance at which all idea of collusion was strictly excluded.

We formed the chain as usual around the table and without touching it. Once during the séance we noticed (in the darkness) that the table was raised, and, after a little time, Colonel B., who was on the immediate left of the medium, found that it was coming outside the circle over his arm which was joined to Sambor's; after which we heard it placed on the ground behind these two people, but with less noise than a table of this size would have made if it had been thrown; we then heard it moved in various directions and subsequently stop still.. When the candle was lighted we discovered that this table was placed on the ground, with its feet in the air, and taking up the entire space between Sambor and Colonel B. and the wall of the room, or, to be exact, the stove.

It seemed to me very unlikely that this transference could have been effected by means of the feet and head of the medium—even admitting that he had his feet free all the time, which is doubtful—without striking the head of one of the spectators. But, except a slight blow felt on the head of one of us, no one was in any way injured. I repeat that these transferences of heavy tables in such conditions seem to me outside the domain of prestidigitation.

I have witnessed this phenomenon many times, always without the medium leaving his chair. In some cases these transferences have been executed with remarkable rapidity. On other occasions a table, which went out of the circle between the medium and M. A., re-entered it by passing (in the air) between Sambor and M. B. At the séance of December 10th (22nd) (at my house) this phenomenon had this remarkable feature that it was produced (in darkness) without our perceiving it. The table, it is true, was rather small and light, and half of it had been removed, because it was broken at the commencement of the séance (the remaining half weighed nearly twelve pounds), but I ought to add that a nickel lamp was hanging almost over the middle of the circle, and it is certainly curious that this was not touched during the movement.

Luminous Apparitions

These were very frequent with Sambor some years ago. We saw a luminous spot suddenly rise in the darkness and shine for one or two seconds; we then saw a kind of vapour or smoke become detached from it, and the whole disappeared. I have no decided opinion as to this phenomenon, but have often asked myself if it could not be produced by means of some substance with which the medium had coated his hair, which he often rubbed during the séance with one of his hands without breaking the chain (he made, however, the same movement without any "light" appearing as the result).

Since then these apparitions have changed their character. At present they are generally small bluish or greenish specks, which suddenly shine out in the darkness, describing zigzag paths in the air, then disappearing. Provided that the medium's hands—as was almost always the case—were firmly held when the phenomenon was produced, I am inclined to regard the evidence here as conclusive.

I think, however, that I was mistaken in saying just now that "these greenish points" have a later origin than the luminous apparitions of Sambor of a different character. If my memory serves me, some were witnessed at the commencement of his career. What I mean is, that at present "these greenish points" are, I think, almost the only phenomenon of this character presented by Sambor.

Several observers have often had occasion to notice an evident connection between the luminous apparitions and the movement of objects.

For example, a luminous point has been seen to detach itself from the medium and go towards a guitar which was placed on the table, the cords of which then sounded.

The reader will find further on, in the account of the

very remarkable experiment of Dr. Pogorelsky, the mention of a luminous star whose appearance coincided with a case of the " passage of matter through matter."

At a séance at which I was present, a small musical box (with handle) began playing a tune while flying about in the midst of the circle, and some of its movements were accompanied by those of a luminous spot (December 1897).

Passages of Matter through Matter and Knots like Zöllner's

I come now to the most striking class of Sambor's phenomena, and that which is, in my opinion, the most calculated to produce conviction. It is the most striking because nothing more impresses the mind than facts which tend to make one believe that the action of one of the most immutable and evident laws of nature, such as that of the impenetrability of matter, can be temporarily suspended. It is the most convincing, because this particular phenemenon has on several occasions been produced through Sambor in conditions which, if they do not absolutely eliminate all possibility of error, render it improbable to a degree which almost amounts to absolute certainty.

This same phenomenon, moreover, presents the indisputable advantage that the experimental observation of it is much less difficult, and the sources of error much less numerous, than in other branches of psychic phenomena.

When it is a question of movement of objects, the certainty that these movements are not due to any known cause, is only the result of a series of other certainties, often difficult to realise. The control of the hands only is not sufficient. It must be made impossible for the medium to obtain the result wished by the aid of his feet and head, or by means of threads, or any instrument whatever, and when all these sources of error are undoubtedly eliminated there remains the hypothesis of collusion.

On the other hand, if I wish to obtain, for example, a

wooden ring or a chair passed over the medium's hand whilst I hold his hand in mine, it is sufficient for this experiment to be regarded as satisfactory for three very simple conditions to be observed :—

1. I must be certain that the ring or the chair that is to be used in the experiment is not a "trick" article;

2. I must hold the medium's hand in my own in such a way that it cannot escape from me, even for a quarter of a second;

3. If the experiment is successful, I must be convinced that there was no substitution of the ring or the chair.

Apart from that, the position of the medium's feet and head, the presence or absence of threads or hooks, the questions of darkness or light, do not play any part. It would, doubtless, be preferable that this phenomenon should take place in a lighted room ; but it is by no means a *sine qua non* condition, and it must be agreed that when the experimenter can confine his attention to the hand only of the medium, it is much more easy to maintain an unflagging observation.

It seems to me that the necessity for this observation, to which Messrs. Podmore and Hodgson assign no value, is not always appreciated in an experiment of this character. As a matter of fact, the question to be solved is the following : granted that the experimenter holds one of the medium's hands firmly in his own, is it possible for this hand to become free and then to resume its former position without the experimenter perceiving it?

Well, I know nothing that allows me to regard such a thing as possible. I fully admit that when the hands are placed one over the other on the table, one of them can be liberated—even, perhaps, if the sitter next to the medium gives all necessary attention to the experiment, and all the more so if his attention is distracted. But that is not the question. The majority, if not all, of the experiments of the "passage of matter through matter" have taken place with Sambor in quite different conditions:

the chain of hands did not touch the table, and the medium's hands were firmly held.[1]

Some years ago it happened very frequently at the séances with Sambor in Petersburg, that when his hands were held a chair was threaded upon his arm without the medium's hands being released by his neighbours. These phenomena happened in 1894 and 1896; they have almost ceased since that time, and now only occur very seldom.

Here, for example, is an extract from a report made by me of a séance which took place in the offices of *Rebus* on November 3rd (15th), 1894.

"The séance commenced at a quarter to nine; fourteen persons were present, excluding the medium. At the commencement of the séance M. Sch. controlled the medium on the right and M. N. on the left. After Sambor had struggled a good deal in the darkness, two cane chairs (called Thonet chairs) came and linked themselves over the right and left arms of the medium's neighbour, which all present verified in the light. The sitter on Sambor's right declared that he had held his hand all the time. According to M. Sch., after Sambor had made a violent movement, his hand escaped for a second from the hand of the controller, but it was immediately caught again, convincing himself that the chair was not there, but he distinctly felt a chair near to his right arm and pushed it back."

On another occasion (at the same period) I was seated at the medium's right hand. The séance took place in darkness. Sambor was struggling terribly; I fully believe that once he fell on to the floor (he has become much calmer since). In spite of all my efforts his hand once escaped mine; I caught it again and convinced myself that there was no chair on his arm (at least I was so persuaded at that moment, which ought to be sufficient),

---

[1] I may remind readers that the criticisms directed against certain experiments made with Eusapia were based on the real or supposed circumstance that her hands were not held in the strict sense of the word Dr. Hodgson was careful to state this.

I did not again loose his hand. Colonel M., who was on Sambor's left, did not loose his hold at all; half-an-hour afterwards we lighted up and saw two chairs hanging round the medium's arm: one on the right and another on the left.

The following is an account of another séance where the same phenomenon took place in a dull light, it is true. (*Rebus*, No. 47, 1894.)

Séance held October 30th (November 12th), 1894

(At the commencement of the report some phenomena are described which are not of great interest.)

" The third part of the séance began, and took place by the light of a candle placed inside the stove (the opening of which was not closed). Five minutes after the chain had been formed the medium began to move and to rise from his chair, then he sat down and got up again. Immediately afterwards the controller on the left of the medium declared that a chair was suspended from his arm, and guaranteed that he had not ceased holding the medium's hand for one moment. The third part of the séance did not last more than fifteen minutes. The medium was controlled by MM. Narbout and Panaieff.

" The fourth part of the séance, which lasted nearly half-an-hour, began in the light, but a quarter of an hour afterwards the medium declared that he was very tired, and asked that the light might be reduced: in order to accede to his request we closed the opening of the stove in which the candle had been placed. The medium was controlled by MM. Narbout and Vassilieff; the latter, whose hand was tied to that of the medium, greatly desired a chair to be suspended from his arm also. Soon after the opening of the stove had been closed the medium began to move, to groan loudly, and to throw himself this way and that, and five minutes afterwards said, ' Give me more light.' We had hardly opened the door of the stove when the medium rose up, while his controllers did the same, and it was found that the controller on the right had two chairs on his arm, and M. Vassilieff, who was on the left, and whose hand was tied to the medium's, one only. This controller declared that he had felt the chair pass, so to speak, through his arm and rest upon it until it was suspended from it." [1]

The official account of this séance is signed by all who were present.

I remember that some one who was present at a séance with Sambor told me of a similar impression, but I am not quite certain if it was M. Vassilieff. I believe, however, that it was.

Here is a similar instance.

At the séance of November 3rd (15th), 1894, which has already been mentioned, after one of the intervals, my cousin, M. Ch., was seated on the medium's left, and M. Vassilieff on his right; M. Ch.'s hand was tied to Sambor's. In these conditions a chair was placed around M. Vassilieff's arm, who maintained, as did also M. Ch., that he had not released his hold of the medium's hand for one moment. We lighted the candle, and I examined the chair myself without finding anything suspicious. (*Rebus*, No. 47, 1894.)

I am not able to say precisely, at this distance of time, how long this experiment lasted, but I am under the impression that it did not last longer than half-an-hour at the outside, and perhaps much less.

Cases of this sort are, I repeat, numerous, and I could quote others.

Let us see if the phenomenon in question can be rationally explained.

The first explanation—that of a surreptitious liberation of one of the medium's hands—has already been discussed above. I repeat once more that, seeing the perfect way in which Sambor's hands are generally held, it seems to me untenable, and in any case it is for the sceptics to prove the contrary.[2]

---

[1] Unfortunately I was not present at the séance in question.

[2] It might, with extreme strictness, be objected that although Sambor was never opposed to my holding his hand in the manner described above,

Another analogous explanation would be the following: when the chair used in the experiment is a cane chair, it may be that the medium succeeds in slipping through the back of the chair and making it rise to the height of his arms: if then his left hand, let us say, is loosed by the control, he can make the chair appear on his right arm without his right hand being liberated. To do this he would have to draw his left arm, set free for the moment, through the back of the chair, and throw this chair over his head on to his right arm. In order to refute this explanation I will content myself by observing that this also necessitates our assuming the possibility of liberating one hand unobserved: that this is absolutely excluded in cases such as those which I have quoted above, in which three chairs were suspended from the medium's two arms; in which one of Sambor's hands was tied to one of his neighbour's, the chair becoming suspended from the other arm; in which the back of the chair was such that a man could not pass through it;[1] in which, lastly, the chairs were not "trick" chairs, previously subjected by the medium to any manipulations.

This explanation cannot, strictly speaking, be considered as absolutely excluded from the séances previously described—in fact, they took place, as I have said, in the offices of *Rebus*, the spiritualistic newspaper of St. Petersburg; where, at that time, Sambor was living, and this circumstance may, in the eyes of some, affect the value of the experiments in question. It should be noted that the chairs used formed part of the furniture of the office; that Sambor was only in Petersburg for a short time, and I do not see what manipulations he could have effected on these cane chairs.

An hypothesis of this character is therefore very improbable: it even becomes quite valueless, since similar pheno-

it does not necessarily follow that his hands were always thus held. To this I reply that I could see the manner in which his hands were held at a number of séances where there was observed what seemed to be the passing of matter through matter, and I have always considered the control of the hands as good.

[1] I have been present at one or two cases of this kind.

mena were produced at séances with Sambor, with other objects which cannot lend themselves to any suspicion.

Thus I brought to this same séance of November 15, 1894, which has already been mentioned several times, a wooden ring bought by myself and marked.

Well, this ring was placed (I ought to say it threaded itself) on M. Vassilieff's arm, when he was holding one of the medium's hands. (*Rebus*, No. 47, 1894.)

It is true that unfortunately this fact lost, in my eyes, a part of its value, seeing that it happened after I had left, but I should not have mentioned it in *Rebus* at that time if I had not been convinced, by questioning some of those present, that it really took place.

Here, again, is the account of two very interesting experiments described, the first by Dr. Pogorelsky, the other by Dr. Fisher, Vice-President of the Russian Society of Experimental Psychology.

Dr. Pogorelski was kind enough to communicate to me in the month of May 1899 an account of his remarkable experiment. I reproduce it here with some abbreviations:—

"During the winter of 1895–1896," he states, "S. F. Sambor gave some séances at the Spiritist Club at St. Petersburg, in the editorial offices of *Rebus* at 65, Nevsky. At one of these séances I was sitting by the side of Sambor and held his left hand with my right, in my own special manner—that is to say, by passing all the fingers of my hand between those of his hand. At one of these séances a cane chair was found suspended by the opening at the back on my arm. I was particularly interested in this phenomenon (the luminous apparitions which were then produced with Sambor already interested me a little), and I wanted to verify this experiment in conditions which seemed, to me at least, convincing.

" For this purpose I arranged to hold some séances at my residence, 40 Liteinaia ; these séances taking place in my study, a very large room, but not in the presence of professed spiritists—quite the contrary. I invited anti-spiritists exclusively, or else people who had not heard the subject mentioned. Moreover, I authorised those whom I knew to bring any one they chose, so that the company was half changed at each séance, and there were always new faces. The majority of these persons were scarcely known to me, and unknown to each other, except, of course, to those who had introduced them.

"At these three séances the number present varied from twelve or fifteen to twenty-two persons of both sexes. There were doctors, lawyers, engineers, mathematicians, officers, public officials, an author, some ladies, and some young girls."

(Dr. Pogorelski mentions several names.)

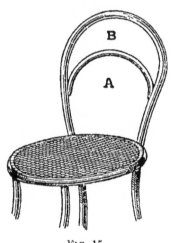

Fig. 15.

"The séances were held once a week in March and April 1896.

"The conditions of the experiments were perfect darkness and singing.[1] I only had one cane chair in my rooms, so before the experiment we borrowed some from a person we knew, Mme. Elizabeth P. Levtchenko.

She lent us altogether three chairs: one for the medium, and two for his neighbours on either side. These chairs were of beechwood with plaited seats, and the backs formed of two arches with two openings. A (large) and B (smaller).

Only an arm could pass through B; whereas a man could slip through A if he were thin and very adroit, and then not without great difficulty.[2]

During the second part of the séance of April 4th (16th), 1896, to the best of my recollection I was sitting on one side of the medium, the engineer T. on the other. Suddenly I

---

[1] Generally we simply sang at Sambor's séances; on other occasions a musical box played.

[2] It must be stated that Sambor is tall of stature, although rather thin.

felt a blow on my right arm (close to the shoulder), and I felt a chair passed on to my right arm by the opening B. As I held Sambor's hands in my usual way (by interlacing the fingers) it was impossible for our hands to become separated, even for a hundredth part of a second, without my feeling it. Moreover, if that had happened—that is to say, if Sambor had removed his hand—it would have been impossible in the darkness to put it back in the same place without changing the order of the fingers, and without my feeling it. Finally, there could be here no question of the hypothesis of his slipping through the opening A. For—without taking account of other considerations (how could he have freed his hand from that of F.?)—that would have served no purpose, because in this case my arm would then have been passed through A. and not through B.

"We lighted the candle and verified this fact. Then the usual long discussions began, and not only the medium was suspected, but myself, as having taken part in a hoax.

"Then with the permission of Sambor I thought of trying the following experiment:—

"We placed Sambor between M. Maxime W., a solicitor and a violent sceptic, whom all who knew regarded as an honest man and a gentleman, which is the reason he was chosen as controller. He was sitting on Sambor's left, and Mlle. O. on his right. She was a young girl of twenty years of age at the most, very healthy, of perfect constitution, well built but slightly nervous, and was what is called a sensitive. She has self-control, is not timid nor superstitious, does not believe in spiritualism, and had sat next to Sambor at previous séances. She was not nervous at his touchings or at his way of knocking with his fist on her knees."

Dr. Pogorelsky then stated that he tied M. W.'s right hand to Sambor's left, by means of a linen ribbon about half an inch wide and nearly ten yards long, by placing first of all the fingers of one hand between the fingers of the other and rolling the ribbon round the hands and fingers and making many knots. These ligatures not

2 I

only made it impossible to separate the hands, but even for the fingers to move. Seals were placed on the ends of the ribbon.

"The candle being extinguished, we awaited the result. In order to make Sambor feel at ease, I naturally told everybody beforehand that the experiment might not be successful; that this would not be a proof to the contrary seeing that séances were not always successful. At the end of not more than ten minutes Sambor's usual disturbance commenced: he began to let himself slip off his chair on to the floor, to groan, to knock with his fist on his knees, to rise up, &c. This time there were few lights, not more than one or two. Suddenly Mlle. O. cried out that she felt the chair on her left arm.

"She solemnly declared that she had not released Sambor's right hand for a second. But unfortunately her hand was not sealed to Sambor's, which would have made the experiment much more decisive, and everybody declared with one voice that it was not convincing. M. W. and myself categorically insisted that the chair should be threaded on M. W.'s arm. In his half-entranced condition Sambor asked us all to insist, saying, 'Pray all, pray that the chair pass on to W.'s side.'

"Everybody cried out, 'We ask it, we ask it,' and in the twinkling of an eye, I do not know if half a minute had elapsed from the time when we began to call out 'We ask it,' M. W., in a voice choking with fright, cried out: 'Gentlemen, the chair is on my arm, I feel it'; and Mlle. O. declared that the chair had disappeared from her arm.

"One detail: myself and several other persons, but not all, saw at that moment something like a luminous flash that passed from Mlle. O. to W.

"After W.'s exclamation that the chair had been threaded on to his arm, everybody requested that it should remain there, which it did.

"We turned up the light and everybody crowded round Sambor and W., who were inseparably bound together. The chair was found hanging from W.'s arm by the opening A. The seals and ligatures were intact, and it was only with difficulty that we undid them."

Dr. Pogorelsky draws from this experiment the conclusion that Sambor's right hand not having been tied to Mlle. O.'s left hand, the hypothesis of Sambor passing through the opening A. from the back of the chair could not be regarded as excluded "with mathematical certainty"; but that if we took into consideration the fact that Mlle. O.'s fingers were indissolubly united to Sambor's, at the time of the appearance of the chair on her arm, as well as during the transport of this chair on to M. W.'s arm, and also the rapidity of this removal, there could be no question that in this experiment, we have a genuine case of the passing of matter through matter "à la Zöllner."

For my part, I accept this conclusion.

CHAPTER XXXVI

PROFESSOR C. RICHET'S OBSERVATIONS AT THE VILLA CARMEN [1]

WE shall devote this chapter to the study of the materialisations which were produced at the Villa Carmen in Algiers, the residence of General and Mme. Noel.

These facts have been much talked of because they were witnessed by the eminent professor of physiology at the Faculty of Medicine in Paris and Honorary President of La Société Universelle d'Études Psychiques, M. Charles Richet, who went to Algiers expressly for the purpose of studying them.

But whatever may be the scientific authority possessed by those who dare to express an opinion in favour of certain facts and declare that they have been proved, there will be found men without any authority or scientific standing who will not hesitate flatly to deny the statements made without bringing forward proofs, or make puerile objections to definite, scientific, and documentary evidence of men of science of indisputable authority.

In these discussions there is evident prejudice on the part of those who do not seek the truth, but who desire, at any price, to deny certain facts which are unpalatable to their narrow minds.

These objections, as regards the observations made by M. Richet at the Villa Carmen, have been reduced to nothing, as will be proved by the following investigation. We will quote Professor Richet's own words,[2] in which he meets all these objections.

---

[1] Where modifications have been deemed advisable in the English rendering of the translation of original documents in this and other chapters, they have been unhesitatingly adopted.

[2] See *Annals of Psychical Science*, April 1906.

"Everything that Dr. Z. announces as to the fraud or frauds at the Villa Carmen really rests on the following :—

"He was able to exhibit on the stage of a theatre an individual who, covered with a white sheet, played the part of a phantom, exactly as in *Les Cloches de Corneville;* and the simple-minded public immediately concluded from this that the phenomena of the Villa Carmen were fraudulent.

"Dr. Z. was not obliged to draw very heavily on his imagination in order to exhibit so cheap a phantom at the Université Populaire of Algiers. He even wished to exhibit luminous phenomena by employing phosphorated oil, but his chemical knowledge was not sufficient to enable him to prepare it successfully.

"The whole scene, which excited the audience and took place in impressive silence, had this element of spice that the actor who played the part of the phantom was the former coachman of General Noel, a man named Areski, who had been dismissed by the General.

"How the coachman Areski managed to intervene, we are told by Dr. Z. It was simply by entering the séance room with us, by a process which does not seem at all mysterious, that is to say, by examining, along with us, the carpet, the bath, and the furniture ; then, when attention was diverted to another quarter, he slipped into the cabinet and hid behind the curtain.

"Now, I declare formally and solemnly that during the séances—about twenty in number—at which I was present, *Areski was not once permitted to enter the séance room.* His actions had inspired us with sufficient distrust of him to cause us to take care to keep him completely away. I will add that it would have been just as impossible for him to leave the cabinet as to enter it, and that of all imaginable hypotheses of deception, that of Areski or any other person entering or leaving the cabinet without our knowledge is by far the most absurd. It is even so impossible that I have difficulty in believing that any person of common sense could be found capable of crediting it.

"This is mere kitchen or stable gossip which I should have passed over in contemptuous silence if, in his feverish desire for self-advertisement, Dr. Z. had not revealed to the universe this tattle of a discharged servant.

"There remain the two other confessions, or so-called confessions, which Dr. Z. has obtained after an inquiry probably greatly prolonged. He tells us first that a doctor, whose name he has the modesty not to give, had played a farce on Mme. Noel by getting some one to learn by heart a ridiculous English phrase, and to give it out as a proof of supposed mediumistic power. I declare that I did not know the smallest portion of this story, that I have never mentioned it in my account, that I am in no way responsible for what may have been said by others, and that, if it is true, I am very sorry both for the doctor who consented to play such a despicable part, and for Mme. Noel whose hospitality was thus abused.

"As to the so-called confession of Mlle. Marthe B., which, according to Dr. Z., consists merely in saying that there is a trap-door in the séance room.

"(1) *Mlle. Marthe B. has never written or said that there was a trap-door;*

"(2) *There is no trap-door.*

"We must, however, draw one conclusion as to the objections which, after six months' reflection, reinforced by extorted confessions, inquiries and counter inquiries, backstairs talk, &c., have been raised against the facts of which I have given an account. This consists in the five following assertions:—

"1. An individual dressed up in a white sheet can amuse himself by playing the phantom on the stage.

"2. This individual may be General Noel's coachman.

"3. General Noel's coachman asserts that he has freely entered the séance room with us, whereas that statement is without foundation.

"4. A doctor played a trick on Mme. Noel two years ago by teaching eleven words of English to an individual who does not know English.

"5. Mlle. Marthe B. is reported to have said that everything was done by means of a trap-door, whereas she has not said it, and there is no trap-door.

"I confess, for my part, that in treating seriously of these phenomena, their strangeness had, in spite of all proofs, occasioned some doubts in my mind, and I have not neglected to express them fully and forcibly. But now, in view of the poverty of the objections which could be brought against them, many of these doubts have disappeared.

"The existence of this trap-door—concerning which a lawyer in Algiers wrote me a touching letter, which I shall publish if need be—is formally refuted by the following certificate :—

"'EMILE LOWE, *Architect*, S.N.
Boulevard Laferrière, 1.

"'I, the undersigned, Emile Lowe, expert architect at Algiers, hereby certify that I have visited and examined the interior and exterior of the room known as the séance-room at the Villa Carmen, Rue Darwin, at Mustapha, belonging to General Noel.

"'This villa and its outhouses were built to my plans and under my direction in 1893 for M. Battistini.

"'The room in question occupies the whole of the first and only floor of a little pavilion to the right of the entrance to the property and was formerly used as a laundry; it is covered by a terrace-roof in bricks and cement on double T-irons, and is built of masonry. The ground-floor is used as a coach-house, and is separated from the first-floor by a floor also of double T-iron, filled in with bricks and cement nine inches thick.

"'In these two floors, which are visible throughout their whole extent between the four walls, there exists no opening or trap-door whatever.

"'The coach-house is entered from the Rue Darwin and from the platform forming the entrance to the property; it is also lighted by a ventilator under the ceiling in the wall facing the garden, and in full view.

"'The room on the first-floor is lighted by two large windows, one of which looks on to the Rue Darwin and the other on to the entrance platform. Access to the room is obtained by a door looking on to the garden. In the party wall, which is completely visible from the interior and from the next garden, there is no opening.

"'In consequence I certify that there does not exist, and never has existed, any other opening than those above mentioned.

"'I have also ascertained that the building is in the same state in which I built it, and that no repairs have been executed for more than six months.

"' EMILE LOWE.

"'ALGIERS, *March* 16, 1906.

"' Signature seen and legalised by me at
Algiers, March 16, 1906.
For the Mayor: Adjoint Delegate.
(Signature illegible).'"

We here give in full, by the kind permission of Professor Richet, the account which he has published on these phenomena.

I

General and Mme. Noel have, during the last year or two, published various notices concerning these singular facts in the *Revue scientifique et morale du spiritisme*, edited by M. Delanne. But I will make no allusion whatever to these recitals, and will dwell only upon those facts which I myself witnessed.[1]

The persons who were present at these experiments were General and Mme. Noel, Mme. X., a lady whom I know, and who knows General and Mme. Noel, but who wishes to withhold her name; M. Gabriel Delanne, and

---

[1] See *Annals of Psychical Science*, October 1905.

the three daughters of M. B., a retired military officer: Marthe (aged 19 years), Paulette (aged 16 years), Maïa (aged 14 years). Marthe was engaged to be married to Maurice Noel, the son of General and Mme. Noel, who died last year in the Congo.

It is highly probable that the greater part of the phenomena which were forthcoming was due to the influence of Marthe as medium; for the various persons I have mentioned were seated outside the curtains of the cabinet where the materialisations were produced, whilst Marthe was always inside the cabinet behind the curtains. On two occasions during these experiments another person was also seated inside the cabinet with Marthe : a person named Ninon, who exercises the profession of chiromancer; but her rôle was practically nil, for she was only twice present. A negress, one of Mme. Noel's servants, a girl of 22, named Aïscha, also took part sometimes in the séances as a *soi-disant* medium, being then seated behind the curtains. But her rôle appears also to have been a very unimportant one; for several most important phenomena were forthcoming when Marthe was quite alone in the cabinet—without either Aïscha or Ninon.

The room in which these experiments took place is a small kiosk situated in the garden of the Villa Carmen. This kiosk or pavilion is entirely separated from any habitation; it is composed of one room only, and is built over a stable and coach-house. This room has two windows and one entrance door. One of the windows looks out on the street and is five yards above the street. The other window looks out on a stone staircase which leads from the garden to the street. The garden slopes down abruptly from the Rue Fontaine-Bleue to the Rue Darwin. The door looks out on the garden. Each of the two windows is blocked up and covered with canvas nailed to the wall. Over this canvas there is a thick tapestry curtain which is also nailed to the wall. The floor of the room consists of flagstones cemented together. A kind of linoleum is nailed on the floor; near the séance cabinet this linoleum is covered with a thin felt carpet.

The séance cabinet is made by a canopy in one of the corners of the room, which forms a triangle, the hypotenuse A, B of which measures 3 yards. The height of the canopy is 7 feet; that of the room is 9 feet 6 inches. There is therefore a space of 2 feet 6 inches between the canopy and the ceiling.

The triangle is closed by a very thick, dark, tapestry curtain. The curtain runs on a rod by means of brass rings.

In front of the curtain, leaving barely sufficient space to pass between it and the curtain, is a round table of

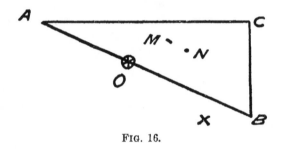

FIG. 16.

black wood, around which we were seated nearly always in the following order:—

Looking at the curtain, and beginning from the spectator's right, there were seated around the table successively: Maïa, Mme. X., myself, Paulette, G. Delanne, Mme. Noel, General Noel.

Before every sitting I examined the room minutely and thoroughly—the canopy, the curtains, the chairs (lifting them up), a bath and an old trunk which were in a corner of the room—and I am able to certify that no one was hidden in the room when the séance began. Moreover, as the curtains over the windows were securely nailed to the wall, as there was no trap or secret panel in the walls, I am quite certainly able to affirm that no one could enter the room during the séance.

The séances were held by the light of a candle placed in a red photographic lantern which stood on a shelf at a height of 6 feet 9 inches above the floor.

Finally, I will note that the curtain had an opening, and was so made that the right side was longer than the left side. When the curtain was fully opened, and the eyes became accustomed to the feeble light, we were able to distinguish the hands and faces of the mediums and their garments. At the same time, it was rather difficult to recognise them even when the opening was at its maximum. On the contrary, in the room itself, outside the cabinet, at a distance of one yard to one and a half yards, the various sitters could be easily recognised.

After several preliminary operations, on which I will not dwell, Marthe and Aïscha seated themselves in the cabinet: Marthe to the left, Aïscha to the right, and the curtain was closed.

The séances took place either at four o'clock in the afternoon or at eight o'clock in the evening. They lasted from two to three hours. At the close of each séance I examined the room as thoroughly and minutely as before the séance.

II

All the experiments conducted at the Villa Carmen cannot be described here in detail; for the detailed report of these experiments, written by me immediately after each séance, would be too lengthy and tedious. It will perhaps be sufficient if I set forth methodically a few essential facts, choosing those which appear to have the greatest significance.

I said further back that it was not possible to suppose the presence of some individual concealed in the séance room, or of some one entering the room during the séance, in order to explain the presence of a new personage appearing beside the medium.

I will establish, first of all, that the personage in question is neither an image reflected in a mirror, nor a doll, nor a lay-figure. In fact, it possesses all the attributes of life. I have seen it leave the séance cabinet, walk about, go and come. I have heard its breathing and its voice; I have touched its hand several times: that hand was warm and jointed. I have been able, through the drapery with which the hand was covered, to feel the wrist, the bones of the wrist and of the metacarpus, which yielded to the pressure of my hand-clasp.

Therefore, the only fraud possible—and it is absolutely impossible to suppose any other — must consist in the so-called phantom being the medium disguised. For reasons which I will give in detail further on, I consider this hypothesis extremely difficult, if not impossible, to admit. But before entering on this discussion, I will relate in full the following experience, which proves undoubtedly that the phantom—or the form which was before our eyes—possesses some of the essential attributes of life.

On Friday, September 1st, Marthe and Aïscha were seated behind the curtain. In front of the curtain were the usual sitters: General Noel, Mme. Noel, M. D., Paulette B., myself, Mme. X., and Maïa B. I had prepared a bottle containing some clear baryta water, and arranged in such a way that by blowing through a tube made of india-rubber it was possible to make the expired air bubble in the baryta water. After the production of several phenomena, the details of which I will not enlarge upon, Bien Boa (this is the name by which the phantom calls itself) asked to be permitted to try the experiment of the baryta. At the same time, he bent forward, outside the curtain, and through the opening he thus made in bending forward, I distinguished clearly Aïscha seated far away from B. B. and Marthe. I could not see Marthe's face very well; but I recognised the skirt and chemisette she was wearing, and I saw her hands. M. Delanne, who was nearer the cabinet than I was, affirms he saw Marthe's face.

B. B. bent forward, as I said. The General took the tube of baryta from my hands and handed it to B. B., who tried to blow through it. During the whole time this experiment was going on, I distinguished clearly the entire form of Marthe, who was seated far in the background. M. Delanne remarked aloud to me that he distinguished

Marthe completely; and, as the capital point of the experiment lay precisely in a thorough and complete view of Marthe, all my attention was devoted to her. At the same time we heard B. B. trying hard to blow through the tube; but he did it badly, and his respiration, instead of passing through the tube, passed outside it, consequently there was no gurgling or bubbling of the water.

For some time B. B. made fruitless efforts, and we heard his blowing.

Then the General explained to him that he must make the liquid bubble, which can only occur when the expired air is made to pass through the tube. At last B. B. succeeded; he blew strongly, and I heard the bubbling, which lasted for about half a minute; then he made a sign with his head that he was fatigued and could not go on any longer, and he passed the tube of baryta to me: I observed that the liquid had become quite white.

I desire to point out: (1) That my eyes did not leave the tube, and that it left my hands to pass into those of the General and B. B.; also that I saw the tube all the time near the mouth of B. B., while the expired gas was bubbling through the baryta water, and that immediately afterwards there was carbonate of baryta, as I observed by the sufficient light of the room, without the tube having left my sight. (2) That at various times I was able to see, behind B. B., the form of Marthe; her hands I saw very clearly, her face with less certainty, but at all events the whole outline of her face, although it was too indistinct to be able to recognise the features.

Following upon this extraordinary and exciting experiment there occurred an incident which was rather comical; for comical things sometimes get strangely confused with serious matters. After the persons present had assured themselves that there was carbonic acid formed (white carbonate of baryta), they became so enthusiastic that they broke out into applause, crying, "Bravo!" Then B. B., who had disappeared behind the curtain, reappeared three separate times, showing his head and saluting, like an actor returning to the stage in response to the applause of the audience.

It should also be noted that while B. B. was blowing into the tube, M. Delanne remarked to me aloud that the form of Marthe could be perfectly distinguished behind B. B., and he made this observation at three different times, while B. B. was blowing.

It results from these facts that the phantom of B. B. possesses all the attributes of life. It walks, speaks, moves, and breathes like a human being. Its body is resistant and has a certain muscular strength. It is neither a lay-figure nor a doll, nor an image reflected by a mirror; it is like a living being; and there are reasons for resolutely setting aside every other supposition than one or the other of these two hypotheses: either that of a phantom having the attributes of life, or that of a living person playing the part of a phantom.

The following phenomenon appeared to me to be of prime importance.

The experiment was made under the same conditions as the others, except that Mme. X. was not present. It was on Tuesday, August 29th, and it was on that day that the photograph was taken.

After the photograph had been taken the curtain closed again. In the diagram the triangle A, C, B re-presents the cabinet in which Marthe was sitting at M and Aïscha at N; A, B is the curtain, with an opening at O, by which the form of B. B. comes out and returns.

Scarcely had B. B. re-entered at O, when I saw, with-out any movement whatever of the curtain, a white light at X, on the ground, outside the curtain, between the table and the curtain. I half rose, in order to look over the table; I saw as it were a white luminous ball floating over the ground; then, rising straight upwards, very rapidly, as though issuing from a trap-door, appeared B. B. He appeared to me to be of no great height; he was clad in a drapery, and, I think, had something like a *caftan* with a girdle at the waist. He was then placed between the table and the curtain, being *born*, so to speak, out of the flooring outside the curtain (which had not stirred). The curtain is nailed to the wall all along the angle B, so that a living person, in order to leave the cabinet by that way, would have no other means than to crawl along the floor and pass under the curtain. But the coming out was sudden, and the luminous spot on the floor preceded the appearance of B. B. outside the curtain, and he raised himself up (developing his form rapidly in a straight line.)[1] Then B. B. tried, as it seemed to me, to come among us, but he had a limping, hesitating gait. I could not say whether he walked or glided. At one moment he reeled, as though about to fall, limping with one leg, which seemed unable to support him (I give my own impression). Then he went towards the opening of the curtains. Then, without, as far as I believe, opening the curtains, he suddenly sank down, disappeared into the ground, and, at the same time, a sound of clac, clac was heard, like the noise of a body thrown on to the ground. A very little time afterwards (two, three, or four minutes), at the very feet of the General, in the opening of the curtains, we again saw the same white ball (his head ?) on the ground ; it mounted rapidly, quite straight, rose to the height of a man, then suddenly sank down to the ground, with the same noise, clac, clac, of a body falling on to the ground. The General felt the shock of the limbs, which, in falling, struck his leg with some violence.

It appeared to me that this experiment was decisive ; for the formation of a luminous spot on the ground, which then changes into a living and walking being, cannot, seemingly, be produced by any trick. To suppose that Marthe, disguised as B. B., could, by gliding under the curtain and then rising upright, give the appearance of a white spot rising in a straight line, seems to me impossible ; all the more so as, the next day, perhaps to show me the difference, B. B. again appeared in front of the curtain, behind which he had formed, placing him-

---

[1] These last words are not in my notes. I add them in order to render intelligible the notes hastily written and sometimes obscure.

self on all fours, as we say, and then rising to his feet.
There was no possible analogy between the two modes of
procedure.

Several times, for instance three times on Thursday,
August 24th, I saw him plunge himself straight into the
ground. "He suddenly became shorter, and under our
eyes disappeared into the ground; then raised himself
again suddenly in a vertical line. The head, with the
turban and the black moustache, and as it were the indication of eyes, grew, and gradually rose, until it nearly
overtopped the canopy. At certain moments it was
obliged to lean and bend, *because of the great height
which it assumed*. Then, suddenly, the head sank, sank
right down to the ground and disappeared. B. B. did this
three times in succession. In trying to compare this
phenomenon to something, I can find nothing better than
the figure in a Jack-in-the-box, which comes out all of a
sudden. But I do not know of anything resembling that
vanishing into the earth in a straight line, so that at one
moment it seems as though only the head was above the
ground and that there was no longer a body."

Important as this last experience was, three times
repeated, it seems to me less decisive than the preceding
experiment, the birth by means of a white spot on the
ground outside the curtain; in fact, in the case of the
body sinking in a straight line into the ground, one might
suppose that by extraordinary efforts of clever gymnastics
some very skilful person, by dislocating his joints, could
draw himself backwards while allowing his head to lower
itself in front until it touched the ground, so as to give
the impression of a head descending in a straight line to the
ground. (But how could the appearance of the drapery be
caused to disappear?)

It would have been for me a matter of considerable
importance to feel the hand, or the body, or any portion of
the drapery *melt* in my hand. I ought to say that I have
in vain, at various times, asked insistently for this experience. B. B. indeed promised to give it to me, but I have
had nothing, absolutely nothing, of the sort. However,

the fact of his thus forming himself and disappearing permits the supposition that this is not impossible. If this is so, there is no doubt that it would be a decisive experiment for the hypothesis of a tactile hallucination, or even illusion, on my part is out of the question.

In any case, there remains this fact of considerable value, namely, that a living body was formed, outside the curtain, before our eyes, issuing from and returning into the ground.

I was so convinced that this living body could not come from the curtain that I at first supposed the possibility (although an absurd one) of there being a trapdoor. On the day after this experiment of August 29th, I minutely examined the flagstones, and the coach-house and stable immediately under that part of the kiosk. The ceiling of this stable, a very high one, is whitewashed, and covered with spiders' webs, which had not been disturbed for a very long time, when, with the help of a ladder, I examined the ceiling of the stable.

Now I pass over some other facts, to which I shall have occasion to return when I discuss the reality of these phenomena, and come to the photographs.

III

Study of the Photographs taken at Villa Carmen

These photographs, taken by the flash-light obtained from a mixture of chlorate of potash and magnesium, were taken simultaneously by Mme. X. with a kodak, by M. Delanne with a stereoscopic camera, and by myself with a Richard stereoscopic verascope; so that, in certain cases, there were five plates taken simultaneously at one single flash of magnesium. This excludes all possibility of photographic fraud. Moreover, the negatives were developed by Messrs. R. and M., optical instrument makers

2 K

at Algiers, who were absolutely ignorant of the nature of the negatives which I submitted to them.[1]

On Fig. 17 (kodak) and Fig. 18 (Richard stereoscopic verascope) there is seen a large form enveloped in white drapery, floating in the opening of the curtain. To the left there is clearly defined the back of the chair on which Aïscha is seated, with Aïscha's left shoulder in a good light. The smallest details can be distinguished of the design of the cotton check in which she is dressed. The photograph of the phantom taken with the kodak is much clearer than that of the one taken with the verascope. It can be seen that this drapery is of a stuff sufficiently fine and transparent to allow of the appearance through it, in a vertical black line, of the dark curtain. Behind this fine drapery appear the forms of the elbow, arm, and hand ; a very long hand, scarcely formed, of which the extremities of the fingers, as though they were not covered with drapery, *seem to lose themselves in a sort of mist of white vapour with indeterminate outlines.* Above, the whole of the face is not seen, but only the lower part of it; a head leaning forward, of which only the very short chin is seen, hidden by a thick black beard which covers the whole of the mouth, and above which only the end of the nose can be distinguished; unfortunately the photograph stops there, and is cut transversely by a streak which does not allow the eyes to be seen at all, and crossing the face at the lower extremity of the nose. The neck is bare, with a short black ribbon (?) and various indistinct ornaments which are beneath the white drapery. Below the phantom, and to its left, there can be distinguished a sleeve which appears more or less empty, and something like the form of a bodice. The white brilliance of the phantom illuminated by the magnesium is so strong that the table of black wood is illuminated by it, and its reflection is seen as in a polished surface. The opening of the curtain is also, to a

---

[1] At the moment of writing this article I do not know to what extent all the details which I give may be visible in the annexed plates. All that I can say is that they appear very clearly on the photographs which I have before my eyes, and which I shall be happy to show to those who may desire to see them.

Fig. 17.

FIG. 18.

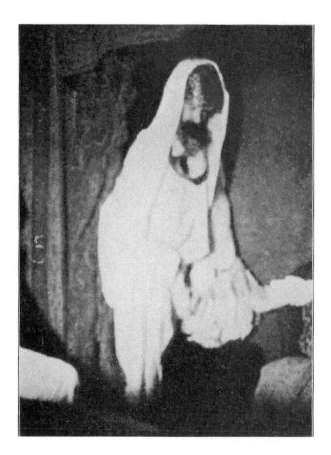

FIG. 19.

certain distance, illuminated by it. The curtain is, however, slightly pushed back and thrown over to the left.

The stereoscopic picture (Fig. 18) adds certain interesting details; everything is confirmed, notably the cloudy, indistinct form of the left hand of the phantom enveloped in the drapery. The clouds which terminate the hand are in front of the curtain. The difference in precision will also be noted between the white drapery, the contours of which cannot be distinguished, and the clear outlines of Aïscha's shoulder. B. B.'s face is very deeply sunk into the drapery, which seems to form in front of it, as though to protect it, a long tunnel, at the bottom of which the face is, as it were, hidden. Between the face and the drapery there are ornaments, bands, stuffs, of which the nature cannot be distinguished, but which truly seem very complicated. At the bottom, to the left, a small angular projection reveals the sleeve of Marthe, who is seen to be placed much further in the background. That only the end of the sleeve is seen, is because the angle at which I took the verascopic photograph was not the same as that at which the Kodak photograph was taken. What is remarkable in this photograph is the extreme thinness of the drapery, contrasting with the comparative thickness of B. B.'s veil in the other photographs.

Fig. 19 is verascopic only. It was taken on Tuesday, August 29th, when Mme. X., who took the kodak photographs, was absent. Various interesting things can be distinguished. First of all, Aïscha appears very clearly photographed. We see her black face, her features, her skin with its metallic lustre; her head is turned backwards, and she is looking towards B. B., her eyes turned to the right without moving her head. The whole of the canopy is seen, for unfortunately the photograph was taken a little too high up. At any rate, every one can thus see for himself the conditions under which the experiment took place.

As regards B. B., he is clearly seen at the right side of the curtain. He has his head covered by a sort of helmet with some metallic ornamentation, and over this helmet a turban, and falling over the ears a sort of chin-piece, which is only clearly seen to the right, and which covers the right cheek and ear, and seems to be applied to the cheek under the helmet. From the turban the drapery descends, floating and forming a sort of pendentive. The left arm, of which nothing can be distinguished, is enveloped in a thick drapery extending towards Marthe and completely hiding her. In fact, B. B. had informed us that, as Marthe feared the magnesium light, he would take care to hide her eyes and face during the taking of the photograph. The drapery which covers the body falls straight down, but is caught up, as it were, in small bunches at the upper part. Below these bunches, clothing the neck, and forming a sort of cape, is a series of singular ornaments, the nature of which is difficult to determine.

. The face itself of B. B. is rather indistinct—faint, when compared with the clear, accentuated face of Aïscha. The nose is long; the eyes are open, as it seems, and a very thick black moustache, which appears as though glued on to the upper lip, forms the base of the face. This moustache, as it falls, conceals the chin.

It will be noticed, also, that the outlines of the drapery are faint, cloudy, vapoury, and that this undecided form contrasts curiously with the precise and hard limits of the outline of the handkerchief which we had put round Aïscha's head in order to recognise her easily in the darkness, as also it contrasts with the clear outlines of the curtain—so clear indeed that at one point we can see a black thread which stands out from the frayed curtain.

I will also call attention to the strange shape of the drapery, which is as though hanging from the left hand of B. B. It is like a sort of white cloud descending from the hand and covering the head and body of Marthe. In fact, thanks to the relief given by the double plate, we can clearly see the white pendentive which descends from the turban placed in front of the arm. The arm stands out clearly from the body, and at the place where the hand would be there is a thick drapery which falls down. Nothing is less like an ordinary garment than this vestment, which is composed of three portions—a white robe with bunches at the top falling straight down over the body, a turban put on over a helmet with a pendentive quite detached from the robe and issuing from the turban, and finally this mass of white draperies covering the wrist and hand of B. B. (which are not seen), and masking, as it falls in the form of a thick veil, the place where Marthe is, or, rather, ought to be.

Another observation ought to be made, namely, that there is in front and above, over the right portion of the curtain, and much in advance of the curtain, as indicated by the stereoscopic relief, a white luminous spot, a sort of white twig with an efflorescent offshoot. This is not a photographic error, for it occurs on both plates. It is possible that this spot is due to a portion of the magnesium being projected in front of the objective at the' time of the explosion. But I do not think so, for there was nothing of the kind to our knowledge. In previous photographs which Mme. Noel showed me, I have seen these *fluidic* spots (effluvia?) between the two mediums with an identical appearance. It is, however, possible that these effluvia may have affected the plate before the magnesium flash, for I took care to leave the camera open for some time before the flash; the red light was not sufficient to affect the plate, even after a long exposure.

Figs. 20, 21, and 22 are certainly the best (except Fig. 21, kodak, which was taken *after* Fig. 20, and when the apparatus was not properly readjusted).

In Fig. 20 we see a little of Aïscha (the right side) and the arm-chair in which she is sitting, also her robe. Then, at her side, Marthe is seen, seated; neither her face nor her hands can be distinguished, but her skirt, chemisette, and waist-belt are seen, also the left arm stretched out towards Aïscha. B. B. is at the side of the curtain, and standing up.

The face of B. B. is clearer than in Fig. 19. The nose is shorter. There is not only a moustache, but perhaps also a beard. The helmet is very large. It has metallic reflections, so that it is apparently of metal. (It is interesting to note that in the previous experiments—those at least at which I was present—B. B. had only a turban.) The helmet comes down almost to the eyes, to the level of the eyebrows, which it overlaps, and it is so high that its height exceeds, by about one-third, the distance from the eyebrows to the chin. This great height 'of the helmet, surmounted by a rounded protuberance at the upper part, like certain old mediæval helmets, is better seen in Fig. 21 than in Fig. 20. The ears are completely hidden and invisible. The drapery covers the helmet, and thence falls over the shoulders and in front of the breast. This drapery is behind the curtain, the fringes of which are outlined upon it. Below the head is the chin-piece, which seems to have fallen down, and hangs in front of the breast; and there are perhaps also some indistinct ornaments below the neck. The drapery at the upper part to the left of the head has fringes which stand out. These fringes are much better seen in the stereoscopic view, Fig. 22, in which also we clearly distinguish the metallic appearance of the helmet, which projects boldly in front of the eyes. But what appears to be fully evident in this stereoscopic view is the arrangement of the perspective : in the foreground the fringe of the curtain; a little behind this the head of B. B., and the drapery which covers his turban and falls straight from his head; then, in the background, Marthe, separated very evidently from B. B. by a tolerably wide empty space. The drapery does not fall down to the ground, it stops short, becoming thinner (like a shawl covering a person's shoulders), and below, between the curtain and Marthe's black skirt, there are seen two things like straight sticks, serving as supports to this strange personage. The drapery is white, and appears to be of another tissue, much denser than that of Fig. 17.

In Fig. 22 there can be seen a singular appearance of the drapery at the point where it covers the head of Marthe. There it is altogether misty, and is in the background, as also is Marthe's head, so that the appearance is that of a sort of luminous, misty column issuing

FIG. 20.

FIG. 21.

FIG. 22.

from Marthe's head, and masking it, so as to form a drapery, which ascends and loses itself at the left side of B. B. As for the curtain, it seems to bulge out a very little, being pushed forward by B. B.'s back.

I have little to say as to the other personages in Fig. 22. Aïscha is at her usual place, her black lustrous skin shows up well, likewise the handkerchief knotted on her head. Her jet-black hands are seen crossed; it can also be observed that she is looking towards B. B. Around the table are seen, near the curtain, General Noel in profile, then Mme. Noel, who is shading her eyes in order not to be blinded by the magnesium light, then M. Delanne, who is taking a photograph.

With regard to Marthe, whose presence it is so important to confirm, neither her head nor feet are seen; only her clothes are shown, but they are easily distinguished; the left arm is towards Aïscha. It looks as though Marthe had taken Aïscha by the neck, passing her hand behind Aïscha's neck. One would be tempted to believe at first that it is the thin hand of Marthe which is in front of Aïscha's neck; but this would be a mistake, for what is to be seen on Aïscha's neck is a coloured handkerchief which she wore tied round her neck; Marthe's hand is not visible. The sleeve, however, *appears to be empty;* it has strange bends, as though, being empty, it had been fastened by a pin to Aïscha's chair. And yet, on looking more closely, we find that the sleeve is not *entirely* empty. Apart from this, the rest of Marthe's body, under the clothing that covers it, is perfectly normal. The robe is full; one can make out that there are knees in front, and that there is a waist under the belt, which is very clearly seen. The chemisette, with guipure in the form of a collar, is evidently not very ample, but Marthe is so very slender that this is not surprising, and we know the fashion of chemisettes with pendentives coming down in front of the breast. Above the belt there is also seen a small black border, which is the upper part of the skirt. There remains, however, this singular circumstance, that Marthe's right arm is not seen at all.

Lastly, if we compare Figs. 17, 19, and 20 with each other, we see that the height of B. B. is very different in Fig. 17 on the one hand, and in Figs. 19 and 20 on the other. In Fig. 17 he is much taller, as is easy to see by taking as a point of comparison the top of the chair on which Aïscha is sitting.

IV

Discussions and Conclusions

In the first place, I shall present no theory, and shall not even attempt to theorise concerning these strange phenomena. It is a heavy enough task even to analyse their reality.

It is therefore solely a question of deciding whether or not there was any deception.[1]

If we had to judge by reasons of a psychological order, and not by reasons of a material order, there could be no question of deception. The integrity, irreproachable and unquestionable, of Marthe B., the fiancée of Maurice Noel, the General's son, could never be called in question.

Moreover, before the mediumistic faculties of Marthe had been discovered, there had already been phenomena of materialisation at the Villa Carmen, due to two other mediums, and the form of B. B. had manifested also with these mediums.

Lastly, as the materialisations took place in the cabinet with Ninon or Aïscha generally at the side of Marthe, we should also have to assume the complicity of Marthe, Ninon, and Aïscha, who look upon one another, it seems to me, if not with suspicion, at least with no very great goodwill.

To suppose that Marthe, the daughter of an officer, and the fiancée of the General's son, should concert with a negress and a palmist to practise an odious deception

---

[1] Do I need to apologise to General and Mme. Noel, and to Mlle. Marthe B., for discussing with perfect freedom their good faith and their sagacity? They all three know how great is my respect for them, and my profound gratitude. But the duty of the scientist in such a case is not the same as that of the friend.

on General and Mme. Noel for six months, is absurd. For it could not be a matter of unconscious fraud. It would need, to bring in this helmet, these draperies, this turban, this false moustache, a whole apparatus of great complexity, which Marthe could not conceal from her two sisters in the small villa in which they live, and the deliberate and prolonged complicity of Paulette and Maïa would have to be added to that of Ninon and Aïscha. Such a conspiracy, so skilfully carried on, would be impossible; and the loyalty, purity, and simplicity of mind of Marthe could not be simulated with such astuteness that the most incredulous are constrained to believe in them.

But it is not upon such ground that we shall discuss the matter. We shall suppose, on the contrary—although it is the reverse of good sense and truth and probability— that Marthe may be cheating, that she is a skilful conjurer, agile and resourceful. We have to find out whether this suppleness and agility could throw us off the scent.

The reason why I dwell so much on Marthe's personality is because all deception proceeding from other persons should be set aside : (1) There are no trap-doors in the room ; (2) the room is searched carefully every time, and no person could remain hidden in it unknown to us ; (3) no person could enter it without our knowledge ; (4) the persons in the room, and whom we can see and hear during the whole time of the experiments, could not intervene directly for the mechanical production of the phenomena, which take place behind the curtain and at a distance from them; (5) Aïscha, who can, moreover, be seen very distinctly in almost all the experiments, does not come into question, for she is always some distance away from the form of B. B.; and besides, in several experiments, B. B. showed himself without Aïscha being in the cabinet, or even in the room.

In fact, I repeat, every other hypothesis of fraud must be resolutely set aside which is not that of deception, most artfully managed, on the part of Marthe B.

Even this deception could only consist in disguising

herself as B. B.; bringing in under her dress a helmet and various draperies, a false beard, and complicated ornaments, and disrobing, in the little cabinet in which she was seated beside Aïscha, in order to put on the drapery she had hidden, and put upon the chair on which she sat a sort of mannikin or lay-figure, with gloves and apparatus for simulating her body, her knees, her arms, her face; and finally, taking all these objects again, the drapery, and the lay-figure, and hiding them afresh under her dress—all this in the presence, and by the side of, Aïscha.

Now, this hiding away of a quantity of apparatus is manifestly impossible; for, as we all of us observed, Marthe's bodice was only a very thin muslin chemisette. She is frail, with small arms, and a very slender waist. After the séance this chemisette is soaked with perspiration. Moreover, it fastens behind with hooks, difficult to undo, and equally so to fasten again. It is therefore not in her bodice that she can hide all these draperies and other paraphernalia which appear with B. B. Is it in her dress? But she wears very short dresses, very clinging, which completely outline her form. She goes and comes, runs, mounts staircases quickly, both before and after the séance. The voluminous draperies which surround B. B. could not be hidden by her under that thin tunic.

Even if she could succeed in this, still nothing would be explained. For besides the draperies she would also have to hide the lay-figure on which to arrange her own clothes, so as to give the appearance of a Marthe seated on a chair, an appearance so striking that it is only from excess of scrupulousness that I do not say I distinctly recognised her in the person seated beside Aïscha, behind B. B., who is seen moving. In fact, I repeat again, B. B. is like a living being; he is neither a lay-figure nor a doll; and, if he is not a phantom, it could only be Marthe.

But still, in defiance of the evidence, let us assume this also. Let us suppose that Marthe, whom we have never searched, nor bound, could bring in on her person all the apparatus necessary to serve for her disguise, is it possible that she could have made use of them?

Now, I answer boldly, No.

(1) In certain cases the drapery appeared, shook, and moved, almost at the same time that Mme. Noel was in the cabinet. On August 31st, scarcely half a minute after Mme. Noel had left the cabinet, we saw appearing in the opening of the curtains the helmet of B. B., and some floating drapery. On August 29th I distinguished very clearly, beyond possibility of dispute, Marthe and Aïscha seated side by side. Then the curtain was drawn sharply, and I saw a large white drapery, as though enveloping an arm, placed very high up, which drew the curtain and disappeared with the speed of lightning.

(2) It is not sufficient to cause the drapery to appear; it must also be made to disappear. Now most frequently other persons—for instance, Mme. X., sometimes also Mme. Noel—entered the cabinet unexpectedly, and never noticed anything of a suspicious nature. The draperies and B. B. disappeared as rapidly as they had come.

(3) It appears to me to be absolutely impossible to produce the phenomenon of the luminous spot, arising out of the ground and giving birth to a living being. No agility, not even that of a professed gymnast, could produce this impression, which struck me as a categorical proof.

(4) In the photographs there are clearly seen three personages when Aïscha and Marthe were alone in the cabinet. It is impossible to pretend that Marthe had disguised herself as B. B., leaving a lay-figure in her place, and put on, while quite nude, the draperies and the helmet. For then where would her legs and body be? The head is erect and the bust vertical.

(5) Certain details of the photographs are characteristic: the great height of the form in Fig. 17; the faintness and cloudiness of outline; the large hand and the drapery scarcely materialised of Fig. 17; the cloud covering the face of Marthe in Figs. 20 and 21; the different aspect of the draperies in the different photo-

graphs; sometimes a turban, with pendentives, sometimes fringes, &c.

Such are the extremely powerful reasons which militate in favour of the reality of these phenomena. But I do not conceal from myself the force of some objections; it would be childish not to bring them forward in all their force. Why does the body and sleeve of Marthe in Fig. 20 seem empty? Why do we not see Marthe's right hand? Why, in all these photographs, do we never see Marthe's face clearly, as clearly as we see the face of Aïscha, for instance? Why is darkness necessary at that point? Why is the face of B. B. so similar to the face that Marthe might have, if she had stuck a coarse black moustache on to her upper lip? Why, after having promised that his hand should melt away in mine, was I never able to obtain anything of the sort, when I declared that this experience would be for me the *experimentum crucis*, the fundamental one? Why was I not permitted to touch and hold B. B. when he was walking about, around us, in the room?

These are certainly very serious objections, but it is allowable to suppose that the phenomenon, so mysterious, almost miraculous, which we call *materialisation*, is accompanied by a sort of disaggregation (?) of the pre-existing matter, so that the new matter formed is formed at the expense of the old, and that the medium *empties herself*, so to speak, in order to constitute the new being which emanates from her, and which cannot be touched without harm to the medium.

If Marthe were really a clever conjurer, if she were mistress of such prodigious cunning, she would certainly have understood that the empty sleeve nailed to Aïscha's chair would give the impression of an empty sleeve. All the more so as nothing would have been easier than to conceal this sleeve, like the rest of her body, behind the drapery. I am not afraid of saying that the emptiness of this sleeve, far from demonstrating the presence of fraud, establishes, on the contrary, that there was no fraud; also it seems to speak in favour of a sort of material disaggregation of the medium which she herself was incapable of suspecting.

But I do not wish to go any further into theory at present. I do not even wish to hazard an affirmation of the phenomenon.

In spite of all the proofs which I have given, in spite of all that I have seen and touched, in spite of the photographs, conclusive as they are, I cannot make up my mind to admit this fact of materialisation; it is too much to ask of a physiologist to expect him to accept, even after much experimentation, a fact so extraordinary and improbable, and I shall not yield so easily, even to evidence.

However, I have thought it my duty to mention these facts, in the same way as Sir William Crookes thought it his duty, in more difficult times, to report the history of Katie King. After all, it may be that I have been deceived. But the explanation of such an error would be of considerable importance. And then—need I say it ?—I do not believe that I have been deceived. I am convinced that I have been present at realities, not at deceptions.

Certainly I cannot say in what materialisation consists; I am only ready to maintain that there is something profoundly mysterious in it, which will change from top to bottom our ideas on nature and on life.

CHAPTER XXXVII

EXPERIMENTS MADE WITH EUSAPIA PALADINO AT GENOA BY PROFESSOR MORSELLI

WE shall in this chapter consider the very complete study made on the phenomena produced through Eusapia Paladino at Genoa by Professor Morselli.[1]

Eusapia Paladino is mainly a physical medium; and if students of psychical matters have preferred to go to her, it is because she has consented to hold sittings under the control of men of science, and has accepted, up to certain limits imposed by the form of her mediumship, unusual conditions of experiment; she has also submitted to examination which no medium had ever previously permitted. In this respect Eusapia's attitude is worthy of praise, and her position as a medium ought to be regarded with less distrust.

Intellectual mediumship, which takes place through subjective psychological processes in the medium, is not susceptible of scientific investigation except by consummate psychologists; and of these there are, in truth, not too many, and moreover psychology, although dabbled in by fashionable dilettantism, is not a study within the reach of all. Physical mediumship, on the other hand, is manifested in objective, tangible, visible facts, which can therefore be perceived by the senses of the sitters, and ascertained and, up to a certain point, measured by mechanical means and apparatus. Physical mediumship, therefore, comes within the scope of experimental research, under which name we include also the simple observation of phenomena as they occur naturally and spontaneously, and the analysis of their causes.

[1] *Annals of Psychical Science*, vol. v. p. 327.

There can no longer be any doubt as to the reality of Eusapia's phenomena. They have now been seen by too many persons under excellent conditions of verification, with the full certainty that the medium had not her hands and feet free, and that many of the phenomena occurred at a distance which excluded all possibility of deception; and there are now too many trustworthy men, accustomed to observe and experiment, who say that they have become convinced that Eusapia's mediumship is genuine.

We have now got far beyond the time when her phenomena could be explained by the exchange of hands and feet in the dark; the method of inquiry into her phenomena is very different, and so is her attitude in the sittings, especially when she is watched by persons not bound by preconceptions and by fear of trickery, and in whom she has confidence. In fact, none of the most celebrated mediums are accredited by so many explicit declarations by scientific men of the foremost rank; no one, from Home and F. Cook onward, has allowed the introduction into the sittings of scientific instruments and methods with so much tolerance as Paladino.

The general public, on reading the accounts of the sittings, cannot always form a precise and complete conception of the conditions under which the phenomena are witnessed. Each phenomenon would require such minute particulars as to every element of fact, as to the position and gestures of the medium, the chain formed by the observers, the psychic state of each of them, the control for verification, the development, duration, and intensity of the manifestations, the preparations and consecutive circumstances, &c., that the description would become perfectly unreadable, and impossible to grasp as a complete mental picture. Luigi Barzini has done admirably, but not all of Eusapia's sittings can hope to have such an able and readable chronicler.

It follows that the public distrusts the accounts, or is not convinced by them; and many sceptics, every time that phenomena are related, recommence their usual

eternal questionings, dictated by doubt. Everything is
an occasion for incredulity to those who obstinately
remain, or pose as, sceptics: the control of the hands,
the position of the feet, the attitude of the head, the
distance of the object, the attention of the two watchers
to right and left, the convulsions of the medium, the
emotions of the spectators, the degree of light. This last
point especially arrests the doubters; we feel them always
turning to the question of darkness, as though the séances
were always held in the dark, and as though students,
especially after long practice, were incapable of making
use of their senses and of their perceptive centres, simply
because there was no light!

It is useless to reply exhaustively to such objectors;
they return to the charge and repeat their remarks as
though they had made new discoveries, and as though
they alone, the incredulous who have not seen, possessed
the key of the secret.

Many say: "I will believe when I see it," and this is
all well and good; meanwhile they believe, without verification, that Nansen reached 86° 4′ north latitude, but
not that I have been present at a real levitation of a
table or at a visible or tangible materialisation of a hand.
They are within their rights, but Eusapia cannot be at
every one's service, and her mediumistic phenomena cannot serve as a theatrical show.

Some put forward a condition for their belief; they
appeal to the criterion of authority, and say that they
will believe when such and such a man of science, "that
man, who is above all suspicion," shall have made certain
of the matter. Well, while I was and declared myself a
sceptic in regard to spiritism and psychism, people did
me the honour to point me out as a judge to whom appeal
might be made, and this was said and printed in 1892.
When, however, I admitted that I had seen and touched
the reality of mediumistic facts at the Minerva Club, I
lost my position with doubters as an "authority above
suspicion," and in 1902 a brilliant journalist, engaged in
a superficial anti-spiritistic campaign, dethroned me from

this position, though not much to my regret, and invoked the superior authority, &c., &c., of Professor Blaserna of Rome.

I am convinced that Blaserna, if he had been present, as I was, at about thirty sittings with Eusapia (not at one or two only, which are not enough for a serious judgment), would have seen, touched, and perceived with his senses that which I have seen, touched, and perceived with mine, and that even he, the distinguished secretary of the *Accademia dei Lincei*, would end by losing the confidence of the obstinate deniers.

Neither I nor Blaserna, nor any one else, can change the substance of facts, when hundreds of persons endowed with senses and brains, not different from our own in morphology and function, assert and confirm each other in the assertion that they have not been the victims either of deceptions or of illusions. It is time that there was an end of this negationist attitude *à outrance*, of this habit of constantly casting the shadow of doubt and directing the smile of sarcasm, I will not say upon the moral respectability (for in science all are subject to caution), but upon the common sense of the observers who make assertions.

Eusapia, like other individuals endowed with her meta-psychical powers, would certainly have taken another empirical direction, if, as was the case with Stainton Moses and Mme. d'Esperance, she had been left to herself (I ought to say, however, that she is completely lacking in initiative). But she was discovered and developed between 1872 and 1882 by Signor Damiani, an ardent spiritist, who, on his return from England, where he had learned the American technique of spiritism, introduced it into Naples and rendered it automatic in Eusapia. M. Chiaia, who succeeded Damiani, simply followed in the same track.

It is true that, given the nature of the experiments, there is nothing much better to be done; but, at all events, it might be said that the spiritists fear to detach themselves from their antiquated and crude paraphernalia. Eusapia is therefore automatically bound to this "technique," and cannot free herself from it; but this is not to be charged entirely against her. It is the whole history of spiritism that is summed up in her, and she is not to blame.

On the other hand, there seems to be some reason for the habitual technique of spiritism. Take, for example, the darkness or the feeble light or the red light. It is not "psychic" phenomena alone which require this condition; is it not also demanded for the impression of images on a photographic plate? Have not certain chemical combinations in the laboratory to be made in the dark? And does not the night bring about changes in the functions of organisms, animal as well as vegetable? It is no wonder, therefore, to a man of science who knows these facts, if the mediumistic, or metapsychic, or bio-dynamic force (the name is of no importance) is inhibited or neutralised by light, especially for the production of the important phenomena of materialisation.

Even as seen in the light of historical analogy we may find justification for the rigid character of spiritistic phenomena; the table, the dark cabinet, &c., are like the earthen pot of Papias, with regard to our modern locomotive, or as the rude electrostatic machine of a hundred and fifty years ago in comparison with our present stupendous dynamos!

Some make the objection (and I was once one of them) that mediums, beginning with Eusapia, should be subjected to more scientific vigilance, by surrounding them with recording apparatus to register every movement, to measure their efforts, to take away every doubt as to fraud.

I must premise that the traditional technique of the sittings being accepted as necessary, the "control" entrusted to two attentive observers, one on each side, appears to be sufficient; the spiritists maintain this, and Eusapia requires it. Barzini and I did not find it difficult to hold and watch the lady's hands and feet; after a little practice we learned to hold these extremities without allowing them to escape, and at the same time to watch her head (which was always visible) and to be attentive to the phenomena.   It is not every one who succeeds in this multiple work, muscular, mental, and tactile, but I am certain that every time that the control devolved on me, Eusapia has never, except for one or two naïve attempts, carried out the supposed trick of substitution of hands (by which, moreover, not one-twentieth part of her phenomena could be explained); nor could she, as some have absurdly supposed, caress my forehead, pull my moustache, or sound trumpets with her feet.

Moreover, the "control" adopted at spiritistic séances is somewhat ridiculous; it tires those who carry it out, and certainly hinders Eusapia from giving new and spontaneous manifestations of her mediumship, which might be very fine.   I should like to have the more remarkable phenomena of materialisation with the medium at liberty; I have had them, and very surprising ones, with Eusapia fixed and bound, but who knows what energy she might be able to externalise if she were left to the automatism of her sub-consciousness ?

It is true that every modification of the habitual technique is a check on deceit, but it is also an impediment and sometimes a complete hindrance to mediumistic phenomena.   Those who demand scientific "control" do not consider that mediumship, whatever be its origin and nature, is not a mechanical function like that of a physical apparatus; it is based on psychism, and it cannot be claimed that the actions of consciousness, of automatism, or of the sub-consciousness will take place under fixed conditions to which only a machine of iron or of wood can be indifferent !   It is as though a living physiologist should claim to study a functional act of the living and thinking person, such as the poetic or amorous frenzy, by surrounding the poet who creates, or the lover who loves, with his complicated paraphernalia of " control."   Is it likely that he would accomplish the end aimed at by an experiment so ill-conceived ?

No; physical facts have their proper conditions for production, but they cannot be discharged at our pleasure, like an arquebus or an electrical pile.

In about thirty sittings I have seen Paladino perform several hundred phenomena. One or two sittings turned out, it is true, not very interesting, especially to those who, being acquainted with her powers and having been present at the simpler and more elementary phenomena (movements of the table, touching with invisible hands, &c.), expected and hoped for higher and more complex manifestations. But there were sittings, though rare even for Eusapia, which compensated for all the tiresomeness of the long evenings passed in fruitless and unsatisfactory waiting, in which the summit of Paladino's mediumship was reached, and we witnessed the exceptional phenomena of full materialisations, of veritable apparitions.

In general, however, all who are merely curious, and many students of metapsychic facts, have not patience, do not know how to wait, and want to see without delay the astonishing things described in spiritistic works, which they know it to be possible for Eusapia to perform. The impatience of those who form new circles, however, is harmful to the spontaneity of the phenomena, because, although transformed into mechanical or material action, these phenomena are bio-psychical in their origin; the more important ones occur especially when they are not asked for or expected. Contrary to what is often said about Paladino's sittings, these have to take place in conditions of the greatest mental calmness.

Moreover, the medium has not always the power to do what is desired of her, whence arises that tendency to conscious or unconscious simulation, about which such an outcry is made; while, by reason of her scanty education, Eusapia has very little inventive faculty, even in her subconsciousness, which must, according to my observations, almost always act by receiving from the superior or lucid portion of the consciousness the idea of the impulse to be acted upon or of the direction to be given to such impulse. The medium, being a psychically abnormal person (a "hysteric"), is suggestionable, and very often certain phenomena are performed immediately after they have been spoken of or asked for by the sitters; in such cases the idea of the phenomenon, perceived by the waking or semi-waking consciousness of Eusapia, descends or (so to speak) plunges into her sub-consciousness, in which is elaborated the still unknown bio-psychic dynamism of mediumship, and from thence it is released and emerges in the form of mechanical action at a distance, of luminous or materialisation phenomena, &c.

In this connection it is important to define the mental state of the medium during the phenomena. I will only say here ₍that whereas for the minor phenomena (raps, movements of the table, levitations, &c.), Eusapia can be seen to be awake and attentive, although very soon her attention is restricted to certain groups of perceptions, yet in the case of the major phenomena, those of greater significance in the spiritist doctrine and more novel to the observer (such as strong action at a distance, the apparition of forms or phantasms) it is necessary that her consciousness should be obscured in "trance," and her will in suspense. It is only then that we have the automatic discharge of the energies which we call mediumistic, accumulated in her nervous centres; then only do we enter into the mysterious and surprising region of true "spiritism." In the work which I have promised and announced, I shall give all the fruits of my observations and experiments on the physio-psychological state of the medium, on the symptoms and gradations of her "trance," and on the various auto-suggestive processes put into operation by Eusapia during the sittings; I hope to show that in order to thoroughly understand and appreciate metapsychical phenomena we need to be psychologists, and not merely physicists or photographers or dilettanti in curiosities and the "marvellous."

The mediumistic phenomena of Eusapia, as I have observed them, are very various and intense in the physical sphere, but very poor in the intellectual one; and this, for me, is a great blow to the spiritistic doctrine, since the scientific conclusion to be drawn from it, though little acceptable to systematic spiritists, is that the phenomena are due exclusively to the action of the mediums and are proportional to the psychic or sub-psychic elements existing in their brain by individual acquisition or by cumulative heredity.

To reduce somewhat to order the intricate tangle of spiritistic psychic manifestations, many classifications have been adopted.

Some are merely empirical, grouping the phenomena according to their outward characters without pretending to touch their inward nature. Crookes commenced in this prudent way when he set forth by "classes" his famous experiments of 1870–74; Gibier followed in his studies on Slade, and so did the Milan Commission of 1892, and De Rochas in his studies on Eusapia, Aksakoff, and Gyel in the excellent synthetic *résumés* of spiritism, &c.

Other classifications are of a theoretical nature, or attempts to arrange the phenomena according to their inward nature, whether real or conjectural; and among these the first place is merited by that daring attempt (yet, in my opinion, lacking in positive basis) of the great psychist, F. W. H. Myers (*Human Personality*, vol. ii. p. 506 *et seq.*). Myers has achieved by his studies and by his devotion a monumental and admirable work; but he has claimed too much in trying to connect the most "spiritual" and exceptional facts of "spiritism" with the most elementary facts of biology and psychology; he has not succeeded in filling up the enormous, dark, and still unfathomable gulf which separates and distinguishes them from each other.

I also shall try elsewhere to construct a co-ordinated and complete scheme of mediumistic nomenclature; but I shall take care to keep on the firm ground of observation. In these articles I shall content myself with grouping in a clear and easily comprehensible manner the phenomena of Eusapia which have been observed by myself. I do not deny that Eusapia, like other mediums, may have given other and more decided manifestations of her mediumship in sittings at which I was not present, and may in the future give new and different ones, and perhaps more convincing in favour of the "spiritistic" hypothesis. Nor do I deny that she may, in further experiments or sittings, and before other observers, show herself incapable of producing the phenomena witnessed and verified by me; not so much because Eusapia is not always in possession of equal bio-psychic-dynamic powers, as because the study of mediumistic forces, but just commenced, has in store for science surprises which cannot be foreseen.

OBJECTIVE PHENOMENA

The greater number of those who at present interest themselves in spiritism, either for or against, have been greatly impressed by the movements of the table produced by Paladino; the spiritists, and those who consider that the existence of "psychical forces" is now proved, use them to demonstrate the reality of these forces; the incredulous, to bring up all the objections and doubts, and all the more or less inconsistent hypotheses which have been put forth in explanation of this very evident and real phenomenon. But this typtokinesis, to give it a Greek name, forms the ABC of Paladino's manifestations; and when one has had the chances which I have had to witness the apparition of phantasms, the phenomenon of the moving table, while preserving its high importance as an objective fact which can be actually verified by photography, loses much of its striking character so much wondered at by the anti-psychists, and takes its proper place among the much more numerous and complex objective or physical effects of Eusapia's mediumship. I shall rapidly review the principal classes of phenomena, giving little more than the names, and keeping to the scheme of classification most commonly adopted in reports and treatises on psychical subjects. But every classification has the fault of artificiality, and thus the following groupings must be understood rather as expressing their outward form of production than as denoting their substantial dynamical affinities; such a division according to intrinsic character can only be made after longer and more mature experience.

The first class includes mechanical phenomena with production of motion in objects by contact with the person of the medium, but with effects disproportionate to the expenditure of ordinary nervo-muscular force on the part of the medium herself. Maxwell calls them "parakinesis," and Eusapia produces them both in darkness and in the light, always, be it understood, under secure "control."

1. *Oscillations and movements of the table without significance.*—These are the initial and elementary facts of all the complicated phenomena of spiritism. I have felt them under my hands, and have also seen them with my eyes, hundreds of times, since from beginning to end of each séance with Eusapia the table is constantly, every little while, shaking, raising itself on one side or the other, oscillating, and then becoming quiet again without anything else happening.

2. *Movements and beatings of the table having a significance.*—These also are very frequent, and those corresponding to the conventional language used by Paladino (two blows "no," three blows "yes," &c.), regulate for the most part the proceedings of the sitting, order or consent to changes in the chain, ask for modifications of the light, &c. It is true that in Eusapia's séances this typtology (which we never encouraged in the purely spiritistic sense) is reduced to very little in comparison with the marvellous communications of a personal or of a philosophical-social character given by other mediums. In compensation, Eusapia's table has a very rich language which I may call mimetic, which has been well described by L. Barzini, and which resembles the mimicry of a child.

3. *Complete lifting of the table (improperly called "levitation" by empirical spiritists).*—It is frequently seen at the sittings that the table is completely lifted from the floor when the hands of the medium, placed upon it, do not make any effort whatever, and cannot contribute to it; and the phenomenon has several times been recorded by photography in an incontestable manner; I shall reproduce some of the photographs in my book.

4. *Movements of various objects barely touched by the hands or body of the medium.*—Eusapia, laying her hands lightly on chairs or other articles of furniture, and objects of various weights, succeeds in imparting to them movements of displacement, of lifting, or of rotation on their own axis, which are not to be explained with certainty by the very light pressure exercised by her.

5. *Movements, undulations, and swellings of the curtains of the cabinet.*—I place this very curious phenomenon here because the black curtains of the cabinet are as a rule in contact with the medium's seat, and often fall over her back. The curtains move, swell outwards from within the cabinet, come forward, draw back, open and close, without Eusapia being able to do this with her hands and feet, which are always kept under strict control.

6. *Movements and swelling out of the medium's clothes.*—This phenomenon, upon which the Cambridge Commission erroneously based a proclamation that Eusapia cheated, is, on the contrary, by our direct observation, genuine; it takes place mostly in full light and while Eusapia's feet are closely watched; the impression formed is as though supernumerary limbs, invisible but palpable, were formed under the medium's skirt.

The second class is only the first in more perfect form, or mechanical effects produced without any contact with the person of the medium, at a distance which may vary from an inch or two to a yard or more. They are the most disputed, because they are incomprehensible according to the ordinary laws of physics, which teach that a mechanical force must act directly on the resistance offered by material bodies; and yet this telekinesis is one of the things most frequently seen at Paladino's sittings. I will mention summarily the principal phenomena of this class.

7. *Oscillations and movements of the table without contact.*—We have verified this several times; all of us, including Eusapia, raised our hands from the surface of the table, and the latter continued to give proof of its ability to move by itself.

8. *Independent liftings of the table.*—This is a pheno-menon one prefers to photograph. We saw in full light the table raised to the height of our heads while we were standing up in the middle of the room. I have also been present at veritable *pas seuls* of the table by full gas-light, when the medium was secured within the cabinet.

9. *Undulations, swellings, and movements of the curtain of the cabinet.*—These happen also when the medium is evidently at a distance—for instance, when she is lying down and bound firmly within the cabinet; one would say that invisible persons were raising the curtain with their hands, drawing it one way to open it and another way to close it, &c.

10. *Movements occasioned in material objects by the hands being voluntarily turned towards them, but at a distance.*—This impressive phenomenon usually occurs in the light and at the close of the sitting. It is veritable exter-nalisation of motricity, as described by Colonel de Rochas, and Barzini has given a very effective description of it.

11. *Spontaneous movements and displacement of differ-ent objects at various distances from the medium.*—Seats are seen and heard to move, also tables, utensils, musical instruments, &c.; in short, the whole apparatus usual at spiritistic séances, at such a distance from the medium as to render absurd the hypothesis of deception; I have seen such phenomena occur even at a distance of two or three yards.

12. *Bringing of distant objects on to the table.*—These are phenomena in which Eusapia appears to take great pleasure. Objects of every kind, even when placed (and this is always to be understood) in positions easily verifi-able, acquire under her mediumistic influence an apparent power of self-movement, as though they were alive. I shall narrate elsewhere some astonishing examples. I ought, however, to say that very often there was some connection between the objects so moved and the curtains of the cabinet, which perform a very important part in the phenomena of Paladino, as though invisible hands were behind them.

13. *Displacement of the seats of the experimenters.*—This is another phenomenon highly pleasing to that jester "John King." Several times I was pulled violently on my chair, back towards the cabinet, to receive special manifestations of a personal character. Sometimes we felt our chairs pulled from beneath us, &c.

14. *Appropriate movements of mechanical instruments placed at a distance.*—These really multitudinous phenomena relate, for instance, to the apparently spontaneous setting in action of musical instruments (mandoline, zither, pianoforte, trumpet, &c.), or other small mechanical articles (carillons, metronome, dynamometer, &c.), at a distance from Eusapia. These occurred at almost every sitting. Here I may mention the mysterious opening and closing of the electric circuit of the lights by means of unperceived manipulations of the pear-shaped switches contained in the pocket of one of the sitters.

The third class of mechanical phenomena relates to the alteration of the weight of bodies. I ought, however, to state that to me they seemed to be the least certain of the phenomena, although other observers guarantee their authenticity.

15. *Spontaneous changes of weight in a scale.*—I have not seen the phenomenon of the letter-weigher, reported as genuine by Colonel de Rochas; but we were present at the oscillation in the arm of a weighing-machine when it was not visibly pressed by Eusapia, though she was near to the platform; this phenomenon, however, appeared doubtful.

16. *Change of weight in the body of the medium.*—As to this also, though it occurred under my eyes, I have no scientific certainty, and I only mention it to encourage students to make further researches.

17. *Raising of the medium's body in the air.*—This is the real "levitation" which is narrated to have been performed by certain saints: Home was levitated up to the ceiling! It sometimes happens that Eusapia is lifted bodily, together with her chair, and, to her great alarm,

deposited on the table. I have only once seen this "miracle," contrary to the law of gravitation, and had the impression that it was genuine at the beginning, but was unconsciously aided in its completion by the two guardians; it would be well to see it again and study it carefully.

A curious class which has been little studied up to now is that of the mediumistic effects which I will call those of thermal radiation; it consists of few but interesting phenomena.

18. *Wind from the cabinet.*—This is very frequent, and is felt at almost every sitting; it is a veritable current of air, which comes from within the cabinet and behind the medium.

19. *Intense cold.*—This is usually announced by the two controllers, and is the prelude to many manifestations : on certain evenings it becomes perceptible to all the persons forming the chain. It may perhaps be symbolical of the cold of the "sepulchres" which open to let the "defunct" come forth. Certainly it is impressive and is not hallucinatory.

20. *Radiations from the head and body of the medium.* —On putting the hand to Eusapia's head, especially where she has a breach in the bone caused by an old fall, and sometimes also at her hands, one feels a sensible "breath," now warm, now cool. I need not say that this phenomenon (of which I shall speak later at length) is significant as regards the hypothesis of new nervous forces.

The class of acoustic phenomena is already partly comprised in the first three, since very often movements at a distance are rendered perceptible by noises, sounds, rubbing over the floor, &c., of the objects and instruments set in motion. But there are also other special phenomena of this class.

21. *Blows, raps, and other sounds in the table.*—Of the famous "raps" of Anglo-American spiritism hundreds have been heard at Eusapia's sittings. Some have the

intensity of blows delivered by a powerful but invisible
fist. Others (and not the least mysterious) take place in
the joints of the wood.

22. *Blows and raps at a distance from the medium.*—
These are very often heard within the cabinet, or on the
seats of the two guardians and their neighbours, on the
furniture, on the walls, in the cabinet, &c.

23. *Sounds of musical instruments.*—I have already
alluded to these; we have had them under such conditions
as to exclude all action of visible and tangible hands; the
trumpets emit their harsh sound in the air, the strings
of the mandolines and zithers vibrate, the keys of the
pianoforte give detached notes; and all this without any
one visibly touching them. But they are never really
musical sounds, in my experience, nor harmonic chords, still
less airs of some melody; at the best they are rhythms in
measured time.

24. *Sounds of hands, feet, &c.*—In various cases the
clapping of hands is heard, either behind the curtain or
in the air of the room. Once or twice we seemed to hear
footsteps within the cabinet.

25. *Sounds of human voices.*—This is a very rare
phenomenon, and consists in hearing the "voices" of the
discarnate. I only perceived it once under conditions
which were not convincing; but this is not the place to
relate the particulars of my extraordinary spiritistic adventure (the apparent materialisation of a disincarnate
being who was very dear to me).

I pass on to a class of manifestations not less impressive and which, according to spiritists, go to prove
the action of occult "intelligences" by producing lasting
effects on inert matter. Eusapia, being uneducated, gives
very few of these phenomena.

26. *Mysterious signs left at a distance.*—These consist
in signs or marks found on the table, on the cuffs of the
sitters, or on the wall, and seem to be made with pencil.
They do not appear to me sufficiently certain to merit
attention.

27. *Direct writing.*—This is supposed to be writing made directly by the "spirits" without the apparent action of hands, whether done with visible writing instruments (pencil or crayon) or without. But Eusapia is illiterate and cannot write, and in all the sittings at which I was present only two or three times did there appear signs of writing which might be taken for badly formed letters. The spirits evoked by the Apulian countrywoman seemed also to be very ignorant; and this appears to me to be a very grave objection to the spiritistic hypothesis.

28. *Impressions in plastic substances.*—This is a favourite phenomenon with students of psychical matters, and Eusapia gives good examples of it, although sometimes under circumstances suggestive of doubt. They are impressions of fingers, palms, hands, fists, feet, and also of faces, generally in full profile or half profile; these faces have a certain resemblance to a Eusapia grown old, and in fact are said to be reproductions of the face of "John King," her father in a former life. At our sittings we obtained many such impressions, and as to the greater part of them, we are certain that there was no deception.

29. *Apports.*—These figure as phenomena of the very foremost rank in the history and doings of the most famous mediums. The phenomenon is one of the greatest significance for the spiritist doctrine of the disaggregation and reconstitution of matter, for it consists in the unexpected appearance on the table or in the room of objects (such as flowers, branches, leaves, iron nails, coins, stones, &c.) coming from a distance and penetrating through doors and walls. This phenomenon was reported two or three times during our sittings, but I frankly confess that I was not convinced of it, which does not imply that under better observation it might not be real also in the case of Paladino, as it seems to have been through the agency of other mediums.

30. *Knotting and unknotting of a piece of string, cords, &c., in the dark cabinet as well as on the person*

of Eusapia.—I have seen this phenomenon on several occasions.

We now come to the higher ranges of phenomena, to those which constitute the true basis of spiritism; I refer to the category of materialisations. This is a case of creation *ex novo*, by the use of the vital fluid or spirit of the medium, of forms more or less organised, having the physical characteristics assigned by us to matter, that is, of being resistant to the sense of touch and muscular pressure (tangible), and of being sometimes endowed with light of their own (luminous), but for the most part only capable of arresting exterior rays of light (thus rendering themselves visible).

The first sub-class is that of solid materialisations, which I will call mediumistic stereosis or plasmation.

31. *Touching, feeling, and grasping by invisible hands.*—These form a very common phenomenon at the dark séances, or by a faint light, or a red light; and they are really human hands which touch, press, grasp, pull, push, pat lightly, strike, pull the sitters' beards or hair, take off their spectacles, &c. Some of those to whom such contacts were new have been caused to shudder, and really the first time they cause quite an impression.

32. *Organisations of solid forms having the characteristics of human limbs.*—These are usually hands, arms, shoulders (?), and even heads, which are felt behind the curtain, and seem to be pieces or fragments of a being which is in process of formation; occasionally they give the tangible impression of the whole of a person. On being grasped through the curtain they usually withdraw hastily; but sometimes they remain long enough to allow themselves to be handled, especially the faces. The invisible mouth also makes movements indicative of kissing, biting, &c., usually under cover of the stuff.

33. *Organisation of hands, naked and distinguishable to the touch.*—At certain times we felt ourselves touched by real human hands, having the character of members of a living being; we felt the skin, the warmth, the movable fingers, &c. On grasping them one felt the

impression of hands dissolving away, as though composed of semi-fluid substance.

34. *Complicated actions of materialised forms, tangible but invisible.*—These hands, arms, heads, and half persons, while remaining imperceptible to the sight even on looking into the cabinet, behind the curtains, advance towards the sitters, touch and feel them, embrace, grasp, draw them nearer, or push them away, caress and kiss them, with all the movements of living and real persons. They also execute still more complex actions, both in the shade of the cabinet and in front of it, with the interposition of the curtain, which is swelled out and projected for the purpose on to the table or towards the seats of those near, even though out of the chain; and also in full freedom in the very midst of the sitters, so that some of those present feel themselves invisibly pushed against, pressed, their pockets searched, &c. This last astonishing manifestation (of those previously mentioned I am quite certain) occurred very rarely, and only in complete darkness or by a very faint light which did not allow anything to be clearly seen, so that, though I was present one evening when it occurred, I cannot remove from my mind all uncertainty and should require fuller and more convincing demonstration. Some of those present believed that they recognised and "identified" these invisible forms, by means of impressions of touch and feeling through the curtains. But, in the cases at which I was present, the identification does not sustain, as I shall show, a critical analysis of the psychological origin of the phenomenon; the latter, however, remains real and authentic, though incomprehensible.

I collect into one small group the elementary luminous phenomena, self-visible or visible by exterior light, but not organised.

35. *Appearance of luminous points.*—These are the celebrated "spirit lights"; Eusapia produces them from time to time, but not with the intensity of other mediums whom I have seen. They are indefinable glow-lights, sometimes like very bright globules of light, sometimes

veritable "tongues of fire," like those figured on the heads of the Apostles. They have not been photographed, as far as I know; but they are very evident, sometimes multiple, and running together into one; it is impossible as well as absurd for those who have once seen them, to compare them with artificial phosphorescent effects, not to speak of identifying them with the latter.

36. *Appearance of whitish clouds or mists.*—These do not seem to be endowed with light of their own, since they can only be discerned in a dim light, outside the curtains, or within the cabinet; sometimes they surround Eusapia's head, or rise over her body when she lies down inside the cabinet.

I place the visible materialisations last, because they appear to be formed by a very subtle substance or matter emanating from the person of the medium and composed of particles or molecules which obstruct ordinary light ("teleplastic").

37. *Formation of dark prolongations of the body of the medium.*—These are the supernumerary members seen and described by all those who had previously experimented with Paladino. Visible in half light or in very faint light, and when the actual hands of Eusapia are also in full view and well guarded, these neo-plastic appendages perform many of the phenomena above described (touching and feeling of those near, blows on the chairs, movement of objects, &c.). I shall give drawings of them

38. *Forms having the appearance of arms and hands coming out of the cabinet.*—This manifestation is not rare, and has been already mentioned by those who were present at previous sittings with Eusapia. Being short-sighted, I was not always able to see them distinctly, but my perception, even when indistinct, has always corresponded with what has been seen more clearly by others present who have been endowed with better sight.

39. *Appearance of hands.*—These are among the more common and recognised spiritistic manifestations. The hands usually appear with indistinct or evanescent outlines, of a whitish colour, almost transparent, and with

2 M

elongated fingers (the drawings I shall give will be very expressive). I have perceived them very clearly every time that I was in a position favourable for seeing them; and they were certainly not the medium's hands, which were simultaneously watched, and also visible to all, above the table.

40. *Appearance of obscure forms of indeterminate character or not very evident.*—These are "incomplete materialisations." Sometimes there are seen, advancing and disappearing in the half light, black globes (heads?), indefinable shadowy appendages (arms? fists?); sometimes shadows with crooked profiles which may be conjectured to be bearded ("John King"); and again on the semi-luminous background there appear blackish shapes, flat, and seeming as though transparent, strangely formed, and gesticulating in an uncouth manner. They manifested to me in particular at the sittings of 1901 and 1902, and I perceived them so distinctly (as confirmed by my companions) that I was able, as will be seen, to draw them one by one.

41. *Appearance of forms having determinate and personal characteristics, unknown to any of the sitters.*—We are now at the end, because these are the "complete materialisations" and constitute the apex of Eusapia's mediumship up to the present (other mediums, including Florence Cook and Mme. d'Espérance, have given much more marvellous and truly incredible ones). I have seen these supreme phenomena a few times only, for they are rare events in Eusapia's mediumship. They are well-delineated faces, heads, and half busts of personages, mostly unknown, not recognised by any one present, or who are identified and named by taking advantage of the notions belonging to the traditional history of spiritism. If this is so, I must have seen the same phantasms which the celebrated Sir William Crookes saw, and, moreover, had under his hands; that is to say, there re-appeared at our séances with Eusapia the spirit guide of Florence Cook, "Katie King," who, moreover, is a relative of "John King"! I will publish the curious portrait which I sketched at once in pencil.

42. *Appearance of forms having a personality known to one of the sitters.*—Besides seeing some personal forms tangibly materialised, I must also have been present at a real spirit evocation! On this occasion the apparition was somewhat doubtfully identified and named by living members of his family present at the sitting; but with regard to myself, I did not gain from this extraordinary event in my "spiritistic" experience that impression of obvious certainty which the man of science, the psychologist who studies this very new branch of science, and is habituated to the rules of the strict positive method, is obliged to impose upon himself and has the right to claim from others.

I do not desire to dwell at present on this part of Paladino's phenomena; the space which has been assigned to me will not permit of descriptions or discussions, but only of a pure and simple synthetic *résumé* of my personal experiences.

Thus, in the phenomena in which Paladino's mediumship manifests itself, we have, according to my provisional scheme, nine classes and thirty-nine orders of manifestations; I may possibly have forgotten one or two, and perhaps have grouped together several which ought to have been classed separately; certainly I did not see all that were possible, and other observers may add some which are unknown to me. All this is very different from the simple lifting of the table, or the trick of exchanging hands or withdrawing the feet.

CHAPTER XXXVIII

METHOD OF EXPERIMENTATION IN PSYCHICAL PHENOMENA

GENERAL ARRANGEMENTS, SPONTANEOUS PHENOMENA, FRAUD IN PSYCHICAL EXPERIMENTS

PSYCHICAL phenomena are essentially different from chemical, physical, or other phenomena, scientifically observed, by their nature, the manner in which they can be known and the re-agents which reveal them to our observation. It is therefore necessary that the method employed in studying them should also be special.

In the study of chemical phenomena the experimenter deals with bodies which, in the same conditions, are always identical. When he combines these different bodies, it is always possible, in a general manner, to forecast, almost certainly, the result of the experiment undertaken.

In the study of physical phenomena the conditions are a little more delicate. The physicist employs instruments more or less accurate, but always constructed on experimental data; the working of these instruments, however perfect it may be, still demands certain conditions which do not always depend upon the experimenter.

Every one knows, for example, that an electrical machine is affected by the hygrometric conditions of the air; but, in addition, there are conditions in which the output of the same machine is variable, and in the present condition of science we are not able to determine the cause. In the same way photography (in which the chemical action of light on the sensitive plate is combined with the physical phenomenon of refraction of luminous rays and the operation of a physical apparatus, the camera) often affords the experimenters some un-expected surprises.

More delicate still is the experimentation with psychical phenomena; here the reagent is not an inert body; the instrument is not an insensible mechanism; it is a human being, endowed with all physiological sensibility.

If we first of all examine this very delicate instrument which constitutes the necessary subject for experiment, we find him exceedingly variable. He varies, first of all, by reason of his characteristic nature, which is necessi-tated by his race, his physical, intellectual, and moral development; in the second place, by his temperament, the result of various pre-dispositions derived from his ancestors. To these causes of variability which exist between the different subjects must be added others which cause the same subject not to be identical with himself at different periods of his existence. The more or less perfect state of health, down to a state of illness, causes infinite changes in the faculties of the subject, as well as in his physical vigour and intellectual capacity. Even in the state of good health many passing pheno-mena exercise a considerable influence on our dispositions at the moment. Digestion, sleep, fatigue, only to mention a few of them, have an action on our whole being that cannot be denied.

Another cause of variability of the subject consists in the sentiments awakened in him by the persons in whose presence he is. You will observe that it is not necessary that the subject should know the persons beforehand. This feeling of attraction or repulsion, pleasure or dislike, which we nearly always experience at the sight of a person, even a stranger, a feeling which later changes into sympathy or antipathy, is infallibly experienced by the subject, sometimes unknown to himself, and this feeling, even when unconscious, exercises in many ways an action on his psychical condition. We can understand this influence better if we remember that our subjects are sensi-tives, that is to say, persons of very great impressionability, of a sensitiveness more than normally developed.

We have seen up to now the internal influences that affect the subject—that is to say, the causes of variability in himself; but the whole external world, the objects and the persons surrounding him, also exercise on him an influence not less important.

Everything which acts on the physical being, the temperature, atmospheric pressure, meteorological phenomena, find their echo in his psychic state. We spoke just now of the action of the feelings of sympathy or antipathy which he may experience for persons in whose presence he finds himself. There is also an altogether different influence which acts on the subject from without inwards: an action produced by certain persons quite unconsciously, but which is capable of greatly affecting the conditions and faculties of the subject. It is therefore not surprising if some subjects are powerless to produce certain phenomena or to succeed with an experiment, in the presence of a certain person, or, if sometimes, unconsciously, though quite distinctly, the subject asks that a certain person shall not be present at the experiments. We need not see in this fact, which has given rise to discussions of every description, either caprice on the part of the subject, or reason to suspect his good faith, but simply the evidence of a natural influence unfavourable to the production of the phenomena.

The experimenter who, in other sciences, only takes what may be termed an anonymous part in the experiments—that is to say, who represents merely the sum of his knowledge and of his ability—exercises in experiments with psychic phenomena a real, personal influence. Like the subject himself, but, as we shall see later, in varying degrees, according to the nature of the experiments in which he is engaged, he takes an active part in the production of the phenomena.

First of all, in the same way as each of the sitters, he arouses in the subject feelings of sympathy or antipathy, and these feelings are of all the more importance as the part taken by the experimenter is greater. With regard to these feelings which the experimenter arouses in the subject, it should be observed that sometimes, for a certain time, the latter experiences curiosity or a certain fear, which proceeds from his believing himself to be in the presence of a mysterious power. These feelings of curiosity or of fear may be very useful in the direction of the experiments, and we must learn to take advantage of them; but we must never lose sight of the fact that these feelings are only transitory, and that, after a certain time, they are infallibly transformed into attraction or repulsion, sympathy or antipathy, and that, in consequence of this transformation, the subject may become powerless to produce the smallest phenomenon, or he may refuse in future to lend himself to new experiments. The experimenter ought, therefore, to watch his subject attentively, and, in many cases, he can moderate his impressions and give to his ideas a direction at once reasonable and useful.

After the feelings awakened spontaneously in the subject in regard to the experimenter, we must examine the direct action of the psychic forces on each of them. There may be harmony between the qualities and the natures of the two psychic forces present. In this case, if one of them is better directed, or is superior to the other, it may conduct, train, and use the latter for the realisation of the phenomenon sought for. If these two psychic forces, without being absolutely harmonious, are not too different from each other, and if that of the experimenter is superior to that of the subject, the former can dominate the latter, and by the combination obtain good effects; but if these two forces are absolutely opposed, the experiments will be completely impossible for this experimenter with that subject, and it would be better to give up the attempt.

It is to that cause that we must attribute the fact frequently observed that some subjects, who have given evident proof of psychic qualities, seem suddenly to have lost all their faculties and to be unable to give any result when they are with another experimenter. Doubtless, in certain cases, the operator may be responsible for the non-success, for an inexperienced or ignorant experimenter may not know how to use a subject, even in the most favourable conditions; but there are also cases in which, in spite of experience and knowledge, the results would be nil, because the psychic force of the experimenter cannot harmonise with that of the subject.

As the experimenter takes an active part in the production of certain phenomena, it is very clear that, especially in these experiments, we must take account of all the internal and external conditions whose influence on the subject we have already studied. Thus, states of illness, fatigue, or overwork, leading to a depression of the physical powers, and, at the same time, to a diminution of the energy of the will; transitory physiological disturbances, like those which result from digestion or want of food, fatigue or sleep, disturbances which affect the nervous centres, either directly or through the circulation, must be taken into account in relation to this class of experiments.

The experimenter in psychical research ought to present a certain number of natural and acquired qualities which are absolutely indispensable to success. He must direct the experiments and the subjects; the latter will not be always easy to manage. Their nervous and impressionable nature usually renders them whimsical and capricious. If phenomena of some interest are obtained with them, it often happens that they become vain, appropriating all the honour, and becoming more and more exacting, thinking themselves indispensable. In addition to the natural mobility of their mind, the fact must not be lost sight of that, for the most part, they are not led, as we are, by interest in psychical research. When the attraction of the novelty has worn off, when their curiosity has been more or less satisfied, they begin to grow tired of the experiments; they put less goodwill and energy into them, sometimes they refuse to continue them.

It is for the experimenter to forestall and overcome these difficulties by trying to ascertain beforehand the tendencies of his different subjects. He must certainly not give in to all their whims, which might become innumerable and render all work impossible; but he must also not rebuff them, so that he obtains their co-operation only through fear. He must, during the experiments, know how to make himself accessible to his subjects, amusing them and making himself agreeable to them; he must so contrive that each new experiment awakens in them a fresh interest, and urges them on to emulation. It is necessary for this that the experimenter should have a deep knowledge of psycho-physiology, together with tact, versatility, and prudence, so as to enable him to acquire the necessary authority over his subjects.

In spite of that, difficulties will not fail sometimes to arise, whether they be obstacles springing from the general condition of the experiments or troubles arising from the unwillingness or inexperience of the subjects. Untiring patience will alone enable the experimenter to triumph over these difficulties; he should never allow himself to show the annoyances or disappointments which may be caused by badly managed or fruitless experiments. But, though he ought to appear imperturbable, the experimenter ought to be a very careful and able observer—he ought to give proof of a sagacity and attention continuously maintained; all his senses ought to be constantly awake and perfectly exercised, in order to seize the slightest symptoms which might pass unperceived by less experienced persons.

In order to direct the experiments properly, he must exercise on the subjects and on all who take part, or are present as spectators, an absolute and incontestable authority, but which will have all the greater force the less it is felt. Good manners, dignity, the esteem which he ought to enjoy, united with the qualities we have enumerated, will assure to the experimenter this authority, which will be enhanced by the acquired and scientific qualities of which we shall speak.

Numerous and extensive scientific attainments are, in fact, indispensable in order properly to direct the study of psychic phenomena. A deep knowledge of psycho-physiology is necessary in order to discover the subjects, discern their aptitudes, know how to use and direct them. Hypnology furnishes the means of action by which the subjects can be influenced, at the same time as it enables them to be completely protected from all the difficulties and dangers which might result to them from experiments made without due precaution or the cause of which was left to chance. In combination with a perfect knowledge of nervous pathology, this science also enables us to discover the slightest trace of simulation or trickery which may be mixed with the experiments and falsify the results. Finally, at every moment, the physical and chemical sciences, the most delicate mechanical apparatus, ought to be employed, the better to observe and analyse, control, and register the phenomena experimented upon.

After having examined the conditions requisite for good experimentation in so far as the subjects and operators are concerned, we have likewise to consider the various methods that may be applied to the different categories of the phenomena which we may have to study.

Methodical classification of the phenomena is indispensable, because they are so different in their nature and manifestation that it is impossible to study them without equally varying the means of examination and control.

Spontaneous Phenomena

In the first place, we have to examine the method to be followed in the observation of spontaneous phenomena.

We call spontaneous phenomena those which occur without the actual intervention of the experimenter; and they must be subdivided into phenomena which are produced without conscious intervention of the subject, and phenomena caused by the subject either consciously or even voluntarily.

As regards the observation of haunted houses in particular, it is of special interest that these phenomena should be observed by persons accustomed to experimenting in psychical phenomena; that is the only way to avoid the exaggerations of too credulous minds, or the prejudiced negations of persons who are not even willing to take the trouble to observe them.

That is why the Société Universelle d'Études Psychiques has asked for information from its correspondents on the appearance of these phenomena, and, as soon as it receives information, sends a committee to make a careful inquiry on the spot.

Here are the rules which the observers ought to follow when they receive information of a fact of this character, and when they are at the place where the phenomena occur.

Two eventualities are possible:—

(*a*) The phenomena are no longer produced ;

(*b*) The phenomena continue.

(*a*) *The phenomena are no longer produced.*—The first care of the observers should be to interrogate the witnesses, and divide these witnesses into three categories:—

(1) The witnesses who have heard immediately the account of the phenomena;

(2) The witnesses who have seen them ;

(3) The witnesses who have taken part in them.

The witnesses of the first category are evidently the least important. Nevertheless, their personal worth may give the greater value to their testimony; for example, the doctor, the vicar, or the notary of a village, who have interrogated the eye-witnesses immediately after the events, can often give us a much more accurate idea than those who saw and reported one or two days later.

The witnesses mentioned in the second category, those who saw the phenomena, are very important. The investigators will take every care to question them and note their replies.

Some of the witnesses will have seen the whole of the phenomena; others will only have seen a part. In both cases the investigator will take every care to make them say, with all possible accuracy and precision, all that they saw.

In order to do that, it is necessary to eliminate all the remarks and explanations that the witnesses are too much tempted to add to their statements.

It is necessary to note the bare facts of what they saw, without neglecting any. The smallest fact, precisely stated, is of greater importance than the longest explanation the witnesses can give.

In the third category—the witnesses who have taken part in the phenomena — we have persons still better placed to observe them well, and consequently their depositions are still more important.

Among these we include all those who have ascertained the phenomena otherwise than by seeing and hearing: those, for example, who have been touched by the objects set in motion; those who restored to their places the articles that have been displaced and have seen them moved again; those who have shut up in a cupboard or in a room some articles that have afterwards been found displaced or removed, on condition that they have been able to testify that no one else could get at the objects to remove them ; and, lastly, those who have repaired the damage caused by the force operating.

All this evidence being collected and immediately noted, the investigator ought to observe for himself the marks left by the phenomena. He must look for the traces of the contacts, rubbings, blows, &c., left on the furniture or on the walls; for marks on the floor or on the dust caused by the movement of the furniture.

Articles damaged or broken should be specially examined, and this will be of the greater importance, particularly if the investigator can arrive before the objects have been picked up, replaced, or, more important still, repaired.

From these traces we endeavour to determine the intensity of the force manifested ; the direction of this force and its starting-point; the form and nature of the material object which has left the traces.

These marks should be correctly measured in their dimensions and their relative distances from each other;

further, if it is possible, those which are most important should be sketched or photographed.

Possessed of these important documents, the investigator should first of all seek to ascertain whether the phenomena observed could be produced by any ordinary cause, the instability of certain objects, a shaking of the house coming from without ; he will pass successively in review all the atmospheric forces, air-currents, wind, temperature, electricity.

Having, as a rule, rapidly eliminated all these causes, he will look for trickery, by inquiry, if any person present, or near, could, from within or without, produce all the facts that have been ascertained.

If the phenomena cannot be attributed to any of these ordinary causes, since the facts have ceased to occur, he must now look for the cause of the cessation of the phenomena. He will carefully note all the persons who have left the house, and whose departure coincided with the cessation of the phenomena. He will then see if the phenomena have not coincided with the sickness of any person and their cessation with his return to health.

Finally, he ought to examine separately and minutely all the persons living in the house, and all those who have been present at the phenomena. This examination ought to turn particularly on the state of their nervous system, and on their psycho-physiology and pathology. The examination of their nervous equilibrium and projection of force by means of the sthenometer, if it can be done, would be of the utmost importance.

If the result should point to the probability of a certain person being the medium, a special examination of that person may be made ; and, if the supposed medium has left the house, he should be traced, so as not to lose sight of him.

Very frequently the people of the house or family will show great fright and agitation at the phenomena occurring around them. The investigator will then make it his duty to reassure them, to tell them that though the phenomena may be exceptional they are natural ; to explain them to them, as far as they are able to understand. If the medium has left the house, they can be told that the phenomena will probably not occur again.

In case the medium has not left the house, or if he has not been recognised, the inhabitants should be reassured as to the innocent character of the phenomena, and requested to inform the investigator without delay if the phenomena occur again. They will make no difficulty when they are made to understand that it will be easy by observing the phenomena at the moment of their manifestation to discover the medium, and to put an end to them by summary removal of the cause.

(b) *Persistent phenomena.* — The first care of the observer should be to verify the phenomena themselves at the time of their production.

First of all, it must be observed that it is infinitely preferable to have, at least, two persons to verify these phenomena; in fact, whilst the attention of one observer is drawn to one point, it is necessary that the persons present, and often other parts of the room, should be at the same time watched by another observer.

There are some useful processes to employ for the observation of these phenomena. Granting that some of them often happen in the dark, or, at least, in a dim light, each investigator ought to be provided with one or two small pocket electric lamps, giving a light at any moment, and sometimes enabling him to see the phenomenon at the very time of its production and, at the same time, to detect the attitude of the persons present when the phenomenon is manifested.

In the second place, photography ought to be made use of. Photography offers advantages which differ somewhat from those of the electric light. With the instantaneous light the eye perceives immediately and simultaneously a number of objects which may not be within the range of the camera. On the other hand, the photographic plate will preserve for an indefinite period the exact picture of all the objects which have been found within its range.

It will therefore be useful to employ both processes and to obtain as many photographic proofs as possible. This can be done by employing as many cameras as possible pointing in different directions, and always, be it understood, by means of an instantaneous flash-light.

In the third place, it will be useful to employ also for the verification of the phenomena, various other mechanical processes which will be suggested to the investigators by the circumstances and arrangement of the place. A portable electric bell will often be useful by allowing the arrangement of contacts to give warning of the displacement of certain objects.

After having thus verified the phenomena, it is necessary to notice the conditions in which they are produced.

Conditions of place.—These include careful examination and an exact description of the house, and particularly of the apartment; photographs should be taken of both.

Conditions of time.—Note the hour of the day or night when the phenomena usually occur and the time of their greatest intensity; also the exact duration of the various phenomena observed.

Physical conditions.—Light or darkness, temperature, atmospheric conditions, which seem to favour the production of the phenomena.

We must then pass to the study of the cause of the phenomena. This cause ought to be considered as a force. We shall try, according to the observations made and the principles of mechanics, to determine its seat, direction, and intensity.

As in the first case, it is necessary to make a methodical examination of all the persons in the house and all those who have been present at the manifestations. Among those persons we must note those who have *always* been present when the phenomena are produced, and seek to ascertain if there are any in whose presence they occurred with greater intensity.

Having, by this successive analysis, selected a small number of subjects, we must endeavour, if it is possible, to experimentally eliminate each subject by removing them in succession from the place where the phenomena occur. It will thus be quite easy to determine which person's presence is necessary for their production.

It is of great importance that the investigators should let nothing be known to the inmates of the family as to the result of their investigations concerning the persons or their suspicion as to the one who is the cause, if they think they have discovered him. They should continue their observations, watching the supposed medium very carefully, but without any one being able to perceive this.

When the investigators have discovered the medium, they must first of all express the hope to the inhabitants of the house that the phenomena will cease; then under some pretext they will remove the medium. If everything becomes orderly again, they will have proof that they have not been mistaken.

When they arrive at this point, the rôle of the investigators is not yet ended. In removing the medium they will be careful not to lose trace of him, because they will need to examine him further.

The medium may be absolutely unconscious of being one, and unaware that he is the active agent in the production of the phenomena; but if he knows that the phenomena have ceased in his absence, especially if similar phenomena have occurred at the place to which he has removed since his arrival, he may become aware of the relation existing between his presence and the manifestations.

The duty of the investigators then is to remove his fears; they should make him understand that these manifestations depend upon a special condition which is temporary. They should endeavour to get him to entrust himself to a committee of serious experimenters in whom he can place complete confidence, who will experiment with him as to these mediumistic faculties. They should show that this methodical experimentation will put an end to the spontaneous manifestations of an abnormal power; the experiment will demonstrate, in fact, that the mediums, who exercise their faculties in a scientific group, are no longer subject to the spontaneous and incoherent manifestations we are now studying.

The dominant characteristics of spontaneous phenomena is that they cannot be produced at one's pleasure. At the most we can place ourselves in conditions which appear the most favourable for their production; it is necessary then to wait with an imperturbable patience. If we try to do more, to hasten them or make them appear by any excitation whatever, they will be infallibly impaired, transformed in some manner, and the investigator will lose the greatest part of their value. The experimenter ought here to limit his part to that of an observer; but he ought to make use of all the qualities we have already recognised as indispensable in those who would devote themselves to these researches. He ought to employ all his sagacity, experience, and scientific knowledge in careful observation. He ought not let pass any accessory circumstances, which to the unlearned may appear insignificant, but which are capable of enlightening him as to the value, origin, nature, or consequences of the phenomenon observed.

When the phenomena occur unknown to the subject through whom they are produced, this subject, the generating agent of the force which gives rise to the phenomena, may pass unperceived, and, for the time being, remain unknown to the witnesses, and even to the experimenters.

In facts of this category, as regards the phenomenon, the experimenter has no action to exert on it. But it must not be forgotten that if he cannot provoke it voluntarily, he can involuntarily cause it to cease or impede its progress. The first thing, therefore, is to observe the phenomenon in itself, in its slightest details, which ought to be noted with rigorous exactitude. In the course of this observation the experimenter should take every care not to impede the progress of the phenomenon, and also not to run the risk of modifying it, which might happen, even involuntarily. The danger of exercising an involuntary influence on the phenomenon is all the

2 N

more to be feared here, because the experimenter does not
yet know the cause or the active subject, and because if he
does not exercise extreme prudence and circumspection
he may influence one or the other.

In order to avoid this difficulty he must observe in
silence, without departing from the utmost impassiveness,
whatever may be the surprises he may experience in the ·
course of this observation. It is evidently necessary also
to demand from all those present, as far as possible, the
same silence and the same calmness. It is, above all,
necessary to forbid, during the whole time of the experiment, all remarks as to the phenomenon or its progress,
as well as all expressions of opinion concerning its probable
cause or consequences.

Whilst considering the phenomenon in itself, the
experimenter will apply himself to the most careful
observation of all the persons present, but taking care
that this constant and rigorous surveillance is concealed,
and especially that it is unperceived by the persons to
whom it is directed. The experimenter ought thus to be
able to discover the principal factor in the production of
the phenomenon, the agent who produces it, the subject
who brings into play or transmits the forces necessary for
its manifestation.

There may be only one subject, and he may be some
person present, but the fact must not be lost sight of that
the symptoms of his condition as the active subject may
be absolutely latent. In other cases the phenomenon
may be produced by the influence of the forces collected
from several subjects present; it may be that these various
subjects take an almost equal part in the manifestation
by joining forces of the same nature and the same intensity;
it may be that one of those present, possessing in himself a
force superior to that of the others, plays the part of principal
active subject and draws from the energy of the persons
around powers which he lacks and thereby becomes the
sole director of the progress of the phenomenon.

It may also happen that the subject directing the
manifestation may be more or less distant. One of the

subjects present then collects around him all the forces
necessary for the action, but unconsciously allows himself
to be directed by the impulse of what comes to him from
without.

It must not be forgotten that the experimenter himself
may be at the same time the active subject, and that
entirely unconsciously. This may be the case in two
ways, which we shall indicate; either because he alone
produces and directs the force which gives rise to the
phenomenon, or because he assembles and directs the
scattered forces emitted by those present.

The experimenter may, in this case also, come to discover that he is himself the active subject, but he can
only arrive at this deduction by way of elimination, and
consequently generally after long observations. This
search for the active subject, which brings the psychic
forces into play, is very important in the study of these
phenomena, because, once the subject has been really
ascertained, the study of the phenomenon itself becomes
much more easy and more precise. The rational and
scientific method will therefore be to seek first of all to
discover this subject, without neglecting, be it understood,
the observation of the events which may occur in the
course of this research.

Whoever may be the active subject, whether he be
known or is still unknown, and whatever may be his
action, more or less direct, upon the phenomena, when
we are observing spontaneous phenomena, the first rule
is not to disturb them, in order to observe them in all
their completeness. We must, therefore, take account of
the ease with which these phenomena may be impeded.

The investigators, like the spectators, may act directly
or indirectly on the phenomena; directly, by exercising
an action differing from, or even contrary to, that of the
subject, or again, by acting in any manner on the subject;
this action may have the effect either of modifying his
powers, or of impressing his nervous system, or of divert-
ing his attention, or of isolating him from the point at
which the phenomenon is manifested; indirectly, by

acting on the instrument by means of which the phenomenon is manifested, or by interrupting the communication
between the subject and the instrument.

The effect of these different actions may be manifested
in several ways. The conditions being no longer favourable for their production, the phenomenon commenced
may be interrupted, or may become more and more
feeble until it becomes insignificant, or it may be arrested
suddenly. If the phenomenon has not yet begun to manifest itself, we may be in apparently favourable conditions,
that is to say, identical with those in which we have
already observed the phenomenon, but we wait in vain—
nothing happens.

It is necessary in these different cases to verify with
the most rigorous exactitude the prevailing conditions.
If the obstacle proves to be some external circumstances
(heat, light, noise, &c.) which are within our control,
it must be remedied. If the obstacle comes from the
action of a spectator or the subject, it is sometimes sufficient to separate them from each other as far as the room
will permit. But if this action is too intense or too much
opposed to the production of the phenomena, if, as sometimes happens, it is augmented by an auto-suggestion on
the part of the subject, it may become necessary to completely remove the person who forms an obstacle to the
experiment.

Hitherto we have seen how an operator may, by inexperience or overlooking precautions, prevent the production of psychical phenomena. There is a much
greater danger to avoid, because it exposes us to more
unpleasant consequences—that is, to cause the phenomena to deviate from their normal course and falsify the
results.

When experimenters seek in vain to study a phenomenon or to perform an experiment, they can at most
only lose their time, and yet for those who know how
to observe, experiments, even negative ones, always give
rise to very instructive observations; but if it happens
that, involuntarily and unconsciously, we modify or change

a phenomenon, the results of the experiments thus falsified may become the source of new errors, and it is necessary to begin again later on a whole series of similar labours in order to arrive at the origin of the error committed.

It should be pointed out that we may arrive at false results in two ways: either the observation is erroneous from the commencement and may not rest on any real foundation; or a real phenomenon had been observed at the beginning, but the observer, without being aware of the fact, has caused it to deviate from its normal course during the manifestation. A phenomenon real in its origin, may thus have been artificially changed and appear altogether different from what it would have been but for the external influence which is exercised upon it. Such an observation would be without value, and the conclusions we should draw would only lead us into error.

We shall suppose that the observer knows the active subject; if he did not know him at the commencement of the observation he has been able to discover him. It must not be forgotten that in certain cases the subject is himself ignorant of the part he plays in the production of the phenomena. Under these circumstances he must not be informed of the influence he exercises; it is better to let him think that the phenomenon is the result of a collective action, and that he does not play a preponderant part. Without making the active subject known or bringing him into prominence, it is the duty of the observer from this time on to keep his attention fixed on him in a very special manner.

FRAUD IN PSYCHICAL EXPERIMENTS

It is necessary to have constantly before the mind the possibility of fraud. Considered in itself fraud may be complete or partial.

Complete fraud extends to a whole series of experiments, to an entire séance. There may be at first sight the appearance of real phenomena, but if we examine them closely, and if we go to the bottom of the matter, we perceive that there is nothing but illusion, that they are imitated or simulated. It is evident that if we are dealing with a subject incapable of producing the slightest psychical phenomenon, and who wishes to deceive the observers, we can only have a series of simulations and a totally fraudulent séance. But it is not necessary to believe that the proof of total fraud necessarily implies that we are in the presence of a subject of that class. It may very well be that even with a good subject, capable of producing highly interesting phenomena, after a long wait for manifestations, which, from one cause or another, cannot be produced, we get only simulated phenomena.

With regard to partial fraud, it is always a real medium in whose presence we observe it, because it is produced in a séance where real phenomena have already been obtained. Either the real phenomena cease to occur at a certain time, and are replaced by imitated phenomena, or else we obtain at will a whole category of real phenomena; but when we wish to go forward to more complicated manifestations, or simply pass on to different phenomena, which in the circumstances are more difficult to obtain, we only obtain, instead of these, simulated phenomena which are sometimes mixed with authentic ones.

Considered from the subject's point of view, fraud may be :—

(1) Conscious and voluntary;
(2) Conscious and involuntary;
(3) Totally unconscious.

Conscious and voluntary fraud does not give occasion for any useful scientific observation. It can only teach the experimenters the better to put themselves on guard against the unscrupulous subjects who might still seek to lead them into error. Subjects who make a profession of lending themselves to psychical experiments, or who derive profit from their reputation and from séances for which they are solicited, sometimes deliberately try to deceive. They make their preparations beforehand, practise the imitation of certain phenomena, and carefully hide instruments, more or less rudimentary, which they use with great dexterity, such as imperceptible threads, springs or wires, by means of which they sometimes produce a great illusion. Or they may even have an accomplice who assists them in their operations, which are in no way scientific, by communicating with them in the conventional manner. Thus, for example, a thought-reader will guess the most complicated figures, words, and phrases proposed by the spectators. It is finally discovered that the bandage with which his eyes are covered allows the subject to see his companion's foot, and that an imperceptible movement of this foot indicates to him the figures or the letters he ought to name.

When it is only a question of experiments made by a conjurer on the stage, the matter is not important, because it is only a question of amusing the public, and the operator is performing his part and giving an illusion accepted as such in advance. It is not the same thing when he gives a serious séance : and it is evident that subjects who thus lend themselves to a habitual and premeditated fraud, ought to be completely excluded from all scientific experimentation.

By the side of these premeditated frauds, got up by individuals who have no other object than to deceive, we also sometimes observe conscious, and, up to a certain point, voluntary frauds on the part of subjects who, under other circumstances, show themselves sincere and capable of taking part in scientific experiments. That happens especially when a subject is overworked, when he is asked to make experiments which are repugnant or distasteful to him, or again when evident distrust is manifested which wounds his susceptibilities and irritates him. These subjects ought not to be completely rejected, for they may be very good, but we should act towards them with much skill and tact; we must know how to avoid the causes which lead them to simulation, and, in every case, watch them in a much more rigorous manner by observing the precautions which I will indicate further on.

Conscious and involuntary fraud, as well as totally unconscious fraud, comes from subjects who are true mediums and who have real aptitude for psychical experiments. These two classes of fraud differ only in this, that in the first the subject is in a less profound mediumistic state, which enables him to know all that is happening around him and what he himself accomplishes. It is clear that we have here a mixed and transitory condition, such as is but seldom observed. In every case, the characteristics of conscious and involuntary fraud are the same as those of unconscious fraud and we can study them together.

It must not be forgotten that in psycho-physiology the subject is a very complicated being, with whom we cannot obtain a given phenomenon at will, even if it has already been obtained in similar conditions. We have already seen that we have to take into account a great number of factors, and in the first place the psychical state of the subject at the moment, which may be influenced by causes of which we have been able to discover and study a certain number, but of which others have completely escaped us.

The subject is not always master of his impressions; he cannot go at will into any physical or moral state asked for. And further, he is often ignorant himself as to what conditions of his psychical being are most favourable for obtaining the results expected.

These conditions, for the most part, are produced in him unawares, without his seeking them : whilst his efforts, on the contrary, may raise an obstacle to them.

The mere fact of his submitting to experiments may lead the sensitive, in spite of himself, and without his knowledge, to simulate a phenomenon which is not spontaneously produced, or to intensify it.

In mediumistic states hyperæsthesia is usually observed which may occur with regard to all the possible sensations, singly or together, and may make certain impressions unpleasant or even painful. The subject, under this first influence, often executes involuntarily some disordered movements without even suspecting it. Later on, under certain influences, he is dominated by the thought of the phenomenon asked of him, and these movements follow the motor images of his thought. According to psychological laws, all thought is accompanied by a muscular action: in a general way the muscles begin to contract, in accordance with the different movements necessary for the accomplishment of the act thought of: the result is that the hand always moves automatically in the direction of our thoughts. This action is reflex, instantaneous, and executed in a more or less complete manner, if the subject does not oppose it by an act of the will, or if there is no mechanical obstacle in the way. Even in this latter case the attempt at contraction at least exists in the different muscles.

We can observe it by feeling or we can even register it with certain apparatus, and the subject is aware of it by his muscular sense. The result is that in psychical experiments, in which the thought and will of the subject ought to be directed to, or be influenced by, an object or a person, sympathetic movements often if not always accompany the phenomenon.

There is still another cause for the movements observed in the subject when we expect a phenomenon or see it produced. It seems to be proved that most frequently the effort made by a subject in the active mediumistic state in order to produce a dynamic phenomenon is painful, or, at least, difficult. First of all there is a cutaneous hyperæsthesia, then a pain which accompanies the excessive expenditure of the nervous forces and which is proportionate to the special effort demanded. It is therefore quite natural that the subject, especially in the states in which he is unconscious and powerless to control his automatic movements, seeks to avoid pain and to effect the physical action by means which are less painful to him.

In the mediumistic experiments on the externalisation of motricity, the force of the medium is often in part borrowed from the bystanders: this decomposition of the force occasions also movements which the observers are, in most cases, unable to explain.

Unconscious fraud may be clumsy or artless, but as a rule it closely resembles real phenomena; it seems to be skilful and well arranged and premeditated. We know that generally instinctive actions are performed with remarkable precision and cleverness; they are more perfect in their execution than voluntary actions: unconscious fraud partakes of all these qualities. Unconscious fraud does not leave any recollection, when the subject has returned to his normal state, of the fraudulent means employed; but he can often remember the effects produced by these means, just as he may also have forgotten the effect produced, as well as the mechanism which produced it.

We cannot leave this question of fraud without speaking of one very frequent cause of fraud, although its mechanism seems at first sight very complicated—namely, fraud which results from suggestions. We must remember, in the first place, that the mediums or subjects placed by any means in a mediumistic state are very sensitive to mental suggestion. The thoughts and will of the persons who take part in the experiment exercise on the subject an influence of which he is not conscious, but which is none the less considerable.

Now, the spectators and witnesses of a psychical experiment may act thus on the subject in several different ways. Persons are sometimes admitted to these experiments who have no knowledge of such phenomena. Often they bring doubts based on the physical laws which they know and which they believe to be absolute, and on the difficulty of admitting anything to be scientific which is outside the narrow range of ancient knowledge. This doubt, which resolves itself into a conviction of the impossibility of carrying out the experiment, seems to arouse the opposition of the subject, as though he was personally interested in convincing the spectators, and was thus challenged to succeed. The subject vaguely perceives this hostility, which distracts his attention and takes away a part of the faculties which he ought to bring into play. He thus finds himself directly impelled to help out, by fraudulent means, the result which is expected.

In other cases the suggestion of fraud is still more direct. Certain persons, while desirous of being present at psychical experiments, experience an aversion for these phenomena which develops into actual hostility. These feelings of prejudice are sometimes such that they unconsciously lead to actual bad faith in the observation of the experiments. These persons, understanding nothing of the nature of psychical experiments, use every means to counteract them. They are often more insistent than any one else to be present at the experiments; all the same it is sometimes wrong to admit them. But as they are convinced that these phenomena do not exist, their secret desire is always to catch the subjects in the very act of trickery. These persons think of all the possible means that can be employed by the subject to introduce fraud into the experiments, and, far from recognising that the subject is unconscious and seeking to prevent him from making use of simulation, they make it easy for him and induce it in every possible manner. These experimenters seem to rejoice when the subject has fallen into their trap and simulates a phenomenon; they do not take into account that the subject is unconscious of the way in which the phenomena are produced, that he instinctively seeks the easiest and least troublesome means of attaining the desired end. In this case the experimenters alone are responsible for the fraud, because they have made a real mental suggestion to the subject from which he is unable to escape.

These considerations on the manner in which fraud is produced, and on the part which the subject may take in it, lead us to deduce the line of conduct which the experimenter ought to follow. If he suspects any trickery whatever at any part of the experiment, his first care ought to be to hide his impression and to let nothing be seen of what he has been able to discover; but he should redouble his attention and seek first of all to decide in what category of fraud he can place it. Then he should

seek by all possible means to prevent the fraud being
produced, but always indirectly, in order not to disclose
the process employed by the subject. It must not be
forgotten, in fact, that the subject, who may be irrespon-
sible, will be immediately lost for experimental purposes,
even if he is a good subject, from the simple fact that he
will be denounced or unmasked when making use of some
deception of slight importance.

There are many ways of watching the subject and of
making it impossible for him to employ such or such
fraudulent means. One of the best methods is to pretend
to watch particularly one of the experimenters other than
the subject. We then have perfect liberty for taking
precautions which render the suspected fraud impossible
without implicating the subject.

Particular Observation of the Subjects or Mediums and Verification of the Phenomena

Now that the experimenter has ascertained the sincerity of the subject and thus eliminated the principal
causes of error, we will see how he ought to pursue his
observations.

The subject himself must, in the first place, be specially
studied during the course of the experiment.

We must find out whether his will comes into play
in the production of the phenomena. This question can
be divided into two : can he produce, stop, or direct them
at will ? Is it possible for him to vary the nature, form,
or intensity of them ?

What is the precise condition of the subject during the
production of the phenomena ? Is he in a hypnotic state,
an active or passive mediumistic state, or in a mixed state,
and, finally, what are the symptoms presented ?

It is well also to determine the degree of psychical
force which the subject is obliged to expend for the production of the phenomenon. Does he only utilise his own
physical or psychical forces, or does he seem to draw

them in part, either from the sitters or from any dynamic source whatever?

In what way does the subject bring these various forces into play? Does he use his limbs or muscles, or his glance to direct them? How does he communicate them—immediately or mediately, and, in the latter case, what are the intermediaries employed?

We do not find many subjects capable of producing indifferently various kinds of psychical phenomena. Each subject exhibits special faculties which are personal to him, and which enable him to produce a certain phenomenon. If we ask him to perform other experiments we shall obtain nothing, or only some insignificant phenomena, even with a subject excellently endowed in his own speciality.

We do indeed sometimes meet with subjects capable of carrying on several different classes of experiments, but even with them we easily recognise their special dominant faculties.

We can develop by exercise the faculties which subjects naturally possess; but it must not be forgotten that the laws of the development of psychic faculties teach us:

1. That we cannot develop several different faculties simultaneously in the same subject without detracting from the perfection of the experiments;

2. That one faculty, when specially cultivated, is developed to the detriment of others;

3. That there is, consequently, every inducement to cultivate the special dominant faculty in each subject, by which we shall succeed in producing much more important phenomena, and more complete and interesting experiments.

We conclude from all this that it is very important that the experimenter should seek to ascertain as quickly as possible the special dominant faculty of the subject with whom he operates.

The experimenter ought not to confine his observation to the subject only, but he ought carefully to note all the circumstances of the experiment and the concomitant phenomena. We have seen, in the course of this study, the influence exercised by the persons who surround the subject, and the physical and atmospherical conditions.

Taking these various influences in the order of their importance, the experimenter will therefore now have to direct his attention to the persons who take part in the experiment and all those who are present.

From the commencement of the séance, and before even beginning the experiments, the operator should by a rapid glance make a summary diagnosis of the psychological condition of the persons present, aided by the information which he has been able to gather as to their antecedents from the psychological and experimental point of view, which he ought never to neglect.

Those present are naturally divided into two categories: those who take some part or other in the experiments, and those who are present merely as spectators. Both ought to be carefully observed. It is necessary also to note carefully those who have previously been in relation with the subject; to know as far as possible what have been their mutual relations; and if some persons have already been present at experiments with him, what observations have been made with regard to them.

It is necessary, first of all, to ascertain the physiological modifications which may occur in the condition of each person in particular; traces of fatigue or nervousness, tendency to sleep; torpor, and sometimes complete sleep; unconscious or convulsive movements; any sensations whatever, painful or unpleasant, which may be perceived by the person himself.

It is also very important to note the influence which the subject may exercise on these different phenomena, and to ascertain if there exists a sort of parallelism between the states through which the subject passes and those which are observed in some other person present. We know that the subject may unconsciously place a spectator in the passive mediumistic state; this point ought never to be forgotten, because the subject may directly utilise by himself, or indirectly, the new faculties which are thus developed in a spectator, who becomes in consequence a secondary subject.

Finally, after having ended the experiments, the investigator should interrogate the persons present, and especially those who seem to present some physiological modifications, and he will note the subjective phenomena which they mention: nervousness, fatigue, somnolence, &c. In the case of certain persons, the observation of whom is of particular interest, it will be well, as far as possible, to take, before and after the séance, the condition of their forces by the dynamometer and sthenometer.

It is also necessary to take account of the physical and atmospheric conditions in which the experiment takes place, because, as we have demonstrated some years ago, these conditions exercise an influence on certain phenomena. The barometric pressure, the temperature, the general condition of the atmosphere ought to be taken, and it should be observed whether the place where the experiment takes place is more or less protected from these influences. In the room in which the experiment takes place, we should note the temperature, natural or artificial light (its source, intensity, colour), the dimensions of the room, its shape, and the principal objects in it.

The séance is ended, but the investigator's duty is not finished. He ought first, in concert with the sitters, witnesses, or experimenters, to write an account of all that has happened, and which can be confirmed by all. Then he will assemble separately and immediately the observers and experimenters—that is to say, those who have the necessary knowledge and experience in this class of phenomena to be able to appreciate their value and importance.

It is then particularly that it must not be forgotten that no one should, under any pretext, utter any observation on or any explanation whatever of the phenomena observed, in the presence of the subject or any person who may have been an active agent. When these different persons, as well as those who may have been present at the experiments as witnesses or out of curiosity, have withdrawn, the immediate impressions of the observers and experimenters must be collected and carefully recorded.

Later, that is to say, one or two days afterwards, the experimenters must be again assembled, and, having before them the notes taken during and after the séance, they should discuss certain points, and try as far as possible to interpret the phenomena observed. They should always endeavour to draw practical conclusions as to the procedure to be followed in subsequent experiments, and, comparing the phenomena observed with those already known, they should at least classify them with scientific method. In this way we can be certain that all the experiments, of whatever kind, will always have a useful bearing on science.

CHAPTER XXXIX

METHOD OF EXPERIMENTATION—INDUCED
PHENOMENA

EXPERIMENTATION WITH INDUCED PHENOMENA

IN the second part of this study, we have to examine the
special rules which ought to be applied to experiments in
regard to the different psychical phenomena which can be
induced. Every experiment ought to have for its end, and
for its result, either to search more deeply into that which
is already known, or to find out something new. An experiment undertaken merely out of curiosity does not
deserve the name of a scientific experiment.

If each experimenter were to consider as null all that
has been done before him and recommence on his own
account the work of his predecessors, no scientific progress
would be possible. The first experiments made in any
line whatever ought to serve as bases for subsequent experiments, not that these latter should be only servile
imitations of them, but the results acquired, the deductions made, even the negative results and the lack of
success enable us to discover the rules useful for
methodical experimentation. That is why every well-
conducted experiment deserves to be taken into consideration, because it ought to contribute to the progress
of human knowledge.

Psychical phenomena have appeared up to now so
various that it was scarcely possible to submit them to
methodical experimentation. However, it seems to us,
from the whole of the experiments of which we have
collected the results and from those which we have made
ourselves, that it is possible to divide them, from the

experimental point of view, into four groups in order to
facilitate their study.

We will therefore examine successively how the experiments ought to be conducted for the study of the
following phenomena :—

(1) Mental suggestion and transmission of thought;
(2) Lucidity;
(3) Externalisation of sensibility;
(4) Externalisation of force.

We must repeat that this is only a purely experimental division, hence essentially conventional; but it
has in our eyes this advantage, that we can bring the
majority of psychical phenomena, which it is possible
to induce for experiment, into one or other of these
categories.

MENTAL SUGGESTION AND TRANSMISSION OF THOUGHT

We must clearly distinguish, first of all, the two kinds
of experiments which, though presenting some apparent
resemblances, are absolutely different in practice.

In mental suggestion the experimenter does not
transmit to the subject the idea of the act to be accomplished, the subject is ignorant during a great part of the
experiment of what we wish to lead him to do. If he
happens, more or less rapidly, to guess the object of the
suggestion, it is by a simple association of ideas. The
experimenter splits up the act to be accomplished into
a series of partial movements, and it is these movements
that he imposes on the subject successively, as though he
were accomplishing them himself.

In order to walk, for example, he will first of all
incline the body of the subject to the side to which he
wishes to lead him; then he will make him raise his leg,
advance his foot in the direction desired, and so on. In
order to make him avoid obstacles, he will make him turn
or swerve to the right or left, then he will stop him when
he arrives at the end.

In the same way, if he is required to take up an

article, he will first make him raise his forearm, then carry this arm in the desired direction, hold out his hand and take hold of the object.

The most complicated movements and acts will thus be dissected and the experimenter will successively contract the different groups of muscles, as he would do himself if he were carrying out the movement.

For the transmission of thought, the mode of action and mode of reception are alike absolutely different. The phenomenon of thought-transmission consists essentially in this, that an idea emitted by the will of the active subject, whom we call in this case the suggester, is perceived by the passive or receptive subject, who, just now, was the one to whom the suggestion was made.

The idea may be absolutely independent of any act or any motor phenomenon; while, on the other hand, it may also involve the execution of a more or less complex action.

In this case the transmission of thought becomes almost necessarily more or less multiple. We have, first of all, the idea of the act itself; in the second place, there is the will not to accomplish or to accomplish the act. The transmission of thought may be stopped there, and leave the subject to choose the way to be followed in order to arrive at the desired end; but we may also go further, and, without acting on the motor organs of the subject, suggest to him the idea of the means by which he will realise the act demanded of him. The subject will, in this case, always have present to the mind the definite or partial act which he is to carry out.

From all that we have said, it will be seen that in both cases, whether of mental suggestion or of the transmission of thought, in spite of mechanical differences, the suggester, and the person to whom the suggestion is made, both take an active part in the experiment.

They can, therefore, both train themselves separately, and it is even necessary for the perfect success of the experiments that they should do so.

The suggester ought, for mental suggestion, to accustom

himself to split up any act into partial, well-defined movements.

The difficulty consists in knowing how to combine the successive impulses, sufficiently strongly, in a single direction towards the desired end. This can be accomplished by a little training; the mechanism consists, first of all, in energetically fixing in the mind the act to be suggested, and, at the same time, in arranging in the mind the plan of the different movements by which the subject must accomplish it. This first operation the suggestioner accomplishes in himself, without entering into communication with the subject. After this he must not consider the end, except in a general way; he must voluntarily make dominant in his mind the idea of partial impulsions, by awaking in himself a vivid mental representation of the sensations he experiences in personally accomplishing the movements suggested; in order to do this he must know how to keep away all other thoughts and all disturbing influences from without.

For thought-transmission the operator ought first of all to apply himself to gaining a thorough knowledge of his subject. The subjects must be divided into various categories, according to which of the senses is, by nature or training, especially refined or delicate. Each, in fact, has the habit of giving to his thought a form which corresponds to one of the three senses of sight, hearing, or touch.

The representation by the sight of an idea may be made in three different ways, so that we can distinguish three categories of individuals of the visual type. If we take as example the idea of an object, or of an animal or vegetable, some will represent the object as it exists in nature, with its proper forms, dimensions, and colour. Others will make a mental representation of the image of the object: one will see simply its outline and form: an artist will see particularly its colour and shades; the photographer will perceive the picture in the special tone of a photograph. The third class of visuals, including especially educated men and writers, will have before their eyes the written or printed word which denotes the object.

With the last named, the word which comes first to the mind of the subject in order to express it is that of the language which he employs most habitually; but if one of these subjects is very familiar with several languages, so as to speak them fluently, his idea will take body, or, if you will, he will think in the language he was using at the moment the idea dawned in his mind. Thus a Latin scholar, while engaged in reading a Latin text, will think in Latin; a Frenchman, conversing with an Englishman in his own language, will feel his thought manifesting under the form of the English word which represents it.

If we now consider the auditory category, that is to say, those in whom the sense of hearing predominates for the representation of the thought, we find in the same way that they must be divided into several groups. Some will perceive, for a certain class of objects, the noise peculiar to the object: the sound of the voice for men, the cry for animals, the resonance for objects. The most important group represents the idea by the sound of the spoken word which expresses it. Here we should make the same remark on the subject of different languages that we made for the image of the written word, the auditive representation of the thought by the spoken word following exactly the same rules.

In the category of the subjects in whom the sense of touch predominates, we find a still more limited number of individuals: it is rarer, in fact, to identify the idea with the tactile sensation given by the object. Nevertheless we must refer to this category the idea of movement which is inseparable from certain objects, and the sensation of which may be the first one awakened. Finally, special account must be taken of the motor sensation which accompanies the pronunciation of the spoken word; it is that sensation which in certain subjects specially represents the idea.

It is indispensable, for any one who wishes to succeed in transmitting his thought, not only to know all these details, but to practise giving body to his thought under all these forms. In fact, in making experiments of thought-transmission with a subject, the first important thing will be to know to which of the different groups mentioned the subject belongs, in order to transmit to him the thought in the form in which it is most easily perceptible to him.

It is quite evident that the experiment will be much more easily carried out if the suggester and the subject belong to the same category; and, on the other hand, it may sometimes be found impossible to succeed with the experiment if the subject belongs to an absolutely different group and the suggester has not been able to give this identical form to his thought.

It also follows that experiments with certain subjects which have not succeeded with one operator, may be quite successful with another, without there being any trickery or collusion between them.

In the same way as the suggestioner can, as we have seen, practise mental suggestion and thought-transmission, the subject may also train himself for the same experiments. He will commence by accustoming himself to isolate himself from all his surroundings, freeing himself from all disturbing elements, making, so to speak, a void in his thoughts so that nothing may hinder the penetration of the suggestion into his mind. Then he will exercise himself, for mental suggestion, in splitting up actions into successive movements, and, in the case of the transmission of thought, in cultivating the natural faculty of mental representation which he possesses.

After this training, which each of the experimenters can undertake separately, they will practise again together. Here we must recommend the suggester to adopt a well-reasoned method, but which once adopted will remain permanent. It is, in fact, of the highest importance to act always in the same manner with the same subject.

One should commence with exceedingly simple suggestions, and repeat them a great number of times;

varying them, and gradually making them more complicated, but only in proportion as the more simple ones succeed without difficulty, and as the sensibility of the subject is developed.

Finally, in every case, the experimental séance must not be too greatly prolonged; when the suggester or the subject becomes fatigued, the experiments must be suspended. In the same way if, for any cause, it is seen that either of the operators is indisposed and that the attempts are fatiguing or unsuccessful, the experiments should be stopped and resumed on another occasion.

Experiments in Lucidity

The phenomenon of lucidity consists essentially in a subject having knowledge of facts which are outside the range of his normal senses. It is therefore necessary to separate from the phenomenon of lucidity those effects of apparent lucidity which may arise from transmission of thought. This knowledge may apply either to facts which happened some long time since, or to present events, or finally to events only destined to happen in the more or less distant future. These conditions may give a very considerable interest to the phenomenon, but they do not change its nature.

There are two ways of experimenting on lucidity; the first consists in experiments known, in England particularly, under the name of visions in the crystal. The second consists in researches on somnambulistic lucidity with a hypnotic subject.

The procedure to be employed and the rules to be followed in these two experiments are absolutely different : we shall examine them successively.

The experiments of vision in the crystal are simple, easy to carry out, within the reach of every one; but the results are also much less important and of less interest.

There are, first of all, some general conditions which concern the environment of the subject. The place in which the experiment is made ought to be as quiet and isolated as possible, so that no outside noises distract the subject. It is especially necessary to avoid any sudden and unexpected noises which may divert his attention.

Only a small number of persons must be present, and they must not be close to the subject, and, above all, not in front of him. They must remain absolutely silent and motionless.

The person who lends himself to the experiment ought to turn his back to the light. If the light is an artificial one it must be placed high enough for the rays to pass over the head of the subject. The subject should be comfortably seated before a table covered by preference with a dark-coloured cloth, and on the table, right in front of him, should be placed the object which is to serve as a mirror.

A number of different objects may be employed—a glass filled with water, a carafe. The English have invented a small apparatus which is very convenient for this experiment; it consists of a very transparent glass ball with no defect; it is generally of the size of a small orange, and it is placed on a small support made of black wood. The subject should look very attentively at the centre of the object, whatever it may be, and wait, motionless, and in silence. At first he will see on the brilliant surface the reflection of the surrounding objects. He must not keep his eyes on these, but fix them on the centre of the globe. This fixity of attention on a brilliant object ends by the sight becoming fatigued and the view is disturbed. It is then that the imagination is brought into play. When the gazer is a sensitive, the rainbow-coloured rays which traverse the transparent ball soon take an appearance of clouds of different colours, and as the least movement changes the direction of the rays which come to the eyes, these clouds seem to be animated with various movements. At the same time, the subject falls into a superficial hypnotic state, which renders him susceptible to hallucinations. Then he begins to perceive in the transparent globe the formation of various pictures.

These pictures appear in a variable manner according

to the subjects. More frequently they are first of all indefinite forms with undecided outlines, then a part of the picture begins to clear, and the subject recognises and describes each part successively. He seems to follow the development of a photographic plate. When the image is developed in this way, it generally remains for some time; the subject has full time in which to examine it, to recognise it, and describe it in the slightest details. Then it is effaced a little at a time and slowly: the subject remains for a while without observing anything, then another picture is formed in the same way.

With other subjects the appearance of the pictures forms in an altogether different way. In the centre of a cloud that at first seems to fill the transparent globe, there appears suddenly a form to which they at once find a resemblance. These visions are most frequently partial, and less complete than the preceding: the subject describes a face or a head of a man or an animal, sometimes a landscape, but the rapidity with which the pictures succeed each other prevents them from completely developing, and does not allow the subject to specify the details.

All these pictures are evidently only a play of the subject's imagination, which creates an hallucination out of nothing. Nevertheless, there are in this vision two mechanisms which must be clearly distinguished. The transparent globe receives and reflects the picture, but the refraction distorts it. When it is this irregular image that is utilised by the subject in order to form the vision, a consequent hallucination may still be produced, it is true, but the phenomenon presents much less interest. In the second process of which we have spoken, a real hallucination is, on the contrary, immediately formed. Setting aside the reflected pictures, the subject's sight is fatigued and disturbed by the brilliant surface; then this surface combined with the dark background seen transparently forms a cloud; then as the mind is concentrated on this fixed point, not presenting any regular outline, the hallucination is produced.

With regard to the value of these hallucinations, it must be recognised that most frequently they are solely composed of reminiscences — that is to say, of images drawn from the visual memory of the subject. Thus it is that a subject will recognise a site, a monument, an object which he may have seen in his travels, or else a landscape, a house, the aspect of which was familiar to him in his childhood; or it may be a picture or an engraving which had caught his eye a short time previously.

All this, we see, is quite insignificant, and is not worth stopping to consider. The phenomenon only becomes interesting when a telepathic hallucination occurs—that is to say, one which originates in a mental transmission, coming from a person present or absent, and especially when this hallucination is due to a faculty of lucidity which is revealed in the subject. These cases are rare, it must be admitted, but they sometimes present themselves; that is not less incontestable, and they suffice to draw our attention to this class of experiment.

It must not be forgotten that the subject who thus undergoes an hallucination, and especially a telepathic hallucination, is necessarily brought into a certain state of hypnosis, usually light, it is true. But the fact must not be lost sight of that many of these subjects thus placed before a brilliant object, on which they fix their gaze attentively for some time, are disposed to fall into a more profound hypnotic state, which is caused by fascination. Some subjects are very quickly fascinated and go to sleep very shortly after they are placed in front of the crystal. Others only reach the hypnotic sleep after having already undergone one or more hallucinations.

The experimenter ought therefore to constantly watch the condition of the subject; he should know how to direct the fascination and the hypnotic condition, if it is produced, in the most useful manner, and then to take all the usual precautions in bringing the subject back to the normal state when the experiment is terminated.

This precaution taken he must also know how to

direct the experiment, in order to give it the importance it ought to have, and to draw from it what is of value. For that he must, after placing the subject before the brilliant object, simply indicate to him what he ought to do, and then leave him motionless and silent, taking care that nothing occurs to disturb him. He must refrain from questioning him at this time, and not allow any one present to speak to him.

The subject ought to describe very minutely all that he observes, first before the formation of the pictures, and then successively their progressive development and their slightest details. At this time only, and if he finds that the subject gives a too summary description, the experimenter may question him, and ask him to specify certain points. Then, as the pictures appear and disappear, he will carefully note, without adding or taking away anything, all that the subject may say.

The experiment ended, the experimenter should question the subject in a methodical manner on the different visions he has seen. First he ought to inquire whether the objects seen and described by the subject had been seen by him shortly before the experiment, and if they were present to his memory at the time. But the pictures may also refer to more distant recollections, to his impressions of childhood. The subject may not think in any way of these things at the time of the experiment, but the sight of the objects may immediately recall the remembrance. There is in that case an evocation of recollections existing in the sub-consciousness, and this in itself is interesting.

There may also exist certain dissimilarities between the real object the subject has remembered and the picture of his vision. However, the similarity is sufficient for him not to have any doubt that the picture is certainly that of the object present in his memory, but a play of the imagination has superposed several recollections and made an incorrect picture.

Again, the subject may not be at all conscious that

the object which was seen by him in the vision had been previously known to him.

In this case, the subject must be given time to collect his thoughts, and assisted in searching his memory and in noting also the doubts and uncertainties that may come from his sub-consciousness.

Finally, if it seems proved that the object of vision is not in the recollections of the subject, all those present must be questioned in turn, care being taken to follow exactly the same method. If there is any connection between the visions of the subject and the pictures which are in the memory of one of the sitters, it ought to be carefully noted whether these pictures were actually present in his thoughts; or if the recollection had been immediately awakened by the description given by the subject; or if he had been compelled to dig and search into old memories to find the partly effaced traces.

But if we do not find either in the memory of the subject or in that of those present anything in connection with the visions obtained, we must specify and preserve with the greatest care the exact description. In this case, again, the subject and witnesses should be again questioned several days afterwards and with the notes taken during the experiment. It will sometimes happen, in fact, that only after a certain time is a recollection found that exactly fits in with the description given by the subject. I have also known a subject recognise several days after the experiment, in a shop, a picture of which he had seen the vision in the crystal. He did not at all remember having seen this picture previously, but he had passed the same shop several times and the picture might have caught his eye unconsciously.

After having thus rigorously eliminated the most simple phenomena of conscious or sub-conscious memory, if we are led to think that the subject has really had a telepathic hallucination, we must turn our researches and inquiry towards the object or the place of the vision.

Here, again, three cases present themselves; if the picture seen in the crystal only represents an inanimate

scene, we must confine ourselves to verifying the greater
or less correctness of the picture or the scene represented.
If we find some divergence between the objects and the
description which has been given, we must find out whether
this description does not correspond more exactly with a
previous condition of the places described. If the picture
seen in the crystal represented an animated scene or an
event, beside the question of exactitude which will be the
subject of investigation as in the preceding case, there is
the question of time, which may very considerably affect
the importance of the vision. If the fact has happened
exactly at the time when the vision took place, we may
regard it in the same manner as an inanimate picture and
its authenticity will be verified in exactly the same way,
without giving rise to any other special observation. In
the contrary case, the observers will have to take a completely different line of conduct, according as the vision
is connected with a past or a future event.

If the event is past, it should be noted whether it is
recent or long past, and particularly if it could in any way
whatever come to the knowledge either of the medium
himself or of any person present at the experiment.

We may then, while admitting the possibility of other
explanations, interpret it, in the first case, as a phenomenon due to the sub-consciousness of the subject; in
the second case, as a transmission of thought, which
may itself be complicated also by an action of the sub-
consciousness.

If, in the case of a past event, it can be thoroughly
proved that it was not normally known either to the
subject or to any one present at the vision, we must try
to find out what connection there has been between
the subject and the various persons who took part in
the scene described; also, if it is possible, we should
find out whether one of the actors in this scene, at the
moment when it occurred, thought of the subject or
experienced a more or less intense feeling with regard
to him (telepathy).

If the scene perceived in the crystal has not yet taken

place, but is to occur later, this can be known either by
indications given by the subject, or by the very circumstances described.   Two cases can again be presented
here; either the subject indicates in one way or another
the time when the event seen ought to take place; or
he may simply describe what he sees, without assigning
any time for its realisation.   In both cases we carefully
record in writing, word for word, all the details given
by the subject.   Of this account two or three copies
ought to be made immediately, and signed by every one
present at the experiment.   Each of these copies, signed
and sealed in a special manner, should be handed to a person who will give a receipt bearing the date of the deposit.
Then, all the persons who have been present at the experiment, including the subject, should pledge themselves, as
far as possible, to preserve silence on what has been revealed
to them by the vision, and particularly not to say anything about it to persons who take part in the event
forecasted by the subject; all this for the purpose of avoiding suggestions which might arise.   The subsequent procedure will vary according as the date of the event is
fixed, or remains indefinite.   In the first case, we endeavour to enable some experimenters, and preferably those
who have been present at the experiment, to be present
at the realisation of the vision, in order that they may
note the details with scientific exactitude.

In the second case, everything possible should be done
in order to secure as rigorous a verification as possible when
the event occurs.   After this has been done, the official
report of the experiment should be opened in the presence
of those who were present at the vision, and of those who
were witnesses of its realisation.

As we have just seen, in the experiments of visions in
the crystal, we succeed sometimes in obtaining real phenomena of lucidity; but it must be remembered that this is
rare.   The phenomena of somnambulistic lucidity present
similar results, but the progress of the experiment is
absolutely different.

Hypnotic lucidity is only observed in the somnam-

bulistic state, and only in the third degree of somnambulism, or again in the active mediumistic condition—that
is to say, in all cases, in a deep hypnotic condition. Most
frequently it is in the somnambulistic state that we meet
with this phenomenon, so that it is commonly called
somnambulistic lucidity.

It results from this, that to experiment with lucidity
we must first of all have a subject capable of reaching the
third degree of somnambulism. Such subjects are not
frequently met with, and besides, all subjects who can be
put into a state of deep somnambulism are not lucid.

Lucidity is a special faculty, personal to the subject;
but if this faculty cannot be given to a subject who does
not possess it, it frequently happens that a really lucid
subject shows this faculty at first only in a very feeble
degree, and possesses it, so to speak, in a latent state. An
observer, experienced in psychical studies, will, however,
discover it in him, and will know how to develop it by
practice based on methodical and scientific training.

It would be absurd to ask a subject at once, even
though he showed the most evident disposition towards
lucidity, to produce immediately the most complete experiments and the most extraordinary phenomena. Nevertheless, that is the mistake into which a number of persons
fall, who have the reputation of being scientific, and who,
up to a certain point, deserve it in one branch of science
or another. But when they come to experiment in
psychical science, they seem to lose all notion of logic;
or rather they bring to psychical science a real hatred,
which arises from the fear of finding something marvellous
which will upset some classical scientific principle; and
by an extraordinary consequence, these enemies of the
marvellous, when experimenting with a psychical phenomenon, treat it as though it were a question of something
supernatural. If we speak to them of a lucid subject, they
demand that he should read to them a Hebrew text of
which he does not know the first word, or that he should
tell them at once, being in Paris, what is happening in
London, Berlin, or Vienna. That is as absurd as wishing

to make a pupil, in whom one has recognised a beautiful voice and some taste for music, play a leading part at the opera without study or preliminary rehearsals.

Let us seek, therefore, to do away with this misapprehension, and to bring good faith and scientific method to bear on all the experiments.

In order to experiment with lucidity the subject must first of all be placed in a deep state of hypnosis. To perform successful experiments in these states of deep sleep, the subject must be thoroughly known. We must not imagine that some general hypnotic knowledge is sufficient, such as would enable us to make use of a suggestion in all its forms and to modify at will the condition of the subject. When we wish to start on delicate experiments we must know the disposition and the personal faculties of the subject we have in hand, which demands a very particular and deep study of each subject. The training must be complete, that is to say, we must from the first accustom the subject to be methodically placed in the hypnotic state most favourable to the development of the faculties we wish to study.

At the same time, we must ascertain what are the processes which best suit his sensibility and temperament; in what manner we must direct and how far we must push the hypnotic state in order to obtain all that we expect of him. We must conduct this training with much prudence and gentleness in order not to repel the subject, and not to lose sight of the fact that auto-suggestions awakened inadvertently or from want of precautions may blunt the faculties of the subject and endanger the success of the experiments.

The subject ought always to be used by the same experimenter, who alone ought to take him in hand; he alone ought to direct the hypnotic training, and later he himself ought also to develop in the subject the faculties on which he wishes to experiment. A subject who is in the hands of several experimenters, however rigorous the method followed, will necessarily experience the influence of several different methods of operation. The hypnotic training might be carried to a certain point, but it would never reach the highest degree that might be expected; with regard to these psychical faculties, not only could they not acquire their full development, but they would risk being damaged. These experiments being made in a state of deep sleep, care must be taken to conform exactly to the method we shall give further on when putting the subject to sleep, directing his sleep, and inducing awakening, so that no discomfort or unpleasant effects may result from the experiments.

We have to consider, in the second place, how we must proceed in order to develop the faculty of lucidity in a subject. We can, without doubt, meet with subjects in whom lucidity has spontaneously developed in such a manner that they at once reach the highest degree, or in whom the faculty has already been exercised in special circumstances; but this rarely happens. Most frequently, it is for the experimenter to direct and develop the tendencies which he discovers in his subject. We need only remember that it is a natural faculty, which must be cultivated in the subject, like any other intellectual or physical faculty—that is to say, it must be exercised at first on the most simple things and gradually be employed for more complex ones.

We must start from the principle, that objects are more easily known than facts, and that the subject will always have much greater facility in dealing with what concerns or is known to the experimenter, because of the latter's presence and the influence he exerts. We must, therefore, first of all exercise the lucidity of the subject on objects belonging to the experimenter and such as are familiar to him, afterwards on actions recently performed by him. We cannot too frequently repeat that great patience must be exercised in these experiments; this rule is not confined to psychical experiments, but as they are less known and less practised than others, the majority of experimenters are led to imitate young pupils, who when they have scarcely entered the laboratory, think that they can succeed in all they undertake. Yet great patience

2 P

and exactitude in manipulation are needed in order to succeed with delicate experiments in chemistry, physics, or microbe culture, and we cannot reasonably accord less to a much more complex science like experimental psychology.

We must not, therefore, be afraid to repeat the same experiments, until they have become absolutely familiar to the subject, and he carries them out without difficulty.

We have now to examine the third question: How the experiments must be carried on. We have already seen how an observer ought to set about experimenting for himself; we have now to see how an experiment is to be conducted in order to show it to other people, who, most frequently, are not accustomed to psychical phenomena. We will state, first of all, three general rules, from which the details of the procedure to be followed in the experiments will easily be deduced :—

(1) Only make experiments in the presence of persons of good faith;

(2) Always settle beforehand, and in writing, all the details of the experiment to be performed;

(3) On no pretext allow a spectator to interfere with the experiment, either to alter it, to stop it, or to intervene in any manner whatever, no matter what the result obtained.

To try to make an experiment before persons who have an interest in its non-success, and who will deny through prejudice an evident result, or persons too flippant to follow a scientific experiment seriously, is loss of time.

Apart from this circumstance, it is to the interest both of witnesses and of the experimenters that the result of the experiment shall be clear and well controlled. If it is simply a question of recognising an object brought by a spectator, we must make the subject give some exact details, and have the identity of the object recognised by several witnesses and by the experimenter. If we wish to make a subject read a number, a phrase, or a letter enclosed in an envelope, it is absolutely necessary to avoid all discussion, always idle and ridiculous, of the possibility of opening the envelope. There is a very simple process for preventing this, by means of a thread which is passed through the envelope at four different points, the knot being imbedded in the wax of a seal on the flap. If this sealing is well done, no one can possibly ascertain the contents of the envelope by physical means, without leaving evident traces.

If the experiment refers to a fact which has happened at a distance, all the subject says must be noted very exactly in writing; this account, in duplicate, will be signed by all the witnesses; then the verification of the fact will in the same way be recorded in writing, but by other witnesses who have no knowledge of the report of the experiment.

During the experiment itself, it is for the experimenter to assign to each of the sitters the place he is to occupy, according to the exigencies of the experiment. None of the witnesses should approach the subject, and they must be forbidden to speak a word to him or the experimenter; they must also abstain from all remarks during the experiment.

It will be noticed that we have insisted on details, apparently insignificant; but it must be recognised that when taken into account they will give indisputable value to the observations; further, it is to the interest of science that the largest possible number of experiments should be conducted in a uniform manner. Without doubt, in many cases, it will be absolutely impossible to observe all these conditions, but if they are present in the mind, we can endeavour to come as near to them as possible.

EXTERNALISATION OF SENSIBILITY

The externalisation of sensibility is a phenomenon observed in a deep state of hypnosis. We think that it is in the active mediumistic state alone that it presents itself, but authors are not agreed upon this point; perhaps this is because the active mediumistic state, like the somnambulistic state, presents several different degrees, and consequently has not always been recognised.

The externalisation of sensibility is a rather rare

phenomenon. It is developed spontaneously in certain subjects—that is to say, the subject being placed in the necessary condition of hypnosis, namely, in one of the first phases of the active mediumistic state, we notice not only cutaneous anæsthesia but also the development of sensitive external layers. Most frequently, in these conditions, the phenomenon is not very marked ; it remains more or less vague and, in any case, scarcely amenable to a rigorously controlled experiment.

In order to experiment scientifically on externalisation of sensibility we must transfer the sensibility of the subject to an object; a glass of water lends itself best to the different tests by which we can control the phenomenon.

We therefore place a glass of water between the hands of a subject who has been previously sent to sleep, and make passes from the head and shoulders of the subject down his arms and ending at the glass of water held between his hands. The experiment shows that it is sometimes necessary to continue these passes for some time, five minutes, or even longer. From time to time we must test the cutaneous sensibility of the subject, and it is only when we find absolute anæsthesia that we can proceed with the research on externalised sensibility.

With some subjects, probably even the greater number, it is necessary, in addition to the passes, to give verbal suggestions with the object, first of producing cutaneous sensibility, and then of transferring the sensibility to the object chosen for the experiment. It must not be thought that the suggestions thus made at all diminish the value of the experiment. In fact, suggestions made at that time have only one aim : to bring about the production of the phenomenon. Once the transfer of the sensibility is effected, all precautions will be taken that no new suggestion shall occur. At this moment the entire interest of the experiment consists in the observation of the fact of externalisation of sensibility; the mechanism by which the phenomenon is produced is immaterial, and we have sufficient·means of verification to prove whether the externalisation of sensibility really exists, apart from voluntary or involuntary suggestion, or auto-suggestion.

The subject being thus prepared, precaution must be taken to bandage his eyes. It is necessary to employ a special bandage for this purpose, or rather a mask, which ought to fulfil the following conditions:—

1. To cover the eyes without pressure, and to cover them with very closely woven black cloth folded several times ;

2. To fill up the whole of the hollows between the cheek-bones and the bridge of the nose, fitting the bandage close to the cheeks so that no ray of light can penetrate from below. These conditions can easily be realised. For persons who have some knowledge of hypnotism, the bandage is only an accessory, because we observe at the same time undeniable signs of the subject's hypnotic condition ; but the subject's eyes should not, under any pretext, be bandaged with a handkerchief or napkin, for these bandages sometimes allow the subject to see within a certain range and lead to useless and fruitless discussions; it would be better in that case to work without any bandage and to take other precautions.

We can then commence the experiment, and we must not lose sight of what is the end and import of it, namely, to demonstrate that the sensibility of the subject is projected and transferred to the water in the glass, so that if any action whatever is exercised on the water in this glass, the subject will experience sensations corresponding to that action. We know very well that if we suggest to a subject in a somnambulistic state any sensation whatever, he will experience this sensation; we can suggest a pain to a subject, as we can take it away by suggestion; we can suggest to a subject a sensation of pricking or burning, of heat or cold, but this is not the question here. We insist on this point, because, on the one hand, certain experimenters fall into the mistake of making suggestions; and, on the other hand, suggestion, voluntary or involuntary, is the great objection raised by those who wish to deny the reality of the phenomenon of externalisation of sensibility.

In order to conduct the experiment properly, we must therefore avoid all direct suggestion; for this purpose the witnesses of the experiment require to be silent and motionless, and they should direct their attention solely to what is happening under their eyes. The experimenter should himself assign to the witnesses the places they should occupy, in such a way that they can easily see the slightest movements of the subject, as well as all that is done by the operator; but he must not place them too near the subject or allow them to approach him, because here, as in all experiments made in hypnotic states, the subject is affected by influences from another person near to him, which may alter his condition and prejudice the success of the experiments.

The operator will himself make the experiments in perfect silence. It is quite easy to recognise the cutaneous anæsthesia of the subject by pinching or pricking the skin with a needle at different parts. He must not forget that certain subjects have, at all times, even in a waking state, more or less extensive zones of cutaneous anæsthesia. The sensibility of the subject must therefore be tested at several different parts of the body, some distance apart, if the cutaneous sensibility has not been tested before the experiment, and the parts where it is intact ascertained. During all these tests, as during those which follow, the subject's face must be attentively watched, because it is well to notice the exact moment when the sensation is perceived, as shown by a slight contraction of the features, before even he has time to report it by speech.

In addition to suggestion, which might have arisen from the experimenter or those present having thoughtlessly mentioned beforehand in the subject's presence the test which is being applied, there may also be produced in the subject auto-suggestions which will cause him to experience sensations similar to those that are the subject of the experiment but without externalisation of the sensibility really taking place.

In order to avoid these auto-suggestions, care must be taken not to speak before the subject, whether in the waking or sleeping state, of the nature of the experiments to be performed. His consent must simply have been obtained to an experiment while he is in a hypnotic state, and the subject, who should have entire confidence in the operator, should not ask for further explanations, knowing that they might be detrimental to success.

We have supposed in this experiment that the sensibility of the subject has been transferred to the glass of water, consequently the principal and most interesting point of the experiment is to ascertain if the phenomenon has occurred. In order to do this the point of the pin is slightly pressed into the surface of the liquid; if the externalisation really exists the face of the subject will immediately show signs of pain, sometimes also a shrinking movement of the arms is noticed, a spontaneous and natural movement when pricking is felt. Sometimes the subject will speak of this sensation, either of his own accord or in answer to questions.

If the phenomenon occurs thus, it may be objected that this was simulation or auto-suggestion on the part of the subject. We shall see by what experiments we can answer these objections.

The objection of simulation can only be made in two cases :—

1. If we have neglected to make an accurate diagnosis of the hypnotic state in which the subject is, and to verify, before the witnesses of the experiment, the undeniable signs, impossible to imitate, which are characteristic of this state;

2. If we have to do with persons who have not the most elementary notions of hypnology.

It lies with us to avoid the first case, and it is an elementary duty for the experimenter to make a diagnosis of the subject's condition. On the second supposition we would advise those who wish to take part in the supervision of psychical phenomena to begin by learning hypnology.

The objection of simulation has therefore no value, and, moreover, we shall see that it would also be reduced to nothing by the same means of control by which auto-suggestion is eliminated.

The subject holds the glass of water between his hands, and we find that he experiences a pricking sensation when we press the point of the needle into the water.

As we know that there is often considerable hyper-æsthesia of the organs of sense in subjects in a hypnotic state, it might be said that the subject hears the movement of the hand which is raised and lowered in order to press the needle into the water. There is a very simple means of ascertaining this.

Exactly the same gesture is made, with the pin in the hand, around the glass of water; if it is noticed that the subject expresses the sensation only when we prick the water with the pin, we can no longer say that there is an auto-suggestion due to hearing the movement, because the latter is exactly the same in both cases. But it may still be said that the subject saw the movement of the hand through the eyelids and the bandages.

We will reply to this objection in the following manner. After the subject has submitted to several tests with the glass of water, if the sensibility is thoroughly projected, it is no longer necessary for him to hold the glass of water in his hands; we can take it from him, another person can hold it, we can place it on a table, and if we do not remove it too far the phenomenon is produced in the same manner. We then place the glass of water on the table behind the chair in which the subject is seated: the operator again makes the gesture of pricking, either around the glass or over it, but without touching the surface of the water, and from time to time by the same movement he will bring the needle down to the water.

If, in these conditions, the subject again expresses sensation when the needle touches the water and absolutely nothing in the other cases, it must necessarily be concluded that there is a connection between the contact of the water with the pin and the sensation perceived. It is absolutely impossible for the subject to see, by this arrangement, what happens behind him; it is also impossible for him to hear a difference in movement when the hand holding the pin is raised or lowered around the glass, whether the pin penetrates the water or whether it remains clear of the surface.

Lastly, we have to examine the objection which consists of explaining the phenomenon of the externalisation of sensibility by mental suggestion. This objection seems, it is true, capable of explaining all the phenomena and to be a very embarrassing one. Nevertheless, it is not impossible for us to reply to it. This objection can only come from persons having some knowledge of hypnotic and psychical phenomena, and it is much easier to reply by some decisive facts to persons who know something than to the ignorant. When the experimenter pricks the water with a pin, either in front of or behind the subject, there is the possibility of an involuntary mental suggestion on his part; if the same action is performed by an assistant or by some person, other than the experimenter himself, there is still possibility of a mental transmission, because the subject may receive a suggestion from any person who has knowledge of the action which should influence him.

We have two methods of avoiding this objection. The first consists in using a small automatic apparatus to press the pin into the water; this sets in motion a lever which supports the point, without either the experimenter or any one present being able to know the time when the contact takes place. The experimenter meanwhile confines himself to recording with the same apparatus the precise moment when the subject experiences the sensation. It is sufficient, then, to ascertain if the two events have taken place simultaneously.

We can again use the phenomenon of delay of sensation in the subject, which occurs when this sensation comes to him through several organisms. For this purpose we form a chain of three, four, or five persons; the one who is at the extreme end holds the subject's hand, the person at the other extremity holds the glass of water. The persons who form the chain do not see either when the needle is plunged into the water or the time when the subject experiences the sensation. There is then evidenced a delay in the sensation, proportionate to the number of persons who form the chain. If mental suggestion had been the cause of the phenomenon, it would have been as rapid in this case as when the subject held the glass of water himself.

When we have made all these experiments with the precautions indicated, we have demonstrated the reality of the phenomenon of projection of sensibility. We can then vary the experiment in different ways: by trying, for example, if the sensibility at different points of the subject's body is externalised in the same degree, or by transferring this sensibility to other persons or to different objects, and noting the substances which appear most favourable to the phenomenon. All this can be done by conforming in a general way to the same rules.

It now remains for us to see what special precautions are to be taken in order that the subject may not suffer any pain or annoyance from the experiments to which he submits.

The hypnotic state demands particular precautions which will be the object of special study in the following chapter; we will not, therefore, now speak of the general rules which are common to all deep hypnotic states.

We do not know exactly what happens in the sensations experienced by the subject in these conditions, but we ought to act as though the sensations which he experiences by the intermediary of the sensitised object were as strong as those which he would have experienced if the action had been performed directly on him, and as though this projected sensibility could produce the same general reactions as the direct excitation of his organism. We should therefore never make too violent tests; this is also why the experimenter should always make the tests himself. Among those present at an experiment there are always some sceptics, and sceptics so illogical that they always wish to force the experiment under the pretext of seeing what the subject will do. Prudence is therefore indispensable, particularly when we wish to make some fresh test.

In addition to violent tests which we ought to avoid, there are also some which have a special action on the subject, because of the hypnotic state in which he is. We know, in fact, that certain actions, insignificant in the case of a subject in a waking state, cause violent reactions in a hypnotised subject. In the present case experience has shown that if, after having transferred the sensibility of a subject into a vase containing a saturated saline solution, we cause the liquid to crystallise, the subject may be thrown into a cataleptic state. We therefore take special precautions, in view of the possibility of this phenomenon, when we make experiments of this character.

When we have transferred the sensibility of a subject into a glass of water, if we absorb a portion of this water by a sponge, the experiment demonstrates that the subject seems to experience very pronounced suffering. This experiment must therefore always be conducted with many precautions : care must be taken, as long as it continues, to watch the subject carefully, and it is expedient not to prolong it unduly. Further, observation leads us to believe that abrupt movements or transformations in the liquid to which the sensibility of the subject has been transferred, such as the upsetting of the liquid, certain chemical combinations, boiling, &c., may produce in the subject violent sensations or more or less dangerous crises. The conclusion, therefore, is that much prudence should be brought to bear on this class of experiment.

After the experiments, danger may consist either in certain objects remaining in relation with the sensibility of the subject, who in consequence may be exposed to injuries; or it may be that the subject has retained in himself, independently of the objects, disturbances of his normal sensibility. To avoid these two drawbacks it is necessary, first of all, after each part of the experiment, to liberate the sensibility of the subject from every object which may have received it; and, in the second place, before ending the séance to bring the subject completely back to his normal sensibility. These two results are surely and easily obtained by means of suggestions, and it is well to add the suggestion that he should forget all the modifications of sensibility which have been produced during sleep.

EXTERNALISATION OF FORCE

We now come to some rarer psychical phenomena, the conditions of which are yet little known, and consequently difficult to obtain. These experiments must be divided into two groups which have absolutely different aims: the first has for its object simply to demonstrate the existence of psychic force; others endeavour to determine what are the different phenomena that this force can produce, and what are the conditions in which these phenomena can take place with the greatest intensity.

The experiments of the first category are very easily carried out; they are simple, but they are also very limited. In order to demonstrate the existence of psychic force, we simply need a special instrument. In order that these experiments may be of value it is necessary that this instrument should contain any magnetised needle or induction bobbin of solenoid of any description, or any part that can receive an electric current, or that contains in itself a current which can be modified by the electricity which is developed in all living organism; and those conditions are realised in the sthenometer. When we have thus an instrument which cannot be influenced by electricity, light, or heat, we have only to guard it from the air and from any tremors which might be communicated to it.

For experiments of the second category, the difficulties are much greater. Here we have to investigate the phenomena that can be produced through certain subjects endowed with absolutely abnormal faculties, either a psychical force of very considerable intensity, or simply a very great facility in projecting and directing these forces.

The conditions of these phenomena are all the more difficult to define, because if they have been sometimes methodically observed, in the greater number of cases, they have presented themselves in a fortuitous manner and amid surroundings unfavourable for scientific observation. We are therefore reduced to act in an almost empirical manner, and to reproduce as exactly as possible the conditions in which these phenomena have been obtained.

We know, in the first place, that the presence of a medium is necessary—that is to say, from our point of view, a subject capable of being placed in an active mediumistic state. Sometimes, it is true, experiments are undertaken without making choice of a medium beforehand. If we obtain some results under these conditions, it is really because there is a medium among the experimenters.

It is necessary that there should not be a very large number of experimenters; four or five persons seem to give the best conditions; we may go up to eight as the maximum. This maximum figure ought to include all persons present at the experiment, whether they take direct part in it or remain as simple spectators. It is evident that it is necessary to eliminate rigorously every person who does not wish to undertake a serious scientific observation of the phenomena, or who refuses to submit to the conditions of the experiment, such persons, for example, as only regard them as a pastime and who would be disposed to turn them into a joke.

The experimenters ought, as far as possible, to be in a sparsely furnished, closed room, moderately illuminated. They must then place themselves round a small table, about which they can all sit; and they should either place their hands open and flat on the edge of the table, or form a chain, by holding each other's hands without touching the table in the midst of them.

It may be asked why we need this table, which must make the experiment look like a farce or anything rather than a scientific experiment.

We reply that we confine ourselves to describing the arrangement in which the phenomena are most frequently manifested; that, wishing to reproduce these phenomena, we cannot do better, in order to have every chance of success, than to place ourselves in the same conditions; that it is precisely because we place ourselves above all prejudices, and accept indifferently all objects, whatever they may be, which are presented to us as favourable to the end in view, that, up to the present, we have found nothing better than the table, but we should be ready to substitute any other object which could be proved to have contributed to the manifestation of the phenomena. Moreover, since the majority of mediums, whom we are compelled to take as they are, usually make use of a table, the table may be useful to fix and maintain their attention, and thus to put them in the frame of mind most favourable to the manifestation of their faculties. Although the phenomena are produced around the medium, most frequently in an unexpected manner, and by means of all sorts of objects, it very frequently happens that it is by means of the table that the first effects of the psychic force are manifested.

These reasons are sufficient, until we are more certain as to the laws which govern these phenomena, to cause us to adopt the rules previously followed by other experimenters. A part of the psychic force employed for the manifestation of the phenomena seems to emanate from the whole of the experimenters—this force seems to require to be, as far as possible, equalised, and that is why we advise, in the arrangement of the experimenters, that the two sexes should be alternated, or rather the sensitives alternated with those who are less sensitive.

It may happen that the medium, when he is known, gives some indications as to the arrangements to be made for the experiment, or asks for some alteration in the arrangements already made. We should, as far as possible, accede to such indications, provided that they do not interfere with scientific observation and place no obstacle in the way of the control.

The séance ought to be directed by a person chosen as having the greatest authority and competence in this class of experiment. This director should have entire charge of the order and nature of the experiments, as well as of all the methods of control to be employed; in fact, it is on the certainty and rigour of his scientific observation that the value of the results which may be obtained will depend. The other experimenters ought then to submit themselves to all the arrangements judged to be useful by the director, whose authority should extend to the slightest details of the experiment.

It is well as a rule to demand silence during the experiments; however, as the period of waiting may be rather long, we can, in certain cases, tolerate a serious and calm conversation among the experimenters, but they should particularly avoid prejudging or discussing in any way the phenomena which they are expecting; the conversation should therefore turn on some other subject. Moreover, in this class of experiments, patience is absolutely indispensable in the experimenters, the phenomena sometimes being very long in making their appearance; therefore, the director of the séance should sustain the attention of the experimenters and encourage them to wait patiently.

It may be that we are working with a medium chosen beforehand; or that a group of experimenters has simply met in the hope of finding among them the necessary medium.

In this latter case, the director of the séance, by attentively observing all the experimenters, should look out for symptoms which may indicate that one of them is a medium.

When he has discovered him, he will endeavour to study him, without however making him known to the other experimenters, because it is often useful, at least at the commencement, that the subject himself should be ignorant as long as possible of the influence he exercises on the phenomena obtained.

It is better only to make use of one medium at a time, in order not to mix or impede the phenomena which take place or the forces which are brought into play. Also when we discover several mediums among the experimenters, it is necessary to make some pretext for dividing the experiments, and to admit to each séance only one medium at a time.

When we have discovered the subject who is to act as medium, it is not necessary to persist in seeking to obtain a particular class of phenomena. We must at first ask nothing from him, and leave him alone, contenting ourselves with observing and waiting for the phenomena which may be manifested. If the subject shows a tendency to lend himself to certain classes of experiments, or the desire to see certain manifestations produced, we must not oppose him, because, most frequently, he will thus show the special faculties which he possesses.

After the discovery of the medium, the most important thing to be ascertained is the class of phenomena which he is capable of producing. Once the capacities of the subject are established, we can indirectly suggest the various phenomena of this class that we may desire to observe.

We must endeavour before all else to obtain clear and precise facts; then, by the supervision to which we submit these phenomena, we can assure ourselves that they are really produced by a psychic force; that is to say, by a force other than the known physical forces—in short, that they cannot be attributed to any trickery on the part of the subject.

In a previous chapter we have studied the different classes of fraud on the part of subjects with which we may have to deal, we have therefore no need to return to this point here. We need only repeat that if we believe we perceive any trickery we should not be in a hurry to unmask it, and at once to confound the subject, as a less experienced observer would do who was ignorant of what a subject is and what psychical phenomena are. We must only watch the medium more carefully, and, if we see that the fraud is voluntary and constant, abandon this subject as being unable to serve for serious experiments and seek for another; if, on the contrary, we see that the fraud is involuntary and only passing, there is no reason to part with the medium; it is sufficient to bring more attention and patience to bear on the observation of the phenomena. It is in this case particularly that we shall find great advantage in the use of registration apparatus and the most delicate instruments, with which we shall easily distinguish doubtful results from those which may be conclusive.

Finally, we must know how to limit very definitely the compass of the experiments which we undertake. In the present condition of our knowledge what we have to establish scientifically is :—

(1) If the medium is able, in certain conditions, to produce authentic psychical phenomena.

(2) What are the phenomena which this medium can produce?

(3) What are the conditions in which we can observe these phenomena?

By conducting experiments in this way, and confining ourselves to drawing these conclusions, they will have an indisputable scientific value, and will be of unquestionable utility in advancing our knowledge.

CHAPTER XL

METHOD OF EXPERIMENTING

General Rules

We have studied up to now the different categories into which we can divide all psychical phenomena; it would therefore appear that our task is at an end. It seems to us, however, that our study of the method of experimenting on psychical phenomena ought to be completed by a final chapter. In fact, we have found that some experimenters are hindered in their studies by the vague fear of what would happen to their subjects from experiments of this class. On the other hand, many persons who would be very good subjects, mediums even, are afraid to lend themselves to these experiments, under the pretext that they are often dangerous, or, at least, unfavourable to their health.

We have now to examine what foundation there is for these fears, and to study the real or even imaginary dangers which are feared by the subjects and experimenters.

The best things, if badly done, present certain disadvantages. There is not an exercise, recommended on the score of health, such as gymnastics, cycling, or any other, in which we may not hurt ourselves if we go to work imprudently or without experience. Even a simple bath, however necessary to health, may make us ill if we do not observe the well-known rules with regard to temperature, digestion, &c.

It is the same with hypnotism : badly done, it presents disadvantages and dangers ; well done, it is much less dangerous than a simple ride in a carriage or on a bicycle.

We consider hypnotism here because we believe that

the mediumistic states, and, in general, all the states in which psychical phenomena are produced, are varieties of the hypnotic conditions, and to those who dispute this opinion we say that, at least from the psychological point of view, they can be compared with them.

We will divide our subject methodically, and examine in order:—

(1) The immediate dangers to the subject which may result from hypnotic sleep.

(2) The more remote dangers to the subject, resulting from hypnotic sleep.

(3) The dangers that are not due to hypnotic sleep itself, but to suggestions.

(4) The dangers which may exist the hypnotiser.

(5) The rules to be followed in order to avoid all the inconveniences or dangers which may exist.

Immediate dangers to the subject resulting from hypnotic sleep.—It is evidently only a question here as to hypnotic states which are so deep that the subject is put to sleep; because in the lighter states, such as waking somnambulism, as also in the case of suggestions made in the waking state, there is no real cause for apprehension on the part of either subjects or experimenters.

The first objection often made by subjects whom it is proposed to send to sleep is: "I fear that I shall not be able to wake up again." Whence comes this fear? Does it rest on any serious foundation? It is not the sleep in itself that provokes this fear, because no one ever thinks of not going to sleep at night for fear of not waking up the next morning. It therefore arises from the fact that the hypnotic sleep is an induced sleep, and the general public assimilate this provoked sleep with another induced sleep, but a very different one, of which they have also heard, namely, that produced by chloroform.

The chloroform sleep is dangerous, and a large number of accidents have been known to arise from this anæsthetic agent. The chloroform sleep, like that due to opium, morphia, chloral, &c., is nothing else than a real poisoning. Chloroform acts on the brain, lungs, and heart, and if the action produced on one of these organs is too strong, poisoning supervenes.

It is quite different with hypnotic sleep. Hypnotism introduces no poison into the organism, and cannot therefore exert an injurious action on any organ. Hypnotic sleep, from the physiological point of view, is exactly similar to natural sleep, and is just as little liable to cause any accident. One may die in bed as one may at table, or when out walking, or in a chair; but one always dies from an illness or an accident; never from sleep, whether natural or hypnotic.

It is sometimes also feared that hypnotic experiments may produce convulsive attacks. It is certain that a large number of subjects in whom hypnotic phenomena are easily obtained are hysterical persons. Those subjects who are accustomed to have nervous attacks under all circumstances and at all times of the day may also have them during hypnotic experiments. Further, as most frequently these attacks come on under the influence of emotion or vexation, if hypnotic experiments excite or disturb them, they may bring on nervous attacks. But it must not be forgotten that the best remedy for convulsive fits is the hypnotic treatment. Hypnosis is the true process for the cure of the nervous attacks, because it is the only treatment by which we can fight them in their origin and in their causes. It is also the best means by which we can master and stop the convulsions themselves at the moment of their appearance.

There is therefore no occasion to fear that any nervous convulsions whatever are produced by hypnotic experiments. If the subject has a disposition to such convulsions, not only can they be arrested, but they can be cured by this very means of hypnosis, provided one knows how to use it.

Dreams or attacks of delirium may be produced during hypnotic sleep, sometimes accompanied by hallucinations, in which the subject sees persons who may be either sympathetic or disagreeable to him; sometimes a vague remembrance of these hallucinations persists after the waking. It will be sufficient for us to say that this delirium and these hallucinations ought to be regarded as of the same nature as nervous fits, of which they are only a modification. The hypnotiser ought therefore to stop them and drive them away by the same procedure by which he combats the convulsive attacks.

Can hypnotic sleep be prolonged beyond the will of the hypnotiser, and may he experience any difficulty in waking up the sleeping subject? This is the fear expressed by some experimenters, but it is more chimerical than real. If the sleep thus prolonged were a lethargic or cataleptic fit, it would come within the category of nervous convulsions of which we have previously spoken, and it can and ought to be efficaciously fought by hypnotic suggestion. If not, the hypnotiser would have to be one of small experience and forgetful of the most elementary rules of hypnotic practice, if he experienced any difficulty in awaking his subject; and, even in this case, if an experienced hypnotiser were present, he would always be able to restore the subject to his normal state.

It is also advisable, in order to reassure certain people who fabricate imaginary dangers, to remind them of the laws which govern the memory in the hypnotic states. The fundamental law is this: in the waking state the remembrance of what has passed in the deep hypnotic states does not exist; but in the deep hypnotic states the subject preserves the memory of what has happened both in the waking and in the corresponding hypnotic conditions. We have not to concern ourselves here with the special laws which govern the memory in the different hypnotic states as related one to another; the general law is sufficient to show that hypnosis does not in any way enfeeble the normal memory. The hypnotic condition passes like a dream, or even like a beneficial sleep, without exercising the slightest injurious action on any of the intellectual faculties.

Some subjects, after having been hypnotised, complain of fatigue or of pain in the head. This may arise from several causes: most frequently it is because the subject

himself has resisted the sleep; he has therefore had a
struggle with the hypnotiser, and it is this effort that has
made him tired and caused him to suffer. In other cases it
is because the hypnotiser has tried to go too fast, and has
not exercised sufficient gentleness and moderation in sending the subject to sleep; he can avoid this inconvenience
by following a little more patiently the rules we shall give
further on. Nor should the operator forget that the resistance of the subject is sometimes unconscious; it is for him
to recognise this and to employ indirect means to overcome it without causing the subject to become needlessly
fatigued.

Dangers to the Subject, subsequent to Hypnotic Sleep

We have now to examine the possible dangers to the
subject, after the hypnotic sleep is over.

We find here again the same prejudice, which causes
the fear that the employment of hypnotism may bring on
convulsive fits or lead to an aggravation of the hysteria. It
is indeed difficult to understand how such a fear can arise in
the mind of any one who sees the state of calm, comfort,
and peaceable repose peculiar to hypnotic sleep. But
it must also be remarked that the majority of those who
express this fear have never seen people seriously hypnotised, and are quite ignorant as to what scientific hypnotism
is. Therefore, the whole of their reasoning is only based
on a fantastic idea of hypnotism due to their imagination.

We must repeat here what we have already said
before: it is certain that many hypnotic experiments are
made with hysterical subjects. Such persons are often
subject to convulsions, which seize them unexpectedly
under the influence of many different causes—annoyances,
fears, digestive trouble, &c. It may therefore happen
with these sufferers that a convulsive fit may come on at
a longer or shorter period after a hypnotic séance; but
that is no reason for saying that this fit is the result of
being hypnotised, any more than if it occurred after a
walk it would be correct to ascribe it to the exercise.

We have admitted that these attacks, brought on by an accidental cause, quite apart from hypnotism, may by chance happen after a hypnotic séance; well, even that is going too far, and we must hasten to add a correction. This coincidence can, in fact, only occur after the first séances, and if the hypnotiser has not yet secured sufficient influence over his subject. In fact, if the hypnotising is properly carried out, whether by a doctor or by an experienced hypnotiser, a few séances will be sufficient to stop these fits and prevent their return. For hypnotism and hypnotic suggestion are the best treatment for neurotic trouble and for the nervous or convulsive attacks which arise from them.

It is superfluous, after what has been said, to add anything on the subject of the fear, sometimes expressed, that hypnosis will aggravate hysteria, since the hypnotic treatment is the rational one for hysteria. Hypnotism employed in an experimental manner does not prevent the making of suggestions appropriate to the treatment of the malady; it can therefore only be useful to the subject in every way, and never injurious.

There may sometimes occur after hypnotic sleep hallucinations which arise from two different causes. Either this hallucination is only the return and the reproduction of a hallucination which occurred during the hypnotic sleep; or else it is the result of fortuitous or involuntary suggestion made during hypnosis. In either case it is difficult to admit that such hallucinations can have any serious consequences. But we would, and can, avoid even the least discomforts which might result from hypnotic experiments. That is easily done; for hallucinations are produced during the course of hypnotic sleep. We can cause them to vanish immediately by a contrary suggestion; further, we can prevent their future return by a preventive suggestion. In the second place, by keeping a strict watch upon everything that might produce suggestions during hypnosis, we can easily avoid producing them; we must also not forget that accidental suggestions may be made apart from ourselves, whether by witnesses of the experiment or by circumstances that might produce auto-suggestions on the part of the subject, and we shall be able to prevent them by making the subject impervious to them by a positive suggestion.

One of the principal objections which many persons make to hypnotic experiments is that, by thus accustoming the subject to being hypnotised, we may develop in him a sensitiveness to hypnotic influence, so that in the future he may be hypnotised too easily. This question deserves to be considered from two points of view.

The subjects with whom experiments in the deeper states of hypnosis can be successfully carried out, and the only ones with whom we are now concerned, must be classed in two categories : those who are very easily hypnotised, who at once, from the first séances, fall into deep hypnotic states, and are consequently strongly open to suggestion; and those who reach this condition after a certain training. With regard to the first class, we must not ascribe the facility with which they are hypnotised to the séances regularly held, whether experimental or therapeutic, since they possess this sensibility beforehand. Training can only regulate it, limit it, and protect them from the inconveniences to which they might be exposed through it. With regard to the second class, since this sensibility is developed by the hypnotiser himself, it will be very easy for him to direct it properly and to make use of it in order to give the useful and preventive suggestions of which we shall presently speak.

The examination of what might be feared from the development of hypnotic sensibility will indicate at the same time the means for remedying it.

The first thing that might be feared from hypnotic training is that it renders the subject easily hypnotised by any person; this, however, would only be harmful if the subject could be hypnotised at any time against his will. In this case the subject will be afraid of being placed at the mercy of any hypnotiser, and the dangers which may result from this circumstance may be ranged under four heads :—

1. The abuse that the hypnotiser may make of the state of sleep in which the subject is placed to injure him in any way.

2. The suggestions that he may impose on him and which may lead to culpable actions.

3. The simple impulses that he can give to the ideas and actions of the subject, and which are not in accordance with his own wishes and intentions.

4. A certain tendency to accept the will of the hypnotiser, resulting from the habit of receiving suggestions, which place the subject, even in the waking state, in a condition of comparative dependence, and which would be painful to him if the hypnotiser did not completely possess his confidence and sympathy.[1]

The second thing that might be feared from hypnotic training is the spontaneous involuntary sleep, produced by the sight of brilliant objects, lights, flames, metallic articles or crystals.

These attacks of sleep may have two disadvantages :—

(1) If produced unexpectedly in certain circumstances they may cause accidents.

(2) The fit of sleep may be prolonged for some time if an experienced hypnotiser is not at hand to dissipate it.

We shall see that all these objections and fears, in themselves very legitimate, fall to the ground of themselves. In fact, the hypnotiser who trains a subject will not fail to protect him from all harm by two preventive suggestions which he will give him in any case, and particularly in proportion as his hypnotic sensitiveness develops. These suggestions consist :—

1. In forbidding him to allow himself to be hypnotised by any hypnotiser or suggester, except the hypnotiser himself or some other person specially designated by him to do so.

---

[1] All this, however, enters into the question of the relation between hypnotism and jurisprudence, a question which we discussed in detail at the Neurological Congress at Brussels in 1897, and at the International Congress on Hypnotism at Paris in 1900. See the *Proceedings* of each Congress.

This restriction specially refers to the therapeutic use of hypnotism; in fact, the doctor who treats a patient by hypnotism, although it is his duty to protect him from all the dangers of which we speak, ought not to expose him to the deprivation of the benefits of hypnotic treatment, if an accidental circumstance prevents him from applying it himself. This is why he makes the preventive suggestion, reserving to himself the possibility of naming a successor or a substitute.

2. The second preventive suggestion consists in prohibiting him from allowing himself to be sent to sleep by any object that is not directly employed by the hypnotiser himself for the purpose of inducing hypnosis.

Thus, therefore, when this elementary precaution is taken, and it ought always to be taken, whether in therapeutical or in experimental hypnotism, there remain absolutely no dangers or fears which can be raised as objections to the development of hypnotic sensitiveness. I will even go further and say that this proves that hypnotism is essentially useful because it is necessary to the whole class of subjects of which we have been speaking, who exhibit great and spontaneous hypnotic sensitiveness, and no one can know in advance whether he does not come within this category. These subjects who, by their peculiar nature, may be suddenly exposed to the dangers we have enumerated are definitely protected by preventive suggestions made to them in the course of hypnotic séances. If some subjects complain that hypnotism produces in them agitation, nervous excitement, insomnia, these objections will not detain us long, because these phenomena only arise from the fear which the subject has of hypnotism. This fear disappears immediately when the subject has experienced for himself the calm and comfort which result from hypnosis, and, moreover, all these momentary effects will rapidly disappear under appropriate suggestions.

Sometimes subjects complain of pain in the head after séances; these pains are produced when the subject resists the hypnotiser and makes efforts, more or less conscious,

not to go to sleep; the headache is due to the fatigue
arising from this struggle. This result is no longer produced when the subject gives himself up without resistance. Moreover, as soon as a suggestionable condition is
produced, however slight, the hypnotiser should take
advantage of it to drive away the headache and prevent
its recurrence.

Dangers which do not proceed from Sleep but from Suggestion

We have first of all to consider auto-suggestion, which
may be divided into three categories.

The first is that of auto-suggestion, which may be
developed in the subject during sleep, in hypnotic experiments. The hypnotiser can always very easily perceive auto-suggestions of this kind and can easily stop
their development.

Independently of the experiments made by the hypnotiser, auto-suggestion may also be developed in the subject
either from experiences of an accidental sensation, or the
sight of an object which had caught his eyes before the
sleep.

In the third place, auto-suggestions may arise through
the prolongation of an idea existing previous to the sleep
and not confessed to the hypnotiser.

It is not always so easy for the hypnotiser to perceive
the development of these two last kinds of auto-suggestion; and therefore he ought to be warned of their
possibility in order to watch for them and combat them.

Experimental suggestions ought always to be made
directly by the hypnotiser, and to be strictly limited to
the duration of the experiment. The majority ought to
be carried out under the eyes of the experimenter, and
he should be careful to neutralise them completely at the
close of the séance. However, in certain cases, one is led
by the experiments themselves to make suggestions, the
effect of which will be prolonged for some time after the
séance, or even may only be realised some time afterwards.

In the last case, especially, the suggestion ought to be very exactly defined, so that nothing can be added to the suggestion that had been made, and that its effect may completely cease immediately the experiment is at an end.

When a doctor or a psychologist devotes himself to hypnotic experiments, it is his duty to make use of the power that he acquires and the sensibility developed, for the good of the subject. He may therefore often have to make suggestions to the subject, for a purpose which the subject himself will indicate, or even which the hypnotiser may propose, because he can see that they may be useful. In the use of these suggestions, though very good in themselves, there are two dangers to be avoided.

The subject, yielding to impressions or ill-considered desires, is not always sufficiently rational to appreciate for himself the import of the suggestions made to him. In this case, which we may compare with simulation on his part, he deceives the hypnotiser in order to induce him to make a suggestion that is bad for him.

The psychologist ought to know how to find out the real bent of the subject, he should act prudently and without going directly against the subject's wish; he must understand where his mistake lies, and lead him to desire for himself the suggestion that is good for him.

In the second case, the subject is sincere and asks for a suggestion that he really believes will be useful to him. But the psychologist possesses a knowledge and an experience which enable him to see better and further than the subject; he knows all the importance and the consequences of a suggestion, and, as he is invested with the confidence of the subject, he ought to judge for himself if what he asks for is really in his interest.

He must never forget in this case that a suggestion that is very good in itself, at the moment when it is asked for by the subject, may only be so temporarily; the ideas and feelings of the subject may change, the circumstances may no longer be the same; but the subject ought never to have to regret the influence produced by a suggestion that has been made to him, and the possibility must

therefore be foreseen that, although good at first, a suggestion might afterwards become harmful to him. This
is easy to avoid by taking care, in all cases where there
may be the slightest doubt, to make only temporary and
conditional suggestions.

Precautions to be taken for the Hypnotiser

We have so far considered the dangers and harm to
the subject which may arise from hypnotic experiments ;
these are the only ones of which we habitually think. It
is no less true that there may also be dangers to the
experimenter, and we must pass them rapidly in review.

We have seen at the commencement of this chapter
that no serious accident can result from the regular and
scientific use of hypnotism. But, unfortunately, unpleasant coincidences, although quite accidental, may present themselves ; and it is just these coincidences that
very often cause the public to fear the most inoffensive
things and inconsiderately expose themselves to danger.
The majority of people, in fact, do not see very far, and
always think they find the cause of an event in the facts
which accompany it or immediately precede it. Therefore, in the eyes of the public, the hypnotiser is responsible for everything that happens during the hypnosis or
immediately after the experiments, even if these events
have nothing at all to do with hypnotism.

The hypnotiser ought therefore to foresee all that may
happen, and the apparent cause to which any accident may
be ascribed, and the most elementary prudence compels
him, if there is the least danger, to abstain from all
experiment and to refuse to hypnotise. So much for the
accidents which ignorance or prejudice may attribute to
the use of hypnotic sleep.

But there are more real inconveniences and annoyances
with which he may with some reason be reproached.

First of all, there are hallucinations or unpleasant
dreams that may present themselves during hypnosis,
the recollection of which may persist after the awaking ;

even if the recollection of them is effaced, these hallucinations may leave a painful impression, a sadness in the subject's mind. He must avoid that at once by repressing these hallucinations or at least by effacing their effects before awakening the subject.

Another class of hallucinations which may be produced during hypnosis, and against which he must guard, are those by which the subject takes the persons present for persons known to him, and the hypnotiser himself for some one else. In general, these hallucinatory visions cause the subject to see persons who arouse to some extent his sympathy, or more frequently still, his antipathy; so that they are most frequently disagreeable to the subject. These hallucinations must be foreseen and prevented from developing, as soon as the first signs of them are observed; if any occur before they can be prevented, or accidentally, the subject must at least be caused to forget them on waking.

In the third place, there are ideas and feelings, not hallucinatory, which may arise in the subject; whether they relate to other persons or to the hypnotiser himself, they may do harm if special care is not taken. This is a very delicate point, demanding much tact and skill on the part of the hypnotiser. He ought always to direct his subject with gentleness and prudence, and by his general bearing try to gain his confidence, at the same preserving full authority over him.

Lastly, another danger may result for the hypnotiser through the bad faith of the hypnotised subject; whether it be trickery or absolute simulation on the subject's part; or whether, impelled by motives which it is not always easy to unravel, he makes use of the circumstances to attempt blackmail, or simply to throw out calumnies or malevolent insinuations with regard to the hypnotiser. In order to avoid all annoyance the hypnotiser will always have this possibility present in his mind; he will always have an absolute guarantee in all cases by never hypnotising except before witnesses, in case he has the slightest doubt as to his subject.

*Rules that ought to be followed in the Use of Hypnotism
and in Psychical Experiments*

We have so far examined the ill-consequences and
dangers which may accompany experimental hypnotism;
on the one hand, in order to learn how to avoid them, and
on the other, to reply to objections which may be raised.

It now remains for us to give the rules which every
experimenter ought to follow in making use of hypnotism,
by which he will at the same time avoid the ill-consequences which we have set forth and obtain the most
satisfactory results from these experiments.

1. Before undertaking any experiment, he should study
his subject well from the physical and moral point of view.
In order to do this he must himself first of all gain all the
information he can, but never accept the same without
personal verification. By a serious and close examination
he should ascertain precisely his physiological or patho-
logical state. His psychical and moral state will also be
determined by several special tests.

2. He should put his subject to sleep gently, without
abruptness, by following a regular and well-determined
method, but not always the same method; for he should
vary and select the method employed according to: (1)
The subject. (2) His condition. (3) The end which it is
desired to attain.

3. The preliminary examination of the subject will
enable him to foresee the attacks which may come on. At
the same time that he sends him to sleep and throughout
the whole of the experiment he will be careful to prevent
them from developing, by stopping them at the commencement. If necessary, during the first séances, he must
frequently awaken the subject and put him to sleep again
several times over. After a few well-conducted séances,
the danger of the attacks will be entirely obviated, and no
further precaution will be needed.

4. Fatigue must also be prevented by suggestion; not
that the fatigue can be the result of hypnosis, but it may
come through auto-suggestion. He will also dissipate by

suggestion any fatigue that may have existed before the séance, and the auto-suggestion that fatigue may be produced can also be prevented. Agitation, or any discomfort, and the headache which generally occurs as the result of resistance, more or less conscious on the part of the subject, can also be provided against, as well as dreams and insomnia.

5. The séances should not be prolonged at the beginning, but should instead be held frequently. If it is desired to obtain important results in the experiments undertaken, séances must, at first, be held regularly.

6. For the awakening, suggestion accompanied by slow and moderate movements should be employed. When the subject is well trained, the awakening may be rapid, but it should never be sudden; in all cases it will have been prepared for by suggestions previously made to the subject. When the deeper hypnotic states have been reached by several successive stages, the return must be made through the same phases.

7. The experimenter should provide against the very acute suggestionability which may be developed in the subject; for this purpose he must remain sole possessor of the hypnotic power acquired over the subject. But he must provide for the possibility of the subject being compelled, in his own interests, to have recourse to another hypnotiser; he must reserve the power of designating very precisely a substitute who can hypnotise and make suggestions to the subject.

8. He should provide against auto-hypnotism of the subject by circumstances similar to those which accompany the experiment, and particularly against auto-hypnotisms produced by the sight of a brilliant or luminous object; he should also prevent auto-suggestions of any character which might subsequently be developed in the subject.

9. In the majority of cases at the beginning, and particularly with subjects of an hysterical tendency, he should only send them to sleep in the presence of trustworthy witnesses.

10. He should never allow himself to make suggestions outside of those made in view of the end desired by the subject, or in his interests, and should always obtain his consent beforehand to experimental suggestions.

11. He should find out as quickly as possible the special faculties of the subject, and specially cultivate in him the kind of experiment for which he is adapted. He must not forget, in fact, that if he tries to develop different faculties in the subject, this will generally be detrimental to those which he spontaneously possesses.

12. There should be a regular gradation in the most important and complex experiments. When it is noticed that any experiment fatigues the subject, the fatigue should be dispelled by suggestion before waking.

13. Always remember that the hypnotiser is the sole judge of the experiments that he can make with his subject, and the conditions in which they ought to be carried out. Never, therefore, be influenced by the wishes or by the doubts or objections of witnesses, who ought never to be permitted to interfere in the experiments.

14. When experiments are concerned, bring a much greater prudence to bear than in any other use of hypnotism; never depart from the general rules, and only make experiments to which the subject consents.

15. Always act in such a manner that neither the experiments nor the after effects can be injurious or unpleasant to the subject. On the contrary, so manage that the subject always gains some good from hypnotism.

16. Bear in mind the very great influence that the suggestions may have on the life of the subject, on his physical as well as on his moral state.

17. Whatever may be the circumstances, if the subject is suffering, whether or not it is possible to cure him, he can always be relieved. Whatever wishes the subject may express, only consent to suggestions which may be useful to him, and lead him to desire them. So arrange that the subject can only desire real physical and moral good from hypnotism and suggestion, and from all the experiments made upon him.

2 R

If these rules we have formulated are followed precisely we think that no one, however strict he may be, can deny that under these circumstances such experiments are quite legitimate.

We hope, therefore, that in the last part of this study we have dispelled certain prejudices by examining fearlessly and without reticence, all the objections which it seemed to us could possibly be raised.

Investigators may thus go forward with their experiments with greater security, and, at the same time, these experiments, by being carried on with more rigorous and scientific precision, will have a greater influence on the development of our knowledge.

CHAPTER XLI

A GENERAL CONSIDERATION OF PSYCHICAL PHENOMENA

CONCLUSION

LET us now consider the inferences resulting from the facts which we have studied, and what conclusions may be logically drawn from them.

We have been able to recognise the authenticity of a certain number of facts of thought-transmission, of telepathy. These phenomena demonstrate the possibility of a mental communication from one mind to another, outside the usual channels of our normal senses.

Related to this category of phenomena are abnormal dreams, crystal-gazing, clairaudience, typtology, and automatic writing.

Other facts prove to us the perception of certain thoughts or knowledge which previously existed in another mind, even at a comparatively distant period. This phenomenon, which may be explained in various ways, seems to prove that an indestructible impression is left of every thought conceived by the mind.

The act of thinking would, therefore, appear to result in the creation of an immaterial and permanent entity, which survives, not only the act itself, but also the person who has produced it, and which is able to produce indefinite results and to be perceived under certain special conditions.

This permanence of thought and of all mental activity has moral consequences of the greatest importance, which we shall study and expound in another work.

These phenomena of thought-transmission, telepathy and perception of a mental act do not take place in a normal state, but require special conditions, of which one of the principal is a peculiar state in the subjects, which may be compared with hypnotic conditions.

Lucidity, of which we have seen examples of rigorously demonstrated authenticity, proves to us that certain subjects possess a peculiar faculty which enables them to perceive a whole series of mental thought phenomena and of material facts which are outside the range of their normal senses. Further, by means of these perceptions, which are very clear and trustworthy and which are not disturbed by any extraneous influence, these subjects are able to draw accurate deductions, which result from the inflexible logical connection between facts. It therefore follows that if no new element springs up outside the anticipated facts arising from those already in process of completion, the previsions of the subject are realised. The lucidity of subjects is therefore variable, and all the greater when they have been capable of foreseeing the largest number of those elements which may influence the order of events, and of drawing the logical conclusions.

Lucidity not only depends on a special faculty in certain subjects, but is only manifested in them when they are in a particular condition allied to hypnotic states.

Connected with the phenomenon of lucidity are crystal-gazing, clairaudience, automatic writing, typtology, predictions, and somnambulistic visions.

With the externalisation of sensibility we arrive at another order of phenomena. The human organism, by projecting certain of its faculties, seems to have extensions which go beyond the limits of the material body which we perceive by our ordinary senses.

But is this faculty of perceiving sensations at a distance as extraordinary as it appeared at first, so much so indeed that many serious minds for a long time refused to believe it?

Let us remark at the outset that the externalisation of sensibility is only the momentary extension of the normal faculty of touch.

To those who find it too extraordinary that the nervous

papillæ of a sense organ should perceive at a distance the sensation of impression by certain objects, I would remark that they admit without doubt that the sense of smell can be exercised at a distance, that the sense of hearing perceives impressions of sound at a great distance from the object producing it, that the sense of sight perceives visual impressions at a still greater distance.

And if they reply that imperceptible particles of odoriferous bodies come directly in contact with the papillæ of the olfactory nerve, that there are special vibratory waves which directly cause vibrations in the auditory nerve or strike on the retina; I will reply that there is nothing to prove that there do not likewise exist special waves or vibrations which emanate from all bodies, and which are perceptible only to the sense of touch, and only then when it is raised to a degree of special exaltation through a certain hypnotic condition.

This hypothesis is the more admissible because we do not know why certain slow vibrations impress the auditory nerve and not the retina, whilst some more rapid vibrations do not impress the auditory nerve but are perceived by the retina. Do we not also know of some vibrations which give neither sonorous nor luminous impressions, and yet produce chemical effects? There may, therefore, also be vibrations of another order which are not perceived by any other means that we know, but which may be perceived by the sense of touch in certain special conditions.

The externalisation of sensibility leads us by analogy to the externalisation of force, because here again it seems that we observe an extension of certain faculties of the organism beyond the limits of the material body.

The externalisation of force is observed first of all by the action of the organism on the needle of the sthenometer. It is manifested in the phenomena of movement of objects without contact, levitation of objects or of the medium, raps or knocks made at a distance, and hauntings.

All these phenomena are only observed in the presence

of a subject endowed with special faculties—a medium, and when the subject is placed in a condition other than the normal one. Sometimes it is necessary for the medium to receive the co-operation of other persons; he would appear to act as an accumulator of a force which he himself possesses in a high degree, but which he is sometimes able to supplement by drawing from other organisms, and which he condenses and then directs himself.

Not only is this externalised force intimately connected with the medium's presence, but it would appear that the medium directs it himself by means of his corporeal limbs. Thus we see the medium make movements which absolutely synchronise with the displacements of objects which are beyond his reach. This also explains why, if we ask the medium to set an object in motion without contact, we frequently see him advance his hands towards the object as though he would take hold of it.

This movement has frequently led to the suspicion of fraudulent intention on the part of the medium. It is nothing of the sort, it is an automatic movement, perhaps useful or even necessary, because it seems that the medium exerts his externalised force by means of an invisible member, which seems to be the prolongation of his normal limb, or at any rate he directs this force by the movement of his muscles. If the object to be displaced is sufficiently distant to be beyond the reach of the medium's hand, we may allow him freely to stretch out his arm and extend his hand; we shall thus see him put the object in motion, though it was impossible for him to touch it, and we shall find that the displacements of this object coincided exactly with the movements of his arm and hand.

Darkness seems to be a condition which facilitates the development of the externalised force. Many mediums ask for darkness, or at least for a very faint light, and it is noticeable that the greater the development of force required by the phenomenon desired, the more complete must be the darkness. This is also why the majority of mediums demand, in addition to the general darkness of the room, the provision of an even darker cabinet, which is formed by enclosing a corner of the room within curtains.

In this cabinet, and in the still deeper shadow of these curtains, are placed the articles which are to serve for the demonstration of the phenomenon. The medium remains outside the curtain, consequently the greater darkness of the cabinet cannot serve to conceal any fraud, but we nearly always find that the manifestations of the force are more energetic inside the cabinet, where no one is, than outside, and if an object, originally placed in this cabinet, comes out through the influence of the medium's force, we see it move with greater difficulty when it is clear of the curtain and is in a brighter light.

Modifications of matter are phenomena which are manifested through certain mediums, at the same time as the phenomena of motricity.

We cannot refuse to admit the existence of these phenomena which have been witnessed: (1) A large number of times; (2) in conditions of absolute and rigorously scientific control; (3) by men whose authority and scientific competence do not allow us to doubt the veracity of their testimony.

These phenomena include the passing of certain solid bodies through other solid bodies.

With regard to this phenomenon we must remember that it was believed, even lately, that certain opaque bodies cannot be traversed by luminous rays capable of projecting on a photographic plate the shadows of objects placed behind them, and à fortiori we believed that our retina could never perceive the objects placed behind these opaque bodies. The discovery of the X-rays has demonstrated to us that our conception of matter, and in particular of that property of bodies which we call opacity, must be entirely modified. Our present ideas on the impenetrability of matter may very probably one day be found to be quite erroneous and have to be similarly modified.

We will also place in this category :—

1. Apparitions which leave material traces of their presence.

2. Impressions obtained by certain mediums in wax, clay, or putty.

3. The tactile sensation of invisible bodies perceived by experimenters.

4. Partial or total materialisations.

5. Finally, the apparition of phantoms which can be touched or photographed.

These phenomena depend not only on the presence of the medium, but also on his will.

The medium knows the phenomena which he is going to produce: he makes efforts to realise them: his efforts synchronise with their realisation.

The phantoms produced by mediums possess force and form.

With regard to the force, the medium, as in the phenomenon of the externalisation of motricity, accumulates and condenses the force that he draws from the spectators along with his own, and puts it into operation by his will.

He may be all the more aided by the group around him if he feels between the different persons of the group a sympathetic current which favourably influences him, and if he finds in this circle other persons who are endowed with a greater faculty of externalisation of force; and, finally, if the wish to assist in producing the phenomena of externalisation is general in the circle.

With regard to the form, it depends both on the idea in the medium's mind and the dominant idea among the persons composing the circle.

Therefore the materialisation has more chances of being complete, durable, and perfect, when the idea conceived by the circle is perceived in one and the same manner by all the members of the circle; when it is stronger, more precise, and more homogeneous in their minds.

The medium is therefore more especially a collector who gathers, concentrates, and condenses the thought of the persons surrounding him together with his own, which thought probably plays a predominant part in the formation of the image.

While going as far as possible in the scientific study and in the interpretation of the mechanism of these phenomena, we ought to maintain, with regard to their explanation and cause, that attitude of prudent reserve which caused Pio Foà to say:—

"*There are some superb humilities, and it has appeared to certain thinkers that the word* Ignorabimus! *was one of these. This affirmation of a definite limit of our knowledge seems superb in its humility. We may prefer the word* Ignoramus: *at all events it does not take away from us the hope, and with that the power, of extending the domain of the knowable, although from every discovery there arises the evidence of new gaps in our knowledge, just as occurs with a body illuminated on one side, which, in proportion as it becomes more voluminous throws also a larger cone of shadow. The Jacobin of the old order cried out, 'With each step of science God recedes a step.' If 'God' is the synthetic expression (and, let us say, the author) of the cosmic law, with each step that science takes His domain extends and proves itself to be ever more clearly infinite.*"

What we find, in fact, is that with every discovery we make the extent of our ignorance appears more clearly before our eyes. Each time the light of science enables us to clear up some obscure point of the unknown, we see better the frailty of human theories and we understand more clearly how feeble is the intelligence of man in the presence of the Infinite.